The Spirit of the Age

# *Anamnesis*

*Anamnesis* means remembrance or reminiscence, the collection and recollection of what has been lost, forgotten, or effaced. It is therefore a matter of the very old, of what has made us who we are. But *anamnesis* is also a work that transforms its subject, always producing something new. To recollect the old, to produce the new: that is the task of *Anamnesis*.

**a re.press series**

# The Spirit of the Age:
# Hegel and the Fate of Thinking

Paul Ashton, Toula Nicolacopoulos and
George Vassilacopoulos, editors

re.press Melbourne 2008

## re.press

PO Box 75, Seddon, 3011, Melbourne, Australia
http://www.re-press.org

© re.press 2008

This work is 'Open Access', published under a creative commons license which means that you are free to copy, distribute, display, and perform the work as long as you clearly attribute the work to the authors, that you do not use this work for any commercial gain in any form whatsoever and that you in no way alter, transform or build on the work outside of its use in normal academic scholarship without express permission of the author (or their executors) *and* the publisher of this volume. For any reuse or distribution, you must make clear to others the license terms of this work. For more information see the details of the creative commons licence at this website:
http://creativecommons.org/licenses/by-nc-nd/2.5/

British Library Cataloguing-in-Publication Data
*A catalogue record for this book is available from the British Library*

Library of Congress Cataloguing-in-Publication Data
*A catalogue record for this book is available from the Library of Congress*

National Library of Australia Cataloguing-in-Publication Data

The spirit of the age : Hegel and the fate of thinking

Bibliography.
ISBN: 9780980305265 (pbk.) :

1. Hegel, Georg Wilhelm Friedrich, 1770-1831.
2. Philosophy, German—19th century. 3. Philosophy.
I. Ashton, Paul, 1974-. II. Nicolacopoulos, Toula.
III. Vassilacopoulos, George. (Series : Anamnesis).

Designed and Typeset by *A&R*
Typeset in *Baskerville*

Printed on-demand in Australia, the United Kingdom and the United States. This book is produced sustainably using plantation timber, and printed in the destination market on demand reducing wastage and excess transport.

*To the memory of a dedicated student of Hegel
and a source of inspiration*

H. S. Harris (1926-2007)

# Contents

| | | |
|---|---|---|
| *Acknowledgements* | *page* | ix |
| *Abbreviations* | | xi |

## INTRODUCTION

1  *The Spirit of the Age and the Fate of Philosophical Thinking* — 3
   Paul Ashton, Toula Nicolacopoulos & George Vassilacopoulos

2  *Would Hegel Be A 'Hegelian' Today?* — 7
   H. S. Harris

## RIGHT AND WORLD

3  *Dialectical Reason and Necessary Conflict: Understanding and the Nature of Terror* — 21
   Angelica Nuzzo

4  *Hegel Today: Towards a Tragic Conception of Intercultural Conflicts* — 38
   Karin de Boer

5  *Hegel's Theory of Moral Action, its Place in his System and the 'Highest' Right of the Subject* — 52
   David Rose

6  *Hegel's Science of Logic and the 'Sociality of Reason'* — 72
   Jorge Armando Reyes Escobar

## LOGIC AND IDEALISM

7  *The Relevance of Hegel's Logic* — 107
   John W. Burbidge

8  *Hegel and the Becoming of Essence* — 118
   David Gray Carlson

9  *Hegel, Idealism and God: Philosophy as the Self-Correcting Appropriation of the Norms of Life and Thought* — 133
   Paul Redding

## HEGEL AND THE TRADITION

10 *Being and Implication: On Hegel and the Greeks*  153
   Andrew Haas

11 *Kierkegaard's Ethical Stage in Hegel's Logical Categories:*
   *Actual Possibility, Reality and Necessity*  172
   María J. Binetti

12 *Sein und Geist: Heidegger's Confrontation with Hegel's Phenomenology*  185
   Robert Sinnerbrink

13 *Hegel, Derrida and the Subject*  205
   Simon Lumsden

14 *Agamben, Hegel, and the State of Exception*  223
   Wendell Kisner

## ENCOUNTERING THE SPECULATIVE

15 *The Ego as World: Speculative Justification and the Role of*
   *the Thinker in Hegel's Philosophy*  259
   Toula Nicolacopoulos and George Vassilacopoulos

16 *Gathering and Dispersing: The Absolute Spirit in Hegel's Philosophy*  292
   George Vassilacopoulos

17 *The Beginning Before the Beginning:*
   *Hegel and the Activation of Philosophy*  314
   Paul Ashton

*Bibliography*  343
*Contributors*  358

# Acknowledgements

It is difficult to know who to thank for a project like this one because it is almost impossible to identify where it starts and ends. Nonetheless, we shall name a few active participants who have directly contributed to the production process or offered intellectual support in one form or another: A. J. Bartlett, Justin Clemens, Jim Devin, Claire Rafferty and the anonymous reviewers. We thank the contributors for their work, as well as those who responded to our initial call for papers but did not make the final volume due to the sheer number of responses.

We would also like to thank Bill Sampson for the use of his artwork *Trophy of the 51st Attack* (photograph by Bill Bachman) which appears on the cover of this volume, and MARS Gallery in Melbourne for making this possible.

Finally this book is a co-production with the open access journal *Cosmos and History: The Journal of Natural and Social Philosophy* (C&H) and we thank the editorial board for their co-operation.

Paul Ashton<br>
Toula Nicolacopoulos<br>
George Vassilacopoulos<br>
<br>
Melbourne, 14 November 2007<br>
— The 176th Anniversary of Hegel's Death

# Abbreviations

Hegel's works are cited by either page, section (§) or paragraph (¶) number; Hegel's remarks (Anmerkungen) to his sections are cited by an accompanying 'R' (e.g. EL §140 R); Hegel's additions (Zusätze) with an 'A' (e.g. EN § 140 A). When a citation is made of additions, remarks and sections at the same time they will be separated with a comma. For example (EL § 140, R, A) would refer to a citation of the section, its remark and the addition. Where there are multiple additions to a single section a number will be placed after the 'A' (e.g. EL § 136 A2). Citation of texts with pages appear thus: (LA 257) or (LHP III 87). When a German edition is cited it follows the English citation if one is given, e.g. for example (SL 47/WL I 31). The German volume numbers follow the abbreviation in roman numerals.

*German Editions of Hegel's Work*

| | |
|---|---|
| GW | *Gesammelte Werke*, Hamburg, Felix Meiner Verlag, 1968-. |
| W | *Werke in zwanzing Bänden*, Eva Moldenhauer and Karl Markus (eds.), Frankfurt am Main, Suhrkamp Verlag, 1969. |
| WL | *Wissenschaft der Logik*, Georg Lasson, (ed.), Hamburg, Felix Meiner, 1975. |
| PG | *Phänomenologie des Geistes*, H.-F. Wessels and H. Clairmont (eds.), Hamburg, Felix Meiner Verlag, 1988. |

*English Editions of Hegel's Work*

| | |
|---|---|
| D | *The Difference Between Fichte's and Schelling's System of Philosophy*, trans. H. S. Harris and Walter Cerf, Albany, State University of New York Press, 1977. |
| EL | *The Encyclopaedia Logic (1830), with the Zusätze: Part I of the Encyclopaedia of Philosophical Sciences with the Zusätze*, trans. Theodore F. Geraets, W. A. Suchting, and H. S. Harris, Indianapolis, Hackett, 1991. |

| | |
|---|---|
| EPM | *Philosophy of Mind: Being Part Three of the Encyclopaedia of the Philosophical Sciences (1830), Together with the Zusätze*, M. J. Inwood (ed.), trans. William Wallace and A. V. Miller with revisions and commentary by M. J. Inwood, Oxford, Oxford, 2007. |
| | *Philosophy of Mind: Being Part Three of the Encyclopaedia of the Philosophical Sciences (1830), Together with the Zusätze*, trans. William Wallace and A. V. Miller, Oxford, Oxford, 1971. |
| EPN | *Philosophy of Nature: Being Part Two of the Encyclopaedia of the Philosophical Sciences, 1830*, trans. M. J. Petry, 3 vols., London, George Allen & Unwin, 1970. |
| | *Philosophy of Nature: Being Part Two of the Encyclopaedia of the Philosophical Sciences, 1830*, trans. A.V. Miller, Oxford, Clarendon Press, 1970. |
| ILHP | *Introduction to the Lectures on the History of Philosophy*, trans. T. M. Knox and A. V. Miller, Oxford, Oxford University Press, 1987. |
| JS | *The Jena System, 1804-5: Logic and Metaphysics*, trans. John W. Burbidge and George di Giovanni, Kingston, McGill-Queen's University Press, 1986. |
| LA | *Aesthetics: Lectures on Fine Art*, trans. T. M. Knox, 2 vols., Oxford, Oxford, 1998. |
| LHP I | *Lectures on the History of Philosophy*, trans. E. S. Haldane and Frances H. Simson, vol. I Greek Philosophy to Plato, 3 vols., Lincoln, University of Nebraska Press, 1995. |
| LHP II | *Lectures on the History of Philosophy*, trans. E. S. Haldane and Frances H. Simson, vol. II Plato and the Platonists, 3 vols., Lincoln, University of Nebraska Press, 1995. |
| LHP III | *Lectures on the History of Philosophy*, trans. E. S. Haldane and Frances H. Simson, vol. III Medieval and Modern Philosophy, 3 vols., Lincoln, University of Nebraska Press, 1995. |
| LHP 25-6 II | *Lectures on the History of Philosophy 1825-6*, Robert F. Brown (ed.), trans. R. F. Brown and J. M. Stewart with the assistance of H. S. Harris, vol. 2 Greek Philosophy, Oxford, Oxford, 2006. |
| LHP 25-6 III | *Lectures on the History of Philosophy: The Lectures of 1825-1826*, trans. Robert F. Brown, J. M. Stewart, and H. S. Harris, vol. 3 Medieval and Modern Philosophy, Berkeley, University of California Press, 1990. |

| | |
|---|---|
| LNR | *Lectures on Natural Right and Political Science: The First Philosophy of Right: Heidelberg, 1817-1818, with Additions From the Lectures of 1818-1819*, trans. J. Michael Stewart and Peter C. Hodgson, Berkeley, University of California Press, 1995. |
| LPH | *The Philosophy of History*, trans. J. Sibree, New York, Dover Publications, 1956. |
| LPR I, II, III | *Lectures on the Philosophy of Religion*, trans. R.F. Brown, P.C. Hodgson, and J.M. Stewart, 3 vols., Berkeley, University of California Press, 1984. |
| NL | 'On the Scientific Ways of Treating Natural Law, on its Place in Practical Philosophy, and its Relation to the Positive Sciences of Right', in Laurence Dickey and H. B. Nisbet (eds.), *Political Writings*, trans. H. B. Nisbet, Cambridge, Cambridge, 1999, pp. 102-80. |
| PR | *Elements of the Philosophy of Right*, Allen Wood (ed.), trans. H. B. Nisbet, Cambridge, Cambridge University Press, 1996. |
| | *The Philosophy of Right*, trans. T. M. Knox, New York, Oxford, 1980. |
| PS | *The Phenomenology of Spirit*, trans. A.V. Miller, New York, Oxford, 1977. |
| RH | *Reason in History: A General Introduction to the Philosophy of History*, trans. Hartman Robert S., New York, Liberal Arts Press, 1953. |
| SEL | *System of Ethical Life (1802/3) and First Philosophy of Spirit (part III of the System of Speculative Philosophy 1803/4)*, trans. H. S. Harris and T. M. Knox, Albany, State University of New York Press, 1979. |
| SL | *Science of Logic*, trans. A.V. Miller, New Jersey, Humanities Press, 1997. |

*Abbreviations of Works by Other Philosophers*

| | |
|---|---|
| BT | Heidegger, Martin, *Being and Time*, trans. Joan Stambaugh, New York, State University of New York Press, 1996. |
| GA 32 | Heidegger, Martin, *Hegels Phänomenologie des Geistes*, Frankfurt an Main, Klostermann, 1980. |
| HCE | Heidegger, Martin, 'Hegel's Concept of Experience', *Off the Beaten Track*, ed. and trans. Julian Young and Kenneth Haynes, Cambridge, Cambridge University, 2002. |

| | |
|---|---|
| HPS | Heidegger, Martin, *Hegel's Phenomenology of Spirit*, trans. P. Emad and K. Maly, Bloomington, Indiana, 1994. |
| HS | Agamben, Giorgio, *Homo Sacer: Sovereign Power and Bare Life*, trans. Daniel Heller-Roazen, Stanford, Stanford University Press, 1998. |
| ID | Heidegger, Martin, *Identity and Difference*, trans. J. Stambaugh, Chicago, University of Chicago, 2002. |
| JP | Søren Kierkegaard, *Journals and Papers*, trans. Howard V. Hong and Edna H. Hong, 7 vols., Bloomington, Indiana University Press, 1967-78. |
| KW | Søren Kierkegaard, *Kierkegaard's Writings*, trans. Howard V. Hong and Edna H. Hong, 24 vols., Princeton University Press, 1978-98. |
| *Meta.* | Aristtole, *Metaphysics*, 1048b18-34, in *The Basic Works of Aristotle*, ed. and trans. W. D. Ross, New York, Random House, 1941. |
| Pap | Søren Kierkegaard, *Søren Kierkegaard's Papirer*, P. A. Heiberg, V. Kuhr and E. Torsting (eds.), 2nd ed., 20 vols., København, Gyldendalske Boghandel Nordisk Forlag, 1909-1948. |
| PM | Heidegger, Martin, *Pathmarks*, William McNeill (ed.), Cambridge, Cambridge University, 1998. |
| SE | Agamben, Giorgio, *State of Exception*, trans. K. Attell Chicago, The University of Chicago Press, 2005. |
| SV | Søren Kierkegaard, Samlede Værker, A. B. Drachmann, J. L. Heiberg and H. O. Lange (eds.), 15 vols., Gyldendalske Boghandel Nordisk Forlag, København, 1920-1936 (superscript indicationn the edition). |

*introduction*

# I

# The Spirit of the Age and the Fate of Philosophical Thinking

Paul Ashton, Toula Nicolacopoulos & George Vassilacopoulos

> philosophy [...] is entirely identical with its time. (LHP I 54)

If philosophy is identical with its time, is there a sense in which revolutionary philosophers bear the spirit of their own age in so far as they arrive from the future? If so, would this explain why their ideas seem to us so strange and distant yet inexplicably familiar and attractive at the same time? But what is the future in this case? Might it be the *topos* of exile of what mostly belongs to us, to our time; the distant within and the within in the distant. If the revolutionary thinker does indeed come from afar his/her arriving must be the measure of our own distance from the future. Could it be that it is through this arriving that the world manifests itself, that the spirit of the age emerges in an otherwise spiritless age?

Plato is perhaps the paradigm case of the revolutionary philosopher in our sense of the philosopher arriving from the future. According to Hegel, the idea of the just polis that Plato formulated in *The Republic* was the most philosophically thinkable in Plato's time. Even though Plato's ideal was so far from the then given state of affairs that it seemed hardly recognizable to his contemporaries, it was nevertheless out of its thinking that Plato was able to comprehend the rational moment embedded in the sophists' polis in which he lived. Having elaborated his ideal city, a city powerful enough to accommodate the philosopher, Plato was then in a position to cross the abyss between the ideal and the real in order to re-visit and once again embrace his own city as a whole. His thinking showed the city of Athens to be part of the world of the thinkable and in doing so it brought together the ever-changing finite body of the city with its eternal idea.

For this reason the city that condemned the philosopher to death could nonetheless be thought as part of an ongoing becoming that oriented it toward a future. For Plato this future was thought in terms of the polis of justice in which Plato the philosopher dwells conceptually and from which he arrives, albeit invisibly, to be welcomed by those who are prepared to think in the embrace of his thinking. Having arrived from afar in a way that also made it possible for him to dwell in the world in a radically immanent manner, Plato didn't lose himself, like a tourist, amongst the shiny trinkets and the trivialities of market life. Nor did he abandon himself to the shallow wisdom of the local. Rather, as the bearer of the ideal and in so far as he found the strength to withstand the infinite schism between the real and the ideal, his thinking entirely embraced the historical moment of his world and thus allowed the spirit of the age to manifest itself with his thought. Herein lies the determination of Plato's thought as revolutionary philosophy that arrives from the future in its own precise moment.

In this respect Plato the philosopher came to give effect to the conceptual transformative power of the revolutionary practice of his time in a way that Socrates before him was unable to conceive. Plato's thinking grew out of Socrates' failure to convince Athens to re-enact itself in accordance with the principle of radical self-knowing. Although we can say that in his capacity as a revolutionary Socrates also comes from the future, only the philosopher succeeds in thinking what the revolutionary practice announces but fails to achieve. So the thinking of the philosopher takes place in the retreat of the future that the failed revolutionary practice announces. This was the fate of philosophical thinking in Plato's time.

Perhaps Hegel is the Plato of our own era for he too arrives from the future in the sense we have been outlining. He is the thinker of the great schism between the ideal and the real that marks and defines modernity. He is the 'owl of Minerva' that 'spreads its wings only with the falling of dusk' to cross the abyss of the great divide between notion and being in order to address us from the distant (PR 23). His thinking springs out of the future that was announced by the French revolutionaries and that retreated in the failure of this revolution. His thinking was destined to offer a place for the spirit of the age to emerge. His philosophy is the 'inward birth-place of the spirit which will later arrive at actual form' (HP I 55). This is the spirit of utopian violence that is also a violent utopia. Hegel's thought teaches that spirit is the infinitely violent act of separating the universal from the particular, communal love from self-interest. This was Plato's lesson as well. According to Hegel's story, our world is the world of the 'empty self' that unfolds globally and perpetuates itself as an emptying out and hence as a triumphant and narcissistic sinking into the desert of this emptiness. It is out of such sinking that the spirit of communal being arises 'fragrantly' in the 'grey' of the speculative philosopher's utopian vision (LPR III 233 n. 191 & PR 23). It is 'the rose in the cross of the present' (PR 19). Through this vision the philosopher announces the healing power of history. History is the crossing of the abyss by the real that moves towards the ideal, a crossing first performed by the thinker albeit in the reverse direction.

So the philosopher's concern is the schism of the abyss at the heart of our collective being since this schism provides the inescapable context for the unfolding of particular events. Even so, the collapse of the schism is no less inescapable according to the lesson of Hegel's speculative thought. This is a lesson with which many may well disagree but such disagreement typically follows from thematic encounters with what is ultimately a non-thematic thinking. The noteworthy point for our purposes is not whether we should accept or reject the lessons of Hegel's thought, but that ever since Hegel, philosophers are challenged to experience philosophy as such as *the happening of the spirit of the age*.[1] Through its happening, the spirit of the age has explicitly become the age of key Hegelian concepts understood, not as themes, but as happenings of thinking itself, whether of history, the future, manifestation, alienation, recognition, otherness, reconciliation or philosophy. Viewed as this sort of happening we can conclude with H. S. Harris that, whilst it 'is not a very comfortable home that we have made for ourselves in this world', nevertheless Hegel's philosophy

> is the one that shows us that it is our *home* and that we are the ones who have built it. The only comfort that philosophy can add to its amenities must come from our understanding why it is idle to look for comfort in it (H. S. Harris, this collection).

From this perspective the question for us is whether philosophizing today has the power to generate a level of intensity, not so much for the spirit of our own age to emerge clearly and distinctively, but for the spirit of the age to emerge at all. Perhaps, instead, the real issue for the thinkers who come after the revolutionary philosopher is whether we are strong enough to intensify and withstand the intensity that Hegel's thinking has already released. From this perspective to encounter the spirit of the age can be neither to look for it in the developments of the twenty-first century world nor to produce a radically new philosophy. To encounter the spirit of the age can only mean to enter the temple in which the spirit's flame is already alight.

But as we know all too well flames do not only permit us to see; they also pose the risk of going blind. Hegel himself was not very optimistic about the strength and resolve of those around:

> it belongs to the weakness of our time not to be able to bear the greatness, the immensity of the claims made by the human spirit, to feel crushed before them, and to flee from them faint-hearted (LHP II 10).

We have suggested that the fate of those of us who follow the arriving of Hegel, the revolutionary thinker, is to face the challenge of dwelling in his arriving. The fate of philosophers after the arrival of revolutionary philosophy is to play a role much like that of John the Baptist, albeit in relation to what has *already* arrived. But if thinkers today seem destined perpetually to perform the role of announcing the previous arrival of revolutionary thinking, herein lies the danger for thought. Do we announce the thinker's arrival because she/he has arrived or do we consider her/him as having arrived thanks to our announcements? Do we admit to the status of our work as mere footnoting that of revolutionary thinkers?

---

1. On the meaning of 'the spirit of the age' see Löwith, Karl, *From Hegel to Nietzsche: The Revolution in Nineteenth-Century Thought*, trans. David E. Green, New York, Columbia University Press, 1991, p. 201-231.

Does our thinking carry the wisdom of knowing that its place of dwelling is the thought of revolutionary philosophy or do we instead, remaining oblivious to the status of our work, aspire to re-position the work of revolutionary thinking within its confines and thereby imagine ourselves to be safely situated beyond the reach of such thinking? Are we thinkers of the post-Hegelian era more and more evidently not 'able to bear the greatness, the immensity of the claims made by the human spirit'? Is our era the era of a 'faint-hearted' philosophy? These are the questions that motivated us to celebrate 200 years since the publication of *The Phenomenology of Spirit* with the production of this volume. In different ways our contributors have responded to this call for a renewed encounter with Hegel's thought.

* * * * *

We have chosen to begin this volume with an essay by H. S. Harris. This previously unpublished essay is a transcription of the 'Presidential Address' delivered to the Hegel Society of America on 2 October 1980, at Trent University, Peterborough, Ontario. We have included the essay here because Harris in this posthumous publication manages to address in his own distinctive manner many of the central questions that were of concern to us when formulating this collection. The essay fittingly begins the collection as it not only sets an agenda for the volume, but also acknowledges Harris' immense contribution to Hegel Scholarship. Harris remains an inspiration to us as students of Hegel.

2

# Would Hegel Be A 'Hegelian' Today?

## H. S. Harris

If we can have a conference on the announced theme 'Hegel Today', it would seem that many of us must think that there is *something* still alive and relevant to our situation in Hegel's thought. Yet this does not entail that any of us must think that his basic project was valid. It is demonstrated easily, in fact, that some of the most intelligent and dedicated contemporary students of Hegel's work have concluded that his philosophical project was a dialectical illusion generated by *his* historic situation; and that he would never have believed that what he set out to do was achievable, if he had been faced in his maturity with the world that we face.[1]

Thus Emil Fackenheim concluded in the 1960s that 'such are the crises which have befallen the Christian West in the last half-century that it may safely be said that, were he alive today, so realistic a philosopher as Hegel would not be a Hegelian';[2] and Charles Taylor concluded ten years later that 'his actual synthesis is quite dead. That is, no one actually believes his central ontological thesis, that the Universe is posited by a Spirit whose essence is rational Necessity'.[3] Others have arrived at a similar verdict for their own reasons, including our Vice President [Merold Westphal].[4] But at this first conference in Canada I shall con-

---

1. [Editors' Note: The editors of this volume would like to thank Jim Devin, the executor of Harris' papers for making this text available. The text is the 'Presidential Address' delivered on 2 October 1980 to the *Hegel Society of America*, meeting at Trent University, Peterborough, Ontario. The presentation is previously unpublished. This version was transcribed from a typescript of the manuscript by Jim Devin. Readers interested in the work of H. S. Harris should visit the digital repository of selected works, https://www.library.yorku.ca/dspace/handle/123456789/883.]

2. Emil Fackenheim, *The Religious Dimension in Hegel's Thought*, Bloomington, Indiana University Press, 1967, p. 224; cf. also p. 12.

3. Charles Taylor, *Hegel*, Cambridge, Cambridge University Press, 1975, p. 538.

4. Merold Westphal, *History and Truth in Hegel's Phenomenology*, Atlantic Highlands, Humanities Press, 1979, pp. 199-200. It is fair to say, in criticism of Westphal's 'adherence' to Fackenheim's view, that it is internally inconsistent. For if Hegel could believe in the sort of millennium that Westphal ascribes to him, then he was never the hard-headed realist for which Fackenheim takes him. If Westphal agrees

centrate attention—*honoris causa*—upon these two Canadians.

What these critics are saying is both very easy, and very difficult, to refute. Thus, one can refute Taylor's empirical claim that 'no one is a Hegelian today' in the defined sense, by pointing to Clark Butler, who claims that Hegel's diagnosis of his time led to a 'comprehension of God, revolution and their inner identity' which is precisely what *our* time needs because the revolution that began in 1789 is still on going.[5] But Taylor's generalization was plainly intended to cover only thinkers as 'realistic as Hegel' and (in spite of Taylor's own record of youthful protest) one may doubt whether he would be seriously disturbed by the counterexample of one who is prepared to take the 'counter-culture' of the 1950s and 1960s as evidence that the revolution is still on going.

A far more impressive example can be offered in *confirmation* of Fackenheim's thesis, and as the exception that proves the rule for Taylor's. Geoffrey Mure was committed to Hegel's 'central ontological thesis' all his life. But he was too well schooled in the history of philosophy since Kant to affirm it categorically—and too careful a student of Hegel to be as sure as Taylor is, that it was indeed what Hegel meant to affirm. Yet in his *Idealistic Epilogue*, published just before his death in 1979, he validates Fackenheim's thesis that 'From so fragmented a world [as ours] the Hegelian philosophy would be *forced* to flee, as surely as Neoplatonism was forced into flight from Imperial Rome.... such a resort to flight would be tantamount to radical failure'.[6]

Mure's last verdict upon an academic career that began just before the First World War, reads thus:

> The fact is I am sick to death of the spectacle of humanity en masse. I don't doubt that at least from the beginning of this century, perhaps earlier, the human species has declined in quality in inverse proportion to its increase in quantity; declined in thought and action, art and morality, indeed by any standard you can think of except perhaps health and expectation of life. Leaving out black Africa, for which I have no figures, there are now more than three thousand million human beings alive, over-populating this planet by at least 40 percent. The majority of them are not significantly discriminable from one another and are, quite consistently, egalitarian in outlook so far as they have any outlook. The real danger with which the uncontrolled proliferation of mankind threatens us is not starvation. Science for some time will produce a sufficient quantity of food at the expense of its quality to balance Nature's continuing production of more and more inferior human beings. The danger is that, after a little token bloodshed and a great deal of dishonourable appeasement, man will lie flattened under the tyrannies which egalitarianism inevitable begets. The old like me, as they take us to the concentration camp, will cry with Cleopatra, 'The odds is gone, / And there is nothing left remarkable / Beneath the visiting moon'. That is why I shut my eyes and reflected on what an

---

with Fackenheim about *that*—as I do—then he ought to have been driven to re-examine his own interpretation of the supposed final solution reached in the *Phenomenology*.

5. Clark Butler, *G. W. F. Hegel*, Boston, Twayne Publishers, 1977, pp. 9-10. That Butler holds Hegel's central ontological thesis in something like the form in which Taylor states it, is shown—in my opinion—by his declared allegiance to Whitehead's philosophy of nature (see pp. 11, 174-77).

6. Fackenheim, *The Religious Dimension in Hegel's Thought*, p. 236.

individual can be and has been.[7]

If *this* is what the Hegelian '"peace" between faith and philosophy' leads to at the present time, then we may well feel, like Fackenheim, that 'The time is not ripe for the self-elevation of thought to the divine side of the divine-human relation, for *no* time has *this* kind of ripeness'.[8] Mure looks back to the world before 1914 as a time of 'ripeness'. On the other side, Merold Westphal thinks that the author of the *Phenomenology* looked *forward* to a time of 'ripeness' instead of what actually came to pass between 1814 and 1914. Both of them are mistaken in their conception of 'ripeness'. The optimistic Hegel of 1807 did learn indeed that he was mistaken in 1814. But Hegel as a philosopher never *needed* that lesson (if he had needed it, he would after 1814 have denounced the prophetic pretensions, which Westphal claims to find in the *Phenomenology*, as violently after 1814 as he denounced the philosophical prophecies after that date). He lived in *two* times: a time of social hope and a time of social despair (for that is how the century that Mure looks back to with homesick longing appeared to Hegel as it opened). For Hegel personally, the time of social hope was a period in which he was driven as near to despair as he was capable of coming; while the time of social despair was for him personally the moment of success and universal recognition. He well might have come to the conception of philosophy that he held in those last years because of this complex reversal: and his doctrine of the 'ripeness' of his time then might have rested upon the experienced ambivalence of the 'times' in his experience. But in fact he did not come to his view in this way; and the only difference that Hegel's experience of the 'carrousel of time' makes to his concept of its 'ripeness' is that it enables *us* to demonstrate that he was always fully conscious that systematic philosophy as 'time comprehended' is 'absolute', that is to say not dependent upon any time at all. We can show this, because Hegel already maintained in the good time, both that the 'comprehending of one's time' was the highest achievable goal, and that philosophy, because it rises out of its time by comprehending it, cannot presume to give practical advice for its own particular time. We find these two lessons in early texts from successive years (1801-1802); and we find them again, repeated side by side in the bad time to which the Preface of the *Philosophy of Right* was addressed.[9]

---

7. G. R. G. Mure, *Idealist Epilogue*, Oxford, Clarendon Press, 1978, pp. 174-75.

8. Fackenheim, *The Religious Dimension in Hegel's Thought*, p. 240. This is actually the foundation of one of two *extremes* that Fackenheim distinguishes in 'post-Hegelian religious thought'. He says himself that 'philosophic thought must move beyond the extremes of partisan commitments' (p. 241) but he does not say how. He leaves *me*, however, with the impression that the thesis I have quoted represents for him the abiding truth of *this* extreme—cf., p. 49.

9. For 1801-02 compare the 'Resolution' poem (Johannes Hoffmeister, *Dokumente zu Hegel's Entwicklung*, Frommann, Stuttgart, 1936, p. 388): 'Bessers nicht als die Zeit, aber auf's Reste, sie seyne' and the introduction to the essay on the *Constitution of Germany*—'The thoughts contained in this essay can have no aim or effect, when published, save that of promoting the understanding of what is, and therefore a calmer outlook and a moderately tolerant attitude alike in words and in actual contact [with affairs]. For it is not what is that makes us irascible and resentful, but the fact that it is not as it ought to be. But if we recognize that it is as it must be, i.e. that it is not arbitrariness and chance that

One way in which those who say that 'Hegel today would not be a Hegelian'—or that no rational observer of today's world can be one, which is the same thing—plainly contradict themselves, and themselves 'Hegelians' of a sort is here revealed. They all agree with Hegel's definition of philosophy as 'its own time grasped in thoughts'. What they cannot see is how the 'comprehension of one's time' can possibly produce a philosophy that is *out of time* and somehow final. If they could see that, they would agree, I assume, that it is legitimate to be a 'Hegelian today' (and that Hegel himself, the model philosopher from whom they all alike accept the definition of philosophy's problem as comprehension of the time, would *a fortiori* still be a 'Hegelian' today or on any other day). They would agree with this, I think, even though they might not be converted to Hegelianism in the full or systematic sense themselves. (Nothing, I am convinced, ever would convert Fackenheim. The claim that 'there is but one Reason. There is no second super-human Reason. Reason is the divine in man'[10] offends him—upon his interpretation of it—by its *positive* presumption. Upon the interpretation that I shall offer here, it will offend him almost as much by its *negative* presumption—it denies too much; it would require him to give up something too precious to him to be surrendered—namely, his religious faith.)[11]

The solution to the problem of how time finally can be transcended is simpler than one expects. That is why it goes unrecognized. First, to 'comprehend a time' involves comprehending the way in which all previous times are relevant to it. Thus there is at all times a *common structure* in the endeavour to comprehend one's time; and any effort to comprehend a previous time that is known to one is peculiarly relevant to one's own effort in this time. Everything that counts for one as such an effort is 'philosophy'; and in virtue of the fact that it only qualifies as philosophy so far as one can (and has) successfully related it to one's own effort, one must always be able to speak of philosophy as 'perennial', (or as being able to speak of philosophy as 'perennial', (or as being one and the same at all times).[12]

---

make it what it is, then we also recognize that it is as it ought to be. Yet it is hard for the ordinary run of men to rise to the habit of trying to recognize necessity and to think it. Between events and the free interpretation of them they insert a mass of concepts and aims and require what happens to correspond with them. And when doubtless the case is nearly always otherwise, they excuse their concepts on the plea that while what dominated them was necessity what dominated the event was chance. Their concepts are just as restricted as their insight into things, which indeed they interpret as mere isolated events, not as a system of events ruled by a single spirit....' (G. Lasson , ed., *Schriften zur Politik und Rechtsphilosophie*, Leipzig, Meiner, 2nd ed., 1923, p. 5; *Hegel's Political Writings*, trans. T. M. Knox with an introductory essay by Z. A. Pelczynski, Oxford, Clarendon Press, 1964, p. 145[one small revision made to translation]); the relevant passage from the *Preface* of the *Philosophy of Right* is in Lasson, p. 16 (*Hegel's Philosophy of Right*, trans. T. M. Knox, Oxford, Clarendon Press, 1952, p. 11).

10. G. W. F. Hegel, *Einleitung in der Geschichte der Philosophie*, Johannes Hoffmeister (ed.), Leipzig, Meiner, 1940, p. 123 (cf. Fackenheim, *The Religious Dimension in Hegel's Thought*, p. 223).

11. cf. Fackenheim, *The Religious Dimension in Hegel's Thought*, p. 12.

12. Many texts repeat this point at all stages of Hegel's career—from the *Difference* essay (G. W. F. Hegel, *The Difference Between Fichte's and Schelling's System of Philosophy*, trans. H. S. Harris and Walter Cerf, Albany, Sate University of New York Press, 1977, p. 114) to the *Einleitung in der Geschichte der Philosophie* of November 1827. But this last is perhaps the passage that comes closest to saying exactly what I am saying: 'Philosophy is Reason that grasps in the mode of thinking, brings itself to consciousness,

Secondly, Hegel's time is 'ripe' because it is *now* that this comprehension of what philosophy is has been reached. Hegel can be sure that it could not have been reached earlier—no previous time could have reached it—because his concept of spirit as the community of rational inquirers, or as the continuing dialogue of those who are striving to grasp how humanity structures its life-world in its ambiguous pursuit of natural satisfaction 'happiness' and self-expression for contemplative appreciation ('freedom'), presupposes Kant's Copernican revolution—i.e. it presupposes the recognition that real, objective, scientific cognition does not tell us the way things are 'in themselves' but the way they are 'for us'. Because of this *subjective* structure of all finite cognition, the absolute of what [*is*] is 'in and for itself', not the direct or intuitive awareness of what is 'in itself'.

In a sense, of course, this insight was old news. There is a long traditional of 'perennial philosophy' before Hegel.[13] But that earlier tradition depended on the *faith* (or the dogmatic assumption supported by 'proofs' which had only a dialectical validity) that 'what is' is a self-conscious Being, who reveals Himself to us, His finite creatures, truthfully, because He is infinitely good. It was, of course, this great tradition that *una veritas in variis signis varie resplendent* (to borrow a tag from one of the great exponents of the *philosophia perennis*, Nicholas of Cusa) that Hegel wanted to take over. But he wanted both to translate it into post-Kantian terms, and to incorporate the philosophic traditions of unself-conscious naturalism and/or dualism. He could only overcome the Kantian dialectic between these different traditions if he could show that there is a *real* absolute Subject in *human* cognition (not just a 'logical form' furnished with a set of categories peculiarly adapted to make Newton's physics and the sociology of Hobbes and Locke appear as the eternal truth). But what subject is there in our experience for whom the self-positing power of Fichte's Ego can be claimed, without our being required to venture into acts of faith that must inevitably generate 'unbelievers'? Only the human community, as sharing the common duty and delight of knowing the world as its home, and exploring and forever extending its free range of self-expression in that home, can be the subject *for* which the 'order' of nature, and the dialectical disorder of history exists. Thus 'philosophy is the thinking spirit in world-history'; and the self-formative or phenomenological problem of the philosopher is to raise himself to the standpoint of this *real* transcendental subjectivity. From this standpoint the maxim, *homo sum, nihil humani a me alienum puto* will embrace all the ways there are of knowing and relating to the *objective* world,

---

so that it becomes *Gegenstand* [an ob-ject] for itself or knows itself in the form of thought. This producing, the fact that it knows of itself, is thus also one only—just one and the same thinking. Hence there is strictly just *one* philosophy only. Much may be called by the name of philosophy though it is not.—We have nothing of our own [*Spezielles*] before us, for philosophy is the thinking spirit in world-history' (Hegel, *Einleitung in der Geschichte der Philosophie*, pp. 123-24). [For another translation refer to *Hegel's Introduction to the Lectures on the History of Philosophy*, trans. T. M. Knox and A. V. Miller, Oxford, Clarendon Press, 1985, p. 92.]

13. The expression *philosophia perennis* was coined, I think, by the Italian humanist Agostino Steuco, and its most notable popularizer was perhaps Robert, Cardinal Bellarmine—but the concept is medieval and possibly Hellenistic.

as well as to one another; and the true significance of the 'postulate of immortality' will be found precisely in the possibility of obeying the maxim.

That is the easy part; for it is hard to contest the claim that Hegel's *Phenomenology* could not well have been written any sooner than it was. Even to imagine it being written more clearly, by somebody else at that time, becomes difficult when we reflect that nobody we know of understood Hegel's version then and there; and only a scattering of readers seem to have understood it ever since. Yet the conviction that philosophy is the comprehension of one's time is widely shared, and the knowledge that we owe this conviction to Hegel, though not universal among those who share it, is certainly not uncommon.

What is harder to grasp is why Hegel was sure that his own comprehension of what 'comprehending the time' involves would not itself be transcended in some future comprehension of the time. We shall only see why his insight into the problem of what 'comprehending the time' *is* has a colourable claim to be as ultimate as the logical principles of identity, contradiction and excluded middle are in certain modes of formal discourse, when we understand clearly what that insight was. It never ceases to astound me personally—for whom this was almost the first thing I really understood in Hegel, a beacon that has shed light ever more widely on the theoretical puzzles of his work over more than thirty years of studying it since—that in spite of Hegel's perpetual trumpeting about the 'identity' of (Christian) religion and philosophy, Hegel's most crucial debt to the Gospel, is so seldom clearly understood.

The French proverb says '*tout comprendre, c'est tout pardonner*'. This is one of those axioms of '*gesunder Menschenverstand*' that takes on a somewhat Pickwickian sense when it get its proper 'speculative' interpretation. For when we comprehend everything philosophically we do necessarily forgive it. What is *necessary* has minimally to be accepted or recognized rather than forgiven—the 'forgiveness' of what is at all times beyond our power is pointless. Yet Hegel does not characterize even this 'recognition of necessity' as the admission of *justice*: to see that things must be as they are is to see that 'they are as they ought to be'. Thus he makes all recognition of necessity into an anticipation of the rationality of 'forgiveness'; and he does so because forgiveness, whenever it is appropriate, is a higher level of reason than the recognition of justice. In human (or 'spiritual') relations forgiveness is the only *self-sufficient* rationality, for it is what the recognition of necessity properly leads to; and in freeing us from the tyranny of the demand for 'justice', the granting of the pardon shows us that we are indeed free—that freedom is not a 'postulate' but an experience, an actuality to which we can rise at any moment—just as Jesus taught when he counselled us to 'Love your enemies', 'Bless them that persecute you' and so on.

Hegel recognized the three realms of Absolute Spirit as the 'real presence' of the 'Kingdom of God' which the unhellenized Jew, Jesus of Nazareth proclaimed to his people; and he saw that the spirit of charity is 'resurrected' in every man who enters those realms (just as the hellenized Jew, Paul, proclaimed to the Gentiles) because one cannot enter the world of universal human culture without putting the one sided partisanship of practical life behind one. Milton's *Paradise Lost* belongs to the Hegelian Kingdom of God because Shelly, for instance, can recognize the human 'heroism' of Milton's Satan. This kind of recognition does not mean one must 'forgive' everything that one opposes in the ordinary world (as the youthful author of the *Necessity of Atheism* certainly opposed Milton's 'Christianity' for example). Also it is true that, for Hegel—as for Jesus—there is such a thing as the 'sin against the Spirit'—for which there is no forgiveness. I cannot engage to discuss that now, for it seems to me to take several forms and I am not sure I can classify them, still less provide a rational 'phenomenology' for them. But a marvellously clear example is provided by the report—which I am assuming to be true simply because it so providentially apt—that Eichmann claimed that he had tried always to live in accordance with the *Categorical Imperative*. This puts him beyond the range of the prayer 'Father forgive them, for they know not what they do'. He is beyond the range of any of the ambiguous senses of 'not knowing' because the second formula of the *Categorical Imperative* ('always to treat humanity as an *end*, and never as a means only') was the clearest *philosophical* expression of man's rational self-comprehension in practical relations before Hegel. It took Hegel himself several years of hard thinking to see that Jesus had already grasped what 'respect for humanity' involved far better than Kant ever did; and it is the conviction that *he*, Hegel, has finally found a *logical* way to express what Jesus understood that makes him confident that his comprehension of what man's task of self-comprehension is will not be transcended. It is logically impossible to assert as a matter of definite necessity that Hegel's confidence is absolutely warranted. The essence of rational speech requires us to recognize its absolute *freedom* in this direction. One of the reasons why, whether we believe in God or not, we must construct our philosophical logic without speaking of Him (except in non-logical metaphors) is that no word uttered by human tongue or pen can have the absolute finality of 'God's' Word as conceived in the older *philosophia perennis*. But before I let this logical limit trouble *my* confident acceptance of Hegel's 'absolute knowledge' *as* absolute, (at least) what it might mean to 'transcend' the religious definition of man's vocation as 'loving God (the God who *is* Love) and his neighbour as himself.' I confess that I do not know (cannot 'conceive') what a 'transcending' of that formula would be like—i.e., a philosophical doctrine that makes it look as inadequate as Hegel made Kant's moral philosophy look to me beside it. Because Hegel's philosophy has done that for me, I am confident that the new *philosophia perennis* will indeed prove perennial. Since I am thus content to proclaim myself a 'Hegelian today' (in defiance of Charles Taylor), it hardly needs stating that I claim that severest of realists, Hegel, as a Hegelian likewise (in defiance of Emil Fackenheim).

But where does the 'realism' come in? Well, the *Phenomenology* brings the whole range of human moral attitudes, from that of Cain to that of Novalis, within the range of Christian charity, by showing us that the self-conscious appearance of 'charity' itself requires them. Thus it turns '*Father*, forgive them ...' into 'Do you, against whom we trespass, forgive us, as we in turn forgive you'. (The confluence of 'Conscience' with 'The Manifest Religion' shows us *how* we both can and must return from the Hobbesian Terror to the civilly unequal struggle for liberty and equality, in a spirit of fraternity that rests on the clear awareness of our equal helplessness to avoid offence, and of our actual freedom to forgive one another in spite of that. Thus we can also maintain an equal respect for conscience in spite of its inevitable 'badness'.

This general recognition of 'freedom of conscience' can be institutionalized in our public life; and it *is* institutionalized in the modern state. Freedom of conscience cannot be 'perfect' according to *any* concept that conscience can form for itself, because the only conceptual 'perfection' possible here is the recognition that *imperfection is logically inevitable, and morally necessary*. The modern state is thus the only 'perfect' actuality that practical Reason can have, because life must always proceed all the way from the '*unwisdom*' of wealth (the pursuit of material or natural happiness) to the quest for the Hegelian kingdom of God. Free civil life is bound to contain injustice and inequality of opportunity, because neither 'justice' nor 'equality' can be defined in an uncontrovertibly mandatory way; and since our civil existence must contain the 'pursuit of happiness' (the freedom to define human happiness for oneself is the *foundation* of 'conscience'—in other words it is the very earth upon which Jesus once went round forgiving sins, and upon which alone He can be resurrected as the spirit of the community) the modern state necessarily contains the seeds of its own destruction. Whether those seeds will germinate into a struggle for life that finally destroys the ethical bond of our earthly City, philosophy cannot tell us; and the 'actual rationality' of this ignorance arises from the fact that the outcome here depends upon our free use of our own reason. Hegel knew that, far from being spiritually 'perfect', the bourgeois world is utterly 'without wisdom' in its worship of Mammon; and more than forty years before Marx, he saw and said both that the 'Wealth of Nations' is the angel of death for the nations, and that the abstract rationalization of *labour* (with an apparently consequent lightening of the burdens) destroys the concrete rationality of life as human *work*.

Fackenheim remarks that 'Hegel never despaired of the modern bourgeois, Protestant world'. I suspect that, existentially speaking, Hegel sometimes did despair just as—with so much more evident reason—I sometimes do. (For Hegel was a better social logician than I am, and hence much more farsighted, as my remarks about his early analysis of Adam Smith was designed to show). But despair is no more a philosopher's business than hope. The philosopher must look at 'what is' (in and for itself) and show what sort of rationality it actually has. Where the *Begriff* is in *stable equilibrium* its institutional actuality will have the rationality of charity, for the whole community will be agreed about it, and the spirit of mutual respect and forgiveness will make its perceived 'injustices' (various and conflicting as they must be from the different active standpoints that social life offers) bearable for all parties: but so far as the *Begriff* is *in motion* (or 'alienated' or 'for itself the opposite of itself') it will have only the rationality of justice—that is to say we shall be faced with a social *problem*, a conflict that is in the stage of 'judgement', but not yet resolved.[14] This is how the ongoing mechanization of society appeared to Hegel in his own time. He could only analyse the necessity of the process. If he did not despair, it was mainly because war, 'the judgement of God', was always present to save his world. He had seen a war of national preservation save the French Revolution from the egalitarian extremism of the Terror; then Napoleon went down to defeat in the second war—the war for the national salvation of Europe—leaving Hegel in a world that he compared to Imperial Rome because no spiritual star was visible. But he could expect still confidently that a war of national preservation would put things right in the godless conflict of bourgeoisie and proletariat, before the worship of Mammon destroyed the sanctuary of Absolute Spirit from which the new star would be recognized whenever it did finally arise.[15]

This is the only respect in which our situation has significantly developed since Hegel's time. Hegel would not have been surprised to see Jean Juarez and his socialist brothers (including Mussolini) turn into patriotic nationalist in 1914. He also would have been rightly proud of Benedetto Croce's defence of the cultural kingdom in which all are always brothers, and wrongly contemptuous of Bertrand Russell's resolute pacifism. But the awful 'motion of the Concept' from 1914 to 1945 has brought now to birth a world in which the 'rationalization of Labour' has given war quite a new functional meaning. I was nineteen when the bomb was dropped on Hiroshima—Hegel was nineteen when the Bastille fell. And I know that something cataclysmic had happened just as surely as he did. But the difference between us can be estimated from the fact that I did not see the relevance of Hiroshima to the Nuremberg trials then at all. That 'the waging of aggressive war' should be declared a 'crime against humanity' seemed to me absurd. (I then had not read Hegel, but I could see that 'the world's *history* is the court of judgement' without being told.) Yet I see not that the solemn confirma-

---

14. This failure to distinguish between these two levels of 'rationality' is the main reason why Charles Taylor is obliged to conclude that Hegel's ideal of systematic logical necessity cannot be reconciled with his ideal of free self-expression. The 'necessity' of Hegelian logic can only be, in Taylor's view, what Hegel himself calls 'the unbending righteous self-sameness' of Spirit as 'substance', see Hegel, G. W. F., *Phänomenologie des Geistes*, Johannes Hoffmeister (ed.), Hamburg, Meiner 1952, p. 314 [*Phenomenology of Spirit*, trans. A. V. Miller, Oxford, Clarendon Press, 1977, ¶ 439]. But *self-conscious* rationality—Spirit as *Subject* is the *Aufhebung* of this 'righteous self-sameness' in the *free use* of one's Reason. This involves the initial *irrationality* of following one's own 'conscience'—and it only gains a *substantial* rational ground in the community's recognition and forgiveness.

15. Perhaps he was more confident than he should have been. But the expulsion of the Turkish imperial power from Europe, the gradual advance of human rights in Russia, and the eventual downfall of the Russian and Austrian Empires in a war which ended in the proclamation of the Wilsonian principle of national self-determination, all seem to me to testify to the essential soundness of his claim that 'If we were to presuppose a ruler in Europe, who acted according to his whim, and took a notion to make half of his subjects slaves, we should be conscious that this would not work even though he were to use the most extreme force', *Geschichte der Philosophie, Einleitung*, Johannes Hoffmeister, 1940, p. 233—the passage comes from several student transcripts of 1823. In the world of superpowers, computers, and atomic war Hegel would be quick to recognize that the situation has changed. Practical Hegelianism in the shadow of *Nineteen Eighty-four* [1949 (transcriber's addition)] cannot be quite what it was in 1824.

tion of God's 'justice' upon Nazi Germany by a court of bourgeois judges was absolutely appropriate—though it was not the Nazis but their victorious judges who first waged war in a way that made it an evident crime against humanity. (The Nazis had enough genuine crimes against humanity on their conscience without that one, so there is and was—as I saw at the time—no need to be sorry for the leaders who were punished civilly.)

War is only 'the judgement of God' now, in the sense that a world war like the one that Hitler started would be the Last Judgement, literally. By making the Last Judgement present visibly as a technological achievement of our very own, we have driven God from his last vestige of a throne. It is now visibly we who sit in judgement upon ourselves in our history. Can the *Church of Reason*, whose true founder and only father was Hegel, control the *State of Reason* (which the men who followed Jesus, and ultimately Luther and the Reformers founded, but which took its sceptre of sovereign power from Bacon and the scientific Enlightenment)? The control has to be exercised through what Plato called the 'persuasion of necessity by Reason' because that is how the realm of natural necessity is organized into the world of rational freedom. I do not know, and *logically I know why I cannot know*, how our fate will turn out. But there are some relevant things that I do know about it. As a student of Hegel's ethics I can see that it is morally wrong to repine about the egalitarian aspirations of the underprivileged millions on this over-populated planet (as Mure does); and I understand why in the universal community which the economic and technological growth imperative of the scientific Enlightenment created, as the structural context of this problem of over-population, the possibilities of error and the penalties of failure are greater and more terrible than they were in the world of the national communities which 'the judgement of God' could purge and keep healthy by the periodic experience of warfare. The wars that are possible now, are exactly and only what that utilitarian, von Clausewitz, said war is: 'nothing but the prosecution of policy by other means'. A genuine life and death struggle must be avoided because it could prove altogether too final. Because of this Mure's gloomy forebodings about 'appeasement' and 'tyranny' may prove to be correct. But even that outcome will not show that Hegel ought to have despaired of the political world in which 'liberty, equality and fraternity' had for the first time become real possibilities. Rather it was his task to show (as he did), the *meaning* of liberty, the dialectical *ambivalence* of equality, and the *price* of fraternity—respect for the 'conscience' of the Vicar of Bray[16] is such an affront to 'good sense', and the Protestant 'earnestness', that Charles Taylor can suppose that Hegel is being ironic about it!

Philosophy cannot produce the millennium, or even guarantee its continuance supposing—*per impossible*—that it was to produce itself. Rather it is the case that, in the fullness of time (i.e. when we had gained a comprehensive grasp of

---

16. [Transcriber's note: From *The Oxford Encyclopedic English Dictionary*, Oxford, Clarendon Press, 1991—'The Vicar of Bray is the hero of an 18th century song who kept his benefice from the reign of Charles II to the reign of George I by changing his beliefs to suit the times. The song is apparently based on an anecdote of an identified vicar of Bray, Berkshire, in T. Fuller's *Worthies of England* (1662).']

what our rational freedom is and what it *must* aim at) philosophy could show us why there is no millennium. This is the 'self-positing Spirit whose essence is rational necessity' which Taylor says that no one nowadays can believe in. I say that, on the contrary, every rational person today is fully conscious of the negative presence of this spirit (as the *justice* of the 'fate' that we have yet to bring upon ourselves). Few of us have much confidence in its *saving* power, when we contemplate the appalling problems (and costs) of establishing any charitably endurable measure of social justice in the world community as a whole. But we do not therefore have to 'fly from the world'. Mure's claim that the world is already forty percent overpopulated is the measure of his deepest despair here. How can a Hegelian say that what is *ought not* to be, or a Christian borrow the answer of Cain?[17] Those who do not fly from the problem, but regard this despair as selfish and cowardly (as I do) merely see that the cycle of growth has somehow got to be stopped. To believe that *ought implies can* here is to admit the saving capacity of reason, to recognize the positive presence of the Spirit, its existence as moral necessity, i.e., as freedom and as charity It is not a very comfortable home that we have made for ourselves in this world. But the absolute philosophy is the one that shows us that it is our *home*, and that we are the ones who have built it. The only comfort that philosophy can add to its amenities must come from our understanding why it is idle to look for comfort in it. That insight is, indeed, as cold as any comfort Job was offered. But it remains nonetheless the *absolute* truth that '*Ich ist in der Welt zu Hause; wenn es sie kennt, noch mehr wenn es sie begriffen hat*'.[18]

---

17. [Editors' Note: In response to God's question 'where is Abel thy brother?' Cain replied 'Am I my brother's keeper?' Genesis 4:9]

18. [Editors' Note: 'I am at home in the world when I know it, still more so when I have understood it' (Hegel, *Philosophy of Right*, § 4A).]

*right and world*

# 3

# Dialectical Reason and Necessary Conflict: Understanding and the Nature of Terror

Angelica Nuzzo

> War is common and justice strife, and all things come about by way of strife and necessity
> —Heraclitus

> Wenn die Verbrechen sich häufen, werden sie unsichtbar
> —Bertold Brecht

Displaying the immanent structure of rational cognition, dialectic is the philosophical answer that Hegel envisions early on in his philosophical career for the epochal problem posed by the political aftermath of the French Revolution.[1] Dialectic is a strategy for understanding historical conflicts and the transformations that follow periods of deep historical crises such as the one that befalls Europe at the end of the eighteenth century. Viewed in this perspective, dialectic is the solution to the epistemological problem opened by the discontinuous reality of history—it is the key to Hegel's historical hermeneutic. Moreover, since dialectic articulates the inner structure of reason, and *Vernunft* is the framework in which the process of reality in its rationality is inscribed, reason and its dialectic development are ultimately one with the objective reality that philosophy takes on as its peculiar object. In a gesture that continues and radicalizes Kant's critical (self-) investigation of reason, for Hegel *Vernunft* is both organon of philosophical knowledge and its unique content. The actuality of reason is the dynamic field of tensions in which opposite forces are constantly at play; reason is the point of convergence of conflicts and the space of their inevitable resolution. The reality of reason is the reality of the process that produces historical transformations. Viewed in this perspective, dialectic is key to Hegel's understanding of history in the modern world.

---

1. I am grateful to David Kolb for his comments on an earlier version of this essay.

Central to this picture—which can easily be seen as summarizing Hegel's famous claim on the rationality of the actual and the actuality of the rational (PR Preface/W VII 24)—is the idea of change in all the different forms and figures that it can assume logically as well as historically. Since the beginning of Greek philosophy, the idea of change, transformation, and movement—in nature and in human affairs—has not ceased to pose fundamental difficulties to thinking; while the reflection on these difficulties has profoundly shaped the philosophical investigation in its methods, categories, and argumentations. Hegel's dialectical reason is the final answer to the ongoing problem troubling philosophical thinking from the inception of its history. How can the reality of change be thought of or brought to concepts without losing its essential dynamic nature? How can thinking articulate the connection between change and the contradiction that animates it?

These questions, however, do not yet address the problem in its entirety. Another issue must be taken into account. Hegel argues that thought necessarily transforms whatever it thinks. And since in philosophy thinking or reason takes rationality in its actual shapes as its content the philosophical problem of thinking change is ultimately the problem of a form of rationality capable of immanent self-transformation. Truth is not the conceptual grasp of a static object reflectively reproduced in the exact, fixed image yielded by thought. Indeed, this is the way understanding works but *Verstand* is ultimately unable to reach truth. In the form of *Nachdenken*, truth is rather the result of a fundamental 'alteration' (*Veränderung*) (EL § 22/W III 46) in the modality in which the object is given to thought as well as in the structure of the object itself. Once thought, the object is no longer the same; it is forever transformed. Or, alternatively, in thinking its object, thought already thinks something different than what it originally assumed as its content. Hegel's conclusion is that change itself is the true reality of thinking in its actuality—and this is dialectic. Thereby, Kant's transcendental constructivist turn is radicalized yet again by Hegel. He maintains that the object of philosophy is no other than 'the content that has been originally produced and is still being produced in the realm of living spirit and thereby shaped into the *world*—into the external and internal world of consciousness' (EL § 6 R). 'Self-conscious' reason, Hegel argues, is reason 'in its existence'—this equivalence exhausting the realm of what is real or rationally intelligible.[2] Accordingly, dialectic is the dynamic articulation of reason into the objectivity of a world.

But are all forms of thought capable of or indeed amenable to internal transformation, that is, ultimately, to dialectic comprehension? If rational cognition is cognition—and indeed most importantly re-cognition—of change (of historical transformation as well as of reason's own internal transformation), what is the place that Hegel's dialectic grants to the attitude of thought refusing to recognize or undergo change? What is the place that resistance to change or indeed resistance to dialectic comprehension has in Hegel's conception of reason? Or, to

---

2. EL § 6 R: 'selbstbewusste Vernunft' is 'seiende Vernunft.'

put the same point differently: Can we indicate something like an 'Un-Vernunft' (an anti-reason or a moment of 'unreasonableness of reason') operating within the framework of dialectical reason itself and aiming at erasing change and the contradictions that yield change? Clearly, granting the comprehensive, monistic structure of Hegel's system that ultimately follows from the systematic, monistic structure of reason, and granting the dialectic operation by which reason eventually reduces all otherness to itself, the issue that I am thereby raising regards neither the resistance to change that reason encounters on the way to its comprehension of actuality nor an alleged irrational 'rest' to be discovered within Hegelian reason. The search or the desire for a *caput mortuum* of dialectic (within or indeed without the dialectic process) has been the anti-Hegelian inspiration defining projects as different as Adorno's negative dialectic and various postmodern deconstructions. It is not, however, my present concern.[3]

What I am interested in is rather the possibility of bringing Hegelian reason and its dialectic structure to bear on some interesting and disconcerting traits of our present age—the shorthand for which can be indicated as resistance to change and normalization of conflict. The problem is the following: if dialectic logic arises for Hegel from the attempt to give a philosophical account of the fundamental character of the age following the French Revolution, namely, inexorable transformation, 'transition' to new, unknown organizations of the life of spirit, what is the account that this same logic can give of an epoch whose fundamental tendency is to erase change by normalizing it, to make it un-detectable by turning it into a widespread habit? If conflict is necessary, on Hegel's view, because historical transformation is necessary, in what sense is conflict (still) necessary when transformation is impeded and rendered utterly contingent? Does this opposition define a truly alternative scenario or do we rather face two sides of the same coin? How does the characterization of the *necessity* proper to conflict shift when we move from Hegel's to our own historical present?

In discussing these questions I shall proceed in two steps. First, I present Hegel's model of dialectical reason in its relation to un-dialectical thinking (or *Verstand*)—to the shortcomings that prevent it from grasping change and to its different attitudes toward contradiction. Hegel's dialectical reason is both the solution of an ongoing problem in the history of philosophy and the response to a challenge of world history. This latter point occupies the second section of this essay. Given that philosophy's task is the rational comprehension of the historical present, how does our historical present differ from Hegel's and what are the new tasks that our time poses to a philosophy that still wants to be dialectic? After all, the bicentenary of the *Phenomenology of Spirit* calls for a renewed reflection not only on Hegel's philosophy but also on the shape that the world, in which we find ourselves still reflecting on his dialectic, has assumed two hundred years later. Thus, in this section, I briefly outline what I take to be the characters of our historical epoch—characters that I consider relevant in relation to a renewed idea of Hege-

---

3. See also Angelica Nuzzo, 'The End of Hegel's Logic: Absolute Idea as Absolute Method,' in David G. Carlson (ed.), *Hegel's Theory of the Subject*, London, Palgrave Macmillan, 2005, pp. 187-205.

lian rationality. This is also the framework that leads me to assess the challenges that war and terrorism pose today to the project of dialectical reason. My claim is that terrorism is the overarching term summarizing resistance to change and erasure of contradiction, and that these are the forms that un-dialectical thinking assumes in our time. While Hegel's dialectic arises from a historical present that fully displayed contradiction and indeed suffered from it, we are now suffering from the menacing lack of contradiction—from a contradiction that is suffocated and rendered ineffectual. Thus, while reason, for Hegel, has the incumbent task of bringing the 'growing contradiction' of his age to concepts, the challenge of reason in our time it to install contradiction in an indifferent reality and to make consciousness feel it, thereby showing that change is still possible if not necessary. Indeed, for reasons that will emerge from my analysis but curiously never appear in the discussion of such a long-standing topic of many Hegel interpretations, we are now closer than ever before to the risk of an 'end of history'—rooted, as it were, in a possible 'end of reason'. This renders the need for dialectical reason now more pressing than ever before.

## I. GRASPING CHANGE: THE HISTORICAL PROBLEM OF DIALECTICAL REASON

### *Dialectic is Movement: Zeno's Arrow and Heraclitus' Flux*

'War is common and justice strife and all things come about by way of strife and necessity' reads a famous fragment by Heraclitus.[4] On his view, constant transformation constitutes the very essence of reality, the principle to which nothing existing escapes. Change, however, is generated by strife, i.e., by the clash of opposites and their coexistence. To this extent conflict is not only necessary but is promoted to the dignity of a first metaphysical principle next to necessity itself. Opposing Pythagoras who proposed the ideal of a peaceful and harmonious universe as well as Anaximander who saw the warfare of opposites as outright injustice, Heraclitus identifies strife and its necessity with justice. Contradiction does not lead to chaos but to a just order that is the order of universal transformation. Schiller's aphorism, which Hegel takes up in his idea of world-history, has after all a pre-Socratic root: *Weltgeschichte* is *Weltgericht* (PR § 340) because change is strife and strife is justice. Ultimately, Hegel's rejection of Kant's ideal of perpetual peace has the same metaphysical motivation as Heraclitus' polemic stance toward Pythagoras. Contradiction determines the ongoing movement of the historical process the justice of which lies in its self-regulating development.

Significantly, for Heraclitus, change is something that only thought can grasp, while it remains inexplicable (and even undetectable) to the senses. *Gutta cavat lapidem*: for the senses there is no evidence of change in the inexorable corrosion of the stone by the drop of water; the ever-changing river appears to sense perception always the same river. But it is not the same. Thinking grasps the real-

---

4. Heraclitus, B80.

ity of change by grasping its underlying unity or rather its regularity—its *metron* or measure. Thereby Heraclitus solves the paradox that paralyzed Zeno leaving his arrow suspended in an unreal movement, truly, in an unsolvable contradiction. For Heraclitus thinking but not the senses can master contradiction and the movement it engenders. Plato reads a different lesson into Heraclitus' verses and draws from them a different conclusion. He overturns the terms of Heraclitus' problem. Seeing the reality of change confined to the world of the senses (when Heraclitus only tells us that the senses are unable to grasp it), and claiming that knowledge and thinking are only of unmoved, eternal forms (when Heraclitus claims that only thinking can account for the flux of change), Plato concludes that true knowledge of the sensible world is impossible because truth is foreign to it. Since all sensible things are forever flowing, thinking takes refuge in a world itself spared of change.

It is well known that Hegel's presentation of the history of philosophy in its Greek beginnings follows the development of dialectic from its merely subjective forms in the Eleatic school to the recognition of its objectivity in Heraclitus. However, the interpretation of Hegel's position in this regard generally fails to see the crucial point consisting in the essential thematic connection between dialectic and the question of movement. For Hegel, the problem of dialectic is identical with the problem of how change, movement, and the contradiction that brings it about can be grasped in thought. The advancement of dialectic is measured by the position that thinking assumes toward transformation. The issue is whether change is placed in reality or in thinking itself, i.e., in the object or in the subject. For, dialectic is the 'movement of the concept in itself' (W XVIII 295). Significantly, Hegel's argument explains why historically dialectic has met the problem of change as its first and foremost issue. The reason is 'that dialectic is itself this movement or that movement is itself the dialectic of all things' (W XVIII 305). Dialectic and movement are identical. To think movement is to perform movement; is to accept the necessity of thinking through contradictions and in contradictions. This is Hegel's solution of the most original problem in the history of philosophy.

Ultimately, the fact that dialectic itself changes and assumes different forms, hence has a history, is a corollary of Hegel's identification between dialectic and the movement of the concept. Moreover, the philosophical problem of change converges with the issue of how thinking can apprehend its own reality in concepts—a reality that is necessarily subject to change since it is fundamentally historical. As Hegel points out in the preface to the *Philosophy of Right*, despite his search for an unmoved ideality beyond Heraclitus' world of continuous flux, even Plato does not escape this general fate of philosophy. His ideal state is not the portrait of an unmoved idea but the account of a historical moment of crisis and inner transformation in Greek ethical life (PR Preface, W VII 24).

In presenting Heraclitus's philosophy in his *Lectures on the History of Philosophy*, Hegel famously exclaims: 'Here we finally see land'. And he adds: 'There is not a single proposition in Heraclitus that I have not taken up in my logic'

(W XVIII 320). Why is Heraclitus so important in the history of philosophy in general, and for Hegel's own speculative logic in particular? On Hegel's account, Heraclitus solves the *impasse* that paralyzes Zeno's thought in his efforts to deny movement or alternatively to claim that movement as such cannot be thought. What is most relevant, however, is that Hegel puts quite some efforts to make an additional (and not immediately evident) point—a point that interrupts the historical sequence to bring us unexpectedly to Hegel's present. By suggesting that in his antinomies Kant does nothing more than what Zeno has already done with his contradictory propositions or paradoxes (W XVIII 317f), Hegel institutes an important historical parallel. Zeno and Kant on the one hand, Heraclitus and Hegel on the other: the dynamic of dialectical reason solves the static *impasse* of an un-dialectical understanding unable to grasp change and hence stuck in a dead antinomic opposition. In dealing with this ancient phase of philosophy's history Hegel is actually touching on one of the most urgent contemporary issues. How can change (logical, natural as well as historical) be comprehended in concepts? How can logic advance beyond the stalemate between being and nothing, and become, as it were, logic of the real world (or logic of 'objective thinking')? Heraclitus's thesis of the flux of all things is the 'land' on which dialectic finally installs itself.[5] Once it is thought through, the movement of becoming leads to the determinate beginning of dialectic with *Dasein* (See WL W V 113).

Zeno's starting point is the realization that the representation of movement implies contradiction. Movement expresses both the contradiction in the concept and the reality of contradiction; it is contradiction posited as appearance in reality (in time and space) (See W XVIII 307). From this claim Zeno's attempt to a refutation of movement follows. He rightly separates thinking from sense perception. He argues that what is in movement according to the senses does not move according to thinking—in thought the flying arrow is inexorably still. And truth is only in thinking. Hence movement cannot be thought. This conclusion runs opposite to the one reached by Heraclitus (movement exists only for thinking and not for the senses) and already announces the eternal world of Platonic forms.

Hegel's comment on Zeno's conclusion reveals his own solution of the problem of dialectic as immanent movement of the concept: 'It is necessary to think movement so as Zeno thought of it', namely, as something internally contradictory, as the reality of contradiction. And yet, he adds, 'it is necessary to *further bring movement* into this position of movement (*dies Setzen der Bewegung*)' (W XVIII 311 my emphasis). Thinking must learn how to perform movement, how to transform itself. The thought of movement must itself be moving, must embrace the dynamic of the object it thinks.

Thereby Hegel announces the program of his own dialectic-speculative logic. The crucial transformation introduced by his logic over and against traditional *Verstandeslogik* (which includes, in Hegel's critique, formal as well as transcendental logic) regards the method by which the logical development is build as immanent,

---

5. See W V 84 Hegel's comment on Heraclitus with regard to the moment of 'Becoming' in the *Science of Logic*.

self-moving thought-process. The method consists in 'calling to life [...] the dead limbs of logic through spirit' (W V 48). In traditional logic, since the categories 'as fixed determinations fall outside one another and are not held together in organic unity, they are dead forms that do not have in themselves the spirit which alone constitutes their living unity' (W V 41). On Hegel's critique, the categories of formal and transcendental logic are dead, unmoved forms—they have the same status as those political and juridical institutions of the *ancien régime* from which life has forever departed. Their consecrated authority is no longer authority over men's lives or guarantee of meaningfulness in relation to lived practices and cognition. In their dead fixity and unmoved abstract existence, they are nothing but meaningless and useless relics of a long gone past. Hence, in order to claim new meaning to logical form, contradiction and movement must be introduced in pure thinking. Contrary to the traditional view, categories should be seen as 'moments' of an ongoing, fluid process in which they are bound to modify their meaning, to interact with and contradict one another, and finally to constitute the organic unity of a whole.[6] The 'spirit' that alone is able to show the living meaningfulness, that is, the 'actuality' of logical thinking is the force of contradiction, the dynamism labouring on within the process (See also W III 46).

The foregoing look at the history of philosophy makes it clear that the logic of the understanding is flawed, for Hegel, on different counts all going back to its fundamental inability to grasp the movement of contradiction. In addition, that discussion recognizes that such logic has been operative throughout the history of philosophy—from the early Eleatic school up to Kant. On this basis, two further questions must be raised. The first regards the role that the understanding maintains for Hegel once dialectical reason has curbed its structural deficiency and instituted the immanent development of thinking. This is a question that allows for a relatively easy and short answer. The second issue, on the contrary, is much more difficult to address as it leads into the territory of 'speculation' (in the Kantian more than Hegelian sense). However, already by articulating this question we can gain some insight into the role that dialectic may play in our contemporary world. Can one read Hegel's position as claiming that the understanding's un-dialectical logic is defeated once and for all as it is brought under the power of dialectical reason? Or shall we suggest, on the contrary, that the understanding, under specific historical conditions, catching reason off guard so to speak (and maybe exploiting a moment of reason's '*Ohnmacht*')[7] can presumably resume its work displaying yet again its inability to grasp change and even, this time, obstructing real movement and transformation? I will address this latter problem in the next section. Now I turn to a brief discussion of the first point, which, however, I bend already in the direction of the more speculative question.

---

6. I have developed this point in 'Vagueness and Meaning Variance in Hegel's Logic,' forthcoming.

7. The idea of an 'Ohnmacht der Vernunft' can be construed in analogy to the 'Ohnmacht der Natur' in EPN § 250 R and W XI 282.

## Understanding and the Power of Reason

In the conclusion of the '*Vorbegriff*' of the 1830 *Encyclopaedia*, at the end of the general introduction to his speculative logic, Hegel presents three sides of '*das Logische*'—form and content of the incipient discipline of logic. These moments are '(a) the abstract or intellectual (*verständige*), (b) the dialectic or negative-rational (*negativ-vernünftige*), (c) the speculative or positive-rational (*positiv-vernünftige*)' (EL § 79, R). To prevent misinterpretations, Hegel warns us to consider these 'sides' as 'moments of every logical-real formation (*jedes Logisch-Reelle*[*n*])', that is, of every concept and of every truth', not as three distinct 'parts' of the logic itself. Thereby, Hegel makes two different points. First, these three sides do not belong to the logic or the logical element alone. Their validity is much more general, since they are aspects of every reality, every concept, and every truth.[8] Second, they are not to be considered in a succession as offering an anticipation of partition and indicating different parts of the logical discipline. Rather, they coexist in all real formations and are distinct only logically; their status is specifically that of 'moments' of a dynamic process not of static 'parts' of a given whole.

Reduced to '*das Verständige*', the understanding is now fully integrated within the structure and method of Hegel's logic; it is a function or indeed a moment of the broader process of reason. What characterizes this moment is its holding fast to 'fixed determinateness' and to its 'distinction (*Unterschiedenheit*)' against its other. This procedure is now recognized as necessary within the development of each logical-real form. Hegel's point, however, is that although the understanding's fixation of determination is necessary, this moment, being simply a moment, is also necessarily overcome by the specifically dialectical gesture of the 'transition into the opposite' that belongs to reason. There is a contradiction in the understanding's procedure whereby the intellectual abstract moment is lead beyond itself consenting to its own inner *Aufhebung*. As determination is fixed and isolated from the process of reality, it becomes pure indeterminateness because it looses any real possibility of distinction against other. The procedure of fixation is self-defeating; meaning is achieved only in the 'transition' to the opposite (EL § 81). If the problem of dialectic is the problem of grasping change, this is possible only by daring to perform the transition to one's opposite, that is, by taking change upon oneself (as form and not only as content of thinking). This, however, is the first, negative moment of reason: understanding yields to reason or becomes itself reasonable recognizing how untenable its position is. Understanding consents to transform itself into reason. Finally, the positive moment of rationality constitutes the unity of the opposites, the basis of which is precisely that same transition achieved by the negative moment of reason (EL § 82).

Thus, in Hegel's logic, dialectic-speculative reason grasps transformation by leading the understanding to perform the transition into the opposite. The under-

---

8. And notice the insistence on that distributive 'jedes.' This passage is paralleled by the claim that at the end of the logic the absolute idea is established as coextensive with 'all truth' (see A. Nuzzo, 'The End of Hegel's Logic').

standing, on its part, is entirely amenable to such transition. It does not remain fixed to its conceptual untenable fixations but itself consents to the transition into the opposite. Understanding is already defeated or alternatively persuaded by reason and reduced to moment—*das Verständige*. But why is the understanding so easily subjugated to reason; why does it so easily consent to become reasonable and perform the transition to the opposite? After all, this is not what happened in Zeno's or even in Kant's case. To put this point differently: what kind of *necessity* governs the articulation of the three sides of 'every logical-real formation'?

One possible answer is that the understanding, at this point, namely, at the threshold of the logic, has gone through the *Phenomenology of Spirit*, whose result is precisely the standpoint of pure thinking or the element of the logic ('Absolute Knowing').[9] And in pure thinking all 'opposition of consciousness' (W V 43, 57; see also 67f.) has been finally eliminated. Throughout the phenomenological path the understanding has exhausted all its objections to reason (or truth); its opposition is consequently also eliminated. Skepticism has finally turned against itself. But the *Phenomenology* has also presented the succession of spirit's historical figures thereby leading to Hegel's present (and to its final, reflective 'recollection' or *Erinnerung*). This is precisely the historical standpoint that Hegel endorses in the preface to the work.[10] Thus, the systematic standpoint of the logic beyond the opposition of consciousness is also, at the same time, the historical standpoint of Hegel's present—the viewpoint that finally allows for a rational comprehension of the historical change brought forth by the turmoil of 1789 and felt as immediate evidence (*bekannt*) by everyone. At this point in Hegel's system and at this point in history the understanding must yield to the power of reason becoming a consenting 'moment' of its development.

This consideration entails another possible answer to the question of why, in the logic, the understanding yields so easily (or necessarily) to reason: historically, the power of reason—*Macht der Vernunft*—has become too strong to be defied by the understanding's opposition. Indeed, for Zeno and even for Kant reason was still too weak and impotent to sustain the force of contradiction. Blocked by the antinomies, Kantian reason is for Hegel nothing more than understanding. Reason has not yet appeared as an independent, overarching force.

According to these two arguments, the necessity that connects the three sides of every *Logisch-Reelles* is both systematic and historical necessity. Hegel, however, is the first to outline the possibility of a different scenario. While underscoring the mutual dependence of the three sides of every 'logical-real formation', Hegel makes room for the possibility that 'they all be placed under the first moment, *das Verständige*, and hence considered in isolation', and consequently not in their truth. This happened already in traditional logic.[11] But Hegel does not seem to limit this possibility to something that took place in the past. The passage suggests

---

9. See Angelica Nuzzo, 'The Truth of "absolutes Wissen" in Hegel's "Phenomenology of Spirit"', in A. Denker (ed.), *Hegel's Phenomenology of Spirit*, Amherst, Humanities Press, 2003, pp. 265-294.

10. See *Erinnerung* respectively in W III 591 and 19.

11. And Kant was indeed the first to notice that traditional formal logic was not a logic of truth.

that it is always possible that the first moment may take the upper hand, thereby blocking the development of contradiction, the 'transition' to the opposite, and the access to truth. Hegel does also recognize figures and forms of life in which the understanding has become autonomous and has refused to yield to the (not yet so strong) power of reason. Skepticism (EL § 81 A), irony, and the terror of the French Revolution are different examples thereof.

The question is now whether systematically after the *Phenomenology* and the Logic, and historically after Hegel's time, we can think of situations in which the understanding refuses to be reduced to a moment or function of reason's dialectical development, refuses to yield to the contradiction that its fixations produce, and hence makes the crucial 'transition to the opposite' and the constitution of the 'unity' and truth of the opposites impossible for reason to achieve. If this were the case, the *necessity* of the immanent development linking the three sides of all logical-real form would be challenged, and the task of dialectical reason stand in need of important revisions. In this case, a new 'phenomenology of spirit' would be needed to restore the dialectical relation between understanding and reason under new systematic and historical conditions. Finally, notice that the *Macht* or alternatively *Ohnmacht*—of reason or nature—is measured by the capacity to hold fast to the necessity of the concept not allowing contingency to infiltrate its self-development. History is the sphere in which the development of spirit is constantly (and indeed necessarily) met by natural contingency.

The argument has now led us to our second issue.

## II. A DIFFERENT PRESENT: DIALECTICAL REASON, NON-DIALECTICAL UNDERSTANDING, AND THE NATURE OF TERROR

If we read Hegel's solution of the pre-Socratic problem of movement in light of the famous claim of the preface to the *Philosophy of Right* concerning the specific nature of philosophical discourse, we arrive at the same conclusion but we can capture an additional dimension of the argument. Hegel's dialectic arises out of the need to propose a different logic than traditional *Verstandeslogik* because such logic cannot 'see' or grasp conflict, contradiction, and hence historical change. And since these are fundamental features of the modern world, understanding is incapable of giving an account of the dimension of the *Gegenwart*—the historical present or actuality of the world. Thus, if philosophy's task is indeed the comprehension of the *Gegenwart*, that is, the translation of its own time in living thoughts,[12] philosophy becomes impossible under the premises of traditional logic. On Hegel's view, the problem is further complicated by the contradiction that he detects right at the heart of the workings of the understanding: while incapable of comprehending the change produced by conflict, the understanding reveals itself a source of conflict. The understanding is (at least in part) responsible for the problem that it is unable to solve. As shown above, the solution to the understanding's *impasse* is Hegel's idea of *dialectical reason*. *Verstand* is brought

---

12. W VII 26: 'Philosophie ist ihre Zeit in Gedanken erfasst.'

to reason: its autarchic isolation is overcome, and *Verstand* is transformed into '*das Verständige*', into an immanent necessary moment of the development of reason.

Now I want to push this thesis a step further. I shall do so by contextualizing the question of Hegel's dialectic within *our* contemporary world. If the necessity for understanding to yield to reason or to become reasonable by performing the transition into the opposite is (at least in part) historical necessity, the (speculative) question arises of how the understanding may behave under different historical conditions. Under changing historical conditions, understanding may become again an unyielding, resisting power against reason. In this perspective, the argument leads to a philosophical account of *our* historical present and of the new challenges that philosophy faces in *our* time.

It is in this framework that I shall address the question raised above: Can we think of historical situations in which the understanding is no longer so submissive to reason's power or alternatively reason is no longer so powerful as to bend understanding to its dialectic—situations in which the understanding isolates itself again, monopolizing all moments of every logical-real formation, blocking the access to truth,[13] and presenting reason with a renewed opposition? Would this opposition require a new 'phenomenology of contemporary spirit' to allow dialectical reason to resume its work?

## *1807: The 'Need' for a Phenomenology of Spirit*

At the beginning of the new century, Hegel turns to the fossilized world of the *ancient régime* in which the unmoved 'positivity' of old institutions and forms of life is exploded by the irrepressible contradiction at work within reality. It is this contradiction that ushers in the necessity of a new organization of the life of spirit—the birth of a new age. The fragment 'Der immer sich vergrössernde Widerspruch …',[14] probably composed between 1799 and 1800 and placed by many editors at the beginning of Hegel's *Constitution of Germany*, offers at the same time a philosophical diagnosis of the historical crisis faced by Germany at the end of the eighteenth century, and the first emergence of the fundamental terms of his dialectic logic. The philosophical question that Hegel raises herein is: What is change? How shall the philosopher conceptualize the moment of historical transition, the unrest that everyone feels as prevailing dimension of the present, the necessary 'pull' (*Trieb, Drang*) toward the unknown and the new which one must grasp and embrace to be able to survive its unstoppable affirmation? Indeed, unlike the dead fixation of life in 'positive' institutional forms and in their destructive contradictions, the contradiction that shapes transformative processes is the condition of survival—both individual and collective, both personal and national. For the latter contradiction bears within itself the possibility of a way out, that is, the condition of a new beginning. It is relevant to our present ques-

---

13. As Hegel argues in the commented passage of EL § 79 R.
14. In GW V 16-18—with regard to the period of its composition and its editorial history, see the remarks by M. Baum and K.R. Meist.

tion that Hegel distinguishes the destructive and blocked contradiction of the 'positive' from (dialectic) contradiction that moves on toward new (although not necessarily better) developments.

'Der immer sich vergrössernde Widerspruch ...' offers Hegel's philosophical diagnosis of a period of radical change, the phenomenology of a historical crisis, and the assessment of the different directions in which such crisis may develop and resolve. Significantly, however, Hegel does not point to any guaranteed solution to the 'growing contradiction'. Insecurity and the striving for the unknown remain the prevailing tone,[15] the predicament of the age. The fragment indicates in the 'growing contradiction' and the 'need' for its '*Aufhebung*' (GW V 16-17) or '*Widerlegung*' (GW V 18)—its overcoming and refutation—the (logical) structure of change (GW V 16-17). Herein we meet already the fundamental terms of Hegel's dialectic. Contradiction is a real force operating in history; is a force moved by its own inner development. The tension catalyzed in contradiction is the mark of an epoch in which all certainty and security has been shattered and the only hope of survival lies in the acceptance of transformation, in the capacity of facing the negativity in which life is immersed. Knowledge by itself cannot effect transformation although it may be one of the conditions thereof. And not even a pure act of the 'will' (be it individual or collective), nor a social contract or mere revolutionary 'violence' (GW V 16-17) can bring about change. Rather, Hegel seems to suggest that transformation lies somehow in the nature of things, in the inner contradiction that animates the present time once the obstacles to its radicalization and free development are removed and contradiction is let grow to its extreme consequences without being fixated into an unmoved 'absolute' (GW V 16). Contradiction is a force independent of human cognition and will; is the force within which all human activity is rather inscribed. Only 'nature', namely, the recognition and expression of real needs and desires can lead to the articulation and solution of the growing contradiction.[16] Change takes place as contradiction gives raise to a 'need' and thereby to the movement of its own 'refutation'. For, the need that contradiction be overcome—a need that arises once life has met pure negativity and recognized that it can no longer live with it and in it—is already in itself change (GW V 17).

In the 1801 *Differenzschrift*, Hegel famously reflects on the 'need for philosophy' generated by the historical situation of '*Entzweiung*' produced by the fixations of the understanding. Consciousness lives undoubtedly in the 'fractured harmony' of a Heraclitean universe (GW IV 12). Yet, the task of philosophy is not to restore a Pythagorean cosmos. It is rather to recuperate the force of contradiction that has been expelled by that fractured world and engulfed in the positivity of dead forms. Contradiction must become the living force of spirit. 'The task of philosophy consists [...] in positing being and not-being as becoming; in positing separation in the absolute as its appearance; in positing the finite in the infinite as

---

15. See also the 'Unbekannte(s)' in W III 18.
16. See R. Bodei, *Scomposizioni. Forme dell'individuo moderno*, Torino, Einaudi, 1987, p. 19.

life' (GW IV 16). This is, once again, Heraclitus' problem.

In 1807, in the preface to the *Phenomenology of Spirit* Hegel directly addresses his contemporaries. It is to them that he can indeed say that '*it is not difficult to see* that our time is a time of birth and transition to a new epoch' (W III 18 my emphasis)—it is not difficult to see because life provides immediate evidence for this claim in lived, uncontroversial facts. Since the 'growing contradiction' is not the result of philosophical speculation but a hard fact in everybody's life, such contradiction 'is not difficult to see'. Yet, Hegel famously warns that what is known to common sense is still not conceptually grasped, is not yet philosophical knowledge.[17] Far from it: what is most easily seen, felt, and lived in its immediate certainty, is the hardest thing to grasp conceptually, is the real challenge to philosophy. This is precisely the task to be undertaken: to give conceptual, rational form to the mere feeling, perception or indeed 'experience' of change. It is the same problem that Zeno faced in a more abstract form. In the *Phenomenology*, Hegel provides a logic of change that takes consciousness as its concrete object, i.e., as the place in which change occurs and becomes visible as concrete experience.[18] The accepted and indeed unquestionable presupposition is the reality of the historical transformations brought about by the French Revolution—the shattered, fractured reality lived by everyone as that which 'is not difficult to see'. The challenge—or what is instead quite difficult to see—is the philosophical meaning of such presupposition, the meaning that contradiction reveals when translated into speculative concepts.

## 2007: The 'Need for Philosophy' Two Hundred Years Later

But how does philosophical knowledge confront the historical situation in which the presupposition that informs common sense—or indeed the 'spirit of the age'—is quite a different one as now it becomes very difficult even to see or feel that transformation is underway, that contradiction may interrupt the homogeneous surface of everyday life? How can a philosophy that still wants to be dialectic take on the challenge of an epoch that does not show the discontinuity of a revolutionary transition to the unknown new but rather continuous repetition of the same, not *Entzweiung* but (illusory) homogenization of difference and normalization of conflict? What form does change and the philosophical comprehension of change assume in this different setting? Is a 'need for philosophy' still felt? This situation is indeed different from Hegel's. Now the normality of habit does not allow contradiction to 'grow' and hence to produce the 'need' for it to be overcome and refuted. Contradiction cannot be pinpointed; it is so diffuse (or globalized, as it were) that being everywhere it is really nowhere.

Thus, very generally, I shall characterize our age in opposition to Hegel's as

---

17. See the claim in W III 35: 'Das Bekannte überhaupt ist darum, weil es *bekannt* ist, nicht *erkannt*.' The claim is repeated in the preface to the second edition of the *Science of Logic* with regard to the pervasiveness of logical form (W V 22).

18. EL § 25 R; W V 49: in the *Phenomenology* Hegel has offered an 'example' of the logical method 'on a more concrete object, namely, consciousness.'

an age that aims at normalizing conflict and change by neutralizing them into habituation, and at dissolving them by making them all-pervasive. This, in turn, is clearly a corollary of the process of globalization in which contradictions are progressively erased (not solved) and flattened out for the sake of the common, homogenizing imperative of economic profit. This premise sustains, among other things, the troubling idea of terrorism as perpetual state of war to which, in turn, a perpetual war ought to be waged—the two ideas becoming conceptually interchangeable and only politically distinct. The global strife presently designated 'terrorism' is the figure that conflict takes when it becomes so indistinct and indeterminate (in the identification of the 'enemy' as well as in space and time) as to lose the dialectic force that conflicts traditionally have had in producing change through their eventual resolution (in reality as well as in consciousness). Terrorism is indeterminate negation. In its indeterminacy, it refuses any relation to the other—the enemy has no face but may assume any face; it is nowhere in particular because it is a globalized force to be found everywhere; its conflicts extend with no end in time.

By blurring the distinction that sharply opposes 'war' and 'peace' as mutually excluding concepts, terrorism replaces the historical process that ought to negotiate between them—leading from one state to the other by effecting the dialectic 'transition' between them—with an indistinct continuum that resembles the bad infinite reproducing itself or the blocked progression of Zeno's paradoxes. In replacing the contradiction between war and peace, terrorism intends to defy change by positing itself as an indeterminate state with no opposites. Notice that the contradiction is here replaced not solved: in its indeterminateness, the concept of terrorism is not the product of dialectical *Aufhebung*; it is neither the final result of the development of a given contradiction nor the beginning of a new process. On the contrary, the concept of terrorism marks the alternative development imposed by the non-dialectic logic of the understanding whereby contradiction is suffocated by an engulfing indeterminateness and flattened out on an indistinct, uninterrupted surface. Instead of moving on to a higher level in which the opposites (war and peace) receive a new meaning, terrorism marks the regress to a stage in which opposites are simply indistinguishable in their merging into one another (terrorism and counter-terrorism, war and peace). Under these premises, the movement of dialectic logic cannot properly begin. Thinking is stuck in the indeterminateness of being-nothing, unable to unfold the contradiction that necessarily leads to determination. In its isolation, 'becoming' as immediate merging or vanishing of the opposites into each other (W V 83) is nothing more than Zeno's frozen movement that cannot properly—that is, dialectically—advance. The moments of becoming, observes Hegel, 'reciprocally paralyze each other (*paralysieren sich gegenseitig*)' (W V 112).[19] Dialectic advancement is transition to the determination of *Dasein*. Yet, globalization is a virtual state that abstracts from *Dasein*, while terrorism is the globalized war that escapes determination in

---

19. See also W V 113: 'Das Werden ist eine haltungslose Unruhe, die in ein ruhiges Resultat zusammensinkt.'

space and time.

How shall dialectical reason construe its response to the normalizing logic of the understanding? I suggest that it is incumbent on a new 'phenomenology of spirit' to expose the un-dialectical strategy of the understanding in its use of the figure of 'terrorism', and to articulate the response to its avoidance of conflict by producing new forms of valid determination and opposition within the indistinct surface of the globalized world—new forms of localisms but also new forms of global movements alternative to the merely economic ones.

Hegel's critique of the logic of *Verstand* targets the isolation of opposites that are thereby prevented from clashing together and consequently from displaying their higher unity. Currently we see a variation of this strategy at play: the opposites are merged into one another creating an indistinct blur that displays no meaning. No higher unity is possible on this premise but only the forceful substitution of a new arbitrary term. Instead of taking on the challenge of contradiction—the pain of negativity and the 'labor of the concept'—this logic steers away from it with a reverse process that moves from determination back into indeterminateness. Instead of keeping the opposites apart, understanding denies them even the status of opposites by merging them together and erasing all distinction. *Verwirrung* replaces conflict.[20] Contradiction does not receive solution. It simply 'evaporates (*ist verflüchtigt*)' as Hegel aptly observes of the ironic attitude with regard to the opposition of good and evil: good and evil 'do not contradict themselves because all determination and particularization evaporates' (PR § 140 handwritten remark/W VII 280). Contradiction evaporates and is replaced by the complacency of arbitrary substitutions. Terrorism and globalization are examples of such logic of substitution. As such, they should be viewed as shapes or *Gestalten* of a phenomenology of the contemporary world.

What is the function of dialectical reason in a historical situation so configured?[21] In this framework, the chief task of a philosophy that still wants to be dialectical is that of *producing* conflict, of *generating* contradiction against the normalizing work of the understanding, of conferring visibility to contradiction not only at the level of philosophical knowledge but also at the level of common consciousness. Reason should make contradiction felt, should sharpen the opposites as opposites, and reveal them as such to consciousness. The necessity of conflict and hence of transformation must be brought to the fore against the stalling, paralyzing forces of habituation and complacency. Unlike in Hegel's time when reason had (only) to grasp conceptually a change easily detectable by everyone and impenetrable only to the sclerotic *Verstandeslogik*, dialectical reason has now

---

20. Interestingly, Hegel characterizes Socratic irony as '*Verwirrung* rather than solution' of conflict, see PR § 140 handwritten remark/W VII 280.

21. In her 1981 Tanner Lecture on Human Values, 'The Essential Gesture: Writers and Responsibility', (Michigan, University of Michigan, 1981) Nadine Gordimer distinguishes the situations of countries such as South Africa and Nicaragua where 'conflict' is dictating the writer her responsibility, from countries 'where complacency, indifference, accidie and not conflict threaten the human spirit', p. 15. In the latter case, the conflict must be generated with other means.

the additional task of *producing* contradiction for consciousness within a reality whose appearance seems to erase all conflict.

The crucial issue regards the relationship between dialectical reason and an understanding that aims at dissolving contradictions by creating the illusion of normality and continuity. The problem no longer concerns a *Verstand* that cannot see the change that is under everyone's eyes or comprehend the discontinuity that is clearly perceptible within everyone's life—the *bekannt* that is not *erkannt*. Historical discontinuity is now swallowed up by the normality of a seeming continuity with old ways of life; contradiction is erased even at the level of the *bekannt* as the 'positive' reveals unexpected ways of surviving and of taking on new meanings.

In our historical present differences, conflicts, and tensions are rendered inoperative as they are rendered indeterminate. If it is not clear what is the opposite to be negated, negation is no longer *determinate* negation. But if negation loses its determinateness against a specific other, it also loses its rational meaning falling back into merely abstract negation—anything can be considered 'other'. The process of transformation is interrupted—at least until contradiction is allowed to surface or, as Hegel puts it, to 'grow' again. When contradiction is erased before it is able to display the inner tension that unites the opposites, contradiction can no longer be solved. *Verschwinden* of contradiction is not its dialectic *Aufhebung*. It is rather the weakening of dialectic. In this situation, dialectical reason must take on an additional task. It is incumbent on it to counter the dissolving power of the understanding, and to *produce* or *posit* in reality and in consciousness the contradictions that must then be rationally grasped. The 'opposition of consciousness' should be revived precisely as opposition to the lack of opposition, as opposition to widespread indifference. What this means is that a new phenomenology of spirit is now needed in order for dialectic (or dialectic logic) to fulfill its task of comprehension of our historical *Gegenwart*.

To explore the different ways that dialectical reason has to produce contradiction is the further objective of a new 'phenomenology of spirit'. Reason can reveal, by way of deeper analysis, the underlying opposition of forces that understanding tries to mask; it can uncover the lack of contradiction as mere illusion (*Schein*) or powerful ideology; it can create new, unprecedented obstacles to stand against what previously appeared an uninterrupted continuum; it should always aim for conceptual determination against indeterminateness of meaning.

In inscribing the revolutionary terror of 1790 in his *Phenomenology of Spirit*, Hegel characterizes the figure of 'terror' (*Schrecken*) precisely as the 'Furie des Verschwindens' (W III 435f). Terror is the culminating act of universal, abstract freedom. The logic of terror is significantly described as the opposite of dialectic logic (and yet, as such, as one of its figures). Terror is absence of mediation, is negation that in its sheer abstraction aims at the blind and arbitrary dissolution of all determinateness as such. With this figure, spirit falls back into the loss of all meaning proper to a 'meaningless death' (W III 439). But what happens when the terror that defies dialectical thinking instead of a distinct figure or 'moment' within spirit's development is normalized into the pervasive dimension of spirit's historical present? How can such abstract, unmediated negation be in turn meaningfully overcome by dialectical reason?

This is the point in which we presently find ourselves—historically as well as philosophically. This is the open challenge that the present time offers to philosophical thinking. Although I cannot indicate the solution to the problem that our epoch poses to dialectical reason, I can anticipate that from it the very existence of reason depends. We are probably closer than ever before to the 'euthanasia of reason' that Kant saw as a concrete possibility opened up by the antinomies.[22] Hegel's dialectic was the strong response to the *impasse* of a reason still behaving like understanding and trapped in its self-generated antinomies. How can dialectic undermine, today, the efforts of a resurgent unreasonable understanding?

---

22. Immanuel Kant, *Critique of Pure Reason*, trans. Paul Guyer and Allen Wood, New York, Cambridge, 1998, B433.

# 4

# Hegel Today: Towards a Tragic Conception of Intercultural Conflicts

Karin de Boer

I. INTRODUCTION

The intercultural conflicts that confront us today undoubtedly constitute one of the most urgent problems of the contemporary world. These conflicts challenge not only the liberal principles of modern societies, but seem to undermine the paradigm of modernity as such. For it is no longer self-evident that such clashes—in the form of regional, national, or global conflicts—can be resolved by means of democratic procedures, economic measures, repression, expansion, or warfare. If this is true, then the mode of modernity which is ours might have to recognize the inherent limit of the values on which it relies.

There are, of course, many ways in which philosophy could contribute to such a critical self-reflection of modernity. In this article I will do this by drawing on Hegel's conception of tragic conflicts. This choice is likely to meet with suspicion. While, from the 1840s onwards, many philosophers have developed their views through a critical engagement with Hegel, few have drawn on his philosophy to reflect on the socio-political conflicts of their own time. Marx is, of course, among those who set themselves this task. However, Marx's influential reading of Hegel is seriously distorted. Many have followed the early Marx in denouncing Hegel's theoretical philosophy as pseudo-theological metaphysics and his political philosophy as an apology of Prussian absolutism.[1] Although most scholars today agree that these views of Hegel are unwarranted, the re-interpretations of Hegel put forward in the last few decades as yet have had little impact on contemporary critical philosophy.[2] In this respect, the spectre of

---

1. cf. K. Marx, 'Zur Kritik der Hegelschen Rechtsphilosophie. Einleitung' [1844], in S. Landshut (ed.), *Die Frühschriften*, Stuttgart, Alfred Kröner Verlag, 1953, pp. 207-224.

2. I only mention S. Avineri, *Hegel's Theory of the Modern State*, Cambridge, Cambridge University Press, 1972; J. McCumber, 'Contradiction and Resolution in the State, Hegel's Covert View', *Clio*,

Marx's criticism of Hegel continues to haunt contemporary thought.

I consider Hegel's philosophy to contain conceptual resources, the critical potential of which has not yet been sufficiently explored. In this regard, my reading of Hegel shares common ground with the analyses put forward by political philosophers such as Charles Taylor and Axel Honneth. Drawing on texts from Hegel's Jena period, Honneth argues in *The Struggle for Recognition* that persons cannot develop themselves without being granted recognition by others. Social struggles, according to Honneth, aim at establishing structures that facilitate processes of mutual recognition. While Taylor's work focuses on the struggle for recognition enacted by particular cultural communities rather than individuals, he likewise draws on Hegel's political philosophy.[3] Taylor and Honneth agree that the metaphysical conception of reason and world spirit they assign to Hegel must be dismissed.[4]

My approach to Hegel differs from that of Taylor and Honneth in various respects. First, I do not underwrite the strict distinction between Hegel's speculative and political philosophy, because I hold that the latter is deeply informed by the former. I also hold that Hegel's speculative method may well be more pertinent to contemporary critical thought than his actual views on the modern state. Second,

---

vol. 15, no. 4, 1986, pp. 379-390; T. E. Wartenberg, 'Poverty and Class Structure in Hegel's Theory of Civil Society', *Philosophy and Social Criticism*, no. 8, 1981, pp. 169-182; A. Wood, *Hegel's Ethical Thought*, Cambridge, Cambridge University Press, 1990. For an early exception to the traditional view see K.E. Schubarth, 'Über die Unvereinbarkeit der Hegelschen Staatslehre mit der obersten Lebens- und Entwicklungsprinzip des Preussischen Staats' [1839], in: M. Riedel (ed.), *Materialien zu Hegels Rechtsphilosophie*, Band I, Suhrkamp, Frankfurt am Main, 1975, pp. 249-257. D. MacGregor, *Hegel and Marx after the Fall of Communism*, Cardiff, University of Wales Press, 1998, offers an interesting account of the actuality of Hegel's political philosophy not hindered by Marx's criticism of Hegel.

3. C. Taylor, *Hegel and Modern Society*, Cambridge, Cambridge University Press, 1979, pp. 114-118; 'The Politics of Recognition', in: A. Gutmann (ed.), *Multiculturalism: Examining the Politics of Recognition*, New Jersey, Princeton 1994, pp. 25-73. I largely agree with Taylor's analysis of the problems challenging contemporary multicultural societies and his attempt to understand these problems from a Hegelian perspective. In *Hegel and Modern Society*, he rightly points out that the homogenization characteristic of modern societies threatens to deprive people of the means to identify with particular values (pp. 114-118). According to Taylor, we can learn from Hegel that modern society needs 'a ground for differentiation, meaningful to the people concerned, which at the same time does not set the particular communities against each other, but rather knits them together in a larger whole' (p. 117). *Multiculturalism: Examining the Politics of Recognition* further develops this approach in relation to the tension between Francophone and Anglophone communities in Canada. In this essay Taylor argues more specifically that cultural differences be recognized. What has to happen, Taylor holds, is 'a fusion of horizons' (p. 67). Contrary to Taylor, I would argue that any effort at recognition remains tragically entangled with the effort to efface otherness and difference.

4. In *Hegel and Modern Society*, Taylor interprets Hegel's conception of spirit—which, in my view, is Hegel's way of referring to that which we today would call 'culture'—as cosmic spirit (p. 16), larger rational plan (p. 23), and a self-positing God (p. 36) which embodies itself in certain parcels of the universe (p. 26). For this reason, he cannot but attempt to extricate those elements of Hegel's philosophy of right and world history he takes to be relevant today from Hegel's 'ontology of *Geist*' which he considers to be 'close to incredible' (p. 69, cf. p. 111). Although this results in a lucid account of Hegel's conception of the modern state, Taylor discards a conception of spirit that has very little to do with Hegel's philosophy of world history. See also A. Honneth, *The Struggle for Recognition, The Moral Grammar of Social Conflicts*, trans. Joel Anderson, Cambridge, Polity Press, 1995, esp. p. 67.

I take the view that Taylor and Honneth do not sufficiently distinguish themselves from the legacy of the Enlightenment, especially with regard to such ideas as selfhood, autonomy, and progress. Unlike them, I hold that the nature of the current conflicts between contending cultural paradigms cannot be adequately interpreted from within the prevailing paradigm of modernity itself. Although I not deny that Hegel's philosophy is indebted to this paradigm as well, I believe that some of his insights can be deployed to expose precisely its limit. Third, I do not think that the concept of mutual recognition—which is almost completely absent from Hegel's mature political philosophy—grasps the tragic dynamic of conflicts unfolding between individuals or collectives seeking recognition. This is all the more true, I believe, with regard to the dynamic of intercultural conflicts at stake in this article.

Unlike Taylor and Honneth, Chantal Mouffe does not take her bearings from Hegel to analyze socio-political conflicts. Focusing on the antagonistic conflicts unfolding within modern democracies, she argues convincingly that these democracies should attempt to channel rather than suppress the polarization of contending socio-political perspectives.[5] Her recent book *On the Political* by-passes both Marx and Hegel by claiming that 'society is not to be seen as the unfolding of a logic exterior to itself'.[6] I do not think, however, that it is possible—let alone desirable—to sharply distinguish between 'internal' and 'external' logics in this context. Any critical theoretical perspective necessarily differs from the society it intends to interpret, for otherwise it could not provide thought with the means to criticize the paradigm which those who are in power are keen to present as 'proper' to society as such. In my view, Hegel's conception of tragic conflicts provides a philosophical way of comprehending the very antagonistic logic that liberal politics, as Mouffe points out, fails to take into account.[7]

I am aware that a philosophical use of such notions as 'tragedy' and the 'tragic' may seem suspicious as well. These terms are likely to be associated with pessimistic or conservative views concerning the inevitable course of historical

---

5. C. Mouffe, *The Democratic Paradox*, London, Verso, 2000, ch. 3; *On the Political*, London, Routledge 2005. Mouffe's work opposes the self-complacency she assigns to neo-liberalism. Critically reflecting on the liberal tradition from within, Susan Mendus argued already in 1990 that liberals 'respond to pluralism, conflict and loss by constructing a political theory which denies their significance'. They do this, so Mendus, by subordinating the private to the public whenever a conflict between the two emerges (p. 193). The author claims that by repressing conflicts, liberalism creates 'the seeds of a new, and essentially modern, tragic situation' (p. 193) and she illustrates its nature by referring to the fate of Willie Loman in Miller's *Death of a Salesman*. Mendus seems to be primarily concerned with the tragic insofar as it marks the lives of individuals. Although she rightly points to the blindness of liberalism, she does not seem to interpret this blindness itself from a tragic perspective. Whereas she briefly refers to ancient tragedy, she does not refer to Hegel.

6. In *On the Political* Mouffe refers explicitly to Hegel's conception of 'Absolute Spirit', p. 17. While her criticism of Hegel follows Marx's criticism of Hegel, she suggests that Marx's analysis of society in terms of 'forces of production' likewise relies on an external logic.

7. Mouffe's *On the Political* refers to 'the dangers the dominance of liberal logic can bring to the exercise of democracy' (p. 44). It is unclear to me whether she considers this logic to be internal or external to modern societies. If internal, then surely it is not the internal logic she herself puts forward in order to criticize liberalism.

events. If the term 'tragic' is associated with Hegelian dialectics, on the other hand, it might well be considered to entail the necessary resolution of tragic conflicts. In what follows I will argue, however, that Hegel's conception of tragic conflicts cannot be identified with the—predominant—optimistic strand of his philosophy as a whole. By extricating the tragic strand of Hegel's insight into tragic conflicts from this optimistic strand, I hope to provide a philosophical perspective on the tragic polarization of contending paradigms which undercuts the traditional opposition between optimism and pessimism. The same is true, as we will see, of the opposition between universality and particularity. Thus, the conception of the tragic I bring into play does not draw on Hegel's philosophy without modifying its logic.[8] Since the aim of this article is primarily systematic, I will consider only those elements of Hegel's philosophy that bear on the issue of intercultural conflicts. For the same reason, I will disregard the differences between Hegel's early and later works.

## II. THE ORIGIN OF ANCIENT GREECE

Given Hegel's well-known depreciation of Africa and, to a somewhat lesser extent, Asia, it may seem odd to draw on Hegel's philosophy to reflect on the issue of cultural difference and the conflicts to which this difference gives rise. Insofar as world history is concerned, Hegel aligns himself indeed with the most narrow spirit of his time, a choice that can only partly be explained by his limited access to reliable sources.[9] In his *Lectures on the Philosophy of History* Hegel conceives of Africa as falling outside of the domain of world history because he sees the African tribes as completely caught up in nature and hence as incapable of giving rise to spirit proper (LPH 129/99).[10] This view of Africa fits very well, of course, with the idea that world history testifies to the increasing actualization of social, political, and intellectual freedom.

Insofar as *modern* societies are concerned, however, Hegel rather sides with the spirit of tolerance and liberalism inherent in the Enlightenment. Thus, the *Philosophy of Right* maintains that the state must protect the rights of individual human beings regardless of their race, confession or nationality. Insofar as these rights are concerned, particularity does not count:

> It is part of education ... that I am apprehended as a universal person, in which [respect] all are identical. A human being counts as such because he is a human being, not because he is a Jew, Catholic, Protestant, German, Italian, etc. This consciousness ... is of infinite importance (PR § 209 R).

---

8. In my essay 'Tragic Entanglements: Between Hegel and Derrida', *Bulletin of the Hegel Society of Great-Britain*, no. 45, 2003, pp. 34-49, I focus on Hegel's account of tragedy in the *Essay on Natural Law* to achieve the same end.

9. See on this R. Bernasconi, 'Hegel at the Court of the Ashanti', in: S. Barnett (ed.), *Hegel after Derrida*, London, Routledge, pp. 41-63; H. Kimmerle, 'Hegel und Afrika: Das Glas zerspringt', *Hegel-Studien*, no. 28, 1993, pp. 303-325.

10. German page numbers refer to G. W. F. Hegel, *Vorlesungen über die Philosophie der Geschichte [1822/1831]*, E. Moldauer and K.M. Michel (eds.), Frankfurt am Main, Suhrkamp, 1986.

In Hegel's view, the principle of modern civilizations requires that justice abstract from cultural, religious, and racial differences between people. In the *Lectures on the Philosophy of History* he even holds that civilization as such consists in the annulment of natural differences. Thus, Greek culture initially did not rely on 'the natural bond' of patriarchal structures (LPH 277/225), but received vital impulses from the arrival of strangers (LPH 280/227). Greek culture precisely came into its own by 'overcoming' the strangeness (LPH 278/226) to which it owed its initial development:

> Insofar as the origin of its national identity is concerned, we must consider ... the *strangeness* it contained within itself (*die Fremdartigkeit in sich selbst*) as its basic moment... It is only from the strangeness which it contains within itself that [spirit] derives the power to establish itself as spirit. The origin of the history of Greece testifies to this migration and blend of tribes that were partly native and partly completely foreign; and it was precisely Attica, whose people was to attain the highest stage of Greek bloom, that offered asylum to the most diverse tribes and families. Every worldhistorical nation ... has been brought about in this way (LPH 278/226, my own translation).

Whereas Greek civilization owed its life to a heterogeneity constitutive of its own being, it had to efface this internal heterogeneity in order to unfold the totality of its organic moments. According to Hegel, such homogenization constitutes the beginning of any civilization. The particular way in which a civilization achieves this homogenization depends on the particular determination of freedom on which it relies. Modern civilizations seem to have effaced their initial heterogeneity to a much larger extent than ancient Greece; hence the idea of universal rights to which Hegel alludes in the passage of the *Philosophy of Right* just quoted (PR § 209 R).[11] The modern principle of freedom does not imply, however, that the state should treat its subjects as equal in all respects. For freedom is only rational, according to Hegel, if it complies with the organic structure of the society as a whole. This structure may well pose different limits to the freedom of subjects fulfilling different tasks.

## III. TRAGEDY

According to Hegel's *Lectures on the Philosophy of History*, we have seen, the first phase of Greek culture consisted in overcoming its inherent strangeness. Interestingly, Hegel does not interpret the initial 'overcoming' of this foreign element in terms of tragedy. He seems to assume that the tragic conflict between contrary ethical paradigms can only emerge from within a culture that has already constituted itself as a unity. This view corresponds to Hegel's earlier conception of tragic conflicts in the *Phenomenology of Spirit*, which completely disregards the question as to the origin of Greek culture. Clearly, the sections of the *Phenomenology* devoted to Greek ethical life are not so much concerned

---

11. See C. Taylor, *Hegel and Modern Society*, pp. 114-115. Taylor refers to nationalism as a way of enforcing this homogenization.

with tragedy as with the tragic collision between contending ethical paradigms which unfolded within Greek culture. Since, in Hegel's view, Greek tragedies preeminently reflect this collision, he can draw on their content to expose the tragic destiny of Greek culture as such.

Hegel regarded Greek culture as torn apart by the conflict between contrary, yet complementary determinations of justice. His discussion of these determinations in terms of divine law and human law primarily refers, in my view, to the way in which fifth-century city-states such as Athens tried to resolve the conflict between the archaic tradition from which they originated and the new political paradigm they had established. Whereas the former paradigm, relying on such values as kinship, revenge, and pollution, had suited the self-organization of relatively small clans, it could no longer serve as the paradigm of large-scale, urban communities. As this new paradigm, based on the notion of citizenship, came to hold sway over public life, however, it tended to repress elements of the ancient paradigm that many continued to consider as vitally important. Thus, Hegel notes, human law

> is confronted with another power, namely, with divine law. For the ethical power of the state, being the movement of self-conscious action, finds its opposite in the simple and immediate essence of the ethical sphere; ... as actuality in general it finds in that inner essence something other than it is itself (PS ¶ 449/PG 293).

As is well known, Hegel considers the ensuing clash between these contrary paradigms of justice to be exposed pre-eminently by Sophocles' *Antigone*. Whereas Antigone identified one-sidedly with the divine law that obliged her to bury her brother, Creon identified one-sidedly with the law according to which traitors had forfeited their right to be buried. The death of Polyneikes impels either of them to raise a particular, one-sided determination of justice into the ultimate principle of ethical life. Both Creon and Antigone try to disentangle a particular determination of justice from its contrary determination, thus denying their mutual dependence. This mutual exclusion results from the incapacity of both sides to recognize themselves in the other.

Thus, tragic conflicts arise if contending paradigms fail to recognize that the content they posit over against themselves belongs to their own being. Whereas tragedies represent this tragic dynamic by means of individual protagonists, Hegel focuses on the clash between the contending paradigms themselves. Evidently, such clashes cannot come about without individuals who identify with particular principles and act in accordance with them. Yet the logic of tragic conflicts cannot be adequately grasped, in Hegel's view, by referring to such acting individuals alone. In this respect, his approach differs from any theory that takes the individual human being as its starting point.

Since ethical self-consciousness, Hegel notes,

> sees right only on its own side and wrong on the other, the mode of consciousness which belongs to divine law sees in the other side human, arbitrary violence, while the mode of consciousness which is assigned to human law sees in the other the self-will and disobedience of inner autonomy (PS ¶ 466/PG 305).

Hegel emphasizes that the conflict between Antigone and Creon cannot be resolved by subordinating one side to the other:

> The victory of one power and its character, and the defeat of the other side, would thus be only the part and the incomplete work, a work that advances relentlessly toward the equilibrium of both. Only in the subjugation of both sides alike is absolute right accomplished and has the ethical substance manifested itself as the negative power that absorbs both sides (PS ¶ 472/PG 311).[12]

This does not entail, to be sure, that Hegel regarded Greek culture as actually having accomplished such an equilibrium. He seems to interpret the clash between divine law and human law as a particular mode of the basic conflict between particularity and universality. The text suggests that he considered Greek culture to have survived this primordial clash by incorporating elements of the former into the latter. Once this had been achieved, however, the collision between particularity and universality re-emerged as the collision between the sphere of the government—representing human law—and the sphere of the family.[13] In this case, Hegel emphasizes again that the state tends to respond to the threat posed by its contrary—the sphere of particular ends—by repressing its proper force. This repression only increases the polarization of both spheres:

> Human law, of which the community constitutes the universal existence, manhood the general activity, and the government the actual enactment, is, moves, and maintains itself by ... absorbing into itself ... the separation into independent families presided over by womankind, and by keeping them dissolved in the fluid continuity of its own nature (PS ¶ 475/PG 313).

> The community ... can only maintain itself by repressing this spirit of individualism, and, because this spirit is an essential moment, it at once creates this spirit; due to its repressive attitude towards it, it creates this spirit as a hostile principle (PS ¶ 475/PG 314).

According to Hegel, Greek culture could not survive the clash between the spirit of universality represented by the government and the spirit of individualism that came to prevail during the last decades of the fifth century. Yet the actual outcome of this tragic clash is, I think, less relevant to Hegel's conception of tragic conflicts than the logic he considers to underlie any collision between universality and particularity.

The *Phenomenology*, as we have seen, considers two ways in which the city-

---

12. Miller misleadingly translates *Unterwerfung* as 'downfall', cf. '[B]oth sides suffer the same destruction. For neither power has any advantage over the other that would make it a more essential moment of the substance.' (PS ¶ 472/PG 310-11).

13. 'As a moment of the public community, its activity is not confined merely to the underworld, ... but, within the actual nation, it gains an equally public existence and movement. Taken in this form, what was represented as a simple movement of the individualized 'pathos' now acquires a different appearance, and the crime and the ensuing destruction of the community acquire a form that is proper to their existence.' (PS ¶ 475/PG 313). I would like to note that Hegel, when discussing the relation between the state and the family, no longer identifies the latter with the sphere of divine law.

state responded to elements that threatened its purported homogeneity. With regard to both the archaic paradigm of justice and the sphere of the family Hegel holds that the repression of those who identify with particular values entails the re-emergence of the same particularity as an even greater threat to the society as a whole. He would also maintain, however, that this polarization can be overcome if the state comprehends the realm of particular cultural values as one of its necessary moments and if particular communities, for their part, recognize the state as their ultimate principle. Even though Greek culture was not capable of achieving this reconciliation in all respects, Hegel comprehends the resolution of tragic conflicts by assuming that the relation between the contending principles is ultimately asymmetrical.

Yet if we relate Hegel's account of the tragic conflict between the contrary ethical paradigms to his later reflections on the *origin* of Greek culture, it might be argued that the archaic values appealed to by Antigone confronted Greek culture with traces of its immemorial heterogeneity which it was unable to appropriate. Seen in this light, it could not but attempt to efface these traces. Generally, the initial strangeness which a civilization attempts to exclude from itself might well be considered to recur as a force that it can neither completely incorporate nor completely exclude from itself. In the following section I will try to modify Hegel's account of tragic conflicts in such a way that the dynamic that gives rise to tragic conflicts between contrary paradigms does not necessarily result in the incorporation of the one by the other. This can only be done, I believe, by abandoning the dialectical determination of the relation between universality and particularity to which Hegel's own conception of tragic conflicts is bound.

## IV. TRAGEDY TODAY

Just as in Greek culture, many contemporary societies seem to be marked by the tension between, on the one hand, the allegedly universal principles represented by the state and, on the other, particular communities that do not assume these principles as absolute principles. In recent years this tension has developed into the globalizing conflict between Muslim fundamentalism and the democratic world. For the sake of simplicity, however, I will only refer to such intercultural conflicts as unfold within a particular nation.

Evidently, contemporary conflicts between contending cultural paradigms cannot simply be interpreted in terms derived from Greek tragedy. There is, for instance, nothing archaic about the way in which individuals and communities today identify with particular cultural and religious values or with a particular construction of the past. If we wish to connect Hegel's account of tragic conflicts to the contemporary world, it seems to be more worthwhile to do so in terms of the formal distinction between particularity and universality. This would be in line with the way modern societies tend to comprehend themselves. Many modern societies, for which France and Turkey are notable, attempt to control the proper force of particular cultural traditions by subordinating them to the purportedly universal principles of the predominant secular culture represented by the state. Yet it seems increasingly hard to believe that intercultural conflicts can be resolved by means of repression or, conversely, by letting particular communities isolate themselves from the society as a whole. It might be argued, therefore, that neither the repression of cultural differences in the name of universality nor the acceptance of cultural differences in the name of particularity necessarily impedes the polarization between the state and particular cultural minorities.

I do not wish to suggest that Hegel's philosophy offers a satisfying way out of this aporia. Yet I do hold that it contains conceptual means to comprehend the logic of this polarization which contemporary political theories ignore. Although Hegel does not maintain that societies will *actually* be able to reconcile the contrary cultural paradigms that unfold within their bosom, he would neither accept that the particular *in principle* threatens to resist the homogenization advocated by the state. In order to account for this latter possibility, it will be necessary to extricate Hegel's insight into the tragic polarization of contrary determinations from its dialectical framework.

This can be done, I believe, by re-interpreting the asymmetrical relation between universality and particularity as resulting from the effort of two contrary, yet mutually dependent moments to prevail over their contrary, that is, to posit their particular content as universally valid. As we have seen, this symmetry presents itself most clearly in Hegel's reflection on the conflict between Antigone and Creon. Both Antigone and Creon identify with a one-sided determination of justice. Since neither of them is able to recognize the mutual dependence of these contrary determinations, both attempt to posit their own determination of justice as the absolute principle of justice. Seen in this light, the purportedly universal values advocated by the modern state result from its attempt to attribute universal value to its proper principles in the first place, and thus to annul the proper force of its contrary.[14] As long as a modern state, for example, posits the

---

14. This view on the emergence of particular principles does not necessarily entail a relativistic stance on the value that such principles may have. I merely propose, in a Peircean vein, to consider these principles not as they are in themselves (universal or relative), but in view of their possible effects, that is, in view of the tasks they are meant to fulfil. Thus, the Enlightenment deployed such notions as reason, liberty, equality, etc., to throw off the yoke of feudalism and a form of religion considered as repressive. These notions, presented as 'universal', were suited to contest the purportedly universal truths of Christianity and have had an immense impact on the development of the modern world. In the twentieth century, the idea of universal human rights has been developed to fight against forms of oppression characteristic of this particular age. If the *content* of the struggle against oppression changes, the principles at hand not only might lose their original force, but their application might even become counterproductive. The question as to whether 'there exist' universal values seems less relevant to me than the question as to which principles are suited, at a given time, to thwart the polarizing dynamic inherent in human culture as such. Even if the actual deployment of such principles owes its force to the deeply felt and widely shared conviction that they are universally valid, a philosophical reflection on these matters need not take sides in the debate about whether or not some principles are truly universal. Hegel, referring to the existence of monasteries during the Middle Ages, seems to express a similar view in the Introduction to his *Philosophy of Right*: 'If it can be shown that the origin of an institution was entirely expedient and necessary under the specific circumstances of the time, the requirements of the historical viewpoint are fulfilled. But if

sphere of particular moral, cultural, and religious values over against itself, it threatens to deprive its citizens of valuable means to control their selfish impulses and hence to participate in the public realm.[15] Whereas this selfishness constitutes a necessary condition of a liberal economy, it threatens to alienate citizens from the political realm and to reduce their moral freedom.

Once Hegel's dialectical conception of the relation between universality and particularity is redefined in terms of the infinite struggle between contending modes of particularity, his insight into tragic conflicts is suited to comprehend the dynamic of contemporary intercultural conflicts. It seems to me that this modified conception contains three interrelated elements. According to the first element, contrary determinations of a given principle are *mutually dependent*. They are, in other words, entangled to such an extent that neither moment can come into its own as long as it excludes its contrary, for this contrary constitutes one of its proper moments.[16] The second element concerns the *symmetry* of the conflict between contrary determinations. I do not wish to suggest that the contrary determinations themselves are symmetrical in all respects: the term 'symmetry' refers exclusively to the tendency of these determinations to raise themselves into universal principles and to do so by repressing their contrary. The third element concerns the increasing *polarization* that tends to follow from this repression. If the conflict between the contrary determinations of a given principle is symmetrical rather than asymmetrical, then this polarization does not necessarily yield its resolution. The conflict between the state and the particular cultural minorities it harbours is tragic precisely insofar as both attempt—in contrary ways—to annul the entanglement of the one-sided principles to which they adhere, thus depriving themselves of a moment that is vital to their own being. In order to clarify this I will briefly consider the ways in which individual human beings may relate to the entanglement of contrary, yet complementary determinations.

This entanglement entails first of all that I cannot exclusively relate to myself as a human being that has the right to be recognized as such. I find myself at once determined by a particular sex, language, skin, character, descent, and culture, that is, by a particularity that I cannot completely appropriate and of

---

this is supposed to amount to a general justification of the thing itself, the result is precisely the opposite; for since the original circumstances are no longer present, the institution has thereby lost its meaning and its right [to exist].' (PR § 3, 37/30). Hegel's point is here that the historical perspective on socio-political institutions should not transcend its proper limits. Whereas he distinguishes between a historical and a philosophical perspective, I believe that the principle he assigns to the historian is most relevant to contemporary philosophy as well.

15. This is, in my view, the thrust of Hegel's account of civil society in the *Philosophy of Right* (cf. PR §§ 182, 187, 249).

16. In a similar vein, Mouffe argues in *The Democratic Paradox* that modern democracy is constituted by two heterogeneous strands, that is, by the principle of individual liberty on the one hand and the principles of equality and popular sovereignty on the other. On her view, the contingent historical articulation between those two distinct traditions has given rise not only to great achievements, but also to bitter struggles between their proponents (pp. 2-3). Given the actual predominance of the liberalist paradigm, the space for a political struggle between these contending paradigms threatens to decrease. I endorse her view that this development poses a threat to the political as such.

which I cannot control the effects. These particular determinations constitute a strangeness, so to speak, that precedes my efforts at self-identification and that I cannot subordinate to my true identity. This is unsettling. There are, perhaps, three ways of responding to this inherent strangeness.[17] First, I may try to disentangle myself from my particularity by raising a certain content into a universal principle and completely identifying with this principle. By positing myself as a free, rational human being, I at once posit the particularity from which I abstracted over against myself as a hostile principle. Thus, I need no longer be disturbed by the particularity of my sex, skin, and values. In order to annul the threat of the particularity I thus find over against myself, I subsequently try—in vain—to subordinate this particularity to my purportedly universal values.

Second, I may try to annul the disturbing entanglement of contrary determinations by collapsing the established distinction between universality and particularity altogether, that is, by completely identifying with the particularity of my sex, skin, and values. By doing so, my proper particularity no longer conflicts with my effort at self-identification. In this case, I posit my proper particularity over against the particularity of others without acknowledging a universality that transcends these different particularities. Yet it turns out that I cannot completely deprive myself of the universality I thus tried to annul. For insofar as I identify with my particular sex, skin, and values, I make myself vulnerable to the efforts of others violently to reduce me to these particular features—hence sexism, racism, and other kinds of discrimination. I therefore demand not only that my particular sex, skin, and values be recognized as such, but also that I be treated as equal insofar as justice, education, or career are concerned. These contradictory demands cannot be met by a one-sided appeal to either universality or particularity. Yet in order to act I need to adopt one of these contrary determinations as my guiding principle. No policy can be based on two principles at once, even less so if both of them refuse to be subordinated to their counterpart.

---

17. To some extent, the following account is inspired by the interpretation of cultural difference put forward by R. Visker, *The Inhuman Condition: Looking for Difference after Levinas and Heidegger*, Dordrecht, Kluwer Academic Publishers, 2004. Visker, opening up phenomenology to structuralism, psychoanalysis and deconstruction, develops a conception of cultural difference that, in my view, ties in with the conception I develop by starting out from Hegel. This is true in particular of his critical response to Levinas' ethics (see in particular Chs. 1 and 6). Thus, Visker argues that Levinas, focusing one-sidedly on the infinite transcendence of the other, does not account for the excentric attachment of the other—as much as of myself—to particular characteristics such as sex, colour, and cultural tradition. He maintains against Levinas that I do wrong not only by reducing the other to his or her singularizing characteristics, but also by abstracting from the complex and finite relation of the other to these characteristics: 'A person who refuses to be solely recognized as a human being ... does not want to be reduced to his/her ('different') skin-colour, etc., but also refuses to be detached from it—insists on something that ... escapes full understanding, is not possessed, cannot be determined' (p. 181, cf. p. 14). According to Visker's conception of the intersubjective relation, I can neither reduce the face of the other to the particular context out of which it emerges nor, on the other hand, disentangle it from its facticity. This entails that the other does not only confront me with my infinite responsibility, but equally with my proper incapacity to come to terms with a singularity that haunts my attempts to identify with myself (pp. 183, 289).

If these contending modes of particularity depend on one another in such a way that they can neither exclude nor incorporate the other of themselves, then I might try to endure, finally, their unsettling entanglement. In this case, I would not reduce the other to his or her particularity, nor to his or her universality. The irreducible particularity of the other would rather remind me of the irreducible particularity constitutive of my own being. What I would recognize in the other, then, is not so much the universality we are supposed to share, as our utterly precarious attempts to respond to the contradictory demands that the entanglement of contending modes of particularity entails.

Now if the tragic conflict between the predominant culture represented by the state and cultural minorities is interpreted along these lines, it can be traced back to the incapacity of both to endure the entanglement of contending modes of particularity. In order to present its values as universal, the state must efface the particularity from which they emerged. It does this by, first, positing the realm of particularity over against itself, and, second, by trying to subordinate the latter to its purportedly universal ends. The more this fails, the more it turns the realm of particularity into a hostile force. Those who identify with a particular cultural minority, for their part, will tend to react by increasingly identifying with values they consider to hold absolutely, thus equally isolating themselves from the whole. By collapsing the distinction between universality and particularity, the liberal principles adhered to by the state—on which they continue to depend—tend to re-emerge as a hostile force that needs to be resisted rather than embraced.

The tragic perspective on intercultural conflicts of which I have sketched the basic principle entails that contending cultural paradigms will always threaten to oppose their contrary—hence their polarization. It equally entails, however, that those who adhere to contending cultural paradigms can—and must—try to resist this polarizing dynamic by all means. Consequently, modern societies, represented by liberal-democratic governments, should recognize that the negative elements it assigns to particular cultural minorities, such as dogmatism, inequality, and repression, equally belong to their proper cultural tradition and compromise its purported homogeneity from within. It should recognize, moreover, that the repression of these elements, necessary as it may be, tends to entail their re-emergence as a force that perverts its proper paradigm even more. The French government, recently trying to impede the repression of Muslim girls they took to be represented by their headscarves, could only do so by means of a law that many regarded as repressing their freedom of expression. The increasing influence of Christian fundamentalism, especially in the United States, also indicates that pre-modern elements continue to haunt the paradigm of modernity from within, if only by undermining the clear-cut distinction between the private and the public which is crucial to liberal politics.

Thus, depolarization presupposes the capacity of the prevailing cultural paradigm to face the irresolvable tension between the contrary determinations it harbours within itself. On the other hand, modern societies should equally attempt to recognize the positive elements of the cultural paradigm it posits over against itself, such as the emphasis of the latter on values and practices that provide people with concrete means to control their selfish impulses and make sense of their life. In this regard, the attitude of liberal democracies toward cultural paradigms which with it shares a common history—that is, Christianity—need not differ from its attitude toward cultural paradigms it regards as foreign to that history.

Those who identify with a cultural minority, for their part, should not focus exclusively on the elements of modern societies they experience as threats, such as individualism, impiety, and moral corruption. Neither should they blindly identify with the guiding principles of allegedly universal values inherent in their own tradition. Instead, they should try to further develop those elements of their own cultural paradigm that may help individuals and groups to respond to the challenges posed by the contemporary world, elements such as tolerance, piety, decency, or the binding role of religion. This would mean, for example, that those who identify with the cultural paradigm of Islam should try to extricate the productive, non-oppressive elements of their monotheistic tradition from the archaic elements—such as tribalism, the repression of women, honour revenge, or female circumcision—with which this tradition continues to be entangled.[18] While these archaic elements may once have enhanced the effort of a community to stabilize the relation between its members, today the violence reproduced by these very elements by far outweighs the function for which they may have been designed.

If the struggle for recognition undertaken by contending cultural paradigms is considered from a tragic perspective, this struggle only has a chance to succeed if those who adhere to a particular paradigm are willing to recognize the inherent and irresolvable heterogeneity of its constitutive elements. On the basis of this recognition, they should try to enhance those elements of their proper tradition that, given the present circumstances, are likely to decrease oppression, chaos, and alienation. Since the relation between, on the one hand, the predominant culture represented by the state and, on the other, the cultural minorities it hosts is assymmetrical in many respects, it falls primarily to the state to create space for modes of self-reflection intended to thwart polarization. The logic of tragic conflicts does not entail that such a depolarization is actually possible or impossible; the classical categories of modality are not suited for its purpose. This logic only entails that the polarizing dynamic that yields antagonistic conflicts is very difficult to resist, because such a resistance requires first and foremost a radical form of self-criticism. What it requires is the insight that no principle, regardless of its content, guarantees that its effects on human actions will be productive rather than destructive, nor that its productive effects will necessarily prevail.[19]

---

18. This is the aim of, for instance, M. Chebel's *Manifeste pour un islam des Lumières. 27 propositions pour réformer l'islam*, Paris, Hachette, 2004.

19. The dismissal of the possibly destructive effects of the principle one adheres to—and this characterizes the attitude of Antigone, Creon, Oedipus, and many other tragic protagonists—is the source of all ideology. On the other hand, any action requires that one focus on the anticipated positive

This holds true of religion, but no less of capitalism, democracy, or the idea of universal human rights. On this view, one might even have to acknowledge the limit of the principle of individual freedom that has animated not just liberalism, but the history of modernity as such.

Such self-criticism becomes ever more difficult, it seems to me, the larger the scale of the contending cultural paradigms at stake. Individual human beings who, because of the particularity of their skin, sex, or cultural values, are impelled to accommodate the exigencies of contrary cultural paradigms, often find ways to resolve the tragic conflict of which they are the protagonists. One can be a successful accountant—or play soccer—and wear a headscarf in public.[20] Yet cultural paradigms that are meant to protect the interests of large-scale, transnational civilizations are much less likely to impede processes of polarization—the crooked timber they are made of is less easy to bend.

## V. CONCLUSION

I suggested that neither repression nor tolerance necessarily decreases the inherent tension between, on the one hand, the effort at homogenization of the state and, on the other, the resistance of particular minorities against this homogenization. I also suggested, still following Hegel, that this tension turns into a conflict as soon as the state and particular minorities one-sidedly identify with such contrary determinations as reason and faith, progress and tradition, the individual and the community, freedom and culture. In order to comprehend this conflict we can, I have argued, neither rely on the clear-cut opposition between universality and particularity assumed by modernity, nor on Hegel's dialectical subordination of particularity by universality. In both cases, the initial entanglement of contrary determinations is effaced. It is, we have seen, precisely this effacement which induces the polarization of contending cultural paradigms. This effacement also occurs whenever a society—by means of its ethics, politics, or philosophy—clings one-sidedly to relativism or universalism and, accordingly, to multiculturalism or a politics of assimilation. Both perspectives tend to abstract from the contrary moment they contain within themselves. As I see it, contemporary critical philosophy has the task of deconstructing such abstract oppositions wherever they emerge. Even though, in order to achieve this task, it cannot adopt Hegel's speculative science in all respects, I believe that it could greatly profit from the critical force it contains.

---

effects of a particular principle. That is why ideologies are unavoidable. Hence the continuous task of critical philosophy to resist the ideologizing tendency inherent in thought as such.

20. I am aware, of course, that the space for individuals fruitfully to negotiate between contending cultural paradigms largely depends on social and economical conditions. It is the responsibility of the government and local forms of administration to create conditions that enhance the equal access of citizens to this space. As regards the dynamic of exclusion as such—whether on the basis of class, race, culture, or sex—Marx's insights have not lost their pertinence.

5

# Hegel's Theory of Moral Action, its Place in his System and the 'Highest' Right of the Subject

David Rose

## I. INTRODUCTION

There is at present, amongst Hegel scholars and in the interpretative discussions of Hegel's social and political theories, the flavour of old-style 'apology' for his liberal credentials, as though—prior to any attempt to engage with the social ethics he proposes—there exists a real need to prove Hegel holds basic liberal views palatable to the hegemonic, contemporary political worldview.[1] And this almost ubiquitous defensive attitude is present even in the face of a marked absence of convincing, contemporary avowals of the opposite, as though the default starting position is to assume that Hegel is a conservative or reactionary who distrusts the capacity of the modern subjective conscience to interrogate and legitimate social laws, conventions and institutions (that is, right in its broadest sense).[2] The putative motivation for such an understated presentation of Hegel's endorsement of subjective conscience within the limits and requirements of a rational state is perhaps due to two factors: one, the historical, yet false, understanding of Hegel

---

1. The most obvious example of this 'apology' style of writing is to be found in Westphal's attempt to prove beyond doubt that Hegel is a 'reform-minded liberal' (p. 234), see Kenneth Westphal, 'The Basic Context and Structure of Hegel's *Philosophy of Right*', in F. Beiser (ed.), *The Cambridge Companion to Hegel*, Cambridge, Cambridge University Press, 1993. There is putative assumption that conservatism is bad, an attitude which is perhaps mistaken, but I do not have space to elaborate on this here. It is admittedly a 'contested' concept.

2. The most familiar, if one of the least sophisticated, version of this caricature of Hegel is Karl Popper, *The Open Society and its Enemies* vol. 2, 2 vols., 3rd ed., London, Routledge, 1957, chapters 11 and 12. See Walter Kaufmann, 'The Hegel myth and its method', *The Hegel Myths and Legends*, in J. Stewart (ed.), Evanston, Northwestern University Press , 1996 for a comprehensive rebuttal of Popper. The best and most convincing contemporary account of the charge of philosophical conservatism can be found in Ernst Tugendhat, *Self-consciousness and Self-determination*, trans. P. Stern, London, MIT Press, 1986, chapters 13 and 14.

as a conservative[3]; and two, one of the methods for understanding Hegel's ethics is to reconstruct what is left of the modern moral conscience when the philosopher has finished discussing the flaws and contradictions of the Kantian model of moral judgement and motivation.[4] Although this is a fruitful and largely correct approach, it ignores the fact that Hegel's theory of action motivates the critique of transcendentalism rather than merely fills in the hole when one rejects Kantian ethics.[5]

To state clearly and unequivocally what the major claim of this article is, I hold that the critique of 'subjective' moralities in general and the critique of Kantian ethics in particular is neither the sole nor even the main reason for the adoption of an immanent doctrine of ethics. The rejection of Kant is, after all, only the negative part of Hegel's argument which grounds the idea of *Sittlichkeit*. The positive reason resides in the consequences of Hegel's theory of action and the requirements of the concept of recognition. The transition from the moral point of view to social ethics, that is from *Moralität* to *Sittlichkeit*, in Hegel's system is internally motivated by the position adopted in the discussion of a theory of action in the first part of *Moralität* (which, in turn, is a necessary consequence of Hegel's theory of punishment outlined in the latter part of *Abstract Right*), and not just due to the contradictions that arise from the moral point of view itself. It is commonly held that it is Hegel's continued attack on Kantian morality and, above all, on the empty formalism of the categorical imperative that motivates his postulation of an immanent, as opposed to a transcendental, doctrine of duty.[6] Hegel proposes that motivations for right action cannot originate nor be

---

3. M. Jackson, 'Hegel: The Real and the Rational', in J. Stewart (ed.), *The Hegel Myths and Legends*.

4. Stephen Houlgate, 'Hegel's Ethical Thought', *Bulletin of the Hegel Society of Great Britain*, 25, 1-17; Dudley Knowles, *Hegel and the Philosophy of Right*, London, Routledge, 2002, chapter 8; Westphal, Kenneth, 'Hegel's Critique of Kant's Moral World View', *Philosophical Topics*, vol. 19, no. 2, 1991, pp. 133-175; Allen Wood, *Hegel's Ethical Thought*, Cambridge, Cambridge University Press, 1990, chapters 9-10.

5. A second method for the discussion of Hegelian social ethics and the role of the subjective conscience resides in the requirements of freedom as put forward in the introduction to PR, so that the conditions of subjective and objective freedom are traced back to the need for the moral subject to be 'at home' in his or her culture. See Michael Hardimon, *Hegel's Social Philosophy: The Project of Reconciliation*, Cambridge, Cambridge University Press, 1994; Frederick Neuhouser, *Foundations of Hegel's Social Theory: Actualizing Freedom*, London, Harvard University Press, 2000; and Alan Patten, *Hegel's Idea of Freedom*, Oxford, Oxford University Press, 1999. I want to reach the same conclusion, but by approaching the problem in the other direction, that is by showing the direction Hegel takes (from free-will, to abstract right, to *action*, to morality and then to social right) needs to be better understood.

6. For Hegel's criticisms of Kant's moral will, see: NL 102-80, part II; PR §§ 133-140; and EPM §§ 508-512. For the contemporary debate itself, one should refer to Henry Allison, *Kant's Theory of Freedom*, Cambridge, Cambridge University Press, 1990, especially chapter ten; Karl Ameriks, 'The Hegelian Critique of Kantian Morality', in B. den Ouden & M. Marcia (eds.), *New Essays on Kant*, New York, Peter Lang, 1987; Chrsitine Korsgaard, *Creating the Kingdom of Ends*, Cambridge, Cambridge University Press, 1996, chapter three; Onora O'Neill, *Constructions of Reason*, Cambridge, Cambridge University Press, 1989, part two; Timothy O'Hagan, 'On Hegel's Critique of Kant's Moral and Political Philosophy' in S. Priest (ed.), *Hegel's Critique of Kant*, Oxford, Clarendon; 1987; Robert Pippin, *Idealism as Modernism* Cambridge, Cambridge University Press, 1997, part one; Kenneth Westphal, 'Hegel's Critique of Kant's Moral World View', *Philosophical Topics*, vol. 19, no. 2, 1991, pp. 133-175 and

derived from transcendental reason, so the story goes, and so the only alternative is that determinations of the will are to be found in the agent's institutional roles within the rational state: the subject's duties are found embedded in *Sittlichkeit*, his ethical substance or moral fabric.[7] And it is the explicitly social origin of moral motivation which has led to the diverse interpretations and judgements on Hegel's account of the role of the subjective conscience within the rational state which, when coupled with the rejection of the liberal Kantian political programme, ground the accusation of political quietism: if a subject finds liberation through the fulfilment of his social role, then any protest grounded in the moral conscience is seemingly ruled out since to protest is to fail to fulfil one's role. So, alternatively, many Hegel scholars feel the need to celebrate the role of the moral conscience and describe it as a necessary attribute of the rational state and, if it is absent, then neither the individual nor the state is fully free. The aim of this paper is see whether the issue concerning the role of the moral conscience in Hegel's social theory can be answered through an exploration of one of the building blocks in his account of the rational state (that is, his much neglected theory of moral action) and to show the role it has to play in establishing subjective claims at the heart of his social ethics.[8] The ambitious agenda of this piece is, on the one hand, to demonstrate that the concept of *Sittlichkeit* is not only an alternative to transcendental ethics, but is necessarily entailed by the adoption of the modern moral point of view (in much the same way that the realm of 'Abstract Right' requires the realm of morality to make sense of the concepts of crime and coercion, so, too, does 'Morality' require the concept of an immanent doctrine of duty to make sense of free, human action); and, on the other, to show that the challenge that Hegel is, at best, a quietist and, at worst, a reactionary is incompatible with a proper understanding of his political system as a whole and, hence, stress that the moral conscience is a necessary and integral part of the rational state since, otherwise, Hegel's own conditions of free action would not be met.

## II. THE THEORY OF ACTION

My main claim in this section is that Hegel offers, in his mature lectures on right (PR §§ 105-140; EPM §§ 503-12), a hermeneutical theory of action. Acts express something particular about the agent by communicating his or her intention to an ideal other who, to use an apt metaphor, is able to 'read' the inner self from the outer expression.[9] The advantages of this reading reside in its

---

Allen Wood, 'The Emptiness of the Moral Will', *Monist* vol. 72, 1989, pp. 454-483.

7. Such a story does not tell us why other alternatives are not considered: motivations of a moral sense, human nature, pleasure and so on. Of course, Hegel does, see most notably NL & PR §140 R.

8. Knowles, *Hegel and the Philosophy of Right*, pp. 362-63; Michael Quante, *Hegel's Concept of Action*, Cambridge, Cambridge University Press, 2004, p. 1. Quante's own book goes a long way to rectify this neglect.

9. A very good account of this type of theory is Paul Ricoeur, 'The Model of the Text: Meaningful Action Considered as a Text', in *Hermeneutics and the Human Sciences* trans. J. Thompson, Cambridge,

consistency with the Hegelian concepts of recognition and homeliness as well as grounding the necessary existence of the modern, moral conscience implicitly within the fully rational state.

It is pertinent to begin with an idea of what we would expect from a theory of action. In the first instance, a theory of action ought to be able to adequately identify a subset of events properly described as acts from a more general set of occurrences. Hegel, like any theorist of action, starts from the simplest intuition: the subset of events that are properly termed actions are those that are brought about by an agent. So, in its simplest form, a theory of action will identify those events which the agent *does* as actions. The formal way to conceive of an action is any event for which the agent claims responsibility or identifies as his or her own (PR § 115). The idea of *responsibility* put in play at the outset reveals what we should expect from Hegel: he is ultimately interested in the evaluation and justification of actions (moral action), and not just the explication of action (action *per se*).[10] His theory of action arises from a consideration of the responsible subject.

The emphasis on the evaluation of actions is consistent with the claim that Hegel is concerned with full blooded or moral action and not just human action and is supported by the location of his discussion of action within his lectures on right. The transition embodied in the chapter on 'Morality'—that is the systematic developmental and historical transition from *person* to *moral* subject—arises from the requirements of abstract right and, in particular, punishment. For once an individual person has rights and a territory (covering both physical integrity and private possessions), then violations of this legal space require reparation. Intentional behaviour *demands* to be treated differently from accidental damage (a flood), the consequences of animalistic (wild savagery), immature (the infant who decides to colour in one's favourite Persian rug) or neurotic behaviour (kleptomania) (PR § 99 A). The criminal is differentiated from all these other (merely) grammatical subjects due to the responsibility he bears for his own will and our treatment of him depends upon the proper interpretation of an intentional action: to what extent is the criminal responsible and what, then, is the appropriate response. The concepts of 'Abstract right' are inadequate to deal with the proper response to crime and even hard placed to differentiate between crime and deception (PR § 103). Such evaluation requires a theory of action with its explanation of how, when and to what extent the subject is responsible for his or her actions and the 'person' identifies only the individual will, independent of the clan or tribe, which has a given rather than a chosen content. For Hegel, then, a discussion of morality in its broadest sense is entailed by the rights and prohibitions of 'Abstract right' because the discussion of action in that section is formal and at odds with his retributivist justification for punishment (LNR § 56).[11] If ac-

---

Cambridge University Press, 1981.

10. See the introduction to Quante, *Hegel's Concept of Action*.

11. G. W. F. Hegel, *Lectures on Natural Right and Political Science: The First Philosophy of Right: Heidelberg, 1817-1818, with Additions From the Lectures of 1818-1819*, trans. J. Michael Stewart and Peter C. Hodgson, Berkeley, University of California Press, 1995. See David Rose, *Hegel's Philosophy of Right*, London,

tion were merely caused by the content of one's will, then punishment could only be a form of deterrence or rehabilitation. The person who acts due to neurosis or genetic predisposition, that is the person who could not have done otherwise, is not responsible in any robust sense. As such, the aim of punishment practices would be either to protect others from his behaviour (like building a sandbag wall to protect property from a flood) or to change the person's behaviour (as one would domesticate an animal). But, punishment is most rationally comprehended as retribution and such a concept requires the notion of responsibility and moral desert to be rationally grounded (EPM § 503).

Hegel summarizes his theory of moral action in one dense paragraph which sets out the conditions of moral action pertaining to a *subject* as opposed to action pertaining to *a person:*

> The expression of the will as subjective or moral is action. Action contains the following determinations: ($\alpha$) it must be known by me in its externality as mine; ($\beta$) its essential relation to the concept is one of obligation; and ($\gamma$) it has an essential relation to the will of others (PR § 113).

The first determination ($\alpha$) is familiar: an event is an action if the agent's intention plays a causal role and the agent is aware of it. The right of knowledge ($\alpha$) is the condition that the agent must recognize an event as being produced by him or herself for it to be an action as opposed to an event.

Freedom is understood as freedom-in-itself in 'Abstract right': a person is free if he or she can satisfy personal wants and desires even if these wants are immediate inclinations or blind obedience to the dictates of authority. Yet, even within this sphere, it is possible to distinguish actions from mere events: 'Its utterance in deed with this freedom is as action, in the externality of which it only admits as its own, and allows to be imputed to it, so much as it has consciously willed.' (EPM § 503) Only those events admitted as one's own are actions, that is events to which the agent ascribes himself or herself as the author. Such self-ascription is, in the first instance, nothing but the identification of a reason conceived of as an intention in the set of causal conditions necessary for bringing about the event (EPM § 504). Thus, the agent can distinguish between deliberately knocking a man off his ladder ('I wanted to because he had ogled my wife') and involuntarily knocking a man off his ladder ('It wasn't my fault, I tripped on the carpet.')[12] The subject is responsible for the occurrence to which the predicate 'mine' can be attached and which is traceable to the subject's intention. If we can reconstruct a desire and belief as an intention that played a casual role in bringing about the event, then we can identify an action (PR § 115).

However, Hegel wants subjects to be held responsible for their actions in order to distribute praise and blame as demanded by the retributivist theory of

---

Continuum Press, 2007, pp. 69-77.

12. To reinforce this understanding, Hegel distinguishes between the deed and the action. Wood, *Hegel's Ethical Thought*, p. 140 sees no significance in the use of the word 'deed', whereas Quante, *Hegel's Concept of Action*, p. 105 claims that 'deed' captures the event-event characterization of actions and 'action' the moral element ($\alpha + \beta$).

punishment. The first determination of free action on its own is unable to fulfil this goal since it 'fails to cast the agent in his proper role'.[13] Reasons, that is dispositions and beliefs, *cause* an intention which *causes* an action, but the agent just does not feature and it is agents we hold responsible and not their beliefs and dispositions. So, reasons must effect something (viz. an agent) in order to become intentions and since reasons do not always produce the same intention in differing agents, something is missing in the causal explanation in order to make it plausible. Of course, one could cite the agents' differing webs of beliefs as the differentiating factor in diverse responses, but it is still possible for an agent to be moved by beliefs *despite himself*. Cases such as coercion and addiction feature an agent who is in accordance with the standard model ('I believe the robber's gun is loaded and I do not want to die'; 'I am in a state of wanting and I believe that the drug will alleviate this'), but, phenomenologically, these stories do not seem to capture the real nature of human action.[14] It makes intuitive sense to say that 'it was not me' or 'I wasn't acting on my own will' and such statements do have a legal—if not metaphysical—resonance. Coercion and addiction have been problematic for the empiricist model since Hobbes and the only real response is to say that the model of action proposed explains, but does not evaluate the actions of agents in terms of intentions. Evaluation must rest on controversial doctrines such as free-will or responsibility and these concepts play no role in the explanation of action.[15] In other words, there is no way on this simple causal model to distinguish *human* action or *full-blooded* action from *animal* action or *non-intentional* action. The distinction between animal and human action maps neatly onto the Hegelian *person* versus *subject* dichotomy: with the former, the content of the will is given, whereas with the latter the content is chosen and hence is the subject's in the genitive sense. Hegel captures this determination of full-blooded moral action with his second determination (β).

The phenomenology of human action involves reference to the agent and the empiricist model appears to negate this aspiration. To account for cases of coercion and false consciousness, the subject has to freely endorse his or her end for the action to be properly his or her own. Hegel puts this in terms of obligation: the intention is to be known as a good-for-me (β). In the case of coercion, the bank teller has a conflict of goods: self-preservation versus fulfilling his role. The former motivation trumps the latter but the agent is not free because he is not acting from his own will, it is the presence of an external factor which obstructs his free action.

---

13. David Velleman, 'What happens when someone acts?', in *The Possibility of Practical Reason*, Oxford, Oxford University Press, 2002, p. 123.

14. Harry Frankfurt, 'Coercion and Moral Responsibility', in *The Importance of What We Care About*, Cambridge, Cambridge University Press, 1988.

15. 'Hegel regarded the metaphysical conflict between freedom and determinism as basically a pseudo-problem generated by importing mechanical accounts of causality into the domain of action, where they are inappropriate. Understanding and explaining action requires teleological explanation, of both functional and purposive varieties.' Westphal, 'Hegel's Critique of Kant's Moral World View', p. 148.

What is more Hegel's motivation for formalizing a theory of action is, as has already been stated, so that punishment practices can be rationalized. Both of the statements 'I did it' and 'It was an act I brought about in the world' seems to invoke the agent in the causal chain and not just elements (beliefs and dispositions) which can be identified with the agent. The difference between a person and a subject is that he or she must somehow endorse those actions as his or her own. What Hegel recognizes about a pure causal explanation is that it is only partial and cannot, if lauded as the be all and end all of human action, supply the foundations for proper moral evaluation. Hegel's account needs to talk of actions and degrees of agent participation in order to distinguish between cases of coercion, deception and crime. For, although it is able to explain an action, the causal model's explanations are inadequate to ground an evaluative judgement. One needs to move away from the person (a collection of given dispositions and beliefs) to the subject (the agent who is 'at home' with his intentions and motivations):

> Freedom is only present where there is no other for me that is not myself. The natural man, who is determined only by his drives, is not at home with himself; however self-willed he may be, the *content* of his willing and opining is not his own, and his freedom is only a *formal* one (EL § 23 A2).

The natural man (and the person) is akin to the coerced agent and all are 'self-willed': free if he is able to act on the content of his will and not free if he is obstructed from doing so. However, there is no full responsibility since the content of the will is given and ultimately no different from external causes, psychoses, neuroses and the will of others imposed on one. Full blooded human action involves the proper recognition that what one did, one wanted to do and would justify it if asked.

Hegel expresses these very sentiments in his second determination (β). The animal has no choice but to obey its desires, neither does the small child; they bear little responsibility for their actions. Subjective freedom for them—like the person—resides in the satisfaction of the will's desire *whatever* its content may be. Human action is different in that certain desires and preferences are privileged even if they are not so pressing and these can be articulated as values.[16] Furthermore, values need not be exclusively moral since responsibility concerns all self-regarding actions (self-interest, prudence and morality). The process of the rationalization of desires permits the recognition of the 'good' of the subject's purpose, be it moral or prudential, and he perceives it not only as a desire to be satisfied (personal freedom) but a desire worth satisfying (moral freedom). And this means we can now evaluate rather than just explain an action. We identify the role of the agent's intention in the causes bringing about the event, and then are able to say whether or not the action is properly the agent's own if he or she wanted it to be the case (that is, posits it as a purpose). Responsibility requires

---

16. The contemporary characterization would be second-order desires. See Harry Frankfurt, 'Freedom of the will and the concept of a person' and Charles Taylor, 'Responsibility for self' both in G. Watson (ed.), *Free Will*, Oxford, Oxford University Press, 1982.

that subjects self-consciously know and freely choose their purposes for the predicate 'mine' to be attached to the action. An explanation of action requires no real notion of freedom, but an evaluation of action does. In dialogue, the actor would admit what he did as his own and his good and not the good of an alien will acting through him (coercion, false consciousness, and so on).

And the significance of 'homeliness' dovetails with the second consideration of the location of the discussion of action in the lectures. Hegel's theory of action mediates the sections 'Abstract Right' (the recognition and identification of individual persons as rights-bearers with particular desires) and 'Ethical Life' (the positive duties and obligations of the citizen in the rational state). Without the historical and philosophical emergence of the person (a distinct and discrete element of the tribe), there would be no possibility of the subjective freedom of 'I (as individual) want x' and without the immanent doctrine of duties proposed *by Sittlichkeit*, the good-for-me and the good-for-all of the rational social being would not be harmonious and free. The Ancient Greeks had a one-sided existence and were not fully free because the ethical substance they inhabited was, in some sense, not theirs. Their social fabric and values were justified in themselves, but the agents motivated by them took the values as given and natural (LPH 106-7). The subjectivity of the person (this is 'my' good irrespective of the dictates and roles of my social existence) is also one-sided since although the content of one's will is one's own, it is not necessarily rational and if unconstrained by moral concerns would lead to disastrous social atomism (PR § 236 R). The subject, the moral point of view, demands more than the wishes and aspirations of the mere person: he or she is aware that actions have to obey positive obligations, the 'good', to truly express his or her identity to others. Moral freedom is a precondition of social freedom: ethical life is not mine until I as moral agent recognize it as a good and in order to do this, I must be a moral agent who can rationally endorse it. To be 'at home' in one's social fabric is to recognize one's rights and duties as one's own and rational and this requires the capacity of doing or being otherwise, a possibility inconceivable to the Ancient Greeks.

The transition from Person to Moral (in a broad sense) Subject allows one to distinguish between fully free actions and coerced actions:

> Particular self-determination, as the inward self-determination of the will that is for itself, and as a mode of self-determination that is intended to be realized, is known by the subject and is its *purpose*; [it is] a judgment that in its determinacy comprises universal thought. The *disposition* is the universality as belonging to the subject; and, as singled out and set apart on its own account, it is the *maxim* of the subjective will. Once right is enacted, the disposition is of no essential significance for it (LNR § 53).

The identification of me in the action is as a self-willed unit. The responsibility of the agent resides in bringing about those purposes which are his own and trying to falter those that are not. I am responsible for actions that emanate from reasons that are my own.[17] Reasons that are my own are best conceived of as purposes: purposes correspond to what the agent sees as good and the bank teller who gives money to the robber does not see this as a good even if he has a reason playing a causal role in why he gives money to the robber. He can explain why he did it, but he can—intelligibly—state that he did not want to do so because it was contrary to the obligations of his institutional role. And the Kantian resonances in the above quotation cannot be ignored: both the weak-willed bank teller who submits to the robber and the strong-willed one who does not can explain their actions in terms of dispositions (fear and rectitude respectively), but only the latter can separate a maxim worthy of moral approbation.

So, the second determination, (β), is seemingly consistent with Kant and the evaluation of the agent via their intentions. The idea of intentions and obligations resonates with Kant's good will and the voice of conscience, but Hegel does not want the idea of right to rest on the idea of the otherly out there, that is Kant's transcendental idealism.[18] However, at this stage of the argument, the parallels are striking:

> This subjective or 'moral' freedom is what a European especially calls freedom. In virtue of the right thereto a man must possess a personal knowledge of the distinction between good and evil in general: ethical and religious principles shall not merely lay their claim on him as external laws and precepts of authority to be obeyed, but have their assent, recognition, or even justification in his heart, sentiment, conscience, intelligence, etc. The subjectivity of the will in itself is its supreme aim and absolutely essential to it (EPM § 503).

Here, Hegel is offering his own version of the Kantian characterization of Enlightenment, and one cannot fail to see the parallel with Kant's earlier portrayal of the spirit of his age as the 'age of criticism'.[19] It is significant to note that the claim of the Enlightenment is the identifying mark of moral freedom: it is the coming to age of man. To use a traditional analogy, man has grown into maturity and no longer need rely on the dictates of authority or the motivations of immediate inclination (including social character). The subjective ascription of 'good' or value to an end is necessary to free action for Hegel.

Traditionally these two determinations (α + β) have been held to be necessary and sufficient conditions for free action, yet Hegel adds his third determination (γ): the intention has to be capable of reconstruction by others from the objectivity of the act itself. Hegel feels it is necessary to not only retain the traditional concept of the right of knowledge, but also temper it with an objective constraint. One reason he does so is that, ultimately, Kant's picture fails because it cannot generate purposes a priori or resolve conflicting goods, but Hegel does

---

17. This is Taylor's understanding of Hegel's theory of action: the human is a purposive being but one whose purposes are known and endorsed by itself. See Charles Taylor, 'Hegel's concept of Mind', in *Human Agency and Language: Philosophical Papers 1*, Cambridge, Cambridge University Press, 1985.

18. Westphal, 'Hegel's Critique of Kant's Moral World View'.

19. Immanuel Kant, *The Critique of Pure Reason*, trans. J. Meiklejohn & revised V. Politis, London, J M Dent, 1993, pp. Aix-xi.

not introduce his famous Kantian critique here. Instead the reader is offered positive reasons for the adoption of an immanent doctrine of ethics grounded in the Hegelian concept of recognition. It is necessary that others recognize the action as one's own. The action must express the implicit humanity (obligation) rather than appear to be a mere, immediate purpose (wilfulness) and this entails that others must concur with me and my description of the good, otherwise they will continue to treat me under the category of personhood or worse. Intention, therefore, requires recognition by others: 'The implementation of my end therefore has this identity of my will and the will of others within in it—it has a positive reference to the will of others.' (PR § 112) The first-person may be the judge of what is good, but his judgement is constrained by the interpretation of the other. The agent has to be aware that his act ought to accord with the expectations of his form of life, otherwise his intention will be either misdescribed or ignored.

One way to characterize this is to say that the justification of one's good or end involves one in the activity of reason-giving and this activity is, for Hegel, inherently social. Affirming what is substantially right and good is not a matter of external, transcendental standards independent of one's peers, but rests on their recognition of the content of one's will in terms of articulated and shared categories of right.[20] There are no constraints on a will which justifies a good or a purpose to itself, one is able to convince oneself that anything may be good (PR §140 R). Reasons for action require a degree of objectivity for Hegel and this is based on reasons being a justification for all men who share my way of life rather than just for me; that is, an actual reason rather than just wilfulness and, contrary to Kant, one's role, situation and circumstances all constitute reasons for behaviour. In offering reasons, the agent knows if they are good reasons if he can convince others. It follows from this that the agent's description of his intention must harmonize with the other's interpretation of the act. A man unaware of the way in which a certain act will be interpreted, that is how his reasons for action will be reconstructed (the tourist abroad) is not responsible for any offence caused (although he may still be held culpable).[21] Reciprocally, the agent is only fully free when he is aware how his action will be interpreted. The will of others contained in one's own will is this shared scheme of interpretation in and through which we reconstruct intentions.

The rational reformulation of the initial determinations of action (PR § 113) occurs in a later paragraph which reduces the dialectical trinity to a new symmetry of subjective and objective aspects:

> The right of intention is that the universal quality of the action shall have being not only in itself, but shall be known by the agent and thus have been present all along in his subjective will; and conversely, what we may call the right of the objectivity of the action is the right of the action to assert itself as known and willed by the subject

---

20. Neuhouser convincingly traces this element of Hegel's thought back to Rousseau's influence, see *Foundations of Hegel's Social Theory*.

21. His culpability is a legal issue arising form the consideration of what an agent ought to know on setting foot within a state.

as a thinking agent (PR § 120).

Here we find that self-ascription of intentions, or the right of knowledge (α), is combined with the necessary element of modern moral freedom (β) into the 'right of intention' such that the agent will only be held responsible for those actions deliberately brought about by his or her own will, thus ruling out external causality, neurotic behaviour, coercion, deception and false consciousness. However, in order to recognize one's intentions as 'good' or 'rational' requires the reformulation of (γ) into the 'right of objectivity'. An action is—independently of the protestations and affirmations of the agent him or herself—to 'stand in for' or 'represent' the will of the agent in the 'outer' world, just as the word uttered in language is assumed to be a sincere representation of the thought and will of the speaker who is present. If the agent wishes to be understood as a free moral agent, then he or she must be aware that an action requires a commitment to the medium through which others will understand it. So, in order to affirm one's freedom, there must exist a minimum level of expectation which must be met. If the subject's acts are to be the expression of inwardness, then he must be certain that the other is going to reconstruct them faithfully. Both actor and interpreter must, therefore, share a common understanding of the way in which acts are to be rendered intelligible.

The first two determinations of free action are not sufficient to justify an action because, without the moment of certain *recognition* of the moral will, the agent cannot be held fully and morally responsible as demanded by the retributivist theory of punishment. Recognition, it ought to be recalled, is not just granted by the struggle to death, even if that story makes stark what is at stake: I demonstrate to you that I am free over and above my desires by risking the most fundamental drive for the sake of a principle (PS ¶¶ 178-196).[22] Such recognition of one's essential rationality and humanity can alternatively be granted by marriage, whereby the agent sincerely places altruistic and universal needs over particular and egoistic ones (PR § 162). Without the self-certainty granted by knowledge of the inter-subjective categories of the right of objectivity, the subject would be unsure whether or not he has been properly recognized or if his intention can be reconstructed faithfully from his action. In a rational social order, the agent knows the good in question because it is made immediately available to him through fulfilling his roles in the family (parent, child), civil society (worker) and the state (citizen). If I wish to be known as a good father, then my acts must accord with those judgements which accompany a good parent (love, generosity, discipline) and not those which are generally frowned upon (indifference, prodigality, severity). The significance of the right of objectivity resides in the certainty of recognition and one's social fabric is a liberation because it makes possible—and does not inhibit—free moral action.

---

22. G. W. F. Hegel, *The Phenomenology of Spirit*, trans. A.V. Miller, New York, Oxford, 1977. See Alexandre Kojève, *Introduction to the Reading of Hegel*, 2nd ed., trans. J. Nichols, London, Basic Books Inc., 1969 and, for a full discussion of the concept of recognition, see Robert Williams, *Hegel's Ethics of Recognition*, London, University of California Press, 1997.

The conclusions to the all too brief discussion of Hegel's theory of action are not to be underestimated. The right of knowledge (α) is familiar from most theories of action, but the right of intention (α combined with β) makes it obvious that the moral conscience, that is the subject's right to decide his or her good—in which values he or she feels 'at home'—is a necessary condition of the rational state for without it rational, free action would not be possible and Hegel's theory of punishment would be incongruous. Hence, any institutions or practices of the state which motivated citizens without being evaluated by the standards of personal freedom would make it impossible to feel 'at home'. The right of objectivity (γ) sets the limits and conditions of possible subjective endorsement: any deviation from the norm must be justified by familiar standards and not by an appeal to mere wilfulness. One cannot rely on an incoherent noumenal realm to dictate right action and good ends, but one can interrogate one's social roles and meanings for a way to express one's particularity through a universal medium.[23]

And here one should take note of the fact these discussions, prior to any substantial consideration of Kantian or subjective ethics, invite the Hegelian reader to appreciate the moral conscience as necessary and operative in the rational state as well as recognizing that ethical action entails an immanent and not transcendental doctrine of duties, although the latter claim has still to be made apparent. For these points cast light on one of Hegel's most controversial remarks:

> The right to recognize nothing that I do not perceive as rational is the highest right of the subject, but by virtue of its subjective determination, it is at the same time formal; on the other hand, the right of the rational—as the objective—over the subject remains firmly established (PR § 132 R).

Subjective social freedom, the moral conscience of the citizen, is necessary for the subject to feel 'at home' within his or her state and is, hence, the 'highest right'. Yet, if it is unable to generate the 'good' from its own reason, it must rely on the objective freedom of *Sittlichkeit* as those shared meanings and values operative in the practical reasoning of oneself and one's peers coupled with those social practices and material arrangements which make self-determination possible.[24]

## III. THE NECESSITY OF THE RIGHT OF OBJECTIVITY FOR RESPONSIBILITY

In his lecture notes, Hegel introduces the right of objectivity and its relation to the rational order prior to the critique of Kant in particular and subjective moralities in general. The latter arguments are supposed to *support* the already articulated claim that free, moral action is impossible without a medium of immanently shared values and good rather than *ground* it. One could imagine a hand

---

23. Here is a rather playful, but illuminating example. Without the rules of football, the determinations that dictate right action on the field of play (rules and expectations in their broadest sense), Maradona would never have been. Yet, nothing about those rules, expectations and history could have determined what was unique about him.

24. Neuhouser, *Foundations of Hegel's Social Theory*, chapter 5.

being raised in the class room and a courageous student asking Hegel whether he had considered the alternative that right action could be known and willed by the subject from reason alone. To which, the professor would reply with the negative reason for the appropriation of an immanent doctrine of duty: the point by point attack on transcendental morality.[25] It would be pertinent just to offer a brief reminder of these points, as Hegel presents them: one, the subjective will cannot overcome conflicts of duty (whether generated by different kinds of duty or self-interest and duty) (EPM § 508-9); two, the moral point of view has to be constrained because it is infinitely powerful and can posit (or negate) any good whatsoever as universal good.(EPM §§ 510-11; PR § 140); and, three, the subject is unable to generate determinations of the will out of his reflective understanding, its abstractness needs to be overcome by objective determinations (EPM §§ 506, 508; PR § 135).

Hegel is oddly (for once) making an appeal to our intuitive grasp of the phenomenon of moral action. Take the tired and worn out old example of the mother who has to decide whether or not to steal to feed her starving child. The immediate determination of the family, the naturally binding duty of the maternal bond, gives rise to the desire to protect, feed and sustain the child. This is the good-for-mother. Yet, her role in civil society determines that she recognize the rationality of the right to property and this, too, is a good. The universality of good means that these two goods should harmonize, yet the moral conscience is quite able to accept one as right at the expense of the other in one moment, then—in the next second—to reverse such a description. For Hegel, the moral conscience itself cannot decide between conflicting determinations of the will and, if it does so, such a decision is wholly arbitrary and wilful. And if this is the case, then there is no standard by which the agent can be distinguished from the person who acts on a given content of the will (PR § 17). Hegel's solution is to make a demand on one's immanent set of duties and values and ask what it is that gives rise to the conflict in the first place. That a child be fed is a good and that the right of property be respected is a good, so such a society in which a conflict between these two is felt, is *not* rational. The conflict can only be overcome when objective freedom, granted by the institutions of ethical life, eradicates the existence of the mother's need to steal and her subjective freedom can be satisfied. (Through the supply of basic needs as a right (the welfare state) and the eradication of poverty, or legal recognition of her subjective freedom adjudicated in a court.)

Hegel realizes that the abstract nature of the good cannot be created from the top down and theoretically tested. It is not truly possible for the agent to declare what the world ought to be like in all certainty given the dictates of reason. Instead, the moral subject must begin from the existing world and its institutions since the constraint of objectivity involves the idea that the good must be intelligible to these institutions since the judgements of my peers is necessary for my action to be free. Only in such a way can subjective freedom meet the constraint

---

25. See Ameriks, 'The Hegelian Critique of Kantian Morality', and Westphal, 'Hegel's Critique of Kant's Moral World View'.

of objective freedom and, reciprocally, it is this very objective freedom which grants the subject the certainty of recognition he requires to satisfy his actions. Therefore, it is only the ethical person who is truly free:

> The ethical person is conscious of the content of his action as something necessary, something that is valid in and for itself, and this consciousness is so far from diminishing freedom, that, on the contrary, it is only through this consciousness that his abstract freedom becomes a freedom that is actual and rich in content, as distinct from freedom of choice [*Willkür*], a freedom that still lacks content and is merely possible (EL § 158 A).

The objective freedom of ethical life makes possible the satisfaction of rational desires, projects and aspirations and this is an elaboration of the right of objectivity present in the abstract theory of action; a right which renders apparent the requirement of shared categories from which the subjective intention can reliably be reconstructed (as in the case of the mother). Ethical life is the substantial description of the possible determinations of one of its members and is, then, liberation because it purifies and rationalizes the drives of the individual (PR § 19). Objective freedom is freedom because it liberates the subject in three ways: one, from a dependence on immediate drives; two, from having to produce the categories for comprehension (values, rights and duties) for himself *ex nihilo*; and, three, from the need to determine good from his own conscience (PR § 149). The three institutions of modern society—that is, the liberal, bourgeois family, civil society and the modern political state—all combine to fulfil these conditions of objective freedom. It is these determinations of ethical life which constitute the objective freedom of the subject in that they enable him to satisfy his desires, wants and aspirations, to simultaneously pursue the good and to be certain of recognition by the other (EPM § 538). Hegel's claim, then, is that the subject as he has described it in 'Morality' can only be fully free when his or her objective freedom is secured by these modern institutions.[26] *Sittlichkeit* is, in one of its aspects, the world constructed by social reasons for actions.[27] It supplies motivations and obligations for the agent in virtue of his membership and his role in this institutional order and also makes possible recognition of him as a free-self-determining being (PR § 151; EPM § 513).

An immanent doctrine of duties and values overcomes the abstract and formal nature of the 'ought' which results from the subjective will: 'Thus, without any selective reflection, the person performs duty *as his own* and as something which *is*; and in this necessity *he* has himself and his actual freedom' (EG § 514). The member of *Sittlichkeit* can perform his duties—possibly from habit, that is without any 'selective reflection'—because they constitute his identity and he feels 'at home'. It is not how he *should* act, it is how he *does* act (I drive on the left because I am English) and he can be certain of recognition as an agent through

---

26. I have not argued in this essay why it has to be these three institutions, neither do I feel that there are no other alternatives (or, in fact, that these are actually absolutely rational in Hegel's sense). But these remarks cannot be discussed here.

27. It must also be the material conditions necessary for free, self-determining action.

fulfilling the dictates of these roles:

> All these substantial determinations are *duties* which are binding on the will of the individual; for the individual, as subjective and inherently undetermined—or determined in a particular way—is distinct from them and *consequently stands in a relationship to them* as to his own substantial being (PR § 148).

The certain recognition of free action is made possible by the objective social order embedded in institutions coupled with the substantial identity of the agent as a member of these institutions, but the above quotation makes clear that the right of intention is still significant. The modern subject, unlike the Greek citizen, is 'inherently undetermined' and 'distinct' from his 'own substantial being'. According to Hegel, if one is committed to the evaluation of actions (and one must be if one is postulating a retributivist theory of judgement), then this commitment entails an immanent doctrine of duties, values and meanings; that is, *Sittlichkeit*.[28]

## IV. THE DANGERS OF THE PURELY OBJECTIVE WILL

The aim of this paper was to show that Hegel's immanent doctrine of duty arose not just from his rejection of transcendental ethics but also from his own account of human moral action. I believe I have shown above that Hegel's theory of action necessarily requires objective freedom which can only be supplied by *Sittlichkeit* even if I have not gone into the fine details of his account of ethical substance. In justifying this claim it was also hoped that the limits of the moral conscience within the rational state could be delineated and its power described.

The worry, of course, arises from the above quotation where Hegel tells us that *Sittlichkeit* is immediately motivating through habit or second nature 'without any selective reflection' (EPM § 514). The right of the rational, after all, was to be 'firmly established' and it is clear that Hegel's theory of action implicitly involves the notion of *Sittlichkeit* in that the moral agent requires objective determination to be certain of recognition and, hence, to be fully responsible. In order to be recognized as free my action must meet the expectations of my peers, yet this seems to implicitly rule out any abnormal behaviour and protest is, one would assume, always a break from the norm and the expected.[29] It is the objective, rational

---

28. I do not want to give the impression that ethical life is merely a form of life which determines and harmonizes the good, *rather* it is *the* rational order of determinations of the will. The difference can be understood in that the former case holds only that the objective, institutional order coupled with the subjective knowledge of these determinations constrain the actions of the subject within the bounds of intelligibility given *whichever* form of life; or just because humans *happen* to exist in communities. Hegel holds, on the contrary, that objective freedom satisfies the requirements of the subjective will through supplying rational determinations and not just determinations.

29. One immediate Hegelian response would be to invoke an objective, absolutist account of the end of history: man inhabits the purely rational state where social and individual good harmonize and do so due to the rationality of the institutions which exist. Objective freedom meets the requirements of subjective freedom and no conflicts between the two can possibly arise. However, it would be necessary to offer a thorough description of the nature of the end of history, to acknowledge that Hegel's intuitions concerning certain moral problems and our own differ markedly, to admit that it is in no way obvious that modern institutions could deal with future moral problems and, given all

structure of Hegel's account of *Sittlichkeit* which grounds the conservative strains and themes in his work; he lists, interrogates and attempts to actualize the social institutions which existed in the Prussian state and, at each step of the argument, the subjective right—the 'highest' right—of individuals appears to play second fiddle to the role demanded by the institution itself.

Hegel's strongest critic would intimate that the moral conscience described in *Moralität* is negated in *Sittlichkeit* because the right of objectivity determines that deviations from the normal and expected behaviour of citizen, worker and family member are impossible since these roles exhaust the identity of the individual. The duties of the agent in ethical life are to fulfil his or her roles adequately and freedom consists solely in actions which are in accordance with one's duties, that is one's 'substantial identity'. In this way, one can be recognized by one's peers and hence be free. Yet, this is seemingly at the expense of the 'highest' right of subjectivity which, if enacted in opposition to the ethical norm, can be nothing but mere wilfulness.[30]

However, if one is to take seriously the role of the moral theory of action which precedes the account of ethical life, then it is clear that subjectivity still has a role to play in the objective freedom of *Sittlichkeit*. First, if it were true that freedom consisted solely in the fulfilment of one's role within a state that is rational, then there would be no marked difference between Ancient Greek society and our own (LPH 104-7, 444-5). The concept of 'homeliness' derived from the right of intention ($\alpha + \beta$) requires that not only do I act on correct and harmonious determinations of the will, but that I also endorse them as my own. One cannot be coerced into acting freely, for Hegel. Second, within communities that are not fully rational or not even partially so, the subject cannot be free except by resisting the norms and expectations placed on him or her: 'When the existing world of freedom has become unfaithful to the better will, this will no longer finds itself in the duties recognized in this world and must seek to recover in ideal inwardness alone that harmony which it has lost in actuality' (PR § 138 R). The right of intention must be effective on the objective order of things and is so through the necessity that the actualization of social ideality requires self-conscious knowledge: the free, rational state is not one in which the institution of slavery could exist; its rationality cannot be actualized as all persons are to be considered equals in the free, rational state (PR §§ 36, 155). Thus, the right of objectivity requires a subjective will capable of endorsing it; that is, finding it rational *for itself*.

When a child wears a seat-belt he does so to safeguard his personhood, but such a reason is rational only in itself. The child actually acts on another reason: to avoid being shouted at by his mother (personhood). As the child grows, however, he comes to realize that the reason for wearing a seatbelt is to protect himself; that is, he recognizes the good as his own and so he is 'at home' with his social motivation. He is aware that, not only is he reasonable to his mother and

---

these, to reconsider the end of history as purely an objective state of affairs. All of this is well beyond the remit of this paper.

30. Tugendhat, *Self-consciousness and Self-determination*.

her expectations, but also to himself: this is an act which is rational for him not just his mother. He now has self-knowledge of the reason and it is both in itself rational and also for him rational. Only when objective freedom makes possible the satisfaction of desires which can be freely chosen, known and transparent, is the agent fully responsible. Thus, for fully free, responsible action, the right of knowledge is required and individuals stand in a relationship to their substantial identity but remain distinct from it (PR § 148).

Therefore, the right of intention crucial to free action can be inflated into a form of rational legitimation. The rational system of the will's self-determination, for modern man, is self-conscious knowledge of the underlying necessity implicit in the customs and mores of *Sittlichkeit*. To be 'at home' (as required by the right on intention) involves knowing not only what one does but that it is a good for oneself. It is 'customary' to wear a seatbelt, and one wears it without much 'selective reflection,' but, it is possible to actualize the custom; that is, to make apparent its rationality to the knowing subject. The strong critic of Hegel's social philosophy mistakes 'trust' in one's objective order for blind faith. This difference is best illustrated by Hegel's own distinction between reflective (the state) and unreflective trust (the family) and the possibility to articulate one's reasons for action. If I am to save my child from drowning or, on a lesser scale, to provide for the material needs of my family, I cannot truly articulate the reason why I fulfil this role. The best I can manage is 'Because they are my children.' Moreover, someone who demands that I justify my reasons for these actions is simply inhuman, not in the sense of evil, but in the sense that they cannot truly comprehend what it is to be a human being. These reasons, then, are immediate and unreflective and trust in one's family members is based on the same disposition.[31] The reflective trust in the state is open to scrutiny, though; this is the formal requirement of subjective, moral freedom. It is perfectly sensible to demand a justification of a particular law, social duty or more and why I should act in accordance with it. However, agents rarely demand justification and as such express a reflective trust in their state; its laws and institutions are open to legitimation and the state must make scrutiny by the citizen possible, but this need not be carried through every time a demand on the citizen is made. A useful analogy is differentiation in mathematics. All of us are quite happy to use the formula '$nx^{n-1}$', but in order for us to be certain it must be possible for us to carry out the calculation from first-principles. The laws of the state are a type of shorthand of the good, but which must remain possible objects of legitimation even when not perpetually legitimated. The subject has 'trust' in the objective social order and its rationality (EPM § 525; PR, § 147). The 'trust' of the Ancient Greeks was inarticulate and, hence, it was mere social luck that they lived in a rational state. Modern ethical life *makes possible* the satisfaction of subjective freedom, rather than—as many commentators hostile to the Hegelian picture suppose—*determining* the content of subjective freedom. It is no longer a matter of 'luck' that we live in a rational state since without the

---

31. This is perhaps why the abuse of children by their parents is such a reprehensible crime, there is a certain element of inhumanity in it which horrifies us.

subjective endorsement of the morally free agent, the duties of *Sittlichkeit* are not actual duties (PR § 138 R).

The proper consideration of the right of intention seems to put pay to the strong criticism of Hegel's social philosophy, but this idea is rarely the motivation behind the apologist approach of many of his supporters. A more subtle challenge to the relationship between the moral conscience and the state would propose that, if reason giving is inherently social as Hegel holds, then surely the tendency will be—in cases of conflict between individual good and social good— to side with the familiar and conventional. With the stronger form of the challenge, social protest is impossible and irrational, but this is to negate absolutely the 'highest right' of the subject. The weaker form of the challenge does not fully negate the right of knowledge: one is able to deny the determinations of one's role when one cannot endorse its rationality. However, given that this endorsement is a social practice, protest stemming from the moral conscience is ultimately mute since the right of objectivity, that my actions be rational for others, implicitly commits Hegel to conservatism. Endorsement amounts to nothing more than yes-saying: the subject reflects upon his duties and recognizes that they accord with objective determinations. The strong challenge pictured Hegel rather unconvincingly as a strong communitarian who believed agents are identical with (rather than identified with) their roles. The weaker challenge is more persuasive, Hegel appears committed to conservatism which means subjective freedom may be compromised by social pressure because the social nature of reason-giving means the conventional is always by default more persuasive than personal conviction.

The first point to make is simply to admit Hegel is a conservative, that much is clear both from his continued critique of the use of abstract right in political theorizing and in his tinkering with—rather than overhaul of—the Prussian state. However, conservatism may be compatible with central liberal values and does not necessarily commit Hegel to quietism in the face of one's duties in the state. Furthermore, the reasons for his conservatism, especially in the aftermath of the French Revolution, are perhaps justified.

In order to resist the accusation that Hegel's form of rational legitimation is nothing but yes-saying to authority, it would be worthwhile to return to the example of the mother who finds herself unable to fulfil her role without stealing and violating the system of private property. Let us assume that Hegel would see this as an instance of the 'better will' in an 'unfaithful world' (PR § 138 R). On an idealized liberal model, the standards of positive right would be legitimated by an appeal to external values or natural rights. So, the right to life would trump political obligation since civil obedience rests on a duty to comply with political dictates *as long as* they protect and secure external rights and values. If they no longer do so, then the citizen's obligation is null and void. However, for Hegel, there are no external standards of right independent of the social and historical development of ethical life.³² It seems the weaker challenge has some bite: protest when contrary to customary morality is mere wilfulness.

The example of the impoverished mother, though, undermines such an idle reading. The proper understanding of Hegel's theory of action demonstrates that the role of objective freedom and its earlier, abstract cousin—the right of objectivity—is to enable personal self-determination and not to thwart it. Liberation from immediate needs, independence from irrational authorities, the possibility to be self-willed and certain recognition by others are all requirements of self-determination and if they do not obtain, then the subject is not free. The mother is recognized as in the right when she steals because the life of her child ought to be secured and maintained by the objective structures, arrangements and practices of her social existence. Otherwise the world is unfaithful to her better will. The state, for the mother, is irrational because she cannot satisfy her roles as both mother and citizen as she would freely choose to do. She has the subjective right—the highest right—to demand that the state make possible rational self-determination. And protest need not be limited to cases of disharmony between the spheres of ethical life. Historical examples of the need to reject the objective features of a state would include slavery and apartheid since fulfilling one's civil role inhibits one's personal freedom.³³ Such institutions make it impossible for certain agents to fulfil themselves as human beings since other agents cannot recognize what they truly are: they remain identical with their role and, hence, not free.

## V. CONCLUSION

For man to be free—that is, to be *at home* with himself—the content of his will must be *his own*. For the existing social world to be actualized, then the underlying rationality of its dictates and obligations has to be known and endorsed by the thinking subject, but such an endorsement cannot be mere yes-saying. Freedom is formal when I am able to satisfy my desires (personal freedom), but it is substantial when I satisfy desires which are my good. Yet, this does not rule out coercion for my benefit (the child). The will is free when it is substantial, able to be satisfied and *moral*. Without moral freedom, the will of man is no better than the slave or the child or as Hegel tells us, the 'ethical [*sittliche*] will'; that is the ethical will which is not actual because the agent is unaware of its rationality

---

32. Rose, *Hegel's Philosophy of Right*, pp. 16-29.

33. Critically, Hegel's own descriptions of the role of women in the family, the rigidity of social class and the postulation of a hereditary monarch possibly contradict the requirements of equality and careers open to talents which he espouses as necessary for the state to be rational. These, of course, are open to interpretation and I only throw them somewhat glibly in here to demonstrate that, though Hegel's conservatism does not rule out social criticism stemming from the moral conscience, he is often—I believe—guilty of lazy conservatism in describing elements of institutions which are not rational on his own account. Such a discussion is, however, beyond the scope of this paper, but these do illustrate possible areas in which the moral conscience has a proper claim against the duties of the state.

(Ancient Greece) (PR § 26). The purely subjective will is arbitrary, whereas the purely objective will depends on 'luck' to have ethical content.

The two central concepts of the third section of the *Philosophy of Right*—that is, subjective and objective freedom—originate from the rights of knowledge, intention and objectivity of action which characterize the abstract moral will. Objective freedom is necessary for and supplements—which, is to say, ethical life *actualizes*—personal and moral freedom. Without the categories of ethical life, it would be impossible to form judgements concerning the intentions of others. Thus, ethical life is the substantial form of the right of objectivity of an action. Reciprocally, subjective freedom interrogates and justifies objective freedom. If the subject cannot, or is obstructed from, satisfying his rational desires, then he is not free and responsible. He, then, has a legitimate claim against the state arising from his own moral conscience. So long as the claim is unresolved, freedom is unobtainable and the institutions of ethical life are no longer rational. It is this right of knowledge which constitutes the role of the moral will in *Sittlichkeit*. Morality remains an essential element of modern *Sittlichkeit* since, to actualize the rationality of existing social structures, this rationality has to be self-consciously known. Otherwise we are merely 'lucky' citizens like the Ancient Greeks and children with good and rational parents.

# 6

# Hegel's *Science of Logic* and the 'Sociality of Reason'

Jorge Armando Reyes Escobar

This paper is intended to examine the following question: what is the significance of Hegel's *Science of Logic* for social thought? The straightforward inquietude provoking the question is the awareness of the noticeable divergence between the contemporary reappraisals of Hegel's thought from the standpoint of political philosophy and the recent interest on his *Science of Logic*.[1] Both areas of Hegelian scholarship seem to have experienced a growing development in the last two decades, but they hardly meet each other. On the one hand, Jürgen Habermas and Axel Honneth claim that some of the key notions that Hegel yielded between 1801 and 1807 (such as love, ethical life, and spirit) provide elements capable to justify the universal validity of liberal political institutions within the framework of a social notion of agency formed through relations of mutual recognition. From that perspective, they use to regard the *Science of Logic* as a tremendous setback into a metaphysics of consciousness which ultimately wipes out any possibility to grasp the intersubjective dimension of reason[2]. On the other hand, authors like

---

1. Although that inquietude is personal, its significance is very far from being original. In that sense I suppose the accounts provided by Dieter Henrrich ('Logical form and real totality: the authentic conceptual form of Hegel's concept of the state,' in Robert Pippin and Otfried Höffe, (eds.), *Hegel on Ethics and Politics*, Cambridge, Cambridge University Press, p. 241-267), Toula Nicolacopoulos and George Vassilacopoulos (*Hegel and the Logical Structure of Love*, Aldershot, Ashgate, 1999), Richard Dien Winfield (*Overcoming Foundations*, New York, Columbia University Press, 1989), and Allegra de Laurentiis (*Subjects in the Ancient and Modern World*, New York, Palgrave, 2005). All of them have emphasized the importance to understand Hegel's social and political claims from the process of self-determination of the Notion in terms of 'the unity of universal, particular, individual' (Nicolacopoulos and Vassilacopoulos, *Hegel and the Logical Structure of Love*, p. 57). From that perspective my intention is to raise the following question: what is the process through which thinking situates itself as an unity of *meaning* articulated in those three moments. I undertook the research leading to this publication in my capacity as a Research Fellow in the Philosophy Program at the School of Communication, Arts and Critical Enquiry, La Trobe University.

2. It is the position advocated by Axel Honneth, who suggest that we can put into brackets the

Robert Pippin and Terry Pinkard maintain that is possible to combine a reading of Hegel's thought as a support for the 'sociality of reason'[3]—understood as the position advancing the intersubjective constitution of the framework of reference from which is possible to carry on the self-reflection on the conditions of possibility of theoretical discourse, practical mastering of world, and self-description—with an interpretation of his speculative *Logic* as a heir of Kant's transcendental logic devoted to the systematic reconstruction of the of the basic categories at the base of such intersubjective grounding[4].

I agree with the general project outlined by this latter interpretation because I think that there are good reasons to claim that Hegel championed for a social understanding of reason along all the stages of his thought. Nevertheless, as I will try to show, it is a claim that cannot be straightforwardly maintained from the pragmatic awareness of the social embedding of the social practice of asking and giving reasons, but demands us to deal with the crucial requirement opening the *Logic*: the engagement with presuppositionless thinking. Unless we were prone to neglect that demand as if it were an empty shell ready to be discarded in order to legitimate Hegel's *Logic* in a philosophical scene characterized by distrust toward ontological claims, the clarification of what means to be a presuppositionless thinking is indispensable to grasp the general structure of the *Logic*, and likewise to comprehend its significance for social and political thought. The importance of this explanation has been sharply perceived by Ludwig Siep, who stresses the importance of Hegel's *Logic* in the following terms:

> The ontological condition for both [individual self-understanding and communal understanding] is that individual consciousness and rational communal spirit are structured by a conceptual system that has the form of a self-individualizing whole of meanings [...] In the course of a justification of speculative logic vis-à-vis traditional ways of knowing, the emphasis lies on the implicit thesis about the truth of such phenomena. But given a contemporary interest in Hegel's conception of individuality, it seems justified to focus on his analysis of social phenomena. However, the ultimate basis for the synthesis of individual and communal consciousness lies in Hegel's ontological logic.[5]

---

Hegelian system as a whole in order to focus our attention in his understanding of social issues: 'in the writings that have survived from the period before the final system had been worked out [he is referring to the Jena's period] this model is so clearly recognizable in its theoretical principles that *the premises for an independent social theory can be reconstructed from them*' (*The Struggle for Recognition: The Moral Grammar of Social Conflicts*, Cambridge, MIT Press, 1996, p. 6, my italics).

3. The term 'sociality of reason' deliberately echoes the title of the masterful book by Terry Pinkard, *Hegel's Phenomenology. The Sociality of Reason*, Cambridge, Cambridge University Press, 1994.

4. In that sense, Pinkard regards the *Logic* as an explanatory enterprise which applies the basic categories of the logic to the political field. As Pinkard writes: 'the rest of his system —the philosophy of nature, the ethical and political philosophy of absolute spirit— is to be no more than an application both of the program and the general categories of the *Science of Logic*. The other parts of the system display in concrete form the more abstract categorical structures elaborated and defended in the *Science of Logic*.' (*Hegel's Dialectic: The Explanation of Possibility*, Philadelphia, Temple University Press, 1988, p. 8)

5. Ludwig Siep, 'Individuality in Hegel's *Phenomenology of Spirit*, in Ameriks and Sturma (eds.), *The Modern Subject*, Albany, SUNY, 1995, p. 135.

I think that Siep announces the importance of coordinating a *global* interpretation of the *Logic* with Hegel's social and political views. However, after that worthy statement he does not discuss the *Logic* anymore. So, the question still remains: 'how the logical demand of a presuppositionless thinking is related to the sociality of reason?' This paper is intended to examine that question.

So, in the first section will be presented the problems involved with the meaning and plausibility of a discourse developed around the demand of a presuppositionless thinking. Next, in the second section, will be examined the criticisms addressed against the possibility of a presuppositionless thinking as well as the attempt to retort them by means of an interpretation of Hegel's *Logic* along the lines of the methodological enterprise of transcendental philosophy. The proper place of this kind of philosophical reflection in the composition of the *Logic* will be explained in the third section; it will be the more extended part of the paper because in there it will be suggested, on the one hand, that the resources of transcendental philosophy are not enough to activate the demand of presuppositionless thinking because they remain external to the way the *Logic* is addressed to the issue of *meaning*. Nevertheless, on the other hand, I will claim that the encounter with Kant's transcendental philosophy (in particular with the concept of the Originary Synthetic Unity of Apperception—OSUA) is crucial to understand Hegel's concept of self-consciousness as a gathering in which meaning is both unified and dispersed. That explanation will allow us to suggest, in the fourth section, what is the kind of presuppositionless thinking executed in the *Logic*. In particular, I will argue that it is rather the recognition of a ground more than a methodological procedure to bracket off conceptual assumptions. Finally, in the fifth section, it will be explained why most of the interpretations which emphasizes the social character of reason as the pivotal key to account the development of Hegel's philosophy fail to appreciate the recognition of the presuppositionless ground. Therefore, they overlook the interpretative possibility which will be presented a mode of conclusion: the sociality of reason must be understood as a determination reason gives itself through its self-situating in the field of meaning.

I

I want to deem the position from which is possible to raise the question: 'What is the significance of Hegel's *Science of Logic* for social thought?' The rationale behind that mode of questioning does not pursue a merely rhetorical intention but tries to take seriously what *Logic* reminds us: 'In no science is the need to begin with the subject matter itself, without preliminary reflections, felt more strongly than in the science of logic' (SL 42). Even if we are going to approach to that demand keeping in mind a reasonable suspicion about its plausibility, a thoughtful regard of it should take us to ask: 'since logic demands us to engage ourselves in a task "without preliminary reflections", which begins "with the subject matter itself", from where could we be able to understand it in order to eventually compare it to other fields of knowing or experience?' The interrogation is not aimed to prepare the space for an eventual answer pointing out the kind of privileged object capable to perform the function of providing the position from which is possible a proper understanding of the *Logic* and its ramifications, because it does not work as a doctrine about a specific subject-matter which could be defined by means of the aggregate of its determinations, as Hegel puts it forward: 'What we are dealing with in logic is not a thinking *about* something which exists independently as a base for our thinking and apart from it' (SL 50). Of course, along the text we can find explicit propositions stating, for instance, that the *Logic* 'is to be understood as the system of pure reason, as the realm of pure thought' (SL 50). However, those pronouncements are always mediated by wider argumentative contexts reminding us that by themselves the simple assertions of the aim of the *Logic* are of not avail because 'what this subject matter is [...] will be explicated only in the development of the science and cannot be presupposed by it as known beforehand' (SL 75). In sum, the previous interrogation foreshadows anything but the way *Logic* works: as a discourse[6] which is put in motion by the questioning about its own beginning. Perhaps such characterization left us empty-handed if we were expecting a neat definition of the *Logic* under a particular heading: 'epistemology', 'ontology', 'theory of categories', etc., but it will take us to the pertinence of our opening question because it suggests that, in becoming involved in the *Logic*'s work, the question about the meaning of something leaves its place to the question about the ground from which the meaning of something can be understood: 'How is possible at all that some "X" comes to mean "Y" instead of "Z"?' In other words, as soon as we have taken into account the simple suggestion that *Logic* requires us to engage in presuppositionless thinking, the assumed existence of an anchored theoretical framework lending intelligibility to the question 'What is the significance of Hegel's *Science of Logic* for social thought?' becomes bewildered because if we are thinking without presuppositions, then it does not seem plausible to determine at once which is the *beginning*—the process that establishes and holds the whole set of criteria, concepts, and objectives guiding our question—that provides the ground from which both the *meaning* of Hegel's *Science of Logic* and the *meaning* of 'social thought' do appear as a definite set of problems and thesis whose contents are already available for our interpretative exercises.

Nevertheless, that bewilderment is introduced by a demand, the claim of presuppositionless thinking, which hitherto hardly seems to be philosophically plausible because it looks as though Hegel were asking us to get rid of the network of material, practical, and theoretical elements that pervade the situation conditioning the very beginning of its own discourse (of any discourse indeed) in favour of a 'conception of the world as simply existing, seen from no particular perspective, no privileged point of view—as simply there, and hence apprehen-

---

6. I use the word in the second sense provided by the *Oxford English Dictionary* (second edition 1989): 'The act of the understanding, by which it passes from premises to consequences (J.); reasoning, thought, ratiocination; the faculty of reasoning, reason, rationality.'

sible from various points of view'.[7] The problem with such 'view from nowhere' would consist in taking the critical[8] attempt of securing a pure beginning for thinking so far that no longer would be possible to maintain a standpoint from which the more elemental ability to judge could be conceived of.

Along the lines of the interpretation just sketched, putting aside the mere exegetical appreciation of the text, we would not have reasons to take seriously the demand to engage ourselves with the *Logic* without 'preliminary reflections'. Perhaps, at best, if we were eager to concede a benevolent treatment to Hegel, it could be said that the *Logic* undermines unilateral accounts (coming both from empiricism and rationalism) of our relation to the world but, ultimately, it would prove to be unable to actually realize the way our belonging to history, language and society overturns the intelligibility of a presuppositionless thinking. Therefore, under that 'charitable' reading, the efforts to establish a connection between the *Logic* and social issues should be avoided to prevent either an account wherein the alleged 'realm of pure thought' pretends to predetermine from a standpoint without presuppositions the political or ethical meaning of our concrete experiences with others[9], or an approach that, in assuming that there is a linear transition from a purely categorial thought obtained by means of abstraction to the 'existential claims' coming out from the plurality of social world, produces unidimensional models of social explanation inadequate to deal with real process of social change.[10] In sum, thinking in absence of presuppositions seems to be an untenable philosophical request which gets even more precarious when it comes to the field of social thought, either as a reduction of the others to the horizon of pure cognition or as a linear theory of social change.

---

7. Thomas Nagel, *The View From Nowhere*, New York, Oxford University Press, 1989, p. 56.

8. I use here the term 'critical' in the Kantian sense of 'critique' as it appears in the first *Critique*: 'a science of the mere estimation of pure reason, of its sources and boundaries [...] and its utility in regard to speculation would really be only negative, serving not for the amplification but only for the purification of our reason, and for keeping it free of errors.' Immanuel Kant, *Critique of Pure Reason*, (hereafter CPR) Paul Guyer and Allen Wood (eds.), trans. Paul Guyer and Allen Wood, Cambridge, Cambridge University Press, 1998, A11/B25

9. It seems to be a point of view shared by post-Heideggerian criticisms on Hegel. His contention about the possibility and necessity of a logical beginning in terms of presuppositionless thinking allows him to present an ontological model based on the notion of totality, which 'produces both the opposed moments of subjective reflection —the subject and the object— *and* itself as the totality of the medium of reflection.' (Rodolphe Gasché, *The Tain of the Mirror*, Cambridge, Harvard University Press, 1986, p. 62) The social consequence of that notion of totality, powered by presuppositionless thinking, legitimates an image of ethical experience wherein the encounter with the other is always 'comprehended or reduced to an object of cognition or recognition.' (Simon Critchley, *Ethics, Politics, Subjectivity*, London, Verso, 1999, p. 7)

10. It is the position of Hartmann, who summarizes up the 'social impotence' of the *Logic* in the following terms: 'the problem of Hegel's categorial scheme is the linearity of exposition or reconstruction in plural realms. Categories of the social realm —where plurality matters in as much as such categories stand for plural entities and in as much as entities of diverse categorization coexist, such as families, society, and corporations in a state— seem to turn out differently from what we are used to grant because of the linear arrangement.' Klaus Hartmann, 'Hegel: a non-metaphysical view,' in Robert Stern (ed.), *G. W. F. Hegel. Critical Assessments. Volume III. Hegel's* Phenomenology of Spirit *and* Logic, London, Routledge, 1993, p. 254-255.

## II

But why we regard the demand of presuppositionless thinking as impossible? The question seems to be thoughtless once it is put against the background of contemporary philosophy, which has taught us to distrust of the ontological claims of those systems which maintain that it is possible for reflective consciousness detaching itself from its linguistical, historical, and social embodiment to lay down a pure ground from which the totality of the structure of reality can be constituted. In that sense, hermeneutics, phenomenology, post-structuralism, neo-pragmatism, deconstruction, or universal pragmatics, have offered different arguments pointing out a general idea: that embodiment actually works as the condition of possibility of any reflective positioning because the very distinction between what supposedly belongs to the doing of pure thinking, on the one hand, and all the other contingent elements accompanying the use of our reason, on the other, already presupposes our acquaintance with a shared web of meanings providing direction both to our reflective awareness of objects and to our own self understanding.

The inability to make sense of the way in which the reflective attempts to get rid of presuppositions in order to gain a pure realm of thought are themselves conditioned by 'unsuspected horizons' could be condensed in what Gadamer names the *'naïveté of reflection'*, which disregards 'that understanding is not suitably conceived at all as a consciousness of something, since the whole process of understanding itself enters into an event'.[11] Moreover, this *naïveté* would be particularly present in the project of the *Logic* insofar Hegel would have believed that 'the reflective spirit [...] in coming back to itself it is completely at home with itself'.[12] That 'coming back' would represent a model of ontology—with far-reaching aftermaths in ethics and epistemology—in which the process of constitution of meaning of the world is a reflection, a mirroring of the progressive self-understanding of consciousness. Instead of that aseptic starting demanded by the reflective account of ontology, the different voices from the 'constellation' of contemporary philosophy would have showed how meager are the ontological claims of reflective consciousness because, even if such self-reflection is possible, it depends on a previous web of possibilities of meaning

However, at this point of the discussion, it could be contended that Hegel's *Logic* is very far from being an instance of the *'naïveté of reflection'* in desperate need of 'charitable' interpretations in order to survive on the contemporary philosophical landscape. More in particular, one of the possible interpretations and defenses of the program of Hegel's *Logic* could argue that the criticisms on it above sketched sharply overlook that the logical requirement of presuppositionless thinking works more like a methodological movement within an ontological project than like a blatant and dogmatic assertion on the metaphysical nature of

---

11. Hans-Georg Gadamer, *Philosophical Hermeneutics*, trans. David Linge, Berkeley, University of California Press, 1976, p. 125.

12. Gadamer, *Philosophical Hermeneutics*, p. 122.

consciousness. That is to say, we could be able to outline a description of the ontological import of the *Logic*, and then unfolding its methodological requirements in order to show that the global project does not rest on the assumption of the free self-positing of a metaphysical consciousness. This line of interpretation would mean to reformulate the demand of a presuppositionless access to pure beginning along the lines of the transcendental notion of 'conditions of possibility'.

We could begin saying that Hegel's *Logic* aims to make explicit the basic forms of thinking, how they are respectively unrolled and how, in their developing, they become tightly interwoven. From that basis, we could add that just in performing that task, logic is also an ontology because such basic forms of thinking cannot be conceived of as empty devices, whose validity would be severed from the actual content of our experience. Rather, precisely because they are the *basic* forms of thought, they set forth the structure of being. It means that we are able to utter judgments about what is to be accounted as 'the actual content of our experience'—no matter how simple or how skilled such description turns out to be—only because we already make intelligible the meaning of any experience from the logical infrastructure provided by those basic forms of thinking, which Hegel designates 'categories'. So, no matter how heterogeneous, changing and fallible our explanations of experience result, the primary rules specifying what that experience '*is*' (whether it is a cause or an effect, whether it refers to a particular item or to a class of items, etc.) are directly determined by the activity of *thought*. In that way, the aim of Hegel's logic coincides with ontology because the basic categories of thought delineate the essential structure of reality.

Moreover, the accusations of '*naïveté of reflection*' would be nullified because the project hitherto described cannot be accomplished by means of the introduction of a privileged point of view, beyond thinking and reality, from which we could be able to compare the basic categories of thought and the essential structure of reality in order to determine whether the latter actually coincides with the former. Such 'view from nowhere' serving as starting point for the aim of the *Logic* is not conceivable because we are always within the realm of thought; that is, our simplest thinking of something in everyday life already is informed by a set of categories, which 'as impulses [...] are only instinctively active. At first they enter consciousness separately and so are variable and mutually confusing' (SL 37). Therefore, any object or situation (God, cosmos, human subjectivity, the traditions of our community, etc.) contrived to serve as the observatory from which describing the interaction among categories and modes of reality already belongs with that reciprocal influence.

On that account, the closeness between categories and reality would be an insurmountable hindrance to 'the loftier business of logic [which] is to clarify these categories and in them to raise mind to freedom and truth' (SL 37) only if Hegel really were to be blamed for committing the '*naïveté of reflection*', and so that clarification were to demand the real existence of a separated ground providing the conditions of possibility for particular determinate thoughts. But Hegel does not need to do that in order to activate the *Logic* because he only needs transforming the attitude toward the way we usually think in order to introduce a *methodological gaze*, which brackets off the content of our 'variable and mutually confusing' thinking of something, focusing instead to single out the valid structure of the categories involved there. And that stance would deliver a presuppositionless beginning for 'the loftier business of logic' without introducing unacceptable metaphysical claims, which could be reinforced by Houlgate's suggestion of what it means to think in absence of presuppositions: 'It is to say that we may not assume at the outset that such principles are clearly correct and determine in advance what is to count as rational […] To philosophize without presuppositions […] is merely to suspend our familiar assumptions about thought and to look to discover in the course of the science of logic *whether or not* they will prove to be correct'.[13]

Moreover, from this perspective we could intimate the supposition that the real '*naïveté of reflection*' is committed by the positions arguing that the embedding of thinking in passive (that is, pre-reflective) horizons of meaning make totally impossible to conceive—beyond the framework of a 'metaphysics of subjectivity'—a reflective standpoint from which the categories of thought could be clarified. The motives behind that hypothesis are to be found in the apparent inability of some influential trends in contemporary philosophy (in particular, those coming out from hermeneutics and post-Husserlian phenomenology) to think of what the idea of 'conditions of thought' truly demands and supposes. In particular, the criticisms pointing out that the aim of Hegel's *Logic* involves the unsustainable primacy of reflection would fail to realize how the notion of 'beginning' and the notion of 'mediation'—present in the claims stating the different ways reflection is conditioned—are inextricable because the exhibition of the conditioned character of reflection is already pervaded by thinking insofar reflection compels us to search the actual beginning of thought through the getting rid of the presuppositions that maintain the existence of an external, privileged, and given point of view from which the intelligibility of our relation to the world could be explained. To believe that the disclosing of the conditions of possibility of reflection obliterates the logical demand of presuppositionless thinking would mean to treat those conditions as elements totally external to thought; that is to say, as *already always presupposed* elements that only can be indicated but never appropriated by thinking in spite of the fact that they are its condition of possibility.[14] Hegel exposes in the following example the disagreeable consequences of that view: 'With as much truth however we may be said to owe eating to the means of nourishment, so long

---

13. Stephen Houlgate, *The opening of Hegel's Logic: From Being to Infinite*, West Lafayette, Purdue University Press, 2005, p. 30.

14. A similar point is made by William Maker: 'Perhaps the key to demonstrate the authority of reason over what is given to it lies not […] in searching within reason to discover given determinate principles in which modern claims about rational autonomy in thought and action are grounded, but rather in first showing that no givens, either internal or external to reason need necessarily condition or determine it in its operations […] any process of critical reflection which attempts to establish that reason is governed or determined by certain givens (internal or external) is finally aporetic.' (*Philosophy Without Foundations: Rethinking Hegel*, Albany, SUNY, 1994, p. 49)

as we can have no eating without them. If we take this view, eating is certainly represented as ungrateful: it devours that to which it owes itself. Thinking, upon this view of its action, is equally ungrateful' (EL § 12). So, the attempts to avoid an 'ungrateful thinking', which would be the apparently deserved denomination of the presuppositionless endeavour of Hegel's *Logic*, in order to leave room to a 'thinking of the absence'[15] would mean the annihilation of thought just as the efforts to refrain ourselves from the 'ungrateful eating' would take us to starvation and death. Instead of the naïveté affecting those radical positions, Hegel realizes that were the beginning of thinking an 'absolute' and 'pure' position—in the sense of total absence of mediations—there would not be thinking at all but perpetual silence.[16]

## III

Activates the possibility of a presuppositionless thinking the defence, sketched in the previous section, of the Hegelian project of an ontological logic like a transcendental project of disclosing the conditions of possibility of thinking? Well, reasons to think so have been provided. Nevertheless, the advocates of a thinking non-subordinated to the primacy of the ontological language still could argue that that possibility, even if it is conceived of in methodological terms, advances an unacceptable image of thinking based upon the dominion of the modern ideal of self-transparency, which demands the dissolution of any difference and particularity in order to secure a presuppositionless beginning.[17] In turn, these new objections could be met by means of the introduction of exegetical remarks indicating, for instance, that in the *Logic* we already can find severe denunciations of

---

15. The concept is of James R. Mensch, who finds a paradoxical prolongation of the discourse of foundational philosophy in the thought of Heidegger, Levinas and Derrida: 'Apparently engaged in an attack on foundationalism, they nonetheless continue its practice of getting at the basis of the things and of using this basis to account for them. This basis is absence, which is variously named. As we shall see, it appears as the 'lack of intuition,' which Derrida sees as essential for language. It occurs as the 'nothingness,' which Heidegger places at the heart of Dasein. It turns up in the 'beyond being,' which Levinas appeals to in his attempt to differentiate his position from Heidegger's.' (*Postfoundational Penomenology: Husserlian Reflections on Presence and Embodiment*, University Park, Pennsylvania University Press, 2001, p. 8)

16. In that line of thinking would be useful to remind the way Hegel opens the 'Doctrine of Being' demanding an 'absolute beginning,' but at the same time he insists on 'that there is nothing, nothing in heaven or in nature or mind or anywhere else which does not equally contains both immediacy and mediation, so that these two determinations reveal themselves to be *unseparated* and inseparable and the opposition between them to be a nullity.' (SL 68) The Hegelian remark invites us to suppose that the logical demand of presuppositionless thinking is a movement without definitive starts or finals but a continuous effort that cannot be objectified and, therefore, cannot be exhausted in the knowing.

17. For instance, this position is represented by Emmanuel Levinas, who judges the Hegelian project as a never-ending movement of appropriation of difference and the corresponding affirmation of self-consciousness: 'For Sartre, like Hegel, the *oneself* is posited as a *for itself*. The identity of the *I* would thus be reducible to a turning back of *essence* upon itself, a return to itself of essence as both subject and condition of the identification of the Same.' Emmanuel Levinas, *Basic Philosophical Writings*, Peperzak, Critchley, and Bernasconi (eds.) Bloomington, Indiana University Press, p. 84

the *violence* exercised by the external form of reflection against what is regarded as alien to thinking.[18] Probably new counterarguments would be raised, and thereby more subtle defenses of the *Logic* should have to be imagined. But, at the end of the day, who is right? Is the demand of presuppositionless thinking a really *meaning*ful exigency? Those questions are not intended to infuse relativistic or nihilistic overtones in the present discussion. Quite the contrary, they attempt to introduce the following hint: although the arguments presented in the precedent section can be reasonably sound they still do remain external to the actuality of the demand of presuppositionless thinking.

The reason of that claim is not to be found in an alleged absence of clarity, scholarship, erudition, or 'revolutionary' impulses, swaying the efforts to endorse a reading of Hegel's *Logic* in terms of a 'transcendental ontology'.[19] As opposed to that supposition, those interpretations have provided strong reasons vindicating Hegel's *Logic* against traditional and contemporary disapprovals eager to find in that work an anachronistic statement of a pre-critical metaphysics. Nevertheless, I also think that the recent appraisals of Hegel disregard the fact that an approach *exclusively* oriented towards the mere interpretative endeavour of determining what is the most accurate exposition and defense of Hegel's *Logic* in the contemporary philosophical horizon easily can overlook the kind of presuppositionless thinking that *Logic* demands us to engage to. Why? Because if we just assume the legitimacy of the issues, concepts, and frameworks mapping the field of modern philosophy as if they were something *given*[20] authorizing us to use certain exegetical premises, tools and techniques in order to make sense (or to debunk) Hegel's philosophy, then we will have *supposed* therefore that the ground from which we encounter his *Logic* is perfectly a natural and a valid one. The ground I am referring to is not the one of a particular trend of scholarship but the universal ground of *meaning* within which any philosophical position lives. That is

---

18. So, Hegel writes: 'Violence is the *manifestation of power*, or power as *external* [...] Through violence, passive substance is only *posited* as what it is in truth, namely, to be only something posited, just because it is the simple positive, or immediate substance.' (SL 567-568) The violence of external reflection will be overcome in the movement of the Notion.

19. Under the notion of 'transcendental ontology' Alan White (*Absolute Knowledge: Hegel and the Problem of Metaphysics*, Athens, Ohio University Press, 1983, p. 6) presents a defence of Hegel's *Logic* which, I guess, encapsulates the basic features of the view expressed in the prior section: Hegel is not trying to restore the privileges of pre-critical metaphysics by means of the suggestion that does exist a substance, the Absolute, which constitutes the reality and objectivity of the world through its own 'dialectical' development. Rather, Hegel's project follows the pathway opened by Kant's transcendental philosophy and, therefore, his *Logic* is guided by the question about the conditions of possibility of experience, although Hegel, in contrast to Kant, maintained that we could provide a comprehensive system of such conditions of possibility. I agree with him in almost every point of his description of Hegel's system, but, as I will try to suggest, I think that interpretations like White's are not keen to accept the consequences of Hegel's ontological thinking.

20. I will understand the notion of 'the Given' along the lines of the description provided by McDowell: 'The idea of the Given is the idea that the space of justifications and warranties, extends more widely than the conceptual sphere. The extra extent of the space of reasons is supposed to allow it to incorporate non-conceptual impacts from outside the realm of thought.' (John McDowell, *Mind and World*, Cambridge, Harvard University Press, 1996, p. 7.)

to say, we can talk about the *Logic* and claiming that our interpretation is the most reasonable view and yet we can fail to realize that the very mode of our claim already moves within a strong presupposition: the thought is able to determine the *meaning* of judgments in conflict, so that it is capable to evaluate the validity of the reasons in dispute. In other words, in participating in the 'living dialogue' of philosophy we already have supposed that the thought situates itself as the *forum*[21] wherein the subject matter to be presented and evaluated is not an external thing or a psychological event but a chain of reasons that moves 'in the pure ideality of the meaning [which] exists purely for itself, completely detached from all emotional elements of expression'.[22] This *situation* of thinking as a space of meaning makes possible for us to understand Hegel's significance not as a figment of the past dogmatically imposing its authority over us but as a claim whose meaning is intelligible only within an order, which 'is, at one and the same time, that which is given in things as their inner law, the hidden network that determines the way they confront one another, and also that which has no existence except in the grid created by a glance, an examination, a language'.[23] Once we have assumed that the clashing interpretations on Hegel (and, in general, on any other issue) are made possible because they are themselves twined in that order, in that ideality of meaning that thinking has become, the possibility of presuppositionless thinking only could be intelligible insofar it recognizes *the given character of the horizon of meaning as the primordial situation setting the conditions of possibility of any thinking activity*. From that recognition, the presuppositionless' demand can be carried on exclusively under the constrains of a methodological enterprise, which, in a similar venue to Kant's transcendental arguments, is devised to work as a 'regressive argument'[24] that, starting from the assumption that there is knowledge expressed in particular truth-claims about our experience, moves deductively to disclose and validate the necessary conditions of possibility flowing of that knowledge. The presence of that kind of methodological move in the logical endeavour seems to

---

21. I use the terms in the double sense of the word: 'as the place of public discussion' and 'a particular court or jurisdiction.' 'Forum.' Def. 1. Rom. Ant., and 1.b. *Oxford English Dictionary*, second edition, 1989.

22. Hans-Georg Gadamer, *Truth and Method*, trans. Weinsheimer and Marshall, London, Continuum, 2006, p. 394.

23. Michel Foucault, *The Order of Things: An Archaeology of the Human Sciences*, London, Routledge, 2001, p. xxi,

24. In calling 'regressive' the Kantian transcendental arguments, I endorse the interpretation of the issue provided by Karl Ameriks, whose reading 'takes the *Critique* to accept empirical knowledge as a premise to be regressively explained rather than as a conclusion to be established. Peter Strawson, Jonathan Bennett, and Robert Paul Wolff have insisted at length that such an argument is undesirable [...] They all represent the transcendental deduction as basically aiming to *establish* objectivity, i.e. to prove that there is an external and at least partially lawful world, a set of items distinct from one's awareness, and to do this from the minimal premise that one is self-conscious. Whereas these interpretations see the transcendental deduction as showing that one can be self-conscious only if there is an objective world of which one is aware, my interpretation takes Kant essentially to be arguing that for us there is objectivity, and hence empirical knowledge, only if the categories are universally valid.' (Karl Ameriks, *Interpreting Kant's Critiques*, Oxford, Clarendon Press, 2003, p. 54)

find support in Hegel's distinction between thinking in general and comprehensive thinking (which characterizes philosophy)[25]: 'it is one thing to have such feelings and generalized images that have been moulded and permeated by thought, and another thing to have thoughts about them' (EL § 2).

According to that difference, the *Logic* would already take for given that our 'feelings and generalized images permeated by thought' possess meaning within our shared social life even if we don't have 'thoughts about them'. However, this last movement would be legitimate and exigible when those 'feelings and images' were to give place to conflictive claims. In that case, would be required to introduce a methodological bracketing off *within the sphere of meaning* neutralizing the validity of the sociological, scientific, or religious presuppositions involved in thinking in general, in order to exhibit the necessary categories pervading it and how the seemingly contradictory claims arising from that milieu acquire coherence once they are grasped as expressing different moments and articulations of the general entanglement of categories. Along the lines of this interpretation, surely the possibility, extendability, and the degree of the bracketing proposed by Hegel in the *Logic* can be motive for debate (as a matter of fact, there are reasons to claim that contemporary philosophy lives on the rejection of the possibility of such presuppositionless bracketing off). But what absolutely could be regarded as conclusive is the belonging of the demand of presuppositionless thinking to the realm of meaning. Otherwise we would have to acknowledge the inability of Hegel's *Logic* to embrace the results of Kant's Copernican Revolution.

However, in this point arises a problem which will show how the demand of presuppositionless thinking compels us to reflect on the alleged given character of the horizon of meaning as the primordial situation setting the conditions of possibility of any thinking activity. The problem is that Hegel himself refused to understand the development of the *Logic* in terms of a transcendental argument about conditions of possibility of our knowledge:

---

25. Hegel refuses to regard conceptual thinking as an addition to our primal reference to world, a vision which supposes that thought has two levels: the content and the form, and then the main issue is determining how both of them can be connected? How conceptual (reflective) thinking knows that its forms are adequate to the content given in pre-conceptual consciousness? Hegel's answer will insist on the non-existence of a pre-conceptual moment. Even the more basic expressions of experience convey conceptual determinations. Therefore, a third element connecting content and experience is not present: 'the nature, the peculiar essence, that which is genuinely permanent and substantial in the complexity and contingency of appearance and fleeting manifestation, is the notion of the thing, the immanent universal, and that each human being though infinitely unique is so primarily because he is a man, and each individual animal is such individual primarily because it is an animal: if this is true, then it would be impossible to say what such an individual could still be if this foundation were removed, no matter how richly endowed the individual might be with other predicates.' (SL 36-37) Therefore, reflection, and self-reflection, cannot be understood as a turning away from immediacy because such a moment does not exist, we are always in the element of thought. Hegel does not introduce a third term in order to connect content and form because there is no original splitting: 'the pure Notion which is the very heart of things, their simple life-pulse, even of the subjective thinking of them. To focus attention on this logical nature which animates mind, moves and works in it, this is the task.' (SL 37) So, Hegel's enterprise is not introducing mediations. Rather he tries to show that *we are* mediation.

> A second method of apprehending the truth is Reflection, which defines it by intellectual relations of condition and conditioned. But in these two modes the absolute truth has not yet found its appropriate form. The most perfect method of knowledge proceeds in the pure form of thought: and here the attitude of man is one of entire freedom (EL § 3).

It is important to recall that Hegel doesn't deny the validity of transcendental arguments based upon conditions of possibility. On the contrary, the notion of 'conditions of possibility' introduces a determination of reflection which is necessary to show that what appears before thinking is not a self-standing 'representational content' requiring a causal explanation within the framework of a psychological understanding of the cognitive process. Rather, what appears before thinking is the outcome of a reflective mediation which posits a basic distinction between the salient features of appearing and the ground that determines the necessary conditions of that mode of appearing. To put it in terms of the history of philosophy, the transcendental notion of conditions of possibility is the highest expression of Kant's Copernican Revolution, which rejects the idea of a 'ready-made world'[26] and, instead asserts that the world is the 'normative'[27] constitution of the spontaneity of *subjectivity*—a subjectivity understood not in psychological sense but along the lines of the 'Originary Synthetic Unity of Apperception' (OSUA)—, which acts on *a priori* rules to bring the manifold of the intuited under concepts and combine concepts. That action doesn't rest on psychological or anthropological premises; rather it can be traced back to judgments 'so that the understanding in general can be represented as a faculty for judging'.[28]

Far from repudiate the Kantian idea that thinking in general (that is to say, our direct awareness of some state of affairs) can be justified in terms of conditions of possibility outlined through the notion of *discursivity* (the idea that the basic functions of understanding can be identified following the 'leading thread' of the functions of judgment[29]), Hegel recognizes in it an insuperable moment of

---

26. Hilary Putnam, 'Why There Isn't a Ready-made World', in Paul K. Moser, J. D. Trout (eds.), *Contemporary Materialism: A Reader*, London, Routledge, 1995, p. 225.

27. I will employ the term 'normative' in the sense employed by Robert Brandom, who develops a model of rationality wherein the intelligibility of our relation to the world is not based upon the notion of representation (the idea that our intentional states are meaningful *because* they do refer to external objects) but *inference* (which claims that the propositions are meaningful only because they are embedded in a wider *inferential* articulation wherein they can be used as reasons; either as premises or as *normative* because the previously referred inferential articulation of the meaningful addressing to the world requires our ability to employ and identify norms concerning the proper use of inferences: 'The practices that confer propositional and other sorts of conceptual content implicitly contain norms concerning how it is *correct* to use expressions, under what circumstances it is *appropriate* to perform various speech acts, and what the *appropriate* consequences of such performances are.' (Robert Brandom, *Making It Explicit*, Cambridge, Harvard University Press, 1994, p. xiii). According to Brandom this normative notion of reason, based upon the model of inference was already outlined by Kant and eventually developed by Hegel (Brandom, *Making It Explicit*, p. 92).

28. CPR, A69/B94.

29. I take this suggestion about the fate of Kant's deduction of the categories (as well as the translation of *Leitfaden* as 'leading thread') from Béatrice Longuenesse (*Kant on the Human Standpoint*, Cambridge, Cambridge University Press, 2005, p. 81-116), I guess that the problem pointed out by her is

thinking which indwells his own logic:

> The critical philosophy [...] already turned metaphysics into logic [...] Recently, Kant has opposed to what has usually been called logic another, namely, a *transcendental logic*. What has here been called objective logic would correspond in part to what with him is transcendental logic [which] contains the rules of the pure thinking of an *object*, and [...] at the same time it treats of the origin of our cognition so far as this cognition cannot be ascribed to objects (SL 51, 61-62).

The first line of the quotation ('The critical philosophy [...] already turned metaphysics into logic') should provide us a basic guidance to understand the relation between Kant and Hegel: once metaphysics has been turned into logic it is no possible to invoke a supposedly standpoint external to thinking in order to criticize the movement of thinking (which is the main business of logic). Therefore the reasons to put into question the explanations provided by Kant (or by any other thinker) to justify his account of the determination of the world cannot 'begin, like a shot from a pistol, from [...] inner revelation, from faith, intellectual intuition', (SL 67) but they must find their path in the ground of discursivity, what Hegel called in the *Phenomenology* 'the cultivation of the form' (PS ¶ 13),[30] insofar it is the only way our relation to the world owns sense and significance. On the other hand, also in that quotation, we can find the subject matter of the remarks and criticisms that Hegel addresses to Kant: 'the rules of the pure thinking of an *object*;' that is to say, the polemic between both philosophers primarily concerns more to the discursive justification of the proposed rules rendering a meaningful world than to the elucidation of the reaches of empirical knowledge or the socio-historical boundaries of moral judgment[31]. With both provisos in mind we can approach to Hegel's qualification of his own belonging to Kant's Copernican Revolution. He doesn't adheres to the idea of conditions of possibility, but it neither means that he is trying to propose a non-discursive access to a supposed ground beyond our understanding providing meaning to our relation to the world, nor means that he is advocating (at least in the *Science of Logic*) an

---

also one of the problems indicated by Hegel: if we are under the sign of a critique of pure reason, then the determinations produced by it should derive uniquely from thought. But if we posit instead the table of judgments in order to justify that 'the understanding as a whole is a capacity to judge' our critics have all the right to ask us: 'where do you take the justification from?' The Hegelian point will be: the answer to the question 'how are synthetic a priori judgments possible' cannot follow the transcendental model proposed by Kant. The question, instead, must be answered through the immanent justification delivered by speculative philosophy.

30. In the same paragraph, Hegel adds, reinforcing its recognition and adherence of the horizon of discursivity: 'Without this cultivation science lacks Understandability, and looks as if it were the esoteric possession of a few singular individuals [...] Only that which is fully determined is also exoteric, capable of conceptualization, and of being learnt and made everyone's possession.' (This quotation comes from Yovel's translation: G. W. F. Hegel, *Hegel's Preface to the* Phenomenology of Spirit, trans. Yirmiyahu Yovel, Princeton, Princeton University Press, 2005, p. 86)

31. Of course that epistemology and ethics are fields wherein there are strong disagreements between Kant and Hegel, but what I want to suggest is that those dissents largely depend on the way each other situates himself in relation to the basic question about the justification and development of the pure rules of thinking.

intellectual intuition in which intuition and concept are identical. Rather, Hegel's non-adherence to the transcendental language of 'conditions of possibility' signifies that, according to him, Kant's discursive justification of the rules of the pure thinking of an object is unacceptable because it never really offers a justification of its beginning. In other words, Hegel claims that Kant didn't provide a true discursive justification of the logical movement of thinking, which should be able to answer the following question: 'How thinking situates itself in a position from which it can make reference to the other than itself?'[32]

The previous contention seems to misrepresent both the actual Kantian justification of the a priori rules acting on the experience as well as Hegel's explicit recognition and appraisal of that justification. In a different manner: in suggesting that Hegel's criticisms on Kant are addressed to point out the absence of a justification of the ground of transcendental philosophy we would be neglecting the crucial role of Kant's 'Originary Synthetic Unity of Apperception', (OSUA) which works as the highest principle conditioning the possibility of the objectivity of conscious experience.

Briefly explained, OSUA refers to the self-conscious character of experience: the consciousness of something as a determinate something, an object, ultimately depends on the possibility of being conscious that I think of it as a particular object. However, it is crucial to remind that the 'I think' represented by the OSUA is not the inner self-awareness of an empirical ego. Rather, it is a rule imposing unity and order to the gathering of the manifold of the intuited as well as to their combination in concepts. So, the OSUA points out that the experience of an object is an active unity of moments brought together by the normative activity of self-consciousness, which is also a rule-governed working whose principle can be stated as follows: the objectivity of experience rests on its reflective character; that is, in the possibility to be aware of the rules constituting that particular experience. In sum, the OSUA is the basic normative structure governing all the other normative structures determining the differentiations through thinking in general makes reference to the other than itself.

The OSUA no only seems to indicate—against the idea hinted above—that Kant's transcendental philosophy actually does posses a principle of justification of the objectivity of experience but also points out the deepest agreement with He-

---

32. In other words, the question is: 'how thinking can come to recognize what is other than itself and how is able to determine it just as what is other than itself?' Is important to say that the question is not: 'how is possible for thinking to make reference to *otherness*?' If stated in those terms the question would have presupposed in advance the given existence of an otherness as a bundle of being waiting to be determined. And that is just the point rejected by German Idealists (starting from Kant): they claim that philosophy cannot take for granted that there is an absolute otherness opposed to the nature and deeds of consciousness. It's not a kind of skepticism about the external world or other minds because skepticism already involves an 'assertive' moment: the positing of appearance *as mere* appearance in contrast to the real right thing. But critical philosophy rejects the dualism concocted in that position and, instead, claims that consciousness does exist only in its reference to the other than itself. We cannot dismiss that referentiality as a simple additional feature of consciousness because it is the very life of consciousness. So, the question 'how thought's reference to the other than itself is possible?' is a question about the meaning of thinking.

gel, who encountered in that notion of self-consciousness the principle to set free the spontaneity of thinking from any dependence on a given source of meaning:

> It is one of the profoundest and truest insights to be found in the *Critique of Pure Reason* that the *unity* which constitutes the nature of the *Notion* [*Begriff*] is recognized as the *original synthetic* unity of *apperception*, as unity of the *I think*, or of self-consciousness. This proposition [...] demands that we should go beyond the mere *representation* of the relation in which the *I* stands to the *understanding*, or notions stand to a thing and its properties and accidents, and advance to the *thought* of that relation (SL 584).

The reason why Hegel praises the OSUA is because it overcomes the metaphysical positions supposing that meaning comes to life only when is bridged the gulf between an inert item and that *thing* called 'thought' (the bridging relation described by the phrase: 'the mere *representation* of the relation in which the *I* stands to the *understanding*, or notions stand to a thing') through the intervention of the 'tools' provided by the rules and principles of thinking. Instead of that 'non-normative' position, OSUA offers an understanding of thinking as a dynamic field of 'gathering'[33] rules where the relation between consciousness and its other is conceived of in terms of 'recognition' (*Anerkennung*); that is to say, if the meaning of 'thinking' only can be determined through the process of determination of objectivity *qua* objectivity, then the relation between subjectivity and objectivity must be considered otherwise than the model of an one-side foundation. On the contrary, that relation is one of reciprocal co-determination in which, on the one side, consciousness recognizes its own doing in the network of mediations determining the intelligibility of the object. And, on the other side, the object is not a passive and monolithic raw material opposed to conscious activity but a concept, a unity of determinations whose rules of composition impose limits and structure to the active doing of consciousness.[34]

---

33. The general framework from which I attempt to present my position is totally indebted to George Vassilacopoulos. However, my indebtedness to him reaches its peak when the concept of 'gathering' comes to scene. The idea of the gathering refers to the *topos* occupied by the philosopher; a topos which could be described as 'an immanent correlation between the form of the reflecting activity in which the participants engage and the subject matter under consideration in so far as both manifest the finite eternally changeable human collective, or what I shall refer to as 'the gathering-we.'' (Vassilacopoulos, 'Plato's *Republic* and the end of philosophy,' *Philosophical Inquiry*, vol. XIX, no. 1-2, 2007, pp. 34-45.). In the present paper I have tried to present Kant's OSUA as the movement of that gathering expressed in terms of the pure articulation of meaning; a movement whose thought is the basic issue of Hegel's *Logic*.

34. To say it with the language of the *Phenomenology*: consciousness of the world, the consciousness of finite differentiations, must come to recognize self-consciousness as the active pole determining those differentiations. In turn, self-consciousness ought to recognize the consciousness of the world as normatively differentiated and, therefore, as unsurpassable. Self-consciousness cannot engulf the difference of the world by claiming it is only a derivate of its own activity because once the differentiation is posited it acquires 'autonomy' (but not total independence) in taking up a place of its own in the order of reasons. The worldly differentiation is not independent because it only appears by the activity of Notion, of self-consciousness, but the Notion does not just mirror itself in the differentiation because it, in turn, splits itself bringing its own normative structure. So, the *dictum* 'Self-consciousness achieves its satisfaction only in another self-consciousness' (PS, ¶175) primarily is not the formulation of a social theory; rather, it indicates the special kind of reflectivity informing self-consciousness: oth-

In that sense the *Logic* is just 'the *thought* of that relation' of recognition. Its most immediate consequence is to put forward that the rules of the active unity of moments constituting thinking in general are not tools devised to bridge the gap between thought and being because, for a start, there is no such thing as a gulf separating them[35] but the unifying activity—the 'bacchanalian whirl' of the *Phenomenology*—in which the space of meaning is constituted and from which is possible to draw up the distinction between thought and being. That relation in which the thinking and the thought recognizes each other as differentiated moments of the same gathering, of the same active unity,—insofar their unity is brought about by the same basic rule—is the *Notion* (*Begriff*), which can be understood as the motion wherein, at the same time, the rules of objectivity are unified and differentiated. In that sense, the Notion dwells in the space opened by the Kantian OSUA to the extent that both concepts embrace a normative idea of thinking.[36] However both of them refuse to understand thinking as a mere 'syntactical framework for thoughtless contents;'[37] instead, they emphasize that at the

---

erness appears as otherness just because it is already conceptually informed, so it poses a resistance to the attempts of reflective appropriation. In that sense, I think that McDowell ("The apperceptive I and the empirical self", in K. Deligiorgi (ed.), *Hegel New Directions*, Chesham, Acumen, 2006, p. 33-49) has good reasons to claim that directly the other self-consciousness is no other mind; rather it is the differentiation produced by consciousness.

35. So, the OSUA allows us to claim that there is no a primal severing to be re-united; rather, there is a misunderstanding to be dissolved: 'Thinking therefore in its reception and formation of material does not go outside itself; its reception of material and the conforming of itself to it remains a modification of its own self, it does not result in thought becoming the other than itself; and self-conscious determining moreover belongs only to thinking.' (SL 45) In this way, before the question: 'What is the element that constitutes the truth of our normative vocabulary about the world?' The Hegelian answer, following the path opened by the OSUA, would be: nothing. That question becomes a philosophical problem only when we assume that our standpoint, the standpoint of the forms of thought, is an artificial one and, therefore, it needs to recover a 'given' source of validity in order to be really meaningful.

36. Is important to notice that in the first edition of the *Critique* Kant refers to the function of unity of consciousness in terms of the notion (*Begriff*): 'Without consciousness that that which we think is the very same as what we thought a moment before, all reproduction in the series of representations would be in vain [...] this concept consists solely in the consciousness of this unity of the synthesis. The word 'concept' [*Begriff*] itself could already lead us to this remark. For it is this **one** consciousness that unifies the manifold that has been successively intuited, and then also reproduced into one representation' (CPR, A 103).

37. Allegra de Laurentiis, *Subjects in Ancient and Modern World*, p. 70. I think that she has pointed out rightly that 'syntactic framework' is the idea permeating most of the 'transcendental' interpretations of Hegel's *Logic* 'The programmatic rejection of the metaphysical foundations of Hegel's thought in contemporary reconstructions of it is often accompanied by a summary assessment of the Logic as a sort of cabalistic shroud threatening to envelop an otherwise almost intelligible system, rather than providing the key to its disclosure. In this perspective, the role of Hegel's logical and metaphysical categories as foundations of pivotal notions of the system [...] is ignored, the principles of each part of the system are taken as presupposition-less (ultimately dogmatic) beginnings, and Hegel's philosophical contribution is reduced to that of an unduly elaborate social theory or of a prolix epistemology.' (Allegra de Laurentiis, *Subjects in ancient and modern world*, 6-7) By the way, it could seem strange to quote the authority of De Laurentiis since her position is explicitly opposed to Brandom's account of the normative vocabulary we have accepted before as our guide (see note 31 *supra*). Nevertheless I think that it is possible to combine both interpretations: on the one side, I believe that she is totally

very moment consciousness encounters the world it is addressed to a gathering of moments articulated in judgments, and, therefore, in that moment such addressing cannot be justified by means of referring back to an existent being in order to prove the rightness of those judgments. On the contrary, thinking is entirely referred to the rules of composition condensed in the Notion.

Nevertheless, in contrast to Kant's OSUA the Hegelian Notion is not a grammatical subject, the 'I think' accompanying my representations, but the deploying of the self-relating activity which articulates the space of determinations. In order to understand why this difference cannot be interpreted as a Hegelian relapse in the metaphysics of consciousness is crucial to insist on that that self-relation of the Notion means self-differentiation, no introspection, insofar each one of its categories is a development of all the others.[38] So, the self-relating Notion is always speculative because its basic categories refer to its own motion, a motion indicated through the concept of self-consciousness: 'The object, therefore has its objectivity in the *Notion* and this is the *unity of self-consciousness* into which it has been received; consequently its objectivity, or the Notion, is itself none other than the nature of self-consciousness, has no other moments or determinations than the *I itself* (SL 585). The '*I itself* is not a particular and distinctive consciousness, which has the power to gain self-consciousness but an outcome of the self-differentiating activity of thought from which 'thinking in general' can be understood as the gathering, the conceptual articulation of the basic categories of thinking.

If the main contentions of the previous exposition are right, then it would seem reasonable to think, against the hypothesis we have claimed before, that the disagreement between Kant and Hegel—which triggered out the latter's demand of a presuppositionless beginning—consist in that the former lacks of a true discursive justification of the logical movement of thinking, not only that Kant does actually possess an universal principle of justification of the objectivity of experience (the OSUA) but also that such principle is at the base of the Hegelian understanding of self-consciousness (the Notion). So, there would have good reasons to maintain that Hegel's 'own theory of the Notion, and indeed the relation between the Notion and reality [...] should be understood as a direct variation on a crucial Kantian theme, the 'transcendental unity of apperception".[39]

---

right in emphasizing the undeniable importance of Hegel's metaphysical commitments (an importance disregarded by Brandom's starting point of analysis: the social institution of norms). On the other side, however, I guess that De Laurentiis dismisses too fast *the potential* inherent in Brandom's account because his normative pragmatics is not only intended to make explicit the inferential relations conditioning an alleged non-normative realm of referential relations to the world; on the contrary, Brandom recognizes that the biggest challenge of a normative pragmatics is just providing an integral account of both relations. In that sense, the normative *vocabulary* could make explicit how thoughts are 'able to express the essential reality of things.' (EL § 24)

38. In other words, under the concept of the Notion (*Begriff*) Hegel wants to provide an account of a specific historical moment: the moment in which I think myself as subjectivity (or, perhaps would be better, the moment which subjectivity is thought as an 'I'). The Notion is the self-conscious knowledge of myself as subjectivity.

39. Robert Pippin, *Hegel's Idealism: The Satisfactions of Self-consciousness*, Cambridge, Cambridge University Press, 1999, p. 6.

From this point of view, the absolute idealism advocated by the *Logic* could be understood as an holistic attempt to close the gap between mind and world: it does not make sense ascribing the source of our perceptions to supposed 'things in themselves' because in the very moment we try to conceive its causal role in experience we have put in movement the whole of our basic categories. Besides, along the lines of this interpretation, the demand of presuppositionless thinking would mean that, in bridging that gap, thinking comes to be directly aware of the *a priori* categorial determinations involved in the apprehension of any object, no matter the empirical contents of that apprehension.[40]

## IV

The *conclusions* of the interpretation presented above seems to be very appealing because it recovers the lines of continuity between Kant and Hegel in such way that rules out the attempts to constrain the Hegelian identification of the Notion and self-consciousness to the 'mentalist framework' denounced by Habermas.[41] However, I will argue that those conclusions still overlook the force of the main Hegelian criticism to the Kantian presentation of the OSUA as the principle justifying the objectivity of experience: the lack of a self-justification of that grounding; an absence which calls for the activation of presuppositionless thinking in order to recognize that the gathering, the conceptual unity within thinking lives in, justifies itself.

In this sense, I resume to the two basic ideas we have been working with in the previous section: the idea that the OSUA plays the role of the basic principle of justification in Kant's philosophy and the idea that Hegel's Notion directly draws on that model of justification. However, in contrast to the conclusions sketched above, I still contend that is plausible to suggest that the Hegelian criticism on Kant's inability to provide a discursive justification to the question 'How thinking situates itself in a position from which it can make reference to the other than itself?' stands up without necessity of introducing metaphysical assumptions. Moreover, the examination of Hegel's assessments on the subject matter will offer the opportunity to put forward what is the kind of presuppositionless thinking performed by the *Logic*.

On the first hand, let us to quote the following remark that Hegel adds after acknowledging the Kantian legacy on the formulation of the Notion:

> A capital misunderstanding which prevails on this point is that the *natural* principle or the *beginning* which forms the starting point in the *natural* evolution or in the *history*

---

40. "It also seems to be Pippin's position: '[...] the final claim of the *Logic, its Major Thesis*, is that in attempting to render *determinate* any possible object of self-conscious thought, thought comes to understand the 'truth' that it is 'thinking itself', thinking its own activity'." Robert Pippin, *Hegel's Idealism*, p. 6.

41. Habermas contends that after the period of Jena, Hegel did turn back to a mentalist model of self-reflection because 'is still the only model Hegel had available for a higher-level subjectivity to which a higher knowledge could be ascribed,' *Truth and Sustification*, Cambridge, MIT Press, 2003, p. 203.

> of the developing individual, is regarded as the *truth*, and the *first* in the *Notion* [...] But philosophy is not meant to be a narration of happenings but a cognition of what is *true* in them, and further, on the basis of this cognition, to *comprehend* that which, in the narrative, appears as a mere happening (SL 588).

It is an interesting fragment because it appears at the very beginning of the 'Subjective Logic', the moment when both the possibility and necessity to present the Notion as an *activity* able to grasp its own *movements* is being discussed; that is to say, in a moment when, supposedly, we have overcome the point of view of 'thinking in general' in order to enter into the realm of 'comprehensive thinking'. So, why to introduce those warnings once we have accessed to the Notion as 'the *absolute foundation*' (SL 577)? The reason is that Hegel is aware that even if we have gone beyond a conception of thinking as 'the mere *representation* of the relation in which the *I* stands to the *understanding*, or notions stand to a thing' still remains the temptation to think of this other comprehension of thinking as a new privileged object demanding *to be represented as a totally different kind of relation in which the Notion stands to the objects*. In other words, leaving behind the image of the 'I think' as a substantial ego faced to the world of things in order to embrace the Notion as 'the absolute foundation' is not sufficient condition to 'advance to the *thought* of that relation' because—insofar philosophy doesn't realize that the thinking of the Notion demands a change of level: from the relation to objects to the pure relations of meaning within a normative pattern—it is perfectly possible to conceive of the Notion from the standpoint of pictorial thinking: as a particular item (even if that item is a set of rules of synthesis) which relates to the objects of the world in a relation described in terms of condition of possibility but wherein the ultimate ground of that relation remains as a *given* that overwhelms thinking.

On the second hand, that's the temptation that, according to Hegel, Kant has been unable to exorcize it because transcendental philosophy has not 'advance(d) to the *thought* of that relation'. Let us to consider the following extended quotation:

> [...] the statement or definition of a notion expressly includes not only the genus, which itself is, properly speaking, more than a purely abstract universality, but also the *specific determinateness*. If one would but reflect attentively on the meaning of this fact, one would see that *differentiation* must be regarded as an equally essential moment of the Notion. Kant has introduced this consideration by the extremely important thought that there are synthetic judgments *a priori*. This original synthesis of apperception is one of the most profound principles for speculative development; it contains the beginning of a true apprehension of the nature of the Notion and is completely opposed to that empty identity or abstract universality which is not within itself a synthesis. The further development, however, does not fulfil the promise of the beginning. The very expression *synthesis* easily recalls the conception of an *external* unity and *a mere combination* of entities that are *intrinsically separate* (SL 589).

The lengthy quotation could be summarized up in a crucial charge: the Kantian infidelity to the gathering movement of the Notion; that is to say, once Kant has introduced the function of the Notion under the term 'original synthesis of apperception' (the OSUA we have been referring to) he would have been in condition to justify the consciousness' movement from the individuality of the subjectively intuited to the universality of the objectively valid concepts[42] as the to-and-fro motion of gathering and differentiation of thinking which is expressed in the synthetic judgments *a priori*. On the contrary, according to Hegel, Kant behaves toward his own 'speculative development', the OSUA, as if it were a different way to set forth a pole from which the relation of representation can be thought instead of discerning that it is rather a logical structure, the systematic activity of conceptual relations of the forms of thought, which is accountable for the totality of differentiations of judgment, and therefore that it is the relation philosophy must consider in order to 'fulfil the promise of the beginning'.[43]

So, what is the kind of justification the gathering motion of thinking calls for? In the first place we must assess what kind of question has been put forward. If it is 'what is the condition of possibility of the gathering motion of thinking?' we are going to find ourselves with the problem of the ungrounded beginning stated above; that is to say, since thinking is immersed in the gathering motion of the active unity of moments, there is no possibility to establish an external standpoint from which the inquiry could be carried on. Hence, inasmuch any positing of thinking already always belongs to the absolute of the gathering, the terms of the justification demanded must be formulated once again: 'we have to exhibit what the absolute is; but this 'exhibiting' can be neither a determining nor an external reflection from which determinations of the absolute would result; on the contrary, it is the *exposition*, and in fact the *self*-exposition of the absolute and only a *display of what it is*' (SL 530). That is the self-grounding task of the *Logic*: to unfold thinking as an active unity of moments which presupposes no more than its own motion.

This endeavour takes us again to the question on the possibility of a presuppositionless thinking insofar the beginning of the self-justificatory task cannot be caused by the intervention of an external agent (either a prior ground or a predetermined aim) but it is a move prompted by the consciousness of the articu-

---

42. This difficulty is made explicit in CPR, A89-90/B122.

43. In this sense, it could be possible re-evaluate the debate between Kant and Hegel about the boundaries of thinking settled by sensible receptivity. I guess we could interpret that criticism otherwise than pointing out that Hegel is advancing the thesis that thinking is able to create the sensible contents of real world. Rather, what Hegel finds highly unsatisfactory in Kant's conception of the relationship between understanding and sensibility is the following: Kant argues that thinking is unable to gain access to the determinate knowledge of its own rules of operation because it is constrained by the rules of operation that constitute our knowledge of objects of experience (intuition, space and time, and categories). That is, Hegel is not trying to put forward that thinking has the actual faculty to know a supposed 'essence' of things, which would be beyond our sensible experience. The Hegelian objection is addressed to the way Kant makes knowing of thinking dependent upon the same condition which is valid for objects of experience: sensible receptivity. Thus, Kant doesn't realize that, insofar it is the condition of possibility of the constitution of objects of experience, the 'I think' is located in a different *logical* level than possible objects of experience, thereby the rules determining the operation of thinking are not only different, but also they are self-constituted by the own activity of thinking.

lations of thinking as a continuous motion of development. However, if the motion of gathering is admitted as the unique ground of thinking, then the demand of presuppositionless thinking cannot be regarded as a methodological request because the position from which thinking moves does not represent a separate realm demanding the establishment of a via of access. Rather, the absence of presuppositions is a ground which demands to be recognized. In this sense the *Logic* 'presupposes' the conclusion of the *Phenomenology of spirit*: what appears before consciousness is always a conceptual determination insofar the intuitive and transcendental attempts to posit the grounding of appearance in non-conceptual terms are self-deceptive. Therefore, presuppositionless thinking refers to that starting point: the awareness of the world is a relation of recognition between two different conceptual moments belonging to the same self-determining activity.

In this way, the real question on method comes to the fore in trying to establish how the presuppositionless ground can be recognized as such. Hegel's answer states that 'the exposition of what alone can be the true method of philosophical science falls within the treatment of logic itself; for the method is the consciousness of the form of the inner self-movement of the content of logic' (SL 53). From the point of view of contemporary understanding of method, Hegel's definition perhaps could appear awkward because it doesn't deliver the steps to guarantee an 'objective' outcome of the research. In contrast to that view, his concept of 'method' is rather the description of an inflection[44] through which *self-consciousness* grasps itself as the discursive[45] motion wherein the moments belonging to the active unity of the Notion emerge and articulate each other. From this perspective, the understanding of the philosophical beginning must be understood otherwise than a 'starting point' in the sense of an objective situation from which the actual process of thinking is triggered out and from which it must be grasped. On the contrary, the beginning delivered by the method of the *Logic* is already the very activity of self-consciousness from which the discursive differentiations are made (in other words the activity from which is determined what is to be considered as the other from thought) and not a discursive device different to it; in that sense 'the only true method' posits the logical onlooker, self-consciousness itself, in a spiral movement wherein the method 'is not something distinct from its object and content' (SL 54).

If this interpretation holds, there are strong reasons to put into question,

---

44. Perhaps the term 'inflection' could seem to convey Heideggerian overtones because of its proximity to the idea of *Kehre*, Nevertheless, I think that Hegel's suggestion of 'a plastic discourse' makes possible to talk of the making explicit of the categories in terms of an inflection.

45. It is very important to insist on the discursive character of self-consciousness because otherwise, it could not justify its own normative pattern of constitutions of differentiations; in other words, the active unity of moments only can be justified making explicit the rule producing that unity. We could say that discursivity remains as the condition *sine qua non* to liberate thinking from the opposition to consciousness because only if we get rid of the idea that thinking is an activity relating external objects to embrace, instead, a conception of thinking as an ability to judge we are going to be able to assert that science 'contains *thought in so far this is just as much the object in its own self, or the object in its own self in so far as it is equally pure thought*.' (SL 49)

not only the readings of the *Logic* that emphasizes the problems and possibilities involved in the methodological requirements of a presuppositionless thinking, but also those approaches which stress the 'instrumental' role of the *Logic* in the Hegelian system, as if that work were to provide the blueprint of the categories of thought in order to clarify the conceptual misunderstandings of our shared social life; as Houlgate writes: 'The task of the *Logic* for Hegel is thus provide us with a proper understanding of our familiar categories so that we can determine whether or not the way we are used to understanding them is indeed correct'.[46] So, the self-grounding activity of the *Logic* would bridge the gulf between the normative patterns and expectations of our shared social life and the categories by means of the clarification of the authoritative reasons supporting it. Nevertheless at this point we must inquire whether is really necessary clarifying our categories so we can improve our thinking. The ask is pertinent, I guess, because if we agree with Hegel in that 'the categories are instinctively active' (SL 37) then they would not call for improvement unless we harbour doubts about their ability to deal with the world; that is to say, the clarification of our categorial framework would be the rational demand of a presuppositionless thinking only if we were to regard as the beginning of thinking a state of scission wherein thought and being are allegedly opposed, which is just what Hegel rejects in the *Logic*.

On the other hand, if the *Logic* were *exclusively* intended to make explicit the 'instinctive' categories of thought, thus providing a reflective understanding of them which could be eventually applied to our everyday world, then Hegel would have been unable to offer a genuine self-justification of the way the activity of thinking entirely pervades the differentiated structure of being because, insofar the purported self-justificatory endeavour comes *after* the empirical and phenomenal expressions of thinking in general, it only can show that 'we cannot be blamed for believing whatever the [impingements of our spontaneity, our impulses] lead us to believe'.[47] So, the *Logic* would be, at best, a palliative, a mere 'rationalization' of the way we are, but ultimately unable to justify the demarcation between rationality and irrationality.

However, at this moment an objection could be raised against the mode we have put into question the interpretations of the *Logic* in terms of an exercise of clarification. The argument would run along the following lines: the criticisms addressed against those readings are mutually opposed and inconsistent because, in the first case, what is criticized is the inability to recognize that if the categories are instinctively active then they are not in need of a reflective clarification in order to be corrected (a remark which, besides, intimates a dogmatic depiction of thinking); meanwhile, in the second case, what is denounced is just the incapacity to expose the legitimacy of the sources giving birth to the categories. In short, it would be sensible to expect that if an examination of the process of genesis and validity of the categories were necessary and available, then a re-

---

46. Stephen. Houlgate, *The Opening of Hegel's* Logic., p. 11.
47. John. McDowell, *Mind and World*, p. 13.

flective elucidation of the whole of them would be, in Hegel's words, 'the loftier business of logic'.

The objection is perfectly sound if it is posited against the background of the conception of the logical endeavour wherein self-consciousness (which understood *in this context* as the reflective awareness of the framework of categories) is the outcome of the relation between 'thinking in general'—consciousness—and the given source of the meaning of its activity. In that case the reflection on that relation must produce either the awareness of the inner coherence and intelligibility of the different moments of the thinking activity, or the realization of their inadequate or heterogeneous character, thereby the necessity of clarification. In both cases, the rendering of the *Logic*'s project is the representation of an external relation wherein the movement of self-consciousness is conditioned by its attachment to a primal situation whose nature totally differs from the logical structure of its activity. In other words, although the criticized points of view present diverging directions of that project, both of them share a basic assumption: the self-consciousness emerging in the development of the *Logic* is still thought from the point of view of a relation between objects and not as a relation of meaning thoroughly immersed in the motion of thinking. In short, they do still regard the task of the *Logic* as the explanation of a synthesis and not as the discourse describing the gathering—the discursive developing of meaning as an active unity of moments unfolded and recognized by thinking itself.

V

And that is just the prevailing gesture in those interpretations of Hegel's philosophy which immediately point out the social character of his thought without introducing further mediations. In general, they do advocate the thesis that in exercising our ability to judge we already are 'engaged agents' who implicitly presuppose the social, historical and linguistic conceptual frameworks of meaning conditioning the very possibility of any intelligible relation to the world. According to that point of view, which seems to dismiss the foundationalist models of intelligibility since it recognizes the concrete embedding of reason, the logical beginning constructed upon the inner motion of self-consciousness is either a metaphysical denial of the position presented by Hegel himself in his early theological and political writings concerning the social origin of the forms of thought,[48] or a reflective self-justification of thinking which promulgates the basic social intuition of those early writings.

The remarks coming out from the first position could be answered by pointing out the Hegelian appropriation of the Kantian OSUA to formulate his own conception of the Notion. Indeed it is a model of self-consciousness, however it doesn't introduce psychological or substantialist assumptions in the discursive

---

48. It is the position presented by Honneth, who judges the Hegelian system: 'The turn to the philosophy of consciousness [supposedly after 1807] allows Hegel to completely lose sight of the idea of an original intersubjectivity of humankind.' (Axel Honneth, *The Struggle for Recognition*, p. 30)

description of thinking. On the contrary, if, with Habermas, 'post-metaphysical thinking' defines a position which embraces the philosophical task of rational self-reflection putting aside the 'mentalist framework' based upon the transcendentalization of the knowing subject, then a glance at the way *Logic* presents itself as 'the universal which embraces within itself the wealth of the particulars' (SL 58) could be able to put on view the 'post-metaphysical' character of Hegel's thought insofar 'the universal' is not the doing of a metaphysical entity but the discursive unfolding and articulation of the basic categories putting together the active unity of moments informing objectivity.

Nevertheless, being the outlining of the way *Logic* works our focal interest, I would rather prefer to draw attention to the mode in which a defence of Hegel's *Logic* from the accusations of advocating a 'mentalist framework' is attempted from a standpoint that straightforward asserts the social character of reason. In particular, I want to suggest that that strategy is not the best help to lend support to the importance of the *Logic* in the landscape of modern thinking because it does follow a similar path to the represented by the interpretations delineated by Habermas or Honneth. In agree with both of them, those defences do assume that intersubjectivity is the Archimedean point in the constitution of meaning but in contrast to the contemporary representatives of the Critical Theory of Society they do stress that the intersubjective element is not given up by the *Logic*; rather, even if the discussion of social issues is absent in the corpus of the text, this latter is oriented by a decisive social anxiety: to provide a rational model of self-justification apt to ground the binding character of the norms of a post-conventional world. In other words, both sides of the debate presuppose that the only legitimate starting point available for a self-justificatory endeavour is 'the pure intersubjectivity of the relationship of recognition'[49] and the point of disagreement concerns primordially to the extent of the recognition of that starting point along the development of Hegel's thought.

The problem is not the convergence in the presupposition itself but what it implies. For instance, Terry Pinkard explains the movement and structure of the *Logic* taking as starting point the necessity to construct a new ground for the modern forms of life after the collapse of intellectual and political institutions in Europe. In the absence of a shared set of conventional beliefs and principles able to ground the disenchanted and fragmented world of Modernity, the post-conventional justification of the forms of life requires finding a set of reasons which, in principle, can be assessed by any rational subject. The place of *Logic* in this scenery of intellectual distress is to offer reasons supporting the possibility of a secular and universal justification of the social construction of the patterns of rationality:

> In his *Science of Logic*, the first systematic part of the 'system', Hegel attempted to show that thought, taken on its own, could be self-grounding thought. Hegel himself thus took his *Logic* as crucial to his program, not in the sense that it gave him a 'dialectical method' that he could then 'apply' to other areas [...] but in the sense

---

49. Habermas, *Truth and Justification*, p. 193.

that in his view it was crucial for the modern project to show that the enterprise of self grounding goes all the way down, that there is not some 'object of consciousness' that we must simply take as 'given' in order to make the kinds of claims that we do.[50]

In this way, the *Logic* actually is located beyond the metaphysical and mentalist framework denounced by Habermas and Honneth because it extracts its meaning and validity from its belonging to the historical project of providing an epistemological self-grounding demanded by the intersubjective conditions triggered out by Modernity.

So, what is the problem with this interpretation of the *Logic*?

The main problem concerns the status conceded to the recognition of the presuppositionless ground of thinking regarded by Hegel as crucial to activate the method of the *Logic*: the unfolding motion of self-consciousness. Of course, it could be argued that Pinkard's position recognizes the absence of presuppositions required by the logical enterprise insofar there is no an instance of 'givenness' imposing its claims to the social world. On the contrary, the claims of reason operating in it proceed only from the methodological steps and cognitive resources coming out from the critical self-examination of the forms of life. This explanation is right from the point of view offered by history and sociology: the falling down of the authoritative sources of knowledge and action *demand us* to get involved in a project of self-grounding the reasons pervading the form of life we are striving for and its ideal of agency to be fostered. In other words, *given* those ideals and beliefs we develop the appropriate logic to deal with it. However, if that is the way *Logic* works then we have to remain in the perspective of the '*natural* evolution or in the *history*'—as Hegel pointed out in a previous quotation—but we will fail to access to the 'cognition of what is *true*' in those historical happenings. In that way, the main problem with that interpretation is that, in assuming that the historical and social circumstances condition how thinking in general (and in particular 'comprehensive thinking') should be oriented, the methodical identity between the subject matter and the mode of questioning, which ought to activate the *Logic*'s motion, is cancelled because the work of self-consciousness is determined by the contingent unrolling of current affairs.

In order to be fair, we should explain that that determination does not refer to the material contents appearing before consciousness since both parts of the debate reject the existence of a given realm of objects imposing their meaning to consciousness. Rather the conditioning alludes to the way in which the modern historical medium transforms thinking's self-understanding; that is, it is a conditioning on the form of thinking which changes the mode the latter addresses to the world as well as its mode of self-relation. It means, on the first hand, that thinking can no more think of itself as an entirely free activity constituting the objective validity of the field of external things but it must learn to regard that determinative process as a rule-governed procedure embedded in the linguistic

---

50. Pinkard, *Hegel's Phenomenology*, p. 270.

practices of a form of life. On the other hand, that awareness also overhauls thinking's self-understanding because debunks the representation of thinking as a self-transparent activity able to freely create its own positions. Instead, the consciousness of its belonging to the historical medium forces thinking to understand itself—its genesis, structure and aims—from the admission of its own finitude. This acceptance, however, does not lead to give up the self-reflective task, as if it were unworkable since the impossibility to secure a pure sphere of thinking. Rather, the self-reflective endeavour finds itself now under a double condition: firstly, it becomes part of a wider epistemological project intended to make explicit the way we cope with the world 'in all the areas of modern life: logic (the science of thought), the philosophy of nature [...] and modern life, with its various institutional structures'.[51] Secondly, within its so designated position ('the science of thought'), self-reflection ought to assume the form of 'a genetic account, tracing the path of consciousness through history'.[52] That double conditioning would set up the development of Modernity's self-justificatory enterprise.

In base to the clarification above presented we can reformulate the thesis claiming that the socially-oriented interpretations of Hegel overlook the actual development and significance of the *Logic*. The problem with those readings is not primarily located in their bias against the suggestion of a pure beginning for the inner motion of self-consciousness but in the consequences of that exegetical stance; a consequence which could be summarized up in the following words: the inability to understand and to carry on Modernity's demand for self-justification. The rationale behind that statement is that, sooner or later, the positions advocating as starting point—but in different degrees—a 'social' interpretation of Hegel's philosophy have to acknowledge that their proposed beginning for self-reflection, the social form of life, is a *given* source of meaning, which appears either as a non-rational source of shared meanings calling for rational organization, or as a 'moral potential that is structurally inherent in communicative relations between subjects',[53] which is to be made explicit through the 'detranscendentalized concept of reason'.[54]

On more time is important to insist on that such 'given' is not referred to an external object opposed to consciousness but to a model of relation of meaning in which the discursive justification of the Notion—understood as the gathering motion of the active unity of moments of thinking—is a development conditioned by a source of intelligibility whose meaningful force is structurally independent of that justification insofar this force is said to provide the communicative medium from which the reflective unfolding of the Notion can be understood.[55]

---

51. Pinkard, *Hegel's Phenomenology*, p. 270.
52. Habermas, *Truth and Justification*, p. 184.
53. Honneth, *The Struggle for Recognition*, p. 67.
54. Honneth, *The Struggle for Recognition*, p. 68.
55. It is the point argued by Habermas in order to claim the impotence of self-reflection to validate modern rationality: 'Even when applied to linguistic phenomena, *self-consciousness* — the basic figure of thought of the philosophy of the subject — does not offer a sound basis for a theory of society. If the subject,

That model of meaning, in which intersubjectivity takes the place of the 'philosophy of consciousness' seems to offer a conception of rationality which not only recovers the non-mentalist elements of Hegel's thought but also reclaim a model of self-justification which avoids the charges of the '*naiveté of reflection*' because it never tries to put aside the intersubjective conditions of possibility of its own doing. However, at the very moment we accept that the *Logic* works, at best, making explicit the given field of intersubjectivity, the forms of thought become a tool useful only to provide exculpations[56]—not justifications—of the kind of rationality we have. Why? Because If the *meaning* of the social character of the normative process of giving and asking reasons within the conceptual space wherein rules of composition are combined and thereby differentiated into different kinds of judgment is depicted as the contingent outcome of specific historical conditions, then reason's claims of validity cannot be ultimately justified because the different paths of any self-reflective endeavour will always take us back to the same extra-conceptual source of meaning: clashes of social forces along history. In that way, the sociality of reason only can be at best 'exculpated': since the processes of secularization, social fragmentation, and scientific understanding of the world foreclosed the possibility of a shared consensus about a self-evident and substantial concept of reason, our models of rationality have no more option than relying on the reconstruction of the conditions of possibility of meaning pervading our concrete social practices. Therefore, we cannot be held responsible for having the kind of rationality we have.

Does it mean the necessity to restore a transcendent metaphysics in order to justify the rationality of our social practices? No. At least the *Logic* does not compel us to do that. It assumes not only the social genesis[57] of the self-justificatory

---

in knowing its objects, relates at the same time to itself, it encounters itself in a double position: both as a single empirical entity in the world and the transcendental subject facing the world as a whole [...] Between these two positions of the subject there is no space left for the symbolically prestructured, linguistically constituted domains of culture, society, and socialized individuals.' (*On the Pragmatics of Communication*, Cambridge, MIT Press, 1998, p. 186, my italics). Of course, if subjectivity is conceived of either as an empirical subject or as a transcendental subject, then the *meaning* of intersubjectivity cannot be made intelligible. But if we assume the standpoint of the logical structure of the subjectivity, i.e. the gathering motion of self-consciousness, then the meaning of the intersubjective medium can be articulated without introducing mentalist assumptions.

56. I take the general idea of exculpation from McDowell (*Mind and World*, p. 8, n. 7) to indicate the relation through which conceptual thinking describes its relation with the *given*: a relation in which we are situated in a position which cannot be understood as a result of the activity of our network of conceptual abilities. Insofar our belonging to that situation is entirely beyond our responsibility we only can be exculpated for be there.

57. This point has been convincingly argued by Maker: 'logic's timelessness is qualified, or mediated, for Hegel repeatedly insists that his task has been undertake the reform of logic which is necessitated because, unlike other domains of philosophy, logic had been hitherto untouched by the indefatigable spirit of the age. 'Logic shows no traces so far of the new spirit which has arisen in the sciences no less than in the world of actuality [SL 26] A glance at the *Philosophy of History* immediately discloses that the 'new spirit' he is talking about is the spirit of freedom, and he holds that this spirit not only pervades the other sciences and actuality, but is most fundamentally philosophical in character.' ('Hegel's Logic of Freedom', in David G. Carlson (ed.), *Hegel's Theory of the Subject*), New York, Palgrave, 2005, p. 2-3) In that sense, Hegel's *Logic* cannot be understood as the formal description

endeavour but also the concrete existence of different disciplines, which have successfully established their particular meanings without necessity of the self-grounding task. To that extent, the *reconstruction* of the *genesis* of the social character of the normative process of giving and asking reasons within the conceptual space wherein rules of composition are combined and thereby differentiated into distinct kinds of judgment as the contingent outcome of specific historical conditions is an intellectual task different to *justifying* the *meaning* of that process as a valid one. This latter task is the business of the *Logic*: to render intelligible how thinking alone is to be held responsible for positioning itself in the space of meaning. From this point of view, Hegel totally agrees with the thesis asserting that reason is social, but he is more concerned in justifying the rationality of that claim by showing the process through which thinking posits itself in conditions to assert that thesis.[58]

I think that this line of exegesis can be supported by a remark introduced by Hegel about the 'posteriority' of the *Logic*: 'the value of logic is only appreciated when it is preceded by experience of the sciences; it then displays itself to mind as the universal truth, not as a *particular* knowledge *alongside* other matters and realities, but as the essential being of all these latter' (SL 58). At first sight that statement is strange because it seems to be at odds with the pure beginning claimed by the logic. Moreover, the recognition of the precedence of the experience of the particular sciences seems to be in plain contradiction with the subsequent claim on the place of the *Logic* 'as the essential being of all these' sciences. Nevertheless, if we keep in mind the suggestion that the *Logic* is aimed to show how the presuppositionless ground can be recognized as such, it becomes clear that its 'value' can be interpreted otherwise than a metaphysical foundation of particular disciplines but as the showing of a process which is already set in motion. That process is the *meaning*, or, maybe better yet, the motion through which thinking comes to situate itself as an activity entirely composed of relations of meaning. In that sense the *Logic* problematizes what other disciplines or philosophical approaches just take for granted as a situation of thought brought about by the necessity to meet the sceptical challenge after the collapse of the traditional sources of practical and cognitive authority and philosophically expressed by Kant's Copernican Revolution: the idea that thinking is the gathering of an active unity of moments which can be reconstructed through the 'leading thread' provided by the logical functions of judgment allowing us to understand our relation to the world and to ourselves under the light of the linguistic terms of 'sense and significance'. It could be appear that that movement is all natural since the modern breaking

---

of a given historical content. Rather, as Vassilacopoulos has detected it, the speculative account of the *Logic* 'identifies a formal description of the content.' (*A Reading of Hegel's Philosophy*, Ph.D. Thesis, Melbourne, La Trobe, 1994, p. 40).

58. In that sense, the position presented in this paper shares the general standpoint of Winfield, who claims that 'Only after that investigation, historically initiated by Hegel in his *Science of Logic*, can one proceed to conceive real structures such as consciousness and intersubjectivity not as epistemological foundations but as topics of the philosophy of reality.' (R.D. Winfield, *Overcoming Foundations*, p. 93)

down of the metaphysical assumptions in which the representational accounts of knowledge and action rested on forecloses the attempts to explain meaning as something given. However, as Jocelyn Benoist has cleverly pointed out[59], this formulation revolves around a non-justified metaphorical displacement to be found in Kant's transposition of the linguistic usage of meaning and signification into our relation to the world.[60]

Here is where the importance of the *Logic* comes to scene because the self-exposition of the gathering movement of the Notion is aimed to justify that metaphorical displacement. But the justification is not intended to disclose a primal ground conditioning thought's ability to conceive itself in terms of relations of meaning. Rather, the *Logic* is the process through which thinking recognizes that its situation in the field of meaning is the outcome of its own doing.

If that suggestion is pertinent, then the self-justificatory enterprise of the *Logic* and its relation to social and political thought considerably changes. In the first place, not only the modern condition of social world does not impose tasks to the *Logic*, as we have insisted on, *but it does not need also to be justified*. To suppose that the way we experience modern social world calls for a logical justification would signify that a particular happening can be experienced as a social or political event only once we have legitimated its belonging to the categories of politics or sociology through the reflective assessments of categories. Instead of that state of affairs Hegel does insist on that the political, social or moral meaning of a par-

---

59. In the article 'L'origine du 'sens': phénoménologie et vérité' ['The origin of meaning: phenomenology and truth'] She remarks the problems and polemics engendered by the *metaphorical* usage of 'meaning' in contemporary philosophy: 'if it is natural for us to talk about our perceptions, our living experiences, and our relation to things and world, and eventually about others and ourselves, in terms of 'meaning' we must remind that there is present the transposition and metaphorical usage. Philosophy, and subsequently common consciousness, transposes that usage into the non-linguistic reality, and thereby, in some manner, the concept of signification seems to be enlarged. The underlying model employed in those statements is clearly a *linguistic* one. Initially, meaning is what is said in a statement. World (or 'reality' in general) becomes a book to be read — or to be interpreted — following a metaphor exerted by Kant.' ['S'il peut nous sembler naturel que l'on parle de nos perceptions, de nos vécus et de notre rapport aux choses et au monde, éventuellement aux autres et à nous-mêmes en termes de 'sens', il faut rappeler qu'il y a là transposition et usage métaphorique. Le modèle subrepticement employé dans de tels énoncés est clairement *linguistique*. Le sens, initialement, c'est ce qui se dit dans un énoncé. Or la philosophie, et éventuellement la conscience commune, transpose cet usage à la réalité non-linguistique, et d'une certaine façon para là-même semble élargir la notion de signification. Le monde (ou le 'réel' en général) devient alors comme un livre à lire — ou à 'interpréter'— suivant une métaphore reprise déjà par Kant.'] (Jocelyn Benoist, *Autour de Husserl: L'ego et la raison*, Paris, Vrin, 1994, p. 268-269). She is thinking in the problematic usage of the concept of meaning in Husserlian phenomenology, but I think that her general argument is useful to understand the philosophical situation of Hegel's *Logic*.

60. That movement can be exemplified by two examples from the *Critique of Pure Reason*. In one of them Kant remarks that the pure concepts of understanding need to be articulated with 'our sensible and empirical intuition' insofar it 'alone can provide them with sense [*Sinn*] and significance [*Bedeutung*].' (CPR, B149). In the other example Kant writs that 'it is also requisite for one to make an abstract concept sensible, i.e., display the object that corresponds to it in intuition, since without this the concept would remain (as one says) without sense, i.e., without significance.' (CPR, A240/B299) In both examples the intelligibility of our relation to the world is displayed upon a linguistic model of meaning, which implies an entire reformulation of the relations between logic and ontology.

ticular event is already experienced as such (as 'feelings and generalized images that have been moulded and permeated by thought') through the judgments provided by political, social or moral criteria and distinctions. So, what *Logic* does is to remind thinking that those distinctions, criteria and methodological orientations are the differentiated expression of its own unifying activity; hence the admonition at the very opening of the *Logic* about the dangers brewing 'when a nation loses its metaphysics, when the spirit which contemplates its own pure essence is no longer a present reality in the life of the nation' (SL 25). The risk is either to suppose that the different ways modern life is articulated and organized is the outcome of anonymous processes devoid of meaning, or to suppose that the rational meaning of those processes is opposed to the meaning expressed in our common social understanding. In both cases we are faced to a social world which could have got rid of pre-modern conceptions of a given source of moral and political meaning (God, the cosmos or the community), embracing instead a post-conventional view of society in which the basic agreements are based upon reasons open to public discussion and revision, and yet assume that the full understanding of those differentiated spheres is an option foreclosed to conscious assessment because individual consciousness has not participated in the constitution of their meaning.

This situation represents a risk because it makes impossible for modern subjects to recognize themselves in the world they live. In other words, at stake here is not only a theoretical issue concerning to the rational grounding of the post-conventional ordering of society against the skeptical attacks, but also a practical difficulty: how the individual subject comes to see her actions as *her own* actions; that is to say, if we are going to explain how the way we are addressed to the world is—as Siep intimated it—a conceptual system articulating the commands coming out from common social life and the claims of individual consciousness, then we need to explain both how the individual commits herself to a normative principle through which she could be able to justify (to herself and to others) the reasons of her action,[61] and how that normative principle is activated by the gathering motion of self-consciousness. This latter point is of the utmost importance because refers to an endeavour which cannot be accomplished by the former part of the task. The clearing up of the rational pattern underlying our attachment to community can indicate the shortcomings and dead ends pervading

---

61. That is the suggestion of Robert Pippin proposes in order to explain the way we become subjects through a rational, self-consciously process: 'In Hegel's account, to pursue an end is to subject oneself to a norm; I pursue an end for a reason, a reason I take to have justifying force. This then raises the central question of the conditions under which my attachment to any such ends, any conferring of value, could be expressive of rational agency.' (Robert Pippin, 'Hegel's ethical rationalism', in Ameriks and Sturma (eds.), *The Modern Subject*, p. 164). I think that Pippin has rightly pointed out that, even if we accept the social formation of individual self-consciousness, we still need to provide an account explaining that an action is rational only if the individual subject has reasons to act the way he does it. However, I guess that the normative pattern Pippin puts forward is not enough to explain the individual attachment to post-conventional practices because we have not explained yet that pattern as a conscious outcome.

the attempts to reconcile the individual consciousness with the whole of society through the affirmation of a one-sided (that is, lacking of differentiations) source of binding normativity (for instance, a communitarian attachment to a religious icon or a deification of ethnicity), but this engagement is unable to deal with the differentiations of meaning; that is, with the disperse judgments coming out and clashing from different areas of life: politics, economics, religion, ethics, etc. If we remain at the level offered by that approach, we must assume those dispersions of meaning as the unavoidable expression of 'the structural overloading of the modern subject',[62] which could be regarded as a cynical conclusion but is said to be the more sensitive solution to that overloading since, as Habermas insists on, 'from a postmetaphysical point of view, we can no longer base our judgments on such an authority [the authority of a speculative philosophical diagnosis]'.[63]

At this point emerges the importance of the second part of the task stated lines above, the task of explaining how the normative principle putting together modern subjectivity is activated by the gathering motion of self-consciousness. Hegel would agree entirely with Habermas about the postmetaphysical impossibility of invoking a speculative philosophy to solve the puzzles and bewilderments faced by modern subjectivity if 'speculative philosophy' is conceived of as an inert substratum creating disparate meanings to be eventually reconciled through a rational process. But certainly, a speculative philosophy, understood as the discursive motion of dispersing and gathering of the Notion, is able to make sense of the way modern subjects can recognize themselves in the modern world insofar it shows that the never-ending process of differentiations of meaning is not to be interpreted as 'the structural overloading of the modern subject', as if it were possible to imagine a *modern* subjectivity exercising *autonomous agency* free from the 'overloads' and 'overtaxes' represented by that conflictive differentiations. Rather, what the *Logic* does is to show that that differentiating activity is the very logical structure that defines our subjectivity: we cannot find what subjectivity means outside the dispersing and gathering movement of the Notion. In sum: I am a *human* subject insofar self-consciousness *differentiates* that universal concept. In that sense the *Logic* not only does not deny the historical, social and moral determinations of human subjectivity, but also allows us to understand how the political and ethical significance of the personal pronoun 'I' can be defended against to the theoretical attempts to reduce it to a mere by-product of anonymous forces just because it is a result of the active situating of self-consciousness in the field of meaning. Only in philosophy is possible to accomplish the task of self-knowledge.

---

62. Habermas, *Truth and Justification*, p. 210.
63. Habermas, *Truth and Justification*, p. 209.

*logic and idealism*

7

# The Relevance of Hegel's Logic

John W. Burbidge

Metaphysical readings of Hegel's Logic have always been popular. McTaggart, for example, claims that Hegel's logic analyzes what happens when categories are predicated of a subject. Because inconsistencies arise between such a thesis and its antithesis, the logic progresses until we have a fully consistent description of a subject. The logical moves through thesis and antithesis to synthesis do not describe reality as it actually is, but rather reflect the way finite and incomplete thought corrects its subjective and limited predications on the way to completeness.[1]

This perspective was taken further by Bradley. For him, the logic is designed to show how all the elements of thought are ultimately interconnected in 'the Absolute'. And we find similar claims in the commentaries of E.E. Harris, Charles Taylor and Clark Butler.[2]

Stephen Houlgate takes another approach; he says that thought simply is being.[3] I find this statement puzzling, however. Is he saying that any act of thinking must be? But then it is not clear why the determinations of thought apply to anything more than the thinking that is doing it. Or is he saying that being, wherever and whenever it is found, is also pure thought? But that sounds almost as preposterous as the earlier talk about an entity called 'the Absolute'.

In that phrase, the definite article suggests something singular and unique. But 'absolute' started out as an adjective. As Kant points out, 'absolute' means two things: that which is isolated from any context that would relativize it—and that is certainly an unhelpful description of ultimate reality. Or it is that which

---

1. John Ellis McTaggart, *A Commentary on Hegel's Logic*, Cambridge, Cambridge University Press, 1910.

2. Francis H. Bradley, *The Principles of Logic*, London, Kegan Paul, Trench, Trübner, 1883, Clark Butler, *Hegel's Logic: Between Dialectic and History*, Evanston, Northwestern University Press, 1997, Errol E. Harris, *An Interpretation of the Logic of Hegel*, Lanham, University Press of America, 1983, Charles Taylor, *Hegel*, Cambridge, Cambridge University Press, 1975.

3. Stephen Houlgate, *An Introduction to Hegel's Philosophy: Freedom, Truth and History*, 2nd ed., Oxford, Blackwell, 2005.

is valid in all respects.[4] Transforming the adjective—which basically means 'that which is not relative'—into a noun seems misplaced. For if the absolute is valid in all respects, then we are ourselves somehow incorporated into its reality, and any claim that, from our finite, involved perspective, we can somehow grasp an objective and comprehensive description of all that is sounds like presumptuous hubris.

My second problem with the metaphysical approach lies in the way it justifies the necessity of the logical progression. The classical British idealists and their successors all suggest that the contradictions and antitheses that drive the logic forward are simply the results of our limited perspective. They are flaws within our natural ways of thinking. And our task is to somehow get beyond these limited perspectives to what is ultimately real. Once we reach our goal, we can cast away the ladder that gets us there. But this implies that, were we to develop suitable intuitive capabilities, we could dispense with the logic altogether. The logic is simply a way we can therapeutically dispose of the impediments that clutter up our everyday existence.

In contrast, Hegel seems to think that the various moments within the logic are significant for understanding the world around us. They are not simply aspects of the way we think, but also of the natural world and historical experience we encounter from day to day. The transition by which 'something' comes to the limit of its capabilities and converts into 'something else' is not just a function of our thinking, but also describes the world of finite things: of rocks and continents, of flowers and dinosaurs, of human beings and the Canadian economy.

On the other hand, for those who think that each of Hegel's categories describes some particular metaphysical reality or principle, one finds it difficult to see how one such principle could ever metamorphose into another one: how the principle that differentiates a substance from its accidents, for example, can be transformed into the principle that differentiates cause from effect. We have, after all, been nurtured within the philosophical heritage of Plato, where metaphysics describes the universal, non-temporal and so unchanging ideas that undergird and explain the changing phenomenal world of every-day. Such metaphysical principles are in some sense eternal and unchanging.

Let me summarize: when we read Hegel's *Logic* primarily as a kind of metaphysics, we come up with something that is not ultimately convincing. We either come up with a metaphysical entity that does not impinge on our normal experience, or we have to abandon any sense of a logically necessary progression. Even more, it is hard to see what relevance such a reading can have for our everyday life—unless we think that we should immerse ourselves in a Buddha-like quest for enlightenment, or go around spouting an incomprehensible explanation of what the world is like, using obscure technical terms in the manner of Alfred North Whitehead.

When I started digging into Hegel's logic, the first thing I encountered was

---

4. Immanuel Kant, *Critique of Pure Reason*, trans. Paul Guyer and Allen Wood, New York, Cambridge, 1998, pp. A324-7/B80-3.

his claim that the logic is thought thinking itself. This is found in Paragraph 19 of the *Encyclopaedia*: 'Logic', he writes, 'is the science *of the pure idea*; that is, the idea in the abstract element of *thinking*'. And he underlines 'thinking' in that last clause. While he does not want to justify his study of logic simply on the basis of its utility, he does allow that it has its uses. For in the accompanying remark he writes: 'The *usefulness* of the logic is a matter of its relationship to the subject, insofar as one gives oneself a certain formation for other purposes. The formation of the subject through logic consists in one becoming proficient in thinking (since this science is the thinking of thinking) and in one's coming to have thoughts in one's head and to know them also as thoughts' (EL § 19).

To be sure he immediately goes on to say that the logic also explores truth in its purity, but he adds that usefulness is nonetheless a proper characteristic of whatever is most excellent, free and independent.

Important to notice in my last citation is Hegel's aside that the science of logic is the 'thinking of thinking'.

Similar expressions can be found in the larger *Science of Logic*. In its introduction, Hegel starts by noting that the logic must not only establish the proper scientific method, but must explore the very concept of what it means to be a science. Its subject matter—that which is to be its most essential content—is '*thinking*, or more precisely *conceptual thinking*', and again he underlines the critical terms. Later in the introduction, just before he says that the logic presents God as he is in his eternal nature before the creation of the world, he points out that 'the logic is to be understood as the system of pure reason, as the realm of pure thoughts'.

The most obvious way of reading all this is to assume that Hegel is going to explore what goes on when we reason—we are going to think about what happens when we think. If he says at the same time that this is the description of God before the creation of the world, he can only mean that God is pure thought—and that whatever happens in our thinking in some way reproduces the inner life of God.

But there is a fly in the ointment. For thinking is never static. We clarify our thoughts and render them more precise and determinate; we find that some thoughts lead on to other thoughts through something we usually call inference or implication. If, instead of relying on simple nouns like 'concepts' or 'thoughts' to describe this reality, we adopt active gerunds like 'conceiving' or 'thinking', we immediately realize that we are immersed in a dynamic that moves and develops. Concepts emerge out of that thinking and disappear back into it again. But this means that, when we talk about such processes, we become vulnerable to the charge of *psychologism*. If we are going to talk about thinking as an activity, we will be simply exploring the way human intellects happen to function.

Indeed, that charge emerged quite quickly. In one of the first, most thorough, and most complimentary reviews of *On Hegel's Logic*,[5] published in the *Owl of*

---

5. John W. Burbidge, *On Hegel's Logic: Fragments of a Commentary*, Atlantic Highlands, Humanities Press, 1981.

*Minerva*,[6] George di Giovanni focused on the fact that, in an effort to clarify the distinction between representation and thought, I had relied on Hegel's discussion of Psychology in the *Philosophy of Spirit*. Representations are based in intuitions, and are thus prey to the contingencies of personal experience. By deriving thinking from representing, I was in danger of removing from the logical discussion the necessity that follows from the inherent determinations or definitions of the concepts themselves.

In my discussion of logical necessity, I had said, 'The claim of absolute necessity for the logical analysis has not been justified in the preceding commentary. ... The reader was invited to refer simply to his own intellectual operations'.[7] And again, 'We have defined pure thought relative to the psychological operations of intelligence; and these are known to us only in the context of the human species'.[8] To these comments, di Giovanni replies: 'To the reader these disclaimers are suspect not because of what they say, but because they are made at all. Either Hegel's Logic has absolute validity *qua* logic, and this has already been established by reflection on its *idea*; or it is not logic at all. No middle position is possible. We are left with the suspicion, therefore, that Burbidge has been trying to validate Hegel's Logic on psychological grounds; and to the extent that this was his intention, he cannot escape the charge of psychologism'.[9]

Psychologism, as a fallacy threatening the objective necessity of logic, was first identified by Gottlob Frege. He drew the same distinction drawn by Hegel: between *Vorstellung* and *Begriff*. Unfortunately that has been lost for his English readers, because his translators have translated *Vorstellung* with 'idea', not 'representation', following in the tradition established by Locke and Hume. Ideas, for Frege as for Hegel, involve images or representations—mental pictures that stem from the idiosyncratic experience of the subject in whom they occur. Thus they provide no established common point of reference to which all people can appeal. 'The idea (*Vorstellung*) is subjective': writes Frege, 'one man's idea is not that of another. There result, as a matter of course, a variety of differences in the ideas (*Vorstellungen*) associated with the same sense. A painter, a horseman, and a zoologist will probably connect different ideas (*Vorstellungen*) with the name 'Bucephalus'. This constitutes an essential distinction between the idea (*Vorstellung*) and the sign's sense, which may be the common property of many people, and so is not a part or mode of the individual mind'.[10]

For Frege, the study of individual minds is psychology, and any attempt to derive logic from what minds do, in the manner of the British empiricists,

---

6. George di Giovanni, 'Burbidge and Hegel on the Logic: On Hegel's Logic, Fragments of a Commentary, by John Burbidge', *The Owl Minerva*, vol. 14, no. 1, 1982, pp. 1-6.

7. Burbidge, *On Hegel's Logic*, p. 204.

8. Burbidge, *On Hegel's Logic*, p. 201.

9. di Giovanni, 'Burbidge and Hegel on the Logic: On Hegel's Logic, Fragments of a Commentary, by John Burbidge', p. 4.

10. Gottlob Frege, 'On Sinn and Bedeuting', in Michael Beaney (ed.), *The Frege Reader*, Oxford, Blackwell, 1997, pp. 151-71, p. 154.

is bedevilled by the contingencies of each person's peculiar mental history. In contrast, concepts persist, are unaffected by particular experiences, and are common to whoever thinks them. In drawing that distinction, however, he placed concepts in an anomalous position. As graduate students back in the fifties, we were told that a critical question for the philosophy of logic was the ontological status of concepts and propositions. Do they exist in some kind of Platonic heaven, simply waiting to be grasped by some perceptive and disciplined thinker? If not, how do they maintain their inviolable character?

For Frege, because concepts are isolated from any contamination by the minds that think them, they persist unchanged and static. With that as his philosophical context, then, it is not surprising that Inwood, in his massive, but seriously flawed, study of Hegel's arguments, insists that 'Concepts and their interrelationships are static in a way that our thinking is not'.[11] It is no wonder that he can find nothing relevant in Hegel's logical discussions.

Yet, even as Frege dismisses psychology, he continues to use psychological terms when talking about concepts. So there are indications, even in Frege's writing, that there may be more to be said about the dynamics of thinking than he allows. For concepts can be *grasped*.[12] 'The grasp of a thought', he commented towards the end of his life, 'presupposes someone who grasps it, who thinks. He is the owner of the thinking, not of the thought. Although the thought does not belong with the contents of the thinker's consciousness, there must be something in his consciousness that is aimed at the thought'.[13]

Throughout *The Foundations of Arithmetic* we find similar references to the intellectual dynamic involved in grasping a thought: 'Often it is only after immense intellectual effort, which may have continued over centuries, that humanity at last succeeds in achieving knowledge of a concept in its pure form, in *stripping off the irrelevant accretions* which veil it from the eye of the mind'.

At one point Frege suggests that this ability to grasp thoughts is improved when we are able to dissociate ourselves from the particular conditions of our native language, with the associations and feelings that have become attached to them: 'It is true that we can express the same thought in different languages; but the psychological trappings, the clothing of the thought, will often be different. This is why the learning of foreign languages is useful for one's logical education. Seeing that the same thought can be worded in different ways, we *learn better to distinguish* the verbal husk from the kernel with which, in any given language, it appears to be organically bound up. This is how the differences between languages can facilitate *our grasp* of what is logical'.[14]

---

11. Michael J. Inwood, *Hegel*, London, Routledge, 1983, p. 310.

12. See Frege's letter to Husserl: 'Thoughts are not mental entities, and thinking is not the mental generation of such entities but the *grasping of thoughts* which are already present objectively' (my italics). Beaney (ed.), *The Frege Reader*, p. 302.

13. See 'Thought' [75] in Beaney (ed.), *The Frege Reader*, p. 342.

14. 'Logic' [154] in Beaney (ed.), *The Frege Reader*, p. 343 (my italics). I was delighted when I discovered this passage, because it fitted with my own attempt to move beyond the relativity of cultures

However, Frege's distinction between our thinking and the thoughts themselves 'which are not mental entities' seems to me to be problematic. Consider what goes on in that process of 'achieving knowledge of a concept in its pure form, … of stripping off the irrelevant accretions', taking as our example the concept 'infinity'. We start by thinking of that which, unlike the finite, has no limits. As beyond any such limit, the infinite can be thought of as a simple 'beyond'. But that has its problems, because it is, to that extent, limited by the fact that it is other than the finite. And as limited, it is itself finite. So we start on a process of moving beyond each limit, only to find that we have only derived another limited thought. When we think back over this dynamic, we come up with a new sense of 'infinite' as that which is this process continually repeated. This is the sense we now associate with mathematical infinity—the fact that any process an be repeated endlessly.

You will have recognized that I have been describing Hegel's analysis of this concept.[15] He suggests that we use this concept of infinite regress not only for mathematics but for qualitative distinctions as well. Whenever any determinate quality comes to an end, the result is simply another determinate quality—and 'infinite' describes the progress or regress by which the dynamic continues on its way.

We now have two or three different definitions of 'infinity'. The abstract 'beyond', the infinity of a recurring mathematical sequence, the infinity of a process where finite things disappear, but never into nothingness, but only into other finite things. Which of these is the pure concept that we are endeavouring to grasp? The logical mathematician would probably prefer the mathematical sequence. But notice that it has emerged only because our thinking has been led to move beyond any determinate number to the next. That thinking dynamic is implicit within our definition of the mathematical term. Thinking has become a component of the thought.

There may be other senses of 'infinity' as well. When we reflect back on the dynamic of an infinite progress or regress, we see that when we consider it as a whole, we have a process in which determinate finite moments are both generated and transcended. Here we are not talking simply about a linear sequence, but a self-contained dynamic that both increases in complexity and at the same time maintains its comprehensive unity. Here we have a quite different sense of 'infinite'. But it, too, has resulted from our thinking about the earlier forms and contains the dynamic of that thinking implicit in its meaning. Thought and thinking are not as isolated as Frege wants to assume. One concept merges into another.

In providing this illustration, I want to suggest that the minds which provide the subject matter of psychology do more than simply represent experiences in retained images or ideas, as the British empiricists have it. The intellect can reflect

---

through an exploration of the way a knowledge of different languages moves us towards concepts. See *On Hegel's Logic*, Chapter 3.

15. See Book 1, Chapter 2, Section C of Hegel's *Science of Logic*.

back over those experiences and extract similarities and common elements; it can distinguish some of those elements from others. In the course of doing so, it starts on a process of distancing itself from the contingent associations and experiences of our original intuitions and of moving toward common, persisting concepts. It is that process of distancing that Hegel traces in his psychology. Nonetheless, for all that reflective thought has removed contingencies when we come to pure thinking, the intellect is still active in generating thoughts. An intellectual dynamic remains. We have made no leap across a nasty broad ditch into some alien genus, some ethereal realm of pure concepts that we simply contemplate. But what we are now thinking has been refined and purified, freed from the contingencies of representation and idiosyncratic experience. In other words, Hegel provides a naturalistic explanation for Frege's distinction between ideas and concepts

I must confess that, in *On Hegel's Logic*, I did not show clearly how Hegel wanted to distinguish the contingencies of representations or ideas from the necessity of concepts. And to this extent I was vulnerable to di Giovanni's attack. But it seemed to me, and it still seems to me, that we have to establish the context within which thought functions if we are to make any sense of Hegel's logic of concepts; and that means that we have to take seriously the dynamic that actual thinking involves.

Hegel identifies three sides to that dynamic, which he calls understanding, dialectical reason and speculative reason. Let me quickly remind you what these kinds of reasoning involve.

The task of understanding is to fix the determinations of a concept—to define it carefully and precisely, and isolate it from the flux of thinking. To do this we must distinguish it from all contingencies and keep its conceptual components separated from other related concepts.

But this has an interesting consequence. For, if we are to get the original concept precisely defined, we need to define as well these related terms—its contraries and its close synonyms—so that the various terms do not become confused. This involves two distinct operations. There is, first of all, distinguishing two contraries that sit within a more general concept or genus. Thus, when we think of the term 'something', we must also define the term 'other'; when we understand 'actual' we must also be clear on 'possible', when we talk about 'subjectivity' we must be aware of what we mean by 'objectivity'.

But there are also close synonyms where we need to discern slightly distinct meanings. In ordinary conversation 'being', 'existence', 'actual', 'real', and 'objective' can frequently substitute for one another. But we find that each one has a subtle character of its own that needs to be marked out precisely if we are to understand the concept (as opposed to our conventional associations) and get it right.

In much philosophical discourse, understanding a term involves abstracting it from its context, and then holding it fixed as an unchanging entity. It then subsists in some kind of static realm, and becomes the basis for Frege's and Inwood's permanent and unchanging concepts. But when we think about the actual process of thinking we are aware that understanding a term introduces a move on to other terms—to those contraries from which it is differentiated, and to those subtle determinations that distinguish it from its close synonyms. This is the process Hegel calls dialectical reason: 'the dialectical moment is the peculiar or typical self-cancelling of these kinds of finite determinations and their passing over into their opposites' (EL § 80). Thought cannot stay fixed with its original isolated terms.

There are several important terms in that definition of dialectic. The first is the term 'self-cancelling'. Hegel is suggesting that when we focus on the original term in its precise definition we find that *it* requires our moving on to the contrary and other determinations. We do not introduce some casual consideration from outside because of our sense of where we want to go. The meanings inherent in the initial concept require that thought move over to an opposite, precisely because the determinations set a limit, and we can understand the limit only if we are clear about what is on the other side.

The second term is one omitted by both translations—by Wallace and the Geraets team: The German modifies self-cancelling (*Sichaufheben*) with the adjective 'eigene'—which means 'typical', 'strange', 'peculiar', or 'particular'. The self cancelling of dialectical thinking does not follow a preordained method or rule. It emerges from the peculiar nature of the concept being thought—from its specific and determinate sense. This is why there can be no discussion of method apart from a consideration of what happens when we actually think. We saw an example of this kind of dialectical move as we went from 'finite' to 'the beyond', and then from there on to 'infinite regress'.

Had we only understanding and dialectical reason, we would be left with nothing but a stream of thoughts, as we move on from thought to thought, each move determined by the specific sense of the preceding concept. But we can do more. We reflect back over what has happened and in a single thought consider both the original term and the opposites that result from its definition. In other words we bring them together and think them as a single thought—as a unity. This means that we can identify what particular senses and meanings bind them together. And we can incorporate those determinations into the characterization or definition of this new thought. 'The *speculative*, or the *positively rational* grasps the unity of the determinations in their opposition, the *affirmative* that is contained in their dissolution and transitions' (EL § 82). This process of speculative reason is also a dynamic one, working from the original meanings and discovering implications and interconnections that integrate the variety of senses. (We saw this happening in the final sense of 'infinity' discussed before.) With this, we set the stage for understanding to start once again fixing the required definition. When understanding isolates that network of meaning, integrates it into a unity and establishes its precise meaning, it generates a new concept.

It is worth recalling here a section of Kant's *Critique of Pure Reason*, particularly in the first edition. In both the Clue to the categories, and their Transcendental Deduction, Kant distinguishes the syntheses of imagination from the unity introduced by the understanding.[16] It is this unity which establishes the particular determinate character of a concept. Unlike Kant, Hegel, in his *Logic* does not rely on imagination as the agent of synthesis. Rather it is reflection on the dialectical transition from one concept to its contrary—that peculiar self-cancelling—that brings together, or synthesizes, the various terms. But understanding a concept involves finding the grounds or reasons that underlie the conceptual synthesis. Once again, the logic follows from the inherent character of the senses being discussed.

Two things need to be highlighted. In the first place, this whole movement follows from the inherent significance of the concepts being thought. It does not reflect anything brought in from the subjectivity of personal experience. This is the point di Giovanni was making in his review.

But the second thing to notice is that it is a movement, a dynamic. Thought *moves* from the original concept to its opposite; thought *brings together* the two terms and integrates them into a unity, using the principle of sufficient reason, thus generating a new network of meanings. This dynamic is inherent in the very nature of reason itself. It is what constitutes the rationality of the logic, and by implication the rationality of the world itself.

How, then, is Hegel, within his psychology, able to make the move from the contingencies of representation to this focusing on pure thought, while retaining the dynamic of intellectual activity? He does so through the working of memory, and in particular mechanical memory. The imagination has introduced signs. And signs refer to that which is common to, or relates, various representations. They have already taken us beyond the specifics of experience to the content that ideas share. Even so, signs retain the contingency and arbitrariness of their initial formation. Memory begins to dilute this contingency, first by attaching a sign to the same content over and over again, so that they become melded to each other. The circumstances of its origin becomes irrelevant. Then, when we say things by heart, we string together a number of signs without paying any attention to their meaning. In this kind of mechanical memory, words simply come out one after another and we pay no attention to the meanings they represent. In other words, we say the words without thinking.

For Hegel, however, this has a dialectical implication, for if we can string off signs without meaning, we can equally well consider meanings without signs. The process becomes inverted. It is this inversion that frees thought finally from the contingencies of representations and experience. For we can now focus on the content of those thoughts and determine them precisely without any reference to the circumstances under which they originated. It is this significance of mechanical memory that had eluded me in my early work, and thus justified di Giovanni's concern.

Hegel's development of a logic based on the dynamic of thinking, it seems to me, has much to say to contemporary discussions.

---

16. Kant, *Critique of Pure Reason*, A76-80/B102-5, A95-30.

Nurtured on Frege's anti-psychologism, with its radical distinction between pure, static concepts and the contingencies of the mind's ideas or representations, modern symbolic logic works only with forms, assuming that concepts can be plugged into the various slots without distortion and without residue. As a result it has moved further and further from the kind of reasoning by which people govern their lives, leaving in its wake freedom for contingent associations to react to, and feed on, rhetoric and emotion. Formal logic has no tools with which it can criticize or assess the natural inferences people make every day, no way of distinguishing when an implication is grounded in the sense being thought, and when it brings in irrelevant considerations. It can identify a modus ponens or a Barbara syllogism; but it cannot distinguish between a syllogism which picks up thoughts only contingently related, and those where meanings are connected through a structure of implication. ('Implication', after all, means drawing out what is implicit.) Within its own sphere, symbolic logic has proven to be a powerful tool for developing a calculus; but by claiming to define exhaustively everything involved in logic proper, it has abandoned any role in governing the way we human beings actualize our rational natures. Ironically, by abandoning the dynamic of concrete reasoning, logic has left the field open for post-modernist deconstruction.

The study of informal logic has moved into that vacancy, and attempted to develop strategies for improving the way people reason. But the most critical criteria for assessing normal reasoning is that of relevance, and informal logicians have found it difficult, if not impossible, to identify what it means for one thought to be relevant to another. By staying within the traditional understanding of concepts as fixed entities, they can only show connections by bringing in contingent and psychological associations, following the practice of the British empiricists, or refer to the expectations of the audience. An Hegelian interest in exploring the dynamic movement inherent in thought could well illuminate what it means to be relevant.

So there is much that Hegel's *Logic* could say to the world of contemporary philosophy. Were we to return to his large three volumed work, we would find hidden in its obscure prose a number of insights into those relationships among concepts that hinge on their objective significance. Even if many of them were to prove conditional, dependent on a particular culture or a particular age, the approach he takes may provide a useful guide for exploring the connections between thoughts in our own culture and our own age. This becomes possible as we stress the role of thought and thinking as providing the foundation of the Logic, and reduce its metaphysical claims to a secondary role. It is because thought requires that we move as we do from concept to concept that the logic builds up its edifice. The fact that this edifice of pure reason captures the core significance of nature and history, revealing their inherent rationality, suggests that our thinking and its dynamic, working within its own inherent necessity, has the capacity of grasping the nature of things. But we need to make sure that we get the horse before the cart. If we do want to draw metaphysical conclusions, we need to start by thinking simply about the nature of pure thought. For it is that logical dynamic, says Hegel, that describes God's nature as he is *before* the creation of nature and finite spirits.

# 8

# Hegel and the Becoming of Essence

## David Gray Carlson

In the *Science of Logic*, Hegel derives essence from being. How precisely does this come about? This is an extraordinarily difficult moment in the interpretation of Hegel's logic. I have found only one essay on the subject. According to Professor Michael Baur:

> Thought finds itself condemned to a perennial and arbitrary interplay of qualitative and quantitative alterations which lack any stable substance or truth of their own. In order to overcome this bad infinite regress, one cannot appeal to yet another kind of external determination, for the mere appeal to another determination as such can only perpetuate the infinite regress. The problem can be overcome only when one succeeds in articulating a kind of relation which is not a relation to Other at all, but rather a kind of self-relation. That is, once the sphere of Being has shown itself in its nullity, one must enter a sphere where all transition is no transition at all.[1]

This is a very nice summary, but it is performed at a very high level of generality. Where in this summary is any reference to the alien terms one finds in the chapter Hegel entitles 'The Becoming of Essence' (*Das Werden des Wesens*)? There, one encounters 'the infinite which is for itself' (*fürsichseiende Unendliche*) (SL 371/ WL I 384), *absolute Indifferenz*, and inverse ratio of the factors (*umgekehrtes Verhältnis ihrer Faktoren*). What do these concepts mean and what role do they play? Furthermore, Hegel insists that an outmoded theory of planetary orbit—the alternation of centripetal and centrifugal force—somehow illustrates the sublation of quality and quantity and the becoming of essence. How does bad astronomy relate to the becoming of essence? Why, when Hegel *knows* centripetal and centrifugal force to be bad astronomy, does he invoke it?

Hegel's logic is a circular chain of necessary progressions. If the chain is broken anywhere, the *Science of Logic* is invalidated and may as well be chucked out the window. Every link of the chain must be inspected for weakness.

---

1. Michael Baur, 'Sublating Kant and the Old Metaphysics: A Reading of the Transition from Being to Essence in Hegel's Logic', *Owl Minerva*, vol. 29, 1998, pp. 139-64, p.139 & p. 146.

My intent in this paper is to examine the exact derivation of essence in the last part of Hegel's analysis of measure. The obscure link in the chain between measure and essence is, in my opinion, a valid one. If Hegel's logic fails, it doesn't fail here. It is possible to endorse the path toward essence through the infinite-for-itself and the inverse ratio of the factors. In the interest of demonstrating how these concepts work, I will first make a few points—quite familiar to veterans of Hegelian logic—about Hegel's method and how it proceeds. Second, I will bring the reader up to speed on the general dynamic of measure—the last subdivision in the realm of being and postern gate to the shadowy realm of essence. Third, I will slow down the discussion to examine the dialectic part of Hegel's theory of measure—real measure. It is here that the sublation of quality and quantity begins to manifest itself. I then examine the troika of absolute indifference, inverse ratio and, finally, essence itself. In these steps essence finally *becomes*. And in the course of this examination, I will try to show why Hegel invokes astronomical theory he knew very well to be decadent. This will allow us to pinpoint the moment when being yields its ghost to the realm of essence.

## I. HEGEL'S LOGICAL METHOD

The prose in Hegel's *Science of Logic* is sibylline,[2] and, in its interpretation, it is always useful to cleave to the fundamentals of Hegel's method. Often Hegel's sentences become clear only upon recalling the exact methodological point one is at.[3]

Hegel's method, as even the non-Hegelians know, proceeds in a triune way. First, the 'understanding' (*Verstand*) makes a one-sided proposition about the absolute, given previous derivations that have previously accrued. Its affirmative proposition, however, always leaves something out as it tries to account for all prior logical progress. The understanding therefore *forgets*.

Dialectical reason *remembers*. It reproaches the understanding for suppressing previously established steps in the interest of making a non-contradictory proposition of the logical progress.[4] But dialectical reason ends up merely replicating

---

2. *See* Theodor W. Adorno, *Negative Dialectics*, trans. E.B. Ashton, New York, Continuum, 2000, p.89. ('In the realm of great philosophy Hegel is no doubt the only one with whom at times one literally does not know and cannot conclusively determine what is being talked about, and with whom there is no guarantee that such a judgment is even possible').

3. *See* David Lamb, 'Teleology: Kant and Hegel', in Stephen Priest (ed.), *Hegel's Critique of Kant*, Oxford, Oxford University Press, 1987, pp. 173 & 175. ('When reading Hegel one must be like a detective and search for clues, for Hegel does not leave the reader with any familiar objects') (footnote omitted).

4. Dialectical reason equates with *experience*. That is, the understanding has made a proposal about the universe. By remembering the past dialectical reason inverts the proposition and reveals it to be the opposite of what it *is*. Dialectical reason is like experience in that 'theory' is shown to be inconsistent with the 'real' world known to exist beyond theory. Kenneth R. Westphal, *Hegel's Epistemological Realism: A Study of the Aim and Method of Hegel's Phenomenology of Spirit*, Dordrecht, Kluwer Academic Publishers, 1989, p. 130; G.W.F. Hegel, *The Jena System, 1804-5: Logic and Metaphysics*, trans. John W. Burbidge and George di Giovanni, Kingston, McGill-Queen's University Press, 1986, p. 53. ('experience, of course, is the conjoining of concept and appearance—that is, the setting in motion of

the one-sided error of the understanding. By affirmatively proposing what the understanding has suppressed, dialectical reason itself suppresses what the understanding has validly discovered.

Speculative reason intervenes to show that the *difference* between the understanding and dialectical reason is what they have in common—negation of the other. In the speculative step, the two extremes of a syllogism reveal their fundamental negativity. Each side is *not* the other. But each side *is* the other. So each side negates itself in negating its other. The negated sides yield their being to a third. This negative surplus is a gain over the prior steps and justifies the adjective 'speculative', in its economic connotation of return on investment.

The three steps repeat themselves over and over until the Logic ends. But as the Logic progresses, the understanding becomes more sophisticated. It makes *affirmative* propositions at first, but it learns to make dialectical propositions in the realm of essence (SL 384/WL II 398).[5] Indeed, in 'The Becoming of Essence', we shall see its newly won dialectical nature already on display. At the end of essence, the understanding abandons its 'negative' correlative point of view and learns to make notional or speculative propositions. In the subjective logic, the previously doubled propositions become triune. The story of the *Science of Logic* is how the understanding *becomes* speculative reason at the end, and how method merges with Being, the very material to which it is applied.

The triune structure repeats itself at the macro-logical level as well as the micro-logical level. The interpreter should expect that the first chapter of, say, measure is relatively *immediate* in its form. The second chapter is dialectical. It constitutes a splitting of the unified premise of the prior chapter. The third chapter resolves the contradiction of the second chapter and unifies the opposites. This pattern may replicate itself many times *within* chapters as well.

Measure itself is *third* to quality and quantity. It is therefore generally speculative compared to its predecessors. Yet measure itself splits in two, leading to the dialectical Doctrine of essence, where reflection is paired with sublated being (*i.e.*, appearance). With this methodology in mind, we approach the becoming of essence through the logic of measure.

## II. MEASURE IN GENERAL

One can visualize Hegel's theory of measure as beginning with a solid 'immediate' sphere—immediate measure, the perfect unity of quality and quantity. A hole develops in this sphere which grows in size until it exactly coincides with the sphere. Measure's positivity is conquered by the negativity which organizes it. When there is a perfect coincidence between the external realm of measure (*i.e.*,

---

indifferent substances, sensations, or whatever you will, whereby they become determinate, existing only in the antithesis').

5. 'The being of the determinations is no longer simply *affirmative* as in the entire sphere of being, but is now a sheer *positedness*, the determinations having the fixed character and significance of being *related* to their unity'; 'Sie sind statt Seiender wie in der ganzen Sphäre des Seins nunmehr schlechthin nur als Gesetzte, schlechthin mit der Bestimmung und Bedeutung, auf ihre Einheit'.

appearance) and the internal, negative organizing centre, we have reached the totalizing regime of essence.

Measure stands for the openness of the universe to determination by an external reflection. This is its quantitative side; 'pure quantity is indifference as open to all determinations provided that these are external to it and that quantity has no immanent connection with them' (SL 375/WL I 344 ).[6] But quantity has yielded to an internal integrity which resists determination by an outside intellect. This is the qualitative side of measure. Measure begins as an *immediate* unity—measure as specific quantity. So conceived, measure is a quantity of a quality, but, if the unity is immediate, the slightest change of quantum produces a different quality and so a different measure. At first measure is brittle.

Yet quality, at this stage, has proved to be an immunity from outside determination (SL 334/WL I 344).[7] In other words, measure is not *just* a quantum, open to externally caused increase and decrease. It is also a quality immune from quantitative change. Quality *survives* a change in quantum. Every measure must have some 'give' to it—this *is* its quality. Measure is no longer so brittle. But neither is it immune from change. Quantity *is* changeability. There must be a range of immunity from change which is nevertheless open to change: 'the quantitative determinateness of anything is thus twofold—namely, it is that to which the quality is tied and also that which can be varied without affecting the quality' (SL 334/WL I 344).[8] This is the stage of specifying measure.

In specifying measure, every measure has a *rule*—a range of quantitative variation within which quality does *not* change. For liquid $H_2O$, its rule would be between 0° and 100° centigrade. Rule is conceived as external to the matter it rules. Yet the specifying measure—the 'ruled matter'—has a quality, indifferent to outside determination, which manifests itself quantitatively.

To illustrate rule and its effect on the specifying measure, take the case of a baby with a fever. The thermometer represents the rule—anything between 37-39° centigrade is a 'normal' temperature. Anything higher is a fever. The baby

---

6. 'die reine Quantität ist die Indifferenz als aller Bestimmung fähig, so aber, daß diese ihr äußerlich [sind] und sie aus sich keinen Zusammenhang mit denselben hat'.

7. 'As a quantum [measure] is an indifferent magnitude open to external determination and capable of increase and decrease. But as a measure it is also distinguished from itself as a quantum, as such an indifferent determination, and is a limitation of that indifferent fluctuation about a limit'; 'Als Quantum ist es gleichgültige Größe, äußerlicher Bestimmung offen und des Auf- und Abgehens am Mehr und Weniger fähig. Aber als Maß ist es zugleich von sich selbst als Quantum, als solcher gleichgültigen Bestimmung, verschieden und eine Beschränkung jenes gleichgültigen Hin-und Hergehens an einer Grenze'.

8. 'die Quantitätsbestimmtheit so an dem Dasein die gedoppelte ist, das eine Mal die, an welche die Qualität gebunden ist, das andere Mal aber die, an der unbeschadet jener hin- und hergegangen werden kann'. Hegel summarizes this opening move succinctly in the *Encyclopaedia Logic*:

'In so far as ... quality and quantity are only in *immediate* unity, to that extent their difference [is] equally immediate. Two cases are then possible. Either the specific quantum or measure is a bare quantum, and the definite being (there-and-then) is capable of an increase or a diminution, without Measure (which to that extent is a *Rule*) being thereby set completely aside. Or the alteration of the quantum is also an alteration of the quality' (EL § 108 R Wallace trans.)

represents specifying measure—the thing we decide to measure. Both the thermometer and the baby have their unique quality and quantity and so two measures face each other. The imposition of rule on the ruled—the thermometer on the child—produces a third thing—the ratio between these two measures. Or, more colloquially, the baby heats up the thermometer but it is equally true that the thermometer cools down the baby. The reported temperature is not strictly speaking the baby's quantum or the thermometer's quantum but is a compromise between the quanta of the baby and the thermometer. All measures are therefore ratios of two other measures. And every measure has something which escapes externalization. Measure has now divided into two--the external and the internal. This is the dialectic realm of real measure.

The two measures are at first indifferent to each other. For example, the specific gravity of gold is 19.3. Specific gravity of gold is the ratio of (a) the density of gold to (b) the density of pure water at its maximum density at 4° C, when both densities are obtained by weighing the substances in air. But gold is indifferent as to whether it is measured against water or measured against some other material. Because gold could have been measured against mercury or fine bordeaux, gold has a *series* of quanta. Properly, gold is all of these quanta. This implies that measure is a *metonym*. One never measures a thing directly; one rather gathers together a series of relations between specifying and specified measures. A thing is finally measured only when *all* its ratios of measure are present. When specifying measure is reduced to series of specified measures, we begin to see quality and quantity in the process of sublation. Measure is the unity of quality and quantity, yet in the centre of the series of measures is a master signifier that organizes everything, even while escaping direct measurement.

## III. THE SUBLATION OF QUALITY AND QUANTITY

In real measure, every measured thing has serial being—the ability to be compared to any other serial being—and a resistance to being *completely* captured in this relation. This seriality Hegel names *elective affinity* (*Wahlverwandtschaft*). The specifying measure reveals itself to be a metonym. It cannot define itself. It can only reveal what it is by interacting with external specified measures, which are ultimately themselves metonyms.

The understanding proposes that affinity is continuity—metonymic things are continuous into their external measures. But dialectical reason protests that affinity is only half the story; something eludes the elective affinities—an empty centre that organizes them. This empty centre Hegel names substrate. The substrate is *discontinuous* with the series of measures *and* continuous at the same time. The substrate is what Hegel calls a true infinite. A true infinite stays what is while becoming something other.[9] So when a thing is measured and measured again,

---

9. *See* EL § 94 R. The true infinite 'consists in being at home with itself in its other, or, if enunciated as a process, in coming to itself in its other'; PS ¶ 161 'infinity means …(a) that it is self-*identical*, but also … *different*; or it is the selfsame which repels itself from itself or sunders itself into two'.

it becomes something external and visible. Yet it stays what it is. The substrate *is* the series of measures. Yet it is also *beyond* the series of measures.

Measure is again split in two. Before there were two measures producing a third—a 'neutrality'. Now we have a different pairing. There is substrate, which is the *beyond* of measure. And there is the *totality* of measure. On the side of measure, continuity and discontinuity are joined in the 'nodal line' (*Knotenlinie*). 'Nodal line' invokes the image of a rope with knots in it. In between the knots, movement up and down the line represents ineffectual quantitative change. To leap over a node represents a qualitative change. The nodal line is illustrated by steam-liquid-ice. Between the nodes of ice and steam, quantitative change can occur without qualitative change in water-as-liquid. But if the temperature is pushed below 0° C or above 100°, radical qualitative change occurs—all at once. None of this has anything to do with the substrate ($H_2O$), which stays what it is while manifesting itself in its measures.

Why must the side of measure be divided into a nodal line? This is the inheritance from immediate measure (specific quantity) and rule. Specific quantity meant that quality can be destroyed by quantitative change. Rule meant that every quality had (and is defined by) a range of indifference to quantitative change. These concepts imply that the substrate can be organized into a series of measures that validly report its *state*. On the side of measure, quantitative change leads to qualitative change—a change in the 'state' of the thing. Thus, a unit of some acid may take two units of *this* alkali to neutralize it or three of *that* alkali; the *quality* of the acid is its quantitative relation to the alkali. If any of the alkali is actually added to the acid, the acid undergoes a qualitative change; it is no longer acid but a neutral product. But the acid's substrate remains what it is regardless of how an external measurer, capable of inflicting change, drives the thing up and down its nodal line of possible qualitative changes. 'Thus there is posited the alternation of specific existences with one another and of these equally with relations remaining merely quantitative—and so on *ad infinitum*' (SL 334/WL I 385).[10]

This leads the understanding to propose that the substrate is the abstract measureless. Measure, as nodal line, stands over against it. Whatever happens on the nodal line side is of no concern to the substrate. Therefore, the nodal line has become purely quantitative vis-a-vis the substrate. That is to say, whatever happens on the nodal line does not change the substrate. The substrate is now immune from qualitative change. All measures of the substrate are strictly quantitative, which is to say indifferently and externally imposed.

What is important to see at this point is that measure is entailed in a duality between the nodal relation of quantity-quality, on the one side, and substrate, on the other. The first side is measure as such—quantity and quality. The second side—the substrate—is something deeper than quantity-quality.[11]

---

10. 'so ist die Abwechslung von spezifischen Existenzen miteinander und derselben ebenso mit bloß quantitativ bleibenden Verhältnissen gesetzt,— so fort ins Unendliche'.

11. John Burbidge provides a different account. He seems to view the nodal line as giving rise to absolutely discontinuous qualities, conceived as distinct neutral compounds. John W. Burbidge, *Real*

The dialectical critique of this position consists in confronting the understanding with what it omitted. Since the nodal line is measure, and since measure is both quality and quantity, the nodal line is itself qualitative. That is to say, there is a qualitative *difference* between measure and substrate. Two indifferent qualities now face each other.

The speculative critique of the prior two positions emphasizes the negativity that they share. The nodal line is *not* qualitative, according to the understanding, but is rather continuous with the substrate. The nodal line *is* qualitative, according to dialectical reason, and therefore *not* quantitative and continuous. The speculative position is that the measureless is *neither* qualitative nor quantitative. This is the measureless in its concrete form. Hegel gives this speculative conclusion the name infinite-for-itself.

I said earlier that speculative reason consists in the sides of a syllogism exhibiting self-negativity. That is precisely what we have in the infinite-for-itself. The two sides of the infinite-for-itself are neither qualitative nor quantitative. Quality and quantity are *for other*. They represent the mere *appearance* of things. The Infinite is now '*for itself*', not for other. Being-for-self was the speculative stage of quality in which being expelled all its content to become quantity. In effect, Measure is now exhibiting its being-for-self. It has expelled its content into the substrate. But the opposite is also true. The substrate has expelled its being into measure. There is a double movement in measure between the measured substrate and its specified measures.[12] The nodal line both *is* and *is not* the substrate.

We now reach the final moves in measure—the moves that constitute 'The Becoming of Essence'. This is an exceptionally difficult chapter, and so our progress must be slow and careful.

## IV. THE BECOMING OF ESSENCE

### A. *Absolute Indifference*

The understanding progressively learns as it proceeds. By now, its immediate

---

*Process: How Logic and Chemistry Combine in Hegel's Philosophy of Nature*, Toronto, University of Toronto Press, 1996, p. 47. This is true so far as it goes, but this leaves out the whole notion of substrate, which stands over from and is immune from (yet related to) the nodal line. Burbidge writes:

> 'Since there is no qualitative boundary the two [neutral com-pounds] share—at least to the extent that thought can anticipate it—they are simply external to each other. So we are far removed from even a minimal account that would enable us to understand the relation. From this perspective no explanation is possible. We cannot conceive what is involved; it is immeasurable' (p. 47 footnote omitted).

Thus, for Burbidge, what is immeasurable is qualitative change 'The transformation of one quality into another is defined as immeasurable' (p. 48). This seems to me off point. There is nothing inconceivable about the measureless. It represents the substrate which is immune from qualitative change through quantitative manipulation. It does not represent a property of qualitative transformations.

12. This doubleness of movement was discovered later by Hegel and appears only in the 1831 revision of the *Science of Logic*. Cinzia Ferrini, 'Framing Hypotheses: Numbers in Nature and the Logic of Measure in the Development of Hegel's System', in Stephen Houlgate (ed.), *Hegel and the Philosophy of Nature*, New York, State University of New York, 1998, pp. 283-310, p. 283.

proposition about the infinite-for-itself is decidedly dialectic in shape. Accordingly, it proposes that the substrate is not to be distinguished from measure.[13]

The *absolute* indifference (*Indifferenz*) of substrate and measure is the product of quality and quantity sublating themselves and yielding their being to the infinite-for-itself. '[T]he indivisible self-subsistent measure' is '*wholly* present in its differentiations' (SL 376/WL I 388).[14] For this reason, absolute indifference is 'concrete, a mediation-with-self through the negation of every determination of being' (SL 375/WL I 388).[15] The understanding, then, has made a *dialectical* proposition about absolute indifference, an important event in the *Bildungsroman* of Absolute Idea.

## B. Inverse Ratio of the Factors

The understanding has proposed that the substrate is a sameness that has difference within it—the difference between substrate and measure. This concreteness was named the substrate's absolute indifference from measure. Dialectical reason reverses the proposition. It proposes that the substrate is a difference which is the same. In other words, there is nothing in the substrate which is not *entirely* present in its measure. But, according to dialectical reason, substrate nevertheless retains its independence from measure. This is the step that Hegel calls the inverse ratio of the factors.

Inverse ratio is a term that hails back to the transition from quantity to measure. An example of quantitative inverse ratio is $xy = 16$. If 16 stays fixed, the increase of $x$ implies the decrease of $y$. The mathematician can determine $y$ by determining $x$. Yet it is not quite true that the variables $x$ and $y$ can be anything the external mathematician would have them be (consistent with multiplying out to 16). Rather, $x$ and $y$ have a moment of immunity from external manipulation; neither $x$ nor $y$ can be made equal to zero. Nor can the mathematician state the highest possible value of $x$ or $y$. This immunity was the quality of quantum re-emerging from its earlier sublation.

In the primitive inverse ratio, the product—16—stays fixed, through the will of the mathematician. This fixity represents quantum's dependence on outside external reflection to determine what it is. Now, at our more advanced stage, the fixed product (16) has become a 'fixed measure' (SL 376/WL I 389).[16] Recall that every measure is in fact a *series* of measures, organized by a measureless substrate. A substrate is not really measured until the *totality of measures* is present. And yet a substrate exists apart from this totality. Hegel's *fixed measure* is therefore the totality of the realm of being. This is substrate's limit. Substrate is the beyond of the

---

13. Rinaldi claims this category is 'nothing else than an analysis and critique—of unexcelled profundity, lucidity and rigor—of the ultimate foundations of Schellingian metaphysics . . . ' Giacomo Rinaldi, *A History and Interpretation of the Logic of Hegel*, Lewiston, E. Mellen Press, 1992, p. 178.

14. 'das untrennbare Selbständige, das in seinen Unterschieden ganz vorhanden ist'.

15. 'das Konkrete, das in ihm selbst durch die Negation aller Bestimmungen des Seins mit sich Vermittelte'.

16. 'Das feste Maß'.

totality of measures. It is different from *and* indifferent to measure and hence is now immune from the external reflection of a measurer. Hegel describes the difference between the *primitive* and *more advanced* inverse ratios as follows: 'here the whole is a real substrate and each of the two sides is posited as having to be itself *in principle* [*an sich*] this whole' (SL 376/WL I 388).[17] In other words, substrate *is* its nodal line. So the sides are the whole and the whole are the sides. Yet the two sides are still different.

Why is measure now an *inverse* ratio? The point here is ultimately simple. Measure is now fixed. The entire series of measures is deemed present and accounted for in the nodal line. It may seem that the series of measures are infinite in number and therefore incapable of completion, but that is not so. Metonyms inherently refer to *context*—a completed idea. Completion is the key to the logic of the inverse ratio of factors. So, conceptually, *every* series is deemed to be present, even though, empirically, we could never gather together all the measures needed to exhaust a substrate's serial being. Each side—nodal line and substrate—purports to be the *whole thing and its organizing other*. Now recall that quantity stands for openness to external manipulation by a measurer. So if the inverse ratio of the factors is the whole thing, a measurer can only add an extra measure by embezzling from the whole a comparable quality and quantity and then presenting it as if it were something new. This is one sense in which the factors are in an *inverse* relation. Something new correlates with something abstracted from the old.

Another way of expressing the completion of fixed measure is to say that any new measure imposed by external reflection is superfluous. It is this surplus that proves the undoing of the realm of being. The fixed measure is simply beyond the influence of an external reflection. In this sense, the passage quoted earlier from Michael Baur's essay is correct.[18] Any added measure is a meaningless surplus that cannot add to our knowledge of the thing.

The sides of the inverse ratio of the factors are quantitative and continuous, but they are still presented as different; it is possible to say that there is a qualitative difference between substrate and measure. Suppose one side puts itself forth as a *quality*. Hegel suggests that the other side must surrender its quality and be merely quantitative. The point is that two qualities meet each other as 'mere oppugnancies', in Shakespearean terms.[19] One must strike the other down. Thus, of the two qualities, Hegel says that 'one of [them] is sublated by the other' (SL 376/WL I 389).[20] But they are unified in a ratio nevertheless. And, Hegel further says, 'neither is separable from the other' (SL 376/WL I 389).[21] So the assertion of one quality at the expense of the other is a useless endeavour. Furthermore, which side is quality and which quantity? The totality, which is both the fixed

---

17. 'daß hier das Ganze ein reales Substrat, und jede der beiden Seiten gesetzt ist, selbst an sich dies Ganze sein zu sollen'.
18. See text accompanying footnote 1.
19. William Shakespeare, Troilus and Cressida Act 1 Scene 3.
20. 'als in deren durch die andere aufgehoben'.
21. 'von der andern untrennbar ist'.

measure and the substrate that organizes it, is indifferent to whether one side is deemed quality and the other quantity. The totality is immune from any schema the external measurer can impose upon it.

## C. Transition into Essence

Absolute indifference and its obverse, the inverse ratio, are not yet essence. Hegel speaks of three deficiencies of these pre-essential stages. The first of these faults is that the determinate being of the substrate is 'groundlessly emerging in it' (SL 377/WL I 390).[22] So far, substrate is a mere 'result and only *in principle* ... a mediation' (SL 376/WL I 390).[23] It still displays a moment of logical *unconnectedness* to its nodal line. No *self*-repulsion is on display, as it will be in essence. This is the *qualitative* fault of the pre-essential stages.

Second, external reflection can indifferently assign to the substrate or to the ratio the role of quality or quantity. Or it can reverse the assignment. This modulation back and forth shows that difference between the sides is imposed externally, whereas essence must be in *and for* itself. This is the *quantitative* fault of the pre-essence stages—that each side can be *determined* to be quality or quantity.

Third, since each of the sides can be assigned a qualitative or quantitative role, each side is inherently already *both* quality and quantity. 'Hence each side is in its own self the totality of the indifference' (SL 378/WL I 390).[24] Each side therefore contains an opposition. This is the speculative fault of the pre-essential stages.

Because each side is the totality, each side can no longer go outside itself. To go into the other is only to go into itself. The pre-essence stages have now passed beyond quantity, which by definition always goes *beyond* itself. Going into the beyond (transition) has now gone into the beyond. Yet if there is no quantity, there can be no quality. Quality isolated is pure being. Pure being is pure nothing, and so quality too sublates itself. The one further step that must be taken 'is to grasp that the reflection of the differences into their unity is not merely the product of the *external* reflection of the subjective thinker, but that it is the very nature of the differences of this unity to sublate themselves' (SL 384/WL I 397).[25]

Hegel identifies the unity of absolute indifference and inverse ratio as 'absolute negativity' (SL 384/WL I 397).[26] This negativity is a truly radical indifference. It is an indifference to being, which is therefore an indifference to itself, and even an indifference 'to its own indifference' (SL 384/WL I 397).[27] Essence repulses itself from itself. It is an active principle, in the nature of pure quantity.

---

22. 'grundlos an ihr hervortretend'.

23. 'Resultat und an sich die Vermittlung'.

24. 'So ist jede Seite an ihr die Totalität der Indifferenz'.

25. 'Was hier noch fehlt, besteht darin, daß diese Reflexion nicht die äußere Reflexion des denkenden, subjektiven Bewußtseins, sondern die eigene Bestimmung der Unterschiede jener Einheit sei, sich aufzuheben'.

26. 'absolute Negativität'.

27. 'gegen ihre eigene Gleichgültigkeit'.

Indeed, at the beginning of essence, Hegel will confirm that, '[i]n the *whole* of logic, essence occupies the same place as quantity does in the sphere of being; absolute indifference to limit' (SL 391/WL II 5)'.[28] Essence is therefore a return to quantity, but in an enriched form—a form which never leaves itself as it repels itself from itself. Quantity, in contrast, has the defect of a *beyond* into which it continues. Essence is a totality with no beyond.

The determination of absolute indifference is 'from every aspect a contradiction' (SL 384/WL I 397).[29] First, it is '*in itself* the totality in which every determination of being is sublated and contained' (SL 384/WL I 397).[30] Yet it implies the inverse ratio of the factors as an externality. It is 'the contradiction of itself and its determinedness' (SL 384/WL I 397).[31] Finally, it is a totality within which its 'determinatenesses have sublated themselves in themselves' (SL 384/WL I 397).[32] The result is *essence*, 'a simple and infinite, negative relation-to-self (SL 384/WL I 397).[33]

That essence is simple is the contribution of the understanding, when it proposed that the substrate and the nodal line were one and the same. That it is infinite is to say that substrate goes outside of itself but remains what it is (though, now that externality has been abolished, 'outside' must be understood as really inside).[34] As simple *and* infinite, the substrate has become essence.

Being has now abolished itself. Being turns out to be 'only a moment of [essence's] repelling' (SL 385/WL I 398).[35] The self-identity toward, which being strived so assiduously '*is* only as the *resulting coming together with itself*' (SL 385/WL I 398).[36] Being is now essence, 'a simple *being-with-self*' (SL 385/WL I 398).[37]

## D. *Centrifugal and Centripetal Force*

By the time we reach the inverse ratio of the factors, measure is *totally present*. Being present, it is a self-sufficient *totality* to which external reflection can add

---

28. 'Das Wesen ist im Ganzen das, was die Quantität in der Sphäre des Seins war; die absolute Gleichgültigkeit gegen die Grenze'.

29. 'nach allen Seiten als der Widerspruch gezeigt'.

30. 'Sie ist an sich die Totalität, in der alle Bestimmungen des Seins aufgehoben und enthalten sind'.

31. 'der Widerspruch ihrer selbst und ihres Bestimmtseins'.

32. 'deren Bestimmtheiten sich an ihnen selbst . . . aufgehoben haben'.

33. 'die einfache und unendliche negative Beziehung auf sich'.

34. Hegel says in the *Encyclopaedia Logic*:
'In the sphere of Essence one category does not pass into another, but refers to another merely. In Being, the form of reference is purely due to our reflection on what takes place: but it is the special and proper characteristic of Essence. In the sphere of Being, when some[thing] becomes another, the some[thing] has vanished. Not so in Essence: here there is no real other, but only diversity, reference of the one to *its* other. The transition of Essence is therefore at the same time no transition: for in the passage of different into different, the different does not vanish: the different terms remain in their relation' (EL § 111 R Wallace trans.).

35. 'nur ein Moment ihres Abstoßens ist'.

36. 'nur ist als das resultierende, unendliche Zusammengehen mit sich'.

37. 'einfaches Sein mit sich'.

nothing. The whole empirical world of measure is now necessary (and yet not sufficient) to measure anything fully. Since a totality is present, externality is cancelled. Any external subdivision or 'analysis' of measure is destructive of the perfect unity it has become.

To illustrate this necessity, Hegel digresses to discuss the orbit of the planets around the sun. Orbit stands for the self-sufficient totality that measure has become. Earlier, building on the insight that measure entails external imposition upon a phenomenon that is partly free and independent of outside observation, Hegel sets forth a hierarchy in the natural sciences in terms of immunity from the imperialism of a measurer.[38] 'The complete, abstract indifference of developed measure ... can only be manifested in the sphere of *mechanics*' (SL 331/ WL I 341).[39] Therefore, planetary orbit is the proper analogy for fixed measure. The orbit of Mars around the sun is supremely indifferent to its measurement by the earthly godfathers of heaven's light. In comparison, measure is less likely to be taken as presenting the totality of, say, organic life and still less of politics or constitutional law—'the realm of spirit' (SL 332/WL I 342).[40]

Planetary orbit is the ideal venue for fixed measure—the realm of the inverse ratio of the factors. According to a discredited theory of astronomy, orbit can be broken down into centripetal and centrifugal force. Hegel knows that this 'analysis' of orbit is self-contradictory. Nevertheless, the false *attempt* to reduce orbit into its constituent parts represents the immunity of the inverse ratio of the factors to a like analysis of a measurer. No analytical 'breakdown' is possible at the level of the inverse relation of the factors. So just as orbit is immune from analysis, so is the inverse ratio.

In the false theory of planetary orbit, centripetal force is what draws the planets toward the centre. Centrifugal force drives the planets away from the centre. Their equilibrium is the elliptical orbit of the planet. Since Newton, however, physicists have identified centrifugal force as *inertia*, which is the very *negation* of force. Centripetal force is gravity—the unified force at work in planetary orbit. In modern physical theory, orbit is the unity of a force and a resistance to force.

Hegel refers to Kepler's Second Law—that planets in an elliptical orbit sweep equal areas with every increment of time.[41] Because the orbit is elliptical, this fact implies that the orbiting planet accelerates as it approaches perihelion—the closest distance to the sun—and decelerates as it approaches aphelion—the farthest distance from the sun. Of this fact, Hegel writes, 'the quantitative side ... has been accurately ascertained by the untiring diligence of observation, and further, it has been reduced to its simple law and formula. Hence all that can properly be

---

38. On this hierarchy, see David Gray Carlson, *A Commentary to Hegel's Science of Logic*, New York, Palgrave, 2007, p. 200-1.

39. 'Die vollständige, abstrakte Gleichgültigkeit des entwickelten Maßes ... kann nur in der Sphäre des Mechanismus statthaben'.

40. 'im Reich des Geistes'.

41. *See* James W. Garrison, 'Metaphysics and Scientific Proof: Newton and Hegel', in Michael John Petry (ed.), *Hegel and Newtonianism*, Kluwer Academic Publishers, Dordrecht, Holland, 1993, pp. 3-16, p. 8.

required of a theory has been accomplished' (SL 380/WL I 393).[42] But for Hegel this is not enough. Theory assumes centripetal and centrifugal force are qualitative, opposed moments. Quantitatively, however, one increases and the other decreases, as the planets, in their evil mixture, pursue their orbits. At some point, the forces reverse in dominance, until the next tipping point is reached.

'[T]his way of representing the matter', Hegel writes, 'is contradicted by the essentially qualitative relation between their respective determinatenesses which makes their separation from each other completely out of the question' (SL 380/WL I 393).[43] Each of the forces only has meaning in relation to the other. Neither can exist on its own.[44] To say, then, that one of the forces preponderates over its fellow is to say that the preponderant force is out of relation with its partner to the extent of the surplus. But this is to say that the surplus does not exist:

> It requires but little consideration to see that if, for example … , the body's centripetal force increases as it approaches perihelion, while the centrifugal force is supposed to decrease proportionately, the [centrifugal force] *would no longer be able* to tear the body away from the former and to set it again at a distance from its central body; on the contrary, for once the former has gained the preponderance, the other is overpowered and the body is carried towards its central body with accelerated velocity (SL 380-1/WL I 394).[45]

Only an alien *third* force could save centripetal or centrifugal force from being overwhelmed. But this is tantamount to saying that the *real* force that guides the planets *sans check* cannot be explained.

The transformation from weakness to strength of one or the other forces implies that 'each side of the inverse relation is in its own self the whole inverse relation' (SL 381/WL I 394).[46] The predominant force implies its opposite, servient force. The servient force has not vanished. 'All that recurs then on either side is the defect characteristic of this inverse relation' (SL 381/WL I 395).[47] Either each force is (wrongly) attributed a self-identical existence free and clear of the other, 'the pair being merely *externally* associated in a motion (as in the parallelogram

---

42. 'Das Quantitative . . . ist durch den unermüdlichen Fleiß des Beobachtens genau bestimmt und dasselbe weiter auf sein einfaches Gesetz und Formel zurückgeführt, somit alles geleistet, was wahrhaft an die Theorie zu fordern ist'.

43. 'Dieser Vorstellung widerspricht aber das Verhältnis ihrer wesentlich qualitativen Bestimmtheiten gegeneinander. Durch diese sind sie schlechthin nicht auseinander-zubringen'..

44. This recalls Hegel's critique of calculus, where $\delta y$ or $\delta x$ were qualitative and meaningless outside the ratio $\delta y/\delta x$.

45. 'Es ist eine sehr einfache Betrachtung, daß, wenn z.B. wie vorgegeben wird, die Zentripetalkraft des Körpers, indem er sich dem Perihelium nähert, zunehmen, die Zentrifugalkraft hingegen um ebensoviel abnehmen soll, die letztere nicht mehr vermöchte, ihn der erstern zu entreißen und von seinem Zentralkörper wieder zu entfernen; im Gegenteil, da die erstere einmal das Übergewicht haben soll, so ist die andere überwältigt, und der Körper wird mit beschleunigter Geschwidigkeit seinem Zentralkörper zugeführt'.

46. 'daß jede der Seiten des umgekehrten Verhältnisses an ihr selbst dies ganze umgekehrten Verhältnis ist'.

47. 'Es rekurriert damit nur an jeder Seite das, was der Mangel an diesem umgekehrten Verhältnis ist'.

of forces)' (SL 381/WL I 395).[48] Or neither side can achieve 'an indifferent, independent subsistence in the face of the other, a subsistence supposedly imparted to it by a *more*' (SL 382/WL I 395).[49]

The idea of intensity cannot help. '[T]his too has its determinateness in quantum and consequently can express only as much force (which is the measure of its existence) as is opposed to it by the opposite force' (SL 382/WL I 395).[50] In other words, intensity is just a way of smuggling in the idea of the quantitative surplus, which is precisely not allowed because the measures are in a zero sum relation at this point. In any case, the sudden shift from predominant to servient implies qualitative change.

Now what has the failed theory of centripetal and centrifugal force to do with the inverse ratio of the factors? Hegel has said that, if centripetal force were predominant, nothing can explain why this force would not sublate centrifugal force once and for all, causing the planet to fly into the sun. Or, when centrifugal force is predominant, nothing can explain why the planets do not to disorder wander. So orbit must be utterly immune from the isolation of either force as a constituent part of the orbit. The orbit will not permit itself to be deconstructed externally in this way. Orbit has 'being in and for self'. Similarly, the inverse ratio of the factors is immune from externality generally. It has a being-for-self that is also a being-in-itself.

With regard to the illegitimate forces, Hegel writes, 'Each of these hypothetical factors vanishes, whether it is supposed to be *beyond* or *equal* to the other' (SL 379/WL I 392)'.[51] Orbit is simply indifferent to these external impositions. Similarly, *any* isolation by external reflection, when faced with a perfect equilibrium, implies their sublation in general. Isolation is the assertion of *pure* being—an impossibility. Qualitative surplus cancels itself, and with it goes quantity. This self-abolition of quality and quantity, Hegel comments paradoxically, 'constitutes itself [as] the sole self-subsistent quality' (SL 379/WL I 392).[52] And, just as orbit is immune from the measurer's intervention, so is the inverse ratio of the factors likewise immune.

Is the argument valid? My conclusion is yes. At the point where the argument is hazarded, the substrate—what organizes measure—was metonymic. It was a negative unity of *all* the measure relations that the thing has with all the other

---

48. 'und mit dem bloß äußerlichen Zusammentreffen derselben zu einer Bewegung, wie im Parallelogramm der Kräfte'. The parallelogram of forces describes the phenomenon that, if two forces exist as vectors, their average vector forms a parallelogram with the original vectors, provided one of the original vectors is multiplied by the imaginary number, $-\sqrt{1}$.

49. 'keine ein gleichgültiges, selbständiges Bestehen gegen die andere erhalten kann, was ihr durch ein Mehr zugeteilt werden sollte'.

50. 'da es selbst in dem Quantum seiene Bestimmtheit hat und damit ebenso nur so viel Kraft äußern kann, d.h. nur insoweit existiert, als es an der entgegengesetzten Kraft sich gegenübersteht hat'.

51. 'Jeder dieser sein sollenden Faktoren verschwindet ebenso, indem er über den andern hinaus, als indem er ihm gleich sein soll'.

52. 'dieser also sich zum einzigen Selbständigen macht'.

things in the world. The thing, being fixed and complete, does not permit quantitative disequilibrium of the measures. The mere attempt of any such surplus to manifest itself is self-destructive. Any such manifestation puts the surplus—a qualitative proposition—in a lethal isolation from the thing. This self-identical thing is thus radically incommensurate with any other thing, including itself. Such an entity destroys itself by its very logic. What is left is the beyond of the realm of quality and quantity—essence. Quality and quantity *have* beyonds. But essence does not. It has swallowed quality and quantity whole and made externality an internality.

CONCLUSION

Every Hegelian could have said in advance that essence comes about because quality and quantity sublate themselves. But how precisely does this unfold in the chapter Hegel names 'The Becoming of Essence'? That is an exceptionally difficult matter, with its use of bad astronomy and invocations of inverse ratios of factors. I have tried, in this paper, to show how this involves setting a substrate over against a completed world of measure. The two sides pass over into each other, and each side becomes not only its other but the unity of itself and its other. This introduces opposition into the sides. Now each side is the totality. External determination can no longer have any bite. Externality itself is sublated, leaving a negative residue that is a totality in and for itself. This is the realm of essence, which bears the cancelled world of measure as merely ideal moments within the totality. Measure becomes the world of appearances, against which essence stands. The fact that essence has been constituted as a totality is vitally important for the sequence that follows measure. Essence is a *totality*; it does not let its other go forth but rather contains it. It is *reflective* in nature. In reflection, 'the negative is thus confined within an enclosed sphere in which, what the one is *not*, is something *determinate*' (SL 639/WL II 282).[53] The insular nature of essence and its very correlativity requires the groundwork in *totality* which emerges in the chapter Hegel names 'The Becoming of Essence'.

---

53. 'das Negative ist somit in einer um Schlossenen Sphäre gehalten, worin das, was das eine nicht ist, ist Bestimmtes ist'.

# 9

# Hegel, Idealism and God: Philosophy as the Self-Correcting Appropriation of the Norms of Life and Thought

Paul Redding

Hegel can be said to have taken philosophical idealism to its most extreme point, the point of *absolute* idealism, and, from the perspective of much contemporary philosophy, this has been enough to damn him.[1] However, an adequate approach to what such a philosophical stance entails, as well as what possibilities it holds for philosophy today, must depend on a clear understanding of the core commitments of idealism itself, and, two hundred years after Hegel finished the earliest of his well-known works, the *Phenomenology of Spirit*, what these commitments amount to is still far from clear. If Bishop Berkeley is taken as the model of idealism, as often seems to be the case among Anglophone philosophers, then idealists would seem to be committed to some combination of his two complementary theses of *subjectivism* and *immaterialism*. However, as recently argued by Frederick Beiser, the trajectory of the German idealist movement from Kant onwards towards Hegel is best seen as a struggle *against* the subjectivism that Berkeley and others had inherited from Descartes.[2] Moreover, when one considers the 'objective' turn within idealism found in the world of Friedrich Schelling, idealism so understood seems more like an attempt to infuse matter with life and spirit, rather than to

---

1. In this, at least, there has been a degree of consensus between 'analytic' and 'continental' stands of twentieth century philosophy, which both oppose idealism in the name of some account of existence that stresses its *materiality*—in analytic philosophy, one that takes the form of a predominant scientific naturalism, and in continental philosophy, one that tends to stress the historical and material nature of the *linguistic ground* of thought (as in the work of Derrida, for example), or, some more generally existentialist sense of 'being' as the ground of thought that is thereby not reducible to it (as in the work of Heidegger). In this essay I am concerned to bring to the surface ways in which the commitments of idealism are in fact *not* subject to the usual objections brought from such philosophical positions.

2. Frederick Beiser, *German Idealism: The Struggle against Subjectivism*, 1781-1801, Cambridge, Harvard University Press, 2002.

eliminate it in the name of something 'immaterial'.[3]

However, if Schelling took idealism in the direction of this acknowledgement of the materiality of the world,[4] Hegel's programmatic statements often seem to take idealism off on a different path. Consider Hegel's claim, for example, that philosophy 'has no other object but God and so is essentially rational theology'. Philosophy, along with art and religion, belongs to what he refers to as 'Absolute Spirit', and these three realms having this same content—God—'differ only in the *forms* in which they bring home to consciousness their object, the Absolute' (LA 101). With claims like these, Hegel seems anything but an advocate of the type of modernizing philosophy that Kant had opened up, or as the type of philosopher intent on acknowledging the fundamental materiality of existence. Nevertheless, one needs to ask exactly what the concept 'God' *means* within a system of absolute idealism. To be an absolute idealist is, presumably, to be an idealist about everything about which one could be a 'realist', and, if one adopts a properly Kantian rather than Berkeleyan starting point, one might get a very different sense of what might be entailed by Hegel's absolute idealism to that given in traditional accounts. For one, it is clear that from Kant's perspective a crucial thing wrong with Berkeley's metaphysics was not so much its *idealist* assumptions as certain of its *realist* ones. That is, what had allowed Berkeley to be 'idealistic' about the material world—his immaterialist reduction of that world to it to a realm of subjective ideas—was his corresponding *realism* about the mental—in particular, his realism about the subjective mind and its contents, and, beyond this, the mind of *God*.[5] But both the individual mind and the mind of God were just the sort of topics that Kant was an *idealist* about, effectively claiming that rather than think of 'the soul' and 'God' as types of referring terms, we should see them as 'ideas' playing 'regulative' roles in our cognitive lives. Read as an 'absolute' idealist in a post-Kantian sense, then, Hegel might be seen as extending such a non-realist approach to both the individual soul and to God. Given the depth to which notions of God and the soul were embedded in early modern philosophy we may

---

3. It should not be surprising, then, that there has emerged within recent philosophy a radical reassessment of the nature and plausibility of Hegel's idealism, for example, as in the influential work of Robert Pippin and Terry Pinkard. See Robert Pippin's seminal *Hegel's Idealism*, Cambridge, Cambridge University Press, 1989, as well as *Modernism as a Philosophical Problem*, Cambridge, Cambridge University Press, 1991, 2nd ed., 1999, and *Idealism as Modernism: Hegelian Variations*, Cambridge, Cambridge University Press, 1997, and Terry Pinkard, *Hegel's Phenomenology: The Sociality of Reason*, Cambridge, Cambridge University Press, 1994, and *German Philosophy 1760–1860: The Legacy of Idealism* Cambridge, Cambridge University Press, 2002. From the side of analytic philosophy, such an interpretation of Hegel has been embraced by Robert Brandom, *Making It Explicit*, Cambridge, Harvard University Press, 1994, *Articulating Reasons*, Cambridge, Harvard University Press, 2000, and *Tales of the Mighty Dead: Historical Essays in the Metaphysics of Intentionality*, Cambridge, Harvard University Press, 2002, and John McDowell, *Mind and World*, second paperback edition with a new introduction, Cambridge, Harvard University Press, 1996.

4. See, for example, the essays collected in Judith Norman and Alistair Welchman, *The New Schelling*, London, Continuum, 2004, for an account of Schelling's approximation to materialism.

5. George Berkeley, *A Treatise Concerning the Principles of Human Knowledge*, Jonathan Dancy (ed.), Oxford, Oxford University Press, 1982.

expect his non-realism about these things to have very significant consequences.

In this essay, from this general starting point I want to consider some of the implications that being an idealist about God might entail, and to consider this in contrast to the more conventional way of extricating God from modern philosophy. I start by examining the relationship between Kant's idealism and the thesis on the basis of which he was thought to be a Berkeleyan, his idealism about *space*, as this can provide a helpful model for understanding exactly what it would be to be an idealist about God.

## IDEALISM AND REALISM ABOUT SPACE AND GOD

Perhaps the most obvious sense in which Kant was an idealist was in his opposition to the 'reality' of time and space,[6] an opposition which has been interpreted by many as suggesting a version of Bekeley's *immaterialism*. The picture motivating this interpretation is, I suggest, something like the following.

- Space and time, Kant thinks, are not real but in 'the mind'.
- But the contents of the empirical world are contents we take to be in space and time.
- Therefore, according to Kant, those contents too are in the mind.

At this level then, that is, at the level of the empirical world, Kant is seen as being a subjectivist and an immaterialist. He may have *supplemented* this Berkeleyan position with realist assumptions about a *second* world—an unknowable world of 'things in themselves'—but *that* world is not the world that we *take* to be 'the world'. The world that we *take* to be the world, the empirical world, is, on this reading of Kant, 'in the mind'.[7]

To the advocates of a non-Berkeleyan interpretation of Kant, such an inference may look no better than one which suggests that because I am conscious of a pain in my left foot, and my left foot is in my left shoe, then I am conscious of a pain in my left shoe. Rather than suggesting a form of Berkeyanism, we can see Kant's attack on the 'reality' of space and time as an attack on the framework that understands space and time *as* 'containers' within which the material world exists, and, in an analogous way, understands *the mind* as a container within which 'representations' exist. But on such a reading, what are we to say about what Kant *is* committing himself to with transcendental idealism? One way of approaching this, I suggest, is to look to the commitments of the concomitant form

---

6. 'I understand by the **transcendental idealism** of all appearances the doctrine that they are all together to be regarded as mere representations and not as things in themselves, and accordingly that space and time are only sensible forms of our intuition, but not determinations given for themselves or conditions of objects as things in themselves. To this idealism is opposed **transcendental realism**, which regards space and time as something given in themselves (independently of our sensibility).' Immanuel Kant, *Critique of Pure Reason*, ed. and trans. Paul Guyer and Allen W. Wood, Cambridge, Cambridge University Press, 1998, A369.

7. On this traditional phenomenalist reading of Kant, and the 'revolutionary' reading of Kant which opposes it see, for example, Graham Bird, *The Revolutionary Kant: A Commentary on the Critique of Pure Reason*, Chicago, Open Court, 2006.

of *realism* to which his idealism was opposed, in this case, that of Newton. And here, Newton's realism about space and time can be seen as relevant precisely because of its connection with his traditionally theistic beliefs about God.[8]

While Kant opposed his transcendental idealist account of space and time to the sort of realist account found in Newton, the *content* that they were respectively idealist and realist about was much the same. Here, Kant was on the side of Newton *qua* instigator of modern physical science, and, concomitantly, against Aristotle, for whom the more basic notion in physics was not that of 'space' but 'place'—*topos*.[9] For Aristotle, place had been a fundamental concept in the explanation of movement because the elements making up the cosmos were all accorded natural 'places' to which they would move if unimpeded. Thus earth had its natural place at the centre of the cosmos, fire, its natural place away from the earth in a layer or shell surrounding it, the layer containing the orbit of the sun, while water and air naturally layered themselves between these two regions, with a fifth element, the *aether*, filling the remaining outer regions. In short, as the derivative term, space, for Aristotle, was just the *finite totality* of qualitatively differentiated *places*.

Central to Newton's achievement had been the application of mathematics—in the first instance, of the constructable space of Euclidean geometry—to physical space, and this necessitated overturning its Aristotelian treatment. As Max Jammer has put it, 'How could Euclidean space, with its homogeneous and infinite lines and planes, possibly fit into the finite and anisotropic Aristotelian universe?'[10] Newton therefore had to transform the available conception of space in order to bring mathematics to bear within a universalized nomological treatment of the behaviour of objects in space, but with this he confronted a host of difficult metaphysical questions.

A long debate over the reality of empty space or 'void-space' had stretched back to Aristotle for whom the very notion itself was contradictory. Simply put, if the 'void' is nothing, how *could* it be real, that is, be *something*.[11] Newton's realist answer to objections to the reality of void space was complex but had a theological dimension.[12] As a variety of commentators have pointed out, Newton seems to

---

8. To simplify I will restrict the discussion to the issue of realism about space rather than both space and time.

9. Aristotle, *Physics*, bk. IV, 208b8–25 and bk. VIII, 261b31–a6. For a helpful discussion of these issues see Benjamin Morison, *On Location: Aristotle's Concept of Place*, Oxford, Oxford University Press, 2002, p. 38.

10. Max Jammer, *Concepts of Space: The History of Theories of Space in Physics*, Cambridge, Cambridge, 1954, p. 26.

11. Later, such an objection was implicit in Descartes' identifying extension as the fundamental property of matter, depriving the notion of an 'empty' extended space of meaning.

12. This had been made explicit in the 'General Scholium' to Book III, added to the second edition of Newtons *Principia* in 1713: 'This most beautiful system of the sun, planets, and comets, could only proceed from the counsel and dominion of an intelligent and powerful Being. ... This Being governs all things, not as the soul of the world, but as Lord over all; and on account of his dominion he is wont to be called *Lord God* pantokrator, or *Universal Ruler* .... He is eternal and infinite; omnipotent and omniscient; that is, his duration reaches from eternity to eternity; his presence from infinity to

have been influenced by the Cambridge neo-platonist Henry More, who, in opposition to Descartes, had insisted that *spirit*, and not just matter, was extended.[13] Combating the 'nullibilists', More equated the empty space *containing* matter with God's extension. Newton's concept of space was not quite the same as More's, but like More, he was to give the thesis of the absolute nature of void-space a profoundly theological basis: far from being 'nothing', space and time were, for Newton, attributes of divine spirit.[14] In turn, Leibniz led the attack against Newton's absolutization of space on grounds that were compatible with the nullibilist hypothesis that 'space' considered in abstraction of everything in it was, in fact, nothing. Leibniz thus used the principle of the identity of indiscernibles to criticize the very idea of thinking of any two points in empty space, or any two moments in empty time, as distinct—an idea needed by Newtonian realism.[15] Accordingly, in contrast to Newton's realism about space and time, Leibniz had treated the ideas of space and time as abstractions from relations among particular substances. *Outside* of these relations, space and time were, in fact, nothing.

These were the disputes that formed the background to Kant's 'transcendentally' idealist treatment of space and time in the *Critique of Pure Reason*. First, Kant was critical of Leibnizian relationalism,[16] and wanted to insist, like Newton, on the difference in analysis employed when one thought of material substances and their properties, on the one hand, and the properties of the ultimately unified

---

infinity; he governs all things and knows all things that are or can be done. ... He endures for ever, and is everywhere present; and by existing always and everywhere, he constitutes duration and space ... In him are all things contained and moved'. F. Cajori (ed.), *Sir Isaac Newton's Mathematical principles of natural philosophy, and his System of the world*, trans. A. Motte, trans. revised F. Cajori, Berkeley, University of California Press, 1962, p. 544.

13. See, for example, Alexandre Koyré, *From the Closed World to the Infinite Universe*, Baltimore, Johns Hopkins Press, 1957, pp. 159–68, Jammer, *Concepts of Space*, pp. 40–7 and 108–12, and Edward Grant, *Much Ado About Nothing: Theories of Space and Vacuum from the Middle Ages to the Scientific Revolution*, Cambridge, Cambridge University Press, 1981, pp. 244–5 and 252–4.

14. Nevertheless, strongly influenced by the mechanist Pierre Gassendi, Newton attempted to avoid the dichotomy of substance and accident that had structured the approach of More and most other participants in the debate to that time. By appealing to the 17th century distinction between a thing's 'nature' and its 'existence', Newton described time and place as 'common affections' characterizing the *existences* of all things, while the substance-accident distinction applied only to those things' *natures*. Thus, while Newton held that God was *extended*, and what we know as empty space just was that divine extension, he could avoid construing space as a necessary property of God—an element of his *essential nature*—an idea that had worrying pantheistic connotations. See in particular, J. E. McGuire, 'Force, Active Principles, and Newton's Invisible Realm', *Ambix*, no. 15, 1968, pp. 154–208, reprinted in J. E. McGuire, *Tradition and Innovation: Newton's Metaphysics of Nature*, Dordrecht, Kluwer, 1995.

15. Next, Leibniz used the principle of sufficient reason to argue against the theological concomitant to Newton's absolutization of space—the idea that God created the material world into some specific spatio-temporal region. Such a view which had God creating the world at some specific point of time, rather than another, portrayed God as acting arbitrarily, because there could *be* no reason for such a decision.

16. More specifically, he objected to Leibniz's relationalism on the basis that it could not account for the phenomenon of incongruent counterparts, and it was here that he appealed strongly to a view something like Newton's absolutism. See, for example, Kant's essay of 1768, 'Concerning the Ultimate Ground of the Differentiation of Directions in Space', in Immanuel Kant, *Theoretical Philosophy, 1755–1770*, ed. and trans. D. Walford and R. Meerbote, Cambridge, Cambridge University Press, 1992.

space that such substances 'occupied', on the other. Here Kant employed his fundamental distinction between 'concepts' and 'intuitions' as forms of representation.[17] While the objects that occupied space were to be understood conceptually as subjects of predication, the space occupied by those objects was to be understood geometrically and hence in terms of the determinations of a distinctly *non-conceptual* form of representation—pure intuition. Thus like Newton, he identified the space of Euclidian geometry with physical space, but he then *opposed* Newton's theologically supported realism, in which Euclidean geometry was regarded as *representing* an independent 'real' space—the space regarded as the extension of God. And with this Kant transformed the very concept of philosophical investigation, shifting the focus of the inquiry away from 'space' itself, about which philosophy has nothing to say, to the *form* in which we finite but rational minds *represent* space.

On Kant's novel understanding of the nature of space, just as the infinite space of the Euclidean geometer is co-constructed as the space within which specific figures are themselves constructed in diagrams, so too do we finite but rational perceivers construct the Euclidean spatio-temporal framework within which we represent the empirical world to ourselves in perceptual experience. It was this type of reversal of perspective that Kant alluded to with the image of Copernicus' reversal of perspective when he transformed the ancient geo-centric picture of the cosmos into the early modern helio-centric one.[18] Just as the ancient cosmologists *mistook* the movement of the earth on which they were located for the movement of the sun, so too, on Kant's account do *realists* about space and time mistake the products of their own representings for the attributes of space and time themselves. But this shift of focus had implications far greater than simply for how Kant understood space and time, it had implications for how philosophy from the Kantian perspective was to deal with the concept of God.

Newton's realist account of space and time, as we have seen, had been predicated on what might be called his 'spiritualist realism'—that is, his belief that ultimately reality was not material nature but a non-material, extended spirit, identified as the traditional Christian God. Significantly, Kant's approach to the concept of God was similarly opposed to such realism in the same way that his approach to space and time had been opposed to Newton's realism in that domain. That is, just as Kant had shifted philosophical analysis away from space itself to the mind's representation of space, so too he shifted philosophy away from the *subject matter* of God, to that of the functioning of the mind's *representation* of God—that is, of the 'idea' of God. Here, Kant interpreted Plato's conception of 'idea' as being as a non-empirical 'pure' concept which belonged to the rational faculty, but instead of primarily functioning in the context of theoretical reason, it now had a central role in the operations of *practical* reason.[19] Thus God was

---

17. Kant, *Critique of Pure Reason*, A19/B33; A320/B376–7.

18. Kant, *Critique of Pure Reason*, B xvi–ii, xii n.

19. Immanuel Kant, *Critique of Practical Reason*, trans. Mary Gregor, Cambridge, Cambridge University Press, 1997, Bk II, Ch. II, section V, 'The Existence of God as a Postulate of Pure Practical Reason'.

eliminated as a relevant subject for theoretical analysis as seen, for example, in Kant's attack on traditional proofs for the existence of God.[20] Ideas could not play a 'constitutive' role in theoretical knowledge, claimed Kant, only a 'regulative' one, mirroring the role they played in practical reason in determining the content of the moral law. But the purely conceptually articulated moral law needed some way of being applied in actual life, and it was here that Kant located the idea of God. In order to be applied, ideas needed to be given *sensibilized* forms, and it was this type of symbolically or analogically expressed idea that formed the traditional picture of God.[21] The traditional theological conception of God, so Kant claimed, has resulted from taking a particular idea (the one associated with forms of explanation employing the disjunctive syllogism) and employing it in a 'constitutive' rather than 'regulative' way. More specifically the traditional theistic concept of God had resulted, he claimed from 'realizing' 'hypostatizing' and 'personalizing' that idea.[22]

With this, Kant initiated a symbolic approach to the content of traditional religious belief that can be recognized not only in near post-Kantians like Schelling and Hegel, but also in more distant ones such as Nietzsche and Durkheim.[23] But while Kant had concentrated on the role of the representation of God within the moral life of the individual subject, Schelling switched attention away from modern individualized life to the very different life-form of the ancient Greek polis, now considering the role of 'the gods' as represented within the public and communal aesthetic practices of the Greeks. Moreover, he claimed to find in the common consciousness of such forms of communal life an awareness that Kant had struggled to establish by philosophical argument in modernity. The Greeks, Schelling asserted, were not concerned with the question of the *existence* of their gods in the way that later became crucial for christian thinkers. The gods had their very being *in* their representations—the myths told within the community as well as the statues, poems, plays and so on that drew their contents from those myths. The Greeks did not then pose the *further* question of how or if those representations did or did not relate to some reality beyond the stories that were told about them.[24]

---

20. Kant, *Critique of Pure Reason*, Second Division, Bk. II, Ch. III, 'The Ideal of Pure Reason'. This attack drew on his separation of matters of existence from that which can be examined in terms of conceptual content, a separation that was *itself* consequent upon the differentiation of concepts and intuitions as functionally different forms of representation.

21. For a comprehensive treatment see Heiner Bielefeldt, *Symbolic Representation in Kant's Practical Philosophy*, Cambridge, Cambridge University Press, 2003.

22. Kant, *Critique of Pure Reason*, A583/B611 n.

23. Many recent interpretations of Nietzsche have tended to stress his relation to Kant. See, for example, Will Dudley, *Hegel, Nietzsche and Philosophy: Thinking Freedom*, Cambridge, Cambridge University Press, 2002, and R. Kevin Hill, *Nietzsche's Critiques: The Kantian Foundations of his Thought*, Oxford, Clarendon Press, 2003. On the influence of late 19$^{th}$ century neo-Kantianism on Durkheim see S. Lukes, *Emile Durkheim: His Life and Work*, Stanford, Stanford University Press, 1973, pp. 54–7. Durkheim's relation to Kantianism is further explored by Warren Schmaus, *Rethinking Durkheim and His Tradition*, Cambridge, Cambridge University Press, 2004.

24. Thus, Schelling criticizes the idea that the reality of the gods can be understood on the model of

The underlying approach was, nevertheless, Kantian, as Schelling interpreted Greek mythology as a realm of representations that gave a peculiarly *figurative* form of representation to that which was represented *discursively* as 'ideas' within the realm of Platonic philosophy. The 'same synthesis of the universal and particular that viewed in themselves are ideas, that is, images of the divine, are, if viewed on the plane of the real, the gods.'[25] The reality of the Greek gods was expressed in what they enabled those who revered them to *do* and the way in which they were enabled to *live*. Thus the whole significance of 'ideas' and their sensibilized 'ideals' was to be found in the role they played in the life of the community. However, this meant that in an account such as Schelling's, ideas could no longer simply be regarded as playing a merely 'regulative' as opposed to 'constitutive' role as in Kant's transcendental idealism. Given their participation in shaping and reproducing an *objective way of life*, this way of life could be thought of as an realm of which those ideas played a 'constitutive' role.[26]

Schelling's approach was the starting point of Hegel's which also exemplified these basic features of Kant's idealist stance to theology, and this, I suggest, is how we should understand Hegel's philosophy as an *extension* of Kant's idealist turn. To be an *absolute idealist* was to shift philosophical attention away from what philosophical *realists* had traditionally taken as fundamental objects or features of reality, to the role played by the representations of such objects or features in the individual and collective life of the community.

## HEGEL ON THE GREEKS AND CHRISTIANITY, NATURE AND SPIRIT

In the context of the type of pre-Christian pagan thought celebrated by the youthful Schelling and (the slightly older) Hegel in their writings of the 1790s, the worldliness and plurality of the Greek gods contrasted with the single, transcendent, omniscient and omnipotent God, the type of Christianity found in Newton.

---

the reality of the objects of the world of experience and understanding. 'Anyone who is still able to ask how such highly cultivated spirits as the Greeks were able to believe in the reality or actuality of the gods ... proves only that he himself has not yet arrived at that stage of cultivation at which precisely the *ideal* is the real and is much more real than the so-called real itself. The Greeks did not at all take the gods to be real in the sense, for example, that common understanding believes in the reality of physical objects.' F. W. J. von Schelling, *Philosophy of Art*, trans. D. W. Stott, Minneapolis, University of Minnesota Press, 1989, p. 35. This coheres with a point made by Robert Pippin in reference to the views of both Nietzsche and Hans Blumenberg. There is no evidence that the Greeks argued about which among the many diverse accounts of the gods was the *true* account. Robert Pippin, 'Truth and Lies in the Early Nietzsche', *Idealism as Modernism: Hegelian Variations*, Cambridge, Cambridge University Press, 1997, pp. 311-329, p. 318.

25. Schelling, *Philosophy of Art*, p. 28.

26. It is because Kant equates the empirical world with the realm of what Anscombe has described as 'brute facts' that 'ideas' cannot be constitutive of the empirical world. (G. E. M. Anscombe, 'On Brute facts', *Analysis*, no. 18, 1958, pp. 69-72.) For Schelling and Hegel, however, who think of the social world as constituted by 'institutional facts', ideas *can* be constitutive, but not constitutive in the sense that Kant had intended when *denying* their constitutive status. On the relevance of this distinction between Kant and Hegel see my *Hegel's Hermeneutics*, Ithaca, Cornell University Press, 1996.

This 'pagan' anti-christian orientation was in turn bound up with features of their *philosophical* position, as in their growing opposition to the way that Fichte had developed Kant's normative concept of the thinking subject, the 'transcendental unity of apperception'.

One of Kant's fundamental ideas had been that thinking itself required the implicit act of ascription of thought by the thinker to herself conceived 'transcendentally', the ascription of all representations to the thinking 'I' that accompanies all thought.[27] In Fichte's development, this notion of a transcendental normative subject had become the concept of the *self-positing* 'absolute I',[28] a conceptual corollary to the god of Newton's natural philosophy—the omnipotent and omniscient god who created the material world *ex nihilo* into the space and time with which he was co-extensive, and who decreed the laws of its operation. The 'paganism' of Schelling and Hegel, then, would be expressed in their conception of the norms of theoretical and practical reason. For example, in the domain of epistemology, such a critique would be directed at a conception of the norm of knowledge as expressed with the phrase 'god's-eye view', presupposing as it does the christian transcendent and omniscient god. But while the early Hegel has shared this pagan characterization of the normative, after his break with Schelling that had been signalled in his well-known remarks in the *Phenomenology*'s Preface (PS ¶ 16), he had incorporated a more conventional Christian theological outlook, the significance of which was to remain disputed among his followers after his death. Eventually, Hegel came to distinguish *two* non-conceptual forms in which gods/norms are represented pre-philosophically: while the Greeks represented their gods artistically, in sensuously presented objective cultural representations such as statues or religious dramas, the christian god came to be represented predominantly in the internalized mode of *memory*—the *memorialized* narrative of the person of Christ (LA 101–4), the god who having become man, had therefore to suffer a fate hitherto unknown to gods, the fate of dying. But in this Christian account, as befitting a god, he returned to life in the form of the *spirit* of the community of followers which was symbolized in the third person of the trinity. This gave the idea of *this* god a complexity and depth within the psychic lives of individuals that had been missing within the sensuous modes of representation of the Greeks. Christians now thought of themselves as carrying their god *within them*, a relation symbolized by the ritual of eating the body and drinking the blood of Christ and which was expressed in the significance given to the phenomenon of individual *conscience*.[29] With this, Hegel reaffirmed the element of *subjectivity* that

---

27. 'The **I think** must **be able** to accompany all my representations, for otherwise something would be represented in me that could not be thought at all, which is as much as to say that the representation would either be impossible or else at least would be nothing for me.' Kant, *Critique of Pure Reason*, B131–2.

28. J. G. Fichte, 'Foundation of the Entire Science of Knowledge', in *The Science of Knowledge*, ed. and trans. Peter Heath and John Lachs, Cambridge, Cambridge University Press, 1982, pp. 93–102.

29. I consider Hegel's account of conscience in relation to that of Fichte in 'Hegel, Fichte and the Pragmatic Contexts of Moral Judgment', in Espen Hammer (ed.), *German Idealism: Historical and Philosophical Perspectives*, London, Routledge, 2007.

was the distinctive trait of modern philosophy which marked it off from that of the ancients.

This turn by the later Hegel from the more pantheistic and polytheistic outlook of his youth to the position fully realized in his Berlin *Lectures on the Philosophy of Religion* is often taken as of a piece with a purported turn to a more conservative *political* outlook of his Berlin period, as is expressed in the *Philosophy of Right*.[30] These are complex questions that cannot be adequately treated here. As is well-known, an ambiguity seems to have marked Hegel's politico-religious position in his Berlin period, an ambiguity that, upon his death, became manifest in the split that developed between the left, humanist and right theist factions among his followers. One consequence of this move away from the pantheism of the early Schelling does need to be confronted, however, as we might think that this pantheistic stance at least seems more compatible with the type of extended Kantian attitude to religion that I have been here treating as the mark of an idealist orientation to God. To the extent that Hegel moved away from this to more conventionally Christian forms of religious culture, does not this undercut the picture being presented of a progressively 'idealist' move away from early modern theo-centric philosophy of, say, Descartes, Newton and Leibniz, and would we not expect to find in pantheism a closer connection to the more 'naturalistic' orientation that is thought of as typical of modern philosophy? To answer to this, I think, is bound up with the issue of what, from the account of idealism that I have been suggesting here, might be perceived as being wrong with the naturalistic de-theologization of philosophy that has since become typical of modernity. And this is bound up with a consideration that was at the core of post-Kantian idealist thought: that of the charge of 'nihilism' brought by Friedrich Jacobi against the developing rationalist-scientific culture when he ignited the 'pantheism' dispute in Germany in the mid 1780s.[31]

Schelling, like many others of his generation, had been attracted to the Spinozism against which Jacobi issued his warnings, but was intent on showing that Spinozism was *not* nihilistic. Rather, he claimed, Spinozism was compatible with the human freedom that was at the centre of Kantian philosophy. But such a reconciliation had to work against the grain of that reading of Spinoza shared by many of his admirers as well as his critics and that identified Spinozism with any type of mechanical materialism. Thus the somewhat mechanistic conception of Spinozism as inherited from the 17th century came to be replaced by a more 'organic' version, especially in the light of the interest that had arisen in the later 18th century in the emerging life sciences. From this point of view, matter was

---

30. Pantheism had been associated with the political radicalism since the English Civil wars of the mid 17th century. On the history of the relation between pantheism and republican politics in the 17th and 18th centuries see Margaret C. Jacob, *The Radical Enlightenment: Pantheists, Freemasons and Republicans*, 2nd revised edition, Lafayette, Cornerstone Books, 2006.

31. F. H. Jacobi, 'On the Doctrine of Spinoza in Letters to Moses Mendelssohn', in *The Main Philosophical Writings and the Novel Allwill*, ed. and trans. G. di Giovanni, Montreal, McGill-Queens University Press, 1994, pp. 173–251, 339–378.

fundamentally *living*.

In *Ideas for a Philosophy of Nature*, written in 1797, Schelling posed what he described as the fundamental philosophical question: 'How a world outside us, how a Nature and with it experience is possible'.[32] Kant had taught that something *as known* had to have a form contributed by the knower, and Schelling seems to be led by this question to the existence of the knower itself, and his answer has to be seen as standing in sharp contrast with the sorts of early modern answers that had come down to the eighteenth century. 'The knower' who had supplied 'the form' of the world had traditionally been conceived as *God*, a conception, as we have seen, still alive in the otherwise 'naturalistic' philosophy of Newton. But for Schelling it was only after the knowing subject had 'disentangled itself from the fetters of nature and her guardianship' that such nature *could be there* as something *knowable for* the knower. Thus this knower is clearly not the divine transcendent knower of Newton, nor that reflected in the idealistic transformation of this in Kant or Fichte, but a much more naturalistically conceived one. Moreover, the idea that this knowing subject must have become 'disentangled' from the world presupposes an earlier state in which the two are presumably 'tangled' together forming an existence that is reducible *neither* to the knowing subject *nor* the known world. For the mind to have 'disentangled itself' from nature there must have been an original unity *to be* disrupted:

> As soon as man sets himself in opposition to the external world ... the first step of philosophy has been taken. With that separation, reflection first begins, he separates from now on what Nature had always united, separates the object from the intuition, the concept from the image, finally (in that he becomes his own *object*) himself from himself.[33]

Schelling's idea of the subject disentangling itself from nature thus needs to be seen in relation to the 'subjects' of Kant and Fichte which still model themselves on a transcendent omnipotent and omniscient god. And his conception of nature breaks with the conceptions of both Kant and Fichte for whom nature stands over against such an ideal knowing subject as the domain of the *knowable*. Schelling, by suggesting a 'prior' state in which subject and object were combined, suggested a conception of nature quite different to the type of nature conceived of only *after* the disentanglement. Schelling's nature was one *immanent* with subjectivity, not abstractly *opposed* to it.

For Hegel too, nature conceived in the way of modern naturalism could not constitute 'the absolute' for essentially the reason that had been given by Schelling. What is taken as an object of knowledge must be conceived in relation to the opposed notion of a subject for whom it is an object. But Schelling, in his more Spinozistic reaction to this, had presupposed the thought of an *original* nature preceding the separation of the subject and object—mind and world—and giv-

---

32. F. W. J. Schelling, *Ideas for a Philosophy of Nature*, trans. E. E. Harris and P. Heath, New York, Cambridge University Press, 1988, p. 10.

33. Schelling, *Ideas for a Philosophy of Nature*, p.10.

ing rise to them both.[34] And the very idea of this original nature was in line with his appeal to a type of 'intellectual intuition' of which we are capable, a form of cognition which combined elements of the conceptual comprehension and intuitive apprehension that Kant had carefully separated. Resisting the idea of intellectual intuition, Hegel was truer to the Kantian origins of idealism. Without any internal distinctions which would be available only on reflection, the 'absolute' to which Schelling appealed, so he famously claimed, could be no more than a 'night in which … all cows are black' (PS ¶ 16).[35] In line with this move away from Schelling's pantheistic conception of an original nature immanent with life and mind, Hegel started to appeal the more conventional christian imagery of 'nature' as an externalization or negation of 'spirit'.

This is easily seen, and has been traditionally seen, as a move away from the early Schelling's more 'naturalist' approach and as a regression back to a more explicitly theo-centric *spiritualist* one. In line with this, much of the left 'young Hegelian' thought, such as that of Ludwig Feuerbach, had manifested a philosophical orientation closer to Schellingian phase of the early Hegel, in contrast to the position of the mature Hegel. However, such a criticism might be put in a different light when one takes note of Hegel's innovative conception of 'spirit', a conception that grounds it in a specific type of embodied social interaction that, following Fichte, he called 'recognition'. Conceiving of spirit as something that existed only *in its* recognition *by* spirit, Hegel's theory of spirit can be seen as thoroughly idealistic, in the sense suggested here. That is, read on the basis of a post-Kantian approach to idealism, Hegel's recourse to 'spirit' would be *anything but* 'spiritualistic' in the conventional sense.

## HEGEL'S RECOGNITIVE CONCEPTION OF ABSOLUTE SPIRIT

Hegel's classic statement on the constitution of spirit by reciprocally presupposing acts of intersubjective recognition appears in the *Phenomenology of Spirit*, chapter 4. From it we learn that recognition by another self-consciousness is a condition for the *existence* of a self-consciousness:

> A self-consciousness exists *for a self-consciousness*. Only so is it in fact self-consciousness; for only in this way does the unity of itself in its otherness become explicit for it.

> Self-consciousness exists in and for itself when, and by the fact that, it so exists for another; that is, it exists only in being acknowledged (PS ¶¶ 177-78).

This is just what it is to be an *idealist* about self-consciousness. Just as Fichte had conceived of rights as only existing in their recognition by others, Hegel extended

---

34. Such an original nature could, of course, no longer be thought of in the way that nature was thought *as object*, as this both presupposed and left out the 'subject' for whom it became an object. Schelling himself moved away from his use of the notion of intellectual intuition in his later writings.

35. While this has standardly been taken as referring to Schelling, H. S. Harris has persuasively argued that this was directed not at Schelling himself but at his followers. See, H. S. Harris, *Hegel's Ladder*, Indianapolis, Hackett, 1997, vol. 1, p. 50-1.

the recognitive approach to the self in *all* its determinations.[36] This does not make selves *unreal* or *fictional*, it simply makes their reality, unlike that of nature, conditional upon their recognition by others. Without this system of recognition, there is no self, just a natural organism.

Clearly, to prevent an infinite regress, recognition must be reciprocal, and it is such a system of reciprocal recognition mediating relations between members of a community that constitutes the 'spirit' within which they can be said to have their existence:

> ... A self-consciousness, in being an object, is just as much 'I' as 'object'. With this, we already have before us the concept of *spirit*. What still lies ahead for consciousness is the experience of what spirit is—this absolute substance which is the unity of the different independent self-consciousnesses which, in their opposition, enjoy perfect freedom and independence: 'I' that is 'We' and 'We' that is 'I' (PS ¶ 177).

While Hegel's conception of the 'recognitive' basis of spirit has become relatively well-known in the context of his approach to what he calls the 'objective spirit' of the concrete socio-political sphere, the systematic importance for the notion of recognition for Hegel's concept of spirit more broadly conceived, and especially for his conception of 'absolute spirit', has been generally less well appreciated.[37] But there is no reason to assume that it applies *there* any less than it applies in the concrete social realm.

Spirit, Hegel tells us, has three forms: 'subjective'; 'objective', and 'absolute'. *Subjective* spirit is spirit in its finite individual form, and the study of subjective spirit might be seen as roughly equivalent to what we now think of as 'philosophy of mind'. In something like the picture found in the thought of the later Wittgenstein, Hegel makes it a condition of mindedness that an individual belongs to a social realm of rule-governed interactions: it is this realm that is where that individual can find the recognition that is a condition of their *being* a self-conscious individual. Thus the study of the conditions of subjective spirit takes us to the realm of *objective* spirit—spirit as it is 'objectified' in those forms of finite, culturally encoded normative (or rule-following) practices and institutions in which an individual 'subjective spirit' engages with others.[38] When Hegel studies 'objective spirit', as he does in the *Philosophy of Right*,[39] he engages with overtly normative phenomena, such as systems of explicitly worked out laws to which members of a community hold themselves, as well as more generally culturally specific and less formalized 'sociologically' normative practices of social life. The subjective and

---

36. See, for example, Robert B. Pippin, 'What is the Question for which Hegel's Theory of Recognition is the Answer?', *European Journal of Philosophy*, vol. 8, no. 2, 2000, pp. 155–72.

37. For a systematic application of the notion of recognition to Hegel's ethical and political thought see Robert R. Williams, *Hegel's Ethics of Recognition*, Berkeley, University of California Press, 1997. I have suggested the broader application of the notion in *Hegel's Hermeneutics*, Ithaca, Cornell University Press, 1996, ch. 7.

38. Objective spirit can thus be thought of as a realm of 'institutional facts' that obtain in virtue of being *recognized* as obtaining.

39. G. W. F. Hegel, *Elements of the Philosophy of Right*, Allen W. Wood (ed.), trans. H. B. Nisbet, Cambridge, Cambridge University Press, 1991.

objectives forms of finite spirit will be mutually presupposing, as the social roles codified in objective spirit will require intentional agents and not merely biological organisms to bear those roles, and individuals can become those agents only by being inducted into social life already structured by those roles.[40] But a *further* level of spirit is required to allow us to think how the structures of subjective and objective spirit can be unified. This is the role of absolute spirit, the level of spirit within which the norms presupposed in subjective and objective spirit are given *explicit* forms of representation.

In the first instance 'absolute spirit' simply refers to a certain subset of the social practices making up objective spirit, specifically, the cultural practices of art, religion and philosophy, spheres of culture with products which will have the type of endurance which allows them to normatively shape the practices of a community and ensure its continuity. In Hegel's account it is clear that there is a development in the medium of these practices from the more sensuous and imagistic through to the more conceptual and linguistic. It is their objectification in this way that gives these products a relative autonomy from the more concrete practices of the culture from which they emerge. Nevertheless, as symbolic products or representations they only exist *as* meaningful in the recognition of subjects whose lives are historically located. But I take the *difference* between absolute and objective spirit to signal that from the point of view of the recognizing *subjects*, these representations are afforded a type of necessity that would be lost were they to be regarded as *merely* the cultural reflections of a particular finite society. This necessity is part of the status they have *as* norms—Kantian 'ideas'—that individuals take as regulative of their interaction and as constitutive of their identities.

As we have noted, Hegel effectively takes over Kant's symbolic approach to religion in modernity, and like Kant he wants to preserve the normative status of religious representation at the same time as divesting those representations of the sort of ontological status they have for believers. This, of course, is a fine line to walk, as the fate of Hegelianism after his death suggests. Does not the 'death of God' have the nihilistic consequence that 'everything is permitted', as Jacobi had charged? Both Kant and Hegel wanted to reply 'no', and both appealed to the normativity of reason itself rather than any other authority to secure the grip of norms on individual lives. This is a central commitment *of* idealism. And while Hegel sought to anchor these norms in historically considered social practices, he nevertheless still wanted to make their grip on individual lives have something of the 'categorical' nature that Kant had found in the categorical imperative. This attempt to integrate normativity with a 'this-worldly' and otherwise naturalistic position, places huge demands on a philosophy, and Hegel's degree of success here is far from clear. For our purposes, however, it may be enough to indicate

---

40. In recent times Robert Brandom has, within the context of analytic philosophy, built an approach to the social and pragmatic conditions of intentionality that attempts to capture Hegel's concept of recognition. See, in particular, Brandom, *Making It Explicit* and *Tales of the Mighty Dead*. For a comparison of Brandom's approach with that of the historical Hegel see my *Analytic Philosophy and the Return of Hegelian Thought*, Cambridge, Cambridge University Press, 2007.

that it is at least equally far from clear that he *fails*, or fails in the way the ways in which he is commonly taken to fail, or fails where *others* have succeeded. And to get some sense on the possibility that Hegel's idealism points in the right direction here, it may be useful to focus on the way that he appeals to aspects of the christian version of religious myth that exemplify aspects of his own way of construing the normativity of reason.

We might start by attempting to grasp the relevance of christianity for Hegel's conception of philosophy by reflecting on the fact that for Aristotle, '*theos*' or 'God', construed as the process of 'thought thinking itself', was effectively an idealization of philosophical thought itself.[41] We should note that such a process in which thought reflects on the conditions and limits of thought *itself* rather than anything *beyond* thought, is also just the way that philosophy is conceived after Kant's Copernican turn. But for Kant, this is conceived from the side of *finite* thinking subjects, not from the side of Aristotle's *theos* construed realistically as a prime mover located at the outer edge of the cosmos and *as* so located as free from the limitations and finitude that characterize the life of humans on earth.[42] If we then think of Aristotle's *theos* as analogous to the first person of the christian trinity, we can see how the movement from the perspective of ancient philosophy to modern philosophy is going to coincide with a movement from the perspective of a transcendent god to one 'fallen' into the realm of objectified living existence on earth. Modern philosophy and religion are going to be characterized by a type of finite subjectivity largely alien to ancient philosophy.

In the theological register, the modern 'consummate' religion of Christianity brought God into the world as an exemplar and thereby subjected him to the sufferings attendant on human life. Analogously, in the context of philosophy, Hegel brings the norms of thought itself into the world where they are objectified in the social life of human communities as a series of finite 'shapes' of consciousness and self-consciousness, all destined, like individuals, to appear in the world, have a short existence, and then die off to be replaced by something different. The recognition of such finitude is, of course, often responded to with skepticism or relativism. To discover that the norms to which we hold ourselves *are* finite can lead to the assumption that 'all is permitted'. But Hegel is clearly opposed to such skepticism. Because even *God* is affected by such finitude, an idea he takes to be at the heart of Christianity, Christian mythology gives expression to a stance which undermines the normative assumptions upon which skepticism makes sense. When, in the *Phenomenology*, Hegel notes that the usual skeptical responses in philosophy vanish 'as soon as Science [philosophy] comes on the scene' and

---

41. Aristotle, *Aristotle XVIII, Metaphysics*, trans. Hugh Tredennick, Harvard, Loeb Classical Library, 1982 book 12, ch. 9. Hegel quotes Aristotle's conception of 'noesis noeseos noesis' at the conclusion of the *Encyclopaedia of the Philosophical Sciences*, (G. W. F. Hegel, *Philosophy of Mind: Part III of the Encyclopaedia of the Philosophical Sciences*, trans. W. Wallace, Oxford, Clarendon Press, 1971, § 577).

42. Of course the Copernican turn destroyed such a *location* for God, hence the type of difficulties for Christian thought in the early modern period that Newton tried to address by his making space an *attribute* of God.

'just because it comes on the scene', the parallel with the christian myth is obvious. Philosophical knowledge is now conceived as no longer transcendent, like the self-consciousness of Aristotle's God, but as having come into the world (having come 'on the scene') like the 'son of God', it 'is itself an appearance'. But what has come on the scene is not yet 'Science in its developed and unfolded truth' (PS ¶ 76), and this points to the peculiarity of philosophy's intersubjective medium—conceptually articulated language.

Philosophy (in contrast to art or religion) can be properly 'scientific' not because it is based in some kind of intuitively certain experience—the sort of primordial intuitive experience Hegel had objected to in Schelling—but because it has a self-transcending character, allowing it at any one time to be not yet 'in its developed and unfolded truth'. Here the special nature of conceptual cognition resides, as Wilfrid Sellars was later to urge, in its self-correcting nature.[43] Having achieved an explicitly conceptual form, philosophical thought can subject itself to the same sort of critical reflection to which thought can subject anything. It is in this way that philosophy is able to free itself from the historical contingency that afflicts the individuals who philosophize, and it is the conceptual nature of philosophy's form of representation that makes its project into that of the 'making explicit' of those norms itself. But this should not be seen as a type of discovery of something belonging to a realm beyond us. The norms must to be those which have come to constitute ourselves as rational beings, they must be *our* norms—hence the *Phenomenology's* retrospective recollection of the complex genealogy seen as constitutive of the modern self. But unlike that which occurs in those who discover their 'roots' in, say, religious or nationalist mythologies, we are meant to come to identity with the norms *qua* norms that are self-correcting, replaceable parts of a process whereby what we hold ourselves to at any one time will, by necessity, be shown to be finite.

I have tried to extricate Hegel from the some of the assumptions normally brought to the very idea of 'absolute idealism', but this is not, of course, to extricate him from *all* the objections traditionally brought against him. Among these, a certain form of criticism extending from the later Schelling and finding expression in Heidegger is critical of Hegel's enlightenment optimism in reason. On this charge, it is *this* aspect of his idealism that implies his inability to come to terms with the depth of the brute *non-rational* materiality of the world. Such a criticism has continued to find adherents in the light of what has seemed to many to be the *failure* of the enlightenment project over the last century. A defence of Hegel here might take its orientation from the considerations of the type just rehearsed, that is, those in which Hegel tries to temper the enlightenment faith in reason with an acknowledgement of the dimension of finitude that is always found in it. But

---

43. Compare Sellars's view that 'empirical knowledge, like its sophisticated extension, science, is rational, not because it has a *foundation* but because it is a self-correcting enterprise which can put *any* claim in jeopardy, though not *all* at once'. Wilfrid Sellars, *Empiricism and the Philosophy of Mind*, with an Introduction by Richard Rorty and a Study Guide by Robert Brandom, Cambridge, Harvard University Press, 1997, p. 79.

whatever form such a defence might take, it is clear that the debate over Hegel must be one that is over the views of the actual philosopher, and not those of the straw man who has been the target of much traditional criticism.

*hegel and the tradition*

10

# Being and Implication:
# On Hegel and the Greeks

Andrew Haas

ei dē to on kai to hen tauton kai mia phusis tō akolouthein
allēlois hōsper archē kai aition...

If being and unity are the same and are one thing in the
sense that they are implied in one another as principle and
cause are...
—Aristotle, Metaphysics, 1003b22-24.

A new concept of being, a *neuer Seinsbegriff*, that 'complies with the meaning of the absolute concept of being' (HPS 141/203)[1]—this is what Heidegger thinks Hegel's *Phenomenology of Spirit* develops. But if this concept is new, it is because it is old, as old as Western metaphysics. And Hegel is merely unfolding the essential motifs of the Greeks, bringing the question *'ti to on'* to completion. The science of the phenomenology of spirit is therefore, *'nothing other than the fundamental-ontology of absolute ontology*, or onto-logy in general' (HPS 141/204).[2]

So what is this new concept of being? It is the concept itself, *der Begriff*. But the concept for Hegel is not simply an abstract idea or category, nor an immedi-

---

1. Martin Heidegger, *Hegel's Phenomenology of Spirit*, trans. P. Emad and K. Maly, Bloomington, Indiana, 1994, p. 141 (henceforth HPS; the corresponding German page number from vol. 32 of the collected works of Heidegger, *Hegels Phänomenologie des Geistes*, Frankfurt an Main, Klostermann, 1980, is given after the slash /).

2. Heidegger continues: insofar as the 'being of beings is determined as *eidos, idea*, idea, and thus related to seeing, knowing, and *logos*', philosophy is always idealism; and the phenomenology of spirit is 'the deliberate, explicit, and absolute justification of idealism' (HPS 141-2/204); see GW IX 132ff. For the interpretation that Hegel's thought is 'not just an epistemological truth; it reflects the ontological one', see Charles Taylor, 'The Opening Arguments of the Phenomenology' in *Hegel*, A. MacIntyre (ed.), Notre Dame, University of Notre Dame, 1972, p. 166. For the view that the Phenomenology 'rests on the difference between knowledge and being', see Jean Hyppolite, *Genesis and Structure of Hegel's Phenomenology of Spirit*, trans. S. Cherniak and J. Heckman, Evanston, Northwestern University, 1974, p. 578.

ate intuition of simple natures, nor is it merely a subjective thought or function of consciousness—for it is just as much concrete and objective, substance and subject—the concept is the absolute idea of absolute spirit. Being is absolute spirit, and the absolute idea is its concept. But if being is the concept, then absolute spirit is the absolute idea. And the phenomenology of spirit is the development of being as the concept; it is the comprehended or conceptual history, *begriffene Geschichte*, of absolute spirit as it comes to absolute knowledge of itself as absolute idea, 'spirit that knows itself as spirit' (PS ¶ 808/GW IX 531).³ Then if the concept is Hegel's new concept of being, history is the concept of the concept, *Begriff des Begriffes* (SL 582/GW XII 11).⁴ As Heidegger insists: if spirit's knowledge is historical history, the concept of being is temporal, and 'the problematic of "being and time" already exists in Hegel' (HPS 144/208).⁵

But what then is the temporality of being, of the historical concept, of the absolute idea of absolute knowledge? For Heidegger, it is that 'being is the essence of time; being, namely, *qua* infinity' (HPS 145/209).⁶ Time is finite; being is infinite—for 'time is *one* appearance of the *simple* essence of being *qua* infinity' (HPS 145/209). Beings appear in time, as temporal, in the 'shape of space' (PS ¶ 169), thanks to the infinity of being, thanks to the concept of infinite history.

Heidegger's thesis in response to the problematic of being and time however, is the exact opposite of Hegel's: being is not the essence of time—rather, 'time is the original essence of being' (HPS 146/211). But is being the essence of time for Hegel? Or is it rather that history is the essence of being? Does the *Phenomenology* not demonstrate that the essence of being is historical spirit? What then happens to time? And to being? Or if Hegel's concept of being is, as Heidegger insists, 'as old as Western philosophy' (HPS 141/204),⁷ as old as the Greeks, must we not look to them in order to think the original meaning of being, and of time?

---

3. As Hyppolite argues: 'Whereas in sensuous certainty the immediate is, in the last chapter it has come to be what it is: it has actualized itself through an internal mediation. In the first chapter, truth and certainty are immediately equal; in the last chapter, certainty, i.e., subjectivity, has posed itself in being, posed itself as truth, and truth, i.e., objectivity, has shown itself to be certainty, self-consciousness', *Genesis and Structure of Hegel's Phenomenology of Spirit*, pp. 81-2.

4. See also F. W. J. Schelling, *System des transzendentalen Idealismus*, Hamburg, Meiner, 1992, p. 15.

5. See also *Being and Time*, trans. J. Stambaugh, New York, SUNY, 1996, §82 (henceforth BT).

6. Heidegger's thesis with respect to being and time is no thesis at all; on the contrary, it is a question, a question that asks for the meaning of being, and its relation to time. Against Hegel, Heidegger is concerned with renewing the question of ontology, the question of being, its *logos*, method and content. Philosophy therefore, as an attempt to raise (or re-raise) being to the status of a question—not find a new answer—'is not a science' (HPS 12/18). The extent to which Heidegger, by raising the question of the meaning of being to the status of a question, fails in this attempt to raise 'the question of the question', is raised by Jacques Derrida, *De l'esprit*, Paris, Galilée, 1987, p. 24. The extent to which the question, or the question of the question, is far more an answer, or an attack, see my *The Irony of Heidegger*, London, Continuum, 2007.

7. Owing to space restrictions, I will limit my consideration of Heidegger's texts to those that explicitly deal with Hegel, as an attempt to do justice to Heidegger's thought with respect to being is beyond the scope of this paper.

## ON HEGEL'S CONCEPT OF BEING

Regardless, Hegel's new concept of being, the concept of the concept, is history. And this is the essence of time. But what is the concept of history? It is neither just one event after another, 'free contingent happening', the empirical fact of change or substantial development, nor the externalization of a self, the kenosis of subjectivity in space and time; rather it is the becoming of being. For the history of the concept of being is the unity, the *Einheit*, of its being and its negation, itself and its other, nothing.[8] And the historical concept of being—itself a *contradictio in adjecto*—the goal of the phenomenology of absolute spirit's absolute knowledge, is the history of the absolute idea, of the becoming of spirit.

Time as historical then, is the truth of the *Phenomenology*—for here the unfolding of the concept of being is a reciprocally necessary movement, the progressive development of absolute spirit. And truth means: conceptual truth, the unity of the philosophical system of science, of the whole of life, of self and other, substance and subject. Indeed, the truth of the concept is double, free from one-sidedness, *Einseitigkeit*. And the Gestalt of the concept therefore, cannot be posited as predication or subsumption, but as *Aufhebung*, the supersession that both preserves and destroys contradiction, the going-under that is a going-over, *Untergang* that is an *Übergang*, a decline that is far more transition. Hegel thus insists that like *aufgeben*, *aufheben* is ambiguous 'to give, like to supersede, two-meanings: a) to give *up*—to view it as lost, destroyed; b) [to *give*]—but even therewith *simultaneously*, to make it into a problem, whose content is not destroy; but which is saved and whose distortion is a difficulty to be solved' (W XI 574).[9] If the truth of the concept is essentially ambiguous, it is because supersession has two-meanings simultaneously—not simply one, nor the other, nor their combination, but both.[10]

The time of the concept then, is 'at the same time;' the Gestalt of *Aufhebung* shows itself to be that of the *zugleich*. In this way, Hegel thinks the temporality of truth—not simply as finite or infinite, true or false, but both simultaneously.

---

8. As Hegel writes in the *Logic*: '*Pure being* and *pure nothing* is therefore the same. What the truth is, is neither being nor nothing, but that being—does not go-over—but has gone-over into nothing, and nothing into being. But the truth is equally not their undifferentiatedness, but that they are *not the same*, that they are *absolutely different*, and equally unseparated and inseparable and that *each immediately vanishes in its opposite*. Their truth is therefore, this *movement* of the immediate vanishing of the one in the other: *becoming*, a movement in which both are differentiated, but through a difference which has equally immediately resolved itself' (SL 82-83/ GW XXI 72); translation modified. For a discussion of the relation between being, nothing and becoming, see for example, Michael Inwood, *A Hegel Dictionary*, London, Blackwell, 1992, p. 44ff.

9. 'Aufgeben, wie Aufheben, doppelsinnig: a) Aufgeben—es als verloren, vernichtet betrachten; b) [Aufgeben]—eben damit aber zugleich es zum Problem machen, dessen Gehalt nicht vernichtet ist, sondern der gerettet und dessen Verkümmerung, Schwierigkeit zu lösen ist', W XI Aphorism 52, p. 574, emphasis and translation AH; cf. SL 116/GW XXI 104.

10. But that which drives the science of phenomenology by refusing to disambiguate the ambiguity of its truth, by resisting any reduction of incompleteness to completeness, or two-sidedness to one-sidedness—this is what Hegel names 'the tremendous power of the negative'. Here the ambiguity (of opposition, *Streit, polemos*) is maintained, kept, preserved—for this is the magical-force, *Zauberkraft*, that returns spirit to being (PS ¶ 32).

And it is this time that allows truth to show itself as temporal, as progressive, self-unfolding; just as it is this time that lets the concept appear as sequential, now one-sided, then two-sided (PS ¶ 5).[11] The ambiguity that simultaneously maintains and destroys ambiguity—this is the temporal truth of the concept. And an ambiguity that was not simultaneous (and simultaneously both ambiguous and non-ambiguous), would be no ambiguity at all. But if ambiguity is the essence of conceptual truth, of that which shows itself in the form of simultaneous time; this time is that of the now: both meanings are now and always. Presence and infinity are the markers of the Hegelian concept—for they are the essential time of its ambiguity. And if the *Phenomenology*, is the science of the concept of being (ontology), it is just as much the science of the temporality of its ambiguity (chronology).

But the problem of the truth of the concept's ambiguity does not stop with onto-chronology; rather, as Hegel insists: '*truth is complete only in the unity of identity with difference*, and hence consists only in this unity' (SL 414/GW XI 30).[12] This however is not simply the abstract or non-conceptual unity of which Hegel accuses everyone, from Parmenides to Leibniz (God as the *monadas monadum*) and Fichte (A=A or I=I)—for it is not the 'original or immediate unity as such' in which, as the saying goes, 'all cows are black'; on the contrary, it is the 'unity of being and nothing', the 'unity of differentiatedness and non-differentiatedness' (PS ¶ 16; SL 74/GW XXI 63).[13] Here, 'all multiplicity is included in the unity' (W XX 243/LHP III 335). And difference is not simply destroyed in indistinguish-

---

11. Hegel uses a multiplicity of metaphors for two-sidedness—just one example: 'the Bacchanalian revel in which no member is not drunk' (PS ¶ 47). I have attempted to think this problem in my, 'The Bacchanalian revel: Hegel and deconstruction', *Man and World*, vol. 30, no. 2, 1997, pp. 217-26.

12. See also, SL 431-443/GW XI 50-64. Here, identity is essentially that which it is only as difference, just as difference is essentially identity. The predicative language therefore, that philosophy has taken up from Aristotle to Kant, is no longer appropriate for Hegel; rather, if philosophy is to direct itself towards science, we must now begin to think and speak according to speculative propositions. As Hegel insists: 'Formally, what has been said can be expressed thus: the general nature of the judgment or proposition, which involves the distinction of subject and predicate, is destroyed by the speculative proposition, and the proposition of identity which the former becomes contains the counter-thrust against that subject-predicate relationship.—This conflict between the general form of a proposition and the unity of the concept which destroys it is similar to the conflict that occurs in rhythm between meter and accent. Rhythm results from the floating center and the unification of the two. So, too, in the philosophical proposition the identification of subject and predicate is not meant to negate the difference between them, which the form of the proposition expresses; their unity, rather, is meant to emerge as a harmony. The form of the proposition is the appearance of the determinate sense, or the accent that distinguishes its fulfillment; but that the predicate expresses the substance, and that the subject itself falls into the universal, this is the *unity* in which the accent dies away' (PS ¶ 61). The beginning is the 'unity of being and nothing; or is non-being which is at the same time being, and being which is at the same time nothing' (SL 73/GW XXI 62).

13. See also LHP III 338/W XX 246. Heidegger's (somehow motivated) assessment is somewhat at odds with Hegel's: 'Even though Western philosophy up to Hegel has basically not gone beyond Parmenides' proposition: *to on to hen*, despite all the transformations, this does not signify a deficiency but a superiority and indicates that in spite of everything, it remains strong enough to preserve its original truth', Martin Heidegger, *Aristotle's Metaphysics Theta 1-3*, trans. W. Brogan and P. Warnek, Bloomington, Indiana, 1995, §3. See also, HPS 93-4/134 and BT, §82(b).

ability and undifferentiatedness, but *aufgehoben* (W XX 255/LHP III 348). The ambiguity of unity therefore shows itself as the 'process of its own becoming' the circular becoming of itself, *Werden seiner selbst*, in which the beginning is the end (PS ¶ 18). And as a unity, the new concept of being is temporally one, a unity or whole, *das Ganze*. As Hegel insists: 'The true is the whole'—for its essence, 'what it is in truth', consists in being its own becoming, *sich selbst Werden, zu sein* (PS ¶ 20 trans. modified). The temporal ambiguity of the concept receives a new determination: as the unity of being and becoming, it is now and then, present and absent, infinite and finite. Thus if the science of the *Phenomenology* is onto-chronology it is also the science of unity (henology); it is onto-heno-chronology.

But we cannot even stop there—for truth must be complete, *vollständig*. And the completion of truth is not a function of time; rather, the concept is one as completely ambiguous. Completeness or incompleteness are ways in which ambiguity shows itself to be one at any time whatsoever, the aspect or *eidos* of time.[14] In addition to its time, now or then, the concept's *Aufhebung* appears as essentially complete or incomplete.[15] In other words, ambiguity's simultaneity,

---

14. Clearly, the linguistic concept of aspect is insufficient for an account of Hegelian (or transcendental, phenomenological, metaphysical) aspect, or for thinking the way in which beings are and are unified at one and the same time, or anytime. But nor is aspect just that which the science of metaphysics has taken as that which shows itself as itself, nor as another, like some kind of perspective or view, symptom or indication, nor an appearance of an appearance, nor that which disappears by appearing, because it is too dimly seen, nor because it is too much or many, but because in showing itself, it shows that it cannot be shown. And nor could it be merely a function of language, reason or time. Rather aspect is implied by unity—and thus can a unified being show its aspect as left or right, up and down, present or absent, relative or absolute, concealed/revealed. But if something could be one or be itself or another at one and the same time, although not in the same way, it is because of aspect. Then the unity of being (or of a being) would have to be aspectually complete or incomplete so that it could show itself in any way whatsoever, could present this face or that, this perspective or that side, so that it could be before or after in this way or another, or even so that it could be something rather than nothing. For the linguistic concept of aspect see, for example, R. Binnick, *Time and the Verb*, Oxford, Oxford University, 1991, or B. Comrie, *Aspect*, Cambridge, Cambridge University, 1976.

15. Aristotle thinks aspect as complete or incomplete through the difference of *peras* and *telos*, limit and end, *kinēsis* and *energeia*, movement and actuality (an aspectual difference that Hegel rearticulates in terms of that which is in itself, *an sich*, for itself, *für sich*, or in and for itself, *an und für sich* (PS ¶ 21 and ¶ 25)—for the difference between actions cannot be taken into account merely through a difference in time. This becomes obvious when attempting to articulate the difference between actions done at the same time ('I ate' and 'I was eating'). But for Aristotle, this difference is one of metaphysical aspect (although the extent to which this difference can be maintained has yet to be established), and the proper place to investigate it is within the *Metaphysics*, the science of being *qua* being, *to on hē on*: 'Since of the actions which have a limit none is an end but all are relative to the end, e.g. the removing of fat, or fat-removal, and the bodily parts themselves when one is making them thin are in movement in this way (i.e. without being already that at which the movement aims), this is not an action or at least not a complete one (for it is not an end); but that movement in which the end is present is an action. E.g. at the same time we are seeing and have seen, are understanding and have understood, are thinking and have thought (while it is not true that at the same time we are learning and have learnt, or are being cured and have been cured). At the same time we are living well and have lived well, and are happy and have been happy. If not, the process would have had to cease, as the process of making think ceases: but, as things are, it does not cease; we are living and have lived. Of these processes, then, we must call the one set movements, and the other actualities. For every movement

must be supplemented in order to show itself as the present (or past or future) system of science. So too philosophy—actually or potentially, as well as always or sometimes—becomes knowing or not. As Hegel insists: the true system of science must understand the diversity of philosophical systems as 'the *progressive* unfolding of truth'—for the *fortschritende Entwicklung der Wahrheit* is the aspectual essence of the concept, aspectually actual as self-moving, being as becoming, complete *qua* incomplete; and its ambiguity exhibits progressive aspect (PS ¶ 2, emphasis added). So too, if absolute spirit appears as an ambiguous *phainomenon* (substance and subject, other-being and being-for-self, *das Andersein und Fürsichsein*); it is because this 'most sublime concept' remains completely incomplete, that is, aspectually complete as incomplete.[16] Thus just as unity is being's other; so too aspect shows itself (*phainesthai*) as the other of time. And if the *Phenomenology of Spirit* is onto-heno-chronology, it is always also the science of aspect (phenomenology); so onto-heno-chrono-phenomenology, or just phenomenology for short.

As a science then, phenomenology remains completely incomplete, finished as unfinished—and the *Phenomenology* is the attempt (essentially unfinished, that is, finished as unfinishable) to lead the individual to knowledge, 'to be able to lay aside the title *love of wisdom* and be *actual wisdom*' (PS ¶ 5, trans. modified; and PS ¶ 28). But as Hegel insists: this attempt is only a goal, *Ziel*; it is only proposed, *vorgesetzt*—for philosophy can only get closer, *näher*, to actual knowing insofar as its actuality consists in never being actualized, or in being actualized as unactualizable.[17] In this (perfectly Socratic) sense, the love of wisdom becomes actual wisdom, knowing that we do not know, not because we do not yet know, but because we cannot know. So too, if the task of raising consciousness through self-consciousness to the position of spirit, like the trajectory of each reader, is always only a task, an *Aufgabe*, it is because it is achieved as unachieved, outstanding as outstanding, complete as incompleteable.[18] It is no surprise then, that the *Phenomenology* ends in complete incompleteness, in the absolutely ambiguous concept, *der*

---

is incomplete—making thin, learning, walking, building; these are movements, and incomplete at that. For it is not true that at the same time a thing is walking and has walked, or is building and has built, or is coming to be and has come to be, or is being moved and has been moved, but what is being moved is different from what has been moved, and what is moving from what has moved. But it is the same thing that at the same time has seen and is seeing, or is thinking and has thought. The latter sort of process, then, I call an actuality, and the former a movement', *Metaphysics*, 1048b18-34, in *The Basic Works of Aristotle*, ed. and trans. W. D. Ross, New York, Random House, 1941, pp. 826-827 (henceforth *Meta*.).

16. As Hegel insists: 'everything turns on grasping and expressing the true, not only as substance, but equally as subject' (PS ¶ 17; see also ¶ 25).

17. Similarly, Hegel insists that 'spirit's insight into what knowing is', into the being of knowledge, is itself only a goal, *Ziel* (PS ¶ 29). As a goal however, a *Ziel*, the end of the *Phenomenology of Spirit* remains essentially uncertain—a goal is both that which is achieved, accomplished, completed, aimed at, a target, boundary, limit or horizon, as well as that which is not achieved, or completed, but left to be completed, hence incomplete. Appropriately, 'goal' means both the end and the beginning of a race. On the one hand, an achieved goal is no longer a goal; on the other hand, the goal is only achieved *qua* goal as unachieved—perhaps unachieveable.

18. On the structure of the task, see Walter Benjamin, 'The Task of the Translator', *Selected Writings*, M. Bullock and M. W. Jennings (eds.), vol. 1, Cambridge, Harvard University, 1996.

*absolute Begriff*, in the four-fold ambiguity of absolute spirit's absolute knowing.[19]

First the time of the absolute concept is that of the past, of recollection, remembering, *Erinnerung*, the memory of spirit's becoming, the self-mediating process that 'is there' as emptied out into time, and presents itself as a 'slow-moving succession of spirits, a gallery of images, each of which, endowed with all the riches of spirit, moves thus slowly just because the self has to penetrate and digest this entire wealth of its substance' (PS ¶ 808).[20] But as Hegel insists: recollection is essentially, inwardizing, *Er-Innerung*, preserving inside that which is lost outside, keeping that which cannot be kept, representing (that is, re-representing, even misrepresenting) past experience as present, present past. Conceptual preservation however, means: that which is preserved is both preserved and destroyed—for *aufbewahren* is as ambiguous as *aufgeben* and *aufheben*. And the goal, *das Ziel* (always just a goal), of the *Phenomenology*, absolute knowing, spirit's recollection of spirits, is only completed insofar as it knows it cannot be complete—the lost *qua* lost cannot be found. For this reason, preservation, *Aufbewahrung*, is on the one hand, historical becoming, contingency, forgetting, the past *qua* past, recollecting *what* is un-recollectable; on the other hand, it is science, ahistorical being, necessary, the past *qua* present, recollecting *that* it is un-recollectable—a recollection that is itself always recollectable, infinitely present. Thus the time of memory, its success and its failure, its success as failure and its failure as success, the ambiguity of the presence of the past, is the time of the *Phenomenology's* absolute concept.

But second, the time of this concept, the ambiguity of memory, of recollection and preservation—this has its other in the aspect of the absolute concept. As Hegel writes: spirit's 'fulfillment consists in perfectly knowing what *it is*'; its completion, *Vollendung*, lies in knowing its substance (PS ¶ 808). But this aspectual completion is itself ambiguous: spirit, on the one hand, knows that it knows itself; on the other hand, it knows that it does not and cannot know itself—an ignorance that it recollects and preserves as ignorance. The speed of its becoming (slow, draggy, sluggish, languid, *träge*), the way in which spirits follow one another in successive time, is just one indication of spirit's incomplete knowledge—for in motion, becoming, emptied out into time, it can never be completely present to knowing. So in the *Phenomenology*, history means that spirit appears with incomplete aspect—but science means that this incompleteness of appearing has

---

19. And this truth is, for Hegel, no longer expressed as subject and predicate, but in a speculative proposition, the absolutely mediated identity of its existence with its essence in which their difference is no longer one of form, but of content (PS ¶ 37, ¶ 61, ¶ 808).

20. Hegel writes: 'Time is the concept itself that *is there* and which presents itself to consciousness as empty intuition; therefore spirit necessarily appears in time, and it appears in time as long as it has not *grasped* its pure concept, that is, has not annulled time. It is the *outer*, intuited pure self which is *not grasped* by the self, the merely intuited concept; insofar as this latter grasps itself, it supersedes its time-form, conceptualizes this intuiting, and is a conceptualized and conceptualizing intuiting. Time therefore appears as the fate and necessity of spirit that is not yet complete within itself' (PS ¶ 801, trans. modified). Thus with respect to spirit: regarded as 'free existence appearing in the form of contingency', spirit is differentiated as history, the becoming in time of spirits; regarded as a conceptual organization, spirits belong to the science of appearing knowledge (PS ¶ 808).

complete aspect. And aspectual ambiguity therefore, the ambiguity of complete incompleteness, is the essence of conceptual history.

Third however, if the absolute concept can show itself temporally and aspectually, it is because it is a unity—not a simple, immediate, one-sided unity of substance or subject, thought and being, or thought and time, but the mediated unity of both, or what Hegel names 'the concept in its truth, namely, in unity with its externalization' (PS ¶ 795 and ¶ 803).[21] Indeed, at the end of the *Phenomenology*, absolute spirit completes itself with the unity of the absolute concept—but this is a unity that ambiguously preserves difference, as well as its difference from difference. Hegel insists: 'In this knowing then, spirit has concluded the movement of its shapes insofar as it is imprisoned with the insurmounted difference of consciousness' (PS ¶ 805, trans. modified). The concept's identity is locked together with difference; unity is burdened with its negation, disunity, and with the historical movement of its own moments. And for this reason, the history of the concept is the unity of historical and scientific knowing—not one, nor the other, nor some third, but the two together, *beide zusammen*, the unifying relationship of both in which neither is alone, that in which subject and substance are one insofar as their difference is preserved (PS ¶ 808). Thus conceptual unity is essentially ambiguous: on the one hand, unitary unity, non-differentiated; on the other hand, differentiated, non-unitary unity.

The time and aspect and unity then, of the absolute concept—but this means, fourth: 'the concept has become the element of existence', the truth of being (PS ¶ 798). So the concept of being as existence, *Dasein*, is both the beginning and the end of the *Phenomenology*. But this also means that the existence of the concept is ambiguous: on the one hand, being means presencing, being-there, being-present, in time, with incomplete aspect, as disunified; on the other hand, it means conceptualizing, being there and here, present and absent, in and out of time, with completely incomplete aspect, as a unity. In this way, 'to be' means 'to conceptualize', *aufheben*. And if asked 'What is?' and 'What is being?', Hegel would respond: the concept is, and the concept of the concept is being. So too with beings—for a being is, is that which it is, and how it is, in relation to its concept; just as being is in relation to its concept. Being then, is both the destruction and preservation of beings. And 'to be' means 'to be ambiguous'; being is ambiguating—or more precisely, ambiguity is Hegel's new concept of being.

## TIME IS THE ESSENCE OF BEING: HEIDEGGER'S HEGEL

For Heidegger however, the thought of being as ambiguity does not dispute, but far more confirms the thesis that, for Hegel, being is the essence of time. And this means that, as '*an appearance* of being', time disappears on the royal road

---

21. As Hegel writes: here, the concept's 'negative attitude to objectivity is just as much positive' (PS ¶ 801). For Heidegger, Hegel is here universalizing Kant's psychologistic-subjectivistic principle of the understanding (HPS 83/118).

to the conceptual history of absolute spirit (HPS 145/209).[22] If Hegel's concept of history then, remains dependent upon what Heidegger calls the common or *vulgäre* understanding of time, it does not supersede but merely repeats the fundamental presuppositions of the Western metaphysical tradition. As Heidegger insists: Hegelian time is not simply the other of space, the number of motion, *arithmos kinēseōs*, with respect to before and after;[23] nor is it some kind of abstract form or empty vessel in which events occur; nor the transcendental schema of the pure concepts of understanding, the representation, *Vorstellung*, which 'mediates the subsumption of the appearances under the category'[24]—rather as the determinate negation, supersession, *Aufhebung* of both, it is coming into being and passing out of being, becoming, transition. As Hegel writes in the *Encyclopedia*: time 'is being, that which *is not* insofar as it *is*, and *is* insofar as it *is not*'; time is the becoming of being. Thus time appears as 'intuited becoming', *angeschaute Werden*, an abstract succession of nows, a movement in which every now is in relation to no-longer-now or not-yet-now.[25] But primarily oriented on the now, only the present is; the past and future, before and after, are not—although as negations, they are posited as essential: 'the being of time is the now', and the being of the now is 'the abstraction of consuming' (BT 431).

In *Being and Time* therefore, Heidegger suggests an interpretation of spirit's progress not as *Aufhebung*, but as *Überwindung*, surmounting, overcoming, conquering, vanquishing (BT 434). For Hegel writes: 'World-history in general is therefore the interpretation of spirit in time, just as the idea interprets itself in nature as space' (Hegel in BT 434, trans modified).[26] The world-history of the 'Lectures on the Philosophy of World-History' however, *Weltgeschichte*, is precisely *not* the conceptual history, *begriffne Geschichte*, of the *Phenomenology of Spirit*. Still Heidegger insists: Hegel's radical formulation of the 'vulgar experience and interpretation of time' (BT 431) is necessary for the *Phenomenology* so that spirit can empty itself out, so that it can self-externalize itself as concrete. The finitude of time, the negation

---

22. Heidegger's interest in the concept of being in Hegel seems in contrast to Nietzsche's: 'We Germans are Hegelians even if there never had been any Hegel, insofar as we (in contrast to all Latins) instinctively attribute a deeper sense and richer value to becoming, to development, than to what "is"—we hardly believe in the justification of the concept "being,"' *The Gay Science*, trans. W. Kaufmann, New York, Random House, 1974, §357; trans. modified.

23. Aristotle, *Physics*, 219b1-2; see BT, §82(a).

24. Immanuel Kant, *Critique of Pure Reason*, trans. N. K. Smith, New York, St. Martin's, 1929, A139/B178. But as Kant warns: 'This schematism of our understanding, in its application to appearances and their mere form, is an art concealed [*eine verborgene Kunst*] in the depths of the human soul, whose real modes of activity nature is hardly likely ever to allow us to discover, and to have open to our gaze', A141/B181. As Augustine writes: 'time is nothing more than distention' of the mind, *Confessions*, trans. J. K. Ryan, Garden City, Doubleday, 1960, Book XI, ch. 26, p. 298.

25. See GW XX § 258-9. For Heidegger, this concept of time is the condition of the possibility of the punctuality of the point, of the being of the point in space (BT § 82(a)). For Catherine Malabou's argument for a 'plasticity of the Hegelian concept of time', that is, for the 'existence of several times', *plusieurs temps*, in the *Phenomenology*, a 'pluralité qui excède la seule distinction entre une temporalité vulgaire et une temporalité originaire', see *L'avenir de Hegel*, Paris, Vrin, 1996, p. 253.

26. See G. W. F. Hegel, *Vorlesungen über die Philosophie der Weltgeschichte I, Die Vernunft in der Geschichte*, Johannes Hoffmeister and Georg Lasson (eds.), Hamburg, Felix Meiner, 1994, p. 154.

of the negation of spirit's in-finity, is the condition of the possibility of any substantial history or *Naturphilosophie* whatsoever—for 'history falls in time', *in die Zeit fällt* (BT 428, trans. modified).²⁷ Indeed, temporality is the power of the finite—but if it is also necessary for spirit, then 'the power of time', is just as much the power of the infinite (GW XX §258n; BT 435). Thus history falls into time so that Hegel can think—as Heidegger notes—the concretion of spirit.

Heidegger then, has two basic questions for Hegel with respect to the connection between spirit and time—and this is no simple denial, refusal or rejection of the unity of subject and substance, nor of the ambiguity of being, but far more an attempt to make these questions questionable. First, what is the origin, the *Ursprung*, of this concept of leveled-down time? And second, is it possible to think the essential constitution of spirit in some way other than '*as* the negating of the negation' (BT 435)?

With respect to the origin of spirit's fall into time, Heidegger quotes Hegel: 'time appears as the very fate and necessity of spirit when it is not in itself complete' (PS ¶ 801; BT 435).²⁸ Indeed, Hegel thinks *that, daß, quid facti*, spirit shows itself in time; but not how, *wie, quid juris*, it does so, with what right the *Phenomenology* asserts that incompleteness necessarily implies the fall. So Heidegger does not dispute that history falls into time, but rather asks: What is the origin of this fate? And for Heidegger, Hegel's thought of the essence of spirit, that it must fall into time in order to become that which it is, in order to preserve its completely incomplete ambiguity, does not answer the question of its origin; but rather far more poses it more profoundly. Hegel therefore fails to raise the question of the origin of falling, of original fallenness, if he cannot think how spirit must be concretized as originally temporal, how the being of history is necessarily constituted by original temporality—for being is not the essence of time; time is the essence of being, and the temporality of time is the origin of the vulgar time into which spirit reveals itself as fallen (and temporality too is that which first makes the existence of us as Dasein, as factially thrown, as fallen, first possible—for the origin of our way of being, existence, is the temporality of time as well).

The essential constitution of spirit therefore can and must be thought in another way, not as the negation of the negation, but as that which first makes negation possible, namely, the 'original *temporalizing* of temporality' (BT 436, trans. modified). Here Heidegger is attempting to think against Hegel's metaphysical fidelity to Spinoza's *omnis determinatio est negatio*, to think the time of that which is determined by negation, as well as the being of determination and negation themselves.²⁹ In other words, if determination needs time, happens in time, has a

---

27. Hegel, *Vorlesungen über die Philosophie der Weltgeschichte I*, p. 153.

28. Unfortunately Stambaugh's translation is here confused and the footnote numbering should be 40, not 38.

29. In fact, F. W. J. Schelling suggests another kind of determination that is not negation: 'with respect to this sort of determination, the saying *determinatio est negatio* does not in any way apply, since this is itself one with the position and concept of essence, thus actually the essence in which essence is', *Über das Wesen der menschlichen Freiheit*, Stuttgart, Reclam, 1964, p. 101; translation AH. For Hegel's discussion of negation in Spinoza, see for example, SL 113/GW XXI 107.

history, then the temporality of time must be presupposed as the essence of being. And negation occurs in time, the temporality of time—for not only *is* it, present or absent, always or not, but that which is negated, even the negation of the negation, and that means that they are temporal as well. Hegel then thinks time as that into which spirit empties itself, but for Heidegger, time is not something into which spirit can be emptied; it is the necessary fate of beings (and spirit is, as well) insofar as they are—for time gives being their way of being, as the temporality of time temporalizes factical existence, now and then, authentically or not, as contingent or necessary or conceptual history. But not just time—aspect as well—for that which lets spirit exist historically remains unthought; the continuous aspect or enduring presence of being, the perdurance or *Austrag* of the concept, its sustained completeness or incompleteness, now and then, sometimes or always—all this remains in the background.[30] And not only time and aspect, but unity too—for the question of being's (spirit's) fate is simultaneously (time) 'the question about beings as such and as a whole' (ID 54). So not merely time and aspect and unity, but being as well—for Hegel thinks spirit as being emptied out into time, as subject and substance, comprehending and conceptualizing its history—but thereby he does not think the being of this being *qua* being. In fact, in thinking being (not as a genus or generality, nor as mere form of human cognition) as spirit, indeterminate immediacy, absolute idea or absolute thinking, 'imperishable *life, self-knowing truth*' (SL 824/GW XII 284), all truth, in thinking the truth of being as essence, and the truth of essence as concept, even in the new concept of being, the concept of the concept, idea of the idea, history—in all this, the question of the being of beings remains far more unquestioned.

This unquestioning and unquestionability of being however, is neither simply a failure of Hegel's, nor of the *Phenomenology* or some other text; it is 'the still unthought unity of the essential nature of metaphysics' (ID 55). And the essence of this unthinking (that Heidegger also calls the forgetting, *Vergessenheit*, of the question of being) is maintained by the 'onto-theological essential-constitution of metaphysics' (ID 56, trans. modified).[31] If Hegel then, belongs to the history of

---

30. Martin Heidegger, *Identity and Difference*, trans. J. Stambaugh, Chicago, University of Chicago, 2002, p. 46 (henceforth ID). And not only being (not just being as another, but being itself, being *qua* being), but the difference between being and beings, and this difference *qua* difference. For if this difference is thought as another, as abstract or absolute, as diversity or multiplicity, as merely qualitative or quantitative, essential or conceptual—if it is interpreted in any of these ways, then *Differenz* as such has been overlooked.

31. See also, for example, BT 2. Werner Marx follows Heidegger in seeing Hegel's metaphysics as part of the tradition of 'Logos philosophy', that is, the thinking that begins with Parmenides identification of thinking and being, and culminates in a 'specifically modern version, authoritatively defined by Kant', the identity of subjectivity and objectivity accessible by spirit through the *noesis* of *nous*—for absolute spirit is nothing more than a modern avatar of Aristotle's divine 'thought thinking thought'. Thus for Marx, insofar as the *Phenomenology* remains rooted in metaphysics, it is onto-theology: 'This power of *nous* and the Logos culminated, for the Greeks, in a philosophy which was understood as "ontology," as a search for the ultimate categorial determinations of the existent, and likewise for those of the highest existent, *theos*, insofar as ontology was always at the same time theology', *Hegel's Phenomenology of Spirit*, trans. P. Heath, Chicago, University of Chicago, 1975, p. xxii.

metaphysics, it is no surprise that he thinks theologically: 'and God has the absolutely undisputed right that the beginning be made with him'—for the beginning of the system of science lies with absolute spirit or God understood as the being of beings, the all-highest truth and absolute ground (ID 53-4; SL 78/GW XXI 68).[32] Nor is it a surprise that the *Phenomenology* begins with ontology, being in general, *das Sein überhaupt*, the indeterminate or simple immediacy, *einfache Unmittelbarkeit*, pure being as the essence of sense-certainty—for here all science says: that it is, *es ist*; 'and its truth contains only the being of the thing' (PS ¶¶ 91, 97, 99, trans. modified).[33] But the onto-theology of metaphysics not only reduces the question of being to an answer (being is the ground of beings), it reduces the multiplicity of answers (ground understood as *hen, logos, idea, hupokeimenon*, substance, subject) to the one God, spirit as the *prōtē archē, ultima ratio, causa sui*—and it leaves unthought therefore, the possibility of thinking the meaning of being, in itself as well as in relation to and difference from beings.[34]

In response then, to the history of Western thought that stretches from the Greeks to Hegel, Heidegger seeks the ground of the onto-theological constitution of metaphysics—and he finds it in the concept of ground, that is, being *qua* ground. As the grounding of the ground, being means letting-laying-out, allowing that which is to arrive and lie before us, *Vorliegenlassen*. To ground means to be that which lets beings be there, present, come to the fore; grounding means letting them come over and show themselves, disclose themselves (as one—and thereby as they are or are not), 'come *forth from* concealment into unconcealment' (PM 333),[35] *alētheia*—not just once, now or then, but always or sometimes (time),

---

32. Hegel is however, critical of Parmenides' onto-theology: 'the said reality in all realities, the *being* in all *determinate being*, which is supposed to express the concept of God, is nothing else than abstract being, which is the same as nothing' (SL 113/GW XXI 107). On the absolute ground, see SL 67/GW XXI 55.

33. As Heidegger notes however: 'it still remains unthought by what unity ontologic and theologic belong together' (ID 60). In other words, the henology of onto-henology has yet to be thought. See also, Heidegger, 'Hegel and the Greeks', *Pathmarks*, William McNeill (ed.), Cambridge, Cambridge University, 1998, p. 328 (henceforth PM). As Hyppolite writes: 'in the *Phenomenology* we have seen the immediate being of the beginning of the book present itself as a *thing*, as *force*, as *life*, and finally as *spirit*', Hyppolite, *Genesis and Structure of Hegel's Phenomenology of Spirit*, p. 580. For Alexandre Kojève, Hegel's *Phenomenology of Spirit* is primarily 'phenomenological anthropology': 'Man is what he is only to the extent that he becomes what he is; his true *Being (Sein)* is *Becoming (Werden), Time, History*; and he *becomes*, he *is* History only in and by *Action* that negates the given [being], the Action of Fighting and of Work', *Introduction to the Reading of Hegel*, trans. J. H. Nichols, Jr., Ithaca, Cornell University, 1969, p. 38. This view seems to be shared by Quentin Lauer: 'It should be obvious from even the very cursory account which we have been able to give of Hegel's system that his philosophy, no matter what its ramifications, is essentially a philosophy of man throughout', *Hegel's Idea of Philosophy*, New York, Fordham University, 1983, p. 15.

34. As Heidegger insists however: 'remaining-unthought constitutes the essence of metaphysics', 'Hegel's Concept of Experience', *Off the Beaten Track*, trans. J. Young and K. Haynes, Cambridge, Cambridge University, 2002, p. 133. For Hegel's discussion of Plato's onto-theology, see for example, LHP II 60/W IXX 83.

35. The origin of the enigma of *alētheia* however, as Heidegger reminds us, lies not with philosophy, but with poetry: 'The oldest evidence of *alētheiē* and *alēthēs*, unconcealment and unconcealed, we find in Homer, and specifically in connection with verbs of saying' (PM 334). Or again: '*alētheia* comes

and repeatedly, continuously (aspect)—for the ground allows beings to remain beings, clears a place for them to endure, maintains an opening for them to stay that which they are throughout change and becoming. And to ground means to let beings be one, as they are in themselves and with others—for grounding is the event of gathering, being the unity (widest and highest, absolute transcendence, *das transcendens schlechthin*) of that which unifies by letting the identity and difference of being and beings be (ID 68-69).[36] Thus if to be, for metaphysics, means to ground and if being is a ground, it is because being means grounding, unifying temporally and aspectually.[37]

## HEGEL AND THE GREEKS

Have we then, come to an understanding of the meaning of the new concept of being? Of being as concept? Or of being as ground? To the meaning of being itself? Is this being *qua* being? Not at all. But as Heidegger argues: 'the new concept of being is the old and ancient concept in its most extreme and total completion', its *äußersten und ganzen Vollendung*. Hegel however, conducts this crucial step: he unfolds, *entfaltet*, the old concept of being, the one as old as Western philosophy in its two main stages (Parmenides/Heraclitus, Plato/Aristotle)—for the fundamental motifs of phenomenology are predetermined, *vorbestimmt*, by the ancient point of departure. The *Phenomenology* then, is 'the last stage in the possible justification' of phenomenology (HPS 141/204-5).

In order to understand the new, we must first return to the old. Heidegger

---

before the history of philosophy' (PM 335). For Werner Marx, Hegel and Heidegger are most at odds with respect to truth: 'The "truth" to which the introductory and preparatory science of phenomenology leads, in the final shape of absolute knowledge, consists in the dialectically assembled system of thought-determinations. This totally manifest truth is the last and most extreme expression of the principle of total lucidity inherent in *logos* and *nous*. Heidegger views the nature of truth as a process in which "hiddenness"—lethe—so passes, within a realm of clearing—aletheia—into "disclosure," as to permeate the latter further in various ways'. Thus, 'if what is shown to knowledge or conceiving is merely a side of Being permeated by hiddenness, or actually "withdrawing" itself from truth proper, we then have a thought running radically counter to the possibility that the self-conceiving concept, the self evolving toward true knowledge, should be able to rediscover itself in the complete movement of thought-determinations, *qua* systematic truth', *Hegel's Phenomenology of Spirit*, p. 107.

36. Heidegger later notes: 'of course not transcendens—despite every metaphysical resonance—scholastic and greek-platonic koinon, rather transcendence as the ecstatic-temporal [*Zeitlichkeit*] temporality [*Temporalität*]; but "horizon"! Being has "thought beyond" ["*überdacht*"] beings. However, transcendence from the truth of being: the event [*das Ereignis*]' (BT 38).

37. As Heidegger writes: 'nothing in this realm lets itself be proved, but something pointed out' (ID 22, trans. modified). In the *Contributions to Philosophy*, Heidegger calls this a 'further-hinting of a hint', *Weiterwinken eines Winkes*—as such, and recognizing that 'the time of "systems" is past', it is neither purposeful nor calculative, neither individual nor communal; rather, is a 'thinking saying of philosophy that would be attempted in an other beginning. This does not describe or explain, does not proclaim or teach. This does not stand over against what is said, but is it itself as the essential-presencing of beyng. This saying gathers beyng's unto a first sounding of its essence, and it itself sounds only out of this essence', trans. P. Emad and K. Maly, Bloomington, Indiana University, 1999, p. 4, trans. modified. An investigation into 'the other beginning' of the *Contributions* is, within the context of this article, not possible.

therefore recalls Hegel's interpretation of the four basic words of Greek philosophy: Parmenides' *hen*, Heraclitus' *logos*, Plato's *idea*, Aristotle's *energeia* (PM 328). For these words 'speak the language of the guiding word, "being," *einai* (*eon*, *ousia*)'—and they do so within the horizon of being as immediate indeterminacy, that which is, the objectivity of objects, abstracted from its relation to the subject. In other words, being is the truth of beings, things; and thoughts must accord with being in order to be true.

For Parmenides then, being is one, the universal—and insofar as being and thinking are the same, the thought of the universal is one with that which is. Here the 'energetic, impetuous soul' strives to grasp and express being. But Hegel insists: this is not the indeterminate infinity, Anaximander's *apeiron*; it is being as the absolutely determined and delimited, *absolut Begrenzende*. And this is the beginning of idealism, the opposite of materialism—for being is not a being, not to be identified with a sensuous thing, but a concept (however indeterminate). Thus being means being one; and being is one insofar as everything is one, *hen panta*, and nothing is not; so to be is to be one; beings and being are one, and one with thought (LHP I 250-3/W XVIII 286-9; PM 329).

But for Heraclitus, being and non-being are the same. So the truth is: nothing and being gathered together through change, *Veränderung*, *Bewegung*—or more precisely, becoming, *Werden*, the unity of opposites insofar as everything is in flux, *panta rhei*. Becoming's gathering of being and nothing is Heraclitus' *logos*—not merely an account of gathering, but the gathering itself (however abstract) into a unity. So in becoming, being and nothing are one—for becoming is the unity of both, that is, the being of being and becoming; it is the 'unity of opposite determinations', that relation or connection, *Verhältnis*, which allows them to be that which they are. As Hegel writes: 'change is unity, relation of both to one, *one* being, this and the other' (W XVIII 327, trans. AH). In this sense, being means becoming, changing, moving, flowing; to be is to become; beings are insofar as they become, change from being to non-being and vice versa, from one to the other—for as the other of the other, *das Andere des Anderen*, each is also the other of itself, and its being consists in being this other, *its* other; becoming means being other.

The essence of becoming however, for Heraclitus, is time—for time is the 'first sensible essence' of being, and the true essence, *wahre Wesen*, of being. As Hegel insists: insofar as becoming shows itself in being and beings, it takes the form of time, *die Form der Zeit*. Indeed time is pure becoming, the essential unity of being and nothing. But this means that 'in time there is no past and future, but only the now'. So to be (or not to be) in time is to be temporal; the unity of being empties itself out into the form of time—for as the essence of becoming, time is the fate and necessity, *Schicksal* and *Notwendigkeit*, *heimarmenē*, of being (LHP I 293/W XVIII 337).

But however much Parmenides thinks being and unity, however much Heraclitus thinks being and unity and time, for Hegel, they do so within the context of a philosophy of nature—the activity of thought, of the subject, consciousness, self-consciousness, spirit, remains passive, content to read the truth of *phusis* like a book. Reason is not free to think, discover, but far more shackled to the world of things. And this means 'the object is for me something essentially free, and I am for myself devoid of subjectivity', *subjektivitätslos* (LHP I 297/W XVIII 342).

With Plato however, a decisive step is taken: being and unity and time (and unified beings in time) are no longer simply functions of nature; they are ideas, principles of reality. The essence of things then shows itself in consciousness, not because it belongs to consciousness, not as simply subjective, but as determinate for nature. Being and unity and time are no longer merely sensible, material, empirical, contingent; they are the supersensible and infinite reality of things, the intellectual or necessary ideas in which reality and thought are conceptualized scientifically 'in *one* unity' (LHP II 1/W IXX 11; PM 330). Nevertheless, the ideas are neither in some kind of transcendent other world, nor just imaginary; they are the ideas of things, the ideal universal look or *eidos* of real unified beings in time (that show themselves to us and that we come to know, so that being and thought are the same). As Hegel writes: the ideas are real; 'they are, and they are alone, being'—for although being and beings exist, the truth of the later are determined by the ideas (LHP II, p. 31; W 19, p. 41; trans. modified).[38] Thus for Hegel, Plato's thought is the dialectical supersession, the *Aufhebung*, of Parmenides and Heraclitus: being, as the becoming of the universal and particular, is the ideal truth of beings insofar as they change, move, become concretely that which they are. So being is an idea, to be is to be ideal, and unified beings are translations of ideal forms in time—for the idea of the unity of being and beings, like the unifying relation of opposites, is the truth of both.

The negation of the sensuous however, by the ideas, means that for Hegel, Plato cannot think the reality of the real, the truth of concrete beings *qua* concrete: being is an idea—but only an idea—and the reality of things is relative, only true in relation to the ideas. And it is not until Aristotle's *Metaphysics*, that being becomes actualized, finds its realization in itself as end, the *telos* of *entelecheia* that is the *logos*. Here being shows itself in beings, not merely as potential, *dynamis*, but as actual, *energeia*; not just in the capacity for self-determination, but in the concrete self-realization of the idea. The idea is actualized however, only insofar as it is the cause of being and unity, beings and unities. But cause must be understood here not simply as *causa*—for although *aitia* means that for the sake of which something is or is done, the reasons or grounds or ends; its primary sense is that of a charge, *crimen*, accusation, guilt, fault, or that which is responsible, so responsibility. And metaphysics is here knowledge of the *aitia* of the whole of being, the totality of beings, that which is universally responsible for the universe—but the *aitia* must be *prōta*; the charges must be firsts, origins. So for first philosophy, *prōtē philosophia*, responsibility means: being first, an origin, the origin of that which is, the origin of being. And being means being charged with being responsible,

---

38. As Hegel later writes: 'it is rather the ideal that is the most real, and it was Plato who perceived that it was the only real, for he characterized the universal or thought as the true, in opposition to what is sensuous' (LHP II 50/W IXX 63).

being implicated in a crime, or by an event, something made or done, *poiein* or *prattein* (PM 330-1; LHP II 149/W IXX 134).

If there is then, a science of being *qua* being, of that which is, insofar as it is; it must seek that which is responsible for being, for it being that which it is, and which is implicated in beings. But what is responsible for being? As Aristotle insists: it cannot simply be the substrate, ground-work, *hupokeimenon*—but if being is spoken in many ways, they all point to *ousia*, substance, as primary essence and cause.[39] In this way, *ousia* is the 'what', *ti*, of a being, that which something is *propter se*, in-itself, *kath' hauto*—not accidentally, but necessarily, actually—and this is expressed by its formula, *logos*, that is, its definition, *horismos*, that which makes it a unified being, this and not that, particular and concrete. And *ousia* is responsible for being, charged with being implicated in beings, for actualizing their potential, for being the final cause of being's becoming that which it essentially is. In this way, the *aitia* are not simply *ideas*, but the real causes of reality, the origins of beings. Thus for Aristotle, being is responsible for beings, for realizing their essence, and as such it takes responsibility for itself.

So being means *ousia*—for 'the question which was raised of old and is raised now and always, and is always the subject of doubt, viz. what being is, is just the question, what is substance?' (*Meta.* 1028b2-4) And what about *ousia*? For it *is* as well. So the discussion of *ousia* means that metaphysics must return to the question of the meaning of being, *ti to on*. And here Aristotle gives us a clue—for he insists: 'being and unity are the same and of one nature insofar as they are implied in one another as origin and cause' (*Meta.* 1003b22-4, trans. mod.).

Indeed, on the one hand, everything that holds for being holds for unity: the theory of one is that of the other; the investigation of being, of being *qua* being, is just as much the investigation of unity, of unity *qua* unity; the aporia of one is that of the other. And if being is said in many ways, likewise for unity, *pollachōs legetai*. As Aristotle writes:

> for 'one man' and 'man' are the same thing, and so are 'existent man' and 'man' and the doubling of the words in 'one man and one *existent* man' does not express anything different (it is clear that the two things are not separated [*ou chōrizetai*] either in coming to be or in ceasing to be); and similarly '*one* existent man' adds nothing to 'existent man', so that it is obvious that the addition in these cases means the same thing, and unity is nothing apart from being; and if, further, the substance of each thing is one in no merely accidental way, and similarly is from its very nature something that *is*:—all this being so, there must be exactly as many species of being as of unity (*Meta.* 1003b26-34).

---

39. *Meta.*, 1004b9, 1028a15. In fact, for Aristotle, there are four original *aitia*, four charges, a fourfold responsibility at the origin: substance, *ousia*, the *logos*, that through which it is that which it is; the matter and substratum, *hulē* and *hupokeimenon*; the origin or beginning of movement, *hē archē tēs kinēseōs*, that good for the sake of which something is, the end of generation and movement, *telos*. These four are responsible for nature, for physical beings, *Phys.* 194b16. But here they are charged with being responsible for the universe, the whole; and they are implicated in everything mortal and immortal, in being and becoming, that which is, was and will be, everywhere and in everyway, as well as in our scientific investigation of beings, *episkepsin tōn ontōn*, *Meta.* 983b2.

The science of the *Metaphysics* then, is neither simply ontology nor henology—for first philosophy is onto-henology; and if the question of the meaning of being has been forgotten, then so too has the question of the meaning of unity (*Meta.* 1004a22).[40]

On the other hand, they have different *logoi*: the meaning of being is *ousia*; the meaning of unity is *horismos*. Indeed beings are insofar as they have the character of apartness, separability, determinability, limitability, boundary, finitude, *chōriston*, thisness, wholeness, particularity, indivisibility, individuality, *tode ti*.[41] A being's essence is *propter se*, in-itself, *kath' hauto*—necessarily, not accidentally—so that 'whatness' is expressed in its formula or definition, *logos* (for example, the human as *zoōn logon echon*, rational animal); but a horizon then separates, *chōrizō*, one being from another, gives each being a place to be, *chōra*, that which it is, and allows for transition, translation, change, movement, becoming. And not only does a being have its horizon, but its horizon too, insofar as it is, has its horizon, the horizon of the horizon. And so too with the horizon of *ousia*. Thus *ousia* can be the meaning of being, that which *to on* is *kath' hauto*, because unity means horizon.

But what then is the relation of being and unity? As Aristotle insists: they imply one another—for being follows from unity, and unity from being, just as essence and horizon are bed-fellows that walk the same path. And as co-implicated origins and causes, being and unity are responsible for the being and unity of beings and unities. Then charged with this responsibility, the most responsible of all responsibilities, there is no presumption of innocence; rather their responsibility is prior to all innocence, to any admission of innocence or guilt; they are most guilty of all (or most innocent), guilty prior. to any guilt, and the charge is undeniable—for at the moment it is made, they have already confessed; and before anything is implied, they have already implicated each other.

## THE IMPLICATION OF BEING

Implication then, from the Greeks to Hegel, is the new old metaphysical concept of being, and of unity. And not just—for time is the unity, that is, the horizon of being; and aspect is the being, that is, essence of unity. To be means to be one because being implies unity; but being is that which it is, namely being, only because unity implies it. And so aspect (complete or incomplete, incompletely complete or completely incomplete) is the horizon of unity; just as time is the essence of being. In this way, the science of metaphysics shows itself as the science of implication, *akolouthology*; it is the investigation of following, attending, not leading, of determining that and how to follow, and not; as well as the study of how implications cannot be followed, if they are to imply, how an essential am-

---

40. See also: 998b20ff, 1001a5-6, 1030b10-11. For the forgetting of being, see BT xixff.

41. *Meta.* 1052b16ff. And even the divine, the prime mover, unmovable and non-sensible substance, thought thinking thought, is only insofar as it is a unity—for its infinity is that finitude or horizon which separates it from mortals. See *Meta.*, Bk. XII. Furthermore, if unity is the *metron* by which beingscan be quantitatively or qualitatively measured, it is because unity is essentially already horizon.

biguity characterizes implication itself.[42] So onto-heno-chrono-phenomenology attends to the implications of being and unity, time and aspect.

What then is this new old concept of being? It is implication. To be means to imply; for being is implicating; being is implication. And insofar as being and unity are the same thing and of one nature, unity too is implication; uniting is implicating, to unify is to imply. But so too with time and aspect—for being and unity are implied temporally and aspectually. And therefore beings can be united in time and with aspect.

But what is the meaning of implication? Perhaps an example will help: *ēthos anthrōpō daimōn*.[43] How can we translate Heraclitus? McKirahan writes: 'a person's character *is* his divinity'.[44] Kahn: 'Man's character *is* his fate'. Kirk, Raven and Schofield: 'Man's character *is* his daimon'.[45] Heidegger: 'the (familiar) abode *is* for man the open region for the presencing of god (the unfamiliar one)'.[46] All of these translations are clearly 'right', but none of them follows the Greek closely enough.[47]

More literally, the words say: 'character human's divine', or switching word order, 'human's character divine'. But what has happened to being here? For in this translation (or non-translation, mistranslation), in what appears as a grammatically erroneous chop-slop string of words, being seems to disappear. Has being then, in fact, disappeared? Must we think and speak and act without being? Is it absent or hiding? And is our task then to make it present or revealed? To allow it to show itself?

Let us rather take a clue from the philologists who remind us: being is im-

---

42. Elsewhere I have suggested that the essence of this ambiguity must be understood as 'uncertainty'; see *The Irony of Heidegger*, especially secs. 1.1, 1.2, 2.2, 2.5, 5.2, 6.2. For a modern scientific understanding of implication, see for example, P. Grice, *Studies in the Way of Words*, Cambridge, Harvard University, 1989. Here Grice is primarily concerned with how 'information' in conventional or non-conventional conversational 'implicatures' might be controlled (according to a kind of 'Cooperative Principle' indebted to Kantian categories) so that which is meant or suggested—in spite of all irony, metaphor, ambiguity—'must be capable of being worked out', p. 31.

43. Fr. 119, Stobaeus Anth. IV, 40, 23, in *The Presocratic Philosophers*, G. S. Kirk, J. E. Raven, M. Schofield (eds.), Cambridge, Cambridge University, 1957, p. 210.

44. Patricia Curd (ed.), *A Presocratics Reader*, trans. Richard D. McKirahan, Indianapolis, Hackett, 1996, p. 40; emphasis added.

45. *The Presocratic Philosophers*, p. 211; emphasis added.

46. Martin Heidegger, 'Letter on Humanism', *Basic Writings*, D. F. Krell (ed.), New York, Harper & Row, 1977, p. 234; emphasis added.

47. As Walter Benjamin insists: Heidegger's thought, in spite of 'all its philosophical packaging', is basically 'only a piece of good translating work', *The Correspondence of Walter Benjamin*, Chicago, University of Chicago, 1994, p. 168. Here however, perhaps what is needed is something more akin to the interlinear version of the holy text; or, as Benjamin writes, citing Pannwitz: 'Our translators, even the very best ones, proceed from a wrong premise. They want to turn Hindi, Greek, English into German instead of turning German into Hindi, Greek, English. Our translators have a far greater reverence for the usage of their own language than for the spirit of the foreign works... The basic error of the translator is that he preserves the state in which his own language happens to be instead of allowing his language to be powerfully affected by the foreign tongue', 'The Task of the Translator', pp. 261-2. Thanks to Helen Lambert for reminding me of this.

plied—it is not merely left out; it was never 'there' to begin with, although nor was it 'not there'. And this is not just negative, as if being is subtracted, erased, nor a negation of the negation that restores or supersedes, nor simply a privation. But nor is it a positing—for being as implication cannot appear or show itself as being, at least without becoming that which it is not.

So granted: our translation fails to do justice to the Greek, whether grammatically correct or incorrect. Phenomenology is akolouthology insofar as it embraces this failure, and attempting to bring it to light, fails to do so. If being is a concept, it is only an implied concept; if it is a ground, only an implied ground. For we are charged with being responsible for this failure, and implicated in the crimes of metaphysics.

The task remains: to think being as implication, as well as unity and time and aspect.

# II

# Kierkegaard's Ethical Stage in Hegel's Logical Categories: Actual Possibility, Reality and Necessity

María J. Binetti

## I. INTRODUCTION

Søren Kierkegaard has interpreted singular existence through the scheme of a triadic dialectic, represented by the three stages of existence: aesthetical, ethical and religious. Each of these stages represents an ascent in subjective becoming verified by a growing differentiation and unification of the self with the world, with itself, and finally with God. Along this ascent, the preceding stage subsists in the following one through a sort of transfiguration or transubstantiation that transcends it without destroying it. More precisely, each of the stages manifests the truth contained *an-sich* in the preceding one around a circular return to the origin, where the point of departure presupposes the totality of development and the arrival point confirms what is eternally stated.

According to this interpretation, the ethical stage represents an intermediary between the aesthetic and the religious ones. This intermediate position has been defined in *Journals and Papers* as 'the dialectical' (Pap I A 239/JP2 1676)[1] between the quiet immediacy of the aesthetics and the reconciling unity of the religious stage. However, the limits and characteristics of this triadic schema may often seem ambiguous and even equivocal. As a matter of fact, Kierkegaard occasionally mentions four stages, and sometimes only two; at times, he opposes ethicalness to religiousness, and at other times he unifies them into a unique ethical-religious stage. According to this ambiguity, we should mention not just

---

1. Søren Kierkegaard, *Søren Kierkegaards Papirer*, P. A. Heiberg, V. Kuhr and E. Torsting (eds.), 2nd ed., 20 vols., København, Gyldendalske Boghandel Nordisk Forlag, 1909-1948 (henceforth Pap, superscript indicates the sub-volume). cf. also *Journals and Papers*, trans. Howard V. Hong and Edna H. Hong, 7 vols., Bloomington, Indiana University Press, 1967-78 (henceforth JP).

one but several meanings of ethics. We nevertheless believe that, if we maintain the triadic structure from which Kierkegaard has interpreted singular existence and we assume the mediating position of ethics, we will be able to reach the speculative core that defines that stage and places it within the schema as a properly dialectical instance of subjective becoming.

G.W.F. Hegel's philosophy also describes a spiritual ascent, dialectically deployed through differentiation and reunification of an absolute subject. As in Kierkegaard, Hegelian thought is founded on an actual inward deepening process, progressing through the reflection of the spirit and ending in self-affirmation, mediated by absolute otherness. In both cases, the self-consciousness must experience its own inner negation, the rending of its inwardness, in order to reach its essential identity.

The following paragraphs aim at showing some logical coincidences between Kierkegaard's existential thought and Hegel's speculative philosophy. In this case, they will circumscribe themselves to Kierkegaard's ethical stage, trying to detect in it the concepts shared with the systematic German philosopher. In this way, I intend to show how 'Hegel has represented one of Kierkegaard's most important sources of inspiration in the development of the stage theory'[2].

## II. ACTUAL IDEALITY AND POSSIBILITY: INTRINSIC BECOMING OF THE SELF

The second part of *Either/Or* is doubtless an exemplary text for the study of Kierkegaard's ethical stage. Ethical subjectivity is generally defined in it as the absolute affirmation of the self by itself through the action of its freedom. While the aesthete maintains his subjectivity in the abstraction of a formally ideal possibility, the ethicist states his possible idea as the effective actuality of a self, at the same time eternal and temporal, finite and infinite. He thus becomes a concrete subject, whose temporal course becomes history and whose factual externality becomes his own intimacy.

From a metaphysical point of view, the becoming of the merely formal or abstract idea into actual or effective ideality indicates an intensification or potentiation of the possible, through which the full actuality of the spirit becomes manifest. Ever since his dissertation, Kierkegaard believed that the idea is concrete in itself, then it is necessary for it to become constantly concrete and thus for him 'in the highest sense motion is the movement of the ideal' (Pap X$^3$ A 524/ JP2 1790). In opposition to the abstract being of immediacy and to the arbitrary becoming of the aesthete is true ideal becoming, through which the essential concretion of the self is revealed.

The intrinsic concretion of the idea constitutes its latent actuality, which necessarily becomes manifest in the finite and the temporal as the intelligible power of the self or as the powerful intelligibility of facts. Because the idea is concrete, its possibility is in itself an *infinitum actu* or an *enérgeia*, capable of deploying the whole

---

2. Jon Stewart, *Kierkegaard's Relations to Hegel Reconsidered*, Cambridge University Press, 2003, p. 231.

concrete content of subjective actuality. The *Concept of Anxiety* refers to this when it states that 'possibility is to be able' (SV² IV 354/KW VIII 49)[3] not mere passiveness or privation but, on the contrary, the intensive vitality and the *nisus formativus* of the actual. Through this 'idea-strength' (Pap XI¹ A 337/JP2 1806), subjectivity reaches existence as a free and conscious development of its ideal essence and the essence exists as deployed concretion. This synthesis of ideality and actuality allows Kierkegaard to state that, in the ethical domain, 'the true ideal is always the actual' (SV² II 227/KW IV 210), because it exercises its power over the finite by revealing itself in it as an essential foundation.

Human action is then the action of the ideal, in which the spirit's eternal power reveals itself through the temporal and contingent particularity contained in it as its own identity. What is reached by the aesthete as an abstract and formally possible infinitude, full of fantasies but impotent, is stated by the ethicist as a power of actuality, permeated with content. Hence for Kierkegaard, 'the more significant an individual is, the easier he will find actuality to be, the more difficult he will find possibility. This is the expression of an ethical view' (Pap IV A 35/JP3 3340). The huge weight of the possible is due to its actual potency, through which the spirit supports the entire universe. The aesthetic possibility is much lighter in comparison, because it does not bear the weight of the actual.

In synthesis, the effective manifestation of the ideal constitutes the ethical task, whose necessity is not extrinsically imposed onto the self but urges it inwardly, as becoming for itself of what is already in itself. The central determination of ethics lies in this conversion of the ideal into the actual that is equally the conversion of the actual into the ideal. Hence Kierkegaard's answer to the question: 'what is then actuality? It is ideality' (SV² VII 313/KW XII 325). But for the ideal and the actual to converge into the one and the same, subjectivity must achieve its potentiation, its own intensification able to deploy the intimacy of facts as well as to deploy itself in factual externality.

The becoming of the ideal into the actual, of the possible into power, describes thus an immanent and circular dynamism, in which what is stated is presupposed in its own positing, and in which the positing resumes the original and eternal foundation of the self. Ethical subjectivity rests wholly upon this immanent and circular dynamism having in itself its own teleology, that is to say, the law of a movement inwardly oriented as a return to a foundation affirmed by it. The ethical is then the affirmation of the self by itself, and the self is thus the absolute, as a result of a process that goes back to itself. Because 'every step forward toward the ideal is a backward step' (Pap X³ A 509/JP2 1789), ethical subjectivity goes back to the origin.

According to Hegel, the idea also presents itself as 'the absolutely active and at the same time actual' (EL § 142), on which the subject's intimate constitution

---

3. cf. Søren Kierkegaard, *Samlede Værker*, A. B. Drachmann, J. L. Heiberg and H. O. Lange (eds.), 15 vols., Gyldendalske Boghandel Nordisk Forlag, København, 1920-1936 (henceforth SV, superscript indicatinon the edition). cf. Also Søren Kierkegaard, *Kierkegaard's Writings*, trans. Howard V. Hong and Edna H. Hong, 24 vols., Princeton University Press, 1978-98 (henceforth KW).

depends. Precisely because the idea is in-itself *potentia, infinitum actu*, it contains the moment of its own actuality as the necessary return of the possible to the intrinsic unity of the absolute. The possibility of the ideal–that on the merely formal level represents an empty and tautological abstraction–is really affirmed as potency in actual effectiveness, through which it mediates with itself.

From a logical point of view, this reintegration of the idea to its own power is expressed in the category of the *essence* as an identity that is self-reflected by the effective manifestation or externalization of itself. What Hegel calls actuality, effectiveness or reality (*Wirklichkeit*) consists in the revealing process of the same and only ideal act that presupposes itself, is mediated in the other, and finally reconciles essence and existence, reflection and immediacy, the inner and the external, in its original unity. The actual is for Hegel this effectualness or realization, operated through an essential *enérgeia* deployed as posited being. The generating core of this essential process resides in the idea of power determining the substance as the ultimate unity of essence and being. Substance is the essence affirmed as absolute potency and creative potency, reflected in itself to return from its own positing.

What in logical terms is defined as the return of essence on itself, is expressed in Hegel's philosophy of the mind as the becoming of freedom seeking recognition and having itself as subject and object, form and content of its action. When consciousness reaches authentic freedom, 'it is itself this actual idea in itself' (PR § 22). Free subjectivity, affirmed in the infinite actuality of the idea, discovers its substance as both the cause and the foundation of its immanent intelligibility.

Whereas immediate aesthetic individuality is determined by an arbitrary and extrinsic content, concrete ethical subjectivity is determined by 'the activity of developing the idea and positing the content as existence, which insofar as it is existence of the idea is actuality' (EL § 482). Concrete existence thus contains the idea as its own fulfilling becoming and, in it, arbitrary will is subordinated to a superior dynamism. The development of the idea, that is in truth the development of existence itself, traces the perfect circularity of a road that goes back on itself with each step forward.

In sum, both Hegel and Kierkegaard believe that from the possible to the actual there is a reflexive internalization process, through which the ideal communicates its power to what exists and what exists manifests the absolute actuality that supports it. This intrinsic becoming of the self is in both cases the work of freedom seeking itself. Ethical subjectivity guarantees the concretion of what the idea is in itself and its own actuality is guaranteed in the idea. This process being a free one, the strength of its actuality lies in decision.

## III. RESOLUTION AS AFFIRMATION OF IDENTITY

When the Stages on Life's Way states that 'a person's total ideality lies first and last in resolution' (SV² VI 119/KW XI 108), they are expressing the intelligible power of freedom, revealed in the concrete action of the self. Resolution concentrates or intensifies to the infinite its own spiritual energy, so that the idea exists there as an actual effectiveness of finitude and the finite exists in it as fulfilled subjectivity. Resolution or decision is thus the primordial category of the ethical stage, as it determines the ideal as the actual and affirms the possible as effective power. In this sense, we must not confuse ethical decision with the aesthete's arbitrary elections determined by finite and temporal objects. On the contrary, the object of resolution is the subject itself, who turns reflectively back on itself to be asserted in its eternal and infinite validity through the mediation of the finite and temporal.

For ethical subjectivity there is only one possibility: its own self, externalized in its concrete situation and at the same time internalized in it. It chooses itself such as it is and in accordance to the conditions of its existence. Its freedom does not oscillate between abstract alternatives but is totally concentrated on the reflexive assumption of its being and its circumstances as the unique possibility of reconciliation. Kierkegaard states clearly that through decision 'the spirit becomes integrated as spirit and now has purely spiritual powers. It perhaps looked easier in possibility, but it has in fact become easier in actuality, because the spirit now is in essential, complete unity with itself' (Pap $X^1$ A 417/JP4 4326). The subject's inner unity coincides with the totality of what exists, so that its power transforms the huge weight of aesthetic abstraction into the light equality of a reconciled self.

Ethical decision should not be mistaken for the choice between good and evil, as an *aut-aut* excluding two objective and abstract terms. On the contrary, resolution is the assumption of the difference between good and evil affirmed by and in itself. The identity of the self contains and overcomes this affirmed opposition, so that freedom is the force of contradiction precisely because it is the force of unity, through a sort of dialectical transcending in which the self maintains and annuls the difference. It is then not a question of subjectivity choosing either good or evil but of reaching the foundation of its contraposition.

Choosing oneself is for Kierkegaard an 'absolute choice' or a 'primordial choice' ($SV^2$ II 236/KW IV 219), because it reflexively relates the self to its own essence, submerges it in its original identity and there it possesses itself as an eternally presupposed actuality effectively posited by itself; eternally produced and at the same time producing itself. The fact that 'the self is a relation that relates itself to itself' ($SV^2$ XI 143/KW XIX 13) indicates the absolute and constitutive character of the relation, whose substantial identity emerges from its own mediation as cause and effect of itself.

When the spirit asserts itself in its essential unity, all its possibilities become a unique power and all representations converge into the only actual ideality, in such a way that then subject is compelled to say: 'I cannot do otherwise; I do it for the sake of the idea, for the sake of meaning, for I cannot live without an idea' ($SV^2$ VI 267/KW XI 253). As a matter of fact–and in the strictest sense of the word– the idea determines the only possible way of existence, outside which the spirit is powerless and in which its power is necessary, because it has power over itself.

In this sense, decision is necessary and Kierkegaard admonishes: 'you shall choose the only one thing needful, but in such a way that there must be no question of any choice [...] The very fact there is no choice expresses the tremendous passion or intensity with which one chooses' (Pap X² A 428/JP2 1261). This immense passion in choice is the huge power that chooses itself. And thus, in necessity, authentic freedom takes place, a freedom that turns the subject into the object itself chosen in an unconditional way. The transcending of formal and abstract freedom coincides in this way with the consciousness of the self as the only alternative.

Choosing oneself is necessary due to the identity of its object as well as to the infinite intensity of its power. But given the fact that in the chosen self multiple immediate, contingent or accidental realities converge, they should be synthesized with that necessity. It would be speculative clumsiness to understand this synthesis as the sum of two opposing things, necessity on the one hand and contingence on the other, the sum of which would result in a third mixed state, the actuality of the self. On the contrary, the synthesis indicates a reflexive and dynamic passage into spiritual identity, in which the contingence of immediacy is assumed and overcome by the necessity of its subjective foundation.

Whoever chooses himself asserts himself absolutely in the multiple, determined and continuous concretion that constitutes his own personal actuality. The ethical conscience freely assumes its external circumstances and its random fortune, and for this reason there is no destiny for it, or rather for it 'what you want to be is—fate' (SV² II 18/KW IV 15), to which we might add that fate is one's own willing, in which the self recognizes the subjective truth of facts. To assume destiny in one's own spiritual becoming does not mean to accept the extrinsic necessity of *fatum* in order not to be carried away by it, but rather to recognize oneself and to recognize it in its intrinsic freedom.

Contingence—the accidental aspect of being—is just as necessary as necessity itself, because it constitute the extrinsic manifestation of essential identity. In Kierkegaard's own terms, contingence is 'the final category, the essential category of transition from the sphere of the idea to actuality' (SV² I 245/KW III 238). As an authentic mediation, in the accidental aspect the idea is expressed as effective force and under its power it acknowledges itself as effect. The movement of decision acknowledges then the infinite subjectivity of finitude, the essential foundation of events, and thus remains in a continuous identification to its externality.

In this sense, the ethical actuality of the self constitutes for Kierkegaard an authentic 'inter-esse' (SV² VII 302/KW XII 314) in which factual existence and ideality, finitude and infinitude, time and eternity are reflected in an absolute way due to that 'essential relation that has become identical to itself' (EL § 142). These are precisely the terms in which Hegel describes the return of the subject upon itself, a return that is the external manifestation and the inward process of the self. From Hegel's point of view, the essential relation is an absolute relation. It is the relation of the absolute with itself, in which effective actuality is resolved as the ultimate and substantial unity of essence and existence, infinitude and finitude, interior and exteriority. That relation expresses the substantial identity of the subject, in the actual revelation or reality of its ideal energy.

The return of the relationship to its identity expresses the deployment of the idea within itself, the reflection or mediation of the subject that, stating in it its own power, proceeds in a necessary way. According to Hegel, necessity 'is the essence that is one and identical to itself; but it is the essence that has a concrete content and that appears in the interior of itself' (EL § 149). Briefly stated, necessity is the work of identity, and it reveals itself both in the substantial potency of the absolute as in its ad extra actuality, through the only and the same movement that proceeds from itself and goes back to itself.

Identity is thus the only real alternative of the subject and, precisely because of this, its necessity is liberating. In necessity, the authentic freedom of a subjective destiny transparent to itself takes place. That 'the truth of necessity is freedom' (EL § 158) means that the penetrated and recognized identity determines the self as positing itself. Freedom is thus the positing by itself of the identity of the subject and the object, of the inner and the outward as the only effective power.

But, as the self integrates in its becoming the whole accidental and contingent content mediating its essentiality, contingence constitutes the immediate manifestation of the essential, presupposed by its own necessity and just as necessary. The immediate existence of the essential encompasses the multiple external conditions, circumstances, determinations, etc, that have to be assumed as moments of the same comprehensive process. In relation to them, necessity determines the instance in which contingence of becoming discovers its true form, the absolute power that moves it and the foundation of its actualization.

In this sense, the actual is for Hegel 'the unity of necessity and the accidental aspect of being' (W VI 213), not as an addition of two different things but as a subjective internal dynamism, which reverses the external inexorable character of facts in the becoming of the self. Through this dynamism, destiny loses its extrinsic compulsion and becomes integrated into the freedom of a subject that has been recovered in its essential identity. Through it, necessity also loses its static rigidity and transforms the temporal course into a same history that liberates the absolute.

If to repeat is to confirm the presupposed identity at the origin of becoming, the process through which the self recovers its essential identity constitutes the authentic repetition that Kierkegaard has so often dealt with. In repetition, one and the same freedom is stated both as subject and object, act and content, beginning and end of its inner reflection. Once the aesthete's immediate consciousness has failed in its attempt to achieve subjectivity, repetition raises the ideal 'to the second power' ($SV^2$ III 291/KW VI 229), in order to see the spirit rise from its own mediation.

## IV. THE INTRINSIC NECESSITY OF DUTY

Resolution is not an arbitrary option but a free necessity, and thus it assumes the form of duty as absolute and unconditional potency of any finite content.

Duty for Kierkegaard designates 'an internal relation; for that which is incumbent upon me, no as this individual with accidental characteristics but in accordance with my true being, certainly has the most intimate relation with myself' (SV$^2$ II 275/KW IV 254). As a relation, it constitutes the essential identity of the subject, through restitution of accidental individuality to its foundation, hence the absolute and unconditional value of duty as eternity characterizing ethics.

Duty is the consciousness of an ideal infinitude that wants to be in the finite, and as every human being possesses it, it is therefore 'the universal' (SV$^2$ II 276/KW IV 255) assigned to each one as their own task. The universality of duty has two meanings. The first one, insofar as its exigency extends to all individuals and determines their essential equality, with themselves and with others. The second one, insofar as its content prescribes the common actions that constitute the social order. In both cases, perhaps the Kierkegaardian pseudonym *Johannes de Silentio* represents the best possible description of ethical universality.

The supreme exigency of duty resides in the substantial identity of the subject, emerging from its own necessity. Kierkegaard's imperative consists thus in the decision itself, in order to grasp the eternal foundation of the self. And given that this power corresponds equally to everybody, Kierkegaard states that 'humanness consists in this: that every human being is granted the capability of being spirit' (Pap IX A 76/JP1 69). If you can, you must and if you must be it, it is because you have the power to achieve it. In this statement there is a conversion of the possible to duty, in which the intimate potentiation of the spirit becomes manifest.

The unconditional appropriation of this one and eternal essence of the self turns temporal becoming into a continuum, because in the face of the immediate fragmentation of phenomena, the ethicist discovers a 'constancy in itself, and the energizing power in this constancy is the same as the law of motion' (SV$^2$ II 108/KW IV 98). Hence, while the aesthete deals with the accidental aspect of events and in it loses his inner unity, ethical subjectivity asserts itself in the divine order of facts, in its immovable foundation that is basically the very origin of becoming, from which the insubstantial appearance of the world is referred to its own absolute inwardness.

As for its content—and precisely because subjective identity does not want to be abstract but concrete—what is due extends to every sphere of life, in order to unconditionally assume those tasks and activities that generally engage human existence. Marriage, work, friendship, vocation, daily occupations, etc. are the object of this due transformation, through which they receive the immovable firmness of a self that accomplishes itself and accomplishes them through its subjectivity. Thus, from the aesthetical to the ethical life, there is no destruction of the former but a circular return–a transfigurative repetition–that discovers in the same the dynamism overcoming the eternal. Thus every particular action of the self is subject to its eternal dynamism, and in this way it becomes the absolute unity of the general and the singular.

These activities are common to all human beings and constitute the social order, and thus Kierkegaard's ethical stage is usually assimilated to a correct civic performance and associated to the Hegelian *Sittlichkeit*. As a matter of fact, ethical subjectivity must accomplish in the existing world the objective and universal order of the spirit, similarly to what Hegel expressed in the *Philosophy of Right*. Nevertheless, for Kierkegaard as well as for Hegel the accomplishment of this order is the manifestation and not the foundation of its ethics. For both of them, ethical life is supported by the universal character of human essence, which transcends individual free will through the reflexive becoming of subjectivity.

From Kierkegaard's point of view, the human being is neither only nor mainly the arbitrariness of its contingent being, but the necessity of a common nature, through which 'the man is *individuum* and as such simultaneously himself and the whole race, and in such a way that the whole race participates in the individual and the individual in the whole race' (SV$^2$ VII 332/KW VIII 28). Participation in the same spiritual nature justifies the objective and universal ethical order, because in it the individual recognizes its immovable substantiality, called upon to unify the contingent particularities of its existence as well as to establish the universal legal status of the social whole.

In an analogous way, Hegel conceives the passing from arbitrary consciousness to the consciousness of duty as the elevation of the spirit to its true content, that is to say, to its universal and necessary foundation, not extrinsic but immanent to subjectivity itself. The ethical constitutes the synthesis or concrete identity of particular individuality and its essential substantiality, an identity in which subjective contingency is transcended without being destroyed. On account of this universal nature, that is not an abstract representation but the very substance of the singular, it reaches its actuality. Through law, the individual elevates its immediate existence to the absolute power of an action that is both singular and general.

Duty is for Hegel subjective action itself, through whose willing and knowing the rational substantiality of the ethical life is stated as the foundation of individuality, while at the same time the individual is essentially encompassed and finds its subsistence in it. Thus the root of ethical life does not reside in the extrinsic determination of law but in 'the pure unconditioned self-determination of the will' (PR § 135), that is to say, in subjective freedom. Precisely because freedom is the necessity of itself, the subjective spirit's self-determination coincides with what is due and it has to become manifest in the objective actuality of ethics.

The *Science of Logic* coincides in that duty expresses the attempt of the finite to transcend itself, retrieving its essential ideality. In this sense, it contains both the limit and the transcending of the limit, and is thus determined as a relation between finitude and infinitude, that is both split and attempt to achieve unity; externalization and reflection in itself. But precisely because free power is assumed as a duty, it always maintains a certain division between the essential and the finite that prevents total unification of the self. In other words, in duty, subjective power discovers an intrinsic difference that turns its possibility into impossibility and the finite into certain death. If 'what has to be, is and is not at the same time' (W III 143), then the forces of the possible are annulled in their own contradiction, and the result is that 'you cannot, precisely because you must' (W III 144-145). Duty does not achieve reconciliation of subjectivity and its failure becomes manifest–according to Hegel–in the bad infinitude of an interminable process.

The solid identity with which ethical life has apparently imposed itself thus far now manifests its intrinsic negativity and claims a transcending dynamism. In Hegel's case, the collapse of subjective affirmation already anticipates the becoming of the concept and the transcending of ethical objectivity in religious and speculative subjectivity. In Kierkegaard's case, the ethical stage confirms–with its collapse–its dialectical position, anticipating authentic reconciliation.

## V. GUILT AS NEGATION OF IDENTITY

If *Either-Or* starts by asserting decision as the identical power of the self, it ends with the edifying statement that 'in relation to God we are always in the wrong' (SV$^2$ II 366/KW IV 339), so that 'the highest expression of an ethical view of life is repentance and I must always repent—but precisely this is a the self-contradiction of the ethical' (Pap IV A 112/JP1 902). Choosing oneself absolutely means choosing oneself as guilty, and in guilt the dialectic of immanence is denied as an impossible self-contradiction. The positing of the self by itself reveals its impotence in repentance and the unity obtained relapses into division.

From a metaphysical point of view, reality of repentance unmasks the constitutive negativity of subjectivity or its essential belonging to evil and to nothingness. Certainly, the self possesses in itself an absolute power and an infinite actuality that it must act, but at the same time it possesses non-being and impotence. We are dealing here with the dialectical constitution of the self, according to which 'insofar as it has the positive aspect, it also has the negative one. Freedom never forgets this dialectical origin of freedom' (Pap V A 90). In this context dialectic refers to a dynamic force whose affirmation is *eo ipso* negation and whose negation remits to a unity transcending difference in such a way that, if freedom has a dialectical origin, it has above all an origin to which it must return. The problem is whether it can achieve this by itself, as its power is annulled in its own contradiction.

The principle of dialectic completely structures subjective actuality and manifests its operative capacity in every sphere of its development. The spirit can never be asserted in a direct way in the case of the aesthete as well as of the ethical and the religious person, but a negation must always come first 'and the more spirit, the more care is taken that the negation is the negation of the very opposite' (Pap XI$^1$ A 152/JP2 2226). In every degree of spiritual intensification the fall and the force of contradiction become deeper. Destiny, guilt, despair, resignation and sin are all names for this negativity that corrodes subjective becoming while driving it forward.

In the ethical stage, dialectical negativity becomes manifest as guilt and repentance. Both reverse the immanent affirmation of the self by itself in impotence. In Kierkegaard's own words: 'the power which is given to a man (in possibility) is altogether dialectical, and the only true expression for a true understanding of himself in possibility is precisely the he has the power to destroy himself, because he, even though he be stronger than the entire world, he nevertheless is not stronger than himself' (Pap V A 16/JP1 46). The infinite power of freedom, precisely because it is possible and dialectical, is an impossibility that annihilates what is due in the contradiction that permeates it. This also means that the self will not reach by itself the positive synthesis of the finite and the infinite, of time and eternity, of being and duty, of relativity and absoluteness, but only through an Other.

Contradiction is evidently the driving force in Hegel's philosophy. It is well known that for Hegel every affirmation is a negation, and that negation is called upon to retrieve original identity. At this point it is much more interesting to confront the Hegelian description of the concept of guilt as a disintegration of ethics. Hegel certainly recognizes in ethical subjectivity an authentic character, which assumes in its singular pathos the universal force of the substantial and achieves in this way a balance with the totality of the actual. Nevertheless, its unity remains in the immediacy of the *an-sich* that has not achieved the *für-sich* of total reflection, and in this way maintains the division it intends to overcome.

Because its possibility is an impossible, when ethical conscience acts, it ipso facto states the duality between divine and human law, and in this separation it perishes, as Abraham's ethical conscience perished in the face of the sacrifice that was demanded of him. Inexorably, 'self-consciousness becomes guilt through action, as guilt is its operating, and operating is its innermost essence'[4]. Freedom manifests in guilt its potency of denial and thus the force of the idea annuls the singular by confronting it with a stranger Other, with a divine law that refutes what is human. The incessant perishing of decision, expressing on the one hand its negation in-itself, asserts on the other hand a transcending dynamism.

In the last resort, the failure of ethical consciousness resides in the immanent attempt of the self for itself, which seeks immediate unity to the absolute without the mediation of a Third, that is to say, without a unifying term that contains identity in its difference. If for Hegel the actual is always a syllogism and for Kierkegaard the division of unity always produces three, in both cases the identity of the I=I does not resist the test of the Other, that ignores contradiction. The perfect circularity of the subjectivity is therefore not closed in itself but in the Difference.

The ethical stage has attempted to assert the self-relationship that is the self together with the synthesis of finitude and infinitude, of time and eternity that it contains. But it has forgotten that 'the relation that relates itself to itself has been established by another, then the relation is indeed the third, but this relation, the third, is yet again a relation and relates itself to that which established the entire

---

4. G. W. F. Hegel, *Phänomenologie des Geistes*, in *Werke in zwanzig Bänden*, Eva Moldenhauer and Karl Markus (eds.), vol. 3, Frankfurt am Main, Suhrkamp Verlag, 1969, p. 346.

relation' (SV² XI 144/KW XIX 13). From a metaphysical point of view, dependency on a third is equivalent to the complete negation of the self and the annihilation of all its efforts. This does not mean that subjectivity is totally powerless, but only that it is powerful by Other and collapses in its recognition.

Ethical life has been lost. Do what it may, it will repent and will always be guilty. Do what it may, reconciliation is impossible for it. Its infinite power is annulled in its own contradiction and its concretion relapses into a new abstraction. However, all that has been lost will come back transfigured, because the power of the Idea is stronger than the self.

## VI. CONCLUSION

During decades, the history of philosophy has kept Kierkegaard and Hegel apart. I believe this has been sadly detrimental to both of them, as their long-standing opposition has swept through the speculative greatness of Kierkegaard's thought and the existential power of Hegel's.

On the one hand, Kierkegaard has been deemed the philosopher of a formally possible and abstract freedom, and in this way the necessary power that impels free action has been concealed. He has been accused of irrationalism, ignoring the central place of the idea as supreme source of intelligibility and sense. His resolution has been mistaken for arbitrary decisionism alien to the internal force of duty that produces it, and his individual for a social abstraction lacking the universal human nature that Kierkegaard attributes to it. Finally, the either/or has been considered the contrary to Hegelian mediation, when it is the infinite dynamism of freedom that presupposes, affirms and overcomes every opposition.

On the other hand, Hegel has been considered the philosopher of rigid abstract understanding, overlooking the fact that he was the first one to demolish the rigid abstractions of the intellect in order to safeguard a rational concreteness that grounds and reverses every opposition. It has been maintained that Hegelian thought has buried contingence, when for it the necessity of the idea is only in the accidental character of facts. The supposed abstraction of the idea only exists in the freedom of individual consciousness and the proclaimed objective order of the social sphere can only be sustained from the point of view of actual subjectivity, also called upon to be transcended by religious form of spirit. If Hegel's system is closed, it is closed in the same instant in which contradiction reappears.

These unfortunate interpretations clearly manifest a logical and existential confusion that this paper has attempted to dispel. In fact, I have tried to show how the internal logic of Kierkegaard's thought coincides with the fundamental dialectical dynamism of Hegel's philosophy. Both of them state that the idea is the real power of subjective becoming, and the existence is the actual concretion of the ideal. The pure *enérgeia* of freedom, which starts as an abstract and aesthetical possibility, realizes itself as the actual concretion of finitude, in which time and contingency are assumed by the eternal and necessary force of duty. The

Kierkegaardian repetition is nothing but this powerful idea, mediating the flux of finite differences in the eternal identity of subject.

Nevertheless, the ethics is just the objective form of the absolute in which subject has assumed the world and the divine, but it is not the own recognition of the Absolute. That is why the ethical subject falls in the contradiction of God. The task of the religious stages consists in the last and definitive mediation, capable of unifying God, individual and neighbour in the perfect syllogism of love. When the absolute difference appears, love will overcome it and the Third will support the circle of unity.

# 12

# *Sein und Geist*: Heidegger's Confrontation with Hegel's Phenomenology

## Robert Sinnerbrink

> The genuine refutation must penetrate the opponent's stronghold and meet him on his own ground; no advantage is gained by attacking him somewhere else and defeating him where he is not.
>
> —Hegel, *Science of Logic*

After a certain period of neglect, philosophical interest in the Hegel-Heidegger relationship has recently intensified in the English-speaking world.[1] While some studies adopt a distinctly Heideggerian perspective concerning Heidegger's critique of Hegel,[2] others launch a Hegelian defence of Hegel against Heidegger's interpretation, seeking to show that Heidegger has simply gone wrong in basic points of Hegel interpretation.[3] Others again adopt a more agnostic view of the

---

1. Recent works on the Hegel-Heidegger relationship include: Rebecca Comay and John McCumber (eds.) *Endings. Questions of Memory in Hegel and Heidegger*, Evanston, Northwestern University Press, 1999; Karin de Boer, *Thinking in the Light of Time: Heidegger's Encounter with Hegel*, Albany, State University of New York Press, 2000; Michael Allen Gillespie, *Hegel, Heidegger, and the Ground of History*, Chicago, Chicago University Press, 1984; David Kolb, *The Critique of Pure Modernity. Hegel, Heidegger, and After*, Chicago, Chicago University Press, 1986; Catherine Malabou, *The Future of Hegel: Plasticity, Temporality, and Dialectic*, trans. Lisabeth During, London, Routledge, 2005; Dennis J. Schmidt, *The Ubiquity of the Finite: Hegel, Heidegger, and the Entitlements of Philosophy*, Cambridge, The MIT Press, 1988. See also Giorgio Agamben, *Language and Death: The Place of Negativity*, trans. K. E. Pinkus with M. Hardt, Minneapolis, University of Minnesota Press, 1991.

2. See, for example Parvis Emad, 'The Place of Hegel in Heidegger's *Being and Time*', *Research in Phenomenology*, no. 13, 1983, pp. 159-173; and David Farrell Krell, 'Hegel, Heidegger, Nietzsche. An Essay in Descensional Reflection', *Nietzsche-Studien*, no. 5, 1976, pp. 255-262.

3. See, for example, Denise Souche-Dagues, 'The Dialogue between Hegel and Heidegger' in Christopher Macann (ed.) *Martin Heidegger: Critical Assessments Volume II: History of Philosophy*, London, Routledge, 1992, pp. 246-276; Robert B. Pippin, 'On Being Anti-Cartesian: Heidegger, Hegel, Subjectivity, and Sociality' in R. B. Pippin, *Idealism as Modernism: Hegelian Variations*, Cambridge, Cambridge University Press, 1997; and Robert R. Williams, 'Hegel and Heidegger' in W. Desmond (ed.) *Hegel and his Critics*, Albany, State University of New York Press, 1989, pp. 135-157.

veracity of Heidegger's reading of Hegel.[4] While all these approaches have merit, I wish to offer a more 'dialogical' approach to the Hegel-Heidegger relationship. Indeed, both Hegel and Heidegger advocated such an approach to the practice of 'originary' philosophical thinking. In the *Science of Logic*, Hegel remarks on the immanent critique that moves beyond mere external refutation in order to confront the problem at issue from within an opposing philosophical standpoint (SL 581).[5] Heidegger, for his part, observes that if a genuine dialogue with Hegel is to occur, 'we are required to be "kindred"' with him in the sense of being '*committed* to the first and last necessities of philosophical inquiry arising from the matter [*Sache*]' (HPS 31).[6] This paper shall therefore attempt to pursue the 'thinking dialogue' between Hegel and Heidegger, a dialogue centred on Heidegger's 'confrontation' [*Auseinandersetzung*] with Hegel's *Phenomenology of Spirit*. In particular, I consider Heidegger's critique of Hegel on the relationship between time and Spirit; Heidegger's interpretation of the *Phenomenology of Spirit* as exemplifying the Cartesian-Fichtean metaphysics of the subject, examining in particular the question of the phenomenological 'we' in Heidegger's reading; and Heidegger's later reflections on Hegel's *Phenomenology* as articulating the modern metaphysics of 'subjectity' [*Subjektität*] that culminates in modern technics. I shall argue that Heidegger forgets those aspects of Hegel's philosophy that make him our philosophical contemporary: Hegel's thinking of intersubjectivity and recognition, his thinking of the historicity of the experience of spirit, and his attempt to sublate modern subject-metaphysics which is also a critique of modernity. The point of this dialogue is to begin a recovery or retrieval of Hegel from Heidegger's critical deconstruction, and to thereby suggest that the future of Hegel—to use Catherine Malabou's resonant phrase—remains for us something still to-come.

## I. HEIDEGGER'S CRITICISM OF HEGEL ON TIME AND SPIRIT

It is significant that Hegel is one of the few figures in *Being and Time* (along with Descartes and Kant) singled out for an explicit critique.[7] In this sense, we could regard Heidegger's brief analysis of Hegel's conception of the relation between time and spirit as a contribution to the task of a 'de-struction' [*Des-struktion*] of the history of ontology.[8] Temporality as such, according to Heidegger, has

---

4. One of the restrictions Karin de Boer imposes in her account of Heidegger's encounter with Hegel is 'to minimize any consideration as to how far Heidegger's interpretations of his predecessors' are correct'. It is hard to see, though, how there can be a genuine 'thinking dialogue' if Heidegger's readings of Hegel are accepted without critical reflection. de Boer, *Thinking in the Light of Time*, p. 5.

5. As evident in my opening quotation from Hegel's greater *Logic*, SL 581.

6. Heidegger, *Hegel's Phenomenology of Spirit*, trans. Parvis Emad and Kenneth Maly, Bloomington, Indiana University Press, 1988, p. 31, (henceforth HPS).

7. Martin Heidegger, *Being and Time*, trans. Joan Stambaugh, Albany, State University of New York, 1996, §82, pp. 391-396, (henceforth BT).

8. On this point Malabou eschews any confrontation between Heidegger and Hegel: 'It is not my purpose here to stage a confrontation between the Hegelian and Heideggerian conceptions of time'. Malabou, *The Future of Hegel*, p. 4. This prompts Derrida, in his lengthy introduction to Malabou's book, to ask a series of probing questions regarding the significance of this demurral. See Jacques

remained unthought or at least distorted and misunderstood within the history of metaphysics, with the sole exception of Kant (BT 20). However, because Kant neglects to pose the fundamental question of Being, and lacks 'a preliminary ontological analytic of the subjectivity of the subject', he was unable to gain proper access to the ontological significance of the problem of temporality (BT 21). Heidegger traces Kant's difficulties back to an appropriation of the Cartesian cogito without a 'fundamental ontology' of Da-sein, and an assumed conception of time centred on the presence of the present. This 'metaphysical' understanding of time is based upon the assumption that the definitive dimension of temporal experience is provided by the familiar perception of the presence of beings encountered in the present.

This presupposition becomes even more acute in the case of Hegel, who is taken to exemplify the 'vulgar' metaphysical conception of time as an infinite sequence of discrete 'Nows' or present moments. Indeed, Hegel's concept of time, according to Heidegger, is 'the most radical way in which the vulgar understanding of time has been given form conceptually' (BT 392). Heidegger thus presents his brief critique of Hegel's 'metaphysical' conception of time and spirit (in §82 of *Being and Time*) as a contrast to the *existential-ontological* interpretation of the originary or ecstatic temporality of Da-sein. Hegel's account of the relationship between time and spirit—that spirit 'falls into' historical time and yet can be sublated or *aufgehoben* by speculative thought—is presented as evidence of how the metaphysical tradition has obliterated the question of temporality in favour of an ontologically inappropriate interpretation of Da-sein as objective presence.

In accordance with Aristotle's demarcation of time within the ontology of nature, Hegel's analysis of time is located in the second part of the *Encyclopaedia*, namely The *Philosophy of Nature*. Heidegger's exposition of paragraphs 254-258 of Hegel's *Encyclopaedia* aims to establish how Hegel's basic conception of time, defined as 'intuited becoming,' privileges the punctual moment of the present—as a Now-Here moment—within the abstract becoming or flux of successive moments. Heidegger argues that the logical conceptualizing of time—as the negation of the negation of the punctuality of space—demonstrates how time has been formalized 'in the most extreme sense' and levelled down to an 'unprecedented degree' (BT 394).

A critical point can immediately be made here concerning Heidegger's claims. Hegel discusses space and time (in the *Philosophy of Nature*) as the most *minimal*, elementary, and *abstract* determinations of nature in general (space presupposes nothing but nature's self-externality while time presupposes nothing but space). Space and time in this abstract sense already acquire a more concrete significance with '*place*' [*Ort*]: the *posited* identity of space and time that is also their posited *contradiction* (EPN § 261). With the category of place, the abstract punctuality of the Now as a present moment is already suspended in relation to the con-

---

Derrida, 'A Time for Farewells: Heidegger (read by) Hegel (read by) Malabou', in Malabou, *The Future of Hegel*, pp. vii-xlvii, esp. pp. xxvii ff.

crete determination of space.⁹ As Hegel remarks: 'The Here is at the same time a Now, for it is the point of duration. This unity of Here and Now is Place' (EPN § 260 A). The extreme formalization of time as a succession of Now moments that Heidegger attributes to Hegel is already challenged at this still relatively simple level of categorical development in Hegel's *Philosophy of Nature*. Although belonging to a somewhat different context, the *Phenomenology of Spirit* (PS ¶¶ 90-110) similarly provides a critical demonstration of the untenability of the abstract punctuality of the Now in the experience of *sense-certainty*. These points cast doubt on Heidegger's presentation of Hegel's conception of time as such.

Nonetheless, Heidegger claims that Hegel's determination of time as the *negation of negation* is the most radical version of the Aristotelian conception of time, but also the most levelled down conception of temporality in Heidegger's originary, existential-ecstatic sense. This *logical formalization* of time is precisely what allows Hegel to make the connection between spirit and its development through historical time: 'Hegel shows the possibility of the historical actualization of spirit "in time" by going back to *the identity of the formal structure of Spirit and time as the negation of a negation*' (BT 396). This is the decisive point in Heidegger's discussion: the identity of time and spirit as sharing the logical structure of the 'negation of the negation' is also their reduction to an empty 'formal-ontological' abstraction that obliterates originary temporality. This reduction makes possible their kinship as well as the ontologically obscure 'actualization' of spirit in time that Hegel describes. In connecting time and spirit in this manner, however, Hegel also leaves unexamined 'the question of whether the constitution of Spirit *as* the negating of negation is possible at all in any other way than on the basis of primordial temporality' (BT 396).

Heidegger insists that this brief discussion of Hegel cannot claim to decide whether 'Hegel's interpretation of time and Spirit and their connection is correct and has an ontologically primordial basis' (BT 396). Nonetheless, I suggest that Heidegger's crucial claim with regard to Hegel deserves further critical engagement. Here I draw attention to Heidegger's compressed discussion of the essence of Hegelian spirit as *the Concept* or *Begriff*. Heidegger defines Hegelian Conceptuality as 'the very form of thinking that thinks itself: Conceiving *itself—as grasping* the non-I' (BT 395). This definition of the Concept is interpreted as the differentiation and comprehension of the difference between the 'I' and the 'non-I': 'the grasping of *this* differentiation, a differentiation of the difference' between I and non-I (BT 395). The Concept thus has the formal structure of the 'negation of a negation'. The 'absolute negativity' of the Concept, for Heidegger, gives 'a logically formalized interpretation of Descartes' *cogito me cogitare rem*' (BT 395). In other words, the Concept comprehends itself in *self-consciousness*: it is the 'conceivedness of the self conceiving itself', the self as it can authentically be, namely

---

9. cf. 'In this way, the *negative* determination in space, the *exclusive* point, no longer only implicitly [or in itself] conforms to the Concept [*Begriff*], but is *posited* and *concrete* within itself, though the total negativity which is time; the point, as thus concrete, is *Place* [*Ort*]', EPN § 260 [trans. mod].

as *free*, a universality that is just as immediately 'individuality' (BT 395).[10]

Heidegger's interpretation of Hegel's Concept of self-consciousness is certainly legitimate in its general outlines: the 'I' *is* the existing Concept, according to Hegel. At the same time, however, Heidegger overlooks that this way of understanding the relationship between the I and the Concept fails to take into account the (logical) *limitations* of the category of *existence*, and moreover ignores the fact that self-consciousness is for Hegel the 'real-philosophical,' finite actualization of the Concept. To make this point clearer, we must consider the relationship between the structure of the Concept and that of the 'I' as subjective spirit. In the *Phenomenology*, Hegel defines the Concept of self-consciousness as comprising three interrelated moments: the *universality* of the pure undifferentiated 'I'; the *particularity* of the mediation through the sensuous object of desire; and the concrete *individuality* of the reflective movement of recognition between self-conscious subjects (PS ¶ 176). While Heidegger accounts for the first moment (the abstract self-identity of the 'I' as I = I) and the second moment (the particularity of self-consciousness as desire), he has no account of the third moment (concrete individuality articulated through intersubjective recognition). Indeed, Heidegger's failure to account for the moment of *concrete individuality* in the Concept of self-consciousness clearly parallels the deficiencies in the Kantian-Fichtean account of self-consciousness that Hegel seeks to overcome through his account of the role of mutual recognition. In this sense, Heidegger, like Kant and Fichte, remains stuck at the *level of reflection* in conceiving of self-consciousness according to an abstract *formalism:* a deficient conception of self-consciousness which fails to unite all three moments of universality, particularity, and the crucial third moment of *individuality* achieved through the process of recognition.

Here we should also distinguish, furthermore, between the infinite structure of the Concept (the absolute, reflexive self-enclosure of the Concept as unitary or unique); and the 'relative' independence of the I, which is self-reflexive only through the *recognition* of the other, a process of 'doubling' or mutual reflection in which the other is both absorbed *and* released, both integrated *and* set free. The character of this process of recognition of and through the other, moreover, necessarily depends on the historically given structures of objective and absolute spirit. For Hegel, the 'I' is *unitary* only by not being *unique* or solitary: it finds its self-identity in otherness only within a plurality that preserves the other. To this extent, the I genuinely does 'fall into time', according to Hegel, insofar as the character of its self-identity depends upon something which it, as finite spirit, can never fully absorb and sublate; it depends upon the historical actuality of objective and absolute spirit as an other of which it is *merely an aspect*, but in which it

---

10. In support of this 'Cartesian-Fichtean' interpretation of the Concept, Heidegger cites Hegel's statements that 'the I is the pure Concept itself which, as concept, has come into *existence* [*Dasein*]' (SL 583), and that the I is '*first*, this pure self-related unity, ... as making abstraction from all determinateness and content and withdrawing into the freedom of unrestricted equality with itself' (SL 583). As I argue presently, these passages are significant in relation to Hegel's parallel between the threefold structure of the Concept and the three aspects (universal, particular, and individual) of the Concept of self-consciousness (see PS ¶ 176).

finds its self-identity and freedom in the sense of being with itself in otherness. Only spirit in its evolving totality fully *realizes* the Concept; in its historical actualization it overcomes time within time itself.

Moreover, by emphasizing the parallel between the formal structure of self-consciousness and the Concept, Heidegger's 'Cartesian' interpretation of self-consciousness, as I shall argue further below, fails to comprehend the *hermeneutic aspects* of Hegel's account of the relation between the 'I' as existing Concept and spirit as self-comprehending totality. Hegel's characterization of the 'I' as existing Concept merely indicates its *formal* structure as a unity of universality, particularity, and individuality. It does not yet disclose those 'real-philosophical' conditions (namely the concrete historical forms of developing recognition) that make possible the determinate actualization of this formal structure (represented by the 'I = I'). Spirit is the concrete or actualized Concept that must appear in historical time, not simply because of the formal structure of the 'negation of the negation' shared by time and spirit, but because finite spirit remains dependent on objective and absolute spirit for its concrete self-identity in otherness. To be sure, spirit as totality is not reducible to subjective spirit as individual self-consciousness. Nonetheless, spirit 'exists' concretely and historically only because there are self-conscious individuals who can acquire adequate self-consciousness within historically developing structures of mutual recognition, work off their natural particularity and inequality in a historical process which progressively discloses spirit in its concrete rationality, and thus (re)produce (objective and absolute) spirit as that which in turn makes possible the finite self-consciousness of these historically situated individuals. Hegel's *Phenomenology* depicts this process as a recollection of the historical-dialectical experience in which spirit recognizes itself within 'comprehended history'—a process of conceptual-historical recollection without which, Hegel tells us, absolute spirit would remain 'lifeless and alone' (PS ¶ 808).

Although Heidegger's brief critical analysis does not claim to do justice to Hegel's broader philosophical project, Hegel is still presented as exemplifying the vulgar metaphysical conception of time. Questions must be asked, however, about the adequacy of Heidegger's interpretation. Why does Heidegger focus on the concept of time taken from the philosophy of nature rather than Hegel's explicit discussions of the historicity of spirit? Moreover, why is Heidegger's discussion in this respect restricted to the most *abstract*, elementary categorization of time in the philosophy of nature?[11] Heidegger ignores the *hermeneutical* dimension of Hegel's procedure in appropriating and conceptualizing categories and models from the history of philosophy; he fails to recognize Hegel's method of simultaneous *exposition* and *critique* in presenting categorical systems within speculative philosophy.[12] It is not surprising that Heidegger finds Hegel to have recapitulated

---

11. In the section on the animal organism in the *Encyclopaedia* Hegel seems to suggest that 'time' (and space) receives more concrete, higher determinations at higher levels of natural organization. The 'subjectivity' of the animal is a 'free time' that, according to inner contingency, 'determines its place'. *Hegel's Philosophy of Nature*, §351, p. 352.

12. See Michael Theunissen's *Sein und Schein. Die Kritische Funktion der Hegelschen Logik*, Frankfurt,

in the Jena Lectures Aristotle's theses on time in the *Physics*, for Hegel hermeneutically appropriates these Aristotelian themes within the philosophy of nature as one aspect of the speculative system. In the paragraphs Heidegger discusses from the 'Mechanism' chapter of the *Encyclopaedia*, for example, Hegel examines the categorical structure of time and space pertinent not only to Aristotle but to *Newtonian mechanics*. The latter remains within the paradigm of the logic of essence that is the subject of Hegel's *critical exposition* in this part of the system (paralleled, for example, by the analysis of the dialectic between force and law in the *Phenomenology*). This discussion, however, cannot provide an adequate example of the essential relationship between time and spirit, for the simple reason that nature occupies a different conceptual/categorical level than spirit, and thus cannot provide the basis for conceptualizing self-conscious spirit in its historical development. In §82 of *Being and Time*, Heidegger overlooks this hermeneutic dimension in Hegel's discussion of time within the philosophy of nature and Hegel's critical exposition of the 'I' as the *finite* actualization of the Concept.

## II. FINITUDE AND INFINITUDE: HEIDEGGER'S READING OF HEGEL'S *PHENOMENOLOGY*

As Denise Souche-Dagues remarks, Heidegger's 'simple refusal' of Hegel in *Being and Time* failed to do justice to the complexity and power of Hegel's speculative thought.[13] Hegelian metaphysics cannot be reduced to a corpus of historically ossified material in need of critical de-struction and ontological re-animation, for Hegel claimed to have achieved the suspension of substance- and subject-metaphysics within the speculative metaphysics of spirit. Heidegger thus embarks upon a different strategy, a dialogical confrontation with Hegel that is part of the project of overcoming metaphysics in the sense of comprehending the underlying question of the metaphysical tradition (the question of Being) and of consequently responding to the forgetting of the ontological difference between Being and beings. In this regard, Hegel is now understood as representing the beginning of the completion or consummation of Western metaphysics (with Nietzsche as the conclusion), a process that must be critically displaced in order to prepare for the possibility of an 'other beginning' of (no-longer-metaphysical) thought.

Heidegger's next sustained engagement with Hegel occurs in the 1930/31

---

Suhrkamp, 1980, for an interpretation of Hegel's *Logic* as involving this movement of simultaneous exposition and critique.

13. As Souche-Dagues suggests in her helpful schema, we can identify three important phases in Heidegger's reading of Hegel: 1) The critique of the 'Hegelian theory of time' in the 1925-26 Marburg lectures and in §82 of *Being and Time*. 2) The 1930/31 lectures on the 'Consciousness' chapters of the PhG and the 1942-43 commentary on the Introduction to the *Phenomenology*. 3) The 1957 lecture on 'The Onto-theological Constitution of Metaphysics,' based on a seminar on the *Science of Logic*, and the accompanying 1957 text on 'The Principle of Identity'. These three moments can also be characterized as marking three distinct attitudes adopted by Heidegger towards Hegel: 1) a simple refusal of the Hegelian problematic, 2) an attempt to assimilate Hegel into Heidegger's own project, and 3) a complicated 'setting at a distance which wants to be an appropriation'. Denise Souche-Dagues, 'The Dialogue between Hegel and Heidegger'. Quotation at pp. 246-247.

lecture series on the opening chapters of the *Phenomenology of Spirit*, a reading that is centred on the problematic of *finitude*. Heidegger takes up this challenge concerning finitude and infinitude in reading the 'Consciousness' and 'Truth of Self-Certainty' chapters of Hegel's *Phenomenology*. It is also pursued and deepened in the later (1942/3) commentary on the 'Introduction' to the *Phenomenology*, the essay entitled 'Hegel's Concept of Experience' published in *Holzwege* in 1950.[14] In his lectures on the *Phenomenology*, Heidegger explicitly situates his critical dialogue with Hegel in the context of the post-Kantian metaphysics of the self-conscious subject. The confrontation between Hegel and Heidegger takes place on the terrain of *the problematic of finitude*, the 'crossing' between Hegel's conceptualization of the infinity of spirit and Heidegger's thinking of the finitude of Being. As Heidegger remarks:

> In our obligation to the first and last inherent necessities of philosophy, we shall try to *encounter* Hegel on *the problematic of finitude*. This means, according to what we said earlier, that through a confrontation with *Hegel's* problematic of infinitude we shall try to create, on the basis of our own inquiry into finitude, *the* kinship needed to reveal the spirit of Hegel's philosophy (HPS 38).

Heidegger's aim here is clear: to continue the task of a critical *Destruktion* of the history of ontology through a confrontation between the Hegelian problematic of finitude and Heidegger's own inquiry into finitude, and in so doing to provide the common problematic for a 'thinking dialogue' with Hegel on the question of Being.

Although Hegel 'ousted finitude from philosophy' by sublating it within the infinitude of reason, this was only an 'incidental finitude', Heidegger claims, a conception inscribed within the metaphysical tradition that Hegel was forced to take up and transmit (HPS 38). As distinct from Kant, with Hegel infinitude becomes a more significant problem than finitude, since the interest of speculative reason is to suspend all oppositions within the rational totality of thought-determinations. In this sense, Heidegger understands the project of post-Kantian idealism to consist in the systematic attempt to overcome the 'relative' knowledge of finite consciousness (in the sense of object-dependent knowledge of otherness) in favour of *the absolute knowledge* of speculative reason (in the sense of a no longer 'relative' or object-dependent self-knowledge). As ab-solving or *detaching* itself from the relativity of consciousness, absolute knowledge *detaches* itself from relative cognition such that consciousness becomes aware of itself or becomes *self-consciousness*. As I shall presently discuss, Heidegger's interpretation of consciousness thus rests on the assumption that the entire phenomenological exposition adopts the standpoint of absolute knowing in the sense of an *absolvent* knowledge that has absolved itself from any dependency on the consciousness of objects (HPS 51). It is only with the *unity* of consciousness and self-consciousness in *reason* that knowledge becomes '*purely unbounded, purely absolved, absolute knowledge*' (HPS

---

14. Heidegger, 'Hegel's Concept of Experience' in *Off the Beaten Track*, ed. and trans. Julian Young and Kenneth Maly, Cambridge, Cambridge University Press, 2002, pp. 86-156, (henceforth HCE).

16). Phenomenology can thus be characterized as 'the *absolute self-presentation of reason (ratio*—logos), whose essence and actuality Hegel finds in *absolute spirit*' (HPS 30).[15]

### a) The Presupposition of the Absolute and the Phenomenological 'We'

A decisive aspect of Heidegger's interpretation of the *Phenomenology* is the claim 'that *Hegel presupposes already at the beginning what he achieves at the end*'—namely absolute knowledge (HPS 30). Absolute knowledge must be presupposed from the outset of the exposition: 'if we do not already from the beginning know in the mode of absolute knowledge', then we cannot truly understand the *Phenomenology* (HPS 33). Hegel, Heidegger continues, presupposes that the absolute is 'with us, in and for itself, all along' (PS ¶ 73). Indeed, Heidegger takes this statement to capture Hegel's fundamental position.

This raises the question: who is the 'we' in Heidegger's reading of Hegel? Heidegger's interpretation presupposes that the *Phenomenology* begins absolutely with the absolute, and consequently that the phenomenological observer is already in possession of absolute knowledge. Indeed, Heidegger insists that we reject interpretations that take the *Phenomenology* to be 'an introduction to philosophy' leading from 'the so-called natural consciousness ... to a genuine speculative philosophical knowledge' (HPS 29). Heidegger's *ontological* interpretation emphasizes, rather, the unfolding of absolute knowledge as a fundamental-ontological presupposition. We must have already abandoned the 'natural attitude' of everyday consciousness, 'not just partially, but totally', if we are properly to understand phenomenological experience (HPS 33).

This abrupt dismissal of any propaedeutic or 'educative' interpretation of the *Phenomenology* as a *Bildungsprozeß* is maintained in the essay 'Hegel's Concept of Experience'. Heidegger again rejects here traditional interpretations of the *Phenomenology* as an 'edificatory' introduction to philosophical science, a propaedeutic for 'natural consciousness' to educate it to the level of philosophical or absolute knowledge: 'in the opinion of philosophy even today, the phenomenology of spirit is an *itinerarium*, a description of a journey, which is escorted by everyday consciousness toward the scientific knowledge of philosophy' (HCE 107). Such approaches, for Heidegger, fail to comprehend the ontological meaning of the *Phenomenology* as the self-presentation of the absolute in its presence (*parousia*) to us (HCE 109). For '[t]he presentation of phenomenal knowledge', Heidegger tells us, 'is not a route which natural consciousness can tread' (HPS 108).[16]

---

15. For Heidegger, Hegel's understanding of reason basically fulfils the traditional conception of the Greek *logos*, via its transformation into the Latin *ratio*, and later development as reason or *Vernunft* in conjunction with the traditional discipline of 'logic'. This explains Hegel presentation of the conceptual and categorical structure of the Absolute, which simultaneously integrates the basic metaphysical positions of the Western tradition from Greek ontology to transcendental idealism, in terms of a 'science of logic'.

16. On the other hand, Heidegger states a few pages later 'that natural consciousness is alive in all shapes of spirit; it lives in each spiritual shape in its own way, including (and especially) that shape of

It is worth mentioning the obvious difficulty that this interpretation is sharply at odds with numerous explicit statements in the text: Hegel describes the phenomenology as a 'ladder' to the standpoint of science [*Wissenschaft*] (PS ¶ 26), as an 'education' of the individual consciousness which repeats the formative path of universal spirit as though 'in a silhouette' (PS ¶ 28), a 'path of *doubt*' or even 'path of *despair*' (PS ¶ 78), and as the 'detailed history of the *education* [*Bildung*] of consciousness itself to the standpoint of Science' (PS ¶ 78). Heidegger's interpretation seems *prima facie* to contradict Hegel's repeated assertions in the *Phenomenology*.

Heidegger's response is to point to the fundamental-ontological significance of the project of phenomenology. In Heidegger's *ontological* interpretation, the phenomenological 'we' has from the outset 'lost the option of being this or that person and thus of being, randomly, an ego' (HPS 48). Rather, Heidegger's reading implies that the phenomenological 'we' is to be understood as a 'subjectivized' version of Heidegger's 'fundamental ontologist' already in possession of absolute knowledge; the 'we' refers to those who have already attained to absolute, fundamental-ontological knowledge of the whole.

Heidegger's fundamental-ontological interpretation of the 'we' can be contrasted, I suggest, with a *historicist-propaedeutic* interpretation, which emphasizes the *historical* character of the process of educative cultivation to the level of Science or *Wissenschaft*. The phenomenological 'we,' on this interpretation, refers to the culturally and historically situated ideal or imputed readers of the *Phenomenology*: philosophically cultivated individuals who desire, but do not yet possess, Science, and are therefore to be educated to the level of speculative philosophy in order to transform their self-understanding [*Besinnung*] as historical subjects of modernity. The *Phenomenology* on this view is a philosophical-historical propaedeutic to Science that has an intrinsically *dialogical* structure: the cognitive claims of a given figure [*Gestalt*] of consciousness are presented by natural consciousness in its 'own voice,' while the structural inadequacies of each cognitive attitude, according to its own standard of truth, emerges for 'us' as phenomenological observers. 'We' can grasp the self-testing of consciousness and the immanent transitions to progressively more complex and integrated figures of consciousness in a manner that ought to be intelligible to the superseded forms of natural consciousness as well, though usually *is not* due to the latter's basic 'unthinking inertia' (PS ¶ 80). Indeed, for Hegel, natural consciousness is typically prone to existential inertia or thoughtlessness, sentimentality, lack of reflection, and historical amnesia concerning its own historical-phenomenological experience (PS ¶ 80). At the conclusion of the phenomenological drama, we realise that we have been observing the philosophico-historical conditions of our *own* experience as dissatisfied modern subjects. Absolute knowledge, as the philosophical self-comprehension of the history of spirit, is the *result* that is also the *ground* of our experience of self-alienated modernity.

---

absolute knowledge which occurs as absolute metaphysics and is at time visible to a few thinkers only' (HCE 112). This remark does not seem reconcilable with Heidegger's claim that natural consciousness is barred from the phenomenological path.

Why assume this historicist-propaedeutic reading of the phenomenological 'we'? One reason is that it avoids the difficulty in Heidegger's ontological interpretation that presupposing absolute knowledge seems to make redundant the project of a phenomenology before it even begins. In Heidegger's interpretation, the *Phenomenology* quickly becomes an absolute ontology or all-consuming science of the absolute, rather than an introduction to the speculative system. If we presuppose that the 'we' is already in possession of absolute knowledge, we also presuppose knowledge of the categories and concepts underlying the figures of consciousness and self-conscious reason depicted in the *Phenomenology*. This means that Hegel's claims concerning what the phenomenology is to perform (to be a 'ladder' to Science, a path towards philosophical self-education, an introduction to the speculative system as a whole) become nonsensical. The presupposition of an absolute standpoint not only renders phenomenology superfluous but makes it collapse before it even begins.

An historicist-propaedeutic interpretation answers this difficulty by pointing out that the immanent phenomenological exposition is precisely what educates 'us' both to recognize the experiences of consciousness as historical figures of spirit and to recognize ourselves within this experience. The phenomenological path of self-consummating scepticism is supposed to be a path that the so-called 'natural consciousness' of the (historically situated) reader can tread, precisely in order to learn that its self-alienation can be overcome *in thought* through the conceptual comprehension of its historico-philosophical experience. The historically achieved level of conceptual-philosophical understanding—what Hegel called the 'reflection philosophy of subjectivity' culminating in Kantian idealism—provides the only 'presupposition' necessary for comprehending the transformation from 'natural' or rather *philosophically naïve* consciousness to the level of speculative thought. As Hegel states, the philosophically naïve reader 'has the right to demand that Science should at least provide him with the ladder to this standpoint, show him this standpoint within himself' (PS ¶ 26); a right based upon the individual's 'absolute independence', the *right of subjectivity* that is one of the distinctive achievements of modernity.[17] The naïve consciousness need not be excluded from phenomenology as a path that it cannot tread. Rather, the modern subject can claim its right of subjectivity in being educated to the standpoint of Science by climbing (and thereby suspending) Hegel's phenomenological ladder.

Heidegger's response to this issue is to point to the inherently *circular* character of the *Phenomenology* that, like all philosophy, 'merely unfolds its *presupposition*' (HPS 36). In this case, it is the absolute knowledge of Being that allows the Being of self-conscious spirit to comprehend itself. Heidegger's strongly 'circular' interpretation, however, faces the problem of accounting for Hegel's *rejection* of the notion that philosophy develops out of a fundamental presupposition (as in Hegel's criticisms of Reinhold's basic presuppositions of philosophizing). For He-

---

17. 'The intelligible form of Science', according to Hegel, 'is the way open and equally accessible to everyone, and consciousness as it approaches Science justly demands that it be able to attain to rational knowledge by way of the ordinary understanding' (PS ¶ 13).

gel, rather, the end emerges out of a process which is itself included in the result. Hegel's fundamental hermeneutical principle is that 'the whole is the true'—the truth emerges as a result of the whole process and the whole process in its self-unfolding is the site of the emergence of truth. The phenomenological exposition is therefore not the unfolding (and legitimation) of the foundational truth of an initial presupposition (such as the absolute knowledge of Being), but rather the path of absolute or self-consummating *skepsis*. It is the unfolding of the *untruth* of whatever presuppositions consciousness makes about itself, the untruth of its own (limited and self-contradictory) standards of knowing and truth; this 'untruth' is thus itself a necessary 'moment' of truth as it is disclosed in the whole developmental movement. Indeed, it is only the failure of the prejudices of natural consciousness that produces the possibility of Science's claim to be philosophical knowledge 'without presuppositions'.

The *Phenomenology* thus presents the demonstration of our 'liberation from the opposition of consciousness' (SL 49), and attainment of the speculative level of pure thought-determinations that is the only 'presupposition' of the *Logic* as such. It is in this sense that Science begins with the matter itself [*Sache selbst*], without any external reflections.[18] Hegel's project in the *Phenomenology* is therefore radically *anti-foundationalist*: Hegel rejects all (Cartesian or Reinholdian) foundationalism in favour of a self-constructing process through which the disparity between knowing and truth is finally overcome. As Hegel remarks, the *Phenomenology* describes the coming-to-be of *Wissenschaft*, a becoming that is 'quite different from the 'foundation' of Science; least of all will it be like the rapturous enthusiasm which, like a shot from a pistol, begins straight away with absolute knowledge, and makes short work of other standpoints by declaring that it takes no notice of them' (PS ¶ 27). In asserting absolute knowledge as the absolute presupposition of the *Phenomenology*, Heidegger appears not to have heeded Hegel's important claim that the absolute as a result is also the ground of the whole process of its own becoming.

### b) *Heidegger on Finitude*

This brings us to the 'crossroads' of which Heidegger speaks in relation to Hegel: the problem of the *infinite* in Hegel's and Heidegger's understanding of *finitude* in relation to the meaning of Being. As Heidegger asks:

> Is the understanding of Being absolvent, and is the absolvent absolute? Or is what Hegel represents as in the *Phenomenology of Spirit* as absolvence merely transcendence in disguise, i.e., finitude? (HPS 65)

Heidegger is concerned to ask whether Being in its essence is *finite* and how this finitude is to be understood with reference to *Being* rather than in relation to *beings*. This is in contrast with what Heidegger takes to be Hegel's conception of

---

18. See Stephen Houlgate's discussion of the significance of Hegel's project of a speculative logic that satisfies the (modern) historical demand for 'free, *self-grounding* thought'. S. Houlgate, *Hegel, Nietzsche, and the Criticism of Metaphysics*, Cambridge, Cambridge University Press, 1986, pp. 41ff.

Being qua *infinity*, in which 'the infinity of absolute knowledge determines the truth of Being', and does so such that 'it has already sublated everything that is finite into itself' (HPS 75). For Heidegger, Hegel's sublation of finitude means that all philosophy moves *in* and *as* this sublation of finitude, which occurs in the process of a *dialectical* movement. Heidegger thus raises the question of the finitude of Being, a question that has hitherto not been raised but which has implicitly 'motivated previous metaphysics' (HPS 75). This is why the confrontation with Hegel over the problem of finitude and infinitude is 'inherently and historically necessary' as well as being a productive precondition for thinking through the question of Being.

Let us turn to Heidegger's account of the Hegelian concept of infinity. Heidegger indicates two aspects to this concept: 1) Hegel's grounding of the problem of Being in the *logos*, manifested in Hegel's 'logical' account of thinking as speculative knowledge or *dialectic*; and 2), the transposition of this logical grounding in Descartes' turn towards the *ego cogito*, manifested in 'Hegel's fundamental thesis', as formulated by Heidegger: 'Substance is in truth subject'[19] (HPS 76-77). Heidegger thus describes the Hegelian concept of infinity as having both a 'logical' and 'subjective' grounding. The *Phenomenology* undertakes the proper 'subjective' grounding of infinity *in* the subject and *as* subject, while the proper 'logical' grounding is developed in the *Science of Logic* (HPS 77). What is the relationship between the 'logical' and the 'subjective' grounding of infinity? On Heidegger's reading, the concept of infinity is 'inherently and necessarily grounded in the second [subjective] one' (HPS 77). The logical meaning of infinity is grounded in the infinite character of self-consciousness, which is in fact the reverse of Hegel's procedure, namely to point to self-consciousness or subjectivity as a 'formal' manifestation of the logical structure of infinity.

We can therefore raise certain questions here about Heidegger's interpretation of infinity and self-consciousness, and his claim that the logical meaning of the infinite is grounded in the structure of self-consciousness (rather than the reverse). Indeed, Hegel's *own* account of the infinite character of self-consciousness emphasizes its *inadequacy* as an exemplification of the true infinite. For it is precisely because of its *subjectivity* that self-consciousness is not the full or complete manifestation of the infinite (understood as self-subsisting independence that incorporates the finite within itself). To be sure, self-consciousness is the 'existing Concept', as previously discussed, but certainly not its full reality or concrete actualization, which is rather *Spirit* in its whole developed articulation. In this case—namely the standpoint of self-consciousness as itself a *Gestalt*, or series of figures in the *Phenomenology*, sublated by Reason—we have the finite (subject) as infinite, but not the infinite (spirit) as finite, that is, articulated as a concrete individuality. The result is an opposition between an abstract self-identity of self-consciousness that attempts to dominate and integrate otherness, an otherness

---

19. We should note in passing that this formulation significantly alters, in a rather one-sided and rigid manner, Hegel's own thesis in the *Phenomenology*: that the True is to be grasped 'not only as Substance, but equally as Subject' (PS ¶ 17).

that is reproduced in this very process such that the opposition between self and other can never be overcome.

For clarification of this point we must turn to Hegel's critique of the 'bad' or 'spurious' infinity of Kantian self-consciousness (and its Fichtean variant) in the *Science of Logic*. Hegel is concerned here in particular with the practical effects of the opposition between finite and infinite within the 'spurious' infinite belonging to the analytic understanding or *Verstand*. The latter—in the form of a 'quantitative progress to infinity which continually surmounts the limit it is powerless to remove, and perpetually falls back into it'—is exalted in the philosophy of reflection as something ultimate and even divine (SL 228). Within the sphere of practical reason, the 'progress to infinity' is likewise exalted in the feeling of the sublime, in which the subject, to quote Kant in the *Critique of Practical Reason*, 'raises himself in thought above the place he occupies in the world of sense, reaching out to infinity' (SL 229). This exaltation of the limitless progress indicates, for Hegel, rather the failure or succumbing of thought: the 'bad' infinite of the Kantian moral subject results in a 'wearisome repetition' in which a limit vanishes and reappears, is displaced into a beyond in order to be overcome, but in being overcome is once again displaced into another beyond, and so on *ad infinitum*. What results from such a endless progression is only the feeling of *impotence* in relation to this unattainable infinite as an *ought-to-be*, an alienation generated by the reflective understanding which attempts, but always fails, to *master* the finite (SL 229).

Hegel's critique of the Kantian account of self-consciousness points to the deleterious moral-practical effects of the opposition between freedom and nature. Within Kant's account, the infinity of outer sensuous intuition is opposed to the infinite of self-consciousness in its abstract universality. The self-conscious subject finds that its freedom lies in its (abstract) self-identity that is defined by excluding and opposing itself to 'the fullness of nature and Geist', which inevitably confronts it as a *beyond* (SL 231). The contradiction that emerges here is the same as that which structures the infinite progression: that between 'a returnedness-into-self which is at the same time immediately an out-of-selfness' (SL 231). The contradiction emerges between a self-identity defined by opposition to an other that is essential to the constitution of this self-identity, but which at the same time contradicts its essential character as a solitary self-relation or *solus ipse*. The result is a perpetual *longing* reminiscent of the self-alienation of the unhappy consciousness and 'beautiful soul' of romanticism: the unsatisfiable desire to overcome the breach between the solitary and self-determining 'void of the ego', and the fullness of sensuous otherness, where the latter is negated by self-consciousness yet still present in the form of an unattainable beyond.

The practical implications of this deficient form of self-identity and universality are highly significant. Hegel argues that the antithesis between finite and infinite—or 'the manifold world and the ego raised to its freedom'—results in a relation of *domination* in which the infinite fails to master the finite. Self-consciousness, in determining itself in its abstract self-identity, proceeds to determine nature and attempts to liberate itself from it: the result is an *objectification of the finite* (nature) and *reification of the infinite* (the free subject) in which the power of the ego over the non-ego (sense and outer nature) is conceived such that morality can and ought to progress while the power of finite sensuousness is diminished (SL 231). The moral project of achieving a perfect adequacy of the free will in relation to the universal moral law is in fact an unending progress to infinity, an achievement that is 'represented as an *absolutely unattainable* beyond' (SL 231). The struggle and meaning of morality is defined precisely through this unattainability of moral truth as an overcoming of the opposition between infinite freedom and finite sensuousness.

The conclusion I want to draw from this analysis is that it is impossible for the logical Concept of infinity in its true sense to be grounded in the infinity of self-consciousness, as Heidegger maintains. Indeed, Hegel's critique of the *subjectivism* of the infinitude of self-consciousness argues explicitly against Heidegger's thesis. For the infinitude of self-consciousness remains a 'bad' infinite mired within an insurmountable opposition to the finite that takes the form of an endless progress towards an unattainable beyond. Heidegger thus misattributes to Hegel the very conception of the spurious infinite that Hegel attempts to overcome.[20]

## III. HEGEL'S CONCEPT OF EXPERIENCE

Heidegger's 1942/43 interpretation of the Introduction to the *Phenomenology*—the essay 'Hegel's Concept of Experience'—is his most intensive treatment of Hegel's philosophy as a whole. Here I shall present a brief analysis with particular reference to the role of the ontological difference. For the critical question is whether Hegel actually does neglect the ontological difference in the exhibiting of the dialectical experience of consciousness, or indeed within the unfolding of dialectical-speculative logic. My aim here as previously is to question Heidegger's reading of Hegel and to suggest that Hegel's thought cannot be so readily sequestered as the culminating phase of modern subject-metaphysics, as Heidegger and his twentieth-century followers will argue.

As Heidegger famously declared, modern philosophy is defined by the search for an absolute foundation for knowledge in 'unconditional self-certainty' (inaugurated by Descartes and critically delimited by Kant). Hegel inherits and completes this search for an absolute or self-grounding knowledge that is grounded in the unconditional self-certainty of self-consciousness. Indeed, Hegel is the first philosopher, Heidegger notes, to fully possess the terrain of self-certain subjectivity once the Cartesian '*fundamentum inconcussum*' is thought of as the absolute itself. With Hegel, the absolute, Heidegger explains, is spirit:

> that which is present to itself [*bei sich*] in the certainty of unconditional self-knowing. Real knowledge of beings as beings now becomes the absolute knowledge of the absolute in its absoluteness (HCE 97).

---

20. Indeed, Heidegger avoids direct reference to the crucial distinction between the infinite of the understanding and the infinite of reason, relying instead on the exposition of the infinite provided in the Jena logic (HPS 77-78).

Heidegger's formulations are certainly legitimate as far as Hegel's claim to develop a system of absolute knowledge is concerned. From an ontological point of view, Heidegger develops in this connection his fundamental thesis concerning the meaning of the *Phenomenology*: that Hegel presupposes the presence or *parousia* of the absolute to us, and that the absolute wills to disclose its Being through (absolute) knowledge. Hegel's aim from the beginning of the *Phenomenology*, Heidegger remarks, is 'to indicate the absolute in its parousia among us' (HCE 98). Indeed, Heidegger takes Hegel's remark—that 'the absolute is from the start in and for itself with us and intends to be with us'—to be the fundamental statement of Hegel's conception of Being (HCE 98). Hegel's conception of Being is articulated in this 'being-with-us *(parousia)*' of the absolute, which is 'in itself already the mode in which the light of truth, the absolute itself, beams [*anstrahlt*] upon us' (HCE 98). The absolute *is* as the ontological horizon of Being in which beings are disclosed to us in their radiant and intelligible presence.

Heidegger then shifts emphasis in order to develop a thesis crucial for his later thinking: that in the course of modern philosophy, from Descartes and Kant to Hegel and Nietzsche, the meaning of Being is progressively *subjectivized* (culminating in the essence of modern technics or *das Ge-stell*). This thesis of a *subjectivization of Being* is a central feature of Heidegger's reading of the *Phenomenology* and of Hegel's crucial role in the completion of Western metaphysics. According to Heidegger, Hegel takes complete possession of the terrain of subjectivity by transforming it into self-knowing and self-willing spirit. Philosophy becomes 'science' or *Wissenschaft* in the absolute metaphysics of Hegel precisely because 'it takes its meaning from the essence of the subject's self-certainty which knows itself unconditionally' (HCE 99). Philosophical science is thus the completion of the Cartesian project of a self-grounding knowledge that has its absolute foundation in the unconditional self-certainty of the knowing subject.

What does Heidegger mean here by the 'subject'? Since Leibniz, Heidegger claims, entities have been understood to be whatever are intelligible as representable for a cognitive subject. The subject, in speculative metaphysics,

> is now that which truly (which now means 'certainly') lies before us, the *subiectum*, the *hypokeimenon*, which philosophy since antiquity has had to recognize as that which presences (HCE 99).

The subject has its Being in the representing relation to the object, and in *being* this representing relationship it also represents itself to itself as *subject*. The mode of Being of the modern metaphysical subject is *self-certainty*, in the sense of a self-conditioned, or rather, *unconditional self-knowing*. This mode of Being as unconditional self-knowing is what Heidegger calls the *subjectity* [*Subjektität*] of the subject:

> The subjectity of the subject is constituted by the subject being a subject, i.e., by the subject being in a subject-object relation. Subjectity consists in unconditional self-knowing (HCE 100).

The Being of the subject is *subjectity* in the form of self-grounding self-knowledge, which Hegel raises to the level of speculative science. This unconditional self-awareness, which for Heidegger is the goal of the *Phenomenology*, articulates the subjectity of the subject and provides the basis for conceptualizing 'being *qua* being' [*das Seiende als Seiende*] as a mode of self-grounding self-knowledge. Interpreting the beingness of beings as *subjectity* means that Being is 'subjectivized'; subjectity in Hegel is now tantamount to 'the absoluteness of the absolute' (HCE 100).

A problem arises here that merits further consideration. How can the subject, whose Being is defined by subjectity, be considered *absolute*? As we saw earlier, the subjectity of the subject is defined in terms of the Being of the subject-object relation, which is thereby raised to the level of unconditional self-knowledge. But the very notion of a subject as 'absolute' seems self-contradictory, since the subject, according to Heidegger, remains inscribed within the paradigm of the subject-object relationship, and thus marked by its 'relative' status, that is, its insurmountable finitude. According to Heidegger, however, absolute knowledge is grounded in the Being of the subject-object relation *qua* subjectity, a move that reduces speculative knowledge to the level of merely 'relative' knowledge. It is not clear, then, how the figure of the subjectity of the subject—given its irreducible finitude and object/other dependence—can at the same time be raised to the level of the 'absoluteness of the absolute', as Heidegger maintains.

A final point to consider in Heidegger's interpretation is the problem of the ontological difference within the *Phenomenology*. According to Heidegger, this fundamental difference between Being and beings provides the un-thought origin and element of metaphysics in its entire history from Plato and Aristotle to Hegel and Nietzsche. This is to be understood as a history of decline [*Verfallsgeschichte*], namely as the *forgetting* of the ontological difference and indeed of the question of Being. Heidegger introduces the ontological difference into his interpretation of Hegel's *Phenomenology*, aligning ontological knowledge with 'Being' and ontic or natural consciousness with knowledge of 'beings'. Hegel's 'natural consciousness' is thus akin to ontic or pre-ontological consciousness that pertains to beings as present to consciousness. Ontological consciousness, on the other hand, describes the ab-solvent standpoint of the phenomenological 'we', those fundamental ontologists who heed the Being of beings in absolute knowledge.

Indeed, Heidegger proceeds to assimilate Hegel's 'natural consciousness' to fallen or inauthentic Da-sein, which covers over any authentic ontological experience of originary temporality or indeed of Being as such (HCE 111-112). As Heidegger remarks:

> In its representation of beings, natural consciousness does not attend to being; nonetheless, it must do so. It cannot help but participate in the representation of the being of beings in general because without the light of being it cannot even be lost *amidst* beings (HCE 111-112).

Here the ontological difference is explicitly invoked in order to clarify Hegel's distinction between the *for-itself* standpoint of consciousness and the *for-us* standpoint of the phenomenological observer. The very possibility of phenomenology is opened up by the ontological difference between beings apprehended by natural consciousness and Being as comprehended by the phenomenological 'we'.

Drawing on the analytic of Da-sein in *Being and Time*, Heidegger interprets Hegel's 'consciousness' as *ontic* or preontological consciousness whose object comprises *beings* taken as *representable*. At the same time, consciousness is also 'ontological consciousness' in the sense of having an awareness of the beingness of beings as *objectivity*. The parallel Heidegger draws here refers to the ontic or preontological understanding belonging to Da-sein in its everyday being-in-the-world; consciousness too has such a preontological understanding even though consciousness only represents the 'beingness of beings' as objective presence. Heidegger thus attempts to absorb Hegelian phenomenology within the project of thinking the difference between Being and beings. Phenomenology is the process of making explicit this implicit difference between ontic and ontological truth, of comprehending the (unthematized) experience of the ontological difference between Being and beings.

Heidegger's theses concerning the ontological meaning of self-consciousness and the subjectivization of the absolute are thus brought together in his interpretation of the dialectical movement of *experience* as naming 'the Being of beings'. Hegel's concept of '*experience*,' according to Heidegger, names 'phenomena, as phenomena, the *on hei on*,' or beings thought in their beingness (HCE 135). 'Experience', Heidegger argues, is thus now a word of *Being* designating the *subjectity of the subject*. Accordingly, the dialectical experience of consciousness involves a comparison between *ontic* preontological knowledge and *ontological* knowledge. A dialogue or *legein* takes place between these two poles in which the claims of ontic and ontological consciousness are heard (HCE 138). This dialogical character of ontic-ontological consciousness prompts Hegel to call the movement of consciousness 'dialectical', where the latter is understood ontologically as the experience of consciousness defined as subjectity: 'Experience is the beingness of beings', Heidegger states, 'which is determined as *subiectum* on the basis of subjectity' (HCE 138).

Heidegger's ontological reading concludes with the 'turning' of natural consciousness towards Being or the presence of the absolute: the inversion of consciousness is construed as returning us—the phenomenological ontologists 'who are attentive, skeptically, to the being of beings' (HCE 153)—to our nature, which consists in our being in the *parousia* of the absolute. As phenomenological ontologists, we allow the ontic-ontological dialogue of experience—the *parousia* of the absolute—to unfold according to its will to be with us or disclose itself in ontological knowledge.

At this point Heidegger articulates the explicit connection between the metaphysics of subjectivity and the modern understanding of Being disclosed within the horizon of the essence of technology. As we have seen, Heidegger argues that the absolute discloses itself as subjectity. This modern understanding of Being as subjectity, which culminates with Hegelian absolute spirit and Nietzschean will to power, determines modernity as the epoch of technics. Heidegger thus connects his critique of metaphysics with the confrontation with modernity: the critical encounter with technology as completed subject-metaphysics is announced through Hegel's interpretation of Being as subjectity. As Heidegger states:

> Within subjectity, every being as such becomes an object. All beings are beings from out of and within steadfast reliability. In the age of subjectity [i.e., modernity], in which the essence of technology is grounded, if nature as being is put in opposition to consciousness, then this nature is only another name for beings as the objects of modern technological objectification which indiscriminately attacks the continued existence of things and men (HCE 144).

What is striking in this analysis is its proximity to Hegel's *own* critique of the subject-metaphysics, or what Hegel elsewhere calls the 'metaphysics of reflection'. Hegel too criticizes the practical effects of the principle of abstract identity and universality that results in the obliteration of particularity, the domination of otherness, and the reification of subjectivity. Modernity, for Heidegger, is the era of subjectity and hence of technological objectification. Modern technology is itself nothing other than natural consciousness that 'has at last made feasible the unlimited, self-assuring production of all beings through the inexorable objectification of each and every thing' (HCE 112). But as we have seen, Hegel's own critique of the subjectivization of the Concept, the 'bad' infinity of the understanding, also emphasizes the domination, reification, and objectification resulting from modern subject-metaphysics. In this sense, Heidegger's critical remarks provide a striking repetition of Hegel's own critical confrontation with modern metaphysics of the subject and its moral-practical implications. In this respect, the dialogue between Hegel and Heidegger finds its shared matter of thinking in the critical confrontation with the metaphysics of modernity.

To conclude, in Heidegger's reading of Hegel's *Phenomenology*, the need to overcome the self-alienation of the unhappy consciousness becomes the need to overcome the objectifying thinking of ontic consciousness in order to return to the *parousia* of the absolute. In Heidegger's confrontation with Hegel, however, the *negativity* of the historical experience of spirit is lost in favour of a recovery of the forgotten 'experience' of the originary question of Being. Instead of Hegel's dynamic historical unfolding of intersubjective spirit we have Heidegger's *Verfallsgeschichte* of a perennial forgetting of Being. Heidegger's confrontation with Hegelian metaphysics thus remains determined by a philosophical metanarrative culminating not in freedom of subjectivity (as for Hegel) but in the nihilism of modern technics.

The main difficulty here, as I have argued, is Heidegger's failure to grasp the *intersubjective* constitution of self-consciousness that provides the basis for Hegel's dialectical interpretation of reason and spirit. For Hegel's lasting legacy for the metaphysics of subjectivity is precisely his move from the abstract self-identity of formal models of self-consciousness (the Kantian and Fichtean 'I = I') towards a conception of social and cultural *intersubjectivity* as a concrete self-identity-in-otherness achieved through mutual recognition. Indeed, Hegel's project is nothing less than an attempt to think the experience of modernity; to comprehend the history and conditions of the formation of modern subjects, and to do so in the most conceptually systematic manner possible.

Heidegger's interpretation, however, neglects this intersubjective dimension of Hegel's *Phenomenology*. This is particularly evident in Heidegger's 'ontological' interpretation of the phenomenological 'we', which equates it with the fundamental ontologist of *Being and Time,* and hence claims that the *Phenomenology* is grounded in a fundamental presupposition—the absolute knowledge of Being. I have argued that this is an implausible interpretation of the project of the *Phenomenology* that fails to do justice to Hegel's attempt to provide a 'presuppositionless' introduction to philosophical science.

In these respects, we could say that the 'thinking dialogue' between Hegel and Heidegger remains perhaps a philosophical monologue. Heidegger's fine ear for the un-thought at the heart of metaphysics—so brilliantly attuned to Kant and profoundly engaged with Nietzsche—seems somewhat deaf in the case of Hegel. For Heidegger fails to heed that the nihilism of metaphysics is not only the forgetting of Being but also the experience of freedom.[21] Nonetheless, the Hegelian and Heideggerian narratives of metaphysics—which mirror and invert one another—still provide a dual horizon for our own questioning of metaphysics and modernity; this is why the dialogue between Hegel and Heidegger remains philosophically important for us today. Genuine dialogue, however, requires reciprocity, an engagement with the other; but perhaps we cannot demand this of a thinker exclusively devoted to the mystery of Being. Hegel once remarked, as though anticipating Heidegger,

> the high sense for the Eternal, the Holy, the Infinite, strides along in the robes of a high priest, on a path that is from the first no path, but has immediate being at its centre, the genius of profound original insight and lofty flashes of inspiration. But just as profundity of this kind still does not reveal the source of essential being, so, too, these sky-rockets of inspiration and not yet the empyrean. True thoughts and scientific insight are only to be won through the labour of the Concept (PS ¶ 70).

---

21. As Heidegger sees more sympathetically in the case of Schelling's attempt to overcome metaphysics. See Martin Heidegger, *Schelling's Treatise on the Essence of Human Freedom*, trans. Joan Stambaugh, Athens/Ohio, Ohio University Press, 1985.

# 13

# Hegel, Derrida and the Subject

## Simon Lumsden

'There has never been The Subject for anyone.... The Subject is a fable.'[1] Within the works of all the major figures in the history of philosophy Derrida argues there are 'aporias, fictions and fabrications' that present as it were internal disruptions within the texts themselves that 'would have at least the virtue of de-simplifying, of "de-homogenizing" the reference to something like The Subject.'[2] This would appear to make the narrative of the history of western metaphysics portrayed by Heidegger decidedly problematic and ostensibly renders the narrative of presence adopted by Deconstruction as itself not an authoritative depiction of the history of philosophy. But this fable of 'the Subject' is nevertheless powerful and an edifice of concepts and method has (rightly or wrongly) grown around it. It is the discourse of mastery, identity and self-knowledge against which Derrida defined his project, terms that have been most often associated in his writing with Hegel's thought.

Despite Derrida's willingness to see fractures and limits in the great works of the canon of philosophy in figures from Plato to Husserl, one can only understand the development of notions such as trace and *différance* and so on in response to a dominating and uniform tendency within the tradition. Deconstruction requires that myth be powerful and real. How would we interpret his early critique of the Hegelian dialectic in 'From Restricted to General Economy' as a totalizing machine unless that myth was clearly taken to be representative of the dominant strain of the philosophical tradition? Without granting the force of this dominant strand Derrida's later turning of the critique of presence back upon Heidegger would be an empty criticism.

Derrida asserts that any 'post-deconstructive' re-conception of the subject would have to be 'a non-coincidence with self' and 'the finite experience of non-

---

1. Jacques Derrida, 'Eating Well' in E. Cadava et al (ed.), *Who Comes After the Subject*, London, Routledge, 1991, p. 102.
2. Derrida, 'Eating Well', p. 102.

identity to self'.[3] It will be argued here that such a description of subjectivity is not so clearly opposed to Hegel's conception of subjectivity which Derrida describes as 'absolute origin, pure will, identity to self, or presence to self of consciousness'.[4] When Hegel is stripped of his metaphysics of presence label considerable continuity of concern between Hegel's project and Derrida's. Of course there are substantive differences between these thinkers and their views of subjectivity diverge but the basis of that divergence is not because Hegel is the avatar of the philosopher of presence.

## I. THE SELF-PRESENT SUBJECT

The debate over and strategy for exiting the metaphysics of the subject has its locus in Heidegger's *Being and Time*. Derrida's discussion of this issue and many of his contemporaries has consistently reinforced the centrality of Heidegger's approach. In *Being and Time* and the lectures contemporaneous with that period the reflective model of subjectivity is largely equated with and indicative of the metaphysical tradition. This reflective subject is a subject that is self-identical, it is disclosed to itself in its reflection, its identity is self-contained and available to it. Dasein does not have this kind of self-relation; what is distinctive for Dasein is that 'in its very being, that Being is an issue for it'.[5] This relation to Being ensures that Dasein's self-relation cannot be self-identical. Its openness to Being is the fundamental condition of its subjectivity. Dasein's self-relation because it is fundamentally other directed cannot be understood as present to itself, it is not capable of anything like full self-disclosure, as the possibilities of its existence are given to it and it must adopt a relation to them: they do not issue from a world under its control. Whatever the differences between Heidegger and Derrida, and there are many, Derrida adopts his fundamental criticism of the metaphysics of presence. This comes out very clearly in a number of Derrida's early works, for example in *Speech and Phenomena*:

> Within the metaphysics of presence, within philosophy as knowledge of the presence of the object, as the being-before-oneself of knowledge in consciousness.... The history of being as presence, as self-presence in absolute knowledge, as consciousness of self in the infinity of *parousia*—this history is closed. The history of presence is closed, for history has never meant anything but the presentation [*Gegenwärtigung*] of Being, the production and recollection of beings in presence, as knowledge and mastery.[6]

This metaphysics of presence aspires to master objective being, it claims that being can be understood in Heidegger's terms ontically, and that being is definable

---

3. 'Eating Well' p. 102-3.
4. 'Eating Well' p. 102-3.
5. Martin Heidegger, *Being and Time*, trans. John Macquarrie and Edward Robinson, Oxford, Blackwell, 1962, p. 31.
6. Jacques Derrida, *Speech and Phenomena*, trans. David B. Allison, Evanston, Northwestern University Press, 1973 102

and knowable. Being is presented *exclusively* as something perceived, intuited and known, and is thereby reduced to an expression of the perceiving and knowing subject. Nothing epitomizes this movement more than Hegel's *aufhebung*, as we will see shortly.

Central to Heidegger's critique of the metaphysics of presence is a model of subjectivity that grounds the enterprise of modern philosophy. This subject has a privileged place in the interpretation of Being as substance

> The motive of this primary orientation toward the subject in modern philosophy is the opinion that this being which we ourselves are is given to the knower first as the only certain thing, that the subject is accessible immediately and with absolute certainty, that is, better known than all objects.[7]

Descartes' seminal move beyond ancient and medieval philosophy was to reformulate their concerns in such a way that rather than truth being disclosed in the world, truth is first to be had in the subject and from there it projects itself out onto the world. In this transition the modern movement is the grounding of meaning in the subject. In this shift of focus being comes to be understood as present-at-hand [*Vorhandensein*], that is available as an object of knowledge to subjectivity. Descartes surmised that such a project was only possible if it was adequately grounded. Heidegger argues that this is not a genuine new beginning just a dogmatic version of ancient philosophy: 'it became a mode of thought, that with the aid of traditional ontological concepts, seeks to gain a positively ontical knowledge of God, the soul and nature'.[8] It appropriates unquestioningly the assumptions of the older metaphysics in its 'turn to the subject' and simply extends this view of the world to the subject itself without even posing 'the question of the being of the subject'.[9] The purpose of this newly grounded subject serves simply to give a better foundation for the project of conceiving all things as objects or potential objects of knowledge. The assumption is that with proper grounding all objects of experience have the potential to be known. The self-present subject understands the mind-world relation as a one-way street of knower to known. There is nothing on this model that is surplus to the objects than the knowledge of them.

Derrida reads the main current of modern philosophy in very similar terms in his reading of Husserl as we saw in the passage of his from *Speech and Phenomena*. In other writings the idea of presence is inflected with a decidedly Hegelian flavour, the notion of *Aufhebung* encapsulates the tendency. The entire motif of presence as mastery, control and containment is explicitly thematized by this notion of *Aufhebung* [sublation]. As Derrida sees it, *Aufhebung* expresses the idea of presence as the positive method of philosophical inquiry. This is why Hegel forms such a neat point of differentiation with the deconstructive enterprise. With the notion of sublation [*Aufhebung*] Hegel appears to turn everything into *vorhanden*, nothing

---

7. Martin Heidegger, *Basic Problems of Phenomenology*, trans. Albert Hofstadter, Bloomington and Indianapolis, Indiana University Press, 1982, p. 123.

8. Heidegger, *Basic Problems of Phenomenology*, p. 124.

9. Heidegger, *Basic Problems of Phenomenology*, p. 124.

is lost every aspect of experience becomes available for the examination of the conscious subject; every object can be internalized. This program of mastering meaning and transforming all otherness into a repeatable and available object for thought requires an agent who can maintain that past, otherness and so on. Hegelian self-consciousness on this view embodies the *Aufhebung* and is unthinkable without it. Here self-consciousness masters itself because that self comes to be identified with the whole.[10] It is the 'unity of concept and consciousness' in Hegel's thought that allows the identification of the subject with the world.

> Truth is here the presence or presentation of essence as *Gewesenheit*, of *wesen* as having-been. Consciousness is the truth of man to the extent that man appears to himself in consciousness in his being-past, in his to-have-been, in his past surpassed and conserved, retained, interiorized and *relevé* [the French translation of *aufheben*].[11]

All meaning in this movement is tied to Man, all the structures of logic, phenomenology, even nature and spirit are all at the very least adumbrations of man. There is a transition from finite man assured of self-certainty in Descartes to a form of self-relation in Hegel that relates to itself in external world by seeing the world as subject.

> What is difficult to think today is an end of man which would not be organized by a dialectics of truth and negativity, an end which would not be a teleology in the first person plural. The we, which articulates natural and philosophical consciousness with each other in the *Phenomenology of Spirit*, assures the proximity to itself of the fixed and central being for which this circular reappropriation is produced. The *we* is the unity of absolute knowledge and anthropology, of God and Man, of ontotheology and Humanism.[12]

## II. EXITING THE METAPHYSICS OF SUBJECTIVITY

Derrida's thought clearly builds on Heidegger's thought, though he has an ambiguous relation to him, one could also add Levinas and others into the mix here as figures instrumental in the development of the positive project of Deconstruction. In contrast Hegel's thought has most often had a kind of central negative function in the development of Deconstruction: he represents the pinnacle of the philosophical tradition, the metaphysics of presence. Hegel's thought is not just content with using the core metaphysical oppositions of the philosophical tradition he tries to resolve them, to collapse the contradictions and determinations of meaning into a unified structure. Hegel's thought is read almost exclusively in terms of the model of presence.

---

10. Jacques Derrida, *Margins of Philosophy*, trans. Alan Bass, Chicago, University of Chicago Press, 1982 p. 73.

11. Derrida, *Margins of Philosophy*, p. 120-1. *Relevé* is the French translation of *aufheben*. See Derrida, *Speech and Phenomena*, p. 15 for a very similar claim about self-consciousness, though the context there concerns language as enabling the preservation and repetition of the object.

12. Derrida, *Margins of Philosophy*, p.121. Referring to Hegel Derrida comments: 'the subject affects itself and is related to itself in the element of ideality', *Of Grammatology*, trans. G. C. Spivak, Baltimore, Johns Hopkins University Press, 1976, p. 12.

> Hegelian idealism consists precisely of a *relève* of the binary oppositions of classical idealism, a resolution of contradiction into a third term that comes in order to *aufheben*, ... while *interning* difference in a self-presence.[13]

*Différance* is explicitly differentiated from Hegelian difference, which is described in the logic as contradiction. The way in which philosophy operates with the binaries of active/passive, real/idea, concept-intuition, heteronomy/autonomy is symbolic of the limitations of the western philosophical tradition. It arranges the world in a way that presents the world as in fact governed by these oppositions. These represent the governing architectonic of meaning.

> And that which I am calling schema or image, that which links the concept to intuition, installs the virile figure at the determinative centre of the subject, Authority and autonomy (for even if autonomy is subject to the law, this subjugation is freedom) are through this schema attributed to man (*homo* and *vir*) rather than to woman, and to the woman rather than to the animal. The virile strength of the adult male, the father, husband or brother ... belongs to the scheme that dominate the concept of the subject. This subject does not just want to master and possess nature actively. In our cultures he accepts sacrifice and eats flesh.[14]

The picture that emerges of Derrida's criticisms of the tradition is that of a system which tries to fix reality, which assumes the categories of thought can make present a given reality. Of course he is not saying that this edifice does in fact get reality wrong because there is some alternate reality that is outside of the edifice of language and metaphysics which we can appeal to for the criteria of knowledge and so on. He is not concerned to undermine our basic knowledge of the world for example, as I have heard someone comment, on the know-how that allows us to get from here to the airport. His claim is focused on the philosophical claim to 'have determined the essential nature of reality'.[15] His primary concern is to show the limitations of that system and a central limitation is its failure to capture the instability and factures that are constitutive of our interpretative schema. Inscribing that instability into philosophy requires a certain destabilizing of the program of the philosophical tradition. *Différance* is more than just pointing out the weaknesses of existing views, and it is more than a matter of collapsing the basis of these binaries. He remarks: 'if there were a definition of *différance*, it would be precisely the limit, the interruption of the Hegelian *relève* wherever it operates'.[16] Such an interruption would prevent the dialectical resolving of contradiction. Deconstruction interrupts the hierarchical resolution. All the basic dualisms of metaphysics presuppose a movement in one way or another of establishing a meaning 'antecedent to *différance*', they are concerned to establish something that

---

13. Jacques Derrida, *Positions*, trans. Alan Bass, Chicago, University of Chicago Press, 1981, p. 43.

14. Derrida, 'Eating Well', p. 114. David Wood argues that Derrida privileges the human over the animal in an unsatisfactory way in this interview. See Wood's *Thinking After Heidegger*, Cambridge, Polity, 2002, especially chapter 9.

15. Gary Gutting, *French Philosophy in the Twentieth Century*, Cambridge, Cambridge University Press, 1999 p. 307.

16. Derrida, *Positions*, pp. 40-1

would govern differences. In contrast to the approach of Hegel, *différance* rather than reconciling dualisms, destabilizes oppositions. *Différance* breaks the economy of negativity. Derrida values the negative but not the economy it serves in Hegel's system.

Philosophy has most often sought to explain difference by examining the basis for them within a transcendental schema, or it has been concerned with how we know objects to be true, establishing a logical structure that organizes them and so on. Derrida similarly is concerned with 'the movement according to which language or any code, any system of referral in general, is constituted "historically" as a weave of differences'.[17] For Derrida philosophy necessarily inadequately articulates the movement by which these meaning systems are transformed. *Différance* presents his alternative to the metaphysical order. Whatever Derrida means by this notion it is clear that the generative power of *différance*, which is the condition for differences, is nothing stable. The language of production, constitution, creation and so on are for him the traditional lexicon of metaphysics; what these terms cannot capture is the inherent instability that 'generates' the various relations constitutive of difference. While *différance* is not straightforwardly equivalent to intersubjectivity, norms, the natural world and so on, neither is it wholly other to the field of determination or the space of reasons that makes up the inhabited world.

We have already seen that *différance* is developed, at least in part, as a counter to Hegelian dialectical thinking. Derrida takes Hegel's logic as the grandest and last philosophical attempt to conceptually reify the generative and transformative process that creates differences.[18] The dialectic and the *Aufhebung* fail in this attempt to arrange the development of difference. Thought, experience and singularity cannot be contained by such a program. Such theorizations cannot capture the inherent instability that generates differences. Whereas Hegel's dialectical system involves the constant process of creating and conflating oppositions Derrida employs a terminology that gestures at that instability. The very distinctions that philosophy uses to neatly demarcate its world (active/passive; concept/intuition; nature/culture and so on) are unable to be mapped onto Derrida's conceptual lexicon.[19]

*Différance* is not animated by these dualisms; it carries within it the sense of both the *active* differentiating that allows any system of meaning determination and the temporal sense of deferring, which is the consequence of this instability. The core distinctions of thought are suspended and delayed because they cannot be equated with or articulate some given world. Since there is no direct access to an originary transcendental domain or to objects themselves our access to the world is always deferred to the interpretative economy in which it moves: 'an element functions and signifies, takes on and conveys meaning, *only by* referring to another past or future element in an economy of traces' (*Positions* 29). *Différance* is

---

17. Derrida, *Margins of Philosophy*, p. 12.
18. Trace has a neat negative similarity to *aufhebung*—see wood p. 28.
19. Derrida, *Positions*, pp. 8-9.

not a new viewpoint from which to examine the world or to correct and realign the core dichotomies of philosophy.

## III. *DIFFÉRANCE* AND THE DIVIDED SELF

Derrida's focus on the general issues of play, the structure of meaning and of language, his emphasis on writing rather than speech for a long time gave many the impression that Derrida was not concerned with revising the traditional model of the subject but in getting rid of it altogether; ours was a world of text without agents and authors. The subject of course exists for him it is just in need of 'resituating'.[20] This resituating of the subject is a necessary effect of *différance*. Derrida describes *différance* as the 'disappearance of any originary presence'. He goes on to unpack what he means by this, describing *différance* as having a doubled character: '*at once* the condition of possibility and the condition of the impossibility of truth'.[21] Derrida illustrates this doubled character with regard to subjectivity in an interview in the 1990's: 'It is because I am not one with my myself that I can speak with the other and address the other'.[22] The subject is not able to be one with itself because the interpretative features that makes up its world and that allow its self relation are not expressions of an essential self-identity, at the same time, it is those interpretative features that allow it to both relate to itself and others. What I hope to do here is examine in a bit more detail why Derrida takes this divided quality of *différance* as the model for subjectivity. And as we shall see while Hegel does not describe his subject as divided in this way it shares many of these features with the Derrridean self.

In the case of the metaphysical tradition there is a clear role for the subject in thinking the relation of what is other to thought. The self-identical subject of this tradition, as we have already seen in the discussion of the metaphysics of presence, ultimately takes a controlling or appropriative position with regard to what is other to it. In contrast Derrida's interests have most often been with what is 'outside' of the subject. While much of Derrida's thought has been concerned with the game, and not the subject playing it, the subject does of course have a place within this play, though discerning what that role is can be difficult as it is intimately bound to the canon of deconstructive terms: *différance*, trace, etc. none of which have meanings that can be explained without reference to the deconstructive project as a whole.

His efforts to rethink the role of the subject came late in his career primarily for strategic reasons. Exiting the metaphysics of subjectivity required first that the entire philosophical system of presence be shown its limitations and transformed.

---

20. Interview with Derrida in Richard Kearney, *Dialogues with Contemporary Continental Thinkers*, Manchester, Manchester University Press, 1984 page 125.

21. Jacques Derrida, *Dissemination*, trans. Barbara Johnson, Chicago, University of Chicago Press, 1981, p. 168.

22. Caputo, *Deconstruction in a Nutshell: A Conversation with Jacques Derrida*, John D. Caputo (ed.), New York, Fordham University Press, 1997, p. 14.

In an important interview in the 1970's Derrida begins to articulate the implications of Deconstruction, in particular the notion of *différance*, for the re-interpretation of subjectivity. He remarks that 'The subject is not present nor above all to itself before *différance*, ... the subject is constituted only in being *divided* from itself'.[23] What is at issue in this divided self could be put like this: 'Feeling responsible for a self that never comes simply from oneself is the sort of self-experience which characterizes the finite subject.'[24] The fundamental self-experience is an experience of the loss of self. The disparate sources that make up one's subjectivity are never merely mine, they are delivered to me; they are not caused by me and they cannot reflect some inner essence. At the same time I must express myself in this language, I have to take responsibility for myself even though the language, norms and values that animates my self-relation are not of my own making. The metaphysical tradition tries to resolve and unify this divided self-relation by establishing an absolute subject or an autonomous subject all of which tries to deny the *irreconcilable heteronomy of our self-relation*. There is not a dichotomy of heteronomy and autonomy, of passive and active; subjectivity hovers between these notions.

This characterization of the subject as fundamentally divided is portrayed by numerous figures in modern philosophy Freud (in the fundamental division of conscious and unconscious), though Saussure and Heidegger are the ones that Derrida focuses on as figures who confronted most forcefully that division. Saussure and Heidegger present overlapping characterizations of subjectivity. In Heidegger's case the subject is presented as divided because of ontological difference. In the case of Saussure he says 'language is not a function of the speaking subject'.[25]

> Language, and in general every semiotic code—which Saussure defines as 'classifications'—are therefore effects, but their cause is not a subject, a substance, or a being somewhere present and outside the movement of *différance*. ... There is no subject who is agent subject and master of difference ... subjectivity like objectivity is an effect of *différance*, an effect inscribed in a system of *différance*.[26]

The subject finds itself in a world that it is not responsible for, it is in Heidegger's language thrown, and the only way in which it can contend with that world and make some place for itself in it is by using the resource of language, a language that the subject is not the cause of but which it must use to understand itself. It is dependent on this system to present itself but it has no independent access to itself other than through that system. There is no given that we can access independent of the interpretative parameters that we are delivered into and at the same time, we (and the world) are not simply identical to semiotic codes and language systems.

---

23. Derrida, *Positions*, p. 29 my emphasis.
24. Rudolf Bernet, 'The Other in Myself', in Critchley and Peter Dews (eds.), *Deconstructive Subjectivities*, New York, SUNY Press, 1996, p. 177
25. Derrida, *Positions*, p. 29.
26. Derrida, *Positions*, p. 28.

What is distinctive about Derrida's approach is that this subject cannot reconcile itself with that world and with the language by which we interpret ourselves and the world we inhabit. The subject is constituted in that division and from this it must establish the basis of its self-experience. This dichotomized subject might be seen as the central problem that humans have to overcome: to reconcile their singularity with the whole, but in Derrida's case he is happy to leave that division unreconciled, as for him 'it is out of this *dislocated* affirmation that something like subject, man or whoever it might be takes shape'.[27] This dislocation is the result of the singularity of the who of subjectivity but is also because *différance* is antecedent but co-extensive with the subject; it can never have a unified form. *Différance* defines the determinative field in which the subject is situated, but the subject has an indetermination at its heart:

> people who fight for their identity must pay attention to the fact that identity is not the self-identity of a thing, this glass for instance, ... but implies a unity within difference. That is the identity of a culture is a way of being different from itself; a culture is different from itself; language is difference from itself; the person is different from itself. ... in the case of culture, person, nation, language, identity is a self-differentiating identity, an identity different from itself, having an opening or gap within itself.[28]

'An identity different from itself' means that its claims about itself cannot be equal to itself, as the plethora, movement and openness of determinations of the subject means it cannot be straightforwardly self-identical, it also excludes the possibility of an alternative domain of truth where this subject can have its identity with certainty. The subject is not self-identical, 'is not one with itself'; because of this the subject can use language, speak to another be open to another, take responsibility. The subject is more than itself; it *is* constituted by what exceeds it.

> consciousness is the effect of forces whose essence, byways, and modalities are not proper to it ... *différance* is the name we give the active moving direction of different forces, and of different forces, that Nietzsche sets up against the entire system of grammar, wherever this system governs culture, philosophy, and science.[29]

Derrida's divided account of subjectivity mirrors as we have seen Heidegger's thrown—throwing distinction. In the case of Heidegger this division is capable of being overcome, for example by resolute action in *Being and Time*. The general point of Derrida's critique of Heidegger is that the language of *eigen* [own] does not allow an escape from a appropriative teleology.[30] Despite Heidegger's plea for Being to presence itself to man and not man to consider himself the determiner of being, Heidegger's privilege of Dasein as the questioner preserves its responsibility as a matter for the single subject. Where Heidegger privileges *Versammlung*,

---

27. Derrida, 'Eating well' p. 100.
28. Caputo, *Deconstruction in a Nutshell*, pp. 13-14.
29. Derrida, *Margins of Philosophy*, p. 17-8
30. See Wood, *Thinking After Heidegger*, chapters 5, 8 and 9.

*gathering, collecting and so on* Derrida privileges disassociation.[31]

We are as subjects *in* the division; it is an originary loss because one can never be that unity rather one exists in a kind of perpetual state of dispossession. The subject is more than just of a divided character, its actual experience of itself is one of loss, it is a failure of self-possession. This loss is originary a 'loss of what one never had'.[32] The very features that allow it to aspire to self-presence, to have knowledge of self, also disallow that self-relation. But in trying to know itself it opens itself to contingency, to the play of *différance* as this is the terrain in which it comes to know itself. Again we see the subject hovering between all the dualisms. The subject in this case 'marks a middle voice between active and passive'.[33] It is not constituted by that division so much as by its desistance, by trying to make itself stable and assert itself on the world but it cannot do that as the resources it draws on to achieve this are unstable. What is critical in understanding why this subject is a loss is again a negative take on reconciliation—the self is not something that will come to be identified with either itself or the whole or tries to create it own world of self-equation by asserting the identity of self and whole. Subjectivity is in the gap between these domains. But we have to give this gap or loss more than just a doubled quality, it is a type of singularity that as with Deleuze is not able to be economized within the negativized and hierarchical conceptual schema.[34] That singularity is not something that we can make available to ourselves as something knowable it is instead instantiated only for example in actions such as taking responsibility.[35]

## IV. HEGEL'S SUBJECT

To bring together Derrida's and Hegel's thought on the issue of subjectivity

---

31. Caputo, *Deconstruction in a Nutshell*, p.14.

32. Jacques Derrida, 'Desistance' introduction to Philippe Lacoue-Labarthe *Typography; Mimesis, Philosophy, Politics*, trans. Christopher Fynsk, Harvard University Press. 1989 p. 16 n. 9; see also his 'eating well', p. 106.

33. Derrida, 'Desistance' p. 5.

34. In thinking subjectivity we should assume the model of *différance* where there never is a definable meaning to the self other than the play of *différance*, and the Singular and transcendent character of the subject. Singularity is not thinkable, in the way it is for example in Deleuze, it remains for Derrida quasi-transcendent, it has to be understood as *ineluctable*.

35. 'It is a singularity that dislocates or divides itself in gathering itself together to answer to the other, whose call somehow precedes its own identification with itself, for to this call I can *only* answer,' Derrida, Eating Well', p.100). He pursues this issue in his later works such as *Aporias* and the *The Gift of Death*. I take this issue up in detail in 'Dialectic and Différance: The Place of Singularity in Hegel and Derrida' in *Philosophy & Social Criticism*, vol. 33, no 6, 2007. One of the decisive implications that Derrida draws from this is for the notion of responsibility. Once the self-identical subject is collapsed then its opposition to what is other to it is also dissipated. Because we are always more than ourselves, this means that even within the very structure of our self-relation the other is inscribed. Derrida following both Heidegger and Levinas argue that this then puts the call of the other prior to any notion of subjectivity, as its relations to others is already inscribed in the language with which its confronts itself. Relations to others presuppose the disruption of self-identity, we relate to the other because of the heterogeneity of self-relation.

is a difficult exercise, particularly because so much of Derrida's iconic reading is built on a Hegel that develops a collection of Heideggerian pre-occupations, we have seen how this takes place. This skewed reading of Hegel in no way undermines the radicality and importance of Derrida's project. What it does demand is a revision of the ground rules by which a proper conversation between Derrida and Hegel on the issue of subjectivity can take place. In order for that conversation to begin we need to set out something of what is at stake in Hegel's view of subjectivity.

The examination of Hegelian subjectivity poses significant difficulties, primarily because Hegel's subject is not fixed and defined in the way that for example Descartes', Kant's and Fichte's are. Hegel nowhere gives a clear view of how his subject should be conceived. Even the well-known discussion of self-consciousness in the *Phenomenology* and its shorter version in the *Encyclopaedia* do not provide a detailed exposition of how we should conceive self-consciousness. Neither do they present an examination of the subject who undergoes the experiences in the *Phenomenology*. Similarly in the *Philosophy of Right* there is no detailed examination of the autonomous subject who underlies and underwrites the moral, economic, social and political spheres that this text examines. Hegel's failure to define his subject is not an oversight. As with many of the core concepts in Hegel's thought it has to be understood socially and historically. That is the subject cannot be defined outside of a determinate socio-historical context because it is something that changes over time; it has no transcendental identity. The character of its self-relation is not something that can be explained outside of the socio-historical conditions in which it is inscribed and those conditions are in constant state of transformation, especially in modernity.

While the Encyclopaedia *Philosophy of Mind* outlines the bare bones of the structure of the I, in terms of self-feeling and self-awareness it does not do so to establish a foundational shape of consciousness upon which Hegel's philosophical system is built. The self-feeling, soul and so on that he discusses there are of only anthropological interest, that is, quasi-natural expressions of Spirit. The discussion of consciousness and self-consciousness (which is where we are to understand his vision of subjectivity) takes places in the *Phenomenology of Spirit* (and in an abbreviated form in the Encyclopaedia discussion of phenomenology). In these discussions the distinctive feature of Hegelian subjectivity is neither natural nor transcendental; the defining character of its self-relation are experiential, social and historical achievements. This means any examination of the subject in Hegel's thought has to look at the general movement of his thought and the nature of his philosophical system as a whole.

The development of Hegel's account of subjectivity is set against the view of subjectivity expressed by Kant and Fichte. Of course other figures are important—particularly Descartes, Aristotle, Spinoza, and Schelling but it is Fichte and Kant that really frame the set of problems that define his philosophical project not just his view of subjectivity. The details of Kant's and Fichte's account of subjectivity are beyond the scope of this essay, my concern here is just to give a very brief account of what Hegel takes to be limited in their respective views and how those limitations influence the development of his thinking on this issue. By looking first at why Hegel describes Kant's categories of experience as subjective and as isolating mind from world we can see why Hegel envisages self-consciousness in the way that he does in the *Phenomenology*. At the same time Hegel finds in Kant's transcendental unity of apperception the resources for re-formulating Kant's own view of subjectivity such that it cannot be considered to be one-sided. Self-consciousness will show itself in Hegel's hands to be necessarily an expression of the objective world.

Hegel argues that the Kantian categories that are constitutive of human experience (the constitutive categories that allow and form subjective experience of the world) are posited as simply belonging to us, they are subjective. The Kantian categories do not determine the object itself, only its phenomenal appearance. The unity of the object is something posited, a combination of categories posited by the I, but not essential to the object considered in itself. The thing-in-itself, in Hegel's view at least, remains thereby something wholly objective, a beyond to which one can have no access because its 'objecthood' belongs only to thinking and not to the object. However, Hegel argues that:

> It does not follow from this that they must therefore be merely something of ours, and not also determinations of ob-jects themselves. But, according to Kant's view, ... the Ego (the knowing subject) furnishes the form and also the material of knowing—the former as *thinking* and the latter as *sensing* subject (EL §42 A3).

The problem for Hegel is that Kant's approach to the categories cannot secure the objectivity of the categories because thought cannot be considered, on these terms, to be self-grounding. Kant's approach to the categories renders thought entirely subjective. The categories in this case could only be understood as 'instruments' with which one attempts to comprehend objects but which remain absolutely distant from their objects. Thought in this case could only have its truth in the object that it is always (and necessarily unsuccessfully) trying to represent. In separating thought from the object Kant renders its explanatory power entirely subjective. On the one hand, the object appears not to have any truth as its unity lies in the thought of it; and on the other, the categories are not true as they are only subjective. The *Phenomenology* demonstrates the inadequacy of thinking in these terms.

Hegel does, however, think Kant's approach can be salvaged by extending the insights of the transcendental unity of apperception.[36] Hegel argues that Kant ignores the potential of the transcendental unity of apperception to connect subject and object. What Hegel sees as revolutionary in the transcendental unity of apperception is not that the categories are validated because they are grounded in the representing activity of any subject, but rather, that apperception is 'a higher principle in which a duality in a unity could be cognized, a cognition

---

36. For an extensive discussion of this issue see Robert Pippin's *Hegel's Idealism*, Cambridge, Cambridge University Press, 1989.

therefore of what is required for truth' (SL 594/GW XII 25). Apperception can overcome the opposition of subject and object; it is as one commentator describes it 'supra-oppositional'.[37]

In apperception, though not (for Kant) in actuality, the object of intuition and perception is at one with the conceptuality that posits its singularity and 'objecthood.' Yet Kant's account of apperception is limited because the thing-in-itself remains beyond what can be known and thereby invalidates any truth for apperception. Hegel argues that with apperception Kant went beyond this merely 'external relation' of concepts to objects. In apperception categories are not 'used' externally, they are not *applied* by consciousness to an intuited entity. In Hegel's account the object is not separable from its conception. In apperception I make the object present to myself precisely because the truth of the object is inseparable from the thought of it. 'Thought sublates the immediacy with which the object at first confronts us and thus converts the object into a positedness; but this its positedness is its being-in-and-for-self, or its objectivity' (SL 585/GW XII 14). Because an object's determinations are conceptual it can express itself as objective, but only through its determinations *in* thought.

Its objectivity is 'none other than the nature of self-consciousness' (SL 585/GW XII 15-16). This is not to say that the thing is determined by the conceptual whim of consciousness, but simply that the comprehension of the object can only be in terms of the manifold of thought determinations. One could not simply reflect on oneself, as consciousness tries to in the opening of the *Phenomenology* and disclose the determinations of one's own self-consciousness in some singular sense. And this is precisely because the conceptuality that is constitutive of consciousness, and the object world of which it is conscious, is not 'visible' in this sense; its meaningfulness overarches this subject-object relation. Self-knowledge is not available through reflection, as it is commonly considered, which assumes it allows access to the mind in the way that the reflection of the mirror presents one's physical appearance.

Fichte's insight into the limitations of the reflective model of consciousness is generally accepted, but his own account of the character of the immediate self-relation, which he presents as the alternative to the reflective model, was never satisfactorily resolved. Fichte's revised notion of subjectivity develops in response to two key problems in Kant's thought: the dualism of concept and intuition and the thing-in-itself. While critical of the thing-in-itself Fichte nevertheless preserves the idea of an external constraint on the I's self-positing. The details of this are extraordinarily complex, the issue that is relevant for our purposes is that Fichte thought the realization of the critical project could only be achieved by showing that knowledge was not given its content by a passively conceived model of intuition. The subject was *active* in the determination of the intuitive component of knowledge as well. In striving against the constraint of the 'real' reason drives itself to further self-determination, this is a process of self-transformation

---

37. David Stern, 'Transcendental Apperception and Subjective Logic', in Ardis B. Collins (ed.), *Hegel on the Modern World*, Albany, State University of New York Press, 1995, p. 170.

that is achieved as consciousness confronts the limitations of its inadequate explanations of the objects of experience.[38] What is problematic for Hegel is that this self-positing and self-transforming subject (which only posits and redefines its knowledge in confrontation with an indeterminate constraint) presupposes an unreconcilable dualism of I and not-I, and so in effect does not overcome the very mind-world dualism that Fichte sought to close.

Hegel builds on the self-positing subject of Fichte, Kant's Transcendental Unity of Apperception (as well as of course Kantian Autonomy) in his reformulation of subjectivity. We can see why it is important for Hegel to overcome the subject-object dualism that Kant's and Fichte's thought left him. The way Hegel does this is by conceiving self-consciousness such that rather than it confronting an absolutely alien world it can see itself in that alien world. That is Hegel reconceives self-consciousness so that rather than the object world standing over and against the conscious subject, the content of experience is not separable from the conditions and categories that allow the experience of objects. The truth of objects is the concept of them and those concepts cannot be seen as being purely subjective or as having a transcendental or naturalistic origin. The way Hegel shows this is an extraordinarily complex process that to a large degree is only disclosed through the entire unfolding of the *Phenomenology of Spirit*. The issue that is of concern here is if that reconceived subject-object relation can be understood as Derrida has described it above as governed by an all consuming *aufhebung* and a self-present subject. The way Derrida describes the nature of Hegelian subjectivity sees it imposing itself on the object world and excluding genuine otherness.

At first glance it might seem as though Derrida's account of Hegelian subjectivity is right, that Hegel resolves the mind-world dualism that Fichte and Kant bestow by creating an expanded version of the subject in which all difference is dissolved. That is the orthodox picture of Hegel's project sounds like fair game for the critique of subjectivity undertaken by Heidegger and Derrida and consequently opens a space for the type of alternative model of subjectivity that Derrida proposes that fractures the hegemony of that subject. The traditional metaphysical picture of Hegel argues that he resolves the problems that we have seen above by reverting to a pre-critical spiritual monism. Hegel on this view was largely seen as resolving the mind-world division by presenting the world as the expression of a cosmic spirit progressively realizing itself in history. There is nothing other than this Spirit's self-expression. What the conscious subject comes to recognize is that its self-consciousness is identical with the whole (determinate Spirit). The progression of the *Phenomenology* coincides with the realization that Spirit determines the world and that self-consciousness is an expression of Spirit, so what it comes to see is that the world which it initially takes to be other is in fact an expression of itself. In effect Spirit is just the subject writ large. Such a metaphysically construed Hegelian subject while it might avoid Kant's and

---

38. I discuss his position in 'Fichte's Striving Subject', *Inquiry: An Interdisciplinary Journal of Philosophy*, vol. 47, no. 2, 2004, pp. 123-142.

Fichte's problems creates far more problems than it answers and is deserving of the kind of criticism Derrida gives it. There is however a far more plausible view of Hegelian subjectivity than this.

The self-conscious subject of the *Phenomenology* is construed such that effectively the entire work is required to describe it. As has already been commented Hegel says comparatively little about the physiological and anthropological basis for self-consciousness. Hegel does not restrict self-consciousness and human subjectivity to a faculty of mind nor does he naturalize it. Hegel was critical of the investigation of the subject in Kant for attempting to present the subject antecedent to the inquiry, and this is a problem with all transcendental approaches. In Hegel's case the subject is conceived as a *result*, or as Pippin describes it as something 'historically achieved',[39] not something we can conceive as Hegel is fond of saying prior to the labour of science. But this means that the subject can have no fixed identity since it is something that is transformed over time. Derrida is, at least in part aware of this, which is why he ties his criticisms of Hegelian subjectivity to the dialectical movement of Hegel's thought, so that Hegel's subject is indistinguishable from the 'totalizing' movement of the Concept. But the dialectic and the Concept as Derrida understands them are weightily metaphysical.

The type of subjectivity at issue in Hegel depends to some degree on the text one is looking at. In the *Philosophy of Right*, at least for part of the text, it is a subject that is transformed through differing and progressive attempts at the realization of freedom, in the *Phenomenology* it is self-consciousness that undergoes changes in its self-understanding as it tries to account for the objects of its experience. In both cases the subject cannot be isolated and examined outside of the progressive and determinate unfolding of the texts. The subject expressed in these works is the result of the complex determination of historical and social forces and the character of self-relation reflects those social and historical changes even if the subjects themselves cannot recognize this. Clearly the subject at issue cannot be understood as presenting an isolatable subject. No single subject is free, freedom is necessarily social and this sociality is also the condition of self-consciousness.

The *Phenomenology of Spirit* begins with a conscious subject who from the outset tries to make various claims to truth. Initially that concern seems primarily epistemological. The method as outlined in the introduction focuses largely on the experience of objects and how the various claims to truth undercut themselves in the experience of the object. But the text is equally a self-examination, indeed the natural consciousness, the text's protagonist, in its examination of the object and its own claims to know progressively shows itself to be an inquiry into itself. The movement of the *Phenomenology* is the self-comprehension of Spirit. That movement and self-comprehension is effected through the one enduring feature of the subject—the negative—outlined in some of the most well known passages of the Preface to the *Phenomenology*.[40] The negative is the key feature of

---

39. Robert Pippin, *The Persistence of Subjectivity*, Cambridge, Cambridge University Press, 2006, p. 12.
40. See for example PS ¶ 32/GW IX 25-6.

this subject and Spirit; it gives them their essential dynamism and capacity for self-transformation.

> Since the Concept is the object's own self, which presents itself as the *coming-to-be of the object*, it is not a passive subject inertly supporting the Accidents; it is, on the contrary, the self-moving Concept which takes its determination back into itself (PS ¶ 60/GW IX 45).

If we look at this passage coupled with his famous account of the negative

> the disparity which exists in consciousness between the I and the substance which is its object is the distinction between them, the negative in general. This can be regarded as the defect of both, though it is their soul or that which moves them. ... the negative is the self (PS ¶ 37/GW IX 28-9).[41]

This is then followed with the famous passage that 'substance shows itself to be essentially Subject' (PS ¶ 37/GW IX 29).

On the face of it Derrida's account seems right: 'the movement of lost presence sets in motion the process of re-appropriation'.[42] The negative seems to accord with this assessment, since the dislocating work of an I, which through its examination of the objects of experience, comes to see that the given determinate character of Spirit is in fact identical with itself. All difference, otherness and so on are therefore simply determined moments of the whole. It appears Hegel replaces the self-sufficiency of the Cartesian subject with a self-sufficient Spirit. Derrida responds to this by refusing the model of home and self-sufficiency and so establishes quasi-transcendental conditions for the necessary transcendence of all systems of thought.[43]

However to read the above quoted passages this way would ignore what we have already seen above—that Hegel's subject and the negativity associated with it have to be understood in light of Hegel's dissatisfaction with Kant's mind-world dualism. Hegel retains what he takes to be the positive features in Kant's subject (autonomy and apperception) and in Fichte's (the self-positing subject). The movement of the negative is not the attempt to recover an originary loss, but is rather the means by which we come to realize that the way in which the world is meaningful has to be understood as self-determined in the widest possible sense of this term. What needs to be stressed is that the *Phenomenology* tries to show how the basis of judgements, the categories of our experience and the reasons we offer for our judgements and actions are necessarily products of a human world. Moreover as the text unfolds we, and the natural consciousness, come to see ourselves not just as products of these conditions but as collectively *producing* the conditions that underlie our judgements and discursive exchanges.[44]

Descartes is often presented as inaugurating modernity in his attempt to

---

41. See also EL §42 A1.

42. Derrida, *Margins of Philosophy*, p. 72.

43. Singularity, for example, is outside the economy of these determinate systems. This singularity is not something I can possess or be at home in, it resists stability and reconciliation.

44. See Pippin's discussion of this in *The Persistence of Subjectivity*, especially chapter 2.

ground thought on his own consciousness, but Hegel's project is of a different order to the extent that the project of grounding thought is shown to be the capacity for thought to be self-transforming.[45] The details of this self-transforming capacity are outside the scope of this paper other than to say that this self-transforming capacity is only possible because of the negative. The basic concepts and categories of experience have to be understood as social and historical achievements. That is Hegel's subject cannot be conceived in the language of social ontology as a foundational/transcendental subject or a foundational/transcendental intersubjectivity. What the *Phenomenology* shows is that conceptions of the subject and human intersubjectivity are the result of progressive changes in human self-understanding. The *Phenomenology* charts a succession of inadequate attempts to explain ourselves and the world, those explanations reveal themselves not just as isolated failures of understanding but show themselves (retrospectively) to be determinate features of self-consciousness. There is no fixed and self-certain subject that is identifiable other than by those historically transformed categories.

There are however numerous occasions in the *Phenomenology* in which absolute claims to *individual* self-determination are presented as the exclusive truth of self and world, the most well known of which are the Lord and Bondsman section and the discussion of conscience. Both these expressions of self-consciousness represent extreme claims to self-certainty that ultimately undermine themselves. That is these attempts to ground all meaning on a basic individual self-certainty show themselves to be unviable forms of self-relation and the text in both cases moves to more adequate expressions of self-consciousness. The *Phenomenology* progresses through the successive undermining of claims to know. The motor of this 'undermining' and transforming is the negative, which as we have seen is the thinking work of the subject. This labour of the negative that the conscious subject undertakes does not reveal a fixed and given whole. Instead what the text shows is progressive changes in human self-understanding, progressive changes in what humans collectively authorize as legitimate ways of understanding the world. The natural consciousness does not of course see it that way until the end of the text.

There is a threefold aspect to the texts unfolding. First as has already been discussed the subject's examination shows a progressive transformation of its knowledge of itself and the world. Second these changes in its knowledge of self and world are inscribed in its self-consciousness.[46] Third that it comes to recognize that the categories and condition which frame its experience of the world (that is the sum total of shapes of consciousness in the *Phenomenology*), which provide the interpretative parameters of all its judgments, are the result of collective human self-determination. What we come to recognize in the end of the *Phenomenology* is that Spirit is essentially self-producing; but importantly this self-determination is not the unfolding of some cosmic spirit but represents collective changes

---

45. Under the conditions of modernity we achieve a self-consciousness that this is the case.

46. For a detailed discussion of this issue see my 'Absolute Knowing', *The Owl of Minerva: Journal of the Hegel Society of America*, vol. 30, no. 1, 1998, pp. 3-32.

in our self-understanding. The dialectical movement of the *Phenomenology* charts these transformations and there is a certain artificiality to the claims to necessity for each transformation. Nevertheless the subject of the *Phenomenology* comes to understand itself in terms of those determinations. In the context of Hegel's dissatisfaction with Kant we can see why Hegel cannot present a world of truth over and against the subject. Instead he takes all the conditions and categories of human meaningfulness as necessarily collectively determined and those conditions are recognized to be the conditions of human self-consciousness. It progressively understands itself in terms of these conditions. In so doing its understands its own essentially self-transcending character. It comes to see the character of its subjectivity not as a singular self-identical subject but in terms of the conditions that are created by the gamut of forces at play in history and society. It comes to recognize that these conditions are inscribed in the very way it is aware of itself and the world.

The path of the *Phenomenology* is one by which the subject comes to understand the relations that underwrite its own thinking as not merely its own. The relations are not self-coincident but reflect the manifold of norms and reasons at play in any social-historical period. Consequently these conditions are unable to be mapped onto the I in any straightforward sense. The subject cannot be self-identical and self-present in the way Derrida describes the Hegelian subject, precisely because as we have seen the norms, concepts and conditions that mediate my relation to myself and the world are always more than what I can conceptually circumscribe at any point in time. Moreover 'this space of reasons' in which this takes place is always in transition and in advance of what a finite subject could know, even though those 'reasons' mediate our self-relation.

# 14

# Agamben, Hegel, and the State of Exception

## Wendell Kisner

INTRODUCTION: THE STATE OF EXCEPTION

Giorgio Agamben's recently published book *State of Exception*[1] takes as its explicit theme the 'state of exception' that had already received considerable attention in many of his earlier publications.[2] In the 'state of exception', the juridical order is suspended. Modern states have used it to justify bypassing that juridical order—an order which requires due process, respecting recognized rights of citizens, the separation of powers, etc.—in cases deemed to be characterized by extreme necessity such as the threat of civil war, revolution, foreign invasion, and now terrorism. Although it has been called by various designations ('martial law' in the US, 'state of siege' in France, etc.), it is essentially characterized by the suspension of law and 'the provisional abolition of the distinction among legislative, executive, and judicial powers' (SE 7). Agamben writes, '[a]lthough the paradigm is, on the one hand (in the state of siege) the extension of the military authority's wartime powers into the civil sphere, and on the other a suspension of the constitution (or of those constitutional norms that protect individual liberties), in time the two models end up merging into a single juridical phenomenon that we call the *state of exception*' (SE 5).

The most notorious modern example was the Nazi regime: when Hitler came into power in Germany he immediately invoked the state of exception in the name of national security and suspended the existing constitution. From that

---

1. Agamben Giorgio, *State of Exception*, trans. K. Attell Chicago, The University of Chicago Press, 2005 (henceforth SE).

2. For instance, *Homo Sacer: Sovereign Power and Bare Life*, trans. Daniel Heller-Roazen, Stanford, Stanford University Press, 1998, pp. 15-29, (henceforth HS) (originally published in Italian in 1995); *Means Without End: Notes on Politics*, trans. Vincenzo Binetti and Cesare Casarino, Minneapolis, University of Minnesota Press, 2000, p. 5 and passim (originally published in Italian in 1996); *The Time that Remains: A Commentary on the Letter to the Romans*, trans. P. Dailey Stanford, Stanford University Press, 2005 (originally published in Italian in 2000), pp. 104-108; and *The Open: Man and Animal*, trans. K. Attell, Stanford, Stanford University Press, 2004, pp. 37-38, (originally published in Italian in 2002).

point forward the entire Nazi regime was carried out within this state of exception. Predictably enough, Agamben caused quite an uproar in the US when he likened the Nazi concentration camps to the Bush administration's use of Guantánamo Bay (and other such camps in Afghanistan and elsewhere) to indefinitely detain people it suspected of 'terrorism'. However, his point was not that the same sorts of atrocities were being committed in the US versions, but rather that insofar as this practice of indefinite detention without recourse to any predetermined juridical order marks out a space in which the rule of law is suspended, they are *formally identical*.[3] As Agamben explained it in an interview,

> But I spoke rather of the prisoners in Guantánamo, and their situation is legally-speaking actually comparable with those in the Nazi camps. The detainees of Guantánamo do not have the status of Prisoners of War, they have absolutely no legal status. They are subject now only to raw power; they have no legal existence. In the Nazi camps, the Jews had to be first fully 'denationalized' and stripped of all the citizenship rights remaining after Nuremberg, after which they were also erased as legal subjects.[4]

The camp then becomes a type, a figure of the state of exception in modernity, in which the 'citizen' disappears into a 'bare life' over whose management the state has taken over and in which the rule of law is suspended.[5] It is not a question of whether or not atrocities will in fact occur in them but rather, given the suspension of the juridical order that the state of exception is, that there is nothing in place to prevent them from occurring. Thus whether it is the US detention camps in Guantánamo Bay, Canada's 'Security Certificate' that sanctions similar indefinite detention, the 'soccer stadium in Bari in which the Italian police temporarily herded Albanian illegal immigrants in 1991', or the New Orleans Centroplex in which hurricane Katrina's victims were corralled, these 'will all have to be considered camps' insofar as in all of them 'an apparently anodyne place (such as the Hotel Arcade near the Paris airport) delimits instead a space in which, for all intents and purposes, the normal rule of law is suspended and in which the fact that atrocities may or may not be committed does not depend on law but rather on the civility and ethical sense of the police that act temporarily as sovereign'.[6]

The camp as such a type is not a localized place, since it can appear at virtually any location and can apply to anyone, citizen or foreigner. Agamben's

---

3. Furthermore, it is not at all clear that the June 29, 2006 court decision (in *Hamdan v. Rumsfeld*) against the Bush administration's use of military tribunals in Guantánamo has any bearing or effect on this, since the practice of indefinite detention was not *itself* called into question at all—a fact Bush himself quickly exploited by explicitly pointing it out to the public.

4. 'Interview with Giorgio Agamben – Life, A Work of Art Without an Author: The State of Exception, the Administration of Disorder and Private Life', Ulrich Raulff (interviewer), *German Law Journal*, no. 5, special ed., 2004, http://www.germanlawjournal.com/article.php?id=437 (retrieved on May 29, 2007).

5. Agamben, Giorgio, *Means Without End: Notes on Politics*, trans. V. Binetti and C. Casarino, Minneapolis, University of Minnesota Press, 2000.

6. Agamben, *Means Without End*, p. 41.

phrase 'dislocating localization' is apropos: 'The political system no longer orders forms of life and juridical norms in a determinate space; rather, it contains within itself a *dislocating localization* that exceeds it and in which virtually every form of life and every norm can be captured'.[7] It marks out the boundaries of a region within which prevails what David Luban called the 'limbo of rightlessness' where both domestic as well as international law are suspended and into which the US Patriot Act, for instance, enables the president to thrust anyone on the planet solely at his own discretion.[8] And although the latter may be the most prominent and visible example today it is not the only one.[9] The state of exception no longer designates an 'exception' in the strict sense of the word, but rather has come to designate the rule: 'The camp intended as a dislocating localization is the hidden matrix of the politics in which we still live, and we must learn to recognize it in all of its metamorphoses'.[10]

Now although the most well-known and perhaps pernicious examples of the state of exception are those imposed by the Right-authoritarian regimes of the twentieth and twenty-first centuries, Agamben cautions us: 'In any case, it is important not to forget that the modern state of exception is a creation of the democratic-revolutionary tradition and not the absolutist one' (SE 5). Though there are ancient roots that Agamben will carefully trace, the state of exception is a modern phenomenon that belongs to the liberal democratic nation-state.

Furthermore, according to Agamben the state of exception is a presupposition of modern politics in general—both that of the Left as well as of the Right. Agamben frustrates any desire for the comfortable sanguinity of relegating the state of exception to the excesses of the Bush administration and other conservative regimes. Revolution likewise must invoke the state of exception insofar as it suspends the state and its juridical order and does so prior to the institution of any new legal order that will establish and preside over future norms. Although he doesn't explicitly mention it, this was precisely Leon Trotsky's problem: once the revolution has overthrown the previously existing juridical order, there is no measure of right and wrong other than the revolutionary party. Insofar as this party acts outside the past juridical order, and insofar as a new order has yet to be established, the party operates—and must operate if it is to operate at all—within the state of exception. Thus Trotsky had to say, 'My party—right or wrong ... I know one cannot be right against the party ... for history has not created other ways for the realization of what is right'.[11] This attitude of course then paved the

---

7. Agamben, *Means Without End*, p. 43.

8. Luban, David, 'The War on Terrorism and the End of Human Rights, in *Philosophy & Public Policy Quarterly*, vol. 22, no. 3, 2002.

9. Canada's 'Bill C-36', for instance, expands the criminal code to include 'preventive arrest' (http://www.justice.gc.ca/en/news/nr/2001/doc_28217.html) and its 'Security Certificate' allows indefinite detention without formal charges or due legal process. Although the latter was recently struck down by the high court, the court nonetheless 'upheld the principle' of security certificates (http://www.cbc.ca/canada/story/2007/02/23/security-certificate.html).

10. Agamben, *Means Without End*, p. 43.

11. Cited in Schapiro, Leonard, *The Communist Party of the Soviet Union*, 2nd ed., New York, Vintage

way for Stalin, a more shrewd strategist, to exile him and eventually have him murdered.

Similarly, Agamben argues that the 'right of resistance' to the state—which includes any presupposition that citizens have a right and/or duty to resist the state when the latter is deemed to be unjust, which in principle can only be done outside the juridical order of the latter—is likewise operative within a state of exception. He cites as a contemporary example the 'draft of the current Italian Constitution' which 'included an article that read, "When the public powers violate the rights and fundamental liberties guaranteed by the Constitution, resistance to oppression is a right and a duty of the citizen"' (SE 10).

Although Agamben argues that the state of exception is the predominant paradigm of contemporary politics, he also maintains that it is only so because it has always been the condition of possibility for any juridical normativity whatsoever:

> In the decision on the state of exception, the norm is suspended or even annulled; but what is at issue in this suspension is, once again, the creation of a situation that makes the application of the norm possible…That is, the state of exception separates the norm from its application in order to make its application possible… (SE 36).

> This space devoid of law seems, for some reason, to be so essential to the juridical order that it must seek in every way to assure itself a relation with it, as if in order to ground itself the juridical order necessarily had to maintain itself in relation with an anomie (SE 51).

Interestingly, he pits against one another two theorists on opposite ends of the political spectrum who explicitly attempted to account for the state of exception: the Nazi jurist Carl Schmitt and Left intellectual Walter Benjamin. Both invoked the state of exception—the former to (ostensibly) protect the state and the civil order, and the latter to justify revolution and the deposing of unjust political orders. In both cases it is a question of violence—an extra-juridical violence brought to bear by the state under threat (Schmitt) or against the state by revolution (Benjamin). Insofar as this violence operates outside any juridical order, it cannot be governed by any predetermined set of legal criteria that could determine in advance what would be a 'legitimate' as opposed to an 'illegitimate' use of violence. Hence the state of exception is itself a kind of 'pure violence' in which the risk cannot be underestimated. Once the existing order is suspended and thereby rendered inoperable, which way it will go is not and cannot be predetermined.

One often enough finds a similar tension emerging in political discussions today: one side concerned with the security of the state and of the civil order against the violence of terrorist acts, and the other concerned with the state's use of these acts as possible excuses for extending state control and its appropriation of resources. It might be interesting to put the debate on different grounds. Rather than debating about whether or not there 'really is' a threat that 'justifies'

---

Books, 1971, p. 288.

military action abroad and the curtailing of civil liberties domestically, it might be interesting to ask how both sides of the debate fare with respect to the state of exception—especially given the fact that insofar as the state of exception is by definition outside the juridical order it may well undermine in advance any normative criteria whereby we might try to determine what 'justification' here would even mean.

With this problem in view Agamben lays out two radically different approaches respectively exemplified by his two chosen theorists:

1) Carl Schmitt's approach is to try to *annex* the state of exception *within* the juridical order itself. The difficulty here is that one then has a juridical order that includes a provision regarding its own suspension (insofar as the state of exception suspends the rule of law), making it difficult to make sense of how a legal order can govern, 'legally', the state of exception in which that very order is deactivated, as well as how any legal limitation can be applied to it. For instance, if it is asserted in a nation's constitution that the state of exception can only be invoked in the most extreme of emergency situations and can last only for a limited period of time, exactly what those 'situations' would look like and exactly how long the time period will be cannot be specified in advance, since these will depend upon the unforeseeable empirical contingencies existing at the time, making it a black hole that swallows up any legal or juridical way of getting out if it. It was precisely this black hole that allowed the Nazi regime to 'temporarily' suspend the Weimar constitution without abrogating it, and then to renew that suspension every four years, thereby creating an indefinitely extended state of exception. In the contemporary context, it is not difficult to imagine a 'terrorist threat' being invoked to justify a similar suspension.

Equally important is Agamben's claim that when the suspension of law is in effect, the decree of the political leader(s) has the so-called 'force of law' which attempts to combine the state of exception and the law in one person—and this, he suggests, is the road to either fascism on the one hand or to a Stalinist-type totalitarianism on the other hand. With perhaps an implicit reference to the US, he writes:

> Indeed, the state of exception has today reached its maximum worldwide deployment. The normative aspect of law can thus be obliterated and contradicted with impunity by a governmental violence that—while ignoring international law externally and producing a permanent state of exception internally—nevertheless still claims to be applying the law (SE 87).

2) Walter Benjamin's approach is to always *separate* the state of exception *from* the juridical order, thereby 'unmasking' (as Agamben puts it) the 'mythico-juridical violence' that attempts to unify them in the service of the authoritarian state (SE 63). Benjamin wrote shortly before his death that 'the tradition of the oppressed teaches us that the 'state of exception' is the rule' (cited in SE 57). Agamben follows Benjamin here and suggests that, because the state of exception is the 'anomic' space from which any legal order emerges at all, it is no longer even possible to return to liberal democracy: 'From the real state of exception in which

we live, it is not possible to return to the state of law, for at issue now are the very concepts of "state" and "law"' (SE 87). Regarding the two possibilities exemplified by Schmitt and Benjamin, he then concludes,

> To live in the state of exception means to experience both of these possibilities and yet, by always separating the two forces, ceaselessly to try to interrupt the working of the machine that is leading the West toward global civil war (SE 87).

And thus:

> The only truly political action, however, is that which severs the nexus between violence and law. And only beginning from the space thus opened will it be possible to pose the question of a possible use of law after the deactivation of a device that, in the state of exception, tied it to life (SE 88).

As mentioned above, beginning from the state of exception, it is not predetermined which way it will go and so the risk is great. Will revolution bring a more just political order or a more oppressive totalitarianism? The state of exception in itself seems to be completely neutral in this regard—no normative imperative can be seen to arise from its black hole, and Agamben, although he evidently sides with the Left revolutionary Benjamin over the Right authoritarian Schmitt, cannot give us (or at any rate does not give us) a sound reason for this decision or any criteria by which we are to make it. The state of exception puts everything up for decision, but it cannot give us any guidance over what decision to make.

Agamben, following Benjamin, wishes to preserve the gap between the state of exception and the juridical order against the annexation of the former by the latter. He provides no reason for doing so other than the suggestion that one road leads to fascism and totalitarianism and the other perhaps opens a future outside of that, but what would bring one to side with Benjamin over Schmitt remains a mystery. Agamben's own alignment with the former seems arbitrary—that is, beyond the commonplace recognition that the Nazis were bad and so the ideas of Schmitt, a Nazi jurist, must be bad as well. One would hope for a stronger reason than that. Hegel may give us one.

## THE HEGELIAN ALTERNATIVE: GETTING OUT OF THE STATE OF EXCEPTION

From the state of exception, as Agamben articulates it, the decision over it, which decision Schmitt identifies with sovereignty, is not presided over by any preexisting juridical order or normative guidelines since all such norms and legalities are suspended. Hence the risk—will it lead to justice or to terror? Or terror in the name of justice? One might perhaps already foresee totalitarianism in the desire to control and preside over the state of exception in advance, a la Schmitt. But one may well also with justification worry about a Stalinist-type bureaucratic state, or perhaps the havoc of a Maoist cultural revolution, resulting from the Benjaminian project of holding open the state of exception. Indeed, this is Hegel's worry.

Hegel presents us with an alternative that neither holds open the state of exception in a constant referral back to it, nor attempts to preside over it in advance. Instead of leaving us with a void in which all decisions are arbitrary, and rather than making of the state of exception a condition of possibility for any juridical order, he shows us that the very negativity of its suspension implies a dialectic which, through its own immanent logic, generates a movement away from it toward the universality of right. Whether or not Hegel's ultimate vision of the state is where we want to end up, or whether that is where we must end up once we start with Hegel, is beyond the scope of this paper.[12] What I wish to examine here is, given the state of exception as an increasingly predominant and global political category and assuming, following Agamben, that the state of exception is the political space in which we live, does Hegel's political philosophy articulate a way out of it that winds up in neither totalitarianism nor undecidability?

A kind of suspension happens at the outset of all of Hegel's major works. The greater *Science of Logic* suspends presuppositions in general in order to think the pure immediacy of being, the *Phenomenology* suspends assumptions about consciousness, etc. But the *Philosophy of Right* suspends all assumptions about the political order, including any juridical structures it may entail, and so is not governed in advance by a predetermined norm. Since, unlike the *Logic* or the *Phenomenology*, it explicitly concerns that political order and any juridical norms emerging from it, this is the place to look in the Hegelian system for something resembling the state of exception.

Hegel is of course writing in the context of the great European Enlightenment discourses of freedom—in particular those of Rousseau and Kant. Rousseau argues that what he calls 'natural freedom' or the liberal conception of freedom articulated earlier by Hobbes and Locke, namely freedom defined primarily as mere absence of restrictions,[13] is inadequate. This impoverished understanding of freedom is replaced in the social state by the 'civil freedom' in which one understands that 'obedience to the law one has prescribed for oneself is liberty'.[14]

---

12. Ample literature is available regarding the relevance and value of the entire Hegelian political philosophy for the modern world, and there are sound arguments against those who, in my view, rather grossly misread Hegel (or don't read him at all) by attributing to him statist tendencies that subordinate individual freedom to the collective order. For instance, see Houlgate, Stephen, *Freedom, Truth and History: An Introduction to Hegel's Philosophy*, New York, Routledge, 1991, pp. 77 ff., and Winfield, Richard, *Overcoming Foundations: Studies in Systematic Philosophy*, New York, Columbia University Press, 1989, pp. 171 ff.

13. Hobbes perhaps gives us the most concise formulation of this understanding of freedom when in the fourteenth chapter of *Leviathan* he writes, 'By *liberty*, is understood, according to the proper signification of the word, the absence of external impediments'. This same definition is repeated in the twenty-first chapter: 'Liberty, or freedom, signifieth, properly, the absence of opposition: by opposition, I mean external impediments of motion; and may be applied no less to irrational and inanimate creatures, than to rational', and hence in the human sphere 'a 'freeman' is he that in those things which by his strength and wit he is able to do, is not hindered to do what he has a will to'. (Hobbes, Thomas, *Leviathan*, http://darkwing.uoregon.edu/%7Erbear/hobbes/leviathan.html, 1651 (retrieved on May 29, 2007).

14. Rousseau, Jean-Jacques, *On the Social Contract*, ed. and trans. Donald Cress, Cambridge, Hackett Publishing Company, 1987, p. 27 (Book I, chapter 8).

However, Rousseau leaves the precise relation of natural freedom to civil freedom unclear—it's not clear exactly how we get from the former to the latter. This is particularly problematic insofar as from the perspective of each the other looks like unfreedom. If I am looking at the world through the lens of natural freedom, civil freedom merely looks like a set of societally-imposed restrictions that is at best a partial sacrifice of freedom for security or at worst a loss of freedom. Hence from this perspective it looks like 'man is born free, and everywhere he is in chains'.[15] Kant doesn't get much further in this regard. He takes freedom to be self-legislation, but this is based on a transcendental moral imperative, and the liberal conception of freedom merely seems to be shoved aside as an irrelevant misunderstanding.

Hegel affirms the Rousseauian and Kantian notions of freedom as self-determination rather than mere absence of restriction, but he does so by beginning from the desire for or gesture towards a sheer absence of restrictions or denial of limits in the liberal conception and then revealing an immanent logic implied in this conception that leads us to the more adequate conception of freedom as self-determination. This 'adequacy' in turn is measured not by a predetermined set of criteria but rather by the logic implied in the concept of freedom itself. Hegel can thereby specify the relation between what Rousseau calls natural and civil freedom, and he can do so without recourse to transcendental structures assumed as given in advance. It is part of the argument of this paper that by thinking such a self-determining structure can one account for the state of exception without either annexing it by the predetermined determinacy of a juridical order along the lines of Schmitt or by positing it as a transcendental structure underlying or always preceding modern liberal democratic structures as that from which they emerge and that to which they invariably return. However, given Agamben's insistence that the state of exception forms the political space in which we live today, and his denial of the relevance of modernist contractual notions,[16] why should we begin with a concept of 'freedom' at all? Given the contemporary geopolitical context, what is there to recommend this beginning?

For Hegel as a philosopher, the centrality of freedom is justified within the entire philosophical system insofar as, beginning without presupposing any underived determinacy in the *Science of Logic*, ontological determinacy in general shows itself to be a self-determining process, and it is this very self-determining process made explicit as such that is freedom. To put it another way, when the self-determining process of reason knows itself as self-determining, it recognizes itself as free. The process of reason becoming self-conscious as freedom is 'history' and therefore 'truth', viz. reason becoming explicit, is historical. It is the universal necessity of the logic in this process of reason becoming explicit, an immanent process of self-determination that submits to its own necessity and is only thereby free, that saves Hegel from historicism or historical relativism without having to

---

15. Rousseau, *On the Social Contract*, p. 17 (Book I, chapter 1).

16. 'All representations of the originary political act as a contract or convention marking the passage from nature to the State in a discrete and definite way must be left wholly behind' (HS 109).

abandon history for ahistoricity. This very process of self-determination leads humanity to the place where it recognizes that thought is self-determining and therefore that it can and must avoid externally imposed determinacy. In other words, humanity thereby comes to recognize a demand that thought be as fully self-critical as possible.

Thus for Hegel the fact that the *Philosophy of Right* begins with freedom is itself ultimately made necessary by the historical post-enlightenment demand that thought become as fully self-critical as possible, which itself requires that no determinacy be dogmatically assumed as merely given in advance and hence underived, which means that we must begin from something like the presuppositionless beginning of Hegel's system that finally gets us to the concept of freedom. And it is of course in the system of philosophy thus generated that the historical demand of the European Enlightenment (that thought be fully self-critical) is itself seen to be a necessity stemming from reason.

## THE POSTMODERN REJECTION OF UNIVERSALITY

We could of course follow postmodern leanings and reject the post-enlightenment demand that thought become as fully self-critical as possible. This demand itself can be historicized and seen as an arbitrary social construction of modern Europe. One might further specify this construction as a masculine requirement for the autonomy of males in a patriarchal system that overlooks the feminine entirely, as premised upon a particular ontology deriving from the peculiarities of modernity, as 'Eurocentric', etc. We then land in the postmodern relativism of multiple language games that suffer from a vacuum of legitimacy.

Badiou currently stands as one of a few voices in the postmodern wilderness advocating the precedence of universality over postmodern relativism and its identity politics, but his 'event' itself, though breaking free of the predetermined variables that make up any historical situation and remaining indiscernible from the perspective of the preestablished set within which the event must appear, nonetheless falls into the same problem of any language game—viz. its criteria of legitimacy are derived from the rules that it itself sets up, and these rules themselves are therefore subject to the contingencies of that particular language game, making them essentially arbitrary and, viewed from outside that particular language game, merely relative again.

This is the problem, for instance, with Badiou's attempt to appropriate St. Paul's militant Christianity as a universal 'truth-procedure' that can be abstracted from the particular content of the Christian belief system. Badiou writes, 'Paul's unprecedented gesture consists in subtracting truth from the communitarian grasp, be it that of a people, a city, an empire, a territory, or a social class'.[17] In this way he looks to Paul for the precedent of overcoming the contingency and relativism with which communitarianism is necessarily burdened. However, he

---

17. Badiou, Alain, *Saint Paul: The Foundation of Universalism*, trans. Ray Brassier, Stanford, Stanford University Press, 2003, p. 5.

also takes what is arguably the central tenet of Christianity—the resurrection of Christ from the dead—to be a 'mere fable', claiming that

> what is important is the subjective gesture grasped in its founding power with respect to the generic conditions of universality. That the content of the fable must be abandoned leaves as its remainder the form of these conditions and, in particular, the ruin of every attempt to assign the discourse of truth to preconstituted historical aggregates.[18]

Formalizing what he takes to be 'Paul's procedure' into a list of 'truth requirements', Badiou then asserts, 'There is not one of these maxims which, setting aside the content of the event, cannot be appropriated for our situation and our philosophical tasks'.[19]

From a Hegelian perspective of course this separation of form from content suggests that the result can only be an abstract universal, landing Badiou in the very abstraction of a universality freed from particular content that he perhaps rightly sees as belonging to capitalism, an empty universality of capital that is left behind by default once truth in general is relegated to postmodern relativism.[20] Hegel opposes to such abstract universality what he calls a 'concrete universal' in which form and content are no longer at odds. But what does Hegel's alternative actually look like? For this we need to take a detour through the opening pages of the *Philosophy of Right* in order to see how Hegel's beginning is relevant to the state of exception and how concrete universality emerges out of it.

## THE OPENING OF HEGEL'S *PHILOSOPHY OF RIGHT*

At the outset of Hegel's *Philosophy of Right*,[21] the derivation of the concept of freedom is assumed (from the *Encyclopedia*). Political philosophy as Hegel understands it must take this concept as given and draw out its implications, but it must start with the most minimal conception of freedom so as to presuppose as little as possible or, more strictly stated, so as to presuppose only those determinacies whose necessity has already been demonstrated. Nonetheless, this might seem to preclude the relevance of the concept of freedom for any discussion of the state of exception insofar as the latter is the suspension of the juridical normativity and so would seem to preclude any such presupposed determinacy.

---

18. Badiou, *Saint Paul*, p. 6.
19. Badiou, *Saint Paul*, p. 15.
20. The 'real unifying factor behind this attempt to promote the cultural virtue of oppressed subsets', Badiou claims, 'is, evidently, monetary abstraction, whose false universality has absolutely no difficulty accommodating the kaleidoscope of communitarianisms' (Badiou, *Saint Paul*, pp. 6-7). Naomi Klein makes the latter point in lay language: the multicultural rainbow merely opens up so many more target markets for capitalists—what she calls a 'market masala'—thereby subjecting all to the same uniform logic (Naomi Klein, *No Logo: Taking Aim at the Brand Bullies*, Vintage Canada, 2000, pp. 115 ff.).
21. Throughout I will be referring to the 1897 Dyde translation of Hegel's *Philosophy of Right* that is available online at http://www.marxists.org/reference/archive/hegel/index.htm (retrieved on May 29, 2007), (henceforth PR).

The fact that Hegel also immediately invokes 'the will' might seem even less promising. However, the 'will' in Hegel is not a metaphysical posit, still less a theological hangover devised to remedy the problem of evil.[22] It is merely the practical side of freedom. When one seeks to actually become free in the world, that is 'willing', and hence

> The distinction between thought and will is only that between a theoretical and a practical relation. They are not two separate faculties. The will is a special way of thinking; it is thought translating itself into reality; it is the impulse of thought to give itself reality (PR § 4 A).

We will have to return to the question of the relevance of Hegel's discourse on freedom to the state of exception. Before we get there, however, our entry into that discourse might be better served by attending to Hegel's remarks on universality that immediately follow:

> Any idea is a universalizing, and this process belongs to thinking. To make something universal is to think. The 'I' is thought and the universal. When I say 'I', I let fall all particularity of character, natural endowment, knowledge, age. The I is empty, a point and simple, but in its simplicity active (PR § 4 A).

To think is to universalize—Hegel takes this to be an inescapable necessity. The *Phenomenology of Spirit* shows that when thought tries to avoid universality and say the absolutely singular and non-universal, it only winds up asserting the most abstract universality (e.g. abstract indicators like 'this', 'now', 'here', etc. that can apply to any content whatsoever) or taking refuge in the further abstraction of wordless pointing.[23] Whether any universal is going to be the same universal across different cultures or historical eras is another question, one not addressed in this passage.

But the further thing to attend to here is that the 'I' or ego *has no content*. It is the sheer vacuity of thought thinking itself in its pure universality. This is not yet a self that is socially constructed with all of the concomitant determinacies involved in it (e.g. those belonging to a particular social class, gender, ethnicity, culture, psychological history, and all the other empirical variables that converge in the self-identity of any particular individual). Rather, it is the *abstraction from* all such determinacy. Insofar as it is an abstraction from any and all determinate content, it cannot be pigeonholed as belonging to any particular variant of the latter.[24] Admittedly, this is precisely an abstract universal, but rather than jettison it in favour of a better conception, Hegel will ask us to first attend to what is implied in it.

One might still ask for the motivating factors. Why would one *want* to make

---

22. E.g. as in Augustine's *On Free Choice of the Will*.

23. See the chapter on 'Sense-Certainty' in the *Phenomenology of Spirit* (Baillie translation), available online at http://www.marxists.org/reference/archive/hegel/index.htm (retrieved on May 29, 2007).

24. E.g. as a universality that is essentially 'masculine' insofar as women were excluded from the independence men enjoyed in patriarchal systems and so are more context-bound, as a Cartesian cogito, etc. These too would be particular determinacies from which abstraction is made in order to think the 'I' as a sheer universal.

such an abstraction? Hegel has his own answer—it is a requirement of the idea of freedom becoming objectively actual that only becomes explicit in the modern era. Insofar as that demand requires abstraction from all particular determinacy in order to first become self-determining and thereby free, however, it requires abstracting from the very historically determinate conditions of its own appearance at a particular time and place in history. This is a point often missed by Hegel's critics who all-too-easily assume that if one can find some historical condition (whether it be related to gender, ethnicity, or any other empirical variable) without which Hegel's system may not have appeared at all, one can then mobilize this condition as the Achilles heel that brings down the entire system—or at least 'situates' it in such a way as to relativize it and thereby take away its claim to universality. But insofar as abstraction is made from all determinacy per se, this abstraction *includes the determinacy of the conditions of this very abstractive move itself*, and hence it cannot be caught short by pointing out some such condition.[25]

For this reason it really doesn't matter *why* one would want to make such an abstraction. The fact remains that we *can* do it, and in such a way that abstraction is made from the enabling conditions of the abstractive move itself. Therefore motivating factors do not enter into it as presupposed determinacies that infect or 'contaminate' the conception. In other words, any such conditions are at most *enabling* but not *determining* conditions. As Winfield put it, 'Although thought has preconditions on which its exercise depends, these preconditions cannot play the role of juridical conditions that determine what counts as valid thought'.[26]

But equally it must not be assumed that this abstraction is a ground or foundation for further propositions about freedom or the political order. It is not a ground or foundation; it is merely a starting point, and one that will be transformed as we follow the immanent logic it implies. Thus we neither remain at this abstract level nor do we return to it. It merely gets us started insofar as the determinacy of particular content is cleared away in order that nothing be merely assumed as given in advance. Were this move not made, then there would be some externally given factor that would determine the development from the outside, and this external determination would undermine freedom. This point becomes more clear in the exposition of this beginning abstraction, but here we might see how any such external determinacy would make *self*-determination at best partial and at worst a sham.

> The will contains [a] the element of pure indeterminateness, i.e., the pure doubling of the I back in thought upon itself. In this process every limit or content, present though it be directly by way of nature, as in want, appetite or impulse, or given in

---

25. Indeed, Hegel sharply criticizes this very kind of reflective thinking that always triumphs in positing a ground or condition for something as if the immediacy of that very ground or condition is not itself at least equally suspect. Such 'criticism' has failed to be fully self-critical insofar as it persists in a certain way of thinking (which Hegel called *Wesenslogik*) that has not itself been critically examined at all. See the sections in Book Two of the greater *Science of Logic* on 'Reflection' (Chapter 1C) and 'Ground' (Chapter 3). As we will see below, this *Wesenslogik* is also precisely the problem with Agamben's conception of the state of exception.

26. Winfield, *Overcoming Foundations*, p. 4.

any specific way, is dissolved. Thus we have the limitless infinitude of absolute abstraction, or universality, the pure thought of itself (PR § 5).

We can put the above point in reverse. Just as the ego is found by abstracting from every determinate content, so also this abstractive move is itself the 'I'. Thus it is not that we first make the abstraction in order to become an ego, but rather that the ego is this abstractive process itself. Hence the ego is the universalizing character of thought. To think is to conceive the universal, which is simultaneously to be an 'I'. Thus rather than positing the abstract individuality of modernity as an immediate given (Descartes), as a product of economic relations (Marx), as an effect of psychological variables (Freud) or as resulting from a history of metaphysical determinations of being (Heidegger), Hegel understands it to be the universalizing character of thought as such made explicit. And it is in this abstraction from content that we find the first determination of freedom: freedom as 'flight from limit' or, as more commonly known, the liberal conception of freedom as absence of restrictions. Thus the very self-identity of the 'I' as the universalizing character of thought contains the concept of freedom in its first form.

The will is simply the activity of this abstraction viewed *as activity*, that is, as practical. Viewed as theoretical, it is the abstraction of thought from content. Just as is the case with so many of Hegel's distinctions, it is a matter of emphasis: abstraction from *content* is the theoretical level of thought, whereas *abstraction* from content is the practical level of the will. Hence the theoretical and the practical are two sides of the same process.

However, it is here in this first shape of freedom as 'negative freedom', the abstraction made from all determinate content, that we come across something in Hegel's text that looks very much like the state of exception with which Agamben is so preoccupied.

## NEGATIVE FREEDOM AS THE STATE OF EXCEPTION

> The will on one side is the possibility of abstraction from every aspect in which the I finds itself or has set itself up. It reckons any content as a limit, and flees from it. This is one of the forms of the self-direction of the will, and is by imaginative thinking insisted upon as of itself freedom. It is the negative side of the will, or freedom as apprehended by the understanding. This freedom is that of the void, which ... becoming actual it assumes both in politics and religion the form of a fanaticism, which would destroy the established social order, remove all individuals suspected of desiring any kind of order, and demolish any organization which then sought to rise out of the ruins. Only in devastation does the negative will feel that it has reality... (PR § 5).

> This phase of will implies that I break loose from everything, give up all ends, and bury myself in abstraction... (PR § 5 A).

What Hegel here calls 'negative freedom' is the liberal concept of freedom as absence of all restriction, the 'absence of external impediments' which Hobbes understood liberty to be, or the 'natural freedom' of Rousseau that wants to throw off the shackles of societally imposed order. It is the most abstract concept of freedom and hence presupposes the least, and hence also for Hegel it is where the philosophy of freedom or political philosophy must begin. However, one cannot help but notice that in its suspension of limit, restriction, order, normativity, etc., it is formally identical to the suspension of juridical normativity that characterizes the state of exception.

In the state of exception any and every juridical order is suspended. Abstraction from all limit in the political sphere is the suspension of the juridical order, over which no predetermined set of norms can preside. This anomie is indeed the space of revolution, as Benjamin rightly saw. The problem emerges, however, when this space is understood as the essence of freedom itself or, to put it in Agamben's language, as the hidden ground of any juridical order whatsoever. More specifically, the problem is not in the state of exception posited merely as a *beginning*, but rather in the state of exception posited as a *ground*.

As such a ground, the state of exception would make possible or underlie any further determinacy that may be added to it or derived from it. It would always remain as the underlying deep structure of any juridical order, which is the function it seems to provide in Agamben's account of it (I will return to this below). To borrow Winfield's phrase, it would be conceived as a 'privileged determiner'.[27] But this is to already posit a determinacy within it that is not necessarily derived from it. In other words, to immediately take the state of exception as the hidden ground of the juridical order is to already make a decision about it, viz., to decide in advance that the state of exception must serve a certain function.

However, we may be able to agree with Agamben that the state of exception provides the space from which the juridical order must emerge insofar as the institution of the latter cannot presuppose any prior normative or juridical order and still be the *institution* of a juridical order (rather than, say, the further development of an already existing juridical order). But we will part company with Agamben's essentially Schmittian hypothesis that any juridical order depends upon the state of exception in determining its limit and thereby also allowing the determination of when and where it is in effect. The first step in that parting of the ways is taken as soon as we attend to the implied determinacy *in the very indeterminacy* of negative freedom. The latter, taken by itself, is 'one-sided'. However, 'as this one-sidedness contains an essential feature, it is not to be discarded' (PR § 5 A).

Now all we have to do is attend to what is implicit in the abstract negative freedom that we have before us. Negative freedom is itself defined as the negation of limit. It is the abstraction from every determinate content, the state of exception that suspends any normative or juridical determinacy. But insofar as negative freedom withdraws from all limitations, it is itself *limited by that very withdrawal*. It appears to be thoroughly negative in its denial of limit, in its insistence upon the absence of restrictions, or in its suspension of normative order. But that

---

27. Winfield, *Overcoming Foundations*, p. 42.

suspension is itself a limit. It cannot, in other words, simply *be* a juridical order. It cannot simply assume some pregiven set of normative standards. Insofar as it cannot do these things, this 'cannot' names a limit—that limit which defines it as the abstraction that it is. To put it another way, the very negativity of its abstractive move and the anomie it brings about *is itself its own positive character*. Hence the absence of all limit *is itself its limit*.

Therefore negative freedom is a standing contradiction: its very character as negation of limit is itself its limit. Alternatively stated, its very flight from all content *is* its content. The abstractive move of the state of exception itself is its own positive character. But this in turn means that negative freedom *negates itself as absence of limits*. It is defined as *absence* of limits. But insofar as this *is* its limit, this negates its character *as* absence of limits. We do not need to merely oppose a better concept of freedom to it, as do Rousseau and Kant. Negative freedom is not negated by *some other* concept of freedom but *by itself*. To put it another way, the state of exception is not overcome by some other juridical order that is imposed upon it or which has to annex it in advance. Rather, its own negativity as the suspension of all normativity/juridicality is itself negated by *the positive character that this very negation is*.

Here we can also see that, rather than posit an external condition not accounted for in the system as its limit or content, abstraction is made from any and all such externally given determinacies. However, abstraction cannot be made from its own character as abstraction. Any attempt to do so merely repeats the abstraction and hence reproduces the same determinacy. As Hegel puts it,

> In that it is the abstraction from all definite character, it has a definite character. Its abstract and one-sided nature constitutes its definite character, its defect and finitude (PR § 6, R).

To understand this positive moment in terms of the will—that is, to understand it in terms of the activity of thought here as this abstractive move, but now with the recognition of its positive character as such—the will in willing to be free of restrictions or limits is no longer merely the vacuity of a will that has nothing to will. It no longer merely wills the void or the empty suspension of the first moment of negative freedom. Rather, in the actualization of freedom that the will is, it has a content to will—namely its own content *as* this negative freedom.

Insofar as it negates all limit, negative freedom is negative. But insofar as this flight from limit is its own limit, it has a positive character. Thus insofar as the will is nothing other than the willing of freedom, the will now wills this positive character. The step is certainly minimal, but a subtle shift has occurred from willing the absence of limit to willing a limit, even if that limit be nothing other than the very willing of the absence of limit. We've moved from a will that wills nothingness to one that wills its own positive character, and hence from willing nothing to willing something.

But this is self-determination in its most germinal form. The abstraction from all limit abstracts from every externally imposed or pregiven determinacy.

But that very movement reveals its own determinacy *as* such abstraction, and hence it is only now in a position to will *itself* as freedom. The limit it now wills is *its own* limit rather than a pregiven one, and hence it has 'given itself' that limit or, to look at it another way, is submitting to the limit that it is. Insofar as it submits to its own limit, it gives its limit to itself or is self-determining. Thus from out of the suspension of law a self-imposed law emerges. This is not yet the fully explicit legal system of a juridical order, of course, but is the minimal limit out of which any such legal order must emerge if it is to be self-determining and thereby free. It is from here that we can get from Rousseau's natural freedom to a freedom defined as 'obedience to the law one has prescribed for oneself'.[28]

We can see from this that if the determinacy of the limit that is self-imposed here is the very abstractive move of negative freedom, then the latter is not simply jettisoned in favour of a better conception. Rather, it is taken up into self-determination as a subordinate aspect that no longer serves as the guiding principle but which nonetheless functions within it. This is the process Hegel famously called *Aufhebung* (a simultaneous negation and preservation) in which a previously dominant determinacy becomes a subordinate 'moment' within a more developed and concrete determinacy. Freedom is now no longer defined solely in terms of a negative flight from limit, but rather as its own positive character that is willed as such. However, since the positive character that is willed as such is the negative moment that abstracts from limit, this negative character still makes itself known.

The shape of freedom we thus have contains both the negative moment of flight from limit as well as the positive moment that wills this as its own character. Hegel understands the unity of these two moments to correspond to freedom defined as 'free choice'. Thus I am free when I can choose whatever I please and I am not forced to accept anything that is not of my choosing. Right away we see the two previously mentioned moments or aspects come to the fore: the negative aspect is seen in the rejection of any externally-imposed limitation that would limit my ability to choose whatever I please. The positive moment is seen in the desire to preserve my freedom of choice. Once again, both flight from limit and willing freedom as that flight from limit are apparent in the structure of choice.

But this structure nonetheless reveals a fatal contradiction. In willing my freedom to choose I reject eternally imposed limits. But in order to exercise my freedom to choose I must choose something. However, what I choose can only be taken from externally given options and so, insofar as I am limited by these options in their empirical number, variety, and availability, I am subject to an externally imposed limit. Thus if I wish to choose the clothes I want to wear, I am limited both by the variety of clothing that is available to me as well as by my own purchasing power, neither of which are determined by my freedom but rather are given independently of whatever I will. True, I may be able to overcome this somewhat by improving my purchasing power (e.g. training to get a better

---

28. Rousseau, *On the Social Contract*, p. 27 (Book I, chapter 8).

job) and by seeking out independent manufacturers or becoming a tailor myself, thereby increasing my options. But no matter how much I am able to maximize my options they will nonetheless be finite and limited, whether that be due to my own limited abilities or to empirical circumstances beyond my control, and these limits will not be of my own choosing but rather will be imposed upon my exercise of choice. In this way freedom as the freedom to choose will always be subject to externally imposed limits and thereby find its freedom compromised—both in the negative sense of flight from limit as well as in the positive sense of the ability to be self-determining.

But it gets worse. The above considerations apply to what we might call the 'objective' side—the particular content that is willed when I make a choice (e.g. the clothing I choose to procure and wear). This side tends to receive the most attention when we think of 'free choice', but whenever I think that I am free when I can choose whatever I please, the question I am not asking is this: What is it that determines what 'I please'? What determines my appetites and desires on the basis of which I then make choices? We might call this the 'subjective' side consisting of desires, appetites, and impulses. The problem, however, is that these are not chosen either—I don't choose to want. Rather, I want, and then on that basis I choose. So my choice is driven by something externally imposed. Merely because it is 'within me' in the sense of residing within my organism in some way does not reduce its external character in the slightest, for its 'externality' consists in the fact that it is not determined by choice but rather determines what choices are made. To put it another way, the externality of 'my own' desires, appetites, and impulses consists in the fact that they do not come from my freedom but rather are imposed upon my freedom, thereby limiting it. Insofar as this limitation is not a self-imposed limit, it compromises freedom just as much as the externally given options mentioned above. In fact, it is precisely these desires, appetites, and impulses that are targeted by advertizing campaigns, making my 'freedom' to 'choose' a commodity a dubious freedom indeed. As Rousseau put it, 'To be driven by appetite alone is slavery'.[29] Because the subjective side is driven by the arbitrariness and capricious character of such impulses and appetites, Hegel calls this way of understanding freedom 'caprice'. Today we might refer to it as a 'consumer model' of freedom.

Thus on both the subjective as well as the objective sides, freedom defined as free choice is saddled by externally imposed limits that are not of its own choosing. What is then left for freedom? If it chooses something, it is immediately subject to limits from within and without. If it does not choose anything, its 'freedom' is merely an empty possibility. Freedom per se seems to have no content whatsoever, making it an empty formal abstraction. It is at this point that the reductionist enters and proclaims freedom to be an illusion. But whether that be due to the reinforcement contingencies of behaviorist theory or the genetically determined 'hard-wired' structures of our neurophysiololgy, the essential point is the same

---

29. Rousseau, *On the Social Contract*, p. 27 (Book I, chapter 8).

as the theological conception of predestination—your choices are only apparent; behind them lurk the real driving forces. Indeed, Hegel agrees with them:

> In the controversy carried on, especially at the time of the metaphysic of Wolf, as to whether the will is really free or our consciousness of its freedom is a delusion, it was this caprice, which was in the minds of both parties. Against the certitude of abstract self-direction, determinism rightly opposed a content, which was externally presented, and not being contained in this certitude came from without. It did not matter whether this 'without' were impulse, imagination, or in general a consciousness so filled that the content was not the peculiar possession of the self-activity as such. Since only the formal element of free self-direction is immanent in caprice, while the other element is something given to it from without, to take caprice as freedom may fairly be named a delusion (PR § 15 R).

The important proviso here of course is that this is not the ultimate and final shape of freedom. Hegel claims that he puts the debate between 'freedom and necessity' to rest, not by 'proving' that we are free empirically, but by showing that the concept of freedom assumed in the debate is itself deficient. Thinking through this deficiency (i.e. the contradiction) will show us a more adequate concept of freedom that is not subject to such a debate. We might also add that once we take the reductionists' way out, that more adequate concept of freedom will likely never be discovered since we will have already given up on the possibility.

The quandary freedom is faced with here leads to the desire to withdraw from any choices made, to suspend one's commitment to them, and thereby to preserve freedom against the externally imposed limits, even though these limits came about through the very exercise of free choice itself. I like to characterize this as the 'Lynyrd Skynyrd' concept of freedom, in reference to the southern rock band and their song 'Freebird' which celebrates a man leaving his companion because he no longer wants to be tied down:

> If I stayed here with you, girl,
> Things just couldn't be the same.
> 'Cause I'm as free as a bird, now,
> And this bird you cannot change.

Liberalism and libertarianism typically embrace this concept of freedom but, unlike the Lynyrd Skynyrd version, include the recognition that freedom can never really get what it wants—to be totally free—and so must resign itself to accepting certain limitations. John Hospers provides an apt characterization of this freedom that must nonetheless accept limitations even when pushed to the libertarian end of the spectrum:

> If I own my life, then it follows that I am free to associate with whom I please. If I own my knowledge and services, it follows that I may ask any compensation I wish for providing them for another, or I may abstain from providing them at all, if I so choose. If I own my own house, it follows that I may decorate it as I please and live in it with whom I please...all that which I own in fact, I may dispose of as I choose in reality. For anyone to attempt to limit my freedom to do so is to violate my rights.

Where do my rights end? Where yours begin.³⁰

However, as soon as we recognize that, in withdrawing from the options chosen—in preserving my freedom to suspend the choices I have made—I am in fact seeking to preserve and protect my freedom from the externalities that seem to threaten it, then a shift in perspective can occur and once again we find ourselves in a similar situation to the one discussed above in which we recognized that the flight from all limit was itself a limit. Here, however, what calls for recognition is the fact that what I am most concerned about in preserving my freedom to choose is freedom, and not so much the particular content of the choices that are made.³¹ It is this move that marks the decisive difference between freedom as self-determination and the consumer model of freedom in which merely multiplying the available options from which to choose is the key issue. We have seen that no matter how much this store of available options is increased, it will always be restricted by limits that are not chosen, and so therefore will always compromise freedom when conceived as free choice. Liberalism and libertarianism accept that compromise and then seek to expand freedom as much as possible within those limits that cannot be overcome or eliminated without also preserving the recognition of everyone's equal right to freedom.

But if we see clearly what the problem is with this conception of freedom, we can see what is needed to alleviate the problem, and then we can also see that the resources for doing so are already there in the concept itself. The problem is this: freedom does not have itself for its content. Its content is instead given externally—on the objective side as the givenness of available options from which to choose, and on the subjective side as the givenness of drives and impulses that determine what options I want or desire. This at first seems to reduce freedom to a vacuous formality that one might easily be tempted to reject entirely—as in the various forms of reductive determinism. On the other hand, one might be tempted to seek recourse in metaphysical speculation and posit a ghost in the machine that would remain free regardless of nature's mechanical necessity. The former gives up freedom, while the latter preserves it by requiring metaphysical commitments.

However, if we merely attend to the problem we can also see that what is needed in order to rectify it is not some additional feature or property. Rather, what is needed is a form of freedom that *has itself for its content*—this alone could avoid the problems that are the direct result of a freedom that relies upon exter-

---

30. John Hospers, 'What Libertarianism Is', in *Social Ethics: Morality and Social Policy*, T. Mappes and J. Zembaty (eds.), New York, McGraw Hill, 2002, p, 321. In order to make this claim to right and thereby defend this conception of freedom, Hospers must presuppose that property rights are already established and inviolable. He reasons that freedom is grounded upon property rights and so, if we are to be free, we must assume property rights. Hegel, on the other hand, requires no such presupposition, and in fact will derive the right to own property from a more developed conception of freedom than the structure of choice.

31. For a more detailed discussion of the deficiency of freedom when defined in terms of choice and the transition out of it, see Stephen Houlgate, *Freedom, Truth and History*, pp 79 ff. The present account of choice is greatly indebted to his interpretation.

nalities for its content. A freedom that had itself for its content would not will external options as its end, nor be motivated by factors that do not stem from freedom itself. Such a freedom can only will itself—a possibility we already saw in the positive character of the first shape of freedom that wants to reject all limitation. But this is precisely what we already have as soon as we recognize that what I am most concerned about in preserving my freedom to choose is freedom, and not so much the particular content of the choices that are made. If this is my primary concern, then I am really willing my freedom, not the externally given content of available options. So too, if this is my primary concern, then I am motivated by something not merely reducible to those drives and impulses that determine my wants and appetites and thereby also the options to be sought. In willing itself, freedom submits to its own necessity, and hereby the age-old dichotomy between freedom and necessity is seen to result from a concept of freedom that has not been sufficiently thought through.

Once freedom wills itself, its content is nothing other than itself and so there is no longer an externality standing over and against it to limit it. But this is a limit nonetheless, since freedom must will itself in order to be free—it cannot 'choose' to do otherwise and still remain freedom. As we saw earlier, insofar as freedom submits to its own limit it is self-determining. The self-determination we now have before us has been purged, as it were, of the vestigial externalities still present in the structure of choice. It is not that our freedom to choose is eliminated and we can no longer make choices. Of course we can. It's just that this no longer defines freedom.

Freedom has here gained a greater degree of concreteness over the merely abstract universality characterizing a will that, in rejecting all limitation, winds up being an empty formality devoid of content. An abstract universal is one that is other than its particular content—the separation of form from content is what makes it abstract. Once we take the step to a will that wills itself, to a freedom that has itself for its content, then we have a concrete universal—the concrete universality in which the form of freedom is the same thing as its content. What the will henceforth must do in order to be free is not to withdraw from all determination but to *determine itself*. A freedom that wills itself universally is what Hegel calls a 'right'.[32] The minimal structure of right is this universal willing of freedom. Initially it shows itself merely as the bare right to be free, but Hegel will then attempt to show that this entails further determinacies such as property, morality, ethical life and, at the macro-level, civil society and the political order of the state. The universality of freedom then will not be an abstract universal that subsumes particular content given to it externally, but rather will be the concrete universal that determines itself further and thereby gains particular content through that self-determination.

---

32. Contra Hospers, we are now in a position to see that the demand to recognize rights and to respect the laws that preserve them is not a restriction that is externally imposed upon freedom but rather is something implied by the character of freedom itself—something we would not be able to see if we followed him by beginning with a pregiven right to own property.

An estimation of Hegel's success in deriving these further determinacies from the concept of freedom on an immanent basis, as well as of the value of his own articulation of these structures, is well beyond the scope of the present paper, and I do not presume that traveling thus far with Hegel necessarily commits us to the remainder of the journey. Sufficient for the purposes outlined here is the demonstration that the state of exception need not leave us in an undecidable limbo between Benjaminian revolution and Schmittian authoritarianism or between socially progressive and regressive alternatives, nor need we be left with the meager hope for an indeterminate post-legal existence after the death of liberal democracy. The universalizing tendency with which we began, having brought about the 'state of exception' in which the juridical order is suspended, has now emerged out of that state into the concrete situation of a free will that wills itself universally. Furthermore, it has done so not through being rescued by something external to its own suspended state nor by a teleologically or eschatologically conceived end point beyond it. Rather, it has emerged out of it through its own immanent dialectic.

At this point we can return to Agamben's account of the state of exception and highlight the transcendental way in which he conceives of it and thereby ensures in advance that it will remain an indeterminacy from which we cannot escape.

## AGAMBEN'S TRANSCENDENTAL WAY OF CONCEIVING THE STATE OF EXCEPTION

I call 'transcendental' any structure that is said to determine other things but is not determined itself in the process. The classic modern sense is that given to it by Kant, for whom the transcendental conditions of possibility for all experience, insofar as they determine that experience, are not themselves determined by the latter and so are not empirical. As Kant put it:

> Reason is present in all the actions of men at all times and under all circumstances, and is always the same; but it is not itself in time, and does not fall into any new state in which it was not before. In respect to new states, it is determining, not determinable. We may not, therefore, ask why reason has not determined itself differently, but only why it has not through its causality determined the appearances differently.[33]

But it is perhaps Hobbes who first gives us transcendence in its modern form insofar as for him the social contract is first made possible by the coercive power that is able to enforce its provisions, and this power is rooted in the sovereign power over life and death that is outside the contract itself—a point not lost on Agamben, whose analysis of the state of exception follows Hobbesian contours (HS 104ff). Because the sovereign power makes the social contract possible, it cannot be itself party to the contract. Hobbesian sovereignty is thereby transcendent—it determines the social order and, for that reason, is not itself determined by that

---

33. Kant, Immanuel, *Critique of Pure Reason*, trans. N.K. Smith, New York, St. Martin's Press, 1929, A556/B584.

order. No longer necessarily referring to something metaphysical or divine, Hobbes gives transcendence its modern secular form and sharpens its definition as well: it is simply that which determines without being itself determined, and it can have either empirical or metaphysical referents. As such it is the sense later inherited by Kant, but it also equally pertains to the 'forms' of Platonism as well as to the divine transcendence of God assumed by Medieval thinkers.

The key point for our purposes, however, is that such transcendental thinking does not have to adopt those specific transcendental determining conditions that Kant or Hobbes privileged. As Winfield has pointed out, any variable can be selected and then elevated to the status of a 'privileged determiner', one that is 'given the privileged role of being the prior condition of all other terms'.[34] From this perspective it matters little whether that privileged determiner be the history of being, language games, cultural context, or the state of exception—in each of these cases, the problem of grounds comes to the fore insofar as, whatever the condition selected to occupy the role of privileged determiner, 'the question naturally arises as to how that condition can have its own determinate character'.[35] And as I will argue below, merely attributing indeterminacy to the privileged determiner does not mitigate the problems involved but, at worst, merely masks them by making it appear to have no need for such justification (a strategy perhaps dating back to Anaximander's *apeiron*).

We already saw Agamben underline the transcendental character of the state of exception ('anomie') as a privileged determiner when he writes that it is 'as if in order to ground itself the juridical order necessarily had to maintain itself in relation with an anomie' (SE 51). In Agamben's account, the state of exception persists within the juridical order—and within any juridical order—as that which grounds it and makes it possible. For him this suggests what a theory of the state of exception should do:

> The essential task of a theory of the state of exception is not simply to clarify whether it has a juridical nature or not, but to define the meaning, place, and modes of its relation to the law (SE 51).

Here we see that Agamben must think of the state of exception and the law as coexisting in a mutual relation. As he further puts it, 'That is to say, everything happens as if both law and logos needed an anomic (or alogical) zone of suspension in order to ground their reference to the world of life' (SE 60). But if we follow Hegel we also see that there is no need to posit a relation between two poles or constructs in this way. The state of exception contains a dialectic which immanently leads to its resolution in the sphere of right, from which the juridical order proceeds. This is neither annexation nor a mutual relation of two structures that creates a 'zone of absolute indeterminacy between anomie and law, in which the sphere of creatures and the juridical order are caught up in a single catastrophe' (SE 60). What does emerge is a political order that does not have

---

34. Winfield, *Overcoming Foundations*, p. 62.
35. Winfield, *Overcoming Foundations*, p. 63.

to 'subsist only by capturing anomie' as if both were posited in advance in some way, but rather one which emerges out of the state of exception without leaving the latter remaining behind as a ground. If we follow the immanent dialectic implied in the state of exception, then from a Hegelian perspective one can actually agree with Agamben's claim, 'For law, this empty space is the state of exception as its constitutive dimension' (SE 60). That is, law is indeed constituted out of the state of exception, but the latter does not persist behind or within the former as a grounding dimension.

According to Agamben, Benjamin 'unmasks' the Schmittian 'attempt of state power to annex anomie through the state of exception' as a juridical fiction, replacing it with 'civil war and revolutionary violence, that is, a human action that has shed every relation to law' (SE 60). However, in siding with Benjamin against Schmitt's program of annexation, Agamben nuances the transcendental character of the state of exception:

> [P]ure violence (which is the name Benjamin gives to human action that neither makes nor preserves law) is not an originary figure of human action that at a certain point is captured and inscribed within the juridical order ... It is, rather, only the stake in the conflict over the state of exception, what results from it and, in this way only, is supposed prior to the law (SE 60).

Although he does not acknowledge it here, in a way Agamben opts for a quasi-Heraclitean ontology of strife (*polemos*) within an open space of conflict, even employing a metaphorics of sport to clarify the contest between revolutionary violence and state authoritarianism as they compete within the void of the state of exception, each remaining a 'stake in the conflict' that results from the latter. Thus the latter, the state of exception itself, remains as transcendental ground or, what is the same thing from a Hegelian perspective, an abyss. Indeed, insofar as the state of exception does not indicate 'that somewhere either beyond or before juridical apparatuses there is an immediate access to something whose fracture and impossible unification are represented by these apparatuses' (SE 87) it is indeed a kind of abyss.

The abyss of its indeterminacy, however, is not sheer indeterminacy per se (e.g. as in the beginning of Hegel's greater *Logic*), but is the specific indeterminacy of the state of exception relative to the juridical order, whether the latter be a preexistent structure or a possible one to come. Agamben himself as much as asserts this in his comparison of the state of exception relative to the juridical order on the one hand with 'being' relative to the *logos* in the Platonic text on the other: 'In both cases, the conflict seems to concern an empty space: on the one hand, anomie, juridical *vacuum*, and, on the other, pure being, devoid of any determination or real predicate' (SE 60 Agamben's emphasis). Once again, however, Agamben's insistence upon transcendental thinking leads him to overlook the determinacies that might be developed immanently based on the implicit determinacy of a specifically juridical 'vacuum', an oversight evident in his own emphasis upon the noun rather than the adjective here—he writes 'juridical *vacuum*' rather than '*juridical* vacuum'.

In other words, the state of exception is indeterminate with respect to law or, as we saw in Hegel's version, to limit, and this gives it a *specific kind* of indeterminacy. But a specific kind of indeterminacy is in fact a determinacy nonetheless. Indeed, its indeterminacy mitigates against seeing that this specific indeterminacy is its very determinate character. Once its determinate character is overlooked, it may appear to readily offer itself as a transcendental privileged determiner insofar as, being indeterminate, it seems to require no account of its own determinacy. Insofar as its specific indeterminacy masks the determinate character of that very indeterminacy, it may well appear to be a kind of ultimate abyss or 'vacuum' beyond which we can venture no further—or, as Hegel saw, it may appear to be the final and ultimate shape of freedom in which the one sided character of indeterminacy is 'exalted' to the 'sole highest place' (PR § 5 A). It is precisely this 'one sided character of indeterminacy' in the state of exception that Agamben does indeed exalt as the ground of law. But as long as we think of it as that which makes the juridical order possible, either because of its sheer indeterminacy or in spite of it, we are still conceiving of it in a transcendental way and will then be left with whatever arbitrary result concludes the contest Agamben leaves us with.

Agamben has been trying to think the state of exception at least since the 1995 publication of *Homo Sacer*, in which we also see the same transcendental way of conceiving of the relation between the state of exception and the juridical order. In this earlier work he is ostensibly addressing what he calls the 'bare life' which, in his account, is placed at the center of the political realm constituting 'the original—if concealed—nucleus of sovereign power' (HS 6). But what is telling for our purposes here is his immediate addition that, with this implication of bare life in political power, it is 'as if politics were the place in which life had to transform itself into good life and in which what had to be politicized were always already bare life' (HS 7). The 'always already' indicates a transcendental structure that remains as an underlying or persisting structure determining any further political development, and so the very possibility of dialectical transformation is ruled out right at the outset of his inquiry.

If there is any doubt whether or not this structure underlying political existence is conceived in a transcendental way, such doubts are quelled as soon as Agamben situates the notion of 'bare life' within the state of exception: 'At once excluding bare life from and capturing it within the political order, the state of exception actually constituted, in its very separateness, the hidden foundation on which the entire political system rested' (HS 9). The past tense here does not refer to an ancient regime that has been superseded, but rather to the process whereby the modern liberal democracy came to be established. This process ultimately reveals, in Agamben's view, 'an inner solidarity between democracy and totalitarianism', a thesis he advances 'with every caution' but which he claims he 'must' advance nonetheless (HS 10). The price one pays for overlooking the possibility of genuine transformation within an autonomous and self-determining political order may be great indeed.

At times Agamben seems to come close to Hegel's immanent account, almost as if he wants a mutually grounding relation without a necessary development that follows from its implicit determinacy:

> The exception does not subtract itself from the rule; rather, the rule, suspending itself, gives rise to the exception and, maintaining itself in relation to the exception, first constitutes itself as a rule (HS 18).

But whereas this may at first seem close to Hegel's derivation of the 'rule' or the juridical order of right from the state of exception, there is a crucial difference: for Hegel that order, having arisen from the unsustainability of the state of exception, no longer needs to 'maintain itself in relation to the exception'. It is the persistence of a privileged determiner as ground that marks the crucial difference between Hegel and Agamben and, more importantly, determines whether humanity gets out of the state of exception or remains mired in its abyssal limbo of rightlessness.

As Richard Winfield has pointed out,[36] Carl Schmitt's attempt to understand the state of exception, and all the attempts to annex the latter into the juridical order that follow from this understanding, consistently make one crucial assumption: it is assumed that the political order is constituted in and through a relation with an exterior. Although this may be understood predominantly in terms of a 'friend-foe opposition' within the context of a plurality of nation-states, the basic gesture is that the political realm is defined in relation to its outside, an outside over which it has no a priori jurisdiction. As Winfield puts it:

> By making such a friend-foe opposition constitutive of political association, Schmitt adopts the novel strategy of advancing a doctrine of politics where the state is a particular body politic irreducibly defined in relation to others. Most traditional political theories address the relations of citizens to one another and their government before turning to international relations and their impact upon the domestic life of each state. Schmitt's first thesis instead suggests that the doctrine of the state must conceive every aspect of politics in terms of the plurality of particular states.[37]

Consequently, Schmitt identifies 'sovereignty with the power to decide when there are situations of emergency or normalcy' and explicitly rejects the 'immanence conception of sovereignty, whose most radical practitioner is Hegel'.[38] This means that 'the objective necessity of the laws must lie not in their content but in a command that assures their competence and authority' and hence according to Schmitt 'the legal order itself rests on a decision that only a sovereign power can make, the decision that determines when a normal situation prevails, first permitting legal norms to have their jurisdiction'.[39]

The state of exception then for Schmitt names this relation to an outside over which the sovereign prevails and must prevail if there is to be a juridical

---

36. Winfield, Richard, 'Rethinking Politics: Carl Schmitt vs. Hegel', in *The Owl of Minerva*, vol. 22, no. 2, 1991, pp. 209-225.
37. Winfield, 'Rethinking Politics', p. 217.
38. Winfield, 'Rethinking Politics', p. 221.
39. Winfield, 'Rethinking Politics', p. 211.

order at all. Agamben recognizes this fundamental assumption in Schmitt when he asserts:

> The 'ordering of space' that is, according to Schmitt, constitutive of the sovereign *nomos* is therefore not only a 'taking of land' (*Landesnahme*)—the determination of a juridical and a territorial ordering (of an *Ordnung* and an *Ortung*)—but above all a 'taking of the outside', an exception (*Ausnahme*) (HS 19).

But then without qualification Agamben seems to immediately embrace this assumption himself:

> Since 'there is no rule that is applicable to chaos', chaos must first be included in the juridical order through the creation of a zone of indistinction between outside and inside, chaos and the normal situation—the state of exception. To refer to something, a rule must both presuppose and yet still establish a relation with what is outside relation (the nonrelational). The relation of exception thus simply expresses the originary formal structure of the juridical relation ... In its archetypal form, the state of exception is therefore the principle of every juridical localization, since only the state of exception opens the space in which the determination of a certain juridical order and a particular territory first becomes possible (HS 19).

Based on this logic, eight years later Agamben will write: '*Being-outside, and yet belonging*: this is the topological structure of the state of exception, and only because the sovereign, who decides on the state of exception, is, in truth, logically defined in his being by the exception, can he too be defined by the oxymoron *ecstasy-belonging*' (SE 35 Agamben's emphasis).[40] However, Winfield shows that this assumption—viz. that the political order is defined in relation to an outside—is both problematic as well as unnecessary and, though he applies this critique to Schmitt, it applies to Agamben as well to the degree that the latter accepts the same assumption. It is the 'unique reflexivity' of the political order that renders such an assumption unnecessary:

> Unlike family participation and civil activity in the economy and courts of law, political engagement involves acting so as to determine the very totality of right within which one's own agency as a citizen proceeds. To participate in self-government, whether as campaigner, voter, or official, is thus to engage in an activity that acts upon itself. By contrast, household activity operates within strictures of family rights and obligations that are never laid down by the acts that conform to them. Similarly, economic activity is always concerned with particular satisfactions and never directed at determining the working of the economy itself.[41]

Precisely due to this reflexivity in which the political order is self-determining, it is not primarily defined in relation to an outside and hence does not first need at its foundation a sovereign that would decide on the state of exception. Indeed, such a sovereign would only serve to undermine the very self-determining char-

---

[40]. It was Heidegger who recalled for us the Greek root combining ek—'outside', with stasis—'to stand', in the word 'ecstasy', which then literally signifies 'to stand outside', and hence in the fevered pitch of ecstasy one is 'outside oneself' or 'beside oneself'. See Heidegger, Martin, *Being and Time*, trans. Joan Stambaugh, New York, State University of New York Press, 1996, pp. 302 ff.

[41]. Winfield, 'Rethinking Politics', p. 221.

acter that gives legitimacy to the political process and assures the 'universality of its aims'.[42]

Winfield's critique of Schmitt is similar to the critique he had earlier leveled against other political theories that in some way always ground the political order on something outside it, e.g. on a pre-political or extra-political realm such as the economy for Marxism, the private interests of individuals for liberalism, or the historically contingent character of a community for communitarianism.[43] However, it is not immediately clear that Agamben would necessarily fall prey to such a critique. Agamben is very emphatic that the state of exception, or the bare life which the former negotiates in producing the political space, is included in the political order *through* its exclusion. It is not that the law comes along and is 'applied' to a life that stands outside it, but rather that the latter is 'abandoned' by law, 'that is, exposed and threatened on the threshold in which life and law, outside and inside, become indistinguishable' (HS 28). We have seen that the state of exception in Agamben's thought is marked by an irreducible ambivalence between inclusion and exclusion—its very inclusion is its exclusion and vice versa, a structure Agamben has been grappling with for some time and is a struggle that can be seen in various ways across many if not all of his writings. Thus the state of exception is not simply something outside the political order on which the latter rests as its foundation. The founding character if the state of exception is more subtle than that—it is the 'dislocating localization' or 'inclusive exclusion' that grounds the political order.

Thus although a Winfieldian critique would no doubt assert that Agamben misses the reflexivity of the political order, we would have to add that if he does so, he does so not so much through a simple external grounding upon something other but rather through the transcendental structure of the included exclusion itself. To put it another way, whereas Winfield looks to the already constituted political realm for its 'interactive' and reflexive structure, a structure which has no need for anything external upon which to base itself, in order to meaningfully address Agamben's argument we have to look at the state of exception *prior* to the political order and trace its development *into* the latter. This reveals the immanent logic implied in its peculiar determinacy, a logic that brings us out of the political limbo which otherwise—that is, when the state of exception is viewed as a transcendental determiner—will always characterize it and will thereby seem to 'always already' found the political order.

## CONCLUSION

Following Hegel, we can agree that the state of exception is indeed the necessary beginning in allowing the very reflexivity Winfield highlights to unfold.

---

42. Winfield, 'Rethinking Politics', p. 221.

43. Winfield, *Overcoming Foundations*, pp. 171 ff. For the specific application of this critique to communitarianism, see also Winfield, Richard, 'Ethical Community without Communitarianism', in *Philosophy Today*, vol. 40, no. 2, 1996, pp. 310 ff.

However, it does not persist behind the scenes as a ground or foundation, nor as a 'zone of indeterminacy' between the outside and the inside that holds open the space in which the juridical order becomes possible. That is, the state of exception is not conceived transcendentally. Rather, the suspension of law that the state of exception is *is itself suspended* in the dialectic that leads us out of it and into the sphere of right. By beginning with this state of exception rather than, following Winfield, simply opposing the Schmittian conception of sovereignty based on it to the reflexivity that is possible in the political order, one can show the necessary genesis of that very reflexivity from the state of exception itself, thereby undermining the Schmittian position as an alternative (which Agamben, due to the transcendental way in which he conceives of it, has to leave open—while hoping that Benjamin wins out in the 'gigantomachy concerning a void') (SE 59 ff).[44] Therefore when Agamben's concludes that 'the task at hand is not to bring the state of exception back within its spatially and temporally defined boundaries in order to then reaffirm the primacy of a norm and of rights that are themselves ultimately grounded in it' (SE 87), we can assert that the sphere of right is precisely *not* 'ultimately grounded in' the state of exception at all and so Agamben fundamentally misconceives the task at hand.

Because the state of exception does not persist within the juridical order as its ground, any Schmittian attempt to annex and preside over the state of exception from the perspective of a predetermined juridical order would fall prey to a Hegelian critique as a regression or a mere misunderstanding. The attempt to dominate the state of exception from the perspective of the juridical order has already turned the state of exception into something else—viz. a regression to arbitrary and irrational rule. It is precisely this arbitrariness and caprice that is exploited by the Bush administration, for instance, when it claims the prerogative of stripping any human being on the planet of all rights and consigning him/her to what Luban calls the 'limbo of rightlessness'.[45] And rather than following Agamben and seeing this as manifesting the hidden ground of modern democracy, most people rightly see it as the regression to arbitrary exercise of power that it is.

On the other hand, the Benjaminian formula of bringing on the state of exception and overturning the state may well look like the mere flight from all limits of negative freedom that Hegel discusses with the French revolution in view. However, to bring on the state of exception a la Benjamin is to open up the beginning of freedom again, from which the dialectic can then take us for-

---

44. Although Agamben apparently identifies the pure violence of Benjaminian revolution with 'being' and the Schmittian strategy of annexing the state of exception into the juridical order with 'the meshes of the logos' (HS 60), a comparison more in keeping with the implicit reference to Plato's *Sophist* here might be to identify pure violence with pure becoming (*dunamis*), a power which by itself lacks direction and so risks self-destruction (for an interesting account of this interplay between power and direction in Plato's text, see Edward Goodwin Ballard, *Man and Technology*, Pittsburgh, Duquesne University Press, 1978, pp. 11 ff.). Agamben's immediate gesture, once again, is to situate both law and *logos* in terms of a ground: 'That is to say, everything happens as if both law and logos needed an anomic (or alogical) zone of suspension in order to ground their reference to the world of life' (SE 60).

45. Luban, 'The War on Terrorism and the End of Human Rights'.

ward and into the universality of right. Whether or not this is a regression or the necessary clearing away of obstacles that prevent the realization of freedom can only be empirically determined with respect to the specific historical context in which such revolution occurs. So Hegel does indeed offer the only viable way out of the state of exception that does not merely leave everything up for grabs. Nor does Hegel attempt to annex the state of exception in advance along lines similar to Schmitt's program. If anything, Hegel eliminates justification for Right-authoritarian invocation of the state of exception insofar as the latter attempts to include the state of exception within its sphere of legitimacy. But *the state* can never return to the state of exception—or to negative freedom—without being a mere regression. This precludes the authoritarian program of Schmitt. Though we cannot make this claim in any a priori way, revolution on the other hand may well—though not necessarily—operate against a state-structure that has replaced self-determining freedom with a mere simulacrum of the latter.

If the state of exception is conceived as a ground that must forever remain situated in relation to the juridical order, however, no such forward movement is possible—we always wind up back again at the *same* determinacy (which is the determinacy of suspended determinacy—still nonetheless a determinacy as we have seen), and so the most Agamben can leave us with is a vague prophesy that

> One day humanity will play with law just as children play with disused objects, not in order to restore them to their canonical use but to free them from it for good. What is found after the law is not a more proper and original use value that precedes the law, but a new use that is born after it' (SE 64).

Agamben seems to see this as the only alternative to a misguided desire to return to a lost origin. But whether we seek a lost origin or a future child-play with law, both still imply the same determinacy of suspended determinacy—and for Hegel the latter is simultaneously the problem with negative freedom as well as the catalyst for progressive movement that gets us out if it.

On the other hand, to follow the Schmittian program in which the juridical order presides over the state of exception is to impose an external authoritarian control over the dialectic of freedom. Because such authority is externally imposed, it effectively blocks the dialectic from unfolding and instead makes the state of exception appear as the space within which the political state operates or as its hidden ground, thereby also concealing its regressive character. Therefore we can get from Benjamin to the universality of freedom and the normativity it generates as self-determination—provided we do not follow Agamben and conceive of the state of exception as a ground—but we cannot do so from Schmitt. This is why the latter leads to totalitarianism—a fact Agamben indicates without being able to provide an explanation.

The problem Agamben has to deal with is that he tries to account for the state of exception from the perspective of the state a la Schmitt and also from the perspective of the oppressed who live under the state a la Benjamin. In both cases, the juridical order appears as predetermined alongside the state of exception, and the problem is to set up or articulate a relation between the two. This invites the positing of one as ground of the other. Indeed, for Agamben the state of exception must be actively maintained in relation to the juridical order: although 'unthinkable' from the perspective of the law, 'this unthinkable thing nevertheless has a decisive strategic relevance for the juridical order and must not be allowed to slip away at any cost' (SE 51). To be sure, Agamben does not necessarily endorse any and every relation or 'strategic relevance' between the state of exception and the juridical order here—for him whether the emergent result is Schmitt's totalitarianism or the quasi-messianic community to come he sees intimated in Benjamin, everything depends upon the kind of relation it is. But by beginning with both as *given* rather than thinking the origin of the juridical order out of the state of exception in terms of the dialectic of freedom as Hegel does, Agamben is misled into the kind of transcendental thinking that looks for essences and grounds rather than the non-foundational thinking that alone can establish non-arbitrary and universal normativity for the political order.

Winfield's critique of communitarianism is instructive in this regard. He argues that the flaw in communitarianism is that it cannot reconcile the universality of its ethical norms with the particularity of its content.[46] If the community establishes its own norms, no normative evaluation can preside over it without being imported from elsewhere and externally imposed, which would thereby undermine its communitarian character. He frames the problem in terms of Wittgenstein's 'language games' in which the rules of each game are internally generated within that game but, viewed from outside that particular language game, the rules are merely arbitrary. If normativity depends upon 'extrinsic foundations', it is for that very reason not a 'communitarian' ethic at all. If it does not depend upon extrinsic foundations, its particular content is arbitrary and contingent, a product of particular historical contingencies. In either case we have an abstract universal that cannot bridge the gap between its universal form and its particular content. This problem is merely repeated in Badiou when he abstracts a formal truth procedure from its particular content, discarding the latter in favour of the former. In a certain way, Agamben's way of conceiving the state of exception as hidden ground also reinstates an abstract universal insofar as this ground remains behind the scenes, as it were, underwriting the juridical order but never actually *becoming* that order, and so the universality of the state of exception always remains other than the juridical order which either seeks to dominate it (Schmitt) or is overthrown by it (Benjamin).

Winfield further argues that the only solution to this problem of abstract universality is to found a community on self-determination. This 'founding', however, is not a *foundation*—it is rather a beginning that progressively determines itself without assuming anything as given in advance upon which it would be based or

---

46. Winfield, Richard, 'Ethical Community without Communitarianism', in *Philosophy Today*, vol. 40, no. 2, 1996, pp. 310 ff.

to which it would return. It is freedom conceived as self-determination that 'owes its measure to nothing but itself, overcoming the gap between legitimating factor and legitimated conduct'[47]—or, to put it in the terms Agamben borrows from Schmitt, between the law-making constituent power and law-preserving constituted power. The contingencies of history and nature—the 'physical, astronomical, chemical, biological, and psychological conditions without which rational agents cannot interact at all, do not thereby prescribe what shape ethical community should have'.[48] To put it another way, these contingencies are enabling but not determining conditions.[49]

But the key element in this 'self-grounding, presuppositionless character that fundamental normativity requires'[50] is that in and of itself, without reference to anything outside the suspension of all normativity—that is, without reference to anything outside the 'state of exception' that alone does not presuppose any predetermined normativity—it implies in itself a logic specifying a normative determinacy that arises out of it. If this is to be the case, the state of exception cannot be a principle or ground that then is situated in relation to something else—be it a juridical order or otherwise—but rather must itself *become* that normative determinacy *through* its own suspension of all normativity. This suspension itself reveals a character specific to it—that of an indeterminate determinacy or a negation of all limit. It is only in submitting to the logic implied by the indeterminate determinacy of the state of exception that it becomes self-determining, viz., that it is subject to the limits imposed by its own structure and so is not subject to an externally imposed measure.

In this way and in this way only, any normativity generated is neither a contingent and thereby also an arbitrary result of historical/cultural circumstances, nor the formal abstraction of a universality that can be conceived outside the determinacy of its particular content (e.g. as ground, principle, truth procedure, etc.). Therefore also in this way and in this way only, its particular content is identical to its universal form and abstract universality is overcome. And finally, in this way and in this way only we neither return to an originary state beyond or before juridical apparatuses nor are we merely left with a humanity that plays with law just as children play with disused objects. We are not left in a political limbo hoping for a good outcome in the contest between revolutionary violence and state authoritarianism as they both spar within the zone of indeterminacy held open by the state of exception. Rather, we have a concrete universal normativity implied by the structure of self-determination that necessarily arises out of the state of exception's own self-negation.

Thus in the context of the view presented here, it is neither mere coincidence nor unreflective habit that the most common immediate reaction to a state-ordered suspension of the juridical order—such as the US under the Bush

---

47. Winfield, 'Ethical Community without Communitarianism', p. 314.
48. Winfield, 'Ethical Community without Communitarianism', p. 314.
49. Winfield, *Overcoming Foundations*, p. 63.
50. Winfield, 'Ethical Community without Communitarianism', p. 314.

administration has attempted in the Guantánamo Bay detention camp—is to demand that the rights of those detained be respected rather than routinely ignored by means of facile justifications.

*encountering the speculative*

# 15

# The Ego as World: Speculative Justification and the Role of the Thinker in Hegel's Philosophy

Toula Nicolacopoulos and George Vassilacopoulos

> to conceive the spiritual spiritually (LHP II 9)

> Aristotle was the first to say that νους is the thought of thought. The result is the thought which is at home with itself, and at the same time embraces the universe, and transforms it into an intelligent world. (LHP III 546)

## I. INTRODUCTION

For Hegel the practice of speculative thought, or 'Science', involves two cycles of justification that are preliminary to the final act of fully realizing Science's notion, that of knowing absolutely. Whereas the first cycle is associated with the *Phenomenology of Spirit* the second concerns the formulation and development of the logical categories in the sections of the *Science of Logic* entitled respectively 'The Doctrine of Being' (Being) and 'The Doctrine of Essence' (Essence). Hegel explains the first phenomenological justificatory cycle in the following terms:

> [T]he individual has the right to demand that Science should at least provide him with the ladder to this standpoint, should show him this standpoint within himself. His right is based on his absolute independence, which he is conscious of possessing in every phase of his knowledge; for in each one, whether recognized by Science or not, and whatever the content may be, the individual is the absolute form, i.e. he is the immediate certainty of himself (PS ¶ 26).

As to the second justificatory cycle, that consisting of Being and Essence, Hegel observes:

> When [...] the notion is called the truth of Being and Essence, we must expect to be

asked why we do not begin with the notion? The answer is that, where knowledge by thought is our aim, we cannot begin with the truth, because the truth, when it forms the beginning, must rest on mere assertion. The truth when it is thought must as such verify itself to thought (EL § 159 A).

Whereas the 'individual', or 'consciousness', requires the phenomenological cycle of justification, it is thought that necessitates the logical cycle. In both instances some sort of verification is sought: in the first Science must verify itself to consciousness whereas in the second it is 'truth' that must verify itself to 'thought'.

Hegel's remarks on the nature and need for these two cycles of justification raise some fundamental questions. For one thing, why is it that the individual has the 'right' to make demands upon Science? Perhaps more importantly, where and how does the individual encounter Science in the first place? One might also ask what it means for truth to verify itself to thought instead of the reverse. In what follows our aim will be to show how the answers to these questions, and indeed the whole issue of justification, are linked to a certain appreciation of the role of the speculative thinker in both the initial appearance and the subsequent development of Science.

## The Question of Justification

By way of introductory observations we can note further that Hegel employs similar terms to speak of the importance of the two justificatory cycles. For example, about the activation of the *Phenomenology of Spirit* phenomenological process he says:

> least of all will it be like the rapturous enthusiasm which, like a shot from a pistol, begins straight away with absolute knowledge, and makes short work of other standpoints by declaring that it takes no notice of them (PS ¶ 27).

So too, when the question of the beginning of Science arises in the *Science of Logic* Hegel once again warns against moving 'like a shot from a pistol' (SL 67). Moreover, the standpoint of Science is similarly represented in relation to the two justificatory cycles. Just as in the *Phenomenology* Science must take into account consciousness' antithetical attitude to its object of knowledge, in the *Science of Logic* it must take into account the inter-relations of logical categories that do not fully conform to the speculative demands of the notion.

The abovementioned remarks draw our attention to the unacceptability of resting on 'mere assertion' to start the speculative project. So, what is the reason for thinking that Science cannot properly begin by presupposing that absolute knowing is the natural orientation of thinking? One might suggest that in so far as Science is philosophy, and philosophy is radical questioning, Science's own justifiedness must be open to questioning. But this sort of response fails to take account of the radical ambitions characterizing the speculative orientation. In assuming a rather vague and free-floating sense of 'philosophy' it does not allow that Science already takes itself to be philosophy *as such* or radically free thinking. If, as we will argue below, speculative thinking takes itself to be free or self-determining in the space of its own freedom, then a legitimate and philosophical questioning of Science must be part of Science's self-orientation. In other words, Science's justificatory processes must be enactments of aspects of the full meaning of the radical freedom that defines speculative thinking. That is, they give rise to Science in so far as they are activated, sustained and completed *by* Science *from within* Science.

So, the legitimacy of raising the question of the justification of Science must have to do with the facts that the thinker is already situated *in* Science and that his or her insights emerge directly from within its space so to speak. It also follows that in so far as Science relies upon the two justificatory cycles it must do so not because *it cannot* begin from the immediate unfolding of the absoluteness of absolute knowledge 'like a shot from a pistol' but, paradoxically, because *it can*. There is nothing from a technical point of view to stop Science from activating its thinking by fully and immediately employing the kind of reflection already incorporated in the already available notion. Indeed, Science could very well have started its project from the section of the *Science of Logic* entitled 'Subjective Logic, or the Doctrine of the Notion'. In doing so, it would have by-passed both the phenomenological process and the thinking involved in the doctrines of Being and Essence. Our claim is that speculative justification is not about *deriving* absolute knowledge that is supposedly initially either known only as a hypothesis, or, not yet known at all. Nor does it rely on an independently justified process that thereby justifies the results it derives. Rather the process of justification is itself justified by what is an already available field of knowing, namely Science. The sort of justification that the speculative demands is itself speculative. Ultimately this means that from the outset the thinker and, consequently, thinking itself is not free-floating but embedded and committed. That Science and everything related to it become an issue at all depend upon the fact that Science 'comes on the scene' (PS ¶ 76) or, in other words, that the thinker already dwells in the 'truth' that the 'Absolute' is (PS ¶ 74).

So the need for justification has to do, not with the absence of absolute knowledge, but with its already achieved presence. For reasons to be explored in some detail below, precisely because Science emerges by fully encountering itself as what it is, namely the mutual embracing of knowing and known, justification becomes an issue as an integral part of the absoluteness of this kind of knowledge. Science's possession of its notion is primordial and irreducible to any kind of original derivation beyond the very problematic that is determined by the appearance of the notion itself. Of course if this reading is correct then the popular hermeneutic idea that the aim of the *Phenomenology* is to lead the unenlightened consciousness to the standpoint of absolute knowledge must be misguided.[1] In our paper we hope to show that to appreciate the radical meaning of justification is to see the speculative purpose often associated with the *Phenomenology* in a new light.

---

1. See, for example, Terry Pinkard, *Hegel's Phenomenology: The Sociality of Reason*, Cambridge, New York and Melbourne, Cambridge University Press, 1996, pp. 16-17.

## Justification and the Thinker's Role and Position in Science

So far we have suggested to appreciate that the logical justification of the notion is the truth of the forms of thinking practiced in Being and Essence, and that the phenomenological justification of Science is the truth of consciousness, we must invoke the idea that, although it could do otherwise, Science refrains from starting immediately from the activation of its already available notion. This refraining on the part of Science becomes Science's place of dwelling so to speak through which it attempts *justifiably* to appropriate what it already is. Starting from the above observation about the appearing of Science, how should we understand the phenomenological and logical dimensions of Science's two-stage process of justification? We will be arguing that the two justificatory cycles are best understood in relation to the thinker's role and position in Science. These must not only be accessible and available from the very beginning, but their very accessibility and availability must themselves be justifiable. To be sure, Hegel attributes a central role to the thinker as is evidenced by the remark in the 'Preface' to his *Phenomenology* that the beginning of philosophy presupposes that consciousness should dwell in the element of 'pure self-recognition' (PS ¶ 26). Indeed, in a number of places throughout the elaboration and discussion of his system Hegel comments strategically on the position of the thinker. Here is one example from an introduction to the lectures on the history of philosophy presented in 1823 and repeated in 1825 and 1827:

> Because the universal is there as objective, I have thought myself in it. I am myself contained in this infinite thing and at the same time have a consciousness of it. Thus at the standpoint of objectivity I remain at the same time at the standpoint of knowing, and I retain this standpoint (ILHP 166).

Again, in the 'Preface' to his *Philosophy of Right* he refers to thinkers as

> those in whom there has once arisen an inner voice bidding them to comprehend, not only to dwell in what is substantive while still retaining subjective freedom, but also to possess subjective freedom while standing not in anything particular and accidental but in what exists absolutely (PR § 12).

The position of the thinker remains central irrespective of whether Hegel is referring to the experience of political freedom and the individual's relationship to the substantiality of his communal being or to the experience of the speculative philosopher. Our argument will be that from 'the moment when Science comes on the scene' (PS ¶ 76) the thinker finds himself or herself dwelling, as a matter of fact, in the element that in turn makes this appearance possible through the thinker's dwelling. Most decisively for the speculative experience, qua speculative dweller the thinker *receives* the absolute commandment 'Know thyself' (EPM § 377). This receiving in turn gives rise to the most primordial emerging of Science, an emerging that is constituted as the vision to think speculatively or purely. Yet it is not enough for the thinker simply to dwell in the necessary element; he or she must also *dwell in this dwelling* in the sense of dwelling freely. Nor is it enough for the thinker merely immediately to receive the command; he or she must also *receive the receiving* as a precondition for actually realizing the command to think speculatively or purely. What is received, as a matter of fact, must also be received freely. These two aspects, dwelling and receiving freely, are necessitated by the fact that the speculative claims consciousness as a self-determining thinker. Whereas the first act of freedom is performed in the *Phenomenology*, the second informs the thinking practiced in 'The Doctrine of Being' and 'The Doctrine of Essence'.

## II. THE APPEARANCE OF SCIENCE AND SPIRIT AS MANIFESTATION

When Science first emerges, it emerges in the world as a radical break from the world's already given orientation. It is therefore a disturbance that takes place unexpectedly. The speculative moment appears and announces itself as this kind of break and it does so by claiming its thinker unconditionally and, from the standpoint of the latter, unexpectedly. The announcement is made *to the thinker* but it also comes *through the thinker* via a process that violently disassociates the thinker from the world in which he or she is otherwise absorbed in order to re-situate him or her in (the world through) absolute knowing.

Here, the thinker is exposed to the challenge of *becoming* a thinker in so far as Science unconditionally permeates and claims his or her being. But as well as belonging to Science in this way, the thinker must also belong to this belonging freely. When in the position of the thinker, one is exposed to a calling that one hears with one's whole being, to an eruptive event whose radical transformative power demands a response. It follows that, rather than being claimed as a thinker for the reason that one already is a thinker independently of the claiming, one is a thinker-to-become in so far as one responds appropriately to having been claimed as a thinker. Ultimately, what matters is the resolve to stay with Science. This is why we can never arrive at the speculative standpoint with the aid of some detached reasoning process or by impartially choosing from amongst a range of alternatives.[2]

Now, the break that the appearance of Science marks between itself and the world also harbours a radical continuity that eventually makes possible the speculative engagement of Science with the world. Because the world and Science are both moments of Spirit their relating is determined by this co-belonging. According to Hegel, the (formal) definition of Spirit (or mind) is that it is manifestation and everything to do with Spirit is manifested within such manifestation. More specifically, Spirit is absolute manifestation since it is ultimately a pure, unqualified, revealing that reveals itself to itself:

> The manifestation of itself to itself is [...] itself the content of mind and not, as it were, only a form externally added to the content; consequently mind, by its mani-

---

2. See Donald P. Verene, *Hegel's Absolute: An Introduction to Reading the Phenomenology of Spirit*, Albany, State University of New York Press, 2007, p. 44.

festation, does not manifest a content different from its form, but manifests its form which expresses the entire content of mind, namely, its self-manifestation (EPM § 383 A).

In the full expression of Spirit as manifestation Spirit's being incorporates thinking that reveals the very notion of manifestation. It thus allows this manifesting being to reveal itself to itself. As this unconditional and self-sustaining revealing, Spirit is apprehended speculatively as a double embracing: being embraces thinking and embraced thinking embraces being. Being and thinking are thus two aspects of this embracing/embraced inter-relation that belong equally to Spirit understood as manifestation in the above radical sense.

This inter-relationship is at the heart of Hegel's account of Reason in terms of the mutual 'encompassing' of the ego and its object:

> The essential and actual truth which reason is, lies in the simple identity of the subjectivity of the notion with its objectivity and universality. The universality of reason, therefore, whilst it signifies that the object, which was only given to consciousness qua consciousness, is now itself universal, permeating and encompassing the ego, also signifies that the pure ego is the pure form which overlaps the object and encompasses it (EPM § 438).

For Hegel then Spirit is the mutual informing of two seemingly antithetical movements. On the one hand, the 'object' is the infinite power (substance) that absolutely embraces the 'ego' that is unable to resist this embracing. On the other, rather than drowning in its absolute passivity, the 'ego' is at once the power (subject) freely to embrace the 'object' that is in turn not in a position to prevent this kind of freedom from realizing itself. The passivity in question is absolute since it can accommodate a freedom whose infinity rests with its power to be informed by passivity without eliminating or being eliminated by it. Both subject and object are expressions of absolute manifestation given that each incorporates the other.

Still, the full expression of Spirit as Reason results from a process that is mediated by the division in Spirit between the object or being and the thinking ego or, in other words, between world and Science. It is as this division that the two moments of Spirit inform or embrace each other, albeit only in principle, that is, only the realm of pure thinking. Disassociated from the world, the thinker thinks the world as thinkable in the absence of the corresponding reflective embracing of this thinking by the world's being.

How should we understand the beginning of philosophy in the light of this fundamental idea of Spirit as (the principle of) Reason and the abovementioned understanding of the position of the thinker in relation to (the principle of) Reason? To answer this question is to offer an interpretation of one of Hegel's more enigmatic observations that in our view is also most fundamental. We are referring to the observation that the 'beginning of philosophy presupposes or requires that consciousness should dwell in this element' of '[p]ure self-recognition in absolute otherness, this Aether as such, [which] is the ground and soil of Science or knowledge in general' (PS ¶ 26). What we want to argue here is that, as the precondition for philosophy, or Science, the abovementioned dwelling of the thinker involves the encompassing (permeating) of consciousness (ego) by the universality of 'pure self-recognition in absolute otherness' (the thinkable object), but also consciousness's potential for encompassing (thinking) pure self-recognition's universality. As we have noted, this principle takes place in the division between thinking and being or, in other words, in the realm of absolute otherness. Moreover, in its capacity as dwelling in the universal, consciousness relates to itself as a universal, that is, as the thinker for whom thinking (philosophy) is an aim to be realized and hence that which must encompass the already encompassing pure self-recognition. Leaving aside for the moment Hegel's reference to 'absolute otherness', we will proceed next to consider how Spirit's self-manifestation incorporates both the moment of pure self-recognition as such and the element of consciousness' dwelling.

*The Meaning of Pure Self-recognition*

The abovementioned reference to 'Aether' is meant to convey the sense that in the case of pure self-recognition we are dealing with the utter simplicity of recognition as such. If we understand 'self-recognition' through this guiding metaphor, we can appreciate that the recognition in question does not happen as the contribution of an external agent. Instead, it is pure or *as such* in that it takes place *within itself* so to speak and does not refer to anything that does not already belong to it qua recognition.

This immanence renders it *immediately* as manifestation. According to Hegel, self-recognition is 'pure spirituality as the universal that has the form of simple immediacy' (PS ¶ 26). Hegel also refers to it as 'this immediacy of Spirit' that is 'the very substance of Spirit' (PS ¶ 26). As immediate manifestation that is not qualified by any specific form, Spirit encounters itself in its purity all at once without having to traverse a distance that might mark some sort of gap to be filled.

Still, given that as self-recognition this universal is living, some difference or otherness must be involved within its already given field of unimpeded operation. Moreover, the difference in question must be related to the particular as such as determined by the specificity of its infinite singularity. This specificity marks an absolute limit within pure self-recognition whose limiting activity intensifies the limitlessness of the latter's immediate self-realization. It is limitless precisely because the substantive universality of pure self-recognition permeates the singularity of the singular qua already permeated. The universal perpetually remains itself whilst simultaneously intensifying and deepening itself through the particular. The particular is not given in terms of an agency that might activate a reflective distance and determination of aims to be realized. In its other Spirit does not detect a loss of itself or some resistance that it must overcome. Rather, it finds itself as always already there. As the substance of Spirit pure self-recognition is a universal, all encompassing and objective condition that is irresistible, infinite life. Hegel also refers to it as the 'free power' that 'could also be called free love and boundless blessedness' since 'it is itself and takes its other within its embrace, but without *doing violence* to it; on the contrary, the universal is, in its other, in peaceful communion with itself' (SL 603).

So, this objective embracing and permeating universal is the truth of the particular. We can say further that the truth of the particular is that it is already gathered with other particulars qua gathered in the already achieved permeating and embracing that the universal is as the 'free power' of gathering as such.[3] This plurality of particulars is necessary in order for the universal not to exhaust itself in the single particular and thereby compromise its universality. At the same time such gathering is not to be understood in terms of some instrumental value or strategic relation between particulars. As the power to gather particulars qua already gathered, the substantive universal is immediate communal being populated by communal singularities. The universal has its being in and as this communality. The substantive communality of this kind of being lays in the fact that it has already claimed particulars, beyond all their concrete specificities, as belonging to it unconditionally. From the standpoint of this radical communality particulars are unconditionally claimed by the communally embracing and permeating universal. Moreover, it is only within the being of each particular qua the purely claimed that specificities, such as personal biographies, become meaningful. Let us proceed to re-conceptualize the idea of pure self-recognition in these more concrete existential terms.

## Pure Self-recognition, Communal Being and the Source of Speculative Thinking

Invoking what he calls a 'community of minds' (PS ¶ 69), Hegel is the thinker of communality as such in the dual sense of thinking *about* communality whilst also being the thinking *of* communality. Here, communality is understood as the immanently thinkable and, hence, the absolute object. Hegel is, therefore, the situated and committed thinker in and of the thinkable. This explains his preoccupation with manifestation and the associated mutual informing of form and content that manifestation implies. From Hegel's perspective, only the historical emergence of such an immediate and purely self-referential communal spirit—a spirit that at once is liberated from specific forms of manifestation, like faith, custom and so on and is the source of the transformative experience associated with the individual's unconditional immersion in it—is capable of supplying the 'ground and soil of Science or knowledge in general' (RH 92).[4] To put the same point differently, only the immediacy and simplicity of communal being's self-referentiality can function as the 'soil' for the growth of knowledge as such. For, if knowledge is the thinking of universals, the 'soil' of this thinking must itself be

---

3. On the significance of gathering for Hegel's absolute see George Vassilacopoulos, 'Gathering and Dispersing: The Absolute Spirit in Hegel's Philosophy', this collection.

4. On these specific forms of manifestation see G. W. F. Hegel, *Reason in History: A General Introduction to the Philosophy of History*, trans. Robert S. Hartman, New York, Liberal Arts Press, 1953, p. 92.

the universal that in its utter simplicity or state of immediacy is substantive or objective communal being in the abovementioned sense.

This said, how is that such a radical reflective standpoint—one directed to the fact of dwelling in the being of pure universality as something that belongs to the thinker's own standpoint of reflection—can be dependent upon a universal characterized by *immediacy*, albeit pure manifestation? In other words, how might this unqualified immediacy immanently transform itself into an absolute object that incorporates reflectiveness? Such a task obviously relies upon there being immanently to the communal immediacy some differentiation that implies a distance or an outside of some sort. Building on Hegel's metaphor we could suggest that there must be a seed of some sort operating in the ground and soil of pure self-recognition. If we think of the question of the activation of speculative thinking in terms of the conditions for the growth of the seed that is to be found in the soil of pure self-recognition, then to understand the source of speculative thinking is to gain a radical appreciation of the role and character of this seed. Let us move on then to identify this seed in the light of our analysis so far.

We can begin by noting that the growth of the seed of pure self-recognition would amount to the transformation of this immediate universal manifestation of communality as a whole into a reflective engagement with its immanent thinking. Moreover, this latter would consist in the dual aim of articulating the notion of manifestation and ultimately achieving manifesting manifestation in this way. In other words, the growth of the seed in question would amount to the activation of the form of communal being that transforms the purely substantive and immediate manifestation of its being into the place of dwelling of the thinker and thereby acting as the embrace of thinking ultimately posits itself as that which thinking is to embrace. Accordingly, we should ask what it would mean for the immediate and universal embracing of communal being to become the absolute object of an immanently posited thinking. Because the universal as such can only be embraced by its notion, in so far as it is possible to supply this notion it would need to be supplied by what belongs to the universal unconditionally and yet is also differentiated from it. The universal would therefore have to differentiate itself from itself by treating its being as self-absence as well. It is manifestation that has yet to manifest itself and so is absent in its manifesting. Moreover, in so far as this self-presence is affirmed as already *immediately* realized in the universal's encounter of itself in the particular—in that it already permeates the particular—the particular must also be capable of functioning as the *topos* of the universal's absence. The universal thus emerges and retreats in the particular since it is in the particular that the universal being is affirmed whilst its notion, or the thinking of its being, is yet to be activated.

It follows from the above that as the *topos* of absencing, the particular must reflectively embrace the universal. So it is the particular qua communal singularity that combines the experience of the infinite antithesis of pure presence—being—that is also absence—notion—and pure absence that is also presence. What is unconditionally present in the particular incorporates into itself the positing of itself as the project of explicit self-appropriation through the particular. What is already unconditionally present yet immediately pure owes its presence to its pure power to be. Moreover, thanks to its purity this power must be retrieved and exercised reflectively through the particular simply because it is there. Communal being must retrieve its power to be what it already is or, in other words, it must retrieve itself as a project. In this inter-relation of the universal and the particular we can discern a certain movement. The universality of immediate communality releases the particular from itself as that which belongs to it unconditionally and it re-claims it by calling upon it to affirm that its unconditional belonging also belongs to its own particular being. In other words it calls upon the particular to become a thinker in order to think the universal.

Without destroying itself then the universal must release the particular and it does so by releasing the particular qua ego since this is the infinitely singular and hence the other of the universal. As the pure thinking of the pure universal the particular ego infinitely expands itself in order to embrace the universality of communal being with the result that manifestation thereby manifests itself. Precisely because what is purely singular is also permeated by the purely universal such permeation releases singularity to be the infinite power of an infinite expansion capable of embracing and dwelling in what initially permeates it thereby acting as the universal's *topos* of dwelling. Infinite passivity thus proves itself to be infinite freedom as well. Here we have the speculative mystery of the infinitely expanding and infinitely contracting communal ego. The truth of the ego is that it is living, that is, pulsating. Such releasing of the free ego transforms passive immersion in substantial communality into the active and visionary dwelling of a thinker.

For Hegel then in providing the thinking that the immediate universality of the pure manifestation of communal being requires, consciousness is 'the universal which has as its content likewise the universal', since the being of consciousness is 'to be as a universal within the universal'. To put the same point in more dramatic terms, as a result of dwelling in the universal before the individual activates his thinking, 'in his particularity [he] has the vision of himself as universal' (ILHP 164, 172). Here Hegel's Spinozism informs the fundamental precondition of his philosophy:

> when man begins to philosophize, the soul must commence by bathing in this ether of the one Substance, in which all that man has held as true has disappeared; this negation of all that is particular, to which every philosopher must have come, is the liberation of the mind and its absolute foundation (LHP III 257-258).

So on our reading when Hegel makes the point that the beginning of philosophy presupposes that consciousness should dwell in the element of the 'Aether as such' of pure self-recognition, he is invoking this link between the immediacy of the pure manifestation of communal being and the demand to think it in the above sense. As the thinking of the universal, philosophy presupposes the dwelling of the thinker in the universal. Still, since thinking is initially encountered as a project, as we noted above, the substantive universal qua what-is-to-be-thought must be encountered as an absence that permeates the being of the thinker. Pure self-recognition is precisely this absence of the universal as manifesting manifestation that both belongs to the universal and is manifested in what is objectively embraced and permeated by the substantive universal, namely the being of the particular. This is manifested manifestation as a project to be realized. The dwelling of consciousness in the absence of the universal that unconditionally fills consciousness' being is thus the precondition of speculative philosophy that is itself understood as the thinking of the universal or manifestation as such. We can conclude that it is the dwelling of consciousness in the terms indicated by the above analysis that supplies the seed for the growth of Science.

## III. MODERNITY AND SPECULATIVE PHILOSOPHY

Let us now consider in some detail the precise way in which the activation and completion of speculative philosophy depend upon the situating of consciousness in the substantive oneness of pure self-recognition that we mentioned in the previous section. To this end we will sketch the outlines of a speculative theory of modernity since Hegel attributes the experience of unqualified, pure communality to western modernity.

### *The New World Order of Atomic Individuality*

Hegel famously relates his own era to the 'sunburst which, in one flash, illuminates the features of the new world' (PS ¶ 11). In what is likely to be an allusion to the French Revolution, this reference to an eruption of sorts announces the arrival in the existing world order of something radically new. In the fullness of its radicality this announcement indicates liberation. The emerging new world, the new form of Spirit, is both liberated, in so far as it emerges from the given order, and the process of liberation from the given order, in so far as it engages in 'dissolving bit by bit the structure of its previous world' (PS ¶ 11).

How might we understand the relationship between speculative philosophy and this complex process of generating historical novelty? To begin with, if we follow Hegel's insistence that Spirit is communal manifestation we can read the old world in terms of a communal being that is determined by specific forms of communal gathering, such as faith, tradition and so on, that Hegel refers to as 'immediate (simple and unreflective) existence'. Now let us suppose that within this world a newly oriented spiritual manifestation emerges and effectively challenges the old by putting into question the very principle of this form of unreflective communal gathering. The emerging of the new must be integrally linked with the collapsing of the old. If unreflective communal being is the power to gather individuals qua already gathered into specific forms of gathering, its collapsing amounts to their release.

Moreover, in their new capacity of having been released from hitherto forms of unreflective communal being the individuals in question are constituted as having turned against the old world. What might such 'liberated individuals' be like? Thinking in purely negative terms we can understand this individuality in its opposition to the gathering of unreflective communal beings. Here is the rather bleak picture that Hegel draws:

> Therewith appears the isolation of the individuals from each other and the whole, their aggressive selfishness and vanity, their seeking of advantage and satisfaction at the expense of the whole. For the inward principle of such isolation (not only produces the content but) the form of subjectivity—selfishness and corruption in the unbound passions and egotistic interests of men (RH 92).

So the liberated individuals experience their being as atomic whereas their collectivity presents in the terms of dispersal. They immerse themselves in their singularity that in turn releases their 'unbound passions and egotistic interests' given that it is unable to expand and become the *topos* of dwelling of communality. Individuals thus lose the power to experience their communal being so much so that the norm is to inter-relate instrumentally. The dispersal of their collective being implicates their atomic individuality in a way that renders the latter seemingly primordial and irreducible. So for Hegel atomic individuality results from the 'violent diremption of mind or spirit into different selves which are [...] in and for themselves and for one another, are independent, absolutely impenetrable, resistant' (EPM § 436 A). Moreover, Hegel links this 'impenetrable, atomic individuality' with the being of 'the person' that he takes to be 'the practical, objective notion, in and for itself' (SL 824).

Accordingly, the dispersal of immediate communal being into the form of personality informs and determines the re-groupings that can proceed as an outcome of the interaction of self-interested subjects. Hobbes is perhaps the first thinker to attempt to make sense of this historically novel situation. He is optimistic because he thinks that, despite their unbound dispersion, the dwellers in the state of nature can come to master their lives when they institute the political state—when they create artificial form out of the formlessness of their situation of total war—purely on the basis of enlightened self-interest. Yet for Hegel, the speculative significance of personality lies in the connection between this impenetrable atomic individuality and its 'real' or concrete expression, namely property ownership (PR § 34-40). Let us consider this connection for a moment.

From the discussion so far it follows that once liberated from the manifestation of specific forms of communal being, the locus of manifestation becomes the individual himself or herself. Consequently, personality, the form of atomic individuality, determines this manifestation. Because manifestation involves the agency of personality that refers to the singularity of the ego, and this singularity in turn presents as *exclusively* atomic individuality, the person's freedom is not infinite despite being the bearer of manifestation. Although self-relating and thus manifesting (free) to this extent, the person cannot also expand infinitely qua thinking being (in the sense analyzed in the previous section) in order thereby to activate the notion of manifestation. In this case manifestation is to some extent contained and determined by singularity. We might say that the person *sinks into himself* and, rather than dwelling in the expansive way we analyzed earlier, the person is instead posited as free-floating. Accordingly, despite being the site of the notion, the atomic individual does not engage his or her speculative subjectivity in so far as he or she does not act as thinking.

This said, the immediate manifestation of personality does not drown itself so to speak in its immediacy; it is not immobile but is already a kind of movement that incorporates otherness precisely because it is atomic. In being atomic, personality is not oriented to the thinking of being but to an immediate unity whose being is devoid of thinking. Consequently, the only available option here is to direct itself to a non-resistant entity whose being is penetrable. In this case, the subject immediately occupies the being in question and thereby appropriates it as its own essence by emerging through it. Here, of course, we are invoking the Hegelian 'thing' that mediates the person's relation to property (PR § 41-71). This is the relation through which the subject's will acquires its being immediately qua occupier of the being of the thing or property owner and thus manifests as immediate atomic individuality. It follows from this association of personality with the property-owning relation that the abovementioned dispersal of atomic individuals refers to the dispersal of individuals qua property-owning beings.

So far we have suggested, firstly, that atomic individuality negates the old world of unreflective communal being and the specific forms of communality that determine it; and, secondly, that this negating is activated by the historical emerging of the atomic individual qua property owner. Now from a speculative standpoint, the negating of the world of unreflective communal being cannot be restricted to the forms of communality being destroyed; it must also implicate the very principle of communality as such. Rather than simply opposing itself to one form of communality that fails to recognize the reflective element of individuality, the negating activity of property-owning atomic individuality is due to its power to appropriate individuality as *exclusively* atomic. Even though historically it arises out of the destruction of traditional forms of communal being, atomic individuality liberates itself by turning against the individuality manifested in terms other than those exclusively dictated by its property-owning being. In other words atomic individuality radicalizes its atomic being by negating communal individuality as such.

*Speculative Being as the Universality of Property-Owning Atomic Individuality*

Next we want to argue that this radical negating accords with a more expansive understanding of individuality. Let us begin by noting that Hegel's abovementioned references to atomic individuality also refer to a further dimension, namely the universal. For Hegel, individuals are in the contradictory relation of being 'impenetrable' and 'at the same time identical with one another, hence not independent, not impenetrable, but, as it were, fused with another' (EPM § 436 A). Similarly, the person is 'none the less, […] not exclusive individuality, but explicitly universality and cognition, and in its other has its own objectivity for its object' (SL 824). It is this relation between the atomic individual and the universal that Hegel characterizes as 'thoroughly speculative' (EPM § 436 A) and giving rise to Spirit that is Reason or the mutual embracing of subject and object as the ultimate act of manifesting manifestation. In other words, the truth of the atomic individuality of personality is to be thinking and qua thinking the individual must have the universal for his or her object.

Now if it is true that fully conceptualized the person is a speculative being in so far as personality, firstly, is atomic or singular individuality that thinks and, secondly, qua thinking expands itself to embrace the universality of communal being as its object then, according to our analysis, it also follows that in so far as he or she experiences the speculative, the person is already embraced by this object as the universal that incorporates within itself the power to be thought. As we argued in the previous section, in permeating and embracing the person, communal being also calls upon or commands him or her to think it. To think communal being is to reconstruct the immediate gathering of communal being as such in a manner that incorporates the mediating element of reflection. In this mutual informing of knowing and known what takes place is the speculative appropriation of both the unreflective communal gathering of the old world and the dispersal of atomic individuals that negates this communality. In this way communal being is liberated from the limitations of *particular forms* of communal manifestation in order to reappear as pure universality—communal being as such—whereas atomic individuality is expanded to serve as the *universality of thinking*.

In the light of the above analysis of speculative or communal personality, how can we make concrete sense of the emergence of communal personality in the new world of atomic individuality and its relationship to the negation that radicalizes the later? In creating its world, atomic individuality repeatedly releases instances of speculative communality whose cumulative effect is absolutely to undermine them as realizable enactments of an alternative world. Each instance of actual negation affirms the radical negating power of atomic individuality. A number of important observations follow from this. First, to recall our analysis so far, speculative communality is manifesting manifestation since, by incorporating reflective or thinking individuality it incorporates the very idea of manifestation. Conversely, in so far as it excludes communal individuality atomic individuality excludes the very idea of manifestation. Yet despite depending on the mediation of the thing, atomic individuality is still manifestation. It follows that atomic individuality is manifestation that excludes the very idea of manifestation. In fact the immediacy that the atomic self-relation exhibits in the property-owning identity is mediated by this act of emptying the speculative out of itself. This act of emptying out is already and, in principle, incorporated in the property owner's appropriation of individuality as exclusively atomic. Hegel refers to this as the 'pure formalism' that characterizes the subjectivity of the modern world.[5]

Second, what exactly is the speculative significance of the radicalization of atomic individuality that, as we argued above, is achieved through the negation of speculative or communal personality? Why not think the reverse, namely that in order to produce the radical result of pure manifesting manifestation it is communal personality that must negate individuality qua exclusively atomic? Here is a possible speculative response. If Spirit, being the unconditional manifesting manifestation of communality, fully and explicitly engages with itself when, for historical reasons, its notion becomes available through the reflective agency of communal personality, then as this inaugural engagement it both announces itself as a vision to be realized and, precisely because it is visionary, it also announces its retreat in its vision as the not-yet. Being visionary as pure manifestation, Spirit's mode of being is pure negation, the 'not' as such. In the absence of Spirit's explicit engagement with its 'not' Spirit would be determined by its self-relation understood in the purely positive terms of a given. Now Spirit's retreat as visionary and its corresponding release as its own negation is nothing short of the release of atomic individuality. The radicalization of atomic individuality through the negation of communal personality is the negation, and hence the radicalization in the abovementioned sense, that Spirit itself is qua visionary.

## *The Vision of Communal Personality and the Retreat of Spirit*

It follows from the above that the vision of communal personality is itself the negation of atomic individuality. If Spirit is self-negating because it is visionary then it also negates its negation for the same reason. In doing so it transforms the latter into the process leading to the realization of the vision. We can now appreciate Hegel's reference to the 'sunburst which, in one flash, illuminates the features of the new world.' In its totality the 'new world' is the vision that announces both the ideal of communal being as an ideal to be realized and its corresponding retreat.

Historically, this dual act of negating is rendered explicit through the mutual informing of political revolution and speculative philosophy. The revolution offers a visionary announcement of the project of communal being (or freedom in solidarity) pointing beyond the world of property-owning atomic individuality. The retreat or failure of the revolution expresses the first instance of Spirit's self-negation. Yet this retreat proves to be unconditional. Ultimately, Spirit retreats in its retreat, thus transforming the space that the retreat is into the *topos* of a more radical encounter with itself. At the same time, in retreating unconditionally Spirit emerges as an absolute arrival, the arriving as such. With the first

---

5. LHP I p. 152. Hegel incorporates the unreflective communal bond as superseded and hence *preserves it as superseded* in his account of civil society, the sphere of atomic individuality, by presenting the immediate loving unity of the family as an individual property-owning unit. So too the reflective bond of solidarity that determines the ethical life of the 'corporations' is preserved as superseded in so far as it is confined to a limited social space rather than acting as a world-determining principle and this expresses the emptying out of speculative individuality that we discussed above.

retreat by emptying itself out of the mutual informing of notion and being that revolutionary communal being takes for granted Spirit prepares the ground for addressing itself on a more fundamental level. With the second by positing itself as the source of the whole speculative problematic concerning the inter-relation of thinking and being it liberates itself from the effects of the first retreat.

Consequently, the vision that is negated as a political project becomes the absolute vision—in the sense of visionary vision or the vision of vision—that, unlike the oppositional posture of revolution, incorporates the totality of the world of atomic individuality that negates it with the effect of negating the negation. Here, failure is speculatively transformed into a new and far more radical announcement of Spirit's arrival by comparison with its political arrival. This arrival of Spirit is absolute precisely because it emerges out of retreat. After all, the retreat of political revolution is not co-extensive with the defeat of the vision of communal being. In this case the critical question does not merely concern *the realization* of the vision but its very meaning and, by extension, the very meaning of the world as the agent that re-produces itself in a visionary manner. In the present context, there is a sense in which vision becomes more significant than reality itself.

### Spirit's Retreat into the Infinitely Expanding Ego

Now the question remains as to the nature and locus of Spirit's unconditional retreat. If by retreating from the concrete world of property-owning atomic individuality Spirit's communal being lands not in some foreign place but in its own *topos* then it lands at the site of its encounter with its pure notion, the very idea of Spirit, as an infinite possibility. This point is crucial for understanding the depth of Spirit's dwelling if it is to encounter itself in a way that gives rise to speculative philosophy. Note, firstly, that Spirit does not encounter its notion as a given. Its *topos* of dwelling does not act as a mirror that immediately reflects an image of itself from which to begin the process of its development. As we have suggested, Spirit already finds itself beyond the limits of the revolution. At the same time, however, it is only by encountering its notion that Spirit encounters itself. How might these two demands that Spirit's radicality poses be simultaneously satisfied? Since Spirit retreats in its retreat without losing itself, it encounters itself as that out of which even its very notion, that of manifesting manifestation, must become an issue. So, in retreating in its retreat Spirit has the vision of its notion as what must become in the dual sense of becoming both the vision that it is and that to which the vision gives expression. As a vision that renders the very meaning of vision—and hence the very meaning of emerging and realizing—an issue, Spirit is not-yet in this radical sense. This is the form that Spirit's second retreat takes through which it deals with the vision qua vision. Basically this means that Spirit deals with itself as the movement from self-givenness to free self-appropriation at the fundamental level of its inaugural encounter with itself. More specifically, because Spirit is 'not' it is absolutely passive with respect to itself and thereby encounters itself thanks to already being infinitely permeated by its notion. Yet it is also the power freely to embrace its visionary notion as a precondition for the notion's realization.

Now, if it is true that by retreating in its retreat Spirit encounters its notion, then Spirit must associate itself with that aspect of its being that concerns the supply of its notion. According to our earlier analysis, the locus of this reflective moment is the communal person's dwelling in Spirit's communal being. As immediately and unconditionally embracing and permeating communal singularities, Spirit encounters itself in visionary terms as a project to be realized. The site of this encounter is communal singularity in its capacity as the power to think and consequently as the bearer of the notion of the universality of communal being. Precisely for this reason whereas the political retreat of communal being is a collective affair, Spirit's retreat in its retreat can, and need, only take place in a single individual. The political retreat empties the singular communal person of the substantive universal communal being's immediate permeating. That is, communal singularity loses sight of its historical mission as a visionary participant in the visionary gathering in communal being as a visionary world-making force. But since it is the communal person qua gathered that provides the gathering with its very notion—and hence with the *topos* of its gathering *as gathering*—the already realized retreat of the gathering from the world takes place *as retreat* in the agent capable of supplying the notion to begin with, that is, in the singularity of the infinitely expanding ego.

The ego thus dwells in the retreat of the retreat that occurs within its own field of awareness as this awareness. That which permeates and embraces the ego retreats unconditionally as this permeating. In doing so, it *posits* the ego as the already permeated. Like the original permeation of communal being, this retreat is no less substantive, objective and universal. In other words the ego cannot resist the universal's emptiness within itself that the retreating communal 'we' activates. Through the retreat because it is already the *topos* of dwelling of the gathering qua gathered, the ego is posited as this *topos* as such. In other words, the ego is posited as immediate pure manifestation or what Hegel calls 'pure self-recognition'—this infinite emptiness that the ego is substantively—made explicit by the retreating 'we'. This is the substantive universal as such within the ego in whose infinite emptiness the ego finds itself dwelling.

Still, precisely because it dwells in the universal in this radical sense, the ego cannot but encounter in its own self the universal that demands that it be thought. In other words, the pure universal already claims the ego as a thinker and, accordingly, the thinker already provides the universal with the vision of its notion that is at once the very notion of the vision. Dwelling in this manner, the thinker is already open to the manifestation of this immediate universality that is encountered as the command to think. Pure self-recognition is activated as a command by this reception of the thinker's dwelling, whereas, as this receiving, the thinker is posited as capable of speculative thinking. Even so, because pure self-recognition and the dwelling of consciousness are both moments of Spirit, in their mutual inter-relation Spirit emerges as the absolute creator of the mutual informing of notion and being. Spirit is both the absolute command and its reception. As such it is the agent that posits the vision of the speculative notion as the originating act of conceptuality. It is in this sense the *topos* from which pure conceptuality is to be activated. This is the primordial freedom of Spirit, or the 'god who impels to self-knowledge' by activating both the absolute commandment 'Know thyself' and its very reception (EPM § 377, A).

Now if Spirit's command is manifested in so far as the thinker receives it, what is the primordial manifestation of the thinker as this receiving and, relatedly, what is the primordial manifestation of the command itself? As this receiving, the infinite singularity of the ego is transformed into an infinite expanding that, as we have already noted, must embrace the empty or pure universality activated by the retreating communal being that embraces it. Indeed, in its most elementary and radically empty expression, the ego takes the form of the thinker qua singular 'I' who utters the 'we'. Hegel's entire philosophy can be understood as an exploration of the very idea of the 'I-we', the thinker's vision of being a universal. From the outset then the thinker emerges as this uttering in whose emptiness all 'that man has held true has disappeared' and out of which emptiness must spring the speculative idea of the world as thinkable (LHP III 258). It follows that one cannot philosophize speculatively in the absence of saying 'we' both prior to the activation of the project and throughout its realization.

We turn next to argue that in keeping with the demands of a presuppositionless Science the idea of the world as thinkable must be available to Science as an indispensable aspect of the very emerging of visionary Science. Indeed on our reading the idea of the world's thinkability and consequent openness to speculative thinking is the precondition of Science in that it defines the 'absolute otherness' that is no less an integral part of Spirit's retreat into pure conceptuality. (Recall that for Hegel the precondition of Science is consciousness' dwelling in the element of 'pure self-recognition in absolute otherness'.)

## IV. ABSOLUTE OTHERNESS AND THE IDEAS OF HISTORY AND NATURE

In the previous section we argued that Spirit's self-negation takes place in the world of property-owning atomic individuality. The formal subject that 'has made itself to be empty' of the speculative inter-relation of thinking and being is none other than property-owning subjectivity. Spirit's moment of 'absolute otherness' is constituted as the world of property owners, this emptying out of the very notion of the speculative. The emptying out in question is absolute since it incorporates being and thinking as forms of the emptying/emptied out inter-relation. In other words, in one and the same act it is being that empties itself of the notion and as this emptying out it is also being that is emptied from the notion since what it empties is its own notion. Accordingly, the site of otherness is not being as the other of the notion but being itself. Here, the notion is transformed into the notion of otherness and being is transformed into the being of otherness. In their mutual informing the notion and being of otherness constitute the realm of 'absolute otherness' that is the 'othering' in otherness itself.

More specifically, on the one hand, in emptying itself from being the notion empties itself as notion and thereby transforms itself into its other, or rather, into the very idea of otherness. Here, it is the *notionless* notion. Consequently, it empties itself from the speculative element of reflection that in the previous sections we associated with the power of the ego to expand infinitely. As this emptying the notion remains implicit and the self is posited as atomic. At the same time, the implicitness of the notion is expressed only in that which is already external to itself—the thing—and, hence, unable immanently to accommodate the element of thinking. In being other to itself in this case, being is the being of otherness. It is beingless and therefore also notionless being. It follows that the immediate unity of the notion of otherness, constituted as the atomic self, and the being of otherness, constituted as the thing, give rise to the property-owning relation in terms of the absolute otherness of the speculative as speculative otherness.

Now, in accordance with our line of argument, the concrete world of absolute otherness mediates the vision of the pure notion of Science that relates to the thinker's receiving of the command to think through the thinker's dwelling in pure self-recognition. Although pure self-recognition is the very idea of Spirit in its immediacy, its purity results from the speculative emptying out that constitutes atomic individuality. This added dimension raises the question of the connection between the thinker's visionary being and his or her concrete participation in the world of property-owning atomic individuality. To put the same question differently, what is the significance for the property-owning world of the fact that the vision of the infinite expansion and embracing of speculative thinking also claims the atomic being of the particular person? These questions turn our attention to the relationship between the vision of speculative thinking that we have been elaborating and the possibility of speculatively thinking the world.

*The Absolute Otherness of the Property-Owning World and History as its Thinkability*

We can begin to address this issue by noting that the very emergence of the vision of Science treats the thinkability of the world as its essence and the world as excluding Science qua the idea of the thinkable—pure self-recognition—and the idea of the thinking of the thinkable. Precisely because, as absolute otherness the property-owning world actively empties itself out of the speculative moment, to the emptied out speculative notion it reveals itself to be the power of the notion's release. It also renders explicit that its act of emptying out is the *topos* in and out of which the vision of the notion emerges. In other words, the notion of pure thinking that is in a sense exiled from the world is the worlds' own notion and hence its *topos* of exile is the world itself as a whole. It is in this sense that Hegel invokes 'pure self-recognition in absolute otherness'.

Now precisely because the world acts in this radically immanent manner in releasing the very notion of thinking the thinkable, the world also releases its power to be the being of thinkability. Consequently, the self-mediation of the world that releases its notion qua notion of the thinkable and its thinking posits the world as the in-itself thinkable. The world is the in-itself-for-the-notion. Speculatively speaking everything in the whole of the property-owning world is gathered in this, and as this, all-inclusive emptying out that explicitly and reflectively happens as what is already the case in the purely conceptual emergence of the notion that belongs to it exclusively, albeit negatively.

Accordingly, Science is the retreating world *as* this retreating, that is, it is the very idea of thinkability emerging in the thinkable world that is empty of its idea. Mediated by the infinite separation of being and thinking the release of the philosophical moment marks the retreat of being into the darkness of its own amnesia, the amnesia of the thinkable. The remembering of the notion that the vision of Science is takes place in the realm of its division from being that the forgetting of the world of absolute otherness is. Speculative philosophy is thus the form of emerging of Spirit as this (di)vision.

To be sure, the implicitness of the world's thinkability directly relates to the absoluteness of Spirit. If the world is unconditionally thinkable then even its own thinkability must be activated out of itself. The world must be the power to know what it is, not by encountering its essence as a given, but by retreating in its essence in order to make knowledge of it a goal to be realized and by surviving this retreat. That is why at the end of the speculative project of thinking the world— Hegel's system—the notion reveals that the forgetting of the world is history understood as the urge and the power of the thinkable actually and explicitly to become thinkable in-and-for-itself. The vision of the notion as the unconditionally thinkable is already the unconscious vision of the world.

But if the above reading is correct, then in having the vision of the notion as the notion of the purely thinkable the thinker must also have the vision of the idea of history. In other words, the thinker must be in a position to acknowledge the mediating role of absolute otherness in terms of the idea of the world being the urge towards becoming thinkable. It follows that from the very beginning the vision of the notion of pure thinkability must also be accompanied by the vision of history as such, or Spirit's release of itself in time through its retreat. If this is the case, then the world of absolute otherness, the global gathering of property-owning persons, is constituted as nothing other than history itself. Here we are not referring to some historical stage to be followed by an other, but to the 'not yet' of the implicit thinkability. This vision of the idea of history renders the world of absolute otherness as one aspect of Spirit's being from the first moment of the emergence of Science.

Ultimately this truth of the world must be revealed with the activation of speculative thinking. Being the idea of the thinkable itself (the absolute object), Science qua vision expresses the idea of Spirit as a whole (manifesting manifestation), that is, the idea of the thinkable-thinking-thought that is fully worked out in the *Science of Logic*. When this comprehensive standpoint of the notion is extended to the thinkable world, the world of absolute otherness emerges as only one moment in the full landscape of the world Spirit. Indeed, it is revealed to be the teleological drive from which being emerges as actually (in and for itself) thinkable, that is, as explicitly releasing the mutual explicit embracing of being and notion (realized Reason). In Hegel's system, this being-notion relation is concretely articulated as the idea of the ethical state. On our analysis, this state refers to the (yet to be) realized Spirit that is perpetually produced by the global gathering of ethical agents who respond to the command to *be as a world absolutely*, a command that is itself activated by the (yet to be) 'achieved community of minds' (PS ¶ 69).[6]

## *Absolute Otherness as the Dwelling of Visionary Spirit in Nature*

We have been arguing that the idea of history must be part of Science's primordial vision but when Hegel discusses absolute knowing at the end of the *Phenomenology* and before the activation of the speculative project he also appeals

---

6. From the above analysis it follows that the received interpretations of the ethical state in terms of the division between civil society and the political state do not take account of the speculative requirements operating in Hegel's *Philosophy of Right*. See, for example, Klaus Hartmann, 'Towards and New Systematic Reading of Hegel's Philosophy of Right', in Z.A. Pelczynski (ed.), *The State and Civil Society: Studies in Hegel's Political Philosophy*, Cambridge, Cambridge University Press, 1984, pp. 114-136; K-H Ilting, 'The Dialectic of Civil Society', in Z.A. Pelczynski (ed.), *The State and Civil Society*, pp. 211-226. On the contrary, the concept of society is one aspect of the realm of absolute otherness whereas that of the ethical state is the speculative vision of communal being that will be released—as the vision that explicitly incorporates the power for its realization—out of the collapse of the global world of absolute otherness. The sovereign political state is another aspect of absolute otherness within which the institutions of civil society can be said to gather. Accordingly, modern liberal institutions, like those that Hegel elaborates in his discussion on civil society, express part of the form of absolute otherness created out of the gathering of property owners. These institutions are in principle global given the formality characterizing the being of personality. Yet, they ultimately emerge within the limited framework of the *particular* political state since the gathering of persons also constitutes the negation of the very idea of the global communality to come, a communality that comprehensively expresses the very idea of world Spirit from the speculative standpoint. (This negation, as we have already argued, results from the emptying out of the speculative moment constituted as the property-owning world.) On this analysis, today's global gathering of property owners perpetuates itself through the negation of its own future. That is, in so far as it takes its own being to be global the gathering of property owners negates the notion and being of communal globality. As this negation the property-owning world is also posited as the dispersal of particulars that results from the denial of the future understood in terms of the speculative universal of communally integrated being in which every form of the particular is also a form of embracing the universal. So the current drive to create global institutions is compromised by the equally decisive drive to negate the very idea of the global in the future. As a result the current reality is that of the dispersal of self-grounding or sovereign particular political states constituted as the international community. The inability of the particulars in question to be informed by the universal is reflected in an ultimately unenforceable international law. So, whereas civil society's economic and legal institutions result from the affirmation of the present of property owners, the sovereign political state results from the denial of the future. Still, since that which is denied belongs to that which acts as the power of denying, the world of absolute otherness denies itself through the mediation of what it denies and thus denies itself as denying. If we understand history as the end result of this infinite or absolute denying, history must be the release of what it already is and, as we have argued, it is the thinkable.

to nature. Like the idea of history, the idea of nature is an integral part of the original vision. Whereas the idea of history invokes Spirit's realization as thinkable, the idea of nature invokes the very emergence of Spirit as purely and perpetually visionary.

The notion's vision of the mutual informing of subject and object—in terms of the commanding (thinkable), receiving (thinking) and realizing (thought) mentioned earlier—also gives rise to the idea of the perpetual vision *as such*. In other words, the execution of the command does not mean that the command and its reception are forgotten. Precisely because what is commanded by the command (the realization of the thinkable as thinkable) is immanently realized, in this capacity it perpetually retrieves the command as its own, thus perpetually positing itself as realizable and hence as visionary. This is because Spirit is both the source of the command and its reception, something that Science qua vision must render explicit in its very emerging pursuant to the mutual informing of its beginning and end. If this is correct then in its notion Spirit's perpetual visionary state is revealed as realized and consequently it is also retrieved as realizable. The movement in question is akin to perpetually encountering oneself for the first time in order to realize oneself and the effect is an intensification of what has already been realized. The being of fully realized Spirit is perpetually teleological in this sense.

How is this primordial and perpetual release of the visionary Spirit, a release that belongs to Spirit itself, possible? It must be the case that the principle of Spirit's self-relating—Spirit's infinite immersion in, and emergence from, itself—emerges from Spirit's infinite outsideness. This latter is the realm of nature that Hegel calls 'indifferent subsistence' (EPN § 248). Spirit's freedom is infinitely and perpetually visionary in so far as its self-awareness is mediated by its emerging from and dwelling in nature or the realm of 'externality'. It follows that in so far as the primordial emergence of Science relies upon the idea of Spirit as visionary this emerging is possible only if Spirit is informed not only by the idea of history but also by the idea of nature.

So at the end of history—the moment when Spirit's perpetual visionary character and its power perpetually to realize its vision become explicit—Spirit's relation to nature must take centre stage. History and historical being presuppose Spirit's primordial relation to nature in this way and it is this relation that is explicitly released with the collapse of history. In this way Spirit moves beyond the limits of historical being to spiritual being. We must say that as spiritual beings our primary relation is not with history but with nature. The primordial emergence of the gathering of the visionary egos who are in a position infinitely to expand with the saying 'we' becomes exclusively a matter between the 'community of minds' and nature. Under these conditions it also becomes possible collectively to retrieve the experience historically introduced by the Greek thinkers who 'presupposed nothing but the heaven above and the earth around.' In Hegel's words, this 'feeling that we are all our own is characterized of free thought—of that voyage into the open, where nothing is below us or above us, and we stand in solitude with ourselves alone' (EL § 31 A).

From the above analysis it follows not only that Science is the vision of the pure idea of thinking but that it is also the mission to think the world in terms of its self-realization qua thinkable (as history) through the awareness of Spirit's speculative relation to nature. This expanded vision makes it possible for Science to encounter itself in its primordial emerging as this vision and mission and thereby to activate its thinking, to undertake each particular stage in its development and immediately move on to the next. Indeed each stage (and each stage within each stage) is from the outset situated in, and mediated by, this panoramic vision. In the light of Science's expanded vision the articulation of the idea of the thinkable—the absolute object—is the first task to be realized. Moreover, once the purely logical process has been undertaken and situated in Science's expanded vision this process leads immediately to a consideration of nature as that from which the visionary power of visionary Science emerges. Moreover, once thinking nature has similarly been elaborated and situated in the expanded vision of Science, thinking leads to the realm of Spirit. So too the realm of Spirit must be thought in a way that reveals the world as the thinkable whose idea has already been worked out in the *Science of Logic*. Thus the (development of the) categories of the *Logic* is the thinker's only guide for conceptualizing Spirit in a way that remains true to the primordial speculative vision.[7]

To summarize, the whole vision and unfolding of the drama of speculative philosophy proceeds as the singularity of the thinker expands to become the universality of thinking the notion of thinking, and consequently of thinking the world of Spirit as the purely thinkable. Philosophy is the encountering in one's singularity of the absolute strangeness of the transformation that makes it possible for the 'I' to think (or say) 'we' and hence to function as the house of the 'we'. Still, precisely because thinking happens here via its exile from being all that is needed for it to occur is a single individual whose infinite philosophical embracing of the 'we' remains unpopulated. The happening of speculative philosophy is therefore not a collective affair; it always involves the strangeness of the expansion of the 'I' and the terror associated with the anxiety of the infinite absence of the 'we' that appears as a shadow in the shadowy realm of the vision that the thinker is. This is why throughout the development of the speculative project the voice of the thinker is the 'I' that repeatedly says 'we'.[8]

---

7. See Toula Nicolacopoulos and George Vassilacopoulos, *Hegel and the Logical Structure of Love: An Essay on Sexualities Family and the Law*, Aldershot, Ashgate, 1999.

8. A fuller articulation of this last point would also tell us something about the origin and the speculative significance of language. The very idea of language is activated by the universality of the infinitely expanding (thinking) ego that utters the 'I-we'. The word as such ('we') emerges as the *topos* of dwelling of the 'community of minds' as a project to be realized. Hegel describes this *topos* as an 'external community'; it is a gathering that is yet to be realized. From this standpoint we can make sense of the poet Yannis Ritsos's appeal that: 'Every word is an outing/to a gathering, one often cancelled/and this is when a word is true: when it insists on the gathering', our translation from Ρίτσος, Γ., 'Το νόημα της απλότητας', *Γιάννης Ρίτσος Ποιήματα, 1941-1958, Τόμος Β*, Αθήνα, Κέδρος, 1979, σ. 453 (Y. Ritsos, 'The Meaning of Simplicity', *Yiannis Ritsosk Poems 1941-1958 Volume B*,

Having completed our account of the thinker's dwelling in pure self-recognition in absolute otherness, we will proceed to explore the implications of our reading for an understanding of role of the phenomenological and logical cycles of justification in the activation of speculative philosophy.

## V. THE PHENOMENOLOGICAL CYCLE OF JUSTIFICATION

We have argued above that consciousness' dwelling in pure self-recognition is characterized by the element of infinite passivity. In this capacity the thinker finds himself or herself already situated in this dwelling; he or she is permeated by the objective or substantive power of the retreat of immediate communal being. The thinker already experiences the singularity of his or her atomic ego as the possibility of infinite expansion (thinking) so that the passivity that determines the finitude of the thinker's singularity is also claimed as infinite freedom. Recall that, according to Hegel, when immersed in pure self-recognition the thinker is posited and preserves himself or herself as 'absolute form' or 'the immediate certainty of oneself' (PS ¶ 26). Qua absolute form the thinker is the exclusive bearer of the vision of speculative thinking. Ultimately it is in and as this infinite and perpetual preserving of the ego as the vision of its universality that the immediate universality of communal being is transformed into the command to know or to think. Moreover, as we have argued, the thinker is transformed into the receiving of the command and thus into the *topos* of the command. This is absolutely elementary for the emergence of Science since 'Science [...] requires that self-consciousness should have raised itself into this Aether in order to be able to live—and [actually] to live—with Science and in Science' (PS ¶ 26).

But, of course, there is the other side to this story, that which calls upon Science to supply the individual qua absolute form with 'the ladder to this standpoint, should show him this standpoint within himself' in conformity with the individual's rightful expectation (PS ¶ 26). In so far as Science claims or embraces the thinker as absolute form—and precisely because one is absolute form—the thinker must be in a position to exercise one's freedom by claiming Science's claim upon one as one's own. When one encounters oneself dwelling in pure self-recognition one can authenticate oneself as the thinker that one is claimed to be by actively dwelling in one's dwelling or by freely embracing what embraces one in one's capacity as free and in this way freely embracing one's own freedom. Now, if, as we have argued, the universality of pure self-recognition embraces the thinker, it acts as absolute object since the thinking it demands does not derive from the outside. Yet such thinking is itself absolute because its own object does not derive from the outside. Accordingly, having already been claimed by absolute content, the thinker in his or her capacity as absolute form must actively and freely affirm the absoluteness of the absolute content of pure self-recognition. Paradoxically this means that the thinker must demand from Science a point of

---

Athens, Kedros, 1979, p. 453). Indeed the uttering of the 'we' is also the transformation of the material naturalness of the sign into the *topos* of emerging of the spiritual as vision.

access from which freely to make his or her entry so to speak into the *topos* that makes Science possible, that is, the *topos* in which he or she already dwells as a matter of fact.

This said, satisfaction of the thinker's demand in the light of his or her absolute form presupposes that he or she has access to some content or object other than that which Science offers (hereafter 'the thinker's second object of reflection'). For in the absence of the availability of another object the thinker would not be in a position *freely* to claim his or her freedom. What sort of object must this be? To answer this question it is worth noting, firstly, that despite dwelling passively and hence immediately in pure self-recognition, taken as a whole the thinker's position is constituted as a *mediated* immediacy. This mediation concerns the thinker's dwelling in Spirit's retreat from the world as well as *in* the world from which Spirit has retreated. Before the retreating Spirit claims the thinker as free, the latter already dwells in the world in which he or she is to be re-introduced reflectively, precisely because he or she is claimed by Science's promise of speculative thinking. The thinker's dwelling in pure self-recognition is not only mediated by the thinker's retreat from his or her world; such dwelling itself mediates the thinker's dwelling in the world, a dwelling that is now experienced as the result of retreating from Science's speculative reflective standpoint. This reappropriation is an act of violence against both Science and consciousness' dwelling in it. Whereas Science is the vision of conceptualizing the world speculatively, the world presents itself to Science as already containing the speculative within it in so far as it accommodates consciousness as free or the individual in his or her capacity as absolute form. To put it differently, even though the thinker has the vision of the freedom of thinking in Science, the world presents itself as the actual *topos* of the freedom of the thinker, his or her natural place of dwelling as a thinker.

Secondly, in both cases the source of thinking is the thinker's own independence or absolute form. Here we have the activation of a movement from one reflective standpoint to the other through which each claims to be the truth of the other and each takes the truth of the other to have collapsed in its own truth. To emphasize again, what makes this possible is that both reflective standpoints—those of Science and the world—present themselves as the appropriate *topos* of the free thinker. In embracing the thinker as thinker both standpoints call upon the thinker to embrace them. In doing so they each claim the form of the speculative as their own. So, the need for the availability of a second object relates to the thinker's resolve to stay where he or she already is, namely in the speculative, rather than to the desirability of choice.

Finally, considering whether there is a *topos* in which the thinker dwells and from which he or she must enter Science as an affirmation of his or her absolute independence in Science we can say with Hegel that this *topos* must be the antithesis of Science. This is the 'standpoint of consciousness which knows objects in their antithesis to itself, and itself in antithesis to them' (PS ¶ 26). So outside of Science, the thinker's second object of reflection is the world defined in terms of consciousness' dichotomous relation(s) to its objects (hereafter 'the subject-object dichotomy'). For Hegel, not only does consciousness dwell in this dichotomy as absolute form but also the subject-object dichotomy appears to be the only antithesis that can be posited to Science. Why should this be the case? Bearing in mind that it is the thinker's dwelling in Science that activates the whole speculative problematic, we can formulate an answer to this question by supposing that in so far as Science claims the thinker, Science must also release him or her into *its own antithesis* as the precondition for freely embracing the resolve to stay with it. So, it seems that qua absolute form the thinker has only two places to dwell in and determining which of the two is the genuine home of his or her speculative freedom is the thinker's first act of freedom.

In the light of our discussion so far two further questions remain regarding our account of the rationale underpinning a phenomenological justificatory cycle. One question relates to the claim that the subject-object dichotomy accommodates consciousness in its capacity as *absolute form*. How is this possible when this latter condition calls for an object whose being is informed by, rather than antithetical to, consciousness' knowing? A second question concerns the link between our discussion of the subject-object dichotomy and that of property-owning atomic individuality that on our earlier analysis constitutes the absolute otherness of pure self-recognition. We will address these two questions in reverse order.

We have argued that the vision of the speculative occurs in the absolute otherness that is constituted by the property-owning world of atomic individuality. In so far as atomic individuality empties itself out of speculative reflection, that is, of the mutual informing of subject and object, it is also posited as this emptying. So from the property-owner's standpoint reflection offers a form of knowing that consciousness' absolute form incorporates whilst remaining external to the object known. Here the source of the subject-object dichotomy presupposes that the object *as such* is the property item whereas the subject *as such* manifests immediately as the property-owning atomic individual.

Yet consciousness remains unaware of the mediating role played by the property-owning atomic individual's release. Consequently it takes itself to be the exclusive source of the awareness that determines its relation to the object. Ultimately this means that consciousness takes the relation of property ownership to be an aspect of the world of the subject-object dichotomy. Consciousness can do so because the role we have attributed here to the property-owning subject is accessible only from the standpoint of Science that is immanently linked to its absolute other. Accordingly, we might say that whereas Science's rivalry with its absolute other—property-owning atomic individuality— mediates the competing claims of Science and the dichotomously related consciousness, the dichotomously related consciousness nevertheless remains unaware of this mediation. For this reason both Science and its absolute other claim awareness (consciousness) for themselves and they both claim it in its capacity as absolute form.

Now from the standpoint of property-owning atomic individuality the challenge is to show that although consciousness is dichotomously related to its object of knowledge it is not also dichotomously related to the manifestation of the subject-object dichotomy itself. Rather, this latter functions as a speculative realm of manifestation that is determined by the external relation of knower and known in which consciousness dwells as absolute form in so far as it supplies the very idea of the dichotomy. In other words consciousness treats the dichotomy itself as its absolute content. It is in this sense that the individual is characterized by 'absolute independence, which he is conscious of possessing in every phase of his knowledge' (PS ¶ 26). We are now also in a position to see why Hegel suggests that 'it makes no difference whether we think of Science as the appearance because it comes on the scene alongside another form of knowledge, or whether we call that other untrue knowledge its manifestation' (PS ¶ 76). Since Science is initially only an appearing, it has yet to incorporate the self-certainty that characterizes consciousness in its capacity as absolute form:

> Science must [...] unite this element of self-certainty with itself, or rather show that and how this element belongs to it. So long as Science lacks this actual dimension, it is only the content as the in-itself, the purpose that is as yet still something inward, not yet Spirit, but only spiritual Substance. This in-itself has to express itself outwardly and become for itself, and this means simply that it has to posit self-consciousness as one with itself (PS ¶ 26).

So, when Science is not yet 'in and for itself' (PS ¶ 76) how is the indispensable positing of self-consciousness' unity to be realized? What is the process by which Science can move from merely being the absolute object that embraces the subject to also being the corresponding embracing of the subject as absolute form? In other words, how is Science supposed to 'turn against' and 'liberate' itself from the other form of knowing that likewise claims the speculative standpoint in so far as it claims consciousness as its own (PS ¶ 76)? In the light of our earlier analysis we can argue that the required process must involve the retreat of what has already retreated. Let us explain. Recall that on our analysis Science emerges as Spirit's retreat from the world as a result of the thinker's dwelling in this retreat. At the same time, in so far as he or she dwells in Spirit's retreat the thinker has already retreated from his or her world. Now in claiming the thinker as free Science presupposes that the thinker's retreat is itself an act of freedom in the light of the failure of the thinker's world to accommodate his or her free agency. Because it initially appears as mere assertion this claim must be justified. If it is true that the thinker whom the absolute object claims as absolute form must embrace the absolute object himself or herself, to activate this embracing the thinker must begin from the recognition that this embracing is otherwise absent. It follows that to activate the embracing in question the thinker must rely upon his or her reflective state of *not embracing*. Now the thinker's non-embracing relation to the object is expressed in terms of the dichotomous inter-relation of the thinker to the object. In this dichotomous relation the thinker has already embraced his or her being as one of neither embracing nor being embraced by the object. Conversely, the thinker embraces and is embraced by the dichotomy and to this extent he or she is free or manifests absolute form.

It follows from the above that to 'posit self-consciousness as one with itself' is to have Science retrieve the thinker from the world *immanently* to the thinker rather than as a simple given. More specifically, since the thinker must freely embrace his or her condition of *already* dwelling in Science, the retrieval in question functions as a process of recollecting. The thinker is in a position to recollect the fact of his or her retreat from the world into Science once the world is shown already to have been unable to accommodate the speculative truth of the thinker's absolute form.

This sums up the significance of the phenomenological process whereby consciousness purifies itself as Science 'liberates' itself (PS ¶ 76). This is a fully speculative process through which the purely negative gives rise to a positive result. It is constituted by consciousness' multiple failed attempts to dwell in the subject-object dichotomy speculatively by thinking this relation. With every failure and collapse of the form of the dichotomy being thought the thinker retreats further into Science in order to reactivate consciousness' dwelling in the dichotomy in ever more radical terms. With this process of determinate negation the aim of consciousness qua absolute form is to collapse the collapsing itself or to complete consciousness' purificatory process that simultaneously amounts to consciousness' ultimate and free retreat into the freedom of Science. The retreat in question can be characterized as free since consciousness has only its *purified* absolute form to retreat into following its phenomenological failure to claim its absolute form for the world. In other words this failure explicitly posits consciousness as what has freely failed. Indeed, consciousness does not itself collapse with the collapse of the dichotomy only because it carries in itself the principle of its freedom—the very idea of absolute form. Its retreat into its own principle permits it to know the collapse as the powerlessness of the dichotomy to accommodate consciousness' freedom.

With the completion of the phenomenological process in the terms just explained—with consciousness' liberation from the element of externality—consciousness retreats into its absolute form teleologically. Being absolute form its aim is to realize its absolute form by producing absolute content as its *topos* of dwelling. Yet the free embracing of this aim affirms that consciousness already dwells in the absolute object that, for reasons already explained, is pure self-recognition in absolute otherness. Having already been initially embraced by the absolute content of communal being, consciousness embraces this embracing—by undergoing the long purificatory phenomenological process—and thereby posits itself as the absolute subject. The realization of this second embracing releases Science as Science 'in and for itself' and thereby makes it possible *justifiably* to begin what was always already open to Science, namely actively to engage the thinker with the command to know.

## VI. THE LOGICAL CYCLE OF JUSTIFICATION

According to our analysis so far, Science fully emerges 'in and for itself' with the completion of the phenomenological process that marks the satisfaction of thinker's demand that Science justify the thinker's dwelling in pure self-recognition and thereby renders possible the thinker's free embracing of this position. In the light of this free embracing the thinker is shown to be the vision of himself or herself as a speculative thinker—qua absolute form, consciousness' particularity emerges as the vision of itself as a universal. So, within the realm of dwelling in pure conceptuality, and as this dwelling, the thinker is the vision of thinking the notion of thinking and, hence, the vision of embracing pure conceptuality as the absolute object that commands pure thinking. In purely conceptual terms this vision is comprised of the pure awareness of the absolute object—the moment of universality—that posits out of itself the command to be embraced—thought—and its reception—the moment of particularity—along with the actual embracing—the moment of individuality. But of course this is the vision of Science itself or Science as vision in relation to whose notion the thinker is the bearer. Now when we turn to the *Science of Logic* we are confronted with the question: 'with what must the Science begin?' (SL 67). In the light of our earlier analysis one might expect the beginning of Science to elaborate the process by which the thinker turns from the *vision* of the notion to the *activation and realization* of the idea of thinking that informs this vision. So what is it that activates the thinking incorporated in the thinker's vision of the notion and, relatedly, of the thinker's vision of himself or herself as a thinker? Here is what Hegel has to say.

> Now starting from this determination of pure knowledge, all that is needed to ensure that the beginning remains immanent in its scientific development is to consider, or rather, ridding oneself of all other reflections and opinions whatever, simply to take up, what is there before us (SL 69).

When the thinker has the vision of pure thinking and has reached the reflective stage of receiving the command to think purely the decision so to speak to begin has already been taken and what remains is to work out the precise starting point. Here is one way of reading Hegel's advice. If the determination of pure knowledge is nothing short of the notion, and if it is the notion that is 'there before us' then, presumably, we must start by simply thinking the thinking that the notion is. A move like this would direct the task of thinking to the realization of the vision of the notion of pure thinking that calls for the activation of the third part of the *Science of Logic*, 'The Doctrine of the Notion'. Yet, according to Hegel, from a speculative standpoint, this is a premature step:

> When [...] the notion is called the truth of Being and Essence, we must expect to be asked why we do not begin with the notion? The answer is that, where knowledge by thought is our aim, we cannot begin with the truth, because the truth, when it forms the beginning, must rest on mere assertion. The truth when it is thought must as such verify itself to thought (EL § 159 A).

So for Hegel the claim that we should not begin with the notion does not rest on the observation that we do not yet know it and, consequently, could not immediately begin to think the thinking it involves. Contrary to first impressions, the concern with Being and Essence proceeds against the background that the notion is already available to the thinker. Accordingly, if the thinker does indeed already dwell in the realm of pure conceptuality as we have argued, the process of thinking the forms of thought involved in Being and Essence must somehow nevertheless result from this engagement with the notion.

This said, we might ask, is there some discrepancy between Hegel's claim and what might seem to follow from our earlier analysis, namely that the thinker should begin the logical process by engaging directly with the already available notion? Can our account of the visionary thinker who freely receives the command to think also explain the necessity to think the forms of thinking involved in Being and Essence as a precondition for moving justifiably to the thinking whose task it is to realize the notion? Indeed we shall argue next that in order to address the command and the vision of the notion as the primordial form of the notion's emerging the thinker must become aware of the necessary role that Being and Essence play in the logical process.[9]

We have argued that in being the vision of thinking the very notion of thinking, the thinker already engages with the notion's emerging in a visionary way. Moreover, the vision of the notion qua vision renders explicit the freedom of the thinker's absolute form as well as the absoluteness of the command to think purely. The commanding of the command to think purely whilst dwelling in the realm of pure conceptuality—something that already permeates the thinker's being—must also be freely received as the command and this can be achieved in so far as the thinker retains the visionary awareness of the notion. Now to make sense of the freedom that the thinker must exercise in this process of receiving the command we must have regard to the idea that both the command and its reception are absolute in that they mutually inform each other and belong to each other in this way. So, the commanding of the command and the receiving of its reception are made explicit through their inter-relation. We want to argue next that this mutual informing is rendered explicit through the thinker's visionary encounter with the notion.

Now, if the command is indeed absolute then it should permeate the thinker, at least substantively or immediately, to begin with. In being immediately commanded the thinker already finds himself or herself in the mode of executing what the command commands. He or she is already in the mode of thinking purely. Yet, if we were to remain exclusively at the level of the command's immediate and, hence, unreflective reception, the command could not be said to command *absolutely* since the commanding *as such* that renders it a command in the first place would remain implicit. More specifically, if the thinker were directly to execute the command he or she would fail to show that the commanding of

---

9. A more extensive defence of this interpretive claim would also elaborate on some interesting implications of our analysis for the way we should understand the logical beginning with the concepts of being, nothing and becoming.

the command implies that the realization of the notion of thinking has yet to be identified and activated. Between the command and its execution there is still the gap of the command's reception. This gap of reception constitutes the freedom through which the thinker affirms what the command commands as a project to be realized.

In the absence of this refrain from an immediate execution of the command, the command would lack force as such—the thinker's thinking would depend upon his or her contingent will. In the light of the absoluteness of the command whose commanding already permeates the thinker, the will to think cannot be contingent. Not only is the thinker permeated by the command; he or she also opens himself to the command that already permeates him, by explicitly receiving it *as* command. Accordingly, the command is commanded and rendered an explicit command as a result of the thinker's free receiving. The command cannot fail to command given that its free receiving expresses the very idea of commanding.

If our analysis is sound, the thinker's receiving as receiving makes explicit the not-yet of the project of thinking the notion that is already incorporated in the command in so far as it commands. Moreover, since explicit reception of the command renders the idea of commanding explicit, to acknowledge this very receiving—to receive the receiving—is to manifest the absoluteness of the command. Now, if the command is indeed absolute in the above speculative sense, then it can only be received by its own idea of commanding in the form of otherness. Otherness is important here, because, as we noted above, the receiving of the command as receiving points to the postponement of the command's demand that it be executed. So there is a sense in which the command must be disobeyed or at least suspended before it can be freely obeyed.

At the same time, the command's absoluteness implies, firstly, that the command incorporates the idea of commanding and, secondly, that the thinker's freedom is no less absolute. If the command emerges qua command in the receiving of the thinker and this receiving provides the command's idea, then as this emerging the command receives its idea and thereby receives the thinker's receiving. In other words the command itself must incorporate the idea of the not-yet of its call to be executed and thus the idea of being received that the thinker's receiving manifests. Conversely, in his or her capacity as receiving the command, the thinker is an absolute receiving since, as we have just suggested, the command incorporates the idea of its own other, namely the receiving. It follows from this inter-relation that the possibility of disobedience—in the sense of suspension of the command's execution—rests on the thinker's prior embrace of his or her obedience to what the command commands in so far as the thinker already fully encounters the notion of pure thinking.

The speculative paradox or mystery here is that the absoluteness of both the command and the thinker's freedom are no less manifested through their own other, disobedience and obedience respectively. The command commands—really happens *as* command—in the open field of its reception, a field whose openness presupposes that the command has not been obeyed. So too, the reception of the command really happens as a receiving in so far as the thinker has already opened himself to *thinking as such* and obeyed the command in this way. So rather than demonstrating that the command is without force and instead of negating the thinker's freedom, disobedience and obedience respectively demonstrate that this inter-relation between the command and its reception is indeed characterized by the absolute power of free love that we mentioned at the outset.

In the light of the above analysis we will attempt now to specify more precisely the link between the idea that the thinker is commanded *immediately* and hence already has access to the notion with the idea that the free reception of the command mediates between the command and its execution. We have noted that the thinker must at once obey and disobey the command to think. He or she must fully encounter the thinking involved in the notion as the precondition for executing this thinking yet without also moving immediately to think the notion. This can be achieved only when by dwelling in pure conceptuality the thinker has the vision of the notion *as* a vision. In so far as the thinker fully encounters the notion in this vision, the command fully permeates the thinker and immediately readies him or her to move on and think the notion. Still, in so far as *the form* of the vision also determines this encounter, the notion is encountered as the not-yet and, whilst obeying the command, the thinker must nevertheless also be preoccupied with its *free* reception.

Now to disobey the command in order to receive it freely is to *refrain* from activating the already available notion that immediately permeates the thinker's thinking. At the same time to refrain from activating the notion is not to preclude the notion's activation. Instead this refraining signals the thinker's readiness to think the notion that is itself the yet to be activated in its capacity as the vision of the notion. It follows that the notion's own readiness to be thought is the truth of the non-activated notion as well as of the notion in the visionary state of the not-yet-activated. It is this truth in the sense that the two ideas of the non-activated notion and of the notion as the not-yet-activated are both integral moments in the thinker's awareness of the notion as ready to be thought. The notion can indeed be activated because it is presupposed as this truth.

Moreover, since the visionary thinker is ready to realize the vision thanks to his or her visionary being—he or she is at once already in the state of the not-yet as well as pointing beyond this state in so far as he or she knows it as the not-yet—the thinker has already prereflectively moved beyond these two moments. That is, he or she is already beyond the forms of thinking that they incorporate in so far as they are incorporated into the thinking of the yet-to-be-activated notion. It follows from this that in order fully to appreciate himself or herself as a free thinker who is ready to think the notion, the thinker must *recollect* the mediating role that he or she must have played to this point. In other words the thinker must now also freely embrace the freedom manifested in receiving the command's receiving by freely recollecting this thinking as the truth of his or her thinking.

Now the truth of thinking with which thinking is already preoccupied must nevertheless spring out of thinking itself. Or in other words the truth of pure conceptuality must be shown to result from pure conceptuality itself. In so far as the notion incorporates other forms of thinking as moments in its thinking, these other forms must be capable of being thought in the abovementioned sense of being recollected in ways that immanently lead to their notion. Basically this means that the thinker must manifest the truth of thinking in the forms of thinking involved in thinking the notion in the two moments in question. These are the moments of Being and Essence in relation to which the notion is the truth. To disobey or suspend the command is initially to disregard what the command commands—the command to think the notion—as well as to disregard that this disregarding belongs to the vision of the notion—the receiving of the command. Here, the thinker must disengage himself or herself from the thinking of the notion whether in the form of actually thinking it or in the form of the vision and the notion thus becomes invisible. With this disengagement 'the Notion is implicit and in germ' in its non-activation (EL § 83). Not only is the *notion* implicit but also the *thinker's thinking* is implicit since it does not manifest the notion's implicitness in the terms of a vision to be realized. In the *Science of Logic* this sort of radical disengagement is worked out in 'The Doctrine of Being' wherein 'pure knowing [...] ceases itself to be knowledge' (SL 69) and thought is thereby revealed as being 'thought [...] in its immediacy' (EL § 83).

Now the activation of the form of thinking that springs from disobeying the command in the abovementioned radical sense ultimately shows that such thinking is not self-sufficient. The exercise of this form of thought demonstrates that disobedience is part of the larger picture of receiving the command to think purely and hence of recognizing the need to obey the command. In rendering explicit the notion's implicitness this process manifests the notion as yet to be realized. In this way the implicitness of the notion is reflectively mediated. Still since this process is the notion's very implicitness, the reflection in question is not yet absolute but remains external.

At the completion of 'The Doctrine of Being' we have 'thought [...] in its reflecting and mediation' that corresponds to 'the being-for-self and show of the Notion' (EL § 83). This is the form of thinking that is practiced in 'The Doctrine of Essence' wherein the 'actual unity of the notion is not realized, but only postulated by reflection' (EL § 112). Now the process of activating and carrying through the forms of thought that are informed by the implicitness of the implicit notion ultimately manifests that which makes possible this reflective practice in the first instance, namely the power actually to think the notion as such. Accordingly, at the completion of 'The Doctrine of Essence' the process by which the thinker recollects his or her becoming a thinker manifests the thinker's being as what he or she already is—the free receiving of the command to think and the infinite power to think the thinking of the notion.

The singularity of the thinker's ego is thus readied for the journey constituting its infinite expansion. This is the point at which 'the I is the pure Notion itself which, as Notion, has come into existence'. The task of thinking the notion's unity may therefore begin *freely* and, hence, justifiably (SL 583).

# 16

# Gathering and Dispersing: The Absolute Spirit in Hegel's Philosophy

George Vassilacopoulos

> The subsistence of the community is its continuous, eternal becoming, which is grounded in the fact that spirit is an eternal process of self-cognition, dividing itself into the finite flashes of light of individual consciousness, and then re-collecting and gathering itself up out of this finitude—inasmuch as it is in the finite consciousness that the process of knowing spirit's essence takes place and that the divine self-consciousness thus arises. Out of the foaming ferment of finitude, spirit rises up fragrantly (LPR III 233 n. 191).[1]

How might the reader of Hegel's system prepare to engage with 'spirit's eternal process of self-cognition'? How might the finitude of one's individual consciousness come to form part of the story of spirit's 'recollecting and gathering itself' so as to ground 'the eternal becoming' of 'the community'? In what follows I elaborate the ideas of gathering and dispersing as a way of preparing to engage with Hegel's absolute spirit.[2]

My purpose is not to develop an argument to the conclusion that we should understand the absolute spirit in terms of its powers of dispersal and gathering but instead immanently to approach the difficult question of the meaning and being of the absolute spirit in Hegel's thought by reflecting through the idea that spirit is the activity and being of gathering through dispersal. To appreciate the role of the absolute spirit by way of preparation for reading Hegel's system I will elaborate its links to the idea of the gathering worked out from three different angles in varying degrees of complexity. In the first section of the paper I approach the tentative formulation of a definition of the absolute spirit by associa-

---

[1]. I would like to thank Paul Ashton for drawing this passage to my attention.

[2]. I would like to express my appreciation to my colleagues Jorge Reyes, Paul Ashton and Toula Nicolacopoulos for our many discussions on this topic.

tion with the idea of 'the gathering-we' and its key manifestations in the history of the western world as a philosophical project. In the second section I approach the absolute spirit's gathering power through the analysis of the implications of the command to finite spirits to 'know thyself' and in the final section I approach the absolute spirit through the gathering and dispersing activity in the logical interrelations of its moments of universality, particularity and individuality. I take the view that this sort of exercise positions the thinker to appreciate the immanent connection between the unfolding of the absolute spirit in Hegel's system and the fundamental work of spirit understood in the terms of the power of gathering and the activity of gathering finite spirits. I contend that in the absence of this positioning the thinker understandably fails to engage fully with the categories of universality, particularity and individuality as a complex differentiated unity that informs the absolute self-determination.[3]

## I. APPROACHING A DEFINITION OF THE ABSOLUTE SPIRIT THROUGH THE MEANING AND BEING OF THE GATHERING-WE

From a speculative perspective 'the gathering-we' is fundamental for humans as thinking beings. For Hegel the gathering-we is the 'community of minds' (PS ¶ 69). For the poet, Tasos Livaditis, it is the 'great mystery': 'the beautiful mystery of being alone, the mystery of the two, or the great mystery of the gathering of us all'.[4] The gathering-we is the 'voyage into the open, where nothing is below or above us, and we stand in solitude with ourselves alone' (EL § 31 A). This aloneness is the universal opening in which the gathering-we unfolds and re-folds as alone. The gathering-we is thus an infinite intensifying in the limitless stillness of its immediacy. It is 'self-moving self-sameness' (PS ¶ 21). The gathering-we is pulsating; it implodes in its formlessness in order to (re)create form out of itself.

### Towards a First Definition of Absolute Spirit

If the gathering-we happens as absolute power it also happens as love. Hegel speaks of 'free power' as 'free love' and 'boundless blessedness' (SL 603). The poetic word insists that 'whatever we don't love does not exist' or that 'we dwell,

---

[3]. To give just one example of a common failing in this regard, Michael Theunissen maintains that the question of the mediation of the particularity of the individual with an objective universal that has not abandoned the universality of inter-subjective relations in favour of the universality of an objective order that has removed all trace of inter-subjectivity remains '*the* unsolved problem of Hegel's philosophy of right' despite Hegel's intentions to the contrary. Michael Theunissen, 'The Repressed Intersubjectivity in Hegel's Philosophy of Right', in Cornell, D., Rosenfeld, M., Carlson, D.G. (eds.), *Hegel and Legal Theory*, New York and London, Routledge, 1991, pp. 3-63, p. 63. Yet because Theunissen's critique presupposes reflective conditions that conflate what I refer to as the absolute power of gathering with the activity of gathering finite beings it is consequently blind to the fact that with the triadic structure of objectivity as a syllogistic unity the objective universality defining the organization of Hegel's ethical state does not erase but coheres with the differentiated universality of inter-subjective relations.

[4]. T. Livadites, *Small Book for Large Dreams* (Greek) Athens, Kethros, 1987, pp. 16-17. Translation from the Greek by Toula Nicolacopoulos and George Vassilacopoulos.

not where we are, but where we love'.[5] As love, the gathering-we is perhaps not only the axiomatic starting point of philosophy but also of communal life itself, as well as their point of return. Moreover, in the absoluteness of its all-embracing aloneness, the happening of the gathering-we is potentially global. That is, in its opening the whole world gathers as the gathering that it is in this most powerful of openings that the gathering-we is. Everything, nature included, is thus a form of gathering that emerges as such in the gathering-we. Indeed the being and the very idea of gathering become an issue in so far as the gathering-we gathers its own gathering by dispersing and embracing its dispersal and in doing so posits the mutual informing of being and notion as a project to be realized. This process of gathering is its infinite power, the aloneness that is perfect and the (hidden) source of any vision of perfection.

So everything belongs to the embracing that the gathering-we is. The gathering-we is so powerful that it even allows divinities to spring from it without destroying itself. The only place of dwelling for the divine is the gathering of the gathering-we that is in a sense more divine than the divine itself. It also destroys the divine without destroying itself since the divine cannot ultimately withstand the power of the gathering. More importantly, the gathering-we does not differentiate between the living and dead, those in the future and those in the present, the human and the non-human. All are particulars that gather in the gathering-we and, as gathered, they are elevated to *places* of gathering. The whole of humanity can gather under one tree just as it can gather in a single death, that of a Palestinian child for instance. What is infinitely singular—that which is gathered in the gathering—is also the power to expand infinitely and to act as the *topos* of the happening of the gathering.

Throughout history we are always situated as gathered in more or less encompassing forms of gathering like the Greek polis, or the Egyptian kingdom. How does one measure the scope, or rather, the intensity of the gathering's encompassing of itself? Everything depends on the degree of power that a gathering-we can generate to embrace itself and thereby gather as the gathering. In order to appreciate this claim we must bear in mind that no gathering is unconditionally given, even though throughout history various forms of the gathering may well be presented as givens. There is something more primordial than an already historically realized gathering. That which is more primordial than the gathering is *the primordial as gathering*. In any of its determinate manifestations the world of gathering and the gathering as a world—gatherings are always worlds—respond, implicitly or explicitly, to the power or vision to gather where the vision is itself a form of gathering.

Still not every gathering is in a position to respond directly to the primordial act of the visionary gathering/gathered. The gathering *as such* becomes an issue only when those who participate in the realized gathering make an issue of

---

5. Graffiti in Athens attributes the first of these quotations to the poet Kostis Palamas. The second is from Thomas Stanley, 'The life', in Colin Burrow (ed.), *Metaphysical Poetry*, London, Penguin, 2006, p. 236.

their capacity to be as gathered and, relatedly, of their capacity to generate and respond to the very idea of gathering in so far as they recollect themselves as the visionary gathered-to-be. This dual act—recollecting the vision from what is already the vision's realized form and projecting the vision's realization in what is already its realized form—is the pulse of the gathering-we, a pulse felt in all forms of gathering irrespective of their degree of comprehensiveness. So, for example, in falling in love with someone one encounters oneself as gathered in the gathering of love that is also the power to create the world of love. In this primordial sense of the gathering/gathered mutuality of the gathering, the power of the gathering-we takes the form of a command—the command to gather as loving and hence to create the world of love. As already gathered in the gathering of love and hence as already received by love, individuals are the receivers of such a command where the commanding is itself activated in and as this receiving. At the same time, once lovers have created the world of love, from within it they retrieve the command by perpetually (re)enacting their world. So the life of the gathering of love is neither simply the world of love nor is it the indeterminate gathering out of which this world springs. This life is the pulse that makes possible a perpetual return, an embracing of the beginning by the end and of the end by the beginning. The gathering is both *anamnesic* and visionary in this way and every form of gathering presupposes that it is a response to the command to gather.

Moreover, since those who gather encounter themselves as already gathered, gatherings always precede those who gather in them. Gatherings can never be reduced to gatherings of aggregated individuals. Individuality is one way of being as gathered in a gathering and of receiving the command to gather. The subjectivity of the individual is this receiving as the already received in the gathering and, as this receiving, subjectivity is the vision of the infinite expansion of its infinite singularity. As this receiving of the command to gather, the subject receives the gathering-we by providing it with the notion of the gathering *as such*. Ultimately it is this singular receiving that activates the commanding of the command and so itself commands the command to command. It is as the bearer of the universality of the notion of the gathering-we that the subject 'in his particularity has the vision of himself as the universal' (ILHP 172). The gathering thus gathers as a project or vision in the *topos* that its own notion is. This *topos* is in turn supplied by the subjectivity of the subject, that is, by the 'I' that is 'thought as a thinker' (EL § 24 A). Here the 'I' is the house so to speak of the visionary 'we'. Accordingly, the gathering-we is the absolute object and the subject is the absolute ego that is embraced in the mutual act of 'unbounded love'. As Hegel puts it 'that the object [...] is itself universal, permeating and encompassing the ego, also signifies that the pure ego is the pure form which overlaps the object and encompasses it' (EPM § 438).

The primordial gathering of the gathered-to-be—the gathering in and through which the idea of gathering is manifested in visionary terms—is the formless, indeterminate gathering that challenges itself to create form out of its very indeterminacy. Understood as this kind of project, participation in such indeterminate gathering involves two elements of experience. One is the experience of primordial communal being that remains unconditioned by any institutional form and a second is the experience of individual agency as free to receive the command and thus as already in and beyond institutions. The formed gathering-we with the power to refer itself to the simplicity of the formless gathering and thereby perpetually to retrieve it is the gathering that is flooded with free individuals who perpetually receive the command and thus perpetually address, and are addressed by, the indeterminate (formless) gathering. This perpetual receiving through retrieving is what animates with life the formed world of gathering that manifests a radical sameness in perpetually renewing itself. The life of the gathering is the pulsating movement between the eternal command and its reception, on the one hand, and the historical world of the formed gathering, on the other. The world of such a realized gathering would be a philosophical world in the speculative sense in so far as it is a world whose being directly addresses and embodies the eternal idea of the gathering as such.

## First Definition of the Absolute Spirit

At this point we can attempt a first and tentative definition of absolute spirit. In its full manifestation the absolute is the self-realizing realized world of gathering. It is the realized gathering that does not sink into the fullness of its realization only to become inert. As fully realized the absolute retrieves the indeterminate gathering without destroying what it has realized. The absolute is thus the visionary power and process of return and projection. It returns to itself as the agent of indeterminacy out of which the gathering, as the already realized project, is released. It is the releasing of the already released. In other words, as the power of releasing its world the absolute is also powerful enough not to be lost in the abyss of its indeterminacy. Out of its indeterminacy it posits its world as the world that has already been realized and as the world that retrieves its realizing. In the absolute's pulsating movement between the realized gathering and the formless gathering the world perpetually opens itself to the eternal command to 'be as a world', that is, to be as the world that is posited in and by the retrieving of the command. As this kind of movement of absolute negativity the absolute manifests as the power to formulate the gathering as the project of the co-belonging of notion and being as well as the realizing realized realization of such co-belonging. Absolute negativity is the pulsating world of the absolute. It is the aloneness of the gathering-we.

## Towards a Second Definition of Absolute Spirit

Unlike gatherings that do not address the notion of gathering at all and so are unable to identify the indeterminate gathering as the source of their world, an already realized (determinate) gathering-we can also be philosophical in so far as it renders explicit the visionary notion that it denies. Such a denial presupposes that the appearance of the indeterminate and visionary gathering amidst the historical being of a realized gathering that ultimately denies the vision renders explicit the project of the notion/being co-belonging of the gathering-we. Due to the radicality of the vision and its denial, the form of the realized gathering is re-appropriated via the mediation of such denial. Here, it is posited as the form of the being of the gathering-we that empties itself out of its notion and this leads to the corresponding emptying out of the notion itself from its own being, that of the realized gathering. It is the realized gathering that produces an infinite distance from itself in that it denies what mostly belongs to it, namely the very idea of gathering. In this sense the realized gathering-we dwells in the emptiness of its being. This mutual emptying out ultimately refers both being and notion to the denied indeterminate gathering in which and as which the visionary project of the notion/being co-belonging first becomes an issue philosophically. Philosophy presupposes the denial of the vision by the realized (determinate) gathering and the corresponding retreat of the indeterminate gathering in its own visionary space. Through this retreat notion and being emerge philosophically as infinitely separated.

Philosophy can only arise in a philosophical world defined in the above terms. It is pure conceptuality, the vision that is empty of being or the thinking of being without being, gathered in a single mind as the *topos* of the gathering of purely visionary concepts. As thinking thought, the thinker expands infinitely to embrace the 'we', albeit only in principle. In this sense his or her embracing remains unpopulated. The philosopher knows that the house that philosophy builds is to become the dwelling of those who arrive through history from the distant future. Philosophy is a welcoming from a far. This is the highest manifestation of the gathering's power to 'submit to infinite pain' (EPM § 382) and withstand its own self as the vortex of otherness. It sinks in the depth of its *kenosis* without loosing itself. In and out of this deepening philosophy emerges as the light of a galaxy out of the cosmic darkness that the gathering itself is. In philosophy the gathering recollects its being as a *thanatology*—as the dying of its death—through which it practices a defiant and visionary emerging of life out of death—that of the notion and history.

In so far as the gathering-we challenges the ultimate given, life itself, the gathering constitutes the (di)vision: *anamnesic* (the philosophical notion) as *amnesic* (political being). The awareness incorporated in such (di)vision is the awareness of history. History is the gathering moving towards itself or the gathering that gathers itself. As history, the gathering dwells in the opening of its aloneness and moves towards opening this opening, towards making this opening happen as a perpetual happening. Its knowledge is the wound that heals itself.[6] The philosophy of the gathering is the announcement of both this healing and is itself a form of healing.

---

6. G.W.F. Hegel, '4 Lectures on the Philosophy of Religion'§ 4, cited in Theunissen, 'The Repressed Intersubjectivity in Hegel's Philosophy of Right', p. 55.

## Second Definition of the Absolute Spirit

We are now ready to attempt a second definition of the absolute. The absolute is not only what withstands its complete realization by reviving the command out of itself but also what survives its complete emptiness that the retreat of the command produces. From a speculative perspective, the absoluteness of the absolute is manifested by this active denying since, far from being destroyed by it, the gathering creates a historically teleological world through this denial and gives rise to the emergence of philosophy as absolute self-knowing. Historically, the absolute as such manifests itself as 'pure self-recognition' in the 'absolute otherness' of the notion/being emptying out—the *kenosis* of *kenosis*. It is in a philosophical world, in this sense of engagement in active self-denial, that the place is created for the emergence of philosophy. What is denied, namely the primordial idea of the command/receiving of the gathered gathering-we retreats in the free being of the philosopher whose receiving activates the thinking of the universal and formless gathering-we. This thinking, as the thinking of the universal (thought), is thinking *as such* or the gathering of concepts together with the concept of gathering. It is the particular that 'has the vision of itself as universal', the thinker who realizes the vision conceptually and, ultimately, invokes the idea of history to become reconciled with the actual world that denies the vision. When it is in the world as philosophical in this last sense, philosophy gives shape both to the very notion of the philosophical, notionless actuality of the present as well as to the fully actual notion of the future.

## The Gathering-We from the Greek Polis to Christianity and the French Revolution

The historical emergence of the indeterminate and visionary gathering is always unexpected and powerful. Its first manifestation was the gathering of Socrates and his friends in ancient Athens. As a democracy that accommodated free individuals, the Greek city was perhaps in a unique position to encounter a philosophical form of the idea of the gathering as such as well as to deny it, as happened when Socrates first introduced into the *polis* a philosophical formulation of the idea of gathering as a project to be realized. Socrates challenged the gathering of the Athenian citizens by positing himself as the bearer of the very idea of the gathering and as the *topos* of gathering for the friends of the philosopher. Here the vision was for the gathering as such to institute itself in response to the command 'know thyself'. In constituting the being of the gathering—its emerging as gathering—such a response was to function as the presupposition for (re)enacting the *polis* and its institutions.

In responding to the philosopher's challenge the *polis* inaugurated the western world as a philosophical world that confronts its gathering-being by undermining the very principle of gathering. In other words, the gathering-we of the *polis* gathers in its inaugural act of rejecting the very principle of gathering when it condemns the philosopher to death. This act marks the radical disassociation of the *polis* from tradition understood as the power of gathering and it does so in a way that makes the distinctively western reflective attitude possible. The philosopher's challenge appears once tradition has lost its integrating power. By turning against the philosopher the already dispersed citizens reconstitute their gathering *as* dispersing or atomic individuals in so far as they reject the philosophical principle of integration.

Ultimately it is in the tension between the being and the idea of gathering that the other great project of the west is activated, that of visionary philosophy. The first master of this project is Plato and his masterpiece is *The Republic*. *The Republic* is a meditation on the very idea of gathering understood in the above terms. On this reading of Plato the indeterminate gathering and its corresponding vision manifest in the embrace of the philosopher whose connection with the *Agathon* enables him to create the *polis* and to function as its ruler. In Plato's ideal *polis* the speculative tension is overcome since everyone responds to the command to 'know thyself' by dwelling in the philosopher's embrace. Such a response makes possible the formation of both the indeterminate gathering-we as well as the institutions of the just *polis* out of this latter. Here for the first time in the west the individual is posited, firstly, as a member of the indeterminate gathering that institutes its sovereign being (emerging) through the sovereign act of responding to the command 'know thyself'—it is sovereign in so far as it incorporates its knowing and hence the principle of its self-institution—and, then, as a citizen of the enacted *polis*.[7]

So we can read Plato's philosophy as responding directly to the eternal command to gather at the notional level. Plato attempts to respond to the command by making sense of the meaning of receiving it wherein the act of making sense is the receiving. In its philosophical expression conceptuality emerges through and as this response. It is the conceptuality that belongs to the gathering as such or the gathering that is speculative since the command and its reception generate the notion/being co-belonging as the task of creating being in knowing and knowing in being. In *The Republic* Plato was able to offer a way of understanding the gathering as command and to articulate the being of the free individuals who have the ability to gather through the reception of the command that the philosopher introduces. He was also able to elaborate the idea of the just *polis* and its institutions as the realization of the gathering as such.

Following the Greeks, a second historical emergence of the gathering-we responds to the Christian command 'love each other'. Here a decisive difference marks the gathering of the community of love from the previous gathering that manifests the idea of Plato's *polis* of justice. Although in both cases there is a supreme source of value—the *Agathon* in relation to justice and the Christian God in relation to love—in the second case it is not one person, the philosopher, but every believer who can be in touch with this source. Consequently, every member of the gathering of believers functions as the *topos* of the indeterminate gathering of love.

---

7. George Vassilacopoulos, 'Plato's *Republic* and the End of Philosophy', *Philosophical Inquiry*, vol. XIX, no.1-2, 2007, pp. 34-45.

This said, the formed gatherings that have been created by the organized churches ultimately have the effect of neutralizing the power of the originating indeterminate gathering of the loving-we to perpetually inform its institutions. Consequently, collectively Christians are unable to retrieve the command in a way that perpetually gives rise to the primordial indeterminate gathering of believers. In the end, the Church-bound Christian becomes the captive of teletourgical formalism and the hierarchical structures of the clergy.

The French Revolution radicalized the universality of equality that the Christian project activated. We can make sense of its emergence in history as the irruption of the formless gathering-we manifesting itself as the unconditional maxim 'be as a world'. For the first time in the history of gathering humans gather in the gathering without appealing to some given, like the platonic Good or the Christian God. Here, the gathering is activated out of itself and moves towards itself. In a single moment it captures the idea of the movement of history as the gathering that gathers itself. With the emerging of this event we enter the third act of the western philosophical project that is also the most explicitly speculative.

The idea of the revolution invokes the command 'be as free and equal in accordance with solidarity' or, in its speculative reformulation, 'be as a world'. In the happening of the infinite aloneness of the indeterminate gathering-we that is a self-activating solidarity, each member of the collective is claimed as the place of dwelling for the other members, that is, as the bearer of the very idea of gathering. Here the subjectivity of the subject is constituted in the dynamic inter-relation of infinite expansion as the embracing of the collective and infinite contraction as being absolutely permeated by the substantive universality of solidarity.

For reasons that we need not go into here, western modernity also gives rise to the negation of this most radical idea of the gathering as such. The idea is negated through the gathering of formal subjects in their capacity as atomic and, hence, dispersed individuals who inter-relate as private property owners dwelling in the externality of the 'things' they each own.[8] In their mutual recognition as persons, the activity of such formal subjects replaces the possibility of infinite expansion at the heart of the command to be as a world with the momentary merging of wills that agree to exchange property items. In this case it becomes impossible for the command of the gathering-we to be heard as a world-transforming power.

The retreat of the abovementioned denied command and its vision opened the space for the emergence of Hegel's philosophy of the 'world Spirit'. Hegel's philosophy, like Plato's before him and unlike any other philosophy after him, is the reception of the last whisper of the eternal command (notion). The receiving that is philosophy is always the receiving of a whispering—that of the retreating gathering-we— that only the thinker is in a position to hear. It is also the last re-opening of the silence of the world (historical being). It teaches that

---

8. See the section titled 'Modernity and Speculative Philosophy', in Toula Nicolacopoulos and George Vassilacopoulos, 'The Ego as World', this collection.

when the gathering gathers the power to command once again no one will fail to receive it.

Moreover, in such a radically philosophical world the production of philosophy will be a thing of the past. The participants of this world will discover that the moment of pure conceptualization has already happened and that their world has already conceptually happened in the happening of this moment. They will be in a position to understand themselves through their past by reading the speculative story of the world Spirit that the philosophers have *already* prepared. On this reading, philosophers like Hegel are the Homers of the people of the future who are the genuine *readers* of philosophy.

## II. APPROACHING THE ABSOLUTE SPIRIT AS THE COMMAND TO 'KNOW THYSELF'

According to Hegel, conceptualization or 'the Notion' 'does not require any external stimulus for its actualization' since 'it embraces the contradiction of simplicity and difference, and therefore its own restless nature impels it to actualize itself' (EPM § 379 A). Hegel suggests that the impelling nature of the absolute that points to its actualization takes the form of a command. He specifically refers to the '"absolute" commandment, *Know Thyself*' and explains:

> Know thyself doesn't have the meaning of a law externally imposed on the human mind by an alien power; on the contrary, the god who impels to self-knowledge is none other than the absolute law of mind itself. Mind is, therefore, in its every act only apprehending itself (EPM § 377 A).

### *The Command of the Absolute and its Reception*

If for the absolute (mind or Notion) the command is not imposed by an alien agent but is part of the fabric of the absolute itself then, from a standpoint that immanently belongs to it, the absolute needs to posit not only itself as the command but also itself as the agent who receives the command. As both the command and its receiving agent the absolute is the simple or the same out of which the difference between the command and its reception is posited. Here we have the difference or contradiction between difference and sameness that is also the sameness of difference and sameness. Being the simple the absolute is immediately universal. At the same time the absolute posits itself as an explicitly self-referential universality when, from its state of immediately being the whole (substance) it also emerges as the power to realize itself as this whole (subject) and hence as not yet being what it already is. In other words, in manifesting itself as the manifestation to become, the absolute creates a disturbance (restlessness) out of the state of tranquility of its immediate universality. Its possibility is thus also its actuality and it realizes this possibility through the creation out of itself of the abovementioned difference between the command and its reception. The absolute is and is not because by being what it is it is also the urge to become. Being both the immediate universal and the urge to become, it is the transforming of itself into its other (the not) and as such it breaks up or negates the universality of its immediate unity.

Nevertheless, since the negating of the absolute's immediate unity belongs to the unity's immediacy, immediate unity is preserved in and as this negating. The immediacy of the immediate is manifested through the negation and as this negation. In and as this self-negating immediacy, the universal preserves and transcends itself by turning itself into a command and at the same time providing itself with the agent of the command's reception. The immediate unity is therefore mediated by its self-manifestation as the power to become what it is. As a command the immediate unity emerges as the whole to become. The command here is infinite. In other words it does not fail to be received and by extension to be absolutely obeyed. Moreover, this implies that the absolute has already, or in principle, become what it is given that as the received command the absolute fully manifests itself both as the whole and as the power to realize itself.

Whereas the agent receiving the universal as a command receives it as what must be realized, in this receiving the universal is *as received* and also *as not receiving itself*. The universal that is received by its other is the 'not yet'. Here we have a differentiation of form and content. Together, the *form* of receiving the universal and the universal's *content* as received manifest the negation of the universal, the not yet. As received and in being received by its other, the universal commands the other to transcend itself in order for the universal to be realized.

Now the agency that functions both as the absolute other of the universal and as the unconditional recipient of the universal command is the finitude of the particular. As the agent receiving the command of the universal, the particular acts as the *topos* of the not yet of the universal. Basically this means that the command commands in and through the particular's receiving. But the particular is in a position to perform the role of receiving the universal in the terms explained so far when it provides the universal with its pure notion without at the same time providing the universal's being. It follows that as the bearer of the notion of the universal the being of the particular is also the negation of the universal—the absolute singularity of the particular. This is the particular that thinks; it is finite mind. In this capacity the particular does not lose itself in its particularity in the process of receiving the command. It is that which thinks or receives the universal of the whole as the universal to become and thus receives itself as the agent of enacting the whole. The particular then is as thinking. In being as thinking in the way just explained, the particular experiences the differentiation of being and thinking as a differentiation that must be overcome.

So the absolute is the immediately realized whole that is also posited as realizable. Through such positing it recaptures itself as realized, albeit only immediately. Once fully realized through the execution of what the command commands, the absolute overcomes the contradiction of simplicity and difference, or substance and subject, without however forgetting their difference. It incorporates itself as realizable by recollecting the command and its receiving. It thus perpetually renews itself as the already realized absolute—that is, as the result of the absolute's circular movement that repeatedly retrieves its beginning and realizes its end. Here what is realized cannot fail also to be as both realizing and realizable.

So it seems that both states of the absolute—its forward movement, through which it posits itself as realizable and ultimately as realized, and its backward movement of recollection from its state of completion—rely upon the mediating power of the moment of the command and its reception. In both of its forms such a state manifests the 'not' at the centre of the absolute. This state is the absolute's power to mediate between its immediate and its mediated states of being the whole. As this power of mediation the absolute is the mutual informing of the infinity of its command with the finitude of its reception.

## *The Absolute Spirit as the Dispersal and Gathering of Finite Spirits*

Hegel observes that 'absolute Spirit [...] opposes to itself another spirit, the finite, the principle of which is to know absolute spirit, in order that absolute spirit may become existent for it' (LHP III 553). The absolute spirit is what withstands the opposition between the infinite command and its finite reception. As being received by the finite, the infinite does not crush the finite. So too, as receiving the infinite, the finite does not distort the infinite. Consequently, as the creator of its own opposition, the absolute already contains in itself that which, when released, posits both its infinite command and finite spirits as the agents of receiving and activating the command through their receiving. It follows that in the absolute's state of being immediately what it must become, finite spirits are already incorporated in some form of gathering—the immediate communal being—that affirms that the absolute is immediately the whole. It is out of this gathering that the absolute posits the command together with finite spirits as the command's recipients. In doing so the absolute posits finite spirits as beings with the appropriate form of agency for receiving its command. Indeed, by positing individualized unities, the absolute posits a form that involves dispersal and so negates the immediate universal communal unity of the agents in question.

Now, as we noted above, the commanding of the command is activated through its being received as a presupposition for the actualization of what is commanded. Significantly for Hegel 'to know absolute spirit', that is, to receive it, is the 'principle' of finite spirit. So finite spirit receives *as receiving*. In other words, finite spirit's whole being is this receiving; the receiving is not just a mere faculty of its agency. Now if the principle of finite spirit is to receive the command 'Know Thyself' and if the being of finite spirit is its receiving the command and activating the commanding, then finite spirit manifests the very principle of finite spirit as such in the specificity of its receiving being. At the same time it also renders explicit the very meaning of the command since the command can be received only by the agent capable of providing its meaning. More specifically, if the command commands me to know myself and if 'know' involves no specification—the like 'know yourself as a patriot'—then I can only know myself as receiver of the command to know that I am already positioned to receive in so far as I provide the very meaning of knowing. So the command manifests as command in the field opened up by the activation of its meaning through the agency of finite spirit.

Now if, as the agent of receiving the command through its specificity, the specific finite spirit provides the meaning of the command *and* the principle of finite spirit, finite spirit must also be the embracing of all finite spirits. This is because in enabling the command to command through its receiving and in thereby receiving the received—the absolute spirit that in already being what it must become has already gathered the finite spirits in itself—the gathered finite spirits must themselves dwell in the single finite spirit as the receiver of the command. This *landing* of the infinite in the finite makes it possible for the finite unconditionally to embrace every particular spirit as *already* gathered by the absolute and hence as *what must be* gathered. That is, it makes it possible for the finite to embrace communal being. Due to its ability to receive the command the singularity of the finite spirit is also an infinite expansion that is the place of dwelling or the gathering of the already gathered finite spirits in their capacity as the gathered to become. This state manifests the power to gather out of which what is commanded is to be realized. In other words what receives the command is what the absolute already *is* and *must become*, namely immediate communal being gathered in the singularity of the 'I'. That it *must become* is manifested in that its bearer is the singular mind whose mode of being is one of dispersal. Here the absolute is the 'I' that is in a position to say 'we'.

In the light of our discussion so far we can now say that the command commands finite spirits to gather since, as already being what it must become, absolute spirit immediately affirms itself by incorporating finite spirits as gathered into its field of self-affirming. For to posit finite spirit as the receiver of the command is simultaneously to manifest *what* the absolute spirit is and *that* it must become what it is. Absolute spirit is affirmed as both in being received as the command by finite spirit. It also follows that finite spirit must itself simultaneously dwell in both moments: it must dwell in the gathering of finite spirits that absolute spirit already incorporates and yet in receiving absolute spirit as command, finite spirit manifests the not yet of the absolute. In this second role as receiver finite spirit dwells in the world of finite spirits that must be gathered and, as the not yet gathered, remain in a state of dispersal or indeterminate gathering. Therefore as command absolute spirit commands finite spirits to re-gather or to become what they already are. In so commanding the infinite is itself the power that gathers or *the gathering* itself.

## III. APPROACHING THE ABSOLUTE SPIRIT THROUGH THE GATHERING AND DISPERSING IN THE LOGICAL STRUCTURE OF UNIVERSALITY, PARTICULARITY AND INDIVIDUALITY

So far the analysis of the notions of gathered and gathering offers a way of appreciating the immanent becoming of absolute spirit. The absolute is always already itself or the whole. But it also must become the whole that it is. This task is made explicit in the self-positing of the absolute as a project to be realized. Here the absolute is realized without however laying to rest the power of realizing. For Hegel this developmental logic concerns the challenge of making sense of the speculative absolute in terms of the relationship between thinking and being. The absolute has being in knowing or, in other words, its mode of being is what Hegel calls 'manifestation'.

> This universality is also its determinate sphere of being. Having a being of its own, the universal is self-particularizing, whilst it still remains self-identical. Hence the special mode of mental being is '*manifestation*'. The spirit is not some one mode or meaning which finds utterance or externality only in a form distinct from itself: it does not manifest or reveal *something*, but its very mode and meaning is this revelation. And thus in its mere possibility mind is at the same moment an infinite, 'absolute', *actuality* (EPM § 383).

Here Hegel invokes the logical categories of universality, particularity and individuality to refer to the absolute's fundamental mode of being and becoming. Drawing upon the inter-relations between these categories we can now re-present the ideas of the gathering, the dispersing and the command in greater depth and with greater precision.

## *The Moment of Universality*

Summarizing our discussion so far we note that the absolute is the realizing of what is always already realized. Precisely because it is already the realized whole it seeks to render itself as the self-realizing whole. Using the terminology of gathering we can say that the absolute is the immediate gathered-gathering that ultimately formulates itself as the gathering-gathered—the gathered that involves the appropriate knowing as gathering—through the reflective moment of self-dispersal.

But what precisely is this original and originating state of the absolute that Hegel refers to as the moment of universality, the moment of utter simplicity or the absolute's infinite equality with itself? In a passage partially cited above Hegel observes:

> The Notion does not require any external stimulus for its actualization; it embraces the contradiction of simplicity and difference, and therefore its own restless nature impels it to actualize itself, to unfold into actuality the difference which, in the Notion itself, is present only in an ideal manner, that is to say, in the contradictory form of differencelessness, and by this removal of its simplicity as of a defect, a one-sidedness, to make itself actually that whole, of which to begin with it contained only the possibility (EPM § 379 A).

Universality is the mode of being of the absolute when the absolute is in its state of immediacy or 'differencelessness'. Here the absolute is affirming but immediately so. In other words, its mode of being is the in-itself. Yet, the absolute is absolute irrespective of its mode of being because it always performs the impossible.

So in the moment of universality the absolute is immediate yet without *sinking into* or *evaporating in* its immediacy and so without moving beyond its immediacy in whatever form. In its state of immediacy the challenge for the absolute is to not lose its absoluteness in the light of its state of immediacy. The immediate absolute must remain an absolute immediacy, that is, an affirming immediacy. Here immediacy is the mode of being that determines mediation or, in other words, 'differencelessness' is the mode of being of the absolute that determines difference.

Being an affirming immediacy the absolute does not go beyond itself into the externality of otherness in order to affirm itself in a mediating way through some return to itself from the state of otherness or self-loss. Even though this is the ultimate aim of the absolute such a move nevertheless presupposes the immanent affirmation of what must be superseded as well as the activation of the superseding process through such affirmation rather than despite it. Precisely because the absolute does not lose itself in its state of immediacy, it is also the power to move beyond to its other moments of self-realization. Of course the reverse is also the case. Because it is the power of moving beyond, it can also affirm itself in its immediacy. Moreover, the absolute is the power to move beyond in so far as it has *already* moved beyond. The task is for this movement to be perpetually recollected from within the moments of its development.

In the light of the above we can say that in order to be both immediate and affirming the absolute must go deeper into what already is the case for it and hence to stay with what it already is. So the reality of the absolute at this point calls not for a transition but for unlimited intensification of its already realized affirmation. It follows that we should understand the immediate as incorporating mediation within itself, albeit without going beyond its own immediacy. The immediate is a return-without-going-beyond. In the mode of being of immediacy the absolute moves with infinite speed in the infinite depth of its immobility.

This said affirmation involves some kind of difference, difference involves otherness and otherness involves mediation. In order for immediate affirmation to be affirming it therefore needs an other, albeit one in whom, as already suggested, the absolute does not lose itself in order to return to itself in a triumphant gesture of accomplishment. It requires of otherness not that it should enable immediacy to pass through it to something else but that it may stay where it already is and thereby traverse the infinity of its remaining where it always already is. This is the realization already involved in what is already realized as intensification or deepening. If the immediate is affirming in so far as it is the infinite power of affirming itself in its absolute other, then moving deeper into itself means moving towards its other *as itself* or itself as *its other*.

How can the immediate be both itself and its other in a way that manifests its power to locate in its other only itself? According to Hegel,

> The universal is free power; it is itself and takes its other within its embrace, but without doing violence to it; on the contrary, the universal is, in its other, in peaceful communion with itself. We have called it free power but it could also be called free love and boundless blessedness, for it bears itself towards its other as towards its own

self; in it, it has returned to itself (SL 603).

Here we have a return without self-loss. As we noted above returning means infinitely intensifying what is already the case or as Hegel says 'boundless blessedness'. What is the other of the universal that the universal is, yet without losing itself? It is the already permeated and embraced particular that the universal permeates and embraces. Thanks to the immediacy that belongs to the other itself the absolute's universal equality with itself retains its immediacy in the particular and thereby affirms this immediacy in and as such retaining. The other of the universal neither expresses the loss of the immediate universal nor offers it a place of dwelling by providing the universal with its notion. The other neither 'expels' the immediate absolute nor 'receives' it. In other words the particular is non-thinking, immediate being. It is the immediate and infinite embraced that the universal immediately and infinitely embraces. In embracing it the universal 'finds' in its other the other as always already embraced by the universal. The universal is the power of life of its other who is already 'living', a power that its other drives to intensification. According to Hegel, 'as parts of the whole, [particular] individuals are like blind men, who are driven forward by the indwelling spirit of the whole' (LHP III 553). From this perspective there is no violence between the universal and its other since the other is always already in the universal's embrace. Let us proceed to explore Hegel's metaphor of 'blindness' in order to further specify the relationship between the universal and its other.

With the immediacy's determination of the mediation the embracing in question is *only* embracing and, correspondingly, the embraced is *only* embraced. Accordingly, the embraced excludes embracing and does not itself embrace the universal in order thereby to transform the embracing into the embraced. What would it mean for the embraced also to embrace the universal? It would offer the very idea of universality and in this way function as the *topos* of the universal. Instead, thinking is excluded here.[9] The universal is thought, but immediately so, since it is not received by the embraced as the agent who thinks or embraces the universal. It follows that the embraced particular does not manifest any form of agency. Moreover, in not reflectively relating to itself it does not make possible its own thematization of its embraced being. This is the essence of its 'blindness'. Being unable to receive thought by thinking it, the embraced being manifests a form of awareness that is blind to thought itself or indeed anything beyond itself. It is an unthinking thought that thought occupies immediately. The embraced being is thus always already open to the universal that in turn, finding itself in the embraced being, takes the particular beyond itself towards the universal. It is in this movement of the universal—of taking beyond as this taking beyond—that the particular is determined as lacking agency.

In contrast, the universal is beyond the particular because it is beyond any particular. In fact, it marks the beyond in a dual sense: it is beyond its embracing

---

9. At this stage thinking is wholly external and derives exclusively from the reflecting 'we' or the philosopher.

of the particular not only because it can also ceaselessly embrace another particular and another but also because the universal is *the world of embracing*. After all, the particular is embraced in the world of embracing. Now this is another way of saying that the universal is the power of gathering the particulars which particulars always already manifest the being of being gathered. It is in the particular as gathered that the universal finds itself. At the same time as the other of the universal in which the universal returns to itself the gathered particular is an individual.

The universal's embracing gathers the particulars as already gathered by the universal. Here, the particular does not recognize itself as gathered and so does not involve itself in acts of gathering. The particular is always already gathered; its being is gathered being. Its being is completely determined by the universality of the always already realized gathering. So the universal is both infinitely (non) divided and the infinite embracing of such (non)division. It is the 'differencelessness' that incorporates difference. Here we have intrinsically communal being as a world, yet without communality understood as the reflective element of the notion that makes manifestation possible. Here the moment of universality is the life of communal being without the happening of the reflective appropriation of such being. Communal being is thus without its happening.

Yet this non-happening is infinitely affirmative. The philosophical task then is to show how the absolute releases its manifestation through the moments of its self-releasing in and through which the absolute recollects itself. Each moment thus becomes a form of the absolute as a whole and the power that releases the other forms. This is why the act of superseding one moment through the release of a second, 'higher', moment also activates the release of the first and a return of the second to the first. It also explains why even in its fully realized state the absolute releases its previous moments in a perpetual movement of recollection as perpetual recreation. In exploding so to speak from its state of immediacy to its state of realized manifestation the absolute also implodes into the primordial state of immediacy in order to reactivate itself through the recollection of the primordial activation.

We referred above to the universal as *the world* of embracing. Indeed the absolute is always a world in the sense of the whole that inter-relates the being and notion of the absolute spirit. (This is why Hegel refers repeatedly to the world spirit that is, of course, spirit as world. It also explains my reformulation of the command to 'know thyself' in terms of the command to 'be as a world'.) Returning to the absolute's immediacy as affirming, note that in this state the inter-relating of notion and being is itself immediate, or unthinking, but it is still an inter-relating and so constitutes a *world*. Following my earlier analysis we can read this world in terms of the idea of gathering, albeit not any particular gathering but the gathering as such that has yet to become reflective. Here, the gathering simply is 'boundless blessedness', to use Hegel's phrase.

## The Moment of Particularity

According to our story so far in the mode of being of universality the absolute is immediately complete and thus infinite. So it must release itself from the simplicity of its completeness into a state of incompleteness or finitude. Being immediate it must release itself *as* immediate that is as the immediate that recognizes that its immediacy is already mediated by its power to be, a power that is itself mediated by the fact that it can be. Consequently the absolute releases itself as a project to be realized, a project that locates its justification and draws its inspiration so to speak from the very completeness of the immediate whole. According to Hegel, as universal in the mode of particularity, the absolute:

> *determines* itself freely; the process by which it makes itself finite is not a transition, for this occurs only in the sphere of being; it is *creative power* as the absolute negativity which relates itself to its own self. As such it differentiates itself internally, and this is a *determining*, because the differentiation is one with the universal. Accordingly, the universal is a process in which it posits the differences themselves as universal and self-related. They thereby become *fixed*, isolated differences (SL 605).

In the mode of being of universality the universal finds itself in the particular but it does not recognize itself in it as the power to be; it simply is being. In a sense such an encounter is also a loss since locating itself in the immediate is itself an immediate locating that excludes the thinking that is associated with the notion of the universal. Still, because it incorporates otherness, the immediate is infinitely affirming and thus nevertheless powerful enough not only to affirm itself in its immediacy but also to affirm itself as the immediate that is able to be.

As far as philosophizing is concerned, this recognition—of immediacy as already being mediated—has already taken place in *our* reflecting on universality. This is the reflecting of the thinker that belongs to the absolute itself. We reflect upon the absolute as immediate without it recognizing our act of thinking. Yet to think the absolute presupposes that it is already received as immediate in the sense explained above. Once we complete our reflection by revealing the affirmingness of the immediate we turn our reflection on itself and thus reveal the immediate as what it always was. That is, we reveal it to be the mediated immediate or being that presupposes its power to be. This basically means that we are ready to receive this being as what it is and thus also to receive ourselves in it. It follows firstly that the abovementioned release of the gathered finite takes place in and through us and, secondly, this process incorporates reflectiveness in the being we reflect upon. In other words the absolute in the mode of being of universality is powerful enough to release itself from its state of immediacy in order to make its state an issue.[10]

Now the moment of particularity manifests its affirmative power as *absolute negation*. With the release of the absolute's immediacy— the release that renders explicit its presupposed power—the absolute is released as the not yet and hence as *the absolutely not*. Because it is itself not it withdraws in and as this not. This is the

---

10. See Toula Nicolacopoulos and Goerge Vassilacopoulos, 'The Ego as World', this collection.

moment of finitude, the moment that, in exhibiting its power to be the absolute, is not yet. But this is also affirmation, the element of recognition in negation that renders the negation absolute since it posits the aim of affirming that the affirmed *is not yet* the affirming affirmed. It is as this *not* that the absolute relates itself to itself. In other words its negativity is absolute because it is also a self-relation.

How exactly does the absolute manifest itself in the mode of being of particularity simultaneously as absolute negativity *and* as self-recognition in the form of a project? Now, the moment of particularity is also the infinite division of the immediacy or simplicity characterizing the moment of universality. As this division the moment of universality is retrieved as an aim to be realized and as a realizable aim. Its realizability has already been demonstrated both in the affirming of the whole that the moment of universality is and through this moment's power of negativity in releasing its immediate being. As such it has shown itself to be the realizable whole that formulates itself as the project that is in the process of realizing itself.

Now the moment of particularity is division, the dispersal of particulars and hence the positing of their singularity, something that the universal has previously absorbed. Even so particularity is not a state of affairs that depends upon the external differentiation of particulars; it is instead the mode of being of the particulars. Particularity is thus the universal condition of particulars and hence the universal itself. So it is a way of gathering the particulars. However, in so far as gathering is also a dispersing, gathering as dispersing is the gathering as the aim to become what it is *not yet*. Transforming dispersal into the gathering-to-be is the absolute power of gathering.

Here the universal re-emerges as a task. The gathering that gathers those that have yet to be gathered—the dispersed ones—is a gathering yet to come. Accordingly the universal cannot yet embrace the particular *as gathered* but only as what must become gathered. An important consequence of this is that in recognizing itself as an aim—that is in recognizing its *not* that dispersal manifests—the universal is transformed into a command. It transforms itself into a task by commanding the particular to be as gathered. Here the infinite blends with the finite. Whereas the command is infinite, its reception is finite. In other words the infinite is precisely received as what must become and hence as what is not. But the universality of dispersing is also the retrieval of the immediate universal and therefore of the universal that has already gathered the particulars. So the universal commands the particular to gather as the immediately and hence already gathered.

From the above it follows that the particular is the gathered-dispersed that manifests its power to gather by receiving the gathering as a command. Moreover, it must recognize, or rather, it is the recognition of dispersal as its mode of being since the particular is already beyond the pure state of immediacy in which it dwells as immediately gathered and thereby manifests its singularity. In so far as this recognition is possible and necessary, in recognizing particularity as the mode of being of the particular the particular is also the recognition of the universal as a command. Drawing on our earlier analysis we can say that the particular must be the power of receiving the command without being crushed by this reception. This involves the particular in thinking since it can only receive the universal as a command and thereby activate the latter's commanding by providing the notion of the universal—the notion of the gathering.

So as thinking, the finite performs the impossible; it survives the reception of the infinite. This is the speculative miracle of finitude, the very idea of the finite. But the finite can only do this *as* gathered. From immediately being gathered the particular moves to the reflecting state of being as immediately gathered. It does this by turning its being into the receiving of the gathering as the command to gather or as the command for it to become what it already is, namely gathered and therefore to receive the command as gatherable. This is also none other than a retrieve of immediate communal being in its entirety—that is as universal—as receiving the command to become or as capable of being communally. Here the particular is the being of communal being, albeit in a thinking manner that provides the notion of the universal in order to receive the universal as command.

In other words the particular receives the command by generating the mutual embracing of being and notion out of itself. It is this being/notion inter-relation that makes possible the universality of the absolute as command in terms of the thinking or receiving of thought. It follows from this that it is the command that commands the realization of the mutual embracing of being and notion. Here we have the explicit genesis of conceptuality, that is, the conceptual emergence of the absolute as manifestation, as the realizable that is also to be realized.

From the above analysis it also follows that two different forms of immediacy characterize the immediate whole in its respective connections with the universal as command and the particular as receiving the command. Even though it is this whole that both commands and receives the command, it nevertheless does so in a way that retains two forms of immediacy as separate and self-subsistent. One is the form of the particular as gathered—in the immediacy of its being the particular provides thinking as the notion of the universal and therefore as gatherable—and the other is the form of the universal as gathering—it is the power to bring about gathering.

Now because the particular receives the universal as command by providing the universal's notion and because the universal commands in this receiving of the particular the commanding of the command is manifested *in the form of the individual*. If this is indeed the case then the realm of particularity or dispersing happens as a command in the particular that incorporates the universal as an individual and thus transforms itself into a totality. What we have here is the logical articulation of the idea of the 'I' that is 'we'. This is perhaps the absolute speculative mystery, the mystery of absolute singularity that in receiving the command of the communal 'we' is transformed into the bearer of the 'we' that commands every single 'I'.

Here of course the totality is the formless gathering whose formlessness manifests as the command to create form out of formlessness. Formlessness concerns the retrieve of the immediate whole as something that must become and this becoming must of course involve the creation of a structured whole. So the formless is the activity of retrieving-positing; it retrieves the whole in order to render it an aim. Still, what is retrieved does the commanding and receiving. This latter is immediate being that must happen as what it is and can only happen in the *topos* of its notion. So the question of the notion/being inter-relation—this, as we noted above, is at the heart of the absolute—becomes explicit here in the realm of the formless gathering. In other words, the realm of the formless gathering posits that which creates being and notion out of itself as self-manifesting, or the absoluteness of the absolute, and through this positing the absolute is itself also posited as an aim to be realized.

It follows from the above analysis that the command is in some sense empty; it is purely a command without commanding something specific. Accordingly, the *what* of the command that is received is the purity of thought in its complete indeterminacy. Moreover, it is received in so far as the particular offers it its notion, the notion of thought, which is none other than pure thinking. The command is thought and commands thinking that is activated as the notion of thinking, that is, as thinking that receives thought. In order for thinking to receive thought it cannot just be a thinking *about* thought; it must be a thinking thought and it is a thinking thought because what is thinking is the being of the particular, the thinking particular, that is in itself universal. In this way thinking already incorporates being and being already incorporates thinking.

## The Moment of Individuality

I have argued that each particular is the *topos* of the gathering and that the gathering takes place as what receives the command to gather. The gathering of particulars is thus a gathering of infinite gatherings. As members of the indeterminate gathering, particular individuals encounter each other as both commanding the other and receiving the command from the other. They greet each other with 'be as a world' or 'know thyself'. For this reason individuals are exactly like one another—the other is like me in that he or she also receives and commands—and yet there is an infinite asymmetry in the inter-relation of individuals in so far one commands and the other receives.

Still, individuality is the mode of being of the absolute as the whole that is both realized and realizing. Since the absolute never remains in the mode of being of an aim to be realized it also never limits itself to the mode of being of the realized that has forgotten its realizing. The realized absolute is the power of infinite construction and infinite deconstruction. It never allows its fully established world of gathering to transform itself into a lifeless given by cutting its ties with its presupposition, namely its very power to be created as a world. So its fullness relates to the fact that it is at once fully realized and also radically yet to be realized. Nevertheless it allows itself to be absorbed in the immediate element of its unity and does not permit the systematization of its difference to become systemic in a way that would empower this difference to destroy its immediate unity.

What follows from the above for our understanding of the logical form and existential manifestation of the realized world of the communal gathering? I have been arguing that the command to be as a world that is linked to the creation of form out of the formless gathering is what commands the gathering to gather. Moreover, since it is the gathering itself that must gather, the formed gathering must be a gathering of gatherings. So too each particular form of gathering must be a particular manifestation of the world of the gathering of gatherings. Not only must the particular forms be gathered as aspects of the universal gathering but also each particular form must realize the gathering of gatherings, that is, each particular form must realize the whole. Accordingly, we might expect the unity of the moments of particularity and universality, the moment of individuality to be a unity of three syllogisms whose form manifests the whole as the gathering of gatherings. In Hegel's system this logical inter-relation will in turn manifest existentially as the moments of the constitution of the ethical state wherein 'each [of these moments] contains the other moments and has them effective in itself' (PR § 272). When we are informed by the ideas of gathering and dispersal we are in a position to appreciate how this existential manifestation of the syllogistic unity results from spirit's 'fragrant rising up' out of the 'foaming ferment of its finitude'.

# 17

# The Beginning Before the Beginning: Hegel and the Activation of Philosophy

Paul Ashton

## INTRODUCTION

The one thing that almost all readers of Hegel agree upon is that for Hegel the question of a properly philosophical beginning, or 'with what must science begin', is of central importance to the activation of his philosophy. The problem of the beginning in Hegel's philosophy is multifarious, there is the beginning of the logic, or the system as a whole, there are new beginnings in each developmental cycle of the system—logic, nature and spirit—and there is the beginning of the *Phenomenology of Spirit*. While not as universally agreed upon, the need for the 'beginning' to be *presuppositionless* is now generally also accepted. However, what has received less attention is the beginning of philosophy *as such*; how or why the philosopher begins—*the beginning before the beginning*.[1]

With Hegel, commentators generally agree that philosophy cannot '*presuppose* its *ob-jects* as given immediately by representation' (EL § 1) and consequently it 'cannot *presuppose* the *method* of cognition [...] with regard to its beginning and advance' (El § 1). Appropriately, given this fundamental starting position, recent commentators have once again begun to recognize the importance of Hegel's systemic texts and in particular the *Science of Logic*.[2] This non-negotiable starting position for philosophy can possibly help us explain the dual tendency within the scholarship on Hegel's work. On the one hand many commentators take a thematic approach, focusing on any number of insights to be found in He-

---

1. I would like to express my sincere gratitude and appreciation to my friends and colleagues Toula Nicolacopoulos, Claire Rafferty and George Vassilacopoulos for their valuable discussion and suggestions regarding this paper.

2. See three recent commentaries on the logic: John W. Burbidge, *Hegel's Systematic Contingency*, Houndmills, Palgrave Macmillan, 2007, David Gray Carlson, *A Commentary to Hegel's Science of Logic*, New York, Palgrave Macmillian, 2007, Stephen Houlgate, *The Opening of Hegel's Logic: From Being to Infinity*, Indiana, Purdue University Press, 2006.

gel—usually from his political philosophy—while avoiding the implications of the speculative logic altogether.[3] On the other hand we find those who try to work through the texts systematically in compliance with Hegel's directive to be presuppositionless. The sheer impenetrability of the Hegelian texts ensures that even the most systematic among the commentaries face unexplainable aporias. However, what is perhaps more revealing are the silences common to both tendencies. On closer inspection of the aspects of Hegel's philosophy upon which the commentaries remain silent, or at least rather laconic, we can find a paradoxical unity. As most readers of Hegel scholarship will have experienced, it is often in the same key areas that the commentaries become silent or vague, regardless of one's perspective. Symptomatic of this are the paradigmatic examples of 'the role the absolute' and 'absolute knowledge'; a consequence of which is that in the two-hundred years since its publication there is no general consensus or 'accepted' reading of the *Phenomenology* or for that matter of the *System*.

However, I want to suggest that the silences found within these two tendencies stem from their continued failure to address the central question of what it means to encounter philosophy as such and Hegel as a philosopher; an omission that interrupts our ability to address the question of the activation of the philosophical project itself or the beginning before the beginning. To this extent, I will attempt to explore the conditions that prepare the ground for a more complete engagement or encounter with Hegel as a 'kindred spirit'.

Possibly the reason that the beginning before the beginning has not become an issue in the literature is that scholars have wisely heeded Hegel's warnings to not be like Scholasticus who tried 'to learn to *swim before he ventured into the water*' (EL § 10 R). Hegel argues that 'to want the nature of cognition clarified *prior* to science is to demand that it be considered *outside* the science; *outside* the science this cannot be accomplished, at least not in a scientific manner and such a manner is alone here in place' (SL 68). There is no doubt that Hegel is rejecting a kind of meta-philosophical perspective, that there exists some space outside of, or for that matter within, philosophy from which to clarify what philosophy is. This does not mean that philosophy cannot consider its own cognitive process, its own movement, but rather it cannot philosophically take account of its own movement prior to, or separate from, the very movement itself. Perhaps an extreme version of this thesis is Hegel's claim in the introduction to the *Phenomenology* that the absolute is 'with us, in and for itself, all along' (PS ¶ 73), for if it were not we would find ourselves trying to cognize something foreign or external to our thinking. If we accept Hegel's understanding that Science cannot take place outside of Science, where and how would such a consideration take place?

An obvious place to look for such a discussion is in Hegel's prefaces and introductions, a part of his work that is not part of the Science itself. What the prefaces and the pre-systemic texts offer us is not a *Science* of the beginning before the beginning—hence the superfluousness of prefaces to *Science*—but a series of

---

3. There are numerous examples of this tendency but perhaps the most cited example is Allen W. Wood, *Hegel's Ethical Thought*, Cambridge, Cambridge University Press, 1990.

reflections *on* philosophy and its conditions of activation that are not themselves the point of activation. There is no doubt that we have a problem here with regard to the beginning; either something is already scientific and thus not in need of a beginning or it is not, and from this perspective the question of how one would even recognize Science if they came across it becomes relevant. However, these texts at best only gesture to such a source of activation in a way that only makes sense to those already *activated* into philosophy and do not give an explicit account of such an activation. Thus even if we accept Hegel's claim that the absolute is there with us from the beginning, we would have to account for how and why we come to recognize what is already there?

*Interests and Wants: How do We Begin?*

The need to introduce the thinker to the scientific standpoint and the coextensive paradox of the supposed impossibility of a completely presuppositionless beginning has been a significant problem for readers of Hegel's system. This has led some commentators, including William Maker, to treat the *Phenomenology* as not properly scientific in itself, and thus not in need of a presuppositionless beginning, in an attempt to ensure a genuinely scientific beginning for the *Logic* (considered as speculative philosophy proper). To this extent, the *Phenomenology* is seen as merely a 'presupposition for presuppositionless science',[4] the fundamental purpose of which is the elimination of the dichotomous perspective of consciousness. More recently Stephen Houlgate has taken a version of this thesis even further in suggesting that the *Phenomenology* is in fact *not* a necessary part of Hegel's philosophy, arguing that: 'the *Phenomenology* does not provide the only possible route into speculative philosophy. Those who are prepared to suspend their ordinary certainties can bypass the *Phenomenology* and proceed directly to the *Logic*'.[5] Thus for Houlgate the requirement here is that one take on or possess the appropriate *attitude* to begin presuppositionless philosophy *qua* speculative logic— that is, beyond the dichotomous perspective of consciousness. Furthermore, it is important that members of the would-be 'we' are 'persuaded to give up their "presuppositions and prejudices"', a persuasion that could take place through 'studying the history of modern philosophy' or even through the engagement with 'true religion'.[6] This rather strong claim suggests that the justificatory role of the *Phenomenology* is both contingent and instrumental.[7] From this position, what

---

4. William Maker, *Philosophy Without Foundations: Rethinking Hegel*, Albany, State University of New York Press, 1994, p. 85.

5. Houlgate, *The Opening of Hegel's Logic*, p. 146.

6. Houlgate, *The Opening of Hegel's Logic*, p. 146.

7. Houlgate carefully defends this argument by drawing on Hegel's claim that 'nothing is needed to begin doing speculative philosophy except "the resolve (*Entschluß*), which can be regarded as arbitrary, that we propose to consider thought as such" (SL 68). Such a resolve requires that one "rid oneself of all other reflections and opinions whatever", and simply "take up *what is there before us*"— namely, the sheer being of thought, or thought as sheer being (SL 68)'. Also instructive here is EL § 78. On this see Houlgate, *The Opening of Hegel's Logic*, p. 145.

places one on the path that activates their philosophical drive so to speak, that annihilates presuppositions, is taken as given. Ignoring the activation of philosophy is no insignificant omission, for why would one without considerable cause seek to rid oneself of the dichotomous perspective of consciousness if, as Hegel informs us, doing so will lead them onto a path of despair (PS ¶ 78) and mean they must suffer the 'violence' of this 'inverted posture' (PS ¶ 26)? Of course on one level we can account for the activation of thinking through a rather mundane or commonsensical 'external' encounter with ideas and institutions in everyday life, but what this ultimately has to do with our encounter with philosophy *as such* is possibly limited or else at least requires some explaining. For that matter, who is this 'we' that has read Hegel's philosophy, who has been walking on its head down the violent highway of despair for two-hundred years now?

If we try to make sense of how these different readings take place and what motivates them—or for that matter what motivates Hegel in his comments regarding the beginning and activation of philosophy—we are struck by the perceptiveness of Kenley Royce Dove's recognition that the 'interpretation of the "we" tends to govern [...] one's view of the *Phenomenology* as a whole'.[8] However, as Dove also recognizes, despite the fact that nearly all commentators 'recognize' the 'need of an explanation' for the 'we', and do in fact offer some explanation, the 'explanations usually provided, are [...] remarkably laconic'.[9] Laconicism is not usually a word one would associate with Hegel scholarship on the *Phenomenology* more generally. For example, one would be reticent to describe Hyppolite's *Genesis and Structure*[10] at 608 pages, Harris' *Hegel's Ladder*[11] at 1567 pages and Pinkard's *Hegel's Phenomenology*[12] at 451 pages, as laconic; yet perhaps with the exception of Hyppolite—who does try to deal with the 'we', even if it does remain

---

8. Kenley R. Dove, 'Hegel's Phenomenological Method', *The Review of Metaphysics*, vol. 23, no. 4, 1970, pp. 615-41, p. 631. The fact that the 'we' plays this governing role is not surprising if we analyse the text. Hegel uses 'we' and its variants 'for us' and 'us' ('*wir*', '*unser*' and '*für uns*') over 180 times throughout every chapter of the *Phenomenology*. For a detailed account of each of these uses and a comprehensive study of the 'we' in Hegel see David M. Parry, *Hegel's Phenomenology of the "We"*, New York, P. Lang, 1988. However, in reading the 'we' strictly in terms of a project of philosophy already taken up, or as already activated, Parry interprets the 'we' simply as the 'reader' of the *Phenomenology* and does not account for what I am suggesting is Hegel's concern in the first place; the activation of philosophy and the 'we' as the dwelling space of the activated philosopher. However, Parry does recognize that there is a need to 'prepare' the 'reader' for the work and this activity must itself be done prior to philosophy understood as Science. This is done through the 'Preface' which is an 'ironic' gesture that functions in terms of what he describes as 'the liar's paradox'. Somehow by being ironic about the status of a preface a would-be thinker can engage with the preconditions in such a way that it does not undermine the phenomenological process as such. However, this strategy is far from convincing and opens up more problems for the would-be philosopher than it solves. For example, an ironic attitude to the text already assumes a level of philosophical engagement.

9. Dove, 'Hegel's Phenomenological Method', p. 629.

10. Jean Hyppolite, *Genesis and Structure of Hegel's Phenomenology of Spirit*, trans. Samuel Cherniak and John Heckman, Evanston, Northwestern University Press, 1974.

11. H. S. Harris, *Hegel's Ladder*, 2 vols., Indianapolis, Hackett, 1997.

12. Terry P. Pinkard, *Hegel's Phenomenology: The Sociality of Reason*, New York, Cambridge University Press, 1996.

largely suggestive—Dove's point is correct in that little is said or made *explicit* with regard to the role of the 'we'.

Accordingly, commentators who read the *Phenomenology* and its beginning in the manner outlined above, such as Houlgate, tend to see the 'we [as simply] the readers and phenomenologists'[13] who take up the task of working through the eradication of the dichotomous perspective of consciousness. Thus the 'readers of the *Phenomenology* are intended to be ordinary people (and philosophers tied to ordinary beliefs) who are unmoved by the modern spirit of philosophical self-criticism and so need to be persuaded that Hegel's presuppositionless, ontological logic is a justified and relevant science'.[14] Accordingly people such as this are typically 'firmly immersed in the world of everyday experience', but if they are to be elevated to the standpoint of Science 'they cannot be bull-headed [and] they must have some interest in what Hegelian speculative philosophy might disclose about the world and be open to what it may show them about their own everyday beliefs'.[15] What prepares the would-be reader of the *Phenomenology* is an 'openness of mind [that] may come from a basic ethical decency and intelligence, or indeed, it may stem from religion.'[16] Thus it is the 'openness of mind' of the consciousness of the would-be philosopher that permits and therefore 'anticipates the perspective of absolute knowing'.[17] But it could be argued that this way of thinking about the character of the 'we' and the anticipation of the perspective of absolute knowledge raises other questions. For example: what would it mean to have an 'interest' in the disclosure of the world, where would such an interest come from and how would one's mind be opened?

If we accept the value of Dove's insight that the 'we' plays a structuring role in the reading of the *Phenomenology* then an interesting comparison with Houlgate's interpretation is that offered by H. S. Harris. While Houlgate and Harris present substantially different readings of the *Phenomenology*—for example, the idea that the *Phenomenology* could be replaced with the study of history or religion is unthinkable for Harris, as the *Phenomenology* is most definitely 'a science in its own right'[18]—they nonetheless maintain similar positions on the 'we'. Like Houlgate, Harris presents the commonsensical view that the 'we' is the 'ordinary consciousness of the present world that wants to comprehend the world of experience philosophically'.[19] However, Harris does acknowledge that this is not just anyone, not just 'educated' people, rather it is the 'educated consciousness of the present

---

13. This statement of Houlgate's could be found in literally dozens of books on Hegel. See Stephen Houlgate, *An Introduction to Hegel's Philosophy: Freedom, Truth and History*, 2nd ed., Oxford, Blackwell, 2005, p. 57.
14. Houlgate, *The Opening of Hegel's Logic*, p. 160.
15. Houlgate, *The Opening of Hegel's Logic*, p. 160.
16. Houlgate, *The Opening of Hegel's Logic*, p. 160.
17. Houlgate, *The Opening of Hegel's Logic*, p. 160.
18. H. S. Harris, *Hegel's Ladder*, vol. 1, 2 vols., Indianapolis, Hackett, 1997, p. 110.
19. Harris, *Hegel's Ladder*, p. 178.

that *wants to be comprehensive*.[20] We can see here that Harris is trying to account for the intersubjectivity of the 'we' and the everydayness of the would-be philosopher, however, we can also see that Harris' position leaves questions unanswered. How or why does the 'we', *qua* 'educated consciousness of the present that *wants to be comprehensive*', come to take up philosophy in this form? In associating this desire '*to be comprehensive*' with 'the natural "desire to know"', as Harris does, the contingency and situatedness of the actualization of the philosophical outlook is missed. Similarly, certain problems arise with the use of language like 'the natural "desire to know"'; for example how does one take account for Hegel's insistence that '[f]reedom of Thought [constitutes …] a first condition' (LHP I 94) of philosophy and that '[t]hought must be for-itself, must come into existence in its freedom, liberate itself from nature and come out of its immersion in mere sense-perception; it must as free, enter within itself and thus arrive at the consciousness of freedom' (LHP I 94)? In responding to a range of 'ontological' readings of the 'we' Harris—and again he is typical of the dominant readings—makes the point that the whole problem of the 'we' is a 'pseudo problem, which exists only for those who […  believe that an] unnatural way of talking is the proper expression of a philosophical consciousness'.[21] Harris continues that 'Hegel obviously means "us" to include anyone who *wants* to share the knowing that will be shown to be "absolute" in the book' the only prerequisite to be one of 'us' is 'that you must already have the sort of knowledge that he himself [Hegel] was endowed with during his own *Bildung*'.[22] That is, to 'be a possible member of the "We" one must know the history of our religious and philosophical culture'.[23]

But if Harris is critical of those who needlessly ontologize the 'we' then he is equally in danger himself of epistemologizing it. There is no doubt that 'absolute knowledge', the achieved cognitive perspective of the 'we', is a knowing and therefore an epistemic stance, but it is equally ontological in that it is *a way of knowing* that takes account of the essential unity of knowing and known, subject and object—that is, a stance taken within the space of the knowing/being mutual informing. Both Harris and Houlgate seem to be suggesting that the would-be philosopher's place in the 'we' is determined by their level of knowledge or intellect and that only when they have reached these heights of thinking—the height of Hegel!—are they capable of becoming a member of the 'we' and beginning the philosophical process. However, both thinkers already acknowledge the limitation of this view when they point to the would-be philosopher as having 'interest' and 'wants'. What their use of the terms 'interest' and 'want' suggests is that these two thinkers already indicate a position beyond the epistemic stance of the philosopher as merely someone who knows, to something ontologically more fundamental: that 'we' have the interest and want to disclose the world, presumably not in a dichotomous sense but speculatively. That is, Harris and Houlgate

---

20. Harris, *Hegel's Ladder*, p. 178.
21. Harris, *Hegel's Ladder*, p. 201 n. 30.
22. Harris, *Hegel's Ladder*, p. 201 n. 30.
23. Harris, *Hegel's Ladder*, p. 178.

already point in the direction of where philosophy comes from and how it is activated before its activation; to a want that is a need.

## THE NEED OF PHILOSOPHY

If we are to address the question of how and where the 'we' that has 'wants' and 'interests' arises, and is constituted, then the question of the *need of philosophy* also arises. In the introductory chapter to the *Difference* essay, the 'Various Forms Occurring in Contemporary Philosophy' (D 85-118), Hegel explicitly addresses the question of 'the need of philosophy'. It has been recognized by many commentators, including the translator H. S. Harris, that this need can be understood as a dual need: 'the need (at this time) for philosophy, *and* what philosophy needs (at this time)'.[24] However, what both of these interpretations possibly miss is the *explicit* meaning of the phrase; by saying 'the need of philosophy' Hegel is drawing attention to the need *of* philosophy (as such), that is, *philosophy's* own need. With this meaning we can also add 'at this time', as although philosophy's need has an eternal dimension, it is nonetheless always situated historically. Thus we can say that what we are dealing with is *philosophy's own need at this time*.

But why is the question of *philosophy's own need at this time* important for us and what do we mean by 'this time' and why is 'this time' important in terms of this *need*? Hegel understands his philosophy as taking place in the space opened up by the rise of modernity, but more specifically Hegel understands his time, and consequently his thought *qua* of 'this time', to be the thought of *revolution*.[25] Thus despite the ambiguous status of the 'future' in Hegel's philosophy, we can see that just as the revolution through its *practice* announces the future, philosophy through its *thinking* gives conceptual form to the future. That is, Hegel's philosophy gives conceptual form to a future already announced through the event of the French Revolution.[26] Read in this way we can see that philosophy comes after the political, giving form to that which has been announced in practice, and that the want and interest of the philosopher, who wants to disclose the world, comes from an announcement that has already taken place. This is why according to Hegel philosophy always 'comes too late' (PR 23).

However, as indicated above, the claim that for Hegel philosophy through its thinking gives conceptual form to the future cannot be made so easily: from

---

24. Harris in G. W. F. Hegel, *The Difference Between Fichte's and Schelling's System of Philosophy*, trans. H. S. Harris and Walter Cerf, Albany, State University of New York Press, 1977, p. 89 n. 7. The second sense of 'need' is not to be confused with what I suggest below because 'need' in this usage is understood as what philosophy needs *in order to be a more satisfactory as a discourse*.

25. See Joachim Ritter: 'there is no other philosophy that is a philosophy of revolution to such a degree and so profoundly, in its innermost drive, as that of Hegel', Joachim Ritter, *Hegel and the French Revolution: Essays on the Philosophy of Right*, Cambridge, MIT Press, 1982, p. 43.

26. Habermas attributes to Hegel's epochal understanding the idea that 'the secular concept of modernity expresses the conviction that the future has already begun', see Jürgen Habermas, *The Philosophical Discourse of Modernity: Twelve Lectures*, trans. Frederick G. Lawrence, Cambridge, MIT Press, 1996, p. 5.

the earliest commentaries the received view has been that Hegel's system has *no* place for the future. For example, the youngest of the Young Hegelians August Cieszkowski in his 1838 work *Prolegomena zur Historiosophie*[27] argued that Hegel's philosophy is essentially contemplative and backward looking and does not take account of the future. Furthermore this early reading, via Marx's eleventh thesis, has been decisive in establishing boundaries for subsequent scholarship on the topic. In its extreme form this reading posits Hegel as a reactionary apologist for the Prussian state, and while this latter view has been demolished in the secondary literature[28] to the extent that no serious thinker accepts this idea today, the same cannot be said for the widely accepted view that Hegel's system has no place for the future. While there have been some attempts more recently to revive the concept of the future in Hegel[29] their impact has been limited. There is of course very good reason for the acceptance of the received view; Hegel repeatedly claims that philosophy arrives on the scene too late, that it ought not issue instructions for future ages and that one is always a thinker of his or her own age. There is no doubt that for Hegel hypothetical speculation on events to come is not and can not be considered philosophical—philosophy is always reflection on what is and never on what ought to be. This of course raises important questions regarding the role of the philosopher and their relation to world in the thinking of freedom and specifically whether we would-be speculative philosophers need philosophy or whether philosophy needs us?

*The Announcement of the Modern Age*

Hegel gives a rather poetic account of the birth of this modern age, the age of revolution, in the preface to his *Phenomenology*:

> it is not difficult to see that ours is a birth-time and a period of transition to a new era. Spirit has broken with the world it has hitherto inhabited and imagined, and is of a mind to submerge it into the past, and in the labour of its own transformation ... The frivolity and boredom which unsettled the established order, the vague foreboding of something unknown, these are the heralds of approaching change. The gradual crumbling that left unaltered the face of the whole is cut short by a sunburst

---

27. See August Cieszkowski, *Prolegomena zur Historiosophie*, Berlin, Veit, 1838. Sections of this text are translated in August Cieszkowski, *Selected Writings of August Cieszkowski*, ed. and trans. Andre Liebich, Cambridge, Cambridge University Press, 1979, August Cieszkowski, 'Prolegomena to Historiosophie', *The Young Hegelians: An Anthology*, ed. and trans. Lawrence S. Stepelevich, Cambridge, Cambridge University Press, 1983, pp. 53-90.

28. See for example chapters 4-8 of Jon Stewart (ed.), *The Hegel Myths and Legends*, Evanston, Northwestern University Press, 1996. In particular see T. M. Knox, 'Hegel and Prussianism', in Jon Stewart (ed.), *The Hegel Myths and Legends*, Evanston, Northwestern University Press, 1996, pp. 70-81.

29. Most notable here is Catherine Malabou, *The Future of Hegel: Plasticity, Temporality, and Dialectic*, trans. Lisabeth During, New York, Routledge, 2004. However, this work, as with many others that try to resurrect the notion of the future in Hegel discuss the future in terms of time and specifically in terms of Heidegger's encounter with Hegel's notion of time. While this focus on temporality is reasonable enough it does prevent the possibility of what I am suggesting here that in some sense the future is already with us.

which, in one flash, illuminates the features of the new world (PS ¶ 11).[30]

However, Hegel reminds us that this new era does not 'come on the scene' ready made, in its full actuality, but rather like a newborn child it comes in its 'immediacy or its Notion'. That is, this new world appears *in time* in its 'principle' or '*simple Notion*' (PS ¶ 12), and this principle is freedom. *Qua* principle, freedom appears as a task to be realized.[31] Thus the French Revolution's proclamation of universal freedom, the 'for all', is a principle lacking embodiment. The living spirit of the collective expression of freedom misfired. Thus 'the experience of what Spirit is' according to Hegel 'still lies ahead for consciousness' and what it is that lies ahead, spirit or freedom actualized, is the 'absolute substance which is the unity of the different independent self-consciousnesses which, in their opposition, enjoy perfect freedom and independence: "I" that is "We" and the "We" that is "I"' (PS ¶ 177). But this is to be expected, for as true *principle* spirit always comes on the scene in its self-loss. Both philosophically and politically speaking, freedom must claim itself as free, for if it were to simply 'come on the scene' ready-made it would not embody its own freedom freely. In this sense cognition of freedom is the principle of the conceptual form, that is of philosophy, and the promise of the future located in the present as a task to be realized. Thus, according to Hegel:

> Through knowledge, Spirit makes manifest a distinction between knowledge and that which is; this knowledge is thus what produces a new form of development. The new forms at first are only special modes of knowledge, and it is thus that a new Philosophy is produced: yet since, it already is a wider kind of spirit, it is the inward birth-place of the spirit which will later arrive at actual form. (LHP I 55)

This is the unique character and *strength* of spirit to survive the separation of its notion from its reality, that is to survive its own division and to create its freedom out of this division. Hence the need of philosophy, spirit's *need*, is to manifest itself out of its self-loss.

> For this reason formally the *essence* of spirit is *freedom*, the concept's [(Notion's)] absolute negativity as identity with itself. In accordance with this formal determination, the spirit *can* abstract from everything external and form its own externality, from its very life; it can endure the negation of its individual immediacy, infinite *pain*, i.e.

---

30. It is interesting to compare this use of 'flash' with a miscellaneous note found in Hegel's hand: 'The subsistence of the community is its continuous, eternal becoming, which is grounded in the fact that spirit is an eternal process of self-cognition, dividing itself into the finite flashes of light of individual consciousness, and then re-collecting and gathering itself up out of this finitude—inasmuch as it is in the finite consciousness that the process of knowing spirit's essence takes place and that the divine self-consciousness thus arises. Out of the foaming ferment of finitude, spirit rises up fragrantly' cited in Georg Wilhelm Friedrich Hegel, *Lectures on the Philosophy of Religion*, P. C. Hodgson (ed.), trans. R. F. Brown, P. C. Hodgson and J. M. Stewart, vol. III The Consummate Religion, 3 vols., Berkeley, University of California Press, 1998, p. 233 n191.

31. See Toula Nicolacopoulos and George Vassilacopoulos, 'Philosophy and Revolution: Badiou's Infidelity to the Event', *Cosmos and History*, vol. 2, no. 1-2, 2006, pp. 210-25, p. 370. In this article the authors read the whole of Western philosophy in these terms. Thus '[s]ince the Greeks, western history can be understood as the yet to be resolved tension between a world that produces the revolutionary idea of the gathering "we" and at the same time constructs itself as the reality that denies the idea its actualization.'

it can maintain itself affirmatively in this negativity and be identical for itself. This possibility is its intrinsic abstract universality, a universality that is for itself (EPM § 382).

If absolute negativity is the essential quality of spirit then we can see how spirit becomes spiritual, present to itself philosophically, out of the division of reality and its principle and thus how and why '[d]ichotomy is the source of *the need of philosophy*' (D 89)—because 'the appearance of the Absolute has become isolated from the Absolute and fixated into independence' (D 89). What is important here is that the image of the whole becomes apparent through the dichotomy, hence 'the appearance [of the Absolute] cannot disown its origin, and must aim to constitute the manifold of its limitations into one whole' (D 89). However, the absolute is no night in which all cows are black, for 'Reason is [not] altogether opposed to opposition and limitation. For the necessary dichotomy is One factor in life[—union, being the other]' (D 90-1). It is for this reason that Hegel suggests that

> [w]hen the might of union vanishes from the life of men and the antitheses lose their living connection and reciprocity and gain independence, the need for philosophy arises. From this point of view the need is contingent. But with respect to the given dichotomy the need is the necessary attempt to suspend the rigidified opposition between subjectivity and objectivity; to comprehend the achieved existence (*das Gewordensein*) of the intellectual and real world as a becoming' (D 91).

Therefore reason, as the infinite activity of becoming, creates a vision of the whole as united in its differentiation, and that in uniting what was rent asunder reason has 'reduced the absolute dichotomy to a relative one, one that is conditioned by the original identity' (D 91). As we can see, according to Hegel the need of philosophy emerges when we experience the divisions of the modern world and that it is through this need that the whole, *qua* spirit, becomes clear for us in its *alienated* being. What needs stressing is that while the 'dichotomy' is situated within specific histories, cultures, and events, for philosophy as such a more fundamental division is present. Hegel argues that the separation of self and world, or subject and object, is in fact the condition for both philosophy and of freedom understood philosophically. This is because for Hegel, freedom makes itself felt philosophically, when a kind of reflective attitude that distances the knowing subject from its known object emerges (LPH I 24 & 94-6). In this sense the Cartesian *cogito* and the Kantian turn to the subject, are radicalizations of an existing division that first emerges in the Greek polis.[32]

Hegel makes the point that the subjectivity of the ancient and modern philosopher is radically different. The 'plasticity' of the ancient self meant that 'one's philosophy determined one's [life] situation. An individual could actually *live* as a philosopher, and this often happened; that is to say, one's outward circumstances were determined in conformity with this purpose of one's inner life' (LHP 25-6 III

---

32. On the relation of philosophizing to the Greek polis see George Vassilacopoulos, 'Plato's *Republic* and the End of Philosophy', *Philosophical Inquiry*, vol. XIX, no. 1-2, 2007, pp. 34-45.

109). However, '[i]n the modern times the relationship is different. Philosophers occupy no specific position in the state; they live in bourgeois circumstances or participate in public life, or in living their private lives they do so in such a way that their private status does not isolate them from other relationships' (LHP 25-6 III 109-10). In the modern world every person is absorbed into the powerful 'universal nexus, based on the understanding' and thus located in the fundamental division in which the 'inner [world within ourselves] and outer [determined by an external order] can coexist as autonomous and independent' (LHP 25-6 III 110). That this outer order can be relegated to an external order, which is in this sense embodied, the philosopher literally lives the dichotomy through which the whole becomes visable, philosophically speaking. Consequently, while Hegel designates several ancient thinkers as 'speculative', genuinely speculative awareness is the awareness inhabited by the modern. Hegel recognizes that 'speculative thinking consists in bringing the thoughts together, and they must be brought together—that is the whole point. The heart and true greatness of Platonic philosophy lies in it bringing-together things that in representation are distinct from one another (being and non-being, one and many, and so forth), so that we are not just passing over from one to the other' (LHP 25-6 II 202). However, the task of gathering for Plato was one thing, but for the modern philosophers, who exist in a more radicalized dispersal, it is altogether another thing and greater speculative strength is required.[33]

## PHILOSOPHY AND THEMATIC THINKING: TWO OBJECTIONS

In taking account of the very force that activates the philosophical project we can see that for Hegel the need of philosophy has two dimensions. On the one hand philosophy needs, or is always retroactively related to, an event that provides the existential conditions or the 'soil' from which philosophy can grow (see PS ¶ 26). On the other hand we can see that philosophy's need is to give conceptual shape to that which *is* so it can *be*—that is to give *conceptual* form to that which will become '*actual* form'. In not taking account of, or treating merely thematically, the beginning before the beginning—and therefore philosophy as the conceptual dwelling space of revolution—many commentators miss the purpose of Hegel's philosophy. For example, in taking up the 'we' as a *theme* or a *problem* in Hegel's thinking, the very possibility of understanding it as the dwelling space of the philosopher opened up by the revolutionary is hidden. Furthermore, given the relation articulated above between philosophy and the political, one may expect thinkers sympathetic to the future announced in the revolution—freedom expressed by and for all—to be more sympathetic, or at least sensitive, to Hegel's

---

33. For an original and sensitive treatment of the power of the formal subject, a subject determined by the 'universal nexus based on the understanding' see Toula Nicolacopoulos, *The Radical Critique of Liberalism: In Memory of a Vision*, Seddon, re.press, 2008, Toula Nicolacopoulos and George Vassilacopoulos, *Hegel and the Logical Structure of Love: An Essay on Sexualities, Family and the Law*, Aldershot, Ashgate, 1999.

project as envisioned in these terms. However, this is not the case. To be sure, some of the most notable examples of a thematic treatment of Hegel's thinking have come from those thinkers informed by the same revolutionary events as Hegel.

This tendency can be found in the work of Habermas who has in turn played a paradigmatic role, if often not specifically acknowledged, in shaping Hegelian scholarship more generally. Habermas sees Hegel's philosophy becoming problematic in at least two ways, both of which from his perspective lead ultimately into conservatism and thus fail to provide the desired or appropriate philosophical grounding for social change. That is, while recognizing that Hegel is indeed the philosopher who first captures the revolutionary spirit of modernity,[34] Habermas believes Hegel ultimately does not and can not sustain this project. Consequently Habermas argues firstly, that in his early work Hegel offers us a radical vision which he later abandons and secondly, that his philosophy relies on the absolute as unwarranted presupposition. While we are using Habermas to engage Hegel on these two points, they are in fact familiar criticisms that any number of thinkers both hostile and sympathetic to Hegel would make.[35]

However, consideration of these criticisms offered by Habermas can potentially make explicit both the role that the relation between philosophy and the political play in the beginning and activation of philosophy for Hegel, and the kind of justification an appropriately presuppositionless beginning requires for Hegel's philosophy to actually be *philosophical*. Furthermore, it will hopefully become clear that by failing to see the appropriate relation between thought and its activation, Habermas may not only fail to understand Hegel's project more broadly, but paradoxically find himself in the position in which his own philosophy can be seen to suffer the very fate that he ascribes to Hegel's. Focusing exclusively on the external dimension of 'the need of philosophy'—or on *the need at this time for philosophy* and *what philosophy needs at this time in order to be reformed* in contradistinction to *philosophy's own need at this time*—Habermas limits the possibilities for establishing an appropriate context to appreciate Hegel's philosophy in its own terms. What is more, the relevance of Habermas' criticisms of Hegel's system are further limited if one takes seriously what *Hegel* considers to be an appropriate context and beginning for philosophical thinking. That is, these criticisms are only criticisms if one accepts the thematic approach to philosophy, because what Habermas presents are criticisms of certain concepts thematically treated. Thus if the presence of the absolute (as with us from the beginning), and the speculative nature of Hegel's 'political' philosophy are understood *speculatively*,

---

34. Recall that Habermas understands and attributes the articulation of modernity—as that period that 'can and will no longer borrow the criteria by which it takes its orientation from models supplied by another epoch; *it has to create its normativity out of itself*—to Hegel. Consequently according to Habermas '[m]odernity sees itself cast back upon itself without any escape' Habermas, *The Philosophical Discourse of Modernity*, p. 7.

35. A well argued example of an alternate reading of the 'we' that rejects the idea of the absolute as there with us from the beginning, a criticism also made by Habermas, is offered by Robert Sinnerbrink in this volume.

that is, in terms of the activation of philosophy and consequently in the context of the aforementioned revolution/philosophy relation—as opposed to Habermas' thematic treatment—, such critical readings can be seen to lack depth and sensitivity.

*Philosophy and the Political*

In characterizing Hegel's *Phenomenology* as 'half-hearted'[36] Habermas goes to the very core of his criticism of Hegel, which is nothing less than a criticism of the very purpose of Hegel's philosophical project as overly idealistic. As stated earlier, Hegel's project is considered by Habermas to be half-hearted or limited for two reasons.[37] Firstly, in presenting the view that would become dominant within Marxist criticism, Habermas argues that Hegel's early pre-*Phenomenological* writings—in particular his *Jena Philosophy of Mind*—'offered a distinctive, systemic basis for the formative process of the spirit, which he later abandoned',[38] in favour of a conservative philosophical system 'which once more devoured the whole world into philosophy'.[39] According to Habermas in Hegel's early writings 'it is not the spirit in the absolute movement of reflecting on itself which manifests itself in, among other things, language, labour, and moral relationships, but rather, it is the dialectical interconnections between linguistic symbolization, labour, and interaction which determine the concept of spirit'.[40] Here we see, in Habermas' eyes, Hegel offering the beginnings of a philosophical discourse that will eventually be developed, by others, into a materialist critical theory and not the idealism of the later Hegel. In this sense Marx is the genuine heir of the early Hegel and it is he who, despite his own shortcomings,[41] develops the so-called 'radical' dimension of Hegel's philosophy against Hegel's own reactionary systematization.

However, the mode of critique offered above does not touch Hegel. For example, when Habermas makes the claim that spirit does not, or should not be understood to manifest itself in the world via 'the absolute movement of reflecting on itself', but rather that we should understand material and social action as that

---

36. Jürgen Habermas, *Knowledge and Human Interests*, trans. Jeremy J. Shapiro, 2nd ed., London, Heinemann, 1981, p. 10.

37. This is not the extent of Habermas' critique of Hegel, rather they are two criticisms that are relevant in terms of this discussion.

38. Jürgen Habermas, 'Labour and Interaction: Remarks on Hegel's Jena Philosophy of Mind', *Theory and Practice*, trans. John Viertel, Boston, Beacon Press, 1973, pp. 142-69, p. 142. While Habermas is drawing on an already emergent trend within Marxism—most notable is perhaps the influence of Lukács—to focus on the works of Hegel that are seen to be still under the influence of his study of political economy, this essay of Habermas' in my view should be recognized as a decisive essay in the development of the understanding of Hegel within the critical Marxist tradition. Also see György Lukács, *The Young Hegel: Studies in the Relations Between Dialectics and Economics*, London, Merlin Press, 1975.

39. Jürgen Habermas, 'On Hegel's Political Writings', *Theory and Practice*, trans. John Viertel, Boston, Beacon Press, 1973, pp. 170-94, p. 194.

40. Habermas, 'Labour and Interaction', p. 143.

41. See Habermas, 'Labour and Interaction', pp. 168-9.

'which determine[s] the concept of spirit'[42] we could be tempted to agree with Habermas, as revolution *is* surely a form of material and social action. However, such agreement from an Hegelian perspective would be futile because this 'view' of Habermas' is formulated without consideration of the philosophical element itself, it is a mode of critique developed without consideration of the emergence and activation of philosophical thinking as such—the event of speculative philosophy. From this perspective we should not understand the relation between philosophy, the political (including the material conditions of a situation) and social change as a series of concepts that one formulates a philosophical position around, rather they should be understood as the very elements which are implicated within, or that become relevant through, the event of philosophy itself. That is, Hegel did not *decide* that philosophy comes after the revolution, or that 'change' is a relevant topic of philosophy. Rather in thinking or encountering the philosophical element as such, the relationship between thinking and change (and for that matter praxis), becomes apparent to the philosopher. What is relevant for philosophy is at the very least initially made relevant in and through thought itself.

Despite the importance that has been attached to these ideas here, it is important to note that there is nothing preventing the thinker from simply producing a philosophy without consideration of the beginning before the beginning or the very event of philosophy itself. On the contrary, it seems natural enough to simply start thinking philosophical thoughts; that is, the world produces situations that strike us as relevant and we simply begin thinking about them in a philosophical manner, the ultimate goal of which is to produce a unique or useful perspective on the problem. However, because of the ease in which we can enter the philosophical process, it could be argued that the challenge for us today is not to think of something important or unique—our culture produces new thoughts all the time—rather the challenge for us as philosophers is to *resist* this path. What is required is that we try to encounter the very activity and activation of thinking itself, so as not to presuppose what is most essential to the philosophical undertaking. More specifically speaking, it is not that we simply *can* just start thinking that is the problem, or even that we *should* resist this particular activity, rather I want to suggest that when a thinker takes the activity of thinking for granted without considering the activation of this thinking, or at least gives up trying to account for it, their thinking becomes limited by this omission and consequently produces concepts shaped by that limitation. According to Hegel, thinking that does not take account of itself remains reflective and consequently produces thoughts—regardless of what may be claimed by the thinker involved—that remain within the shape of 'consciousness' and thus informed by its dichotomous relation. When thought is shaped in 'the way of consciousness' the dichotomous relation between subject and object produces claims that are appropriate to empirical verification. That is, the claims produced either correspond to reality, and are thus labeled 'true', or they do not. It is for this reason that a theory such as Marx's can, on the

---

42. Habermas, 'Labour and Interaction', p. 143.

one hand be disproved in time—as it has more or less been for Habermas—in that it does not adequately correspond empirically to the world as it currently appears. While on the other hand such a theory relies on a rather voluntaristic element with regard to its transformation into praxis.[43] Hence, that Marx produces a theory of revolution and social change, is itself not necessarily related to the *actual* transformation of that theory into practice.

Despite Habermas' critique of Marx's thought, he remains a part of the Marxist tradition in that his thinking is informed by the command that it is no longer adequate for philosophers to merely interpret the world—Hegel is here of course envisioned as the paradigmatic case of an 'interpreter' in this sense—the point is to change it. Despite the 'attractiveness' of a command such as this for the philosopher who wants to be revolutionary—or dwell in the revolutionary space opened up by Hegel—any thought, regardless of the attractiveness of its 'content', produced by a mode of thinking that does not address the fundamental question of the activation of philosophy as such, remains relative to the givenness of its production as a thought. This could explain why we find ourselves today transfixed by the seemingly unanswerable question of how thought can relate to the world that it seeks to change and how the world, considered as a changeable entity, relates to thought without thinking becoming thematic and voluntaristic. After all, this command is a pronouncement in, and is given shape through, philosophical thinking.

Thought of in this way, despite claims made to the contrary, it is not Hegel that produces a philosophy that gives thought too radical a function, that of actually changing the world, but rather Habermas and Marx. Despite this, both philosophical approaches see the French Revolution marking the birth of a new age, an age in which a radical form of freedom has been announced and will eventually be actualized—what philosophy has given *conceptual* form to will eventually become '*actual*' form'. The difference is that for Hegel the world will change to fully embrace the reality of freedom not because we can think how to change the world, as is the case for Marx and Habermas, but because the event of speculative thinking expresses the changeability of the world itself. But if this is the case, then according to Hegel, it follows that the world must have already changed in order for its changeability to be embraced by speculative philosophy, and that philosophy as post-revolutionary can be understood as a *recollection* of this embracing.

### Absolute Knowledge as a Presupposition

According to Hegel the cognitive perspective from which the philosopher recollects is absolute knowledge, a way of thinking that takes place within the unified perspective of the knowing and the known, a perspective that Habermas does not accept Hegel does or can achieve. Thus it is the character of absolute

---

43. It is important to note that Habermas accepts that this is the case for his thinking, but would claim it as a reality for all thought.

knowledge that forms the basis of the second sense in which Habermas thinks that Hegel's philosophy is 'half-hearted'. Reading absolute knowledge epistemologically, Habermas argues that

> there is something half-hearted about the *Phenomenology of Mind*. The standpoint of absolute knowledge is to proceed with immanent necessity from phenomenological experience. But because it is absolute, it does not really need to be justified by the phenomenological self-reflection of mind; and strictly speaking it is not even capable of such justification.[44]

Habermas suggests that 'from the very beginning Hegel presumes as given a knowledge of the Absolute'[45] a presupposition that, regardless of Hegel's critique of (Kantian) knowledge as such, would have to in turn presuppose such a critique because 'the possibility of just this knowledge [of the absolute] would have to be demonstrated according to the criteria of a radicalized critique of knowledge'.[46] However, it could be argued that in epistemologizing the absolute, Habermas fails to understand the role it plays in Hegel's system. In this way Habermas produces a reflective response to absolute knowledge—the cognitive perspective of the 'we'—in much the same as other commentators[47] in that he thinks of absolute knowledge thematically as something that can be 'known' epistemologically rather than as the ontologically constituted dwelling space of the revolutionary thinker. This is why the absolute is with us from the beginning; not because we know something in the way consciousness knows it, but rather that we know it in being claimed by what is, thus philosophy becomes a recollection.

Given this, what requires justification philosophically speaking in Hegel's work is that which is *scientific*—that is, the two *scientific* systems: the *Phenomenology* and the *Encyclopaedic System* including the *Science of Logic*—but not the pre-systemic beginning before the beginning, or the activation of philosophy as such. Justification and necessity—the demands that make a thinking *scientific* in the Hegelian sense—only become necessary or in need of justification themselves within philosophy itself, or rather it is the philosophical process itself that makes justification and necessity an issue for thinking in the first place. The activation of the philosophical project cannot have necessity itself or it would already presuppose the philosophical.

Thus the kind of objections made by Habermas are pre-empted by Hegel in the preface to the *Phenomenology* and also more explicitly in the *Difference* essay when Hegel recognizes that '[o]ne may require of propositions that they be justified. But the justification of these propositions as presuppositions is still not supposed to be philosophy itself, so that the founding and grounding gets going before, and outside of, philosophy' (D 94). Thus philosophy needs to be 'furnished with some sort of vestibule' and this is why, as has been suggested above, that '[t]he

---

44. Habermas, *Knowledge and Human Interests*, p. 10.
45. Habermas, *Knowledge and Human Interests*, p. 10.
46. Habermas, *Knowledge and Human Interests*, p. 10.
47. For a brief account of Harris' objection to the absolute as being with us from the beginning see H. S. Harris, *Hegel: Phenomenology and System*, Indianapolis, Hackett, 1995, pp. 13-4.

need of philosophy can be called the *presupposition* of philosophy' (D 93). But this 'presupposition' is nothing other than the 'need that has come to utterance' (D 93). Accordingly Hegel suggests that the presupposition of philosophy, the *uttered need*, is thus the need 'posited for reflection' and that because of the very nature of reflection 'there must [in fact] be two presuppositions' (D 93). The first presupposition is 'the Absolute itself'[48] that according to Hegel 'is already present'—'how otherwise could it be sought?'—whereas the second presupposition is associated with the philosopher, in that consciousness must have 'stepped out of the totality, that is, it may be taken to be the split into being and not-being, concept and being, finitude and infinity' (D93). Therefore while the absolute must be there with us from the beginning, from the fixed determinate standpoint of the dichotomy 'the absolute synthesis is a beyond, it is the undetermined and the shapeless' (D 93). This is why the philosopher, while dwelling in the already present absolute, begins as the dichotomous figure of consciousness.

It follows from this that 'the task of philosophy consists in uniting these presuppositions: to posit being in non-being, as becoming; to posit dichotomy in the Absolute, as its appearance; to posit the finite in the infinite, as life' (D 93-4). At this point it is worth recalling Hegel's warning against thinking of 'the need' as itself reflective when he makes the point that this kind of language 'is clumsy ... for the need acquires in this way a reflective form' (D 94) that it does not actually have. What is difficult to understand here, but nonetheless underlies the whole of Hegel's thinking and our ability to understand the formation and movement of this thought, is the role of the knowing/being mutual informing. Readings of Hegel's philosophy, like Habermas', that characterize it as overly subjective or hypostatize the absolute[49] tend to under-emphasize the speculative interrelation of being and knowing. Hegel is quite explicit on this mutual informing when he says that:

> Reason is the truth that is in and for itself, and is the simple *identity* of the *subjectivity* of the concept with its *objectivity* and universality. The universality of reason, therefore signifies the *object*, which in consciousness qua consciousness was only given, but is now itself *universal*, permeating and encompassing the I. Equally it signifies the pure *I*, the pure form overarching the object and encompassing it within itself (EPM § 438).

Consequently the so-called unjustified beginning is not the problem it may seem to be, as Hegel's philosophy is concerned with what *is*. Philosophy is activated and sets to work precisely in anticipation of its goal, or in the terms we have outlined here, it sets to work giving conceptual form to that which has already been announced. This is because the Hegelian philosopher encounters the principle of freedom via the force of the revolutionary claims of the era, and the subsequent retreat of these claims from the life-world of the philosopher.

---

48. 'Reason produces [the Absolute], merely by freeing conscious from its limitations. This suspension of the limitations is conditioned by the presupposed unlimitedness' (D 93).

49. Charles Taylor's influential work is also a notable inclusion in this way of thinking. See Charles Taylor, *Hegel*, Cambridge, Cambridge University Press, 1978.

Therefore the requirement for the Hegelian philosopher to *justify* the existence of their object, in this case the manifesting absolute, does not take the same form as the requirement attendant to formal modes of thinking and the thinkers of these modes. Because there is a mutual informing of being and knowing for the speculative philosopher, the lack of externality—an externality to the knowing being relation that is absolute—means that justification takes on a different *form* than it does for the empiricist, metaphysician or critical thinker whom, according to Hegel, presupposes the givenness of their object which includes their mode of cognition and its advance (see EL § 1). This need for justification is determined by the very givenness that is the source of the original demand. Seen in this light the central concern is not to make sense of the absolute per se, but rather that one must allow themselves to be captured by the claim of freedom and claim this claiming as their own. What would be required here from the Hegelian perspective is not an epistemological[50] engagement with the being of the absolute, but rather a dwelling within it as already claimed by the revolutionary spirit of freedom. This does not mean that there is no justification required and that the philosophical enterprise becomes a kind of mystical experience, rather that the kind of justification that needs to take place, a justification that Hegel believes he performs in his *Phenomenology*, is of a wholly different order than what is *expected* by contemporary philosophical discourse. In this sense Hegel's philosophy is of another time. To be sure, the *certainty* of this anticipation and activation is only *known* as justifiably *true* 'by exposition of the system itself' (PS ¶ 17).

If we compare the introduction to Hegel's first published work, the *Difference* essay, to the 'Preface' in the *Phenomenology*—two works that span the time that Habermas considers to be Hegel's more radical period—we can see a striking continuity between the two. To be sure, the similarity relates particularly to Hegel's discussion of the claims and aims of philosophizing itself which seem to be the disputed territory for Habermas. Given this it is reasonable to ask, despite the subtlety and depth of his analysis, why Habermas chooses to focus on unpublished and incomplete lecture manuscripts to simply find what must be considered rather common place insights. The fact that *Hegel* made these observations in the context of spirit/world relations—regardless of the veracity, or lack thereof, of such a way of thinking—seems to lack any kind of necessity for Habermas and indeed adds little to the overall nature of the observations or insights garnered. For has not Marx, as Habermas actually claims, not said much the same things but more poignantly? If these insights extracted from Hegel lack what Habermas acknowledges is what *Hegel* sees as most fundamental, what does Hegel offer us here? In turning Hegel 'the right way up' does Habermas not invite us to see in Hegel what can be seen in just about any thinker of the post-Hegelian period?

It seems that in the criticism of Hegel as a political conservative Habermas wants Hegel to be Marx, and in the criticism of Hegel as dogmatically presupposing the absolute, he wants Hegel to be Kant. However, Hegel is neither of

---

50. According to Habermas 'Hegel replaced the enterprise of epistemology with the phenomenological self-reflection of mind [spirit]' Habermas, *Knowledge and Human Interests*, p. 7.

these thinkers and if we want to encounter Hegel as Hegel—to be kindred with him—we need to meet him somewhere. In the remainder of this essay consideration will be given to the question of what would be involved in encountering Hegel as Hegel and what the conditions of the activation of Hegelian philosophy are according to this encounter. Thus if the issues that have been raised so far have validity, and if certain aporias remain within thinking, then the following questions become relevant for us: how do we take up Hegel?; where do we meet Hegel philosophically?; and how is Hegelian philosophy activated in this light? However, these questions have an added dimension: it would be fair to ask why we are not all Hegelian philosophers already, for didn't the French Revolution as the soil of philosophy announce freedom universally 'for all'? If our 'interest' and 'want' in philosophy comes from our historical claiming as free subjects, why do we not all philosophize *qua* Hegelian? To be sure, as we know, we are certainly *not* all Hegelian philosophers; hence the tendency in the literature to identify 'we' philosophers with an elite that knows. But why and how does one find themselves within the 'we', and what must one *think* to be a philosopher as opposed to a political theorist, a free market entrepreneur or a researcher? Where must our interest lie? To be more explicit, if the commentaries and critiques of Hegel outlined above miss what is most fundamental in Hegel when they approach his thought 'thematically', then the question of how one encounters Hegel's thought *non-thematically* arises.

## THINKING THE THOUGHT THAT GIVES RISE TO PHILOSOPHY

At the beginning of the third part of his lecture series on Nietzsche[51] Heidegger claims that we will only know who Nietzsche '*is* and above all who he *will be*' when we are able to think the thought that gave shape to the phrase 'the will to power'.[52] Heidegger goes on to say that we will never experience who Nietzsche is by an examination of his life history, as a historical figure, a personality or a psychological object; furthermore, we are even unable to encounter Nietzsche as a thinker through a presentation of his writings. In this sense, for Heidegger it is this *one* single thought that destines Nietzsche to be an 'essential thinker' as opposed to a mere 'writer' or 'researcher' who may have many thoughts; for who Nietzsche really *is* can only be understood as the one 'that trod the path of the thought' that led to the saying 'the will to power'. Following Heidegger's approach we might then ask what then is, or should we understand as, Hegel's one great thought, assuming that he is what Heidegger would describe as an 'essential thinker'?

---

51. Martin Heidegger, *Nietzsche: Vol. III: The Will to Power as Knowledge and as Metaphysics & Vol. IV: Nihilism*, David Farrell Krell (ed.), trans. Joan Stambaugh, David Farrell Krell and Frank A. Capuzzi, vol. 3 & 4, 4 vols., San Francisco, HarperSanFrancisco, 1991, p. 3ff.

52. Heidegger links Nietzsche's thought of 'the will to power' with his standing as the last metaphysician. Notwithstanding Heidegger's reading of the history of metaphysics and Hegel as the most radical, and thus the most metaphysical of metaphysicians, Heidegger's account of the encounter with a thinker is instructive.

This question appears to be extremely difficult to answer when one considers the sheer depth and scope of Hegel's field of inquiry. For many, this one great thought would lie in his political philosophy, the field that has the most general appeal in the system, for others it would lie in his bringing forth of history as a key philosophical discipline. Perhaps the only facet of Hegel's philosophical system that most agree his defining moment would not occur in is his *Philosophy of Nature*, however, even this much-maligned aspect of the system has its supporters these days. It seems that Hegel's philosophy contains an almost unlimited number of 'insights' that have shaped thinking in the proceeding centuries; no philosophy of the nineteenth or twentieth century stands apart from Hegel's thinking, untouched by its scope.

It seems reasonable that the one guiding thought, if it is indeed to be the one *singular* thought, should treat a thinker's thinking as a whole, that it should be a thought that unifies that thinking, and that it should single that particular thinker out from all other thinkers. However, one thought that does *not* separate Hegel from other truly great thinkers, but may nonetheless help us in our enquiry, is Hegel's belief that his philosophy is the last philosophical system and that with him *philosophy has come to an end*. If we take Hegel's self-understanding of his philosophy in relation to all others seriously, then we might expect to find some insight to our question in the conclusion to his *Lectures on the History of Philosophy*. Understood in Hegel's terms, the *Lectures* can be considered as the autobiography of philosophy itself. The 'final result' of this autobiographical account of philosophy culminates with the conclusion that:

> The ultimate aim and business of philosophy is to reconcile thought or the Notion with reality [...] The result is the thought which is at home with itself, and at the same time embraces the universe therein, and transforms it into an intelligent world [... This a]bsolute, pure, infinite form is expressed as self-consciousness, the Ego. This is the light that breaks forth on spiritual substance, and shows absolute content and absolute form to be identical;—substance is in itself identical with knowledge [...] *i.e.* it recognizes pure Thought or Being as self-identity (LHP III 545-6 & 550).

In understanding his thought in this way Hegel claims his philosophy as the culmination of the 'only one Philosophy' embodying the 'one principle' (LHP III 552), and thus draws the strong link between his thinking and that of the ancients in that '[t]he philosophy of the ancients had the absolute Idea as its thought' (LHP III 548), and that 'Aristotle was the first to say that *voûs* is the thought of thought' (LHP III 546), or even more explicitly when he approvingly quotes Parmenides:

> Thought, and that on account of which thought is, are the same. For not without that which is, in which it expresses itself (ἐν ᾧ πεΦατιομένον ἐστίν), wilt thou find Thought, seeing that it is nothing and will be nothing outside of that which it is (LHP I 253).

Hegel recognizes that Parmenides' essential claim is that 'Thought produces itself, and what is produced is thought. Thought is thus identical with Being, for there is nothing besides Being, this great affirmation' (LHP I 253) and that this is *the* point of the tradition as a whole. Hegel's one great thought, the thought that he thinks brings the whole of philosophy to a close—the thought that 'reconcile[s] thought or the Notion with reality'—is not *his* thought at all but a thought that comes from the very beginnings of philosophy. Thus we find ourselves in a paradoxical situation, if we try to think the thought that gave rise to Hegel's one great thought we find ourselves in the situation of thinking the thought that leads to the saying that *I have no new thoughts*. What is more, we can understand as Hegel himself does, that his philosophy offers us nothing new in a more general sense; that is, even if we take a thematic approach we can see that Hegel does not offer any new or truly original insights: the absolute, the dialectic, speculative thinking, recognition, the unity of unity and difference, these have all been thought by others prior to Hegel. As Frederick Beiser points out there 'is not a single Hegelian theme that cannot be traced back to his predecessors in Jena'.[53] How then do we think the thought that makes Hegel a genuine and unique thinker if that thought is indeed that *I have no new thoughts*? Furthermore, how can this be the case when we *know* that Hegel is perhaps one of the *most* original, radical and fundamental of thinkers? What does it mean for a fundamental thinker to say I have no new thoughts?

What is easily missed if we follow this investigative approach is that Hegel does not offer any specific theme or *content* of thought that we can identify as unique or original but rather that the thought of the essential unity of thought and being *comes to itself* in *his* thought. Hegel claims that philosophy becomes conscious of itself as the world's principle in his thought; that philosophy has become *self-conscious* and thus has finally realized itself as genuine *Science*, offering us a new *form* of thinking, absolute knowledge.[54] According to Hegel speculative philosophy thinks the world as embodying its own principle, but it is only as *scientific* that philosophy 'knows itself as absolute spirit' (LHP III 552).

If we take seriously Heidegger's claim that what is important for us is not so much to think or even identify the essential thought of a thinker—in Nietzsche's case 'the will to power'—but rather to think the thought that gave shape to the phrase, then we can see in the case of Hegel rather than capturing the phrase 'absolute knowledge' or even to think the 'unity of thought and being', we need to '[tread] the path of thought' as such. But what would be involved in treading

---

53. Frederick C. Beiser, *German Idealism: The Struggle Against Subjectivism, 1781-1801*, Cambridge, Harvard University Press, 2002, p. 10. However, Beiser, erroneously in my view, also suggests that Hegel was wilful in his expropriation of ideas in that he claimed them as his own. If anything Beiser is *underplaying* Hegel's sense of his own philosophy. He did not need to erroneously 'exaggerate' his own 'originality' because he saw himself as the one who *consummated* these ideas or made them philosophical.

54. Recall that in Hegel's usage 'Science' refers to genuinely self-determining philosophy that forms itself as a system. Philosophy is no longer *merely* philosophy in the work of Hegel, that is 'the love of knowing', as knowing is no longer external to its being, it has become '*actual*' knowing' (PS ¶ 5). It is true, as we have said, that others claim the form of the speculative, for example Schelling, but his grasp of the speculative from the Hegelian point of view remains rather intuitive, a point borne out by his continual retreat to the sensual (Art) and the theological (Religion).

the path of this thought? And if Hegel's philosophy is the philosophy that offers us no new thoughts, what would it mean to tread the trodden path anew without stepping in the footsteps that muddy the ground? What is implicit in Heidegger's reflection on Nietzsche becomes relevant to our argument here when he states that what is essential for us, as would-be philosophers, is not a matter of one's *ability* to identify the thought, but rather it is our *willingness* to walk the path; to think the thought that gives rise to the thought. In Hegel's terms we can understand this willingness as the willingness to dwell in absolute knowledge.[55] Absolute knowledge is not the thought but the trodden path, that through Hegel we can see as the path of all true philosophical thinking. What then makes Hegel an essential thinker for us is not *a thought* but that he exposes to us the dwelling place where we, as philosophers, already dwell.

Hegel offers us nothing new in terms of determinate ideas to base our philosophical (or political) project on, but rather shows us the context in which ideas are activated and the dwelling space in which conceptual form is given to the future. This allows us to understand that it is the 'willingness' or the 'want' of the would-be philosopher to dwell in this space that is important, rather than a cognitively achieved height. What has to be noticed is that this space in which the philosopher dwells is the 'we' itself. Understood in terms of the philosopher that expresses his or her *willingness* to embrace the announcement of their freedom by giving conceptual form to it, the 'we' takes on an ontological dimension. This is in contradistinction to the predominantly epistemological reading that characterizes the 'we' in terms of the cognitive capacity of the philosopher. This is why Science *needs* to 'provide [the philosopher] with the ladder to this standpoint [of science, and why it] should show him this standpoint within himself' (PS ¶ 26). If absolute knowledge, as the dwelling place of the philosopher, is understood epistemologically, such a ladder would be superfluous, as Habermas and others have argued.

This analysis of the willingness of the would-be philosopher to activate themselves into the philosophical project and dwell with Hegel in the 'we' is given account by Hegel in the preface to his *Phenomenology* in the following way: '*Pure* self-recognition in absolute otherness, this Aether *as such*, is the ground and soil of Science or *knowledge in general*. The beginning of philosophy presupposes or requires that consciousness should dwell in this *element*' (PS ¶ 26). However, given that this pure self-recognition is 'pure spirituality as the *universal* that has the form of simple immediacy' then this beginning before the beginning, 'achieves its own

---

55. In light of the criticism made earlier that Habermas' and Marx's social theory tends toward 'voluntarism', the use of a term like 'willingness' with relation to Hegel's philosophy needs defending. The 'willingness' of the would-be philosopher discussed in the text above does not introduce a voluntaristic element in the way that I have suggest one potentially exists in Habermas' and Marx's thinking because for Hegel the philosopher always arrives too late—that philosophy is always a recollection—and thus the willingness of the individual to raise themselves into the Aether and dwell philosophically primarily impacts on their own posture as a thinker and not their freedom as theorized. According to Hegel philosophical thinking does not involve itself in politics in this sense, as it does not issue instructions on how the world ought to be.

perfection and transparency only through the movement of its becoming' (PS ¶ 26) which is the movement found firstly in the body of the *Phenomenology* itself. That is, in 'order to be able to live—and [actually] to live—with Science and in Science' the would-be philosopher must 'have raised itself into this Aether' (PS ¶ 26) *before* he or she can think scientifically.

What is important to recognize here is that the individual *qua* philosopher can survive in this Aether and is thus appropriate to it—recall that Science must show 'this standpoint within himself'—because 'the individual is the absolute form [... or] unconditioned *being*' (PS ¶ 26). The philosopher raised into the Aether is appropriate to the task of giving conceptual form to what has been announced in the revolution because, just as with Science that knows that the 'situation in which consciousness knows itself to be at home is [...] one marked by the absence of Spirit' (PS ¶ 26), so too does the revolutionary spirit propelled to philosophy know that the world as it was before the revolution is equally marked by an absence of spirit, the world as it was is no longer habitable. However, the revolution has not fully actualized itself in the world as achieved principle and thus it remains a task for Science to show '*that* and *how* this [spiritual] element belongs to it' (PS ¶ 26). That is, emerging immanently to the political situation of the world itself, out of 'division', so to speak, 'Science lack[s] this *actual* dimension, it is only the content as the *in-itself*, the *purpose* that is as yet still something *inward*, not yet Spirit, but only spiritual Substance. This *in-itself* has to express itself outwardly and become *for-itself*, and this means simply that it has to posit self-consciousness as one with itself' (PS ¶ 26). However, this account assumes a willingness on the part of the philosopher to dwell in Science; but what is the condition of this willingness, what does it mean to be willing in this sense?

## The Kindred Spirit

In the *Difference* essay, which we have already identified as a very important text, Hegel gives an explicit account of the conditions under which an appropriate encounter with philosophy must take: 'The living spirit that dwells in a philosophy demands to be born of a kindred spirit if it is to unveil itself' (D 86). The living spirit, understood in this way, 'brushes past the historical concern which is moved by some interest', past the 'curious collector of information' and the discoverer of 'alien phenomenon' who are not concerned to 'reveal [their] own inwardness'—'spirit itself slipped away between [their] fingers'—and seeks that space where 'there is truth to be had' (D 86). These inferior modes of thinking that Hegel associates with the understanding—the thinking of consciousness situated in the subject/object dichotomy—fail to capture the living spirit the way speculative philosophy does.

To be kindred one must be both '*kin*' and '*re-d*': To be Hegel's kin we must be related, familiar, to be part of his family. But this does not mean that we go along blindly with Hegel, rather to be a member of a family is to be a member of a collective that dwells together. We must dwell together with Hegel. To be 're-d', as with 'kin', means to share the same blood, but re-d also means 'again', 'to return to' or 'go back'—stop—to Hegel, but it also means to 'come after', albeit in terms of, or in opposition to; red is dangerous, forbidden and urgent and finally red is revolution. Accordingly to be kindred with Hegel we must open ourselves to return again to Hegel in order to dwell in the dangerous space of thought so as to conceptualize the world according to its principle.

One of course cannot merely be kindred with Hegel, we must, like Hegel himself, be kindred with the living spirit, for Hegel only exists for us as, and in, the living spirit. Our encounter with Hegel *qua* philosopher is nothing more than an invitation to dwell in the dwelling place of the philosophers for it is through this encounter that the living spirit becomes explicit. Thus, if we must dwell in the dwelling place of philosophers in order to be philosophical then Hegel's *Phenomenology* and *System* become a secondary concern of ours as would-be philosophers. Not secondary in the sense of unimportant, rather secondary in that it is only when one has claimed, or rather has been claimed by, the revolutionary spirit, and activated themselves as a philosopher, that these systematic texts, the architecture of the philosophical, becomes comprehensible to us. We must first raise ourselves into the house of the philosophers, we must learn to dwell philosophically first. To be kindred requires that we willingly claim the revolutionary nature of the living spirit and be committed to dwelling in the claim. A 'claim' is also, of course, a dwelling space itself, but not an unoccupied one, rather it is a place where one 'stakes a claim', and through, which one gains a right or 'title', in this case the right to philosophy.[56]

## CONCLUDING REMARKS: THE TRAGEDY OF HEGELIAN THINKING

If what has been said has value it could be argued that the singular thing that makes Hegel an essential thinker is that he creates the space for us to dwell philosophically and provides a ladder into this Science. It is for this reason that, with Foucault, it is not so easy to 'escape Hegel'[57] because in escaping Hegel it is not his ideas or insights that need overturning or escaping, but the very dwelling space of the philosopher. Thus the consequence of escaping Hegel is to return from the inverted world to the everyday given world, to become a reflective collector of information (D 86), to become a writer or researcher. Nonetheless, people fail to

---

56. When one stakes a claim in the already claimed dwelling space the history and the occupants of the claim become relevant for the claimant. It is for this reason that one cannot honestly claim the title of philosopher without acknowledging and living with those already dwelling in the claim.

57. Michel Foucault, *The Archaeology of Knowledge and the Discourse on Language*, trans. A.M. Sheridan Smith and Rupert Sawyer, New York, Pantheon, 1972, p. 235. 'But truly to escape Hegel involves an exact appreciation of the price we have to pay to detach ourselves from him. It assumes that we are aware of the extent to which Hegel, insidiously perhaps, is close to us; it implies a knowledge, in that which permits us to think against Hegel, of that which remains Hegelian. We have to determine the extent to which our anti-Hegelianism is possibly one of his tricks directed against us, at the end of which he stands, motionless, waiting for us.'

understand the extent to which, 'crushed before [...] the immensity of the claims made by the human spirit' (LHP II 10), today we *have* managed to escape, or rather have *denied* the Hegelian moment within ourselves. This can be seen in the triumph of the 'intellect' over 'reason', of the special sciences (including the social and natural sciences and the formal thinking of analytic philosophy) over speculative philosophy, unfreedom over freedom and the dominance of instrumental thinking, all of which render this abundantly clear. Thus revolution, as a claiming of the 'for all', does not have the power or strength to claim everyone because we are so firmly 'at home in consciousness' and the willingness to leave that which we know so well is not there for us in the way it is for thinkers like Hegel.[58] For thinkers today it is both difficult to find the strength required to be kindred with Hegel, and the claiming that we claim—and claims us—similarly seems to lack the strength to capture us. Thus the task for those of us who are interested and willing to reencounter Hegel, to be kindred with him, and through him encounter the philosophical as such—that is to give conceptual form to the future—is the path of despair and violence, because it is a path that inverts our world.[59]

However, philosophers are always of their time, and our time, being a time of

---

58. Now is not the time to defend this claim, despite this, if Hegel's philosophy is to be comprehensive in the way that is being suggested it must be able to account for the development of thinking after 1830 and consequently the seeming demise of the Hegelian system. A defence which I believe can be made.

59. Hegel cautions us against thinking that our lack of strength to enter philosophy is related to the obscure or difficulty of its language. This is a criticism regularly made of Hegel's philosophy. However, this attitude totally misses the point of why philosophy is difficult. Hegel explains why his thinking is obscure or difficult via Heraclitus: 'The obscurity in the philosophy of Heraclitus lies essentially in the fact that it expresses a profoundly speculative thought, which is always obscure for the understanding. The concept of the idea is in conflict with the understanding and cannot be grasped by it' (LHP 25-6 II 73). In other words only by dwelling in absolute knowledge, by being inverted, can we make sense of that which appears obscure. According to Hegel the only reason that Plato is not labelled obscure as Heraclitus, is because people generally fail to see the truly speculative nature of his writing. Hegel argues that the 'mythic form of the Platonic Dialogues makes [...] them the source of misunderstandings' (LHP 25-6 II 182), that is, there is a tendency in the Plato scholarship to miss the *philosophical* dimension of Plato's thought. There is a failure to differentiate Plato's words that operate 'wholly in the representational mode' (LHP 25-6 II 183), from his philosophical thought. Hegel makes mention of some well worn common misunderstandings such as when in the *Meno* (81c-d) and *Phaedo* (72e-7a) Plato talks of the existence of the human soul before a person's birth: 'But that cannot be found in Plato's philosophy' even though it is 'what Plato's text literally says' (LHP 25-6 II 183). To be sure for Hegel in Plato's philosophy 'the spiritual element belongs to thinking' (LHP 25-6 II 176), thus when Plato 'speaks of the Ideas as a cardinal point, and they are in fact the cardinal point of his philosophy. He speaks of them as independent [*selbständig*], which makes it easy to go on to portray them in the manner of the modern philosophy of the understanding, as separate actualities, as substances, as daemons or as angels; whereas they were indeed more in the nature of philosophical views [*Ansichten*]' (LHP 25-6 II 183).

It is the 'Greek science' presented by Plato and Aristotle 'where objective thought shapes itself into a whole. Plato's thought is pure but concrete—it is the idea or thought, but the thought is inwardly self-determining' (LHP 25-6 II 14). Yet for Hegel Plato's thought remains in abstraction as the 'idea only in its form of its universality', and it is not until Aristotle that thought becomes active, 'that is self-determining through activity' (LHP 25-6 II 14). If what I am suggesting has value the activity that comes to philosophy with Aristotle's thought becomes essential to the development and initiation of thought in the modern period.

darkness, hides from us our ability to occupy or fully dwell in the dwelling space that Hegel has attempted to make explicit through his philosophy—what seemed so apparent to the thinkers in the period after the French Revolution is now less so. The philosopher today finds him or herself tragically caught in a shadow cast from the future, caught between the existing empirical world and the speculative beyond of absolute knowledge.[60] That we cannot easily dwell with Hegel is apparent to all those who try to encounter him philosophically. One possible explanation for this is that the subject of address for great philosophers is the subject of the future, in some sense the speculative philosopher is *from* the future, is a human that has realized their 'nature' in the 'achieved community of minds' (PS ¶ 69), a person who holds thoughts appropriate to another age. That the place in which we encounter Hegel is one of a future cut-off from our empirical everyday being, renders that encounter tragic. In this way we can understand our present being as would-be philosophers, as existing in the shadows of the spirits of the future. However, the business of philosophy is what *is*, not what *ought* to be. But this is no problem for Hegel because spirit as absolute negativity comes on the scene in its simple notion or its principle, it anticipates its actualization as its goal, an actualization that is in the future. To be sure, what *is*, is a shadow cast from the future; Hegel's recollection is a recollection of the future.[61]

---

60. For an exploration of this idea in terms of the Platonic philosopher see Vassilacopoulos, 'Plato's *Republic* and the End of Philosophy'. The language of 'dwelling' has also been taken from this work.

61. As an interesting aside, the famous last lines of the *Phenomenology* are a misquote from Schiller's poem *Die Freundschaft*: 'From the chalice of this realm of spirits / foams forth for Him his own infinitude' (PS ¶ 808). However, what Schiller actually says is '... of this realm of shadows' not spirits. Hegel draws on this passage from Schiller a number of times (usually citing it accurately), most notably in the introduction to the *Science of Logic* where he describes his speculative logic as 'a realm of shadows' (SL 58).

*bibliography*

# Bibliography

Adorno, Theodor W., *Negative Dialectics*, trans. E. B. Ashton, New York, Continuum, 2000.
Agamben, Giorgio, *Language and Death: The Place of Negativity*, trans. K. E. Pinkus with M. Hardt, Minneapolis, University of Minnesota Press, 1991.
Agamben, Giorgio, *Homo Sacer: Sovereign Power and Bare Life*, trans. Daniel Heller-Roazen, Stanford, Stanford University Press, 1998.
Agamben, Giorgio, *Means Without End: Notes on Politics*, trans. Vincenzo Binetti and Cesare Casarino, Minneapolis, University of Minnesota Press, 2000.
Agamben, Giorgio, *The Open: Man and Animal*, trans. K. Attell Stanford, Stanford University Press, 2004.
Agamben, Giorgio, *The Time that Remains: A Commentary on the Letter to the Romans*, trans. P. Dailey Stanford, Stanford University Press, 2005.
Agamben, Giorgio, *State of Exception*, trans. K. Attell, Chicago, The University of Chicago Press, 2005.
Agamben, Giorgio, 'Interview with Giorgio Agamben – Life, A Work of Art Without an Author: The State of Exception, the Administration of Disorder and Private Life', Ulrich Raulff (interviewer), *German Law Journal*, no. 5, special ed., 2004, http://www.germanlawjournal.com/article.php?id=437 (retrieved on May 29, 2007).
Allison, Henry, *Kant's Theory of Freedom*, Cambridge, Cambridge University Press, 1990.
Ameriks, Karl, 'The Hegelian Critique of Kantian Morality', in B. den Ouden and M. Marcia (eds.), *New Essays on Kant*, New York, Peter Lang, 1987.
Ameriks, Karl, *Interpreting Kant's Critiques*, Oxford, Clarendon Press, 2003.
Anscombe, G. E. M., 'On Brute Facts', *Analysis*, no. 18, 1958, pp. 69-72.
Augustine, *Confessions*, trans. J. K. Ryan, Garden City, Doubleday, 1960.
Aristotle, *Metaphysics*, in R. McKeon (ed.), *The Basic Works of Aristotle*, trans. W. D. Ross, New York, Random House, 1941.
Aristotle, *Physics*, in R. McKeon (ed.), *The Basic Works of Aristotle*, trans. W. D. Ross, New York, Random House, 1941.
Aristotle, *Aristotle XVIII, Metaphysics*, trans. Hugh Tredennick, Harvard, Loeb Classical Library, 1982.
Badiou, Alain, *Saint Paul: The Foundation of Universalism*, trans. Ray Brassier,

Stanford, Stanford University Press, 2003.
Ballard, Edward Goodwin, *Man and Technology*, Pittsburgh, Duquesne University Press, 1978.
Baur, Michael, 'Sublating Kant and the Old Metaphysics: A Reading of the Transition from Being to Essence in Hegel's Logic', *Owl Minerva*, vol. 29, 1998, pp. 139-64.
Beaney, Michael (ed.), *The Frege Reader*, Oxford, Blackwell, 1997.
Beiser, Frederick, *German Idealism: The Struggle Against Subjectivism, 1781-1801*, Cambridge, Harvard University Press, 2002.
Benjamin, Walter, *The Correspondence of Walter Benjamin*, Chicago, University of Chicago, 1994.
Benjamin, Walter, 'The Task of the Translator', *Selected Writings*, M. Bullock and M.W. Jennings (eds.), vol. 1, Cambridge, Harvard University, 1996.
Benoist, Jocelyn, *Autour de Husserl. L'ego et la raison*, Paris, Vrin, 1994.
Berkeley, George, *A Treatise Concerning the Principles of Human Knowledge*, Jonathan Dancy (ed.), Oxford, Oxford University Press, 1982.
Bernet, Rudolf, 'The Other in Myself', in Simon Critchley and Peter Dews (eds.), *Deconstructive Subjectivities*, New York, State University of New York Press Press, 1996.
Bielefeldt, Heiner, *Symbolic Representation in Kant's Practical Philosophy*, Cambridge, Cambridge University Press, 2003.
Binnick, Robert, *Time and the Verb*, Oxford, Oxford University, 1991.
Bird, Graham, *The Revolutionary Kant: A Commentary on the Critique of Pure Reason*, Chicago, Open Court, 2006.
Bodei, R., Scomposizioni. Forme dell'individuo moderno, Torino, Einaudi, 1987.
Boer, Karin de, *Thinking in the Light of Time: Heidegger's Encounter with Hegel*, Albany, State University of New York Press, 2000.
Bradley, Francis H., *The Principles of Logic*, London, Kegan Paul, Trench, Trübner, 1883.
Brandom, Robert, *Making It Explicit*, Cambridge, Harvard University Press, 1994.
Brandom, Robert, *Articulating Reasons*, Cambridge, Harvard University Press, 2000.
Brandom, Robert, *Tales of the Mighty Dead: Historical Essays in the Metaphysics of Intentionality*, Cambridge, Harvard University Press, 2002.
Burbidge, John W., *On Hegel's Logic: Fragments of a Commentary*, Atlantic Highlands, Humanities Press, 1981.
Burbidge, John W., *Real Process: How Logic and Chemistry Combine in Hegel's Philosophy of Nature*, Toronto, University of Toronto Press, 1996.
Burbidge, John W., *Hegel's Systematic Contingency*, Houndmills, Palgrave Macmillan, 2007.
Butler, Clark, *Hegel's Logic: Between Dialectic and History*, Evanston, Northwestern University Press, 1997.

Butler, Clark, *G.W.F. Hegel*, Boston, Twayne Publishers, 1977.
Cajori, Florian (ed.), *Sir Isaac Newton's Mathematical principles of natural philosophy, and his System of the world*, trans. A. Motte, trans. revised F. Cajori, Berkeley, University of California Press, 1962.
Carlson, David Gray, *A Commentary to Hegel's Science of Logic*, New York, Palgrave, 2007.
Cieszkowski, August, *Selected Writings of August Cieszkowski*, ed. and trans. Andre Liebich, Cambridge, Cambridge University Press, 1979.
Cieszkowski, August, 'Prolegomena to Historiosophie', in *The Young Hegelians: An Anthology*, ed. and trans. Lawrence S. Stepelevich, Cambridge, Cambridge University Press, 1983, pp. 53-90.
Cieszkowski, August, *Prolegomena zur Historiosophie*, Berlin, Veit, 1838.
Comrie, Bernard, *Aspect*, Cambridge, Cambridge University, 1976.
Comay, Rebecca and John McCumber (eds.), *Endings: Questions of Memory in Hegel and Heidegger*, Evanston, Northwestern University Press, 1999.
Curd, Patricia (ed.), *A Presocratics Reader*, trans. Richard D. McKirahan, Indianapolis, Hackett, 1996.
Derrida, Jacques, *Speech and Phenomena*, trans. David B. Allison, Evanston, Northwestern University Press, 1973.
Derrida, Jacques, *Of Grammatology*, trans. G. C. Spivak, Baltimore, Johns Hopkins University Press, 1976.
Derrida, Jacques, *Writing and Difference*, trans. Alan Bass, Chicago, University of Chicago Press, 1978.
Derrida, Jacques, *Dissemination*, trans. Barbara Johnson, Chicago, University of Chicago Press, 1981.
Derrida, Jacques, *Positions*, trans. Alan Bass, Chicago, University of Chicago Press, 1981.
Derrida, Jacques, *Margins of Philosophy*, trans. Alan Bass, Chicago, University of Chicago Press, 1982.
Derrida, Jacques, *Glas*, trans. John P. Leavey and Richard Rand, Lincoln, University of Nebraska Press, 1986.
Derrida, Jacques, *De l'esprit*, Paris, Galilée, 1987.
Derrida, Jacques, 'Desistance' introduction to Philippe Lacoue-Labarthe, in Philippe Lacoue-Labarthe, *Typography; Mimesis, Philosophy, Politics*, trans. Christopher Fynsk, Harvard University Press. 1989.
Derrida, Jacques, 'Eating Well', in E. Cadava et al. (eds.), *Who Comes After the Subject*, London, Routledge, 1991.
Derrida, Jacques, *Aporias*, trans. Thomas Dutoit, Stanford, Stanford University Press, 1993.
Derrida, Jacques, *The Gift of Death*, trans. David Wills, Chicago, Chicago University Press, 1995.
Derrida, Jacques, *Deconstruction in a Nutshell: A Conversation with Jacques Derrida*, John D. Caputo (ed.), New York, Fordham University Press, 1997.
Derrida, Jacques, 'Preface by Jacques Derrida: A Time for Farewells: Heidegger

(read by) Hegel (read by) Malabou', trans. Joseph D. Cohen, in Catherine Malabou, *The Future of Hegel: Plasticity, Temporality, and Dialectic*, London, Routledge, 2005, pp. vii-xlvii.

Dove, Kenley R., 'Hegel's Phenomenological Method', *The Review of Metaphysics*, vol. 23, no. 4, 1970, pp. 615-41.

Dudley, Will, *Hegel, Nietzsche and Philosophy: Thinking Freedom*, Cambridge, Cambridge University Press, 2002.

Emad, Parvis, 'The Place of Hegel in Heidegger's *Being and Time*', *Research in Phenomenology*, 13, 1983, pp. 159-173.

Fackenheim, Emil, *The Religious Dimension in Hegel's Thought*, Bloomington, Indiana University Press, 1967.

Fichte, J. G., *The Science of Knowledge*, ed. and trans. Peter Heath and John Lachs, Cambridge, Cambridge University Press, 1982.

Frege, Gottlob, 'On Sinn and Bedeuting', in Michael Beaney (ed.), *The Frege Reader*, Oxford, Blackwell, 1997, pp. 151-71.

Ferrini, Cinzia, 'Framing Hypotheses: Numbers in Nature and the Logic of Measure in the Development of Hegel's System', in Stephen Houlgate (ed.), *Hegel and the Philosophy of Nature*, New York, State University of New York, 1998, pp. 283-310.

Foucault, Michel, *The Archaeology of Knowledge and the Discourse on Language*, trans. A.M. Sheridan Smith and Rupert Sawyer, New York, Pantheon, 1972.

Frankfurt, H., 'Coercion and Moral Responsibility', in *The Importance of What We Care About*, Cambridge, Cambridge University Press, 1988.

Frankfurt, H., 'Freedom of the Will and the Concept of a Person', in G. Watson (ed.), *Free Will*, Oxford, Oxford University Press, 1982.

Gadamer, Hans-Georg, *Philosophical Hermeneutics*, trans. David Linge, Berkeley, University of California Press, 1976.

Garrison, James W., 'Metaphysics and Scientific Proof: Newton and Hegel', in Michael John Petry (ed.), *Hegel and Newtonianism*, Kluwer Academic Publishers, Dordrecht, Holland, 1993, pp. 3-16.

Gasché, Rodolphe, *The Tain of the Mirror*, Cambridge, Harvard University Press, 1986.

Gillespie, Michael Allen, *Hegel, Heidegger, and the Ground of History*, Chicago, Chicago University Press, 1984.

Giovanni, George di, 'Burbidge and Hegel on the Logic: On Hegel's Logic, Fragments of a Commentary, by John Burbidge', *The Owl Minerva*, vol. 14, no. 1, 1982, pp. 1-6.

Grant, Edward, *Much Ado About Nothing: Theories of Space and Vacuum from the Middle Ages to the Scientific Revolution*, Cambridge, Cambridge University Press, 1981.

Grice, P., *Studies in the Way of Words*, Cambridge, Harvard University, 1989.

Gordimer, Nadine, 'The Essential Gesture: Writers and Responsibility', *Tanner Lecture on Human Values*, Michigan, University of Michigan, 1981.

Gutting, Gary, *French Philosophy in the Twentieth Century*, Cambridge, Cambridge

University Press, 1999.
Haas, Andrew, 'The Bacchanalian Revel: Hegel and Deconstruction', *Man and World*, vol. 30, no. 2, 1997, pp. 217-26.
Haas, Andrew, *The Irony of Heidegger*, London, Continuum, 2007.
Habermas, Jürgen, 'Labour and Interaction: Remarks on Hegel's Jena Philosophy of Mind', in *Theory and Practice*, trans. John Viertel, Boston, Beacon Press, 1973, pp. 142-69.
Habermas, Jürgen, 'On Hegel's Political Writings', in *Theory and Practice*, trans. John Viertel, Boston, Beacon Press, 1973, pp. 170-94.
Habermas, Jürgen, *Knowledge and Human Interests*, trans. Jeremy J. Shapiro, 2nd ed., London, Heinemann, 1981.
Habermas, Jürgen, *The Philosophical Discourse of Modernity: Twelve Lectures*, trans. Frederick G. Lawrence, Cambridge, MIT Press, 1996.
Habermas, Jürgen, *On the Pragmatics of Communication*, Cambridge, MIT Press, 1998.
Habermas, Jürgen, *Truth and Justification*, Cambridge, MIT Press, 2003.
Hammer, Espen (ed.), *German Idealism: Historical and Philosophical Perspectives*, London, Routledge, 2007.
Hardimon, Michael, *Hegel's Social Philosophy: The Project of Reconciliation*, Cambridge, Cambridge University Press, 1994.
Harris, Errol E., *An Interpretation of the Logic of Hegel*, Lanham, University Press of America, 1983.
Harris, H. S., *Hegel: Phenomenology and System*, Indianapolis, Hackett, 1995.
Harris, H. S., *Hegel's Ladder*, 2 vols., Indianapolis, Hackett, 1997.
Hartmann, Klaus, 'Towards and New Systematic Reading of Hegel's Philosophy of Right', in Z.A. Pelczynski (ed.), *The State and Civil Society: Studies in Hegel's Political Philosophy*, Cambridge, Cambridge University Press, 1984, pp. 114-136.
Hartmann, Klaus, 'Hegel: A Non-metaphysical View,' in Robert Stern (ed.), *G.W.F. Hegel. Critical Assessments: Volume III. Hegel's* Phenomenology of Spirit *and* Logic, London, Routledge, 1993, p. 243-258.
Hegel, G. W. F., *The Philosophy of Right*, trans. S. W. Dyde, http://www.marxists.org/reference/archive/hegel/index.htm, 1897 (retrieved on May 29, 2007).Hegel, G. W. F., *Einleitung in der Geschichte der Philosophie*, Johannes Hoffmeister (ed.), Leipzig, Meiner, 1940.
Hegel, G. W. F., *Phänomenologie des Geistes*, Johannes Hoffmeister (ed.), Hamburg, Meiner 1952.
Hegel, G. W. F., *Reason in History: A General Introduction to the Philosophy of History*, trans. Hartman Robert S., New York, Liberal Arts Press, 1953.
Hegel, G. W. F., *The Philosophy of History*, trans. J. Sibree, New York, Dover Publications, 1956.
Hegel, G. W. F., *Hegel's Political Writings*, translated by T.M. Knox with an introductory essay by Z. A. Pelczynski, Oxford, Clarendon Press, 1964.
Hegel, G. W. F., *Gesammelte Werke*, Hamburg, Felix Meiner Verlag, 1968-.

Hegel, G. W. F., *Werke in zwanzing Bänden*, Eva Moldenhauer and Karl Markus (eds.), Frankfurt am Main, Suhrkamp Verlag, 1969.

Hegel, G. W. F., *Philosophy of Nature: Being Part Two of the Encyclopaedia of the Philosophical Sciences, 1830*, trans. M. J. Petry, 3 vols., London, George Allen & Unwin, 1970.

Hegel, G. W. F., *Philosophy of Nature: Being Part Two of the Encyclopaedia of the Philosophical Sciences, 1830*, trans. A.V. Miller, Oxford, Clarendon Press, 1970.

Hegel, G. W. F., *Early Theological Writings*, trans. T. M. Knox and Richard Kroner, Philadelphia, University of Pennsylvania Press, 1971.

Hegel, G. W. F., *Philosophy of Mind: Being Part Three of the Encyclopaedia of the Philosophical Sciences (1830), Together with the Zusätze*, trans. William Wallace and A. V. Miller, Oxford, Oxford, 1971.

Hegel, G. W. F., *The Difference Between Fichte's and Schelling's System of Philosophy*, trans. H. S. Harris and Walter Cerf, Albany, State University of New York Press, 1977.

Hegel, G. W. F., *Faith and Knowledge*, trans. Walter Cerf and H. S. Harris, Albany, State University of New York Press, 1977.

Hegel, G. W. F., *The Phenomenology of Spirit*, trans. A.V. Miller, New York, Oxford, 1977.

Hegel, G. W. F., *Wissenschaft der Logik. Erster Band. Die objektive Logik (1812/13)*, Friedrich Hogemann und Walter Jaeschke (eds.), Hamburg, Felix Meiner, 1978.

Hegel, G. W. F., *System of Ethical Life (1802/3) and First Philosophy of Spirit (part III of the System of Speculative Philosophy 1803/4)*, trans. H. S. Harris and T. M. Knox, Albany, State University of New York Press, 1979.

Hegel, G. W. F., *Hegel's Philosophy of Subjective Spirit: Being §§ 377-482 of Part Three of The Encyclopaedia of Philosophical Sciences (1830) with Zusätze and Including Two Fragments; 'A Fragment on the Philosophy of Spirit (1822/5)' and 'The Phenomenology of Spirit (Summer Term, 1825)'*, trans. M. J. Petry, 3 vols., Holland, Dordrecht, 1979.

Hegel, G. W. F., *Phänomenologie des Geistes*, W. Bonsiepen and R. Heede (eds.), Hamburg, Felix Meiner, 1980.

Hegel, G. W. F., *The Philosophy of Right*, trans. T. M. Knox, New York, Oxford, 1980.

Hegel, G. W. F., *Wissenschaft der Logik. Zweiter Band. Die subjektive Logik (1816)*, Friedrich Hogemann und Walter Jaeschke (eds.), Hamburg, Felix Meiner, 1981.

Hegel, G. W. F., *Wissenschaft der Logik. Erster Band. Die Lehre vom Sein (1832)*, Friedrich Hogemann und Walter Jaeschke (eds.), Hamburg, Felix Meiner, 1984.

Hegel, G. W. F., *Lectures on the Philosophy of Religion*, trans. R.F. Brown, P.C. Hodgson, and J.M. Stewart, 3 vols., Berkeley, University of California Press, 1984.

Hegel, G. W. F., *Hegel: The Letters*, trans. Clark Butler and Christine Seiler,

Bloomington, Indiana University Press, 1984.
Hegel, G. W. F., *Hegel's Introduction to the Lectures on the History of Philosophy*, trans. T. M. Knox and A.V. Miller, Oxford, Clarendon Press, 1985.
Hegel, G. W. F. and F. W. J. Schelling, 'The Critical Journal, Introduction: On the Essence of Philosophical Criticism Generally, and its Relationship to the Present State of Philosophy', in George di Giovanni and H.S. Harris (eds.), *Between Kant and Hegel: Texts in the Development of Post-Kantian Idealism*, trans. H.S. Harris, Albany, S.U.N.Y., 1985, pp. 272-91.
Hegel, G. W. F., *The Jena System, 1804-5: Logic and Metaphysics*, trans. John W. Burbidge and George di Giovanni, Kingston, McGill-Queen's University Press, 1986.
Hegel, G.W.F., *The Philosophical Propaedeutic*, Michael George and Andrew Vincent (eds.), trans. A.V. Miller, Oxford, Blackwell, 1986.
Hegel, G. W. F., *Introduction to the Lectures on the History of Philosophy*, trans. T. M. Knox and A. V. Miller, Oxford, Oxford University Press, 1987.
Hegel, G. W. F., *Introduction to The Philosophy of History: With Selections From The Philosophy of Right*, trans. Leo Rauch, Indianapolis, Hackett, 1988.
Hegel, G. W. F., *Lectures on the History of Philosophy: The Lectures of 1825-1826*, trans. Robert F. Brown, J. M. Stewart, and H. S. Harris, vol. 3 Medieval and Modern Philosophy, Berkeley, University of California Press, 1990.
Hegel, G.W.F., *Encyclopaedia of the Philosophical Sciences in Outline, and Critical Writings*, Ernst Behler (ed.), trans. Arnold V. Miller, Steven A. Taubeneck, and Diana Behler, New York, Continuum, 1990.
Hegel, G. W. F., *The Encyclopaedia Logic (1830), with the Zusätze: Part I of the Encyclopaedia of Philosophical Sciences with the Zusätze*, trans. Theodore F. Geraets, W. A. Suchting, and H. S. Harris, Indianapolis, Hackett, 1991.
Hegel, G. W. F., *Enzyklopädie der philosophischen Wissenschaften im Grundrisse (1830)*, Wolfgang Bonsiepen und Hans-Christian Lucas (eds.), Hamburg, Felix Meiner, 1992.
Hegel, G. W. F., *Introductory Lectures on Aesthetics*, M. J. Inwood (ed.), trans. Bernard Bosanquet, London, Penguin Books, 1993.
Hegel, G. W. F., *Vorlesungen über die Philosophie der Weltgeschichte I, Die Vernunft in der Geschichte*, Johannes Hoffmeister and Georg Lasson (eds.), Hamburg, Felix Meiner, 1994.
Hegel, G. W. F., *Lectures on the History of Philosophy*, trans. E. S. Haldane and Frances H. Simson, vol. I Greek Philosophy to Plato, 3 vols., Lincoln, University of Nebraska Press, 1995.
Hegel, G. W. F., *Lectures on the History of Philosophy*, trans. E. S. Haldane and Frances H. Simson, vol. II Plato and the Platonists, 3 vols., Lincoln, University of Nebraska Press, 1995.
Hegel, G. W. F., *Lectures on the History of Philosophy*, trans. E. S. Haldane and Frances H. Simson, vol. III Medieval and Modern Philosophy, 3 vols., Lincoln, University of Nebraska Press, 1995.
Hegel, G. W. F., *Lectures on Natural Right and Political Science: The First Philosophy*

of *Right: Heidelberg, 1817-1818, with Additions From the Lectures of 1818-1819,* trans. J. Michael Stewart and Peter C. Hodgson, Berkeley, University of California Press, 1995.

Hegel, G. W. F., *Elements of the Philosophy of Right*, Allen Wood (ed.), trans. H. B. Nisbet, Cambridge, Cambridge University Press, 1996.

Hegel, G. W. F., *Science of Logic*, trans. A.V. Miller, New Jersey, Humanities Press, 1997.

Hegel, G. W. F., *Aesthetics: Lectures on Fine Art*, trans. T. M. Knox, 2 vols., Oxford, Oxford, 1998.

Hegel, G. W. F., *Lectures on the Philosophy of World History: Introduction, Reason in History*, trans. H. B. Nisbet, Cambridge, Cambridge University Press, 1998.

Hegel, G. W. F., 'On the Scientific Ways of Treating Natural Law, on its Place in Practical Philosophy, and its Relation to the Positive Sciences of Right', in Laurence Dickey and H. B. Nisbet (eds.), *Political Writings*, trans. H. B. Nisbet, Cambridge, Cambridge, 1999, pp. 102-80.

Hegel, G. W. F., *Lectures on the History of Philosophy 1825-6*, Robert F. Brown (ed.), trans. R. F. Brown and J. M. Stewart with the assistance of H. S. Harris, vol. 2 Greek Philosophy, Oxford, Oxford, 2006.

Hegel, G. W. F., *Philosophy of Mind: Being Part Three of the Encyclopaedia of the Philosophical Sciences (1830), Together with the Zusätze*, M. J. Inwood (ed.), trans. William Wallace and A. V. Miller with revisions and commentary by M. J. Inwood, Oxford, Oxford, 2007.

Heiddegger, Martin, *Being and Time*, trans. John Macquarrie and Edward Robinson, Oxford, Blackwell, 1962.

Heidegger, Martin, 'Letter on Humanism', in *Basic Writings*, D. F. Krell (ed.), New York, Harper & Row, 1977.

Heidegger, Martin, *Hegels Phänomenologie des Geistes*, Frankfurt an Main, Klostermann, 1980.

Heiddegger, Martin, *Basic Problems of Phenomenology*, trans. Albert Hofstadter, Bloomington, Indiana University Press, 1982.

Heidegger, Martin, *Schelling's Treatise on the Essence of Human Freedom*, trans. Joan Stambaugh, Athens, Ohio University Press, 1985.

Heidegger, Martin, *Nietzsche: Vol. III: The Will to Power as Knowledge and as Metaphysics & Vol. IV: Nihilism*, David Farrell Krell (ed.), trans. Joan Stambaugh, David Farrell Krell and Frank A. Capuzzi, vol. 3 & 4, 4 vols., San Francisco, HarperSanFrancisco, 1991.

Heidegger, Martin, *Hegel's Phenomenology of Spirit*, trans. P. Emad and K. Maly, Bloomington, Indiana, 1994.

Heidegger, Martin, *Aristotle's Metaphysics Theta 1-3*, trans. W. Brogan and P. Warnek, Bloomington, Indiana, 1995.

Heidegger, Martin, *Being and Time*, trans. Joan Stambaugh, New York, State University of New York Press, 1996.

Heidegger, Martin, 'Hegel and the Greeks', trans. Robert Metcalf, in *Pathmarks*,

William McNeill (ed.), Cambridge, Cambridge University, 1998.
Heidegger, Martin, *Pathmarks*, William McNeill (ed.), Cambridge, Cambridge University, 1998.
Heidegger, Martin, *Contributions to Philosophy*, trans. P. Emad and K. Maly, Bloomington, Indiana University, 1999.
Heidegger, Martin, *Identity and Difference*, trans. Joan Stambaugh, Chicago, University of Chicago, 2002.
Heidegger, Martin, 'Hegel's Concept of Experience', *Off the Beaten Track*, ed. and trans. Julian Young and Kenneth Haynes, Cambridge, Cambridge University, 2002.
Henrrich, Dieter 'Logical Form and Real Totality: The Authentic Conceptual Form of Hegel's Concept of the State,' in Robert Pippin and Otfried Höffe, (eds.), *Hegel on Ethics and Politics*, Cambridge, Cambridge University Press, 2004, p. 241-267.
Heraclitus, *The Presocratic Philosophers*, G. S. Kirk, J. E. Raven, M. Schofield (eds.), Cambridge, Cambridge University, 1957.
Hill, R. Kevin, *Nietzsche's Critiques: The Kantian Foundations of his Thought*, Oxford, Clarendon Press, 2003.
Hobbes, Thomas, *Leviathan*, http://darkwing.uoregon.edu/%7Erbear/hobbes/leviathan.html, 1651 (retrieved on May 29, 2007).
Hoffmeister, Johannes, *Dokumente zu Hegel's Entwichlung*, Frommann, Stuttgart, 1936.
Honneth, Axel, *The Struggle for Recognition: The Moral Grammar of Social Conflicts*, Cambridge, MIT Press, 1996.
Hospers, John, 'What Libertarianism Is', in T. Mappes and J. Zembaty (eds.), *Social Ethics: Morality and Social Policy*, New York, McGraw Hill, 2002.
Houlgate, Stephen, *Hegel, Nietzsche, and the Criticism of Metaphysics*, Cambridge, Cambridge University Press, 1986.
Houlgate, Stephen, *Freedom, Truth and History: An Introduction to Hegel's Philosophy*, New York, Routledge, 1991.
Houlgate, S., 'Hegel's Ethical Thought', *Bulletin of the Hegel Society of Great Britain*, no. 25, 1992, pp. 1-17.
Houlgate, Stephen, *An Introduction to Hegel's Philosophy: Freedom, Truth and History*, 2nd ed., Oxford, Blackwell, 2005.
Houlgate, Stephen, *The Opening of Hegel's Logic: From Being to Infinity*, Indiana, Purdue University Press, 2006.
Hyppolite, Jean, *Genesis and Structure of Hegel's Phenomenology of Spirit*, trans. Samuel Cherniak and John Heckman, Evanston, Northwestern University, 1974.
Ilting, K-H, 'The Dialectic of Civil Society', in Z.A. Pelczynski (ed.), *The State and Civil Society*, pp. 211-226.
Inwood, Michael, *Hegel*, London, Routledge, 1983.
Inwood, Michael, *A Hegel Dictionary*, London, Blackwell, 1992.
Jackson, M., 'Hegel: The Real and the Rational', in J. Stewart (ed.), *The Hegel Myths and Legends*, Evanston, Northwestern University Press, 1996.

Jacob, Margaret C., *The Radical Enlightenment: Pantheists, Freemasons and Republicans*, 2nd revised edition, Lafayette, Cornerstone Books, 2006.
Jacobi, F. H., 'On the Doctrine of Spinoza in Letters to Moses Mendelssohn', in *The Main Philosophical Writings and the Novel Allwill*, ed. and trans. G. di Giovanni, Montreal, McGill-Queens University Press, 1994.
Jammer, Max, *Concepts of Space: The History of Theories of Space in Physics*, Cambridge, 1954.
Kant, Immanuel, *Critique of Pure Reason*, trans. N.K. Smith, New York, St. Martin's, 1929.
Kant, Immanuel, *Theoretical Philosophy, 1755–1770*, ed. and trans. D. Walford and R. Meerbote, Cambridge, Cambridge University Press, 1992.
Kant, Immanuel, *Critique of Practical Reason*, trans. Mary Gregor, Cambridge, Cambridge University Press, 1997.
Kant, Immanuel, *Critique of Pure Reason*, trans. N.K. Smith, New York, St. Martin's Press, 1929.
Kant, Immanuel, *Critique of Pure Reason*, trans. Paul Guyer and Allen Wood, New York, Cambridge, 1998.
Kaufmann, W., 'The Hegel Myth and its Method', in J. Stewart (ed.), *The Hegel Myths and Legends*, Evanston, Northwestern University Press, 1996.
Kearney, Richard, *Dialogues with Contemporary Continental Thinkers*, Manchester, Manchester University Press, 1984.
Kierkegaard, Søren, *Søren Kierkegaard's Papirer*, P. A. Heiberg, V. Kuhr and E. Torsting (eds.), 2nd ed., 20 vols., København, Gyldendalske Boghandel Nordisk Forlag, 1909-1948.
Kierkegaard, Søren, *Journals and Papers*, trans. Howard V. Hong and Edna H. Hong, 7 vols., Bloomington, Indiana University Press, 1967-78.
Kierkegaard, Søren, *Samlede Værker*, A. B. Drachmann, J. L. Heiberg and H. O. Lange (eds.), 15 vols., Gyldendalske Boghandel Nordisk Forlag, København, 1920-1936.
Kierkegaard, Søren, *Kierkegaard's Writings*, trans. Howard V. Hong and Edna H. Hong, 24 vols., Princeton University Press, 1978-98.
Klein, Naomi, *No Logo: Taking Aim at the Brand Bullies*, Vintage Canada, 2000.
Knowles, Dudley, *Hegel and the Philosophy of Right*, London, Routledge, 2002.
Kojève, Alexandre, *Introduction to the Reading of Hegel*, trans. J.H. Nichols, Jr., Ithaca, Cornell University, 1969.
Kolb, David, *The Critique of Pure Modernity: Hegel, Heidegger, and After*, Chicago, Chicago University Press, 1986.
Korsgaard, C., *Creating the Kingdom of Ends*, Cambridge, Cambridge University Press, 1996.
Koyré, Alexandre, *From the Closed World to the Infinite Universe*, Baltimore, Johns Hopkins Press, 1957.
Knox, T. M., 'Hegel and Prussianism', in Jon Stewart (ed.), *The Hegel Myths and Legends*, Evanston, Northwestern University Press, 1996, pp. 70-81.
Krell, David Farrell, 'Hegel, Heidegger, Nietzsche: An Essay in Descensional

Reflection', *Nietzsche-Studien*, vol. 5, 1976, pp. 255-262.
Lamb, David, 'Teleology: Kant and Hegel', in Stephen Priest (ed.), *Hegel's Critique of Kant*, Oxford, Oxford University Press, 1987.
Lasson, G. (ed.), *Schriften zur Politik und Rechtsphilosophie*, 2$^{\text{nd}}$ ed., Leipzig, Meiner, 1923.
Lauer, Quentin, *Hegel's Idea of Philosophy*, New York, Fordham University, 1983.
Laurentiis, Allegra de, *Subjects in the Ancient and Modern World*, New York, Palgrave, 2005.
Livadites, T., *Small Book for Large Dreams* (Greek), Athens, Kethros, 1987.
Longuenesse, Béatrice, *Kant on the Human Standpoint*, Cambridge, Cambridge University Press,
Luban, David, 'The War on Terrorism and the End of Human Rights', *Philosophy & Public Policy Quarterly*, vol. 22, no. 3, 2002.
Lukács, György, *The Young Hegel: Studies in the Relations Between Dialectics and Economics*, London, Merlin Press, 1975.
Lukes, S., *Emile Durkheim: His Life and Work*, Stanford, Stanford University Press, 1973.
Lumsden, Simon, 'Absolute Knowing', *The Owl of Minerva: Journal of the Hegel Society of America*, vol. 30, no. 1, 1998, pp. 3-32.
Lumsden, Simon, 'Fichte's Striving Subject', *Inquiry: An Interdisciplinary Journal of Philosophy*, vol. 47, no. 2, 2004, pp. 123-142.
Lumsden, Simon, 'Dialectic and Différance: The Place of Singularity in Hegel and Derrida', *Philosophy & Social Criticism*, vol. 33, no 6, 2007.
Malabou, Catherine, *L'avenir de Hegel*, Paris, Vrin, 1996.
Malabou, Catherine, *The Future of Hegel: Plasticity, Temporality, and Dialectic*, trans. Lisabeth During, New York, Routledge, 2004.
Maker, William, *Philosophy Without Foundations: Rethinking Hegel*, Albany, State University of New York Press, 1994.
Maker, William, 'Hegel's Logic of Freedom', in David G. Carlson, (ed.), *Hegel's Theory of the Subject*, New York, Palgrave, 2005, p. 1-18.
Marx, Werner, *Hegel's Phenomenology of Spirit*, trans. P. Heath, Chicago, University of Chicago, 1975.
McDowell, John, *Mind and World*, Cambridge, Harvard University Press, 1996.
McDowell, John, 'The Apperceptive I and the Empirical Self', in K. Deligiorgi (ed.), *Hegel New Directions*, Chesham, Acumen, 2006, p. 33-49.
McGuire, J. E., 'Force, Active Principles, and Newton's Invisible Realm', *Ambix*, no. 15, 1968, pp. 154-208.
McGuire, J. E., *Tradition and Innovation: Newton's Metaphysics of Nature*, Dordrecht, Kluwer, 1995.
McTaggart, John Ellis, *A Commentary on Hegel's Logic*, Cambridge, Cambridge University Press, 1910.
Mensch, James R., *Postfoundational Phenomenology: Husserlian Reflections on Presence and Embodiment*, University Park, Pennsylvania University Press, 2001.
Morison, Benjamin, *On Location: Aristotle's Concept of Place*, Oxford, Oxford

University Press, 2002.
Mure, G. R. G., *Idealist Epilogue*, Oxford, Clarendon Press, 1978.
Nagel, Thomas, *The View From Nowhere*, New York, Oxford University Press, 1989.
Neuhouser, F., *Foundations of Hegel's Social Theory: Actualizing Freedom*, London, Harvard University Press, 2000.
Nicolacopoulos, Toula, *The Radical Critique of Liberalism: In Memory of a Vision*, Seddon, re.press, 2008.
Nicolacopoulos, Toula and George Vassilacopoulos, *Hegel and the Logical Structure of Love: An Essay on Sexualities, Family and the Law*, Aldershot, Ashgate, 1999.
Nicolacopoulos, Toula and George Vassilacopoulos, 'Philosophy and Revolution: Badiou's Infidelity to the Event', *Cosmos and History*, vol. 2, no. 1-2, 2006, pp. 210-25.
Nietzsche, Friedrich, *The Gay Science*, trans. W. Kaufmann, New York, Random House, 1974.
Norman, Judith and Alistair Welchman (eds.), *The New Schelling*, London, Continuum, 2004.
Nuzzo, Angelica, 'The Truth of "absolutes Wissen" in Hegel's "Phenomenology of Spirit"', in A. Denker (ed.), *Hegel's Phenomenology of Spirit*, Amherst, NY, Humanities Press, 2003, pp. 265-294.
Nuzzo, Angelica, 'The End of Hegel's Logic: Absolute Idea as Absolute Method,' in David G. Carlson (ed.), *Hegel's Theory of the Subject*, London, Palgrave Macmillan, 2005, pp. 187-205.
Nuzzo, Angelica, 'Vagueness and Meaning Variance in Hegel's Logic,' forthcoming.
O'Neill, O., *Constructions of Reason*, Cambridge, Cambridge University Press, 1989.
O'Hagan, T., 'On Hegel's Critique of Kant's Moral and Political Philosophy', in S. Priest (ed.), *Hegel's Critique of Kant*, Oxford, Clarendon, 1987.
Parry, David M., *Hegel's Phenomenology of the "We"*, New York, P. Lang, 1988.
Patten, Alan, *Hegel's Idea of Freedom*, Oxford, Oxford University Press, 1999.
Pinkard, Terry, *Hegel's Dialectic: The Explanation of Possibility*, Philadelphia, Temple University Press, 1988.
Pinkard, Terry, *Hegel's Phenomenology: The Sociality of Reason*, Cambridge, Cambridge University Press, 1994.
Pinkard, Terry, *German Philosophy 1760-1860: The Legacy of Idealism* (Cambridge, Cambridge University Press, 2002.
Pippin, Robert, *Hegel's Idealism*, Cambridge, Cambridge University Press, 1989.
Pippin, Robert, 'Hegel's Ethical Rationalism', in Ameriks and Sturma (eds.), *The Modern Subject*, Albany, State University of New York Press, 1995, p. 149-176.
Pippin, Robert, *Idealism as Modernism: Hegelian Variations*, Cambridge, Cambridge University Press, 1997.
Pippin, Robert, 'On Being Anti-Cartesian: Heidegger, Hegel, Subjectivity,

and Sociality', in Robert Pippin, *Idealism as Modernism: Hegelian Variations*, Cambridge, Cambridge University Press, 1997.
Pippin, Robert 'Truth and Lies in the Early Nietzsche', in Robert Pippin, *Idealism as Modernism: Hegelian Variations*, Cambridge, Cambridge University Press, 1997, pp. 311-329.
Pippin, Robert, *Modernism as a Philosophical Problem*, Cambridge, Cambridge University Press, 1991, 2$^{nd}$ ed., 1999.
Pippin, Robert, 'What is the Question for which Hegel's Theory of Recognition is the Answer?', *European Journal of Philosophy*, vol. 8, no. 2, 2000, pp. 155-72.
Pippin, Robert, *The Persistence of Subjectivity*, Cambridge, Cambridge University Press, 2006.
Popper, K., *The Open Society and its Enemies*, vol. 2, 3$^{rd}$ ed., London, Routledge, 1957.
Priest, Stephen, *Hegel's Critique of Kant*, Oxford, Oxford University Press, 1987.
Quante, Michael, *Hegel's Concept of Action*, Cambridge, Cambridge University Press, 2004.
Redding, Paul, *Hegel's Hermeneutics*, Ithaca, Cornell University Press, 1996.
Redding, Paul, 'Hegel, Fichte and the Pragmatic Contexts of Moral Judgment', in Espen Hammer (ed.), *German Idealism: Historical and Philosophical Perspectives*, London, Routledge, 2007.
Redding, Paul, *Analytic Philosophy and the Return of Hegelian Thought*, Cambridge, Cambridge University Press, 2007.
Ricoeur, P., 'The Model of the Text: Meaningful Action Considered as a Text', in *Hermeneutics and the Human Sciences* trans. J. Thompson, Cambridge, Cambridge University Press, 1981.
Rinaldi, Giacomo, *A History and Interpretation of the Logic of Hegel*, Lewiston, E. Mellen Press, 1992.
Ritsos, Y., 'The Meaning of Simplicity', *Yiannis Ritsosk Poems 1941-1958 Volume B (Greek)*, Athens, Kedros, 1979 (Ρίτσος, Γ., 'Το νόημα της απλότητας', *Γιάννης Ρίτσος Ποιήματα*, 1941-1958, Τόμος Β, Αθήνα, Κέδρος, 1979).
Ritter, Joachim, *Hegel and the French Revolution: Essays on the Philosophy of Right*, Cambridge, MIT Press, 1982.
Rose, D., *Hegel's Philosophy of Right*, London, Continuum Press, 2007.
Rousseau, Jean-Jacques, *On the Social Contract*, ed. and trans. Donald Cress, Cambridge, Hackett Publishing Company, 1987.
Schapiro, Leonard, *The Communist Party of the Soviet Union*, 2$^{nd}$ ed., New York, Vintage Books, 1971.
Schelling, F. W. J. von, *Über das Wesen der menschlichen Freiheit*, Stuttgart, Reclam, 1964.
Schelling, F. W. J. von, *Ideas for a Philosophy of Nature*, trans. E. E. Harris and P. Heath, New York, Cambridge University Press, 1988.
Schelling, F. W. J. von, *Philosophy of Art*, trans. D. W. Stott, Minneapolis, University of Minnesota Press, 1989.
Schelling, F. W. J. von, *System des transzendentalen Idealismus*, Hamburg, Meiner,

1992.

Schmaus, Warren, *Rethinking Durkheim and His Tradition*, Cambridge, Cambridge University Press, 2004.

Schmidt, Dennis J., *The Ubiquity of the Finite: Hegel, Heidegger, and the Entitlements of Philosophy*, Cambridge, The MIT Press, 1988.

Sellars, Wilfrid, *Empiricism and the Philosophy of Mind*, with an Introduction by Richard Rorty and a Study Guide by Robert Brandom, Cambridge, Harvard University Press, 1997.

Siep, Ludwig, 'Individuality in Hegel's *Phenomenology of Spirit*', in Ameriks and Sturma (eds.), *The Modern Subject*, Albany, State University of New York Press, 1995.

Souche-Dagues, Denise, 'The Dialogue between Hegel and Heidegger', in Christopher Macann (ed.), *Martin Heidegger: Critical Assessments Volume II: History of Philosophy*, London, Routledge, 1992, pp. 246-276.

Stanley, Thomas, 'The life', in Colin Burrow (ed.), *Metaphysical Poetry*, London, Penguin, 2006.

Stern, David S., 'Transcendental Apperception and Subjective Logic', in Ardis B. Collins (ed.), *Hegel on the Modern World*, Albany, State University of New York Press, 1995.

Stewart, Jon (ed.), *The Hegel Myths and Legends*, Evanston, Northwestern University Press, 1996.

Stewart, Jon, *Kierkegaard's Relations to Hegel Reconsidered*, Cambridge University Press, 2003.

Taylor, Charles, 'The Opening Arguments of the Phenomenology', in A. MacIntyre (ed.), *Hegel*, Notre Dame, University of Notre Dame, 1972.

Taylor, Charles, *Hegel*, Cambridge, Cambridge University Press, 1975.

Taylor, Charles, 'Hegel's Concept of Mind', in *Human Agency and Language: Philosophical Papers 1*, Cambridge, Cambridge University Press, 1985.

Taylor, C., 'Responsibility for Self', in G. Watson (ed.), *Free Will*, Oxford, Oxford University Press, 1982.

Theunissen, Michael, *Sein und Schein. Die Kritische Funktion der Hegelschen Logik*, Frankfurt, Suhrkamp, 1980.

Michael Theunissen, 'The Repressed Intersubjectivity in Hegel's Philosophy of Right', in Cornell, D., Rosenfeld, M., Carlson, D.G. (eds.), *Hegel and Legal Theory*, New York and London, Routledge, 1991, pp. 3-63.

Tugendhat, E., *Self-consciousness and Self-determination*, trans. P. Stern, London, MIT Press, 1986.

Vassilacopoulos, George, *A Reading of Hegel's Philosophy*, Ph.D. Thesis, Melbourne, La Trobe, 1994.

Vassilacopoulos, George, 'Plato's *Republic* and the End of Philosophy', *Philosophical Inquiry*, vol. XIX, no. 1-2, 2007, pp. 34-45.

Velleman, J., 'What Happens When Someone Acts?', in *The Possibility of Practical Reason*, Oxford, Oxford University Press, 2000.

Verene, Donald P., *Hegel's Absolute: An Introduction to Reading the Phenomenology of*

*Spirit*, Albany, State University of New York Press, 2007.
Westphal, Kenneth R., *Hegel's Epistemological Realism: A Study of the Aim and Method of Hegel's Phenomenology of Spirit*, Dordrecht, Kluwer Academic Publishers, 1989.
Westphal, K., 'The Basic Context and Structure of Hegel's *Philosophy of Right*', in F. Beiser (ed.), *The Cambridge Companion to Hegel*, Cambridge, Cambridge University Press, 1993.
Westphal, K., 'Hegel's Critique of Kant's Moral World View', *Philosophical Topics*, vol. 19, no. 2, 1991, pp. 133-175.
Westphal, Merold, *History and Truth in Hegel's Phenomenology*, Atlantic Highlands, Humanities Press, 1979.
Williams, Robert R., 'Hegel and Heidegger', in W. Desmond (ed.) *Hegel and his Critics*, Albany, State University of New York Press, 1989, pp. 135-157.
Williams, Robert R., *Hegel's Ethics of Recognition*, Berkeley, University of California Press, 1997.
Winfield, Richard, *Overcoming Foundations: Studies in Systematic Philosophy*, New York, Columbia University Press, 1989.
Winfield, Richard, 'Rethinking Politics: Carl Schmitt vs. Hegel, *The Owl of Minerva*, vol. 22, no. 2, 1991, pp. 209-225.
Winfield, Richard, 'Ethical Community without Communitarianism', *Philosophy Today*, vol. 40, no. 2, 1996.
White Alan, *Absolute Knowledge: Hegel and the Problem of Metaphysics*, Athens, Ohio University Press, 1983.
Wood, David, *Thinking After Heidegger*, Cambridge, Polity, 2002.
Wood, Alan W., *Hegel's Ethical Thought*, Cambridge, Cambridge University Press, 1990.

# Contributors

**Paul Ashton** teaches in the Liberal Arts at Victoria University and is a postgraduate student at La Trobe University, both in Melbourne Australia. He is the co-editor of *Cosmos and History: The Journal of Natural Philosophy*, sits on the steering group of *Open Humanities Press* and is an editor of *The Praxis of Alain Badiou* (re.press 2006). His research interests include Hegel, German Idealism, Greek philosophy and Marxism.

**María J. Binetti** is researcher of Conicet (Consejo Nacional de Investigaciones Científicas y Técnicas, Argentina) and professor of Philosophy at the Argentinian Catholic University. She is author of *El poder de la libertad. Introducción a Kierkegaard* (Ciafic, 2006), *La posibilidad necesaria de la libertad* (Universidad de Navarra, 2005), and of numerous articles on Kierkegaardian philosophy. Her current research focuses on Søren Kierkegaard's thought with historical reference to German Idealism and Postmodern philosophy.

**John W. Burbidge** has published extensively on Hegel's philosophy including: *On Hegel's Logic: Fragments of a Commentary* (1981), *Hegel on Logic and Religion* (1992), *Real Process: How Logic and Chemistry Combine in Hegel's Philosophy of Nature* (1996), *Historical Dictionary of Hegelian Philosophy* (2001), *The Logic of Hegel's Logic* (2006), and *Hegel's Systematic Contingency* (2007). He is currently Honorary President of the Hegel Society of Great Britain and a Fellow of the Royal Society of Canada.

**David Gray Carlson** is a professor of law at Benjamin N. Cardozo School of Law in New York and has taught at the University of Miami Law School, George Washington University Law School, and the University of Michigan School of Law. Besides specializing in the American law of debtors and creditors and real property, Carlson studies Hegelian logic and Lacanian psychoanalytic theory. His books include *A Commentary on Hegel's 'Science of Logic'*, (Palgrave 2007), *Hegel's Theory of the Subject* (2006), *Deconstruction and the Possibility of Justice* (1991) (with Drucilla Cornell and Michel Rosenfeld), and *Hegel and Legal Theory* (1991) (with Cornell and Rosenfeld).

# Contributors

**Karin de Boer** is Assistant Professor of Philosophy at the University of Groningen (The Netherlands). She is the author of *Thinking in the Light of Time: Heidegger's Encounter with Hegel* (2000) and of numerous articles on Hegel, Heidegger, and Derrida. Her current research focuses on Hegel's *Science of Logic* and his views on negativity and tragedy.

**Jorge Armando Reyes Escobar** is Associate Professor of philosophy in the Universidad Nacional Autónoma de México. He has written several articles on Gadamer's hermeneutics, and he edited (with Raúl Alcalá) the volume *Gadamer y las Humanidades (Gadamer and Humanities)*. In 2007 he was Visiting Research Fellow in the Philosophy Program at the School of Communication, Arts and Critical Enquiry, La Trobe University.

**Andrew Haas** teaches philosophy at the State University of New York at Stony Brook, USA. He is author of *Hegel and the Problem of Multiplicity* (2000) and *The Irony of Heidegger* (2007); as well as articles on Husserl, Levinas and Derrida. Currently, he is writing a book on metaphysics.

**H. S. (Henry Silton) Harris**, author and educator, was born on 11 April 1926 in Brighton England. He received his B. A. [Literae Humaniores] in classics and philosophy from Oxford University in 1949, his M. A. in 1952 and his Ph.D. (philosophy) in 1954 at the University of Illinois at Urbana-Champaign. Following a teaching career at the University of Illinois and at Ohio State University (1951-1961), Harris joined the Philosophy Department at York University, Toronto in 1962. He served as Academic Dean of Glendon College, 1967-1969 and was awarded the title Distinguished Research Professor in 1984. He was elected to the Royal Society of Canada in 1988; received an Honorary Doctor of Letters from York University in June 2001 and was inducted the same year into York University's Founders' Honour Society in recognition of his contribution to York's early development. He retired from York in 1996 and lived in Victoria British Columbia. Harris was a prolific scholar and an acknowledged authority on the philosophy of Giovanni Gentile and G.W.F. Hegel. He was the author of several books, articles and book chapters on Hegel including H*egel's Development I: Toward the Sunlight (1770-1801)*, published in 1972; *Hegel's Development II: Night Thoughts (Jena 1801-1806)*, published in 1983; and *Hegel's Ladder (Volume 1: The Pilgrimage of Reason; Volume 2: The Odyssey of Spirit)* on Hegel's Phenomenology of Spirit, published in 1997. In addition, Harris prepared several translations with others of Hegel's works to which he added textual notes and introductions including *System of Ethical Life and First Philosophy of Spirit*, (1979), *Lectures on the Philosophy of Religion*, (1984-87) and *Encyclopedia Logic with the Zusätze*, (1991). He was unable to see to press manuscripts on Pre-platonic philosophy, Plato, Dante, Goethe, Blake and Hegel and a large collection of articles on philosophy and literature. Professor Harris died in Victoria on 13 March 2007.

**Wendell Kisner** has been teaching for over seventeen years. His research and instructional interests include Hegel, Nietzsche, Heidegger, Levinas, Plato, Deleuze, Rousseau, Political Philosophy, Environmental Ethics, Globalization, and Technology. He currently teaches online graduate courses at Athabasca University in the Graduate Center for Integrated Studies and resides in Edmonton Alberta with his spouse and a family consisting of two dogs and three cats. He also teaches guitar lessons at his wife's music studio.

**Simon Lumsden** is Senior Lecturer in Philosophy at the University of New South Wales. His research is primarily concerned with German Idealism, Poststructuralism and the relation between these traditions. He has published papers in these areas in journals such as *Inquiry*, *Philosophy and Social Criticism*, *Philosophical Forum*, *International Philosophical Quarterly*, *The Owl of Minerva*, *Topoi* and many other journals. He is currently completing a manuscript concerned with the development of self-consciousness in German Idealism and the critique of the subject in Heidegger and Poststructuralism. His recent research is concerned with Hegel's notion of reconciliation.

**Toula Nicolacopoulos** is a lecturer in the Philosophy Program, La Trobe University, where she teaches Plato, political philosophy and ethics. Her latest book *The Radical Critique of Liberalism* is forthcoming with re.press. She is the co-author of *Hegel And The Logical Structure of Love* and *From Foreigner to Citizen* (Greek) and has written essays on Hegel, Badiou, liberalism, racism, feminism, whiteness and multiculturalism. She is currently writing a book on Ronald Dworkin's liberalism.

**Angelica Nuzzo** (Graduate Center and Brooklyn College, CUNY) has been Fellow at the Radcliffe Institute for Advanced Study at Harvard (2000-01) and recipient of an Alexander von Humboldt Fellowship (2005-06). Among her publications are the forthcoming *Ideal Embodiment: Kant's Theory of Sensibility* (Indiana University Press, 2008), *Kant and the Unity of Reason* (Purdue University Press, 2005), two books on Hegel (*Logica e sistema*, 1996, *Rappresentazione e concetto nella logica della Filosofia del diritto*, 1990), the monograph *System* (2003). Her numerous essays on German Idealism, Modern Philosophy, theory of translation, ethics and globalization appear in such journals as the *Journal of the History of Philosophy*, *Metaphilosophy*, *Journal of Philosophy and Social Criticism*, *Hegel Studien*, *Fichte Studien*.

**Paul Redding** is Professor of Philosophy at the University of Sydney. He is the author of *Hegel's Hermeneutics* (Cornell University Press, 1996); *The Logic of Affect* (Cornell University Press, 1999); and, most recently, *Analytic Philosophy and the Return of Hegelian Thought* (Cambridge University Press, 2007), which examines the revival of Hegelian philosophy within a post-Sellarsian analytic framework offered by Robert Brandom and John McDowell. He is currently working on a book, *Continental Idealism: Leibniz to Nietzsche*, to be published by Routledge in 2009, as well as a project which attempts to extend recent 'post-Kantian' readings of Hegel to an account of Hegel's theology.

**David Rose** is Lecturer in Philosophical Studies at Newcastle University and mainly researches in the ethical and political philosophy of the late modern European philosophical tradition. He published *Hegel's Philosophy of Right* in 2007 and is currently working on a book entitled *Freewill and Continental Philosophy: the death without meaning.*

**Robert Sinnerbrink** is Lecturer in Philosophy at Macquarie University, Sydney, Australia. He is the author of *Understanding Hegelianism* (Acumen, 2007), co-editor of *Critique Today* (Brill, 2006) and a contributing editor of *Recognition, Work, Politics: New Directions in French Critical Theory* (Brill, 2007). He has published numerous articles on European philosophy, social philosophy, and philosophy of film in *Critical Horizons: The International Journal of Philosophical Studies, Social Semiotics, Parrhesia, Literature and Aesthetics, Scan: Journal of Media Arts Culture,* and *Film-Philosophy.*

**George Vassilacopoulos** is a lecturer in the Philosophy Program, La Trobe University where he teaches Greek and contemporary European philosophy. He is the co-author of *Hegel And The Logical Structure of Love* and *From Foreigner to Citizen* (Greek). He has also written on Plato, Hegel, Heidegger, Badiou and on topics including racism, whiteness and multiculturalism. He is currently co-authoring *Indigenous Sovereignty and the Being of the Occupier: Manifesto for a White Australian Philosophy of Origins*. His most recent book, *Gathering and Dispersing: The Western World as a Philosophical Project*, is forthcoming with re.press.